MATHEMATICAL THEORY OF PROGRAM CORRECTNESS

Prentice-Hall International
Series in Computer Science

C. A. R. Hoare, Series Editor

Published

BACKHOUSE, R. C., *Syntax of Programming Languages: Theory and Practice*
de BAKKER, J. W., *Mathematical Theory of Program Correctness*
DUNCAN, F., *Microprocessor Programming and Software Development*
HENDERSON, P., *Functional Programming: Application and Implementation*
JONES, C. B., *Software Development: A Rigorous Approach*
WELSH, J. and ELDER, J., *Introduction to PASCAL*
WELSH, J. and McKEAG, M., *Structured System Programming*

Future Titles

JACKSON, M. A., *System Design*
JOHNSTON, H., *Learning to Program with PASCAL*
NAUR, P., *Studies in Program Analysis and Construction*
PYLE, I. C. and WAND, I., *The ADA Programming Language*
TENNENT, R., *Principles of Programming Languages*
WELSH, J. and ELDER, J., *Sequential and Concurrent Program Structures*

MATHEMATICAL THEORY OF PROGRAM CORRECTNESS

JACO de BAKKER
Mathematical Center and Free University
Amsterdam

with the assistance of

Arie de Bruin / **Jeffery Zucker**
Mathematical Center / Mathematical Center

ENGLEWOOD CLIFFS, NEW JERSEY LONDON NEW DELHI
SINGAPORE SYDNEY TOKYO TORONTO WELLINGTON

Library of Congress Cataloging in Publication Data

BAKKER, JACOBUS WILLEM de.
mathematical theory of program correctness.

Bibliography: p.
Includes index
1. Computer programs—Correctness. 2. Logic, Symbolic and mathematical. I. Title.
QA76.6.B335 001.64'25 80-12451
ISBN 0-13-562132-1

British Library Cataloguing in Publication Data

de BAKKER, J W
mathematical theory of program correctness.

1. Computer programs—Testing
I. Title
001.6'42 QA76.6
ISBN 0-13-562132-1

ISBN 0-13-562132-1

PRENTICE-HALL INTERNATIONAL, INC., *London*
PRENTICE-HALL OF AUSTRALIA PTY., LTD., *Sydney*
PRENTICE-HALL OF CANADA, LTD., *Toronto*
PRENTICE-HALL OF INDIA PRIVATE LIMITED, *New Delhi*
PRENTICE-HALL OF JAPAN, INC., *Tokyo*
PRENTICE-HALL OF SOUTHEAST ASIA PTE., LTD., *Singapore*
PRENTICE-HALL, INC., *Englewood Cliffs, New Jersey*
WHITEHALL BOOKS LIMITED, *Wellington, New Zealand*

Printed in Great Britain by A. Wheaton & Co. Ltd, Exeter

80 81 82 83 84 5 4 3 2 1

for Bas and Jaska

CONTENTS

REFERENCES AND BIBLIOGRAPHICAL NOTES 466

SUBJECT INDEX 491

INDEX OF NOTATIONS 498

PREFACE

Recent years have witnessed major advances both in the semantics of programming languages, and in the methodology of program design and verification. The aim of our book is to bring these two disciplines together by providing a solid mathematical foundation for the techniques of proving program correctness. More specifically, the tools of denotational semantics (Scott, Strachey) are used to justify the proof methods of Floyd, Hoare and Dijkstra which pervade contemporary approaches to program verification.

The book concentrates upon fundamental concepts appearing in ALGOL-like languages (ALGOL 60, PL/I, PASCAL), with emphasis on the algorithmic aspects of these languages, thus paying little attention to data structures. To each of the basic notions – assignment, while statements, recursive procedures, blocks, parameter mechanisms, goto statements – we devote a chapter in which we introduce the concept and its semantics, and then develop its proof theory (definition of correctness, soundness and completeness of an appropriate proof system, and related questions). Apart from chapter 8, all chapters are solely concerned with *partial* correctness (where one abstracts from proving termination). Some topics in the theory of *total* correctness are briefly dealt with in chapter 8.

Besides its emphasis on algorithmic concepts, the book moreover restricts itself to what one might call the classical notions of programming which are, in our opinion, sufficiently well-established to warrant treatment in a textbook. Accordingly, we have excluded all discussion of concurrency or abstract data types, topics which, important as they may be, have not yet achieved sufficient stability in their mathematical theory. The only more modern concept we *do* treat is nondeterminacy, for which a satisfactory theory is indeed available.

Our book is written as a textbook for graduate students, and as a reference work for researchers in theoretical computer science or mathematical logic who are interested in semantics and proof theory of programming languages. It is self-contained, except for one proposition assuming results from recursive function theory. An appendix (by J. I. Zucker) is devoted to the development of the necessary tools to prove this proposition.

As indicated already, we have organized the material – with the exception of chapter 8 – according to the various fundamental programming concepts. Chapters 1 to 4, in which we introduce the basic notions necessary to understand the later chapters, should be studied in the given order. After that, the interdependence of the chapters is no longer linear, but as described in the picture below:

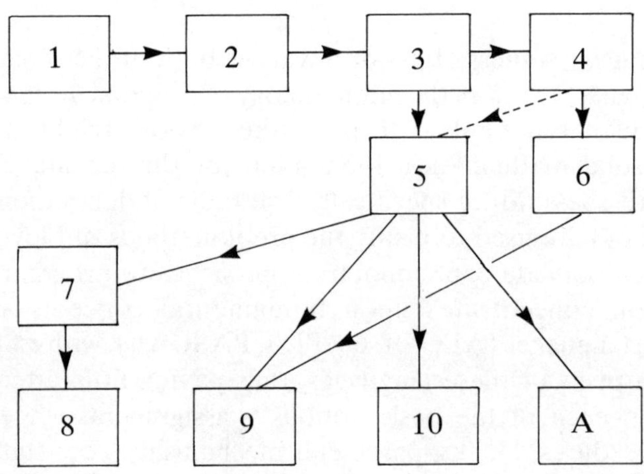

In this picture, "——►" denotes essential, and "----►" non-essential dependence. Note the central role of chapter 5 on recursion, which is fundamental for all of the second half of the book. However, section 5.5 is needed later only in chapter 9.

As to the level of difficulty of the material, we distinguish three categories:

- Basic: chapters 1, 2, 3, 4
- Intermediate: chapters 5.1–5.4, 6, 7, 8.1–8.4, 10
- Advanced: chapters 5.5, 8.5, 9, appendix

For use as a text – say for a one-semester course on the theory of program correctness – we suggest that the instructor cover all of the basic parts, and a selection of the intermediate ones including at least sections 5.1 to 5.4, and chapter 6 or chapter 7. It would probably not be necessary to assume specific prerequisites for a student to attend such a course – apart from some general inclination towards mathematically-oriented arguments – but some prior exposure to the use of assertions in proving program correctness and to elementary mathematical logic would certainly be helpful. We hope to have enhanced the value of the book as a text by the inclusion of many exercises at the end of each chapter.

All references are collected in a separate chapter at the end of the book. This contains a brief outline of the major sources for our work and of related investigations, detailed references for chapters 2 to 10, and the bibliography.

A few words on what have *not* been our objectives in writing this book may now be in order. Firstly, we have not aimed at writing a treatise on denotational semantics in general. We only develop as much of this theory as is necessary to analyze the proof systems which are the main theme of our book. Accordingly, many of its more advanced results are not mentioned at all. Secondly, it is not an introduction to the design of correct programs. It is not so much the correctness of programs, but rather the correctness – or, to use the technical term, the soundness – of the various proof systems which is one of the central concerns of our investigation. Thirdly, though we do cover many of the fundamental concepts in ALGOL-like languages, we are aware of the fact that their union is still a long way from anything like a real programming language. Apart from our very sparse coverage of data structures, we have imposed some further restrictions on the languages considered to ensure that they become amenable to a treatment satisfying the criterion of mathematical rigor which has been our main guiding principle. The most important example of this is that we have no programmer-declared functions inside expressions, thus avoiding all delicate issues concerning side-effects. Lastly, as a remark to the reader with some background in logic, we mention that all our constructs are interpreted over the integers. Hence, we do not deal with the additional problems which arise when the languages considered are interpreted in arbitrary models.

I gratefully acknowledge the comments, inspiration and support I have received from many people in writing this book. Its origin dates back to 1969, when Dana Scott taught me the fundamentals of denotational semantics. Without his lessons, the book would not have been written. I am deeply indebted to Arie de Bruin and Jeffery Zucker for their assistance in preparing the final version. Besides their specific contributions (chapter 10 and the appendix), they have read the whole text, and suggested countless corrections and improvements. Jeff has in particular helped to give many of the advanced sections their final form. Krzysztof Apt and Willem Paul de Roever, my former colleagues at the Mathematical Center, have made various important contributions to the theory of program correctness. Their work has left numerous traces in chapters 6 and 9, and 7 and 8, respectively.

The book grew out of lecture notes for courses I gave at the Free University of Amsterdam. I also used versions of the material for a Unesco

Summer School on the Foundations of Computer Science, and for a course at the Pontificia Universidade Catolica, Rio de Janeiro. Many students from these courses, and colleagues from the Mathematical Center and elsewhere have read and criticized drafts of the text. I want to express my thanks to Ralph-Johan Back, Jan Boon, Peter van Emde Boas, Nissim Francez, Henk Goeman, Theo Janssen, Wiebren de Jonge, Maaret Karttunen, Ruurd Kuiper, Franz Lanzinger, Anton Nijholt, Attendolfo Pereira, Regis Pliuskevicius and Paolo Veloso.

The successive drafts of the book, including the final version in camera-ready form, were produced with great skill by the typing staff of the Mathematical Center. My thanks go first and foremost to Corrie Klein Velderman who did a splendid job in typing most of the preliminary drafts and the final text. I furthermore thank Susan Carolan for her perseverance with the remaining parts, and Aafje van den Berg, Linda Brown, Ria Riechelmann and Malou Sagum for their help at earlier stages.

Finally, I am grateful to Prentice-Hall International for their willingness to include this book in their series in Computer Science, to Ron Decent, Henry Hirschberg and Tony Hoare for their respective shares in its publication, and to Peter Mosses for his reviewing efforts.

JACO DE BAKKER

MATHEMATICAL THEORY
OF
PROGRAM CORRECTNESS

Chapter 1

INTRODUCTION

In this book, we develop a mathematical theory of program correctness. The notion which occupies a central position in our study is that of *partial correctness* of a program S with respect to assertions (conditions which may or may not be satisfied by the program variables) p and q, expressed by the formula

$$\{p\}S\{q\} \tag{1.1}$$

As informal meaning of (1.1) we have that, if p holds before execution of S, and execution of S terminates, then q holds afterwards. Simple examples of partial correctness formulae are

{x=0}x:=x+1{x=1}

or

{x≥0} <u>while</u> x>0 <u>do</u> x:=x-1 <u>od</u> {x=0}

We shall be concerned with a variety of questions about construct (1.1). (Throughout our book, the term "construct" refers to a linguistic entity, i.e. an element of some formal language, such as an expression, statement, assertion, formula etc.) The main ones are:

- What is the exact form of the programs S and assertions p,q which we encounter in (1.1)? That is, we ask for the *syntax* of the languages in which we write S, p and q.
- What is the precise meaning of a formula {p}S{q}; more specifically, when do we say that such a formula is true? For this, we shall have to consider ways of specifying the *semantics* of the statements

occurring in S.

- Can we find satisfactory *proof systems*, i.e. sets of axioms and proof rules such that formal proofs of constructs (1.1) can be given? "Satisfactory" should here be taken in the sense that the systems concerned are *sound* (only true formulae are provable) and *complete* (all true formulae are provable).

The present introduction aims at providing the student with a first orientation in the problem area of our book. Thus, precise definitions should not be expected, and we can well imagine that the uninitiated reader may occasionally encounter remarks which he cannot fully appreciate at this stage. Let us assure him, however, that all matters discussed here return in subsequent chapters where full details will be supplied about notions of which only a sketch is given in this introduction.

1.1. Syntax and semantics

As to syntax, let us mention already that the syntax for assertions remains the same in all of our theory. It is an extension of that of boolean expressions (such as x=1, a[1] > a[2], or (x<y) ∧ (y<z)) in that in the formation of assertions we also use quantifiers (e.g. ∃x[y=x+z]). For the logician, our assertions are the first-order formulae of arithmetic (but for the fact that, from chapter 4 onwards, subscripted variables may also appear in them). For the programs S, we start in chapter 2 with a very simple language consisting only of assignment statements (e.g. x:=x+1), sequential composition (S_1;S_2) and conditionals (<u>if</u> b <u>then</u> S_1 <u>else</u> S_2 <u>fi</u>), and then gradually extend the language in the following chapters with further fundamental constructs such as while statements (<u>while</u> b <u>do</u> S <u>od</u>), recursive procedures (for instance with declarations such as <u>procedure</u> P; <u>if</u> b <u>then</u> S_1;P;S_2 <u>else</u> S_3 <u>fi</u>), blocks (<u>begin</u> <u>new</u> x; S <u>end</u>), nondeterministic statements ($S_1 \cup S_2$), etc. Altogether, however, syntax plays only a very minor role in this book. Usually, its appearance is restricted to the very first part of each chapter, in which we introduce the language construct used to express the concept studied in it, and then continue with the discussion of its semantics and proof theory, which together constitute the main subject matter of our investigation.

For the specification of the meaning of the various constructs studied in our book, we use the method of *denotational* (sometimes also called *mathematical*) semantics. The following remarks may serve as a very first introduction to this method. In general, in the study of the semantics of a language, one is interested in relating the constructs of the language - i.e. entities in the linguistic world- to objects in some other world. In a natural language such as English, the meaning of the word "table" - about which we can say, e.g. that it consists of five letters - is given in terms of its relationship with (some suitable abstraction of) a table as object in the external world, where it might be observed as having four legs. For programming languages, a variety of worlds may be used to attribute meaning to the expressions and statements appearing in them. By way of example, we can view the world of some real computer - its processing unit, memory etc. - as the universe in which to interpret the constructs of the language. Though this is clearly what happens in practice, it is an approach infeasible for theoretical treatment, since the complexity of the system concerned entirely transcends the limits of a rigorous mathematical analysis. Therefore, one has to look for a means of abstracting from this complexity - were it only to do away with the dependency on the idiosyncrasies of a computer of make X, which obviously should not be involved in the definition of a language -, and at least two solutions for this have come forward. The first is to replace the role of a real computer by that of some *abstract* machine, - i.e. a mathematical object endowed with components such as states, a control structure, and maybe further items - and to relate the meaning of a program and its constituent parts to the actions of this machine. The style of semantics we obtain in this way is usually called *operational*; characteristic for it is the appearance of *computation sequences*, i.e. finite or infinite sequences of states which form a trace of the execution of the program by the abstract machine. Advantages of the method of operational semantics - as compared with that of denotational semantics to be introduced in a moment - are, e.g., that one often stays close to what might be called the intuitive semantics of a language as described, say, by the English text of the defining manual. Moreover, an appropriate choice of the abstract machine may lead to a definition which can provide some guidance to the implementer. (An example of exploiting the first advantage will be encountered in chapter 5, where we start with an operational semantics for recursion, and only after that give its denotational semantics.) A possible drawback of the operational approach is that it is still not abstract enough. Too many details of the, however abstract, implementation which are in fact irrelevant for the final outcome of the program - such as how and where to store representations of the objects manipulated - have to be settled. Also, one should realize that, just as we have the familiar fact that many algorithms can express the same function, there are also many ways of organizing the operations of an abstract machine such that they can all be said to express the meaning of a program in a correct way, and what we would like to have is some common abstraction of all these possibilities which is the (unique) meaning of the program rather than a possible implementation. Now such common abstraction is exactly what is provided by the method of denotational semantics, where all use of abstract machines is avoided and, instead, a model is employed which only features mathematical objects such as sets, functions and operators (mappings from functions to functions). Computation sequences have disappeared, i.e. the method is fully *extensional*. Programs are interpreted as functions from (initial) states to (final) states without any use of intermediate states. A further characteristic of the method is the application of various mappings from the entities in the linguistic world to appropriate objects in the mathematical world in such a way that the meaning, or *value*, of a construct is determined in terms of the meanings of its constituent components. (The idea that constructs *denote* values is expressed by the qualification "denotational" for our brand of semantics.) By way of illustration, we discuss some simple examples of the approach; much more about this follows in chapter 2. For our purposes, a *state* is simply a function from integer variables (x,y,...) to integers. Thus, using σ for a typical state, we may have that $\sigma(x)=0$, $\sigma(y)=1$, etc. Let V be the function which maps integer expressions s to their values, which are functions from states to integers. Note that, since the value of an integer expression depends on the (current) values of the integer variables appearing in it, we can determine the value of such an expression only with respect to some state through which these values can be retrieved. Typical examples of definitions involving V are

$$V(x)(\sigma) = \sigma(x)$$
$$V(s_1+s_2)(\sigma) = V(s_1)(\sigma) + V(s_2)(\sigma)$$

From this, taking σ such that $\sigma(x)=0$, $\sigma(y)=1$, we obtain, e.g.

$$V(x)(\sigma) = \sigma(x) = 0$$
$$V(x+y)(\sigma) = V(x)(\sigma) + V(y)(\sigma) = 1$$

Next, let M be the function which maps statements to their values which, as we saw above, are functions from states to states. Thus, $\sigma' = M(S)(\sigma)$ reflects that the initial state σ is transformed by S to the final state σ', where σ and σ' determine the values of the variables before and after execution of S, respectively. Typical clauses in the definition of M are

$$M(x:=s)(\sigma) = \sigma\{V(s)(\sigma)/x\}$$
$$M(S_1;S_2)(\sigma) = M(S_2)(M(S_1)(\sigma))$$

where the notation $\sigma\{V(s)(\sigma)/x\}$ is used for a state which is like σ, but for its value at argument x which is now set to $V(s)(\sigma)$, i.e. to the value of s in σ. Applying this definition, e.g. to the statement x:=x+y, we obtain, for σ as above:

$$\mathcal{M}(x{:=}x{+}y)(\sigma) = \sigma\{1/x\}$$

For assertions, we use the same approach: we introduce a function $\mathcal{T}$ mapping assertions - with respect to some state - to truth-values, and in its definition we encounter clauses such as:

$$\mathcal{T}(s_1{=}s_2)(\sigma) = (\mathcal{V}(s_1)(\sigma) = \mathcal{V}(s_2)(\sigma))$$
$$\mathcal{T}(p_1 \wedge p_2)(\sigma) = \mathcal{T}(p_1)(\sigma) \wedge \mathcal{T}(p_2)(\sigma)$$

Once the functions $\mathcal{V}$, $\mathcal{M}$, $\mathcal{T}$ etc. are known, we can define the meaning of formula (1.1) in terms of these. According to the customary definition of partial correctness, we have that S is partially correct with respect to p and q whenever, for all states σ,σ', if σ (the initial state) satisfies p (i.e. $\mathcal{T}(p)(\sigma)$ holds) and S transforms σ to σ' (the final state), then σ' satisfies q ($\mathcal{T}(q)(\sigma')$ holds). In our formalism, we express this by saying that (1.1) holds whenever, for all σ,σ',

$$\mathcal{T}(p)(\sigma) \wedge \sigma' = \mathcal{M}(S)(\sigma) \Rightarrow \mathcal{T}(q)(\sigma')$$

The discussion so far ignores the problem of possible nontermination. We have not said what to do about, e.g. (*): $\mathcal{M}$(<u>while</u> x>0 <u>do</u> x:=x+1 <u>od</u>)(σ) for some state σ such that σ(x)>0. We see from this example that there are statements S such that the function $\mathcal{M}(S)$ is *partial* in that for some σ no σ' exists such that $\mathcal{M}(S)(\sigma) = \sigma'$. (Correctness of S with respect to p and q where termination is guaranteed is called *total*. Formally, S is totally correct with respect to p and q iff $\forall\sigma[\mathcal{T}(p)(\sigma) \Rightarrow \exists\sigma'[\sigma'=\mathcal{M}(S)(\sigma) \wedge \mathcal{T}(q)(\sigma')]]$.) The usual operational semantics of the while statement in (*) - for σ as indicated - would lead to an infinite computation sequence. In denotational semantics - which, as we saw above, avoids the introduction of such sequences - we have to use other techniques, described at length in chapter 3. Here we only mention that they require a certain mathematical framework involving notions such as partial orderings, chains and their limits, and (least) fixed points of operators. This framework is extended in chapter 5 on recursion, where the notion of *continuity* - which is fundamental in all of our theory - is introduced. Chapter 5 provides in fact a cogent example of the difference between the operational and denotational methods, and of their relative merits. Whereas the operational definition is intuitively satisfactory in that it embodies the customary idea of executing a call of some procedure P by replacing it by its corresponding procedure body - i.e. the statement associated with P in its declaration - , its denotational definition is formulated in terms of the much more abstract concept of least fixed point of some operator associated with that body. However, the latter approach has two distinct advantages. Firstly, it brings into the open questions about the *existence* of certain mathematical entities appearing in the model. More specifically, we shall prove a fundamental theorem stating that each continuous function has a least fixed point, and, as we shall see in chapter 5, this ensures the existence of a function yielding the meaning of a recursive procedure. (In operational semantics, these and similar questions tend to remain hidden. For example, a rigorous justification of the operational semantics of recursion as presented in chapter 5 is only provided using tools as developed in the appendix.) Secondly, we can use it to prove the soundness of a central proof rule for recursive procedures in a rather natural way. On the other hand, we do not know how a *direct* justification of this rule using purely operational means could be given.

By way of conclusion of this first sketch of what denotational semantics is about, we mention a few further notions featured in later chapters. In the treatment of blocks, i.e. of local variable declarations, we encounter *addresses* as an important tool: variables are no longer mapped directly to integers but, instead, to addresses which in turn are mapped to integers. For nondeterminacy, a new partial ordering which is an extension of that of previous chapters is the key to its semantic analysis. Parameters are dealt with - somewhat nonstandardly - by certain syntactic manipulations with the program texts, and for goto statements we use *continuations*: the meaning of a program is then no longer a function, say ϕ, from states to states but, rather, an operator mapping such functions ϕ to ϕ'.

We hope that the preceding discussion has provided the reader with some initial feeling for the flavor of denotational semantics. Of course, in this introduction we could only review a few of the basic characteristics of the method. To summarize, we have seen that language constructs denote values, that for these values we use certain mathematical objects - integers, functions and the like - which are elements of domains endowed with a suitable structure, that the values of programs are state-transforming functions which are defined in a purely extensional manner and, lastly, that the various values are obtained by applying mappings such as V, M, T to the respective constructs in such a way that the meaning of a construct is determined by the meanings of its constituent parts. So much, for the moment, about semantics.

1.2. Proof theory

We now turn to proof theory. Here, the object of study is proof systems, i.e. sets of axioms and proof rules in which formal proofs for partial correctness formulae (1.1) can be derived. By way of example, let us consider a language including assignment statements (of the form x:=s, for s some integer expression), sequential composition ($S_1;S_2$), and while statements (<u>while</u> b <u>do</u> S <u>od</u>). A proof system for this language includes - besides some further rules to be presented in the full treatment in chapters 2 and 3 - an *axiom* for assignment and two *proof rules* corresponding to the other two constructs. As axiom, we have

$$\{p[s/x]\}x:=s\{p\} \tag{1.2}$$

where we use the notation p[s/x] for the assertion which results from p by substituting the expression s for the variable x. E.g. for $p\equiv(x=1)$, we have that $p[x+1/x]\equiv(x+1=1)$. Properly speaking, (1.2) is an axiom *scheme*, with instances such as

$$\{x+1=1\}x:=x+1\{x=1\}$$

The proof rule for sequential composition is

$$\frac{\{p\}S_1\{q\},\{q\}S_2\{r\}}{\{p\}S_1;S_2\{r\}} \tag{1.3}$$

In words, once we have derived $\{p\}S_1\{q\}$ and $\{q\}S_2\{r\}$, we may infer $\{p\}S_1;S_2\{r\}$. Note the role of the *intermediate* assertion q, which holds between execution of S_1 and S_2. As proof rule corresponding to the while statement we have

$$\frac{\{p\wedge b\}S\{p\}}{\{p\}\ \underline{\text{while}}\ b\ \underline{\text{do}}\ S\ \underline{\text{od}}\ \{p\wedge\neg b\}} \tag{1.4}$$

This rule essentially tells us that if an assertion p is an *invariant* of the statement S - for the case that the test b of the while statement is satisfied - then it is also an invariant of while b do S od. Moreover, upon exit from the while statement $\neg b$ holds.

In the analysis of a proof system featuring rules such as (1.2) to (1.4), we have to answer two questions. Firstly, we have to establish the soundness of the system, i.e. we have to verify that only true formulae are provable in it (where "true" is to be taken semantically, i.e. as defined in section 1.1). For this, it is sufficient to show that each axiom is true, and, moreover, for each proof rule we have that its conclusion is true provided its premises are true. Secondly, we want the system to be complete, i.e. such that a formal proof can be derived in it for each true formula. For a system with rules (1.2) to (1.4) as representative components, the soundness question is easy to settle. All rules are intuitively obvious, and rigorous justification of them presents no difficulties. This is no longer the case, however, once further concepts such as recursion and blocks are taken into account. In fact, a good part of the more difficult sections of our book is devoted to a detailed soundness proof for proof rules pertaining to these concepts. For example, already the *definition* of what it means that construct (1.1) is true in a situation where the programs S involve recursive procedures, is not immediate (since, as we shall see in sections 5.4 and 5.5, the definition of section 1.1 is then inadequate).

The issue of completeness is, in general, harder to deal with than that of soundness. (In fact, what we shall obtain is a number of *relative* completeness results; we postpone discussion of the significance of this restriction to section 2.6.) Let us call programs without iteration (in the form of while statements or goto's) or recursion, *straight-line* programs. (Chapters 2,4 and 6 are devoted to them.) For these, completeness of the proof systems concerned can be shown in a straightforward manner. For non-straight-line programs, two sources of complications will be encountered, as we shall now briefly outline. Firstly, the completeness proofs rely on a fundamental proposition stating the expressibility of the notion of *weakest precondition*. For each program S and assertion q, it is possible to find an assertion p such that (i) {p}S{q} is true, and (ii) for any assertion r such that (*) {r}S{q} is true, we have that $r \supset p$. (Note that (i) and (ii) together imply that p is the weakest among all assertions r satisfying (*).) As we shall see later, in the context of the language referred to above, this expressibility result guarantees the existence of appropriate intermediate assertions (cf. rule (1.3)) and invariant assertions (cf. rule (1.4)). The proposition (or its dual for *strongest postconditions*) appears in some form each time we want to show completeness of a proof system. However, in the case of programs involving iteration or recursion, its proof requires tools from recursive function theory which we do not assume to be available in the main text of our book. Therefore, we devote the appendix to an exposition of the framework necessary to prove the proposition for the representative case of a language with parameterless recursive procedures. The second source of problems is the following: in order to obtain a complete proof system dealing with recursion - iteration is essentially simpler in this respect - we need various auxiliary axioms and proof rules for which neither the proof of their soundness, nor their role in the completeness proof could be called natural or intuitively appealing. We have collected our discussion of these difficulties in the advanced parts of our book (sections 5.5, 9.3, 9.4, and the appendix), and recommend the reader to postpone study of this till he has obtained a good understanding of the basic and intermediate parts (see classification in the Preface).

Though the major focus of our investigation is partial correctness and associated semantic and proof-theoretic considerations, there are also a number of further topics dealt with which do not fit under this general heading. Firstly, as a minor point we mention that occasionally some attention is paid to program *equivalence*. E.g., the proof rule for recursion discussed in chapter 5 is general enough to be used for both partial correctness and equivalence proofs. However, our treatment of program equivalence remains scanty; in particular, discussion of full proof systems for equivalence is omitted throughout. Secondly, in chapter 7 we deviate from the general strategy of our book in that, though we do provide a full semantic analysis of nondeterminacy, the ensuing correctness questions are dealt with only through the presentation of a number of rules which, when taken together, do not yet constitute a complete system. Complete proof systems for programs with nondeterminacy are described elsewhere in the literature, albeit in a somewhat different setting (see the references to dynamic logic in the bibliographical notes at the back). We expect that the techniques of section 5.5 can be used to obtain a completeness proof for partial correctness relating to the μ-calculus

- the language of chapter 7 - but we have not investigated this. Lastly, chapter 8 is even more outside the mainstream of our treatise, since it is neither centered around a fundamental programming concept, nor concerned specifically with partial correctness. Nor, as we would like to emphasize, is it concerned with program termination or total correctness in general, but only with various aspects of termination in relation to weakest preconditions. Again, complete proof systems for total correctness are studied elsewhere (cf. the remark just made for chapter 7); they constitute a difficult problem area, and we have not endeavored to touch more than briefly upon questions of termination.

At the end of this introduction, it may be appropriate to devote some comments to the connection between the mathematical theory of program correctness as developed in our book, and the actual practice of program verification. A great deal of attention has been paid in recent years to the issue of program correctness, and we expect that many of our readers have already gained at least some experience with the approach of employing assertions in the design and verification of programs. (We recommend the reader who is not in this position, to consult the excellent books by Alagić and Arbib, Dijkstra, and Manna (see references in the bibliographical chapter) in order to familiarize himself with this approach.) Now it is clearly of essential importance that a proof system used in practical applications be reliable in the sense of the above discussion. When we have shown its soundness, we know that no formal proof can be derived in it of a false correctness formula, and its completeness ensures that when a correctness formula is true, a formal proof of this can indeed be obtained. Thus, our mathematical theory provides the necessary foundation for the use in actual program proving of the proof systems studied in the following chapters. Moreover, in the case that proof systems for partial correctness are used which are variations on the systems investigated below, we are confident that the reader who has mastered the techniques described in our book will be able to apply them to analyze the proof-theoretic properties of these other systems.

This concludes the introduction. We still owe the reader many details of ideas only sketched above. In chapter 2, we make a beginning with the rigorous development of our theory, by presenting its "Basic Concepts".

Chapter 2

BASIC CONCEPTS

2.1. Syntax and semantics of a simple programming language

We start with the introduction of a very simple language which includes some elementary integer and boolean expressions, assignment, sequential composition, and conditional statements. This language will be used as a vehicle to illustrate our major tools; moreover, it will appear that already for this simple case a complete analysis of the ensuing problems isn't all that easy. Thus, we intend to prepare the reader somewhat for the complications he will encounter in subsequent chapters.

Let us consider a small example program: x := x+1. Clearly, if x happens to have the value 0 before execution of this statement, afterwards it will have the value 1. Formally, we shall express this by saying that the formula

$$\{x = 0\}x{:=}x + 1\{x = 1\} \tag{2.1}$$

holds, or, using the technical term we shall reserve for this in the sequel, that (2.1) is *valid*. Another example of a valid formula is

$$\{\underline{\text{true}}\}x{:=}0;y{:=}x + 1\{x = 0 \wedge y = 1\}. \tag{2.2}$$

Observe that the condition preceding this statement (which we shall call the *precondition*) is identically satisfied, whatever the values of the variables. An *invalid* formula is, e.g.,

$$\{x = 0\}x{:=}x + 1\{x = 2\}. \tag{2.3}$$

Also, formulae may be valid but not best possible, as is suggested by the following example:

$$\{x = 0\}x:=x + 1\{x > 0\} \tag{2.4}$$

Moreover, in certain cases it may not be immediately obvious what the *postcondition* (the condition following the statement in the formula) should be corresponding to a given precondition. For example, consider

$$\{\underline{\text{true}}\}x:=x + 1\{?\} \tag{2.5}$$

Though, clearly, $\{\underline{\text{true}}\}x:=1\{x = 1\}$ is valid, it is also clear that $\{\underline{\text{true}}\}x:=x + 1\{x = x+1\}$ is invalid, and the question thus arises as to how to supply the condition which could fill the place of the "?". Altogether we are faced with the following problems:

a. Let S be a statement in our example language, and let p and q be conditions which may or may not be satisfied by the program variables. (In the sequel such conditions will always be referred to by the technical term *assertions*.) Develop a systematic method of assigning meanings (mathematical objects) to the constructs S, p and q. In the terminology of the introduction, we ask for the denotational semantics of these constructs. Moreover, we want to give a precise definition of the validity of correctness formulae {p}S{q}.

b. Investigate the structure of valid correctness formulae. Questions pertaining to this include:
   - (i) For a given assignment statement x:=s and assertion p, determine an assertion q such that {p}x:=s{q} is valid (and dually with the roles of precondition and postcondition interchanged)
   - (ii) Analyze the idea of best possible formulae in the sense as indicated by the contrast between formulae (2.1) and (2.4). This is where the notions of *weakest* precondition and *strongest* postcondition enter our considerations

(iii) What kind of substitutions in correctness formulae do we allow? For example, from {x=0}x:=x+1;y:=2{ x=1 ∧ y=2} we may infer that {z=0}z:=z+1;y:=2{z=1 ∧ y=2} holds, but not that {y=0}y:=y+1;y:=2{y=1 ∧ y=2} holds

(iv) Single out a number of central formulae (axioms) and rules to generate new valid formulae from already given ones (proof rules). Together, these axioms and proof rules should constitute a sound and complete proof system for correctness formulae {p}S{q} in the sense as sketched in the introduction - and made precise in section 2.6.

Apart from the above listed items, an occasional topic which does not belong in this classification will also be dealt with in the present chapter. E.g., we shall also be interested in the *equivalence* of two statements S_1 and S_2, expressed by the formula $S_1 = S_2$. However, such other questions will play only a minor role.

We now turn to the syntax of our example language. We introduce three classes of constructs, *Iexp* (for integer expressions) with typical elements s,t,..., *Bexp* (for boolean expressions) with typical elements b,..., and *Stat* (for statements) with typical elements S,... . In the formation of these constructs we start from certain terminal symbols such as ";", ":=", "if", "then", "else", "fi", "+", "=", etc. Moreover, we have two classes of syntactic entities of which we do not specify the structure (contrary to what is customary in an actual programming language), namely that of *Ivar* (integer variables) and *Icon* (integer constants), with typical elements x,y,z,u,... and m,n,..., respectively. In a language such as ALGOL 60, the first class is included in that of the *identifiers*, whereas for the second class a representation in some number system is provided. We never need any insight into the structure of our integer variables or constants, which is why we omit such specification in our work. All we assume about *Icon* is that it contains the integer constants in *some* representation, be it decimal, octal, binary, the Roman system of numbers, or whatever one prefers. However, in our examples we shall always, for simplicity's sake, use the decimal notation.

Two further remarks are in order to explain our use of variables $s \in \mathit{Iexp}$, $b \in \mathit{Bexp}$, etc. Always, when we say that a syntactic class (such as *Iexp*) has typical elements (such as s,t,...), we allow the indexed or primed variants of these letters just as well as variables over the same set. (With $s,t \in \mathit{Iexp}$ we also have $s_0, s_1, \ldots, s', s'', \ldots, t_0, \ldots \in \mathit{Iexp}$, etc.). Sometimes, we use more than one letter as typical element of a syntactic class. This is the case, e.g., for s and $t \in \mathit{Iexp}$, and x,y,z and $u \in \mathit{Ivar}$. However, no letter is used as a variable for a syntactic class unless specifically indicated in this way. *Only* s and t (and $s_0, \ldots, t', \ldots$, etc.) range over *Iexp*, and not, e.g., r or u. Similarly, only x,y,z and u range over *Ivar*, and not v (let alone X or ξ). These conventions are motivated by the sheer lack of size of the alphabets we have available, thus requiring a careful choice of notation, the more so since, contrary to normal mathematical practice, we shall have to deal with an embarrassingly high number of sets of various (linguistic or mathematical) types, necessitating a systematic and consistent use of letters ranging over them.

We are now ready for our first definition, giving the syntax of our simple example language.

DEFINITION 2.1 (syntax of *Iexp*, *Bexp* and *Stat*). Let *Ivar*, with typical elements x,y,z,u,..., and *Icon*, with typical elements m,n,..., be given sets of symbols. For later use (cf. definition 2.14), we assume the set *Ivar* to be well-ordered.

a. The class *Iexp*, with typical elements s,t,..., is defined by

$$s ::= x \mid m \mid s_1 + s_2 \mid \ldots \mid \underline{\text{if}}\ b\ \underline{\text{then}}\ s_1\ \underline{\text{else}}\ s_2\ \underline{\text{fi}}$$

(Expressions such as $s_1 - s_2$, $s_1 \times s_2, \ldots$ may be added at the position of the ..., if desired.)

b. The class *Bexp*, with typical elements b,..., is defined by

$$b ::= \underline{true} \mid \underline{false} \mid s_1 = s_2 \mid \ldots \mid \neg b \mid b_1 \supset b_2$$

(Expressions such as $s_1 < s_2$,... may be added at the position of the ..., if desired.)

c. The class *Stat*, with typical elements S,..., is defined by

$$S ::= x:=s \mid S_1 ; S_2 \mid \underline{if}\ b\ \underline{then}\ S_1\ \underline{else}\ S_2\ \underline{fi}$$

END 2.1.

For the reader who is not accustomed to the notation of this definition (which is nothing but a small variation on the well-known Backus-Naur formalism as used for instance in the ALGOL 60 report), we give the verbal transliteration of clause a. An integer expression s is defined to be one of the following:

- an integer variable x (i.e. some element of the set *Ivar*)
- an integer constant m (i.e. some element of the set *Icon*)
- some integer expression s_1, followed by a "+" symbol, followed by some integer expression s_2 (not necessarily different from s_1)
- ... (as above, with "+" replaced by "-", etc.)
- an <u>if</u> - symbol, followed by some boolean expression, followed by a <u>then</u> - symbol, followed by some integer expression, followed by an <u>else</u> - symbol, followed by some integer expression, followed by a <u>fi</u> - symbol.

As to the ... in clauses a and b, the idea is that whenever in the sequel one is interested in the treatment of other arithmetic or relational operators than "+" or "=", respectively, it is always immediately clear how to handle them by a straightforward analogy. Since our semantic definitions are always in one-one correspondence with the syntax, we did not want to bother to treat almost identical cases again and again. However, we shall allow ourselves in our examples free use of $-, \times, \ldots, \leq, \ldots$, etc., which, strictly speaking, have not been introduced formally in the syntax.

Examples

1. y, 1, x+y, <u>if</u> x > 0 <u>then</u> x - 1 <u>else</u> y + z <u>fi</u>
2. <u>true</u>, x = y, ¬x > 0 ⊃ x > -1
3. x:=x+1, x:=x+y;y:=x-y,
   <u>if</u> x > 0 <u>then</u> x:=x-1 <u>else</u> y:=y-x <u>fi</u>

As a general comment on the choice of our example language, we add the following. We tried to find some appropriate balance between, on the one hand the wish to include nontrivial concepts and, on the other hand, the strong desire to avoid unnecessary complications. Of course, in later chapters, we shall add various important programming concepts (while statements, subscripted variables, recursive procedures, etc.) to it. However, we do not at all intend to approximate in the end a full-fledged programming language. For example, now that we have integer variables and assignment to them, the theory will hardly benefit from the introduction of boolean variables with corresponding assignment statements. Only small variations - which may be provided by the diligent reader, if he so desires - would then be needed, and their inclusion would detract from the mainstream of the development.

We have not bothered to introduce parentheses in the syntax. Unless specifically stated contrariwise, we agree that parentheses may be added freely in syntactic constructs to increase readability, or, in certain cases, to avoid syntactic (or semantic) ambiguity (see the examples following definition 2.3). Issues of parsing, ambiguity and the like are well understood, treated at length in the literature, and of little interest for our present aims.

Syntactic constructs may be *syntactically identical*, denoted by "≡". Two constructs $x_1, x_2, \ldots, S_1, S_2$ are syntactically identical whenever they consist of the same sequence of symbols. For example, 0+1 ≡ 0+1, x:=x+1 ≡ x:=x+1, but 0+1 ≢ 1+0 and x:=1 ≢ x:=0;x:=x+1. Observe that x ≡ y may or may not be satisfied, depending on whether x and y denote the same or different elements of *Ivar* (x and y are not themselves (sequences of) symbols, but are variables ranging over a set of symbols.) In this and subsequent chapters we shall gradually extend our syntax, without updating each time the definition of syntactic identity. From now on, we assume this notion to be defined once and for all.

After thus having defined the syntax of *Iexp*, *Bexp* and *Stat*, we turn to the definition of their meaning. Expressions such as 0 + 1 or <u>if</u> 0 + 1 = 1 + 0 <u>then</u> 2 + 3 <u>else</u> 4 × 5 <u>fi</u> can be assigned meaning immediately (viz. the integers 1 and 5, respectively). However, as soon as the expressions contain integer variables, this is no longer the case. Without further information we cannot assign meaning to x + 1 or to x + y > z ⊃ u > 0. What additional information do we need? Well, nothing but what in programming practice is called the *current values* of these variables. Where do we find these values? In some memory, be it the store of the computer, a piece of scratch paper, or the human computer's mind. In our mathematical treatment we model this by the introduction of a function called the *state*, typically denoted by σ, which is a function from integer variables to integers. For each integer variable x, we retrieve its current value by applying σ to x as argument, yielding some integer as its value. Also, execution of a statement will result in a change of state.

Besides the class of integers, serving as meaning for integer expressions, we introduce the class of truth-values, which serve the same purpose for boolean expressions.

<u>DEFINITION 2.2</u> (integers, truth-values and states).

a. V is used to denote the set of integers, with typical elements α,...
b. W is used to denote the set of truth-values {tt,ff}, with typical elements β,...
c. Σ is used to denote the set of states, i.e. of all functions from

$Ivar$ to V, and has typical elements σ,... . Thus,

$$\Sigma = Ivar \rightarrow V$$

END 2.2.

Remarks

1. The question might arise as to what is the difference between the sets $Icon$ and V. Without being able to go into this at length, let us offer the following as a tentative explanation. The principal distinction between the two sets is that the first consists of entities of a *linguistic* nature, the second of a *mathematical* one. For the elements of $Icon$ it makes sense to apply, e.g. the operation of concatenation, and to discuss various possible representations for it. For example, the number three might be represented by 3 (decimal) or 11 (binary), or even by III (Roman) or 111 (unary), etc. On the other hand, for the set V the questions will be altogether different. One might start with the characterization of the class of natural numbers through Peano's axioms, and then extend this to the class of all integers by one of the standard methods. Also, mathematical functions such as addition, subtraction etc. are made or assumed to be available with V, which is not necessarily the case for $Icon$. Addition of two integer constants will have to be defined either by establishing a correspondence with the mathematical operation of addition of two integers, as we shall do presently, or by giving an algorithm operating on their representations (which is occasionally preferred in other approaches to semantics). Unfortunately, the distinctions as just indicated get somewhat confused again by the fact that whenever we want to write down a specific element of V, we *are* obliged to use some representation for it, which might, by chance, coincide with the representation selected for the elements of $Icon$ (as will, by the way, indeed be the case in this treatise).

2. Note that for the boolean constants true and false (the linguistic elements) and the truth-values tt and ff (the mathematical elements), we *do* use different representations.
3. In our definition of Σ we encounter for the first time the customary notation for a set of functions. For any two sets C and D, we use $C \to D$ for the set of all functions with C as domain and D as range. Also, we shall use the notation $f: C \to D$ to indicate that f is a function from C to D. Thus, $f: C \to D$ is synonymous with $f \in C \to D$; the latter notation will be used only rarely.

Our next task is to establish a correspondence between Iexp and V, and Bexp and W, respectively, where we use, if necessary, the information on the current values of the variables as stored in the state σ. The technical way of achieving this is to define two functions $\mathcal{V}$ and $\mathcal{W}$ which are, at first glance, functions from Iexp to V and from Bexp to W, but, looking more closely, depend on an additional argument $\sigma \in \Sigma$. Thus, the functions are in fact of the following type:

$$\mathcal{V}: \mathit{Iexp} \to (\Sigma \to V)$$
$$\mathcal{W}: \mathit{Bexp} \to (\Sigma \to W)$$

and it makes sense to write $\mathcal{V}(s)(\sigma) = \alpha$ and $\mathcal{W}(b)(\sigma) = \beta$. The definition of $\mathcal{V}$ and $\mathcal{W}$ will be by induction on the complexity of the arguments s and b. Strictly speaking, we should provide a definition of the complexity of s and b. However, it will be very clear that by defining $\mathcal{V}$ and $\mathcal{W}$ following the syntactic definition of s and b we indeed obtain an exhaustive treatment of all possible cases, which satisfies the requirement that the right-hand sides of the defining equations are either directly given, or involve subexpressions which are of a simpler structure than the expression on the left-hand side.

As indicated already, we assume available together with V and W a number of elementary mathematical functions. More specifically, we assume as given the functions

$+: V \times V \to V$

$=: V \times V \to W$

$\neg: W \to W$

$\Rightarrow: W \times W \to W$

where the meaning of "+" and "=" should be clear, and the meaning of "$\neg$" and "$\Rightarrow$" is given by: $\neg tt = ff$, $\neg ff = tt$, and

$$\Rightarrow(\beta_1,\beta_2) = \begin{cases} tt, & \text{if } \beta_1 = ff \text{ or } \beta_2 = tt \\ ff, & \text{otherwise.} \end{cases}$$

Instead of "$\Rightarrow(\beta_1,\beta_2)$" we shall always write "$\beta_1 \Rightarrow \beta_2$". Mcreover, for any set C we define an <u>if</u>-<u>then</u>-<u>else</u>-<u>fi</u> function: $W \times C \times C \to C$, by putting

$$\underline{\text{if}}\text{-}\underline{\text{then}}\text{-}\underline{\text{else}}\text{-}\underline{\text{fi}}(\beta,c_1,c_2) = \begin{cases} c_1, & \text{if } \beta = tt \\ c_2, & \text{if } \beta = ff. \end{cases}$$

As might be expected, we always write <u>if</u> β <u>then</u> c_1 <u>else</u> c_2 <u>fi</u> for <u>if</u>-<u>then</u>-<u>else</u>-<u>fi</u>(β,c_1,c_2).

Finally, we arrive at our first semantic definition:

<u>DEFINITION 2.3</u> (semantics of $s \in \mathcal{I}exp$ and $b \in \mathcal{B}exp$).

a. $\mathcal{V}(x)(\sigma) = \sigma(x)$

$\mathcal{V}(m)(\sigma) = \alpha$, where α is the integer denoted by the integer constant m (cf. the remark following definition 2.2)

$\mathcal{V}(s_1 + s_2)(\sigma) = \mathcal{V}(s_1)(\sigma) + \mathcal{V}(s_2)(\sigma)$

...

$\mathcal{V}(\underline{\text{if}}\ b\ \underline{\text{then}}\ s_1\ \underline{\text{else}}\ s_2\ \underline{\text{fi}})(\sigma) =$

$\underline{\text{if}}\ \mathcal{W}(b)(\sigma)\ \underline{\text{then}}\ \mathcal{V}(s_1)(\sigma)\ \underline{\text{else}}\ \mathcal{V}(s_2)(\sigma)\ \underline{\text{fi}}$

b. $\mathcal{W}(\underline{\text{true}})(\sigma) = \text{tt}$

$\mathcal{W}(\underline{\text{false}})(\sigma) = \text{ff}$

$\mathcal{W}(s_1 = s_2)(\sigma) = (\mathcal{V}(s_1)(\sigma) = \mathcal{V}(s_2)(\sigma))$

...

$\mathcal{W}(\neg b)(\sigma) = \neg \mathcal{W}(b)(\sigma)$

$\mathcal{W}(b_1 \supset b_2)(\sigma) = \mathcal{W}(b_1)(\sigma) \Rightarrow \mathcal{W}(b_2)(\sigma)$

END 2.3.

Remark. The reader should observe the difference in the three uses of "=" in the third line of clause b. The left-most "=" sign has a priori no meaning whatsoever, and is waiting to be assigned a meaning through our formalism. The second "=" sign is the definitional equality sign (in current mathematical literature also denoted by ":=" (which we always avoid because of its occurrence in assignment statements) or $\overset{\text{df.}}{=}$ (which we usually avoid because we find it too cumbersome)). The third "=" sign is the mathematical function of equality: $V \times V \to W$, assumed to be known in the paragraph immediately preceding the definition.

Examples

1. Assume that σ is such that $\sigma(x) = 3$, $\sigma(y) = 4$.

   $\mathcal{V}(\underline{\text{if}}\ x = y\ \underline{\text{then}}\ x + z\ \underline{\text{else}}\ y + 1\ \underline{\text{fi}})(\sigma) = 5$, for

   a. $\mathcal{W}(x = y)(\sigma) = (\mathcal{V}(x)(\sigma) = \mathcal{V}(y)(\sigma)) = (\sigma(x) = \sigma(y)) = (3 = 4) = \text{ff}$

   b. $\mathcal{V}(y+1)(\sigma) = \mathcal{V}(y)(\sigma) + \mathcal{V}(1)(\sigma) = \sigma(y) + 1 = 4 + 1 = 5$.

2. a. $\mathcal{W}(\neg\underline{\text{true}} \supset \underline{\text{true}})(\sigma) = \text{tt}$, for we can apply the last clause of definition 2.3b, with $b_1 \equiv \neg\underline{\text{true}}$ and $b_2 \equiv \underline{\text{true}}$, for which we have that $\mathcal{W}(b_1)(\sigma) = \text{ff}$ and $\mathcal{W}(b_2)(\sigma) = \text{tt}$, whence $\mathcal{W}(b_1 \supset b_2)(\sigma) = (\text{ff} \Rightarrow \text{tt}) = \text{tt}$

   b. $\mathcal{W}(\neg\underline{\text{true}} \supset \underline{\text{true}})(\sigma) = \text{ff}$, for we can apply the one but last clause of definition 2.3b, with $b = \underline{\text{true}} \supset \underline{\text{true}}$, for which we can easily establish that $\mathcal{W}(b)(\sigma) = \text{tt}$, whence $\mathcal{W}(\neg b)(\sigma) = \text{ff}$

   c. Thus, we see that our syntax is *ambiguous*, allowing more than one parsing for certain expressions, with corresponding difference in meaning. We can remedy this by either appealing to the usual priority conventions about the operators concerned (which we shall mostly do in the sequel) or by adding parentheses (to which we shall occasionally resort below). For the suspicious reader, let us remark that adding parentheses may well be dealt with formally (though, as remarked above, we shall always avoid this) by adding, in the case at hand, the two syntactic clauses s ::= ...| (s) and b ::= ...| (b), and the semantic clauses $\mathcal{V}((s))(\sigma) = \mathcal{V}(s)(\sigma)$ and $\mathcal{W}((b))(\sigma) = \mathcal{W}(b)(\sigma)$. The possibility of ambiguous constructs is now up to the programmer. Exclusion of *all* ambiguity would be achieved by replacing the relevant clauses in the syntax by $s::= \ldots(s_1+s_2) \ldots$, $b::= \ldots(b_1 \supset b_2) \ldots$, etc.

Next, we discuss how to define the meaning of a statement. In general, the effect of a statement will be to change the state. Letting $\mathcal{M}$ stand for the function that maps statements to their meanings, we therefore have as its type:

$$\mathcal{M}: Stat \to (\Sigma \to \Sigma).$$

Before giving the definition, we first need a notational preparation which introduces the notion of variant of a state:

DEFINITION 2.4 (variant of a state). For each $\sigma \in \Sigma$, $x \in Ivar$ and $a \in V$ we write $\sigma\{\alpha/x\}$ for the element of Σ which satisfies, for each $y \in Ivar$,

a. $\sigma\{\alpha/x\}(y) = \alpha$, if $y \equiv x$

b. $\sigma\{\alpha/x\}(y) = \sigma(y)$, if $y \not\equiv x$

END 2.4.

In words, $\sigma\{\alpha/x\}$ is like σ, but for its delivering α when applied to x. The following simple properties of the variant notation will often be employed in the sequel:

LEMMA 2.5.

a. $\sigma\{\sigma(x)/x\} = \sigma$

b. $\sigma\{\alpha_1/x\}\{\alpha_2/x\} = \sigma\{\alpha_2/x\}$

c. $\sigma\{\alpha_1/x\}\{\alpha_2/y\} = \sigma\{\alpha_2/y\}\{\alpha_1/x\}$, for $x \not\equiv y$.

PROOF. We prove only case c, leaving the others as exercise. Let $x \not\equiv y$. In order to show that the two functions $\sigma\{\alpha_1/x\}\{\alpha_2/y\}$ and $\sigma\{\alpha_2/y\}\{\alpha_1/x\}$ are the same, we must prove that they deliver the same value for each $z \in \mathit{Ivar}$.

1. $z \not\equiv x$, $z \not\equiv y$. By definition 2.4b, $\sigma\{\alpha_1/x\}\{\alpha_2/y\}(z) = \sigma\{\alpha_1/x\}(z) = \sigma(z) = \sigma\{\alpha_2/y\}(z) = \sigma\{\alpha_2/y\}\{\alpha_1/x\}(z)$
2. $z \equiv x$. Then $z \not\equiv y$, and by definition 2.4, $\sigma\{\alpha_1/x\}\{\alpha_2/y\}(z) = \sigma\{\alpha_1/x\}(z) = \alpha_1 = \sigma\{\alpha_2/y\}\{\alpha_1/x\}(z)$
3. $z \equiv y$. Similar to 2

END 2.5.

We now give the definition of $\mathcal{M}$:

DEFINITION 2.6 (semantics of $S \in \mathit{Stat}$).

a. $\mathcal{M}(x{:=}s)(\sigma) = \sigma\{\mathcal{V}(s)(\sigma)/x\}$

b. $\mathcal{M}(S_1;S_2)(\sigma) = \mathcal{M}(S_2)(\mathcal{M}(S_1)(\sigma))$

c. $\mathcal{M}(\underline{\text{if}}\ b\ \underline{\text{then}}\ S_1\ \underline{\text{else}}\ S_2\ \underline{\text{fi}})(\sigma) =$

$\quad \underline{\text{if}}\ \mathcal{W}(b)(\sigma)\ \underline{\text{then}}\ \mathcal{M}(S_1)(\sigma)\ \underline{\text{else}}\ \mathcal{M}(S_2)(\sigma)\ \underline{\text{fi}}$

END 2.6.

We see that $\mathcal{M}(x{:=}s)$ transforms σ into some σ' which is like σ, but for the fact that in x it yields $\mathcal{V}(s)(\sigma)$, i.e. the integer which is the value of the right-hand side of the assignment statement. Also, $\mathcal{M}(S_1;S_2)$ is obtained by composing the two functions $\mathcal{M}(S_2)$ and $\mathcal{M}(S_1)$, and $\mathcal{M}(\underline{\text{if}}\ b\ \underline{\text{then}}\ S_1\ \underline{\text{else}}\ S_2\ \underline{\text{fi}})$ should be clear.

Examples

1. M(x:=0; y:=x+1)(σ) = M(y:=x+1)(M(x:=0)(σ)) =
   M(y:=x+1)(σ{V(0)(σ)/x}) = M(y:=x+1)(σ{0/x}) =
   σ{0/x}{V(x+1)(σ{0/x})/y} =
   σ{0/x}{V(x)(σ{0/x}) + V(1)(σ{0/x})/y} =
   σ{0/x}{σ{0/x}(x) + 1/y} = σ{0/x}{0+1/y} = σ{0/x}{1/y}.
2. Let z $\not\equiv$ x, z $\not\equiv$ y and x $\not\equiv$ y. We leave it to the reader to verify that M(z:=x; x:=y; y:=z)(σ{2/x}{3/y}) = σ{3/x}{2/y}{2/z}.

2.2. Correctness formulae and their validity

With definition 2.6 we have settled the question as to what is the meaning of any S ∈ *Stat*. We now turn to the introduction of *correctness formulae* which we use to formally express various properties of the statements in our language. For this purpose, we need a number of preparations. First, it is convenient to have available some additional logical operators besides the operators ¬ and ⊃. Therefore we give

DEFINITION 2.7 (logical operators).

a. $b_1 \vee b_2 \equiv (\neg b_1) \supset b_2$
b. $b_1 \wedge b_2 \equiv \neg((\neg b_1) \vee (\neg b_2))$
c. $b_1 = b_2 \equiv (b_1 \supset b_2) \wedge (b_2 \supset b_1)$
d. $\underline{\text{if}}\ b\ \underline{\text{then}}\ b_1\ \underline{\text{else}}\ b_2\ \underline{\text{fi}} \equiv (b \wedge b_1) \vee ((\neg b) \wedge b_2)$

END 2.7.

We adhere to the usual convention about the priority of the logical operators: ¬, ∧, ∨, ⊃, = in order from highest to lowest priority. We shall not take the trouble to update this definition at later stages, when we shall apply it to the syntactic classes extending *Bexp*. Also, we shall freely use "∧" and "∨" as operators for truth-values in W.

Secondly, by way of preparation for the notion of *validity* to be introduced soon, we discuss a phenomenon which appears when we evaluate a boolean expression b. Three possibilities arise:

a. $\mathcal{W}(b)(\sigma)$ = tt for *all* σ. This is the case, for example, for the following boolean expressions: x+0 = x, b ∧ b = b, $(b_1 \supset b_2) \wedge (b_2 \supset b_3) \supset (b_1 \supset b_3)$, $b_1 \wedge b_2 \supset b_3 = b_1 \supset (b_2 \supset b_3)$, if b then s else s fi = s, if s = t then s else t fi = t, etc.

b. $\mathcal{W}(b)(\sigma)$ = ff, for *all* σ. Examples of such b are: false, x+y ≠ y+x, b ∧ ¬b, etc.

c. $\mathcal{W}(b)(\sigma)$ = tt for some σ, and $\mathcal{W}(b)(\sigma')$ = ff, for some $\sigma' \neq \sigma$. E.g. $\mathcal{W}(x = y)(\sigma\{0/x\}\{0/y\})$ = tt, whereas $\mathcal{W}(x = y)(\sigma\{0/x\}\{1/y\})$ = ff.

We ask the reader to keep this classification of boolean expressions in mind, since it will return in a more general setting below.

We now recall a few of the examples mentioned in the beginning of section 2.1, viz. {x = 0}x:=x+1{x = 1} and {true}x:=x+1{?}. We are interested in a class of syntactic constructs, viz. the class of *assertions* *Assn*, with typical elements p,q,r,..., which we shall use in *correctness formulae* of the form {p}S{q} intended to express that, when p holds before execution of S, then q holds after its execution. Whereas the example {x = 0}x:=x+1{x = 1} suggests that for the class of assertions we might take just the class of boolean expressions, from the other example {true}x:=x+1{?} we may infer that it is convenient to have available a richer class of constructions for *Assn*. We shall extend the class of boolean expressions with the possibility of existential quantification, thus allowing, for any x and p, ∃x[p] as an assertion. Once this is available we can use ∃y[x=y+1] as assertion which takes the place of the "?" above - and which, as we shall see in theorem 2.21, is indeed the best possible postcondition we are looking for. (It should be observed that, according to the meaning to be attributed presently to ∃y[p], we have that ∃y[x=y+1] has the value tt in all states, and we might just as well have taken true as the best possible postcondition. However, in more complex cases dealing with generalized languages such simplification may well be impossible. Also, as we shall see in theorem 2.21, the $\exists y[p]$ formalism allows a direct means of finding the best possible postcondition for a given assignment statement and precondition, and it is therefore useful as well in those cases where the postcondition may be eventually simplified to some element of *Bexp*.)

All this brings us to

DEFINITION 2.8 (syntax of assertions). The class of assertions *Assn*, with typical elements p,q,r,..., is given by

$$p ::= \underline{true} \mid \underline{false} \mid s_1 = s_2 \mid \ldots \mid \neg p \mid p_1 \supset p_2 \mid \exists x[p]$$

END 2.8.

Examples. $\underline{true}$, $x = y$, $\exists y[x = y+1]$, $\neg\exists x[x \neq x]$, etc.

(The reader who would be tempted to replace definition 2.8 by the simpler one $p ::= b \mid \exists x[p]$, should verify that then the fourth example would not qualify as an assertion.)

Convention. Assertions of the form $\exists x_1[\exists x_2[\ldots\exists x_n[p]\ldots]]$, with x_i, $i = 1,\ldots,n$, all different, are usually abbreviated to $\exists x_1,\ldots,x_n[p]$.

Just like boolean expressions, assertions obtain truth-values as their meaning in a given state, i.e. as type of the function $\mathcal{T}$ assigning meaning to assertions one would expect $\mathcal{T}$: *Assn* $\to (\Sigma \to W)$. Somewhat surprisingly, this is not precisely what we do. Instead, we introduce a set $T = \{tt,ff\}$ (which thus coincides with W), and put

$$\mathcal{T}: \mathit{Assn} \to (\Sigma \to T).$$

The reason for this is that in later refinements of the theory the sets W and T are no longer identical, and we anticipate this by already now using different letters.

DEFINITION 2.9 (semantics of assertions).

a. $\mathcal{T}(\underline{\text{true}})(\sigma) = \text{tt}$

b. $\mathcal{T}(\underline{\text{false}})(\sigma) = \text{ff}$

c. $\mathcal{T}(s_1 = s_2)(\sigma) = (\mathcal{V}(s_1)(\sigma) = \mathcal{V}(s_2)(\sigma))$

d. $\mathcal{T}(\neg p)(\sigma) = \neg\mathcal{T}(p)(\sigma)$

e. $\mathcal{T}(p_1 \supset p_2)(\sigma) = \mathcal{T}(p_1)(\sigma) \Rightarrow \mathcal{T}(p_2)(\sigma)$

f. $$\mathcal{T}(\exists x[p])(\sigma) = \begin{cases} \text{tt, if there exists some } \alpha \text{ such that} \\ \qquad \mathcal{T}(p)(\sigma\{\alpha/x\}) = \text{tt} \\ \text{ff, otherwise.} \end{cases}$$

END 2.9.

Cases a to e in this definition should be clear. As example of case f take $\mathcal{T}(\exists y[x=y+1])(\sigma)$, for $x \neq y$. This yields the value tt, since $\mathcal{T}(x=y+1)(\sigma\{\alpha/y\}) = \text{tt}$ for that α which satisfies $\alpha = \mathcal{V}(x-1)(\sigma)$.

At last, we are ready for the introduction of a central notion of our framework, viz. that of correctness formula.

DEFINITION 2.10 (syntax of correctness formulae). The class of correctness formulae *Form* with typical elements f,..., is defined by

$$f ::= p \mid \{p\}S\{q\} \mid s_1 = s_2 \mid f_1 \wedge f_2$$

END 2.10.

According to this definition, correctness formulae are of four kinds:

- Each assertion is a correctness formula. Examples are, besides those encountered above, assertions such as $\underline{\text{if}}$ $\underline{\text{true}}$ $\underline{\text{then}}$ s_1 $\underline{\text{else}}$ s_2 $\underline{\text{fi}}$ $= s_1$, $\exists x[x \neq x]$, $x + y > z$. These three examples suggest that it is possible to distinguish three types of formulae: those which are necessarily true, those which are necessarily false, and those which may or may not be true. This classification was already announced in our remarks on the values of boolean expressions above.
- Each construct {p}S{q} is a correctness formula. Examples are

{x > 0}x:= x+1{x > 1}, {true}x:=x+1{false}, and {x = 0}x:=x+1{y = 1}. In a formula {p}S{q} we call p the *precondition* and q the *postcondition*.

- Examples of formulae of the third kind are: if b then S_1 else S_2 fi; S = if b then S_1;S else S_2;S fi, x:=0 = x:=1, and x:=s;y:=t = y:=t;x:=s.
- Finally, correctness formulae may be composed by conjunction, yielding constructs such as {x = 0}x:=x+1{x = 1} ∧ {x = 1}y:=x+y{∃z[x=1 ∧ y=x+z]}.

The meaning of a correctness formula is given by a function $\mathcal{F}$, of type

$$\mathcal{F}: \mathit{Form} \to (\Sigma \to T)$$

as defined in

DEFINITION 2.11 (semantics of correctness formulae).

a. $\mathcal{F}(p)(\sigma) = \mathcal{T}(p)(\sigma)$
b. $\mathcal{F}(\{p\}S\{q\})(\sigma) = (\mathcal{T}(p)(\sigma) \Rightarrow \mathcal{T}(q)(\mathcal{M}(S)(\sigma)))$
c. $\mathcal{F}(S_1 = S_2)(\sigma) = (\mathcal{M}(S_1)(\sigma) = \mathcal{M}(S_2)(\sigma))$
d. $\mathcal{F}(f_1 \wedge f_2)(\sigma) = \mathcal{F}(f_1)(\sigma) \wedge \mathcal{F}(f_2)(\sigma)$

END 2.11.

Correctness formulae which obtain the value tt for all σ are called *valid*:

DEFINITION 2.12 (validity). Let $f \in \mathit{Form}$. If $\mathcal{F}(f)(\sigma) = tt$ for all σ, we call f valid, and express this by writing

$$\models f$$

END 2.12.

Remark (for the reader with some background in logic). This notion of validity actually corresponds to *arithmetical truth*, i.e. truth in the standard model of arithmetic. It is not the same as the usual notion of (logical) validity which means truth in *arbitrary* models.

Examples of valid correctness formulae are

1. Valid assertions

   a. $\models x + 0 = x$, $\models x + y = y + x$, etc.

   b. $\models p_1 \wedge p_2 = p_2 \wedge p_1$, $\models p \wedge p = p$, $\models (p_1 \supset p_2) \wedge (p_2 \supset p_3) \supset (p_1 \supset p_3)$, $\models p_1 \supset (p_2 \supset p_3) = p_1 \wedge p_2 \supset p_3$, etc.

   c. Let $\forall x[p]$ be short for $\neg\exists x[\neg p]$. Then $\models \forall x \forall y \exists z[x + z = y]$, $\models \forall x[p_1 \supset \exists x[p_2]] = \exists x[p_1] \supset \exists x[p_2]$ (this example is elaborated below), etc.

   d. $\models$ <u>if</u> b <u>then</u> b_1 <u>else</u> b_2 <u>fi</u> $= (b \supset b_1) \wedge (\neg b \supset b_2)$

   $\models$ <u>if</u> <u>true</u> <u>then</u> s_1 <u>else</u> s_2 <u>fi</u> $= s_1$

   $\models$ <u>if</u> <u>false</u> <u>then</u> s_1 <u>else</u> s_2 <u>fi</u> $= s_2$

   $\models$ <u>if</u> b <u>then</u> s <u>else</u> s <u>fi</u> = s

   $\models$ <u>if</u> b <u>then</u> <u>if</u> b <u>then</u> s_1 <u>else</u> s_2 <u>fi</u> <u>else</u> s_3 <u>fi</u> =
   <u>if</u> b <u>then</u> s_1 <u>else</u> s_3 <u>fi</u>

   $\models$ <u>if</u> b <u>then</u> s_1 <u>else</u> <u>if</u> b <u>then</u> s_2 <u>else</u> s_3 <u>fi</u> <u>fi</u> =
   <u>if</u> b <u>then</u> s_1 <u>else</u> s_3 <u>fi</u>

   $\models$ <u>if</u> b <u>then</u> s_1 <u>else</u> s_2 <u>fi</u> = <u>if</u> $\neg$b <u>then</u> s_2 <u>else</u> s_1 <u>fi</u>

   $\models$ <u>if</u> <u>if</u> b <u>then</u> b_1 <u>else</u> b_2 <u>fi</u> <u>then</u> s_1 <u>else</u> s_2 <u>fi</u> =
   <u>if</u> b <u>then</u> <u>if</u> b_1 <u>then</u> s_1 <u>else</u> s_2 <u>fi</u> <u>else</u> <u>if</u> b_2 <u>then</u> s_1 <u>else</u> s_2 <u>fi</u> <u>fi</u>

   $\models$ <u>if</u> b <u>then</u> s_1 <u>else</u> s_2 <u>fi</u> + s = <u>if</u> b <u>then</u> s_1 + s <u>else</u> s_2 + s <u>fi</u>

   $\models$ <u>if</u> s = t <u>then</u> s <u>else</u> t <u>fi</u> = t,

   etc.

A systematic study of the validity of assertions, in particular of the kind as suggested in examples 1a to 1c, is made in (propositional and) predicate logic. Usually, it is intuitively clear why an assertion is valid; formal methods to derive this are available, but not studied in the present treatise which concentrates on the validity of formulae of the second ({p}S{q}) and, to a much lesser extent, of the third kind ($S_1 = S_2$). In the sequel we shall usually not dwell on the reasons why a particular assertion is valid, but assume that the reader is able to verify this on the basis of the definitions, if desired.

We give some of the details of the last example of 1c. To show $\models \forall x[p_1 \supset \exists x[p_2]] = (\exists x[p_1] \supset \exists x[p_2])$, i.e. that $\models \forall x[p_1 \supset \exists x[p_2]] \supset (\exists x[p_1] \supset \exists x[p_2])$, and $\models (\exists x[p_1] \supset \exists x[p_2]) \supset \forall x[p_1 \supset \exists x[p_2]]$. We restrict ourselves to the first subcase, i.e. to showing that $\models \forall x[p_1 \supset \exists x[p_2]] \supset (\exists x[p_1] \supset \exists x[p_2])$, or, equivalently, $\models \forall x[p_1 \supset \exists x[p_2]] \wedge \exists x[p_1] \supset \exists x[p_2]$. Choose some σ, and assume that $T(\forall x[p_1 \supset \exists x[p_2]])(\sigma)$ and $T(\exists x[p_1])(\sigma)$ both hold. To show that $T(\exists x[p_2])(\sigma)$ holds. Since $T(\exists x[p_1])(\sigma)$ holds, $T(p_1)(\sigma\{\alpha'/x\})$ holds for some α'. Since $T(\forall x[p_1 \supset \exists x[p_2]])(\sigma)$ holds, there exists no α'' such that $T(p_1)(\sigma\{\alpha''/x\})$ and $T(\neg\exists x[p_2])(\sigma\{\alpha''/x\})$ both hold. Since $T(p_1)(\sigma\{\alpha'/x\})$ holds, we infer that $T(\neg\exists x[p_2])(\sigma\{\alpha'/x\})$ does not hold, i.e. $T(\exists x[p_2])(\sigma\{\alpha'/x\})$ *does* hold. By definition, $T(\exists x[p_2])(\sigma\{\alpha'/x\})$ holds iff, for some α''', $T(p_2)(\sigma\{\alpha'/x\}\{\alpha'''/x\})$ holds, i.e. iff $T(p_2)(\sigma\{\alpha'''/x\})$ holds, i.e. iff $T(\exists x[p_2])(\sigma)$ holds, as was to be shown.

2. Valid constructs of the form {p}S{q}

$\models$ {x = 0}x:=x+1{x=1}, $\models$ {<u>true</u>}x:=x+1{∃y[x = y+1]}, x ≢ y,

$\models$ {x = 5} <u>if</u> x > 0 <u>then</u> x:=x+y <u>else</u> x:=x-y <u>fi</u> {x = 5+y},

$\models$ {<u>false</u>}S{p}, $\models$ {p}S{<u>true</u>}, $\models$ {x = 0 ∧ y = 1}x:=x+1; y:=y+x{x = 1 ∧ y = 2} etc. We give a few selected details.

a. $\models$ {<u>true</u>}x:=x+1{∃y[x = y+1]}. Assume x ≢ y. By the definitions, we have to show that, for all σ, $T(\underline{true})(\sigma) \Rightarrow T(\exists y[x = y+1])(M(x:=x+1)(\sigma))$, i.e. that $tt \Rightarrow T(\exists y[x = y+1])(\sigma\{V(x+1)(\sigma)/x\})$, or $T(\exists y[x = y+1])(\sigma\{\sigma(x) + 1/x\})$, or $T(x = y+1)(\sigma\{\sigma(x) + 1/x\}\{\alpha/y\})$ for some α. Clearly, it is sufficient to take $\alpha = \sigma(x)$

b. $\models$ {false}S{p}. By the definitions, we have to show that, for all σ, T(false)(σ) ⇒ T(p)(M(S)(σ)), i.e. that ff ⇒ T(p)(M(S)(σ)), which is clearly satisfied.

3. Valid equivalences

a. $\models$ if b then S else S fi = S, etc. (The analogs of many of the examples under 1d may be taken over.)

b. $\models$ x:=y; y:=x = x:=y

$\models$ x:=y; x:=z = x:=z, provided that x ≢ z

$\models$ x:=y; z:=x = x:=y; z:=y

$\models$ x:=y; z:=y = z:=y; x:=y

$\models$ x:=y; z:=u = z:=u; x:=y, provided that x ≢ z, x ≢ u and y ≢ z.

c. $\models$ if b then S_1 else S_2 fi; S = if b then S_1;S else S_2;S fi

$\models$ x:= if b then s_1 else s_2 fi = if b then x:=s_1 else x:=s_2 fi.

Consider, e.g., the second of examples 3b. Take any σ. Then M(x:=y;x:=z)(σ) = M(x:=z)(M(x:=y)(σ)) = M(x:=z)(σ{σ(y)/x}) = σ{σ(y)/x}{σ{σ(y)/x}(z)/x} = (lemma 2.5) σ{σ{σ(y)/x}(z)/x} = (x≢z)σ{σ(z)/x} = M(x:=z)(σ).

4. Valid conjunctions of correctness formulae. Using the observation that $\models f_1 \wedge f_2$ iff $\models f_1$ and $\models f_2$, we may combine any two of the previously listed valid formulae.

By way of contrast, we also list a few invalid correctness formulae: x = y, (x = 0) ⊃ (x = 1), ¬((x = 0) ⊃ (x = 1)), {x = 0}x:=x+1{y = 1}, x:=s;y:=t = y:=t;x:=s, S;if b then S_1 else S_2 fi = if b then S;S_1 else S;S_2 fi, etc.

We discuss two cases.

a. (x = 0) ⊃ (x = 1) and ¬((x = 0) ⊃ (x = 1)). Clearly, $\models$ (x = 0) ⊃ (x = 1) does not hold. However, the reader might be tempted to think that $\models$ ¬((x = 0) ⊃ (x = 1)) *does* hold, i.e. that, for all σ, T(¬((x = 0) ⊃ (x = 1)))(σ) = tt, or that, for all σ, T((x = 0) ⊃ (x = 1))(σ) = ff, which may be simplified to: for all σ, (σ(x) = 0 ⇒ σ(x) = 1) = ff. As counter example, take any σ' such that σ'(x) ≠ 0. Then the implication reduces to ff $\Rightarrow$ ($\sigma'(x) = 1$), i.e. to tt

b. S; <u>if</u> b <u>then</u> S_1 <u>else</u> S_2 <u>fi</u> = <u>if</u> b <u>then</u> S;S_1 <u>else</u> S;S_2 <u>fi</u>. Take S $\equiv$ x:=0, b $\equiv$ x = 0, $S_1 \equiv$ x:=1 and $S_2 \equiv$ x:=2, and choose some σ such that $\sigma(x) \neq 0$.

2.3. The assignment statement

This section is devoted to an analysis of valid {p}S{q} formulae in the case that S is an assignment statement. Two possible ways of attacking this problem arise from the preceding discussions:

- For given p and x:=s, find some q such that $\models$ {p}x:=s{q} holds. Also, we prefer some interesting q, and not, for example, just <u>true</u>.
- For given q and x:=s find some p such that $\models$ {p}x:=s{q} holds. Again, p should not be trivial, such as <u>false</u>.

The two subproblems can indeed be satisfactorily solved, provided one further tool is available, viz. that of *substitution*. In general, substitution is the notion which refers to a linguistic process of replacing, in a certain piece of text, some variable by some expression of appropriate type. At the present stage we are interested in three cases:

- Substitute an integer expression t for an integer variable x in an integer expression s. The result is to be denoted by s[t/x].
- Substitute an integer expression t for an integer variable x in an assertion p. The result is written as p[t/x]; since $\mathit{Bexp} \subseteq \mathit{Assn}$, this also defines b[t/x].
- Substitute an integer variable y for an integer variable x in a statement S (the result written as S[y/x]).

Observe that we do not define S[t/x]. Replacing, for example, in the assignment statement x:=0 the integer variable x by the integer expression t would lead to the syntactically not well-formed construction t:=0. Substitution is fairly straightforward to define, but for one complication which arises through the presence of constructs of the form ∃y[p]. Occurrences of y in such a construct are called *bound*, and we have to make sure that in substitution we only replace *free* (i.e. not bound) occurrences. Moreover, we have to be careful how to treat cases as exemplified by ∃y[x = y+1][s/x]. In general, we expect from substitution that it preserves validity, i.e. we expect that if ⊨ p, then ⊨ p[s/x] holds for arbitrary s. Now, clearly, ⊨ ∃y[x = y+1], but a direct replacement of x by s in this formula leads to a possibly invalid assertion, i.e. we do not necessarily have that ⊨ ∃y[s = y+1]. It is sufficient to take s ≡ y as a counter example. Therefore, we have to avoid that some free occurrence of y in s turns into a bound occurrence as the result of replacing x by s in ∃y[p]. The precaution which is needed here is to first replace ∃y[x = y+1] by the equivalent expression ∃y'[x = y'+1], where y' does not occur free in s, and only then replacing x by s, thus yielding ∃y'[s = y'+1], which is clearly valid again. These considerations motivate the following two definitions.

DEFINITION 2.13 (free and bound occurrences, *ivar*).

a. An occurrence of an integer variable x in an assertion p is bound if it is within a subexpression of p of the form ∃x[p']. Otherwise, occurrences of x in p are free. An integer variable x occurs free in p if it has at least one free occurrence in p.
b. The set of all integer variables occurring in S, s, or b, or occurring *free* in p is denoted by *ivar*(S), *ivar*(s), *ivar*(b), or *ivar*(p), respectively.

END 2.13.

Remarks

1. Note that *ivar*(∃x[p]) = *ivar*(p)\{x}.
2. Notations such as *ivar*(s) ∪ *ivar*(p) or *ivar*(S_1) ∪ *ivar*(S_2) will always be abbreviated to *ivar*(s,p) or *ivar*(S_1,S_2) etc.

Examples. y occurs free and x occurs both free and bound in $(x>0) \supset \exists x[y>x]$. Also, *ivar*(<u>if</u> x>y <u>then</u> z+1 <u>else</u> u+2 <u>fi</u>) = {x,y,z,u}, *ivar*($(x>0) \supset \exists x[y>x]$) = {x,y}, and *ivar*($x+y, \exists z[z>u]$) = {x,y,u}.

<u>DEFINITION 2.14</u> (substitution).

a. $(z:=s)[y/x] \equiv (z[y/x]:=s[y/x])$

$(S_1;S_2)[y/x] \equiv S_1[y/x];\ S_2[y/x]$

(<u>if</u> b <u>then</u> S_1 <u>else</u> S_2 <u>fi</u>)[y/x] ≡ <u>if</u> b[y/x] <u>then</u> $S_1[y/x]$ <u>else</u> $S_2[y/x]$ <u>fi</u>

b. $y[s/x] \equiv \begin{cases} s, & \text{if } y \equiv x \\ y, & \text{if } y \not\equiv x \end{cases}$

$m[s/x] \equiv m$

$(s_1 + s_2)[s/x] \equiv (s_1[s/x] + s_2[s/x])$

(<u>if</u> b <u>then</u> s_1 <u>else</u> s_2 <u>fi</u>)[s/x] ≡ <u>if</u> b[s/x] <u>then</u> $s_1[s/x]$ <u>else</u> $s_2[s/x]$ <u>fi</u>

c. <u>true</u> [s/x] ≡ <u>true</u>, <u>false</u> [s/x] ≡ <u>false</u>,

$(s_1 = s_2)[s/x] \equiv (s_1[s/x] = s_2\ [s/x])$

$(\neg p)[s/x] \equiv \neg(p[s/x])$

$(p_1 \supset p_2)[s/x] \equiv (p_1[s/x] \supset p_2[s/x])$

$\exists y[p][s/x] \equiv \exists y[p]$, if $y \equiv x$

$\equiv \exists y[p[s/x]]$, if $y \not\equiv x$ and $y \notin$ *ivar*(s)

$\equiv \exists y'[p[y'/y][s/x]]$, if $y \not\equiv x$ and $y \in$ *ivar*(s), where y' is the first integer variable such that $y' \not\equiv x$ and $y' \notin$ *ivar*(p,s).

END 2.14.

Remarks

1. The definition of b[s/x] should be immediate from that of p[s/x] and has therefore been omitted
2. The requirement (in the last part of clause c) that y' be the *first* integer variable is imposed to ensure uniqueness of the resulting assertion.

Examples

1. (<u>if</u> x > y+z <u>then</u> x:=x+y <u>else</u> y:=y-z <u>fi</u>)[z/x] ≡
   <u>if</u> z > y+z <u>then</u> z:=z+y <u>else</u> y:=y-z <u>fi</u>
2. (<u>if</u> x > y+z <u>then</u> x+y <u>else</u> y-z <u>fi</u>)[y+z/y] ≡
   <u>if</u> x > ((y+z)+z) <u>then</u> x + (y+z) <u>else</u> (y+z) - z <u>fi</u>
3. ∃y[0 < y ∧ y < x][x+y/x] ≡ ∃y'[0 < y' ∧ y' < x+y], where y' is the first integer variable ≢ x,y

We now have sufficient definitions available for the formulation of

<u>THEOREM 2.15</u> (correctness of assignment statements).

a. ⊨ {p[s/x]}x:=s{p}

b. ⊨ {p}x:=s{∃y[p[y/x] ∧ x = s[y/x]]} *where* y *is some variable such that* y ≢ x, *and* y ∉ *ivar*(p,s)

Note that clause a is a backward rule in that it yields, for each x:=s and postcondition p, a (best possible, see section 2.4) precondition q such that {q}x:=s{p} is valid. Also, clause b is a forward rule yielding, for each precondition p and statement x:=s, the best possible postcondition. The intuition behind these two rules is the following:

a. If p holds with s replacing x before the assignment x:=s, then p holds after the assignment.
b. If p holds before the assignment, then p[y/x] holds after the assignment, where y is some new variable which has the old value of x as its current value. Moreover, for the same y, x = s[y/x] holds.

We precede the proof of the theorem first by a few examples of applying it and then by an auxiliary lemma.

1. ⊨ {(x+0)[0/x]}x:=0{x = 0}, or
   ⊨ {0 = 0}x:=0{x = 0}, which is equivalent to
   ⊨ {<u>true</u>}x:=0{x = 0}

   In words, whatever the precondition, after execution of x:=0 the postcondition x = 0 always holds.

2. $\models$ {(x > y-z)[x-y/x]}x:=x-y{x > y-z}, or

$\models$ {x-y > y-z}x:=x-y{x > y-z}, or

$\models$ {x > 2×y-z}x:=x-y{x > y-z}

3. $\models$ {true}x:=x-y{∃z[true [z/x] ∧ x = (x-y)[z/x]]}, or

$\models$ {true}x:=x-y{∃z[x = z-y]}.

In words, if the precondition doesn't tell us anything about x, then after the execution of x:=x-y we know that for some z (which we choose such that its value equals the value of x before the assignment) we have that x=z-y.

In the auxiliary lemma below, we use the notation $\sigma|$*ivar*(s) (etc.) to denote the function σ, *restricted* to the set *ivar*(s) (which, as we saw above, is a subset of *Ivar*, the domain of σ).

LEMMA 2.16.

a. If $\sigma|$*ivar*(s) = $\sigma'|$*ivar*(s), then $\mathcal{V}$(s)(σ) = $\mathcal{V}$(s)(σ'), and similarly for b and p.

b. If x $\notin$ *ivar*(s), then $\mathcal{V}$(s)($\sigma\{\alpha/x\}$) = $\mathcal{V}$(s)(σ), and similarly for b and p

c. $\mathcal{V}$(s[t/x])(σ) = $\mathcal{V}$(s)($\sigma\{\mathcal{V}(t)(\sigma)/x\}$), and similarly for b and p.

PROOF.

a. The proof proceeds by (simultaneous) induction on the complexity of s and b, and of p.

We prove a few selected subcases.

(i) s ≡ x. Since $\sigma|$*ivar*(x) = $\sigma'|$*ivar*(x), we have that σ(x) = σ'(x), and $\mathcal{V}$(x)(σ) = $\mathcal{V}$(x)(σ') follows.

(ii) s ≡ if b then s_1 else s_2 fi. Then $\mathcal{V}$(s)(σ) = if $\mathcal{W}$(b)(σ) then $\mathcal{V}(s_1)(\sigma)$ else $\mathcal{V}(s_2)(\sigma)$ fi = (ind. hyp. for b and s) if $\mathcal{W}$(b)(σ') then $\mathcal{V}(s_1)(\sigma')$ else $\mathcal{V}(s_2)(\sigma')$ fi = $\mathcal{V}$(s)(σ').

(iii) p ≡ ∃x[p_1]. From the assumption $\sigma|$*ivar*(p) = $\sigma'|$*ivar*(p) we obtain $\sigma|(ivar(p_1)\backslash\{x\})$ = $\sigma'|(ivar(p_1)\backslash\{x\})$, whence, for all α, $\sigma\{\alpha/x\}|ivar(p_1) = \sigma'\{\alpha/x\}|ivar(p_1)$. By the induction hypothesis, $T(p_1)(\sigma\{\alpha/x\}) = T(p_1)(\sigma'\{\alpha/x\})$, and $\exists\alpha[T(p_1)(\sigma\{\alpha/x\})] = \exists\alpha[T(p_1)(\sigma'\{\alpha/x\})]$, i.e. $T(p)(\sigma) = T(p)(\sigma')$, follows.

b. Immediate by part a.

c. The proof again proceeds by (simultaneous) induction on the complexity of s and b, and of p. We treat a few representative subcases. Let $\alpha = V(t)(\sigma)$.

(i) $s \equiv x$. Then $V(s[t/x])(\sigma) = V(t)(\sigma) = \alpha = \sigma\{\alpha/x\}(x) = V(s)(\sigma\{\alpha/x\})$. $s \equiv y$, with $y \not\equiv x$. Then $V(s[t/x])(\sigma) = V(y)(\sigma) = \sigma(y) = \sigma\{\alpha/x\}(y) = V(s)(\sigma\{\alpha/x\})$.

(ii) $p \equiv (s_1 = s_2)$. $T((s_1 = s_2)[t/x])(\sigma) = (V(s_1[t/x])(\sigma) = V(s_2[t/x])(\sigma)) =$ (ind.) $(V(s_1)(\sigma\{\alpha/x\}) = V(s_2)(\sigma\{\alpha/x\})) = T(s_1 = s_2)(\sigma\{\alpha/x\})$.

(iii) $p \equiv \exists y[p_1]$

(α) $x \equiv y$. $T(\exists x[p_1][t/x])(\sigma) = T(\exists x[p_1])(\sigma) = T(\exists x[p_1])(\sigma\{\alpha/x\})$, by part b.

(β) $x \not\equiv y$, and $y \notin ivar(t)$. We only consider the case that $T(\exists y[p_1][t/x])(\sigma) = tt$, leaving the ff-case as an exercise.

$T(\exists y[p_1][t/x])(\sigma) =$ (def. 2.14)
$T(\exists y[p_1[t/x]])(\sigma) =$ (def. 2.9, with α' suitably chosen)
$T(p_1[t/x])(\sigma\{\alpha'/y\}) =$ (induction hypothesis)
$T(p_1)(\sigma\{\alpha'/y\}\{V(t)(\sigma\{\alpha'/y\})/x\}) =$ ($y \notin ivar(t)$ and part b)
$T(p_1)(\sigma\{\alpha'/y\}\{V(t)(\sigma)/x\}) =$ (lemma 2.5)
$T(p_1)(\sigma\{\alpha/x\}\{\alpha'/y\}) =$ (def. 2.9)
$T(\exists y[p_1])(\sigma\{\alpha/x\})$.

(γ) $x \not\equiv y$, and $y \in ivar(t)$. As above, we only consider the tt-case.

$T(\exists y[p_1][t/x])(\sigma) =$ (def. 2.14)
$T(\exists y'[p_1[y'/y][t/x]])(\sigma) =$ (def. 2.9, with α' suitably chosen)

$T(p_1[y'/y][t/x])(\sigma\{\alpha'/y'\})$ = (since p_1 and $p_1[y'/y]$ have the same complexity (which is less than that of $\exists y[p_1]$) we can apply the induction hypothesis; also, since y' does not occur in t, $V(t)(\sigma\{\alpha'/y'\}) = V(t)(\sigma) = \alpha$)

$T(p_1[y'/y])(\sigma\{\alpha'/y'\}\{\alpha/x\})$ = (induction hypothesis)

$T(p_1)(\sigma\{\alpha'/y'\}\{\alpha/x\}\{\sigma\{\alpha'/y'\}\{\alpha/x\}(y')/y\})$ = (lemma 2.5)

$T(p_1)(\sigma\{\alpha/x\}\{\alpha'/y\}\{\alpha'/y'\})$ = ($y' \notin$ *ivar*(p_1) and part b)

$T(p_1)(\sigma\{\alpha/x\}\{\alpha'/y\})$ = (def. 2.9)

$T(\exists y[p_1])(\sigma\{\alpha/x\})$.

END 2.16.

We now give the

PROOF of theorem 2.15.

a. We show that $\models$ {p[s/x]}x:=s{p}, or, by definitions 2.11 and 2.12, that for all σ, $T(p[s/x])(\sigma) \Rightarrow T(p)(M(x:=s)(\sigma))$. By lemma 2.16 and definition 2.6, we may replace this by: for all σ, $T(p)(\sigma\{V(s)(\sigma)/x\}) \Rightarrow T(p)(\sigma\{V(s)(\sigma)/x\})$, which is clearly satisfied.

b. We show that $\models$ {p}x:=s{∃y[p[y/x] ∧ x=s[y/x]]}, where y is some integer variable, $\not\equiv$ x, and such that $y \notin$ *ivar*(s,p). Let $\alpha = V(s)(\sigma)$. From the definitions it follows that we have to prove that for each σ some α' can be found such that $T(p)(\sigma) \Rightarrow T(p[y/x] \wedge x=s[y/x])(\sigma\{\alpha/x\}\{\alpha'/y\})$. We choose $\alpha' = \sigma(x)$. Assume $T(p)(\sigma)$

(i) $T(p[y/x])(\sigma\{\alpha/x\}\{\alpha'/y\})$ = (lemma 2.16c)

$T(p)(\sigma\{\alpha/x\}\{\alpha'/y\}\{\sigma\{\alpha/x\}\{\alpha'/y\}(y)/x\})$ = (lemma 2.5)

$T(p)(\sigma\{\alpha'/x\}\{\alpha'/y\})$ = ($y \notin$ *ivar*(p) and lemma 2.16b)

$T(p)(\sigma\{\sigma(x)/x\})$ = (lemma 2.5)

$T(p)(\sigma)$

(ii) $T(x= s[y/x])(\sigma\{\alpha/x\}\{\alpha'/y\})$ = (def. 2.9 and $x \not\equiv y$)

$(\alpha= V(s[y/x])(\sigma\{\alpha/x\}\{\alpha'/y\}))$ = (lemma 2.16c)

$(\alpha = \mathcal{V}(s)(\sigma\{\alpha/x\}\{\alpha'/y\}\{\sigma\{\alpha/x\}\{\alpha'/y\}(y)/x\}))$ = (lemma 2.5)

$(\alpha = \mathcal{V}(s)(\sigma\{\alpha'/x\}\{\alpha'/y\}))$ = (y $\notin$ *ivar*(s) and lemma 2.16b)

$(\alpha = \mathcal{V}(s)(\sigma\{\sigma(x)/x\}))$ =

$(\alpha = \mathcal{V}(s)(\sigma))$

END 2.15.

With this theorem we have sufficient material to answer the questions of the beginning of this section. In fact, as we shall see in the next section, both the backward rule and the forward rule do yield the best possible results.

2.4. Weakest preconditions and strongest postconditions

We have encountered several times the idea that we are, usually, not interested in just any precondition p such that, for given S and q, $\models$ {p}S{q} holds (and symmetrically for the postcondition case), but in preconditions p and postconditions q which are best possible. We make this idea precise in

DEFINITION 2.17 (weakest preconditions and strongest postconditions).

a. An assertion p is a weakest precondition with respect to statement S and postcondition q whenever the following two requirements are satisfied
   (i) $\models$ {p}S{q}
   (ii) For each r, if $\models$ {r}S{q}, then $\models$ r $\supset$ p.
b. An assertion q is a strongest postcondition with respect to statement S and precondition p whenever the following two requirements are satisfied
   (i) $\models$ {p}S{q}
   (ii) For each r, if $\models$ {p}S{r}, then $\models$ q $\supset$ r.

END 2.17.

Remark. Requirements a(i) and a(ii) determine p uniquely as to its semantics (if p and p' both satisfy a(i) and a(ii) then $\models$ p = p'), but not as to its syntax (if p satisfies a(i) and a(ii), then so does, e.g., p $\wedge$ true). A similar remark applies to q.

For the study of weakest preconditions and strongest postconditions it is convenient to introduce a new syntactic class *Cond* which extends *Assn* with two constructs which play, for each S and p, the role of weakest precondition and strongest postcondition of S with respect to p, respectively. For the usual lack of a sufficient number of symbols, we shall also use p,q,r,... to range over *Cond*. In the sequel, it usually should be clear whether such p ranges over *Assn* or over *Cond*. In cases where this is of importance, we shall explicitly indicate it.

DEFINITION 2.18 (syntax of conditions).
The class of conditions *Cond*, with special elements p,q,r,..., is defined by

$$p ::= \underline{true} \mid \underline{false} \mid s_1 = s_2 \mid \ldots \mid \neg p \mid p_1 \supset p_2 \mid \exists x[p] \mid S \to p \mid p \leftarrow S$$

END 2.18.

Here, S $\to$ p stands for the weakest precondition of S with respect to p, and p $\leftarrow$ S for the strongest postcondition of S with respect to p. We shall use the convention that "$\to$" and "$\leftarrow$" have higher priority than the logical operators. For example, S $\to$ p = q should be parsed as ((S$\to$p)=q). The semantics of *Cond* is given by extending the function T: *Assn* $\to$ ($\Sigma \to$ T) to T: *Cond* $\to$($\Sigma \to$ T), as defined in

DEFINITION 2.19 (semantics of conditions).

a. p $\equiv$ true,..., p $\equiv$ $\exists x[p_1]$. These cases are identical to definition 2.9

b. $T(S \to p)(\sigma) = T(p)(M(S)(\sigma))$

c. $\mathcal{T}(p \leftarrow S)(\sigma) = \begin{cases} tt, & \text{if, for some } \sigma', \mathcal{T}(p)(\sigma') \text{ and } \sigma = \mathcal{M}(S)(\sigma') \\ ff, & \text{otherwise} \end{cases}$

END 2.19.

The extension of *Assn* to *Cond* induces a corresponding extension of the class of correctness formulae *Form* in that each p occurring in a correctness formula may now be taken from *Cond*. We do *not* extend substitution to *Cond*, since we do not know how to define $(S \rightarrow p)[s/x]$ or $(p \leftarrow S)[s/x]$ in a natural way. Accordingly, results which were obtained before which involved substitution in assertions (in particular lemma 2.16 and theorem 2.15) do not extend to analogous results for conditions.

It is not difficult to show that our definition of the meaning of $S \rightarrow p$ and $p \leftarrow S$ indeed satisfies the requirements of definition 2.17.

<u>LEMMA 2.20</u>. For all $p \in$ *Cond*

a. (i) $\models \{S \rightarrow p\} S \{p\}$

(ii) For all $r \in$ *Cond*, if $\models \{r\} S \{p\}$, then $\models r \supset (S \rightarrow p)$

b. (i) $\models \{p\} S \{p \leftarrow S\}$

(ii) For all $r \in$ *Cond*, if $\models \{p\} S \{r\}$, then $\models (p \leftarrow S) \supset r$.

<u>PROOF</u>.

a. (i) By the definitions, we have to show that, for all σ, $\mathcal{T}(S \rightarrow p)(\sigma) \Rightarrow \mathcal{T}(p)(\mathcal{M}(S)(\sigma))$, which, by definition 2.19, is clearly satisfied.

(ii) Choose some r and assume that, for all σ, $\mathcal{T}(r)(\sigma) \Rightarrow \mathcal{T}(p)(\mathcal{M}(S)(\sigma))$. Since, by definition 2.19, this is equivalent to: for all σ, $\mathcal{T}(r)(\sigma) \Rightarrow \mathcal{T}(S \rightarrow p)(\sigma)$, we immediately obtain $\models r \supset (S \rightarrow p)$.

b. (i) We have to show that, for all σ, $\mathcal{T}(p)(\sigma) \Rightarrow \mathcal{T}(p \leftarrow S)(\mathcal{M}(S)(\sigma))$. By definition 2.19, we must show that there exists σ' such that $\mathcal{T}(p)(\sigma')$ and $\sigma'' = \mathcal{M}(S)(\sigma')$. Clearly, it suffices to take $\sigma' = \sigma$.

(ii) Choose some r and assume that, for all σ, $\mathcal{T}(p)(\sigma) \Rightarrow \mathcal{T}(r)(\mathcal{M}(S)(\sigma))$. We have to show that, for all σ, $\mathcal{T}(p\leftarrow S)(\sigma) \Rightarrow \mathcal{T}(r)(\sigma)$. Choose some σ, and assume $\mathcal{T}(p\leftarrow S)(\sigma)$. By definition 2.19, we have that there exists σ' such that $\mathcal{T}(p)(\sigma')$ and $\sigma = \mathcal{M}(S)(\sigma')$. By the assumption on r, if $\mathcal{T}(p)(\sigma')$ then $\mathcal{T}(r)(\mathcal{M}(S)(\sigma'))$, i.e., $\mathcal{T}(r)(\sigma)$, which was to be shown.

END 2.20.

We can now formally state that the results of theorem 2.15 are indeed the best possible:

<u>THEOREM 2.21</u>. For each $p \in \mathcal{Assn}$,

a. $\models (x:=s) \rightarrow p = p[s/x]$

b. $\models p \leftarrow (x:=s) = \exists y[p[y/x] \wedge x=s[y/x]]$

where y is such that $y \not\equiv x$ and $y \notin$ *ivar*(p,s).

<u>PROOF</u>.

a. By the definitions and lemma 2.16, for all σ, $\mathcal{T}((x:=s) \rightarrow p)(\sigma) = \mathcal{T}(p)(\mathcal{M}(x:=s)(\sigma)) = \mathcal{T}(p)(\sigma\{\mathcal{V}(s)(\sigma)/x\}) = \mathcal{T}(p[s/x])(\sigma)$.

b. Choose any σ. We have to prove the equivalence of

(i) There exists σ' such that $\mathcal{T}(p)(\sigma')$ and $\sigma = \sigma'\{\alpha/x\}$, where $\alpha = \mathcal{V}(s)(\sigma')$

(ii) There exists α' such that $\mathcal{T}(p)(\sigma\{\alpha'/y\}\{\alpha'/x\})$ and $\sigma\{\alpha'/y\}(x) = \mathcal{V}(s)(\sigma\{\alpha'/y\}\{\alpha'/x\})$.

(i) $\Rightarrow$ (ii). Take $\alpha' = \sigma'(x)$. $\mathcal{T}(p)(\sigma\{\alpha'/y\}\{\alpha'/x\}) = \mathcal{T}(p)(\sigma'\{\alpha/x\}\{\alpha'/y\}\{\alpha'/x\}) = \mathcal{T}(p)(\sigma'\{\alpha'/x\}\{\alpha'/y\}) =$ ($y \notin$ *ivar*(p)) $\mathcal{T}(p)(\sigma'\{\alpha'/x\}) = \mathcal{T}(p)(\sigma'\{\sigma'(x)/x\}) = \mathcal{T}(p)(\sigma')$, which holds by assumption. Also, $\mathcal{V}(s)(\sigma\{\alpha'/y\}\{\alpha'/x\}) = \mathcal{V}(s)(\sigma') = \alpha = \sigma'\{\alpha/x\}(x) = \sigma'\{\alpha/x\}\{\alpha'/y\}(x) = \sigma\{\alpha'/y\}(x)$

(ii) $\Rightarrow$ (i). Take $\sigma' = \sigma\{\alpha'/x\}$.

(α) $\mathcal{T}(p)(\sigma') = \mathcal{T}(p)(\sigma\{\alpha'/x\}) =$ ($y \notin$ *ivar*(p)) $\mathcal{T}(p)(\sigma\{\alpha'/x\}\{\alpha'/y\})$, which holds by assumption

(β) $\sigma'\{\alpha/x\} = \sigma'\{V(s)(\sigma')/x\} = \sigma\{\alpha'/x\}\{V(s)(\sigma\{\alpha'/x\})/x\} =$
$(y \notin ivar(s))$ $\sigma\{\alpha'/x\}\{V(s)(\sigma\{\alpha'/x\}\{\alpha'/y\})/x\} =$ (assumption)
$\sigma\{\alpha'/x\}\{\sigma\{\alpha'/y\}(x)/x\} =$ $(x \not\equiv y)$ $\sigma\{\alpha'/x\}\{\sigma(x)/x\} = \sigma\{\sigma(x)/x\} =$
σ.

END 2.21.

Our next lemma deals with weakest preconditions and strongest postconditions for the other two types of statements.

LEMMA 2.22. For each $p \in$ *Cond*

a. $\models (S_1;S_2) \to p = S_1 \to (S_2 \to p)$

b. $\models p \leftarrow (S_1;S_2) = (p \leftarrow S_1) \leftarrow S_2$

c. For each $q \in$ *Cond*, $\models \{p\}S_1;S_2\{q\}$ iff $\models \{p\}S_1\{S_2 \to q\}$ iff $\models \{p \leftarrow S_1\}S_2\{q\}$

d. $\models$ <u>if</u> b <u>then</u> S_1 <u>else</u> S_2 <u>fi</u> $\to p =$ <u>if</u> b <u>then</u> $S_1 \to p$ <u>else</u> $S_2 \to p$ <u>fi</u>

e. $\models p \leftarrow$ <u>if</u> b <u>then</u> S_1 <u>else</u> S_2 <u>fi</u> $= ((p \wedge b) \leftarrow S_1) \vee ((p \wedge \neg b) \leftarrow S_2)$.

PROOF. We give some of the details of two subcases, leaving the remainder of the proof as an exercise.

a. For each σ, $T((S_1;S_2) \to p)(\sigma) = T(p)(M(S_1;S_2)(\sigma)) =$
$T(p)(M(S_2)(M(S_1)(\sigma))) = T(S_2 \to p)(M(S_1)(\sigma)) = T(S_1 \to (S_2 \to p))(\sigma)$.

e. Choose any σ. We show the equivalence of

(i) There exists σ' such that $T(p)(\sigma')$ and $\sigma = M($<u>if</u> b <u>then</u> S_1 <u>else</u> S_2 <u>fi</u>$)(\sigma')$

(ii) There exists σ'' such that $T(p \wedge b)(\sigma'')$ and $\sigma = M(S_1)(\sigma'')$, or there exists σ''' such that $T(p \wedge \neg b)(\sigma''')$ and $\sigma = M(S_2)(\sigma''')$.

(i) $\Rightarrow$ (ii). Exercise.

(ii) $\Rightarrow$ (i). Assume that there exists σ'' such that $T(p \wedge b)(\sigma'')$ and $\sigma = M(S_1)(\sigma'')$. Clearly, both $T(p)(\sigma'')$ and $T(b)(\sigma'')$ hold, whence $\sigma = M($<u>if</u> b <u>then</u> S_1 <u>else</u> S_2 <u>fi</u>$)(\sigma'')$ is also satisfied. Thus, we can take $\sigma' = \sigma''$. The other case is exactly analogous

END 2.22.

We close this section with a brief discussion of the following question: under which circumstances are the operators " $\rightarrow$ " and " $\leftarrow$ " inverse to each other?

First we have

LEMMA 2.23. For each $p \in Cond$

a. $\models p \supset (S \rightarrow (p \leftarrow S))$

b. $\models ((S \rightarrow p) \leftarrow S) \supset p$.

PROOF. Immediate from lemma 2.20.
END 2.32.

Secondly, we observe that we have equality in 2.23a or b only if additional assumptions are satisfied. However, even in a simple case such as $S \equiv (x:=0)$ these assumptions do not hold. E.g., take $p \equiv (x=1)$. Then, by theorem 2.21, $\models p \leftarrow S = \exists y[(x=1)[y/x] \wedge x=0[y/x]]$, i.e. $\models p \leftarrow S = \exists y[(y=1) \wedge (x=0)]$, whence, again by theorem 2.21, $\models S \rightarrow (p \leftarrow S) = \exists y[(y=1) \wedge (x=0)][0/x]$, or, equivalently, $\models S \rightarrow (p \leftarrow S) = \exists y[y=1]$. Now it is easy to verify that $\models \exists y[y=1] \supset (x=1)$ does not hold (though, in accordance with lemma 2.23a, $\models (x=1) \supset \exists y[y=1]$ *does* hold). The details of this counter example for case b (where it also works) are left to the reader.

The additional assumptions referred to above are stated in

LEMMA 2.24. For each $p \in Cond$

a. If S is such that, for all σ and σ', if $M(S)(\sigma) = M(S)(\sigma')$ then $\sigma = \sigma'$, then $\models p = (S \rightarrow (p \leftarrow S))$

b. If S is such that, for all σ' there exists some σ such that $M(S)(\sigma) = \sigma'$, then $\models p = ((S \rightarrow p) \leftarrow S)$.

PROOF. Omitted.
END 2.24.

2.5. Inferences and their soundness

An inference is a construct which is used to structure the derivation of valid formulae from valid formulae in the following sense.

DEFINITION 2.26 (inferences and their soundness).

a. An *inference* is a construct of the form $\frac{f_1,\ldots,f_n}{f}$, with f_i, $i = 1,\ldots,n$, and $f \in \mathcal{Form}$.

b. An inference $\frac{f_1,\ldots,f_n}{f}$ is called *sound*, written as

$$\boxed{\frac{f_1,\ldots,f_n}{f}}$$

whenever validity of f_i, $i = 1,\ldots,n$, implies validity of f.

END 2.26.

Thus, $\frac{f_1,\ldots,f_n}{f}$ is sound whenever if, for all i, $i = 1,\ldots,n$ and for all σ, $\mathcal{F}(f_i)(\sigma)$ then, for all σ, $\mathcal{F}(f)(\sigma)$. We list a few examples of sound inferences, some of which we raise to the status of lemma because of their featuring in subsequent applications. In particular, they play a role in the formal proof theory to be dealt with in section 2.6, which is why we call certain of these sound inferences *proof rules*.

Examples

1. $\boxed{\frac{x=0}{x=1}}$

The soundness of this inference should be contrasted with the fact that $\models (x=0) \supset (x=1)$ does not hold. This is a special case of the general phenomenon that, whenever $\models p_1 \supset p_2$, then $\boxed{\frac{p_1}{p_2}}$, but not necessarily conversely. In order to explain this, let us compare the two definitions: $\models p_1 \supset p_2$ holds whenever, for all σ, $\mathcal{T}(p_1)(\sigma) \Rightarrow \mathcal{T}(p_2)(\sigma)$. On the other hand, $\boxed{\frac{p_1}{p_2}}$ holds whenever if, for all σ, $\mathcal{T}(p_1)(\sigma)$ then, for all σ, $\mathcal{T}(p_2)(\sigma)$. We show that the validity of $p_1 \supset p_2$ implies the soundness of $\frac{p_1}{p_2}$. Assume that, for all σ, $\mathcal{T}(p_1)(\sigma) \Rightarrow \mathcal{T}(p_2)(\sigma)$ and that, for all σ, $\mathcal{T}(p_1)(\sigma)$ holds. We have to prove that then, for all σ, $\mathcal{T}(p_2)(\sigma)$ holds. Take any σ_0. By the validity of p_1, $\mathcal{T}(p_1)(\sigma_0)$ holds. By the validity of $p_1 \supset p_2$, $\mathcal{T}(p_2)(\sigma_0)$ follows, as was to be shown. (Note that the same phenomenon may be couched in the language of assertions, viz. as $\models \forall x[p_1 \supset p_2] \supset (\forall x[p_1] \supset \forall x[p_2])$.)

2. $\boxed{\frac{\{p\}S\{q\}}{p \supset (S \rightarrow q)}}$, $\boxed{\frac{\{p\}S\{q\}}{(p \leftarrow S) \supset q}}$

(This is nothing but a reformulation of part of lemma 2.20.)

LEMMA 2.27 (proof rule for sequential composition).

$$\boxed{\frac{\{p\}S_1\{q\} \;,\; \{q\}S_2\{r\}}{\{p\}S_1;S_2\{r\}}}$$

PROOF. Assume, that for all σ, $\mathcal{T}(p)(\sigma) \Rightarrow \mathcal{T}(q)(\mathcal{M}(S_1)(\sigma))$ and, for all σ, $\mathcal{T}(q)(\sigma) \Rightarrow \mathcal{T}(r)(\mathcal{M}(S_2)(\sigma))$. To show that, for all σ, $\mathcal{T}(p)(\sigma) \Rightarrow \mathcal{T}(r)(\mathcal{M}(S_1;S_2)(\sigma))$. Take any σ and assume that $\mathcal{T}(p)(\sigma)$. By the first assumption, $\mathcal{T}(q)(\mathcal{M}(S_1)(\sigma))$. By the second assumption, for $\sigma' = \mathcal{M}(S_1)(\sigma)$, we infer that $\mathcal{T}(r)(\mathcal{M}(S_2)(\sigma'))$, or, equivalently, that

$\mathcal{T}(r)(\mathcal{M}(S_1;S_2)(\sigma))$.

END 2.27.

LEMMA 2.28.

a. (proof rule for conditional statements).

$$\frac{\{p\wedge b\}S_1\{q\},\{p\wedge\neg b\}S_2\{q\}}{\{p\}\ \underline{\text{if}}\ b\ \underline{\text{then}}\ S_1\ \underline{\text{else}}\ S_2\ \underline{\text{fi}}\ \{q\}}$$

b.

$$\frac{\{p\}\ \underline{\text{if}}\ b\ \underline{\text{then}}\ S_1\ \underline{\text{else}}\ S_2\ \underline{\text{fi}}\ \{q\}}{\{p\wedge b\}S_1\{q\}\ \wedge\ \{p\wedge\neg b\}S_2\{q\}}$$

PROOF. Exercise.

END 2.28.

LEMMA 2.29 (rule of consequence).

$$\frac{(p\supset p_1),\{p_1\}S\{q_1\},(q_1\supset q)}{\{p\}S\{q\}}$$

PROOF. Exercise.

END 2.29.

We give two examples of applying these lemmas.

1. We verify that $\models \{x=y\}\ x:=x+y;\ y:=x+y\ \{3\times x = 2\times y\}$
   a. By theorem 2.15, $\models \{3\times x = 2\times(x+y)\}\ y:=x+y\ \{3\times x = 2\times y\}$, i.e. $\models \{x = 2\times y\}\ y:=x+y\ \{3\times x = 2\times y\}$.
   b. Again by theorem 2.15, $\models \{x=y\}\ x:=x+y\ \{x = 2\times y\}$.
   c. By lemma 2.27, the desired result follows from parts a and b.
2. $\models \{x+y > 1\}$ <u>if</u> $x < y$ <u>then</u> $x:=x+y$ <u>else</u> $y:=x+y$ <u>fi</u> $\{1<x \wedge x<2\times y \vee 1<y \wedge y\leq 2\times x\}$. Using the proof rule for the conditional statement, the rule of consequence and theorem 2.15, we see

that it is sufficient to show that

(i) $\models$ x+y>1 $\wedge$ x<y $\supset$ 1<x+y $\wedge$ x+y < 2×y $\vee$
1<y $\wedge$ y $\leq$ 2×(x+y)

(ii) $\models$ x+y>1 $\wedge$ x$\geq$y $\supset$ 1<x $\wedge$ x < 2×(x+y) $\vee$
1<x+y $\wedge$ x+y $\leq$ 2×x

both of which are clearly satisfied.

We conclude this section with a discussion of the effect of substitution on correctness formulae.

LEMMA 2.30 (substitution in correctness formulae, case I). Let p,q $\in$ *Assn*.

$$\frac{\{p\}S\{q\}}{\{p[y/x]\}S[y/x]\{q[y/x]\}}\ \text{, provided that } y \notin \mathit{ivar}(S,q)$$

Before presenting the proof, we exhibit an *unsound* inference which would arise when substitution without constraints were allowed:

$$\frac{\{\underline{true}\}x:=0;\ y:=1\ \{x=0 \wedge y=1\}}{\{\underline{true}\}y:=0;\ y:=1\ \{y=0 \wedge y=1\}}\ .$$

From this example we see - as we will many times in the subsequent chapters - that substitution is a notion which requires considerable care. Unrestricted application may well lead to undesirable (invalid, unsound) results. In fact, the proof of lemma 2.30 is not immediate, either. For the reader who might be tempted to expect that some more or less direct extension of lemma 2.16 would suffice, let us point out that it is not, in general, true that $M(S[y/x])(\sigma) = M(S)(\sigma\{\sigma(y)/x\})$. In fact, we shall present two proofs of lemma 2.30, both of which are non-trivial. The first needs an additional lemma which also has some independent interest.

LEMMA 2.31. For each p $\in$ *Assn* and S $\in$ *Stat* there exist $q_1, q_2 \in$ *Assn* such that

$\models S \rightarrow p = q_1$, with $ivar(q_1) \subseteq ivar(S,p)$

$\models p \leftarrow S = q_2$, with $ivar(q_2) \subseteq ivar(S,p)$.

PROOF. We prove only the weakest precondition case, leaving the other one as exercise. We use induction on the complexity of S.

a. By theorem 2.21, $\models (x:=s) \rightarrow p = p[s/x]$. Clearly, if $p \in \mathit{Assn}$, then $p[s/x] \in \mathit{Assn}$. Also, the free variables of p[s/x] are included in those of x:=s and p.

b. By lemma 2.22, $\models (S_1;S_2) \rightarrow p = S_1 \rightarrow (S_2 \rightarrow p)$. By the induction hypothesis, there exists some $q_2 \in \mathit{Assn}$ such that $ivar(q_2) \subseteq ivar(S_2,p)$, and such that $\models S_2 \rightarrow p = q_2$. Applying the induction hypothesis again, there exists $q_1 \in \mathit{Assn}$, such that $ivar(q_1) \subseteq ivar(S_1,q_2)$, and such that $\models S_1 \rightarrow q_2 = q_1$. Together we have that $\models (S_1;S_2) \rightarrow p = q_1$, and $ivar(q_1) \subseteq ivar(S_1,S_2,p)$.

c. $S \equiv$ <u>if</u> b <u>then</u> S_1 <u>else</u> S_2 <u>fi</u>. Left as an exercise.

END 2.31.

We now give the first

PROOF of lemma 2.30.

a. $S \equiv z:=s$, and $x \equiv z$. We have to show:

If

$$\text{for all } \sigma,\ \mathcal{T}(p)(\sigma) \Rightarrow \mathcal{T}(q)(\sigma\{\mathcal{V}(s)(\sigma)/z\}) \qquad (*)$$

then

$$\text{for all } \sigma,\ \mathcal{T}(p[y/x])(\sigma) \Rightarrow \mathcal{T}(q[y/x])(\sigma\{\mathcal{V}(s[y/x])(\sigma)/y\}). \qquad (**)$$

Let $\alpha = \sigma(y)$. (**) can be rewritten as

$$\text{for all } \sigma,\ \mathcal{T}(p)(\sigma\{\alpha/x\}) \Rightarrow \mathcal{T}(q)(\sigma\{\mathcal{V}(s)(\sigma\{\alpha/x\})/y\}\{\mathcal{V}(s)(\sigma\{\alpha/x\})/x\})$$

or, since $y \notin ivar(q)$, as

$$\text{for all } \sigma,\ \mathcal{T}(p)(\sigma\{\alpha/x\}) \Rightarrow \mathcal{T}(q)(\sigma\{\mathcal{V}(s)(\sigma\{\alpha/x\})/x\}),$$

and this follows easily from (*).

b. $S \equiv z:=s$, and $x \not\equiv z$. This case is a slight variant on part a, and left as exercise.

c. $S \equiv S_1;S_2$. Assume $\models \{p\}S_1;S_2\{q\}$, and let $y \notin ivar(S_1;S_2,q)$. Clearly, $\models \{p\}S_1\{S_2 \to q\}$ and $\models \{S_2 \to q\}S_2\{q\}$. By lemma 2.31, there exists some $r \in \mathit{Assn}$, such that $ivar(r) \subseteq ivar(S_2,q)$, and $\models S_2 \to q = r$. Thus, $\models \{p\}S_1\{r\}$ and $\models \{r\}S_2\{q\}$. Since $y \notin ivar(S_1;S_2,q)$, and $ivar(r) \subseteq ivar(S_2,q)$, also $y \notin ivar(S_1,r)$, and $y \notin ivar(S_2,q)$. Thus, we can apply the induction hypothesis and infer that both $\models \{p[y/x]\}S_1[y/x]\{r[y/x]\}$, and $\models \{r[y/x]\}S_2[y/x]\{q[y/x]\}$. From lemma 2.27 it follows that $\models \{p[y/x]\}S_1[y/x];S_2[y/x]\{q[y/x]\}$, which is equivalent to $\models \{p[y/x]\}(S_1;S_2)[y/x]\{q[y/x]\}$, as was to be shown.

d. $S \equiv$ <u>if</u> b <u>then</u> S_1 <u>else</u> S_2 <u>fi</u>. Exercise.

END 2.30.

For the second proof of lemma 2.30 we again need an auxiliary lemma:

<u>LEMMA 2.32</u>. Let $S \in \mathit{Stat}$, $y,z \notin ivar(S)$, and x, σ and α arbitrary. Then there exist $\bar{\sigma}$ and $\bar{\alpha}$ such that

$$M(S[y/x])(\sigma\{\alpha/y\}) = \bar{\sigma}\{\bar{\alpha}/y\}$$
$$M(S[z/x])(\sigma\{\alpha/z\}) = \bar{\sigma}\{\bar{\alpha}/z\}$$

<u>PROOF</u>. Induction on the complexity of S.

a.(i) $S \equiv u:=s$, $u \not\equiv x$. Then $M(S[y/x])(\sigma\{\alpha/y\}) = M(u:=s[y/x])(\sigma\{\alpha/y\}) = \sigma\{\alpha/y\}\{V(s[y/x])(\sigma\{\alpha/y\})/u\} = \sigma\{\alpha/y\}\{V(s)(\sigma\{\alpha/y\}\{\alpha/x\})/u\} =$ $(y \notin ivar(s))\,\sigma\{\alpha/y\}\{V(s)(\sigma\{\alpha/x\})/u\} = (y \not\equiv u)\,\sigma\{V(s)(\sigma\{\alpha/x\})/u\}\{\alpha/y\}$. From this, it is clear that we may take $\bar{\sigma} = \sigma\{V(s)(\sigma\{\alpha/x\})/u\}$, and $\bar{\alpha} = \alpha$.

(ii) $S \equiv x:=s$. Exercise.

b. $S \equiv S_1;S_2$. By the induction hypothesis, there exists $\bar{\bar{\sigma}}$ and $\bar{\bar{\alpha}}$ such that

$M((S_1;S_2)[y/x])(\sigma\{\alpha/y\}) = M(S_2[y/x])(M(S_1[y/x])(\sigma\{\alpha/y\})) =$
$M(S_2[y/x])(\bar{\bar{\sigma}}\{\bar{\bar{\alpha}}/y\})$

and

$M((S_1;S_2)[z/x])(\sigma\{\alpha/z\}) = M(S_2[z/x])(M(S_1[z/x])(\sigma\{\alpha/z\})) =$
$M(S_2[z/x])(\bar{\bar{\sigma}}\{\bar{\bar{\alpha}}/z\})$.

Another application of the induction hypothesis to $M(S_2[y/x])$ $(\bar{\bar{\sigma}}\{\bar{\bar{\alpha}}/y\})$ and $M(S_2[z/x])(\bar{\bar{\sigma}}\{\bar{\bar{\alpha}}/z\})$ then yields the desired result.

c. $S \equiv$ <u>if</u> b <u>then</u> S_1 <u>else</u> S_2 <u>fi</u>. Exercise.

END 2.32.

The following corollary of this lemma will be used in the second proof of lemma 2.30:

<u>COROLLARY 2.33</u>. Let $S \in$ *Stat*, $y \notin$ *ivar*(S), x, σ and α arbitrary. Then there exist $\bar{\sigma}$ and $\bar{\alpha}$ such that

$$M(S)(\sigma\{\alpha/x\}) = \bar{\sigma}\{\bar{\alpha}/x\}$$
$$M(S[y/x])(\sigma\{\alpha/y\}) = \bar{\sigma}\{\bar{\alpha}/y\}.$$

<u>PROOF</u>. Let u be some integer variable $\notin$ *ivar*(S), and different from x and y. We apply lemma 2.32, with S replaced by S[u/x], x replaced by u, y replaced by x, and z replaced by y. We infer the existence of $\bar{\sigma}$ and $\bar{\alpha}$ such that

$$M(S[u/x][x/u])(\sigma\{\alpha/x\}) = \bar{\sigma}\{\bar{\alpha}/x\}$$
$$M(S[u/x][y/u])(\sigma\{\alpha/y\}) = \bar{\sigma}\{\bar{\alpha}/y\}.$$

Now using the identities $S[u/x][x/u] \equiv S$ and $S[u/x][y/u] \equiv S[y/x]$ (cf. exercise 2.3) we have obtained the desired result.

END 2.33.

This brings us to the second

<u>PROOF</u> of lemma 2.30. Assume that $y \notin$ *ivar*(S,q). We have to show that

from

$$\text{for all } \sigma,\ T(p)(\sigma) \Rightarrow T(q)(M(S)(\sigma)) \qquad (*)$$

it follows that

$$\text{for all } \sigma,\ T(p[y/x])(\sigma) \Rightarrow T(q[y/x])(M(S[y/x])(\sigma)).$$

Choose some σ, let $\alpha = \sigma(y)$, $\sigma_1 = \sigma\{\alpha/x\}$, $\sigma_2 = M(S[y/x])(\sigma)$ $(= M(S[y/x])(\sigma\{\alpha/y\}))$, and assume $T(p)(\sigma_1)$, to show that $T(q[y/x])(\sigma_2)$ holds. By corollary 2.33, there exist $\bar{\sigma}$ and $\bar{\alpha}$ such that $M(S)(\sigma\{\alpha/x\}) = \bar{\sigma}\{\bar{\alpha}/x\})$, $\sigma_2 = \bar{\sigma}\{\bar{\alpha}/y\}$. Replacing, in (*), σ by σ_1, we obtain that $T(q)(\bar{\sigma}\{\bar{\alpha}/x\})$ holds. Now $T(q[y/x])(\sigma_2) = T(q[y/x])(\bar{\sigma}\{\bar{\alpha}/y\})=$ $T(q)(\bar{\sigma}\{\bar{\alpha}/y\}\{\bar{\alpha}/x\}) = (y \notin \mathit{ivar}(q))\ T(q)(\bar{\sigma}\{\bar{\alpha}/x\})$, and we conclude that $T(q[y/x])(\sigma_2)$ indeed holds.
END 2.30 (second proof).

The last proof rule of this section expresses another substitution result which is a variant on lemma 2.30.

LEMMA 2.34 (substitution in correctness formulae, case II). Let $p,q \in \mathit{Assn}$.

$$\frac{\{p\}S\{q\}}{\{p[s/x]\}S\{q[s/x]\}}\ ,\ \text{provided that } \mathit{ivar}(x{:=}s) \cap \mathit{ivar}(S) = \emptyset$$

We precede the proof of this lemma by some definitions and auxiliary facts which will also be employed in a more general setting in later chapters. We are interested in the notion of a function *setting* or *using* a variable:

DEFINITION 2.35 (a function setting or using a variable).
Let $\phi \in \Sigma \to \Sigma$ and $x \in \mathit{Ivar}$.

a. ϕ *sets* x whenever, for some σ, $\phi(\sigma)(x) \neq \sigma(x)$.

b. ϕ *uses* x whenever, for some σ and α, $\phi(\sigma\{\alpha/x\}) \neq \phi(\sigma)\{\alpha/x\}$.

END 2.35.

We shall in fact be more concerned with the negative counterparts of these definitions: ϕ does not set x whenever, for all σ, $\phi(\sigma)(x) = \sigma(x)$; ϕ does not use x whenever, for all σ and α, $\phi(\sigma\{\alpha/x\}) = \phi(\sigma)\{\alpha/x\}$. As basic lemma concerning the first notion we have

LEMMA 2.36.

a. If x does not occur on the left-hand side of any assignment statement in S, then $M(S)$ does not set x.

b. If ϕ sets none of the elements of *ivar*(t), then, for all σ, $V(t)(\sigma) = V(t)(\phi(\sigma))$, and similarly for b and p.

PROOF.

a. Induction on the complexity of S.

 (i) $S \equiv y:=t$. By assumption, $x \not\equiv y$. Thus, for all σ, $M(y:=t)(\sigma)(x) = \sigma\{V(t)(\sigma)/y\}(x) = \sigma(x)$.

 (ii) $S \equiv S_1;S_2$ or $S \equiv$ <u>if</u> b <u>then</u> S_1 <u>else</u> S_2 <u>fi</u>. These cases are clear by induction.

b. Immediate by lemma 2.16a.

END 2.36.

For the second notion we have

LEMMA 2.37.

a. If ϕ does not use x, then ϕ does not set x.

b. If $x \notin$ *ivar*(S), then $M(S)$ does not use x.

PROOF.

a. Assume that ϕ does not use x. Then $\phi(\sigma) = \phi(\sigma\{\sigma(x)/x\}) = \phi(\sigma)\{\sigma(x)/x\}$, whence $\phi(\sigma)(x) = \phi(\sigma)\{\sigma(x)/x\}(x) = \sigma(x)$, and we see that ϕ does not set x.

b. Induction on the complexity of S. Choose any σ and α.

 (i) $S \equiv y:=t$. $M(y:=t)(\sigma\{\alpha/x\}) = \sigma\{\alpha/x\}\{V(t)(\sigma\{\alpha/x\})/y\}$ = (lemma 2.16) $\sigma\{\alpha/x\}\{V(t)(\sigma)/y\}$ = $(x\not\equiv y)$ $\sigma\{V(t)(\sigma)/y\}\{\alpha/x\}$ = $M(y:=t)(\sigma)\{\alpha/x\}$.

(ii) $S \equiv S_1;S_2$ or $S \equiv$ <u>if</u> b <u>then</u> S_1 <u>else</u> S_2 <u>fi</u>. Clear by induction. (Note that, by lemma 2.16, $\mathcal{W}(b)(\sigma) = \mathcal{W}(b)(\sigma\{\alpha/x\}$.)

END 2.37.

Remark. Part a of this lemma may not be reversed: let, for all σ, $\phi(\sigma) = \sigma'$, where $\sigma'(y) = \sigma(x_0)$ for all y and fixed x_0. Then ϕ uses x_0 but does not set x_0. (Choose any σ and $\alpha \neq \sigma(x_0)$. Then $\phi(\sigma\{\alpha/x_0\}) \neq \phi(\sigma)\{\alpha/x_0\}$, since, for any $y \not\equiv x_0$, $\phi(\sigma\{\alpha/x_0\})(y) = \alpha \neq \sigma(x_0) = \phi(\sigma)\{\alpha/x_0\}(y)$.)

We now give the

<u>PROOF</u> of lemma 2.34. Assume that $ivar(x{:=}s) \cap ivar(S) = \emptyset$. We have to show that from

$$\text{for all } \sigma,\ \mathcal{T}(p)(\sigma) \Rightarrow \mathcal{T}(q)(\mathcal{M}(S)(\sigma)) \qquad (*)$$

it follows that

$$\text{for all } \sigma,\ \mathcal{T}(p[s/x])(\sigma) \Rightarrow \mathcal{T}(q[s/x])(\mathcal{M}(S)(\sigma))$$

or, by lemma 2.16, and putting $\mathcal{V}(s)(\sigma) = \alpha$ and $\mathcal{V}(s)(\mathcal{M}(S)(\sigma)) = \alpha'$, that

$$\text{for all } \sigma,\ \mathcal{T}(p)(\sigma\{\alpha/x\}) \Rightarrow \mathcal{T}(q)(\mathcal{M}(S)(\sigma)\{\alpha'/x\}).$$

By lemma 2.36 and the assumptions, $\alpha = \alpha'$. The desired result now follows by replacing, in (*), σ by $\sigma\{\alpha/x\}$, and next applying lemma 2.37.

END 2.34.

2.6 Completeness

Now that we have collected various results about validity of correctness formulae and soundness of inferences (in particular theorems 2.15 and 2.21, and lemmas 2.27 to 2.29) the question arises as to whether we have, in some meaningful sense, gathered *all* the basic facts about our simple programming language. For those properties of the language which are expressible as the validity of formulae {p}S{q}, with $S \in \mathit{Stat}$ and $p,q \in \mathit{Assn}$, this is indeed the case, and the present section is devoted to a discussion of this important result. We shall show that, in a sense to be made precise in a moment, all proofs of the validity of formulae {p}S{q} can be based on the above mentioned theorems and lemmas. For this purpose we introduce the notion of *formal proof* of a correctness formula f with respect to a set of correctness formulae (called the *axioms*) and a set of inferences (called the *proof* rules).

DEFINITION 2.38 (formal proof).
Let there be given a set of correctness formulae Ax, called the set of axioms and a set of inferences Pr, called the set of proof rules. We say that f is *formally provable* from Ax and Pr, denoted by

$$\vdash_{\mathit{Ax},\mathit{Pr}} f$$

whenever there exists $N \geq 1$ and a sequence of correctness formulae $f_1,\ldots,f_N$ (which sequence is called the *formal proof* of f) such that
(i) $f \equiv f_N$
(ii) For each i, $1 \leq i \leq N$, either
  (α) $f_i \in \mathit{Ax}$, or
  (β) There exist $j_1,\ldots,j_{n_i}$, with $1 \leq j_k < i$ for $k = 1,\ldots,n_i$, such that

$$\frac{f_{j_1},\ldots,f_{j_{n_i}}}{f_i} \in \mathit{Pr}.$$

END 2.38.

Remark. Our use of the term proof rule deviates from what is customary in mathematical logic, in that proof rule usually refers to what one might call an inference *scheme*, allowing all its instances as inferences in a formal proof.

In words, $\vdash_{Ax,Pr}$ f if and only if there exists a finite sequence of correctness formulae $f_1,\ldots,f_N$, with f at last element, such that each element in the sequence is either an axiom, or is the conclusion of an inference which has formulae which occur previously in the sequence as premises.

Example (taken from propositional logic).
Let Ax_0 consist of all correctness formulae of the form

(1) $p \supset (q \supset p)$

(2) $(p \supset (q \supset r)) \supset ((p \supset q) \supset (p \supset r))$

and let Pr_0 consist of all inferences of the form

(1) $\frac{p, p \supset q}{q}$.

We show that $\vdash_{Ax_0,Pr_0} p \supset p$, by exhibiting an appropriate sequence of correctness formulae.

1. $f_1 \equiv (p \supset ((p \supset p) \supset p)) \supset ((p \supset (p \supset p)) \supset (p \supset p))$

   (This is the second axiom, with $q \equiv p \supset p$ and $r \equiv p$.)

2. $f_2 \equiv p \supset ((p \supset p) \supset p)$

   (This is the first axiom, with $q \equiv p \supset p$.)

3. $f_3 \equiv (p \supset (p \supset p)) \supset (p \supset p)$

   (Apply the proof rule $\frac{p,\ p \supset q}{q}$, with f_1 and f_2 as premises and f_3 as conclusion.)

4. $f_4 \equiv p \supset (p \supset p)$

   (The first axiom, with $q \equiv p$.)

5. $f_5 \equiv p \supset p$

   (By the proof rule, with f_4 and f_3 as premises and f_5 as conclusion.)

Since $f_5 \equiv p \supset p$, we have indeed established that $\vdash_{Ax_0, Pr_0} p \supset p$.

Remark. The phrase "Let Ax (Pr) consist of all correctness formulae (inferences) of the form $f_1, f_2, \ldots (\frac{f_1,\ldots,f_n}{f}, \frac{f'_1,\ldots,f'_{n'}}{f'}, \ldots)$", will usually be abbreviated in the sequel to "Let Ax (Pr) consist of $f_1, f_2, \ldots (\frac{f_1,\ldots,f_n}{f}, \frac{f'_1,\ldots,f'_{n'}}{f'}, \ldots)$".

Now what do we expect from this notion of formal proof? What we want to do is to capture *all* interesting properties of (a certain class of) correctness formulae through the selection of an appropriate set of axioms Ax and of proof rules Pr. This means that we expect of such a system Ax, Pr that whenever a formula f is valid, it is formally provable with respect to this system. (A system satisfying this requirement is called *complete*.) Moreover, we clearly also want that no *invalid* formula is formally provable. (The system is then called *sound*.) Altogether, we require that

$$\vdash_{Ax, Pr} f \quad \text{iff} \models f.$$

In accordance with our putting the main emphasis in the present treatise on questions concerning formulae f of the form $\{p\}S\{q\}$, we discuss the problem only for f restricted in this way, and do not study the axiomatization of *equivalence* of statements. What we shall do is to exhibit a system Ax, Pr dealing with $\{p\}S\{q\}$ formulae such that, for all $p, q \in Assn$ and $S \in Stat$,

$$\vdash_{Ax, Pr} \{p\}S\{q\} \quad \text{iff} \models \{p\}S\{q\}.$$

DEFINITION 2.39 (formal proof system for formulae $\{p\}S\{q\}$).
Let $p, q, r \in Assn$.

a. The set of axioms Ax consists of

(i) All valid assertions

(ii) $\{p[s/x]\}\ x{:=}s\ \{p\}$

b. The set of proof rules Pr consists of

(i) $$\frac{\{p\}S_1\{q\},\{q\}S_2\{r\}}{\{p\}S_1;S_2\{r\}}$$ (rule of composition)

(ii) $$\frac{\{p\wedge b\}S_1\{q\},\{p\wedge\neg b\}S_2\{q\}}{\{p\}\ \underline{\text{if}}\ b\ \underline{\text{then}}\ S_1\ \underline{\text{else}}\ S_2\ \underline{\text{fi}}\ \{q\}}$$ (rule of conditionals)

(iii) $$\frac{p\supset p_1,\{p_1\}S\{q_1\},q_1\supset q}{\{p\}S\{q\}}$$ (rule of consequence)

END 2.39.

Remarks

1. Observe that $\vdash_{Ax,Pr} p$ iff $\models p$ is satisfied by definition. This may seem a somewhat gratuitous way out of the problem of selecting a number of basic facts about validity (of assertions, in this case), from which all other facts can be inferred. However, there are good reasons for this approach. Firstly, it is known that an axiomatization of validity of assertions is impossible (by Gödel's incompleteness theorem for arithmetic). Secondly, we want to concentrate on the *programming* aspects of our language, and, as remarked already, pay little attention to questions about assertions which do not interact with statements (so that, even if an axiomatization of validity of assertions were to exist, we might not be interested in using it).
2. We emphasize that we restrict p,q,r to *assertions*, and do not allow them to be conditions. Remember that $p[s/x]$ is, in general, undefined for $p \in \mathit{Cond}$, so that, without this restriction, our system would not be wellformed (owing to the presence of the assignment axiom).

We now prove the main theorem of this section:

THEOREM 2.40 (soundness and completeness theorem). Let Ax and Pr be as in definition 2.39. Then, for all $p,q \in \mathit{Assn}$, $S \in \mathit{Stat}$,

$\vdash_{Ax,Pr}\{p\}S\{q\}$ iff $\models \{p\}S\{q\}$

PROOF.

a. (⇒). We show that each formally provable $f \equiv \{p\}S\{q\}$ is valid. Let $f_1,\ldots,f_N$, with $f_N \equiv f$, be a formal proof for f. We prove that, for each $i = 1,\ldots,N$, $\models f_i$ (thus implying that $\models f$). The proof proceeds by showing that f_1 is valid and, for each i, $1 < i \leq N$, if $f_1,\ldots,f_{i-1}$ are valid, then f_i is valid.

(i) i = 1. Clearly, f_1 has to be an axiom and, therefore, is either an assertion which is valid by the definition of Ax, or it has the form $\{p[s/x]\}x:=s\ \{p\}$, which is valid by theorem 2.15.

(ii) Assuming $f_1,\ldots,f_{i-1}$ all valid, we show that f_i is valid. Either f_i is an axiom, in which case its validity follows as in part (i), or there exist $f_{j_1},\ldots,f_{j_{n_i}}$, $1 \leq j_k < i$ for $k = 1,\ldots,n_i$, such that $\frac{f_{j_1},\ldots,f_{j_{n_i}}}{f_i} \in Pr$ (i.e., it is one of the three inferences of definition 2.39b.) By the induction hypothesis, $f_{j_1},\ldots,f_{j_{n_i}}$ are valid. Moreover, the three inferences in Pr are all sound (by lemmas 2.27 to 2.29), so that, in each case, validity of the conclusion, i.e. of f_i, follows.

b. (⇐). Assume that $\models \{p\}S\{q\}$. We show that $\vdash_{Ax,Pr}\{p\}S\{q\}$, by induction on the complexity of S.

(i) $S \equiv x:=s$. We have $\models \{p\}\ x:=s\ \{q\}$, thus, by theorem 2.21,

$\models p \supset q[s/x]$.

Hence, by the definition of Ax,

$\vdash_{Ax,Pr} p \supset q[s/x].$

Also, again by the definition of Ax,

$\vdash_{Ax,Pr}\{q[s/x]\}\ x:=s\ \{q\}.$

Finally, we obviously have that

$\vdash_{Ax,Pr} q \supset q.$

The desired result $\vdash_{Ax,Pr}\{p\}\ x:=s\ \{q\}$ now follows by the rule of consequence. (This is a shorthand - often to be used tacitly in the sequel - for saying that the sequence $f_1 \equiv p \supset q[s/x]$, $f_2 \equiv \{q[s/x]\}\ x:=s\ \{q\}$, $f_3 \equiv q \supset q$, $f_4 \equiv \{p\}\ x:=s\ \{q\}$, constitutes a formal proof for $\{p\}\ x:=s\ \{q\}$. In fact, f_1, f_2 and f_3 are axioms and, moreover, there is an instance of the rule of consequence which has f_1, f_2 and f_3 as premises and f_4 as conclusion.)

(ii) $S \equiv S_1;S_2$. Since $\models \{p\}S_1;S_2\{q\}$, by lemma 2.22c, $\models \{p\}S_1\{S_2 \rightarrow q\}$. Clearly, $\models \{S_2 \rightarrow q\}S_2\{q\}$. By lemma 2.31, there exists $r \in Assn$ such that $\models r = S_2 \rightarrow q$. Thus, we have that $\models \{p\}S_1\{r\}$ and $\models \{r\}S_2\{q\}$. By the induction hypothesis we obtain

$\vdash_{Ax,Pr}\{p\}S_1\{r\}, \qquad \vdash_{Ax,Pr}\{r\}S_2\{q\}.$

The desired result now follows by the composition rule. (The sequence for $\vdash_{Ax,Pr}\{p\}S_1;S_2\{q\}$ is obtained by constructing from the sequences $f_1,\ldots,f_{N_1} \equiv \{p\}S_1\{r\}$ and

$f'_1,\ldots,f'_{N_2} \equiv \{r\}S_2\{q\}$, a new sequence $f_1,\ldots,f_{N_1},f'_1,\ldots,f'_{N_2}$, $f \equiv \{p\}S_1;S_2\{q\}$, which is easily seen to satisfy the requirements. The parts $f_1,\ldots,f_{N_1}$ and $f'_1,\ldots,f'_{N_2}$ are justified by applying the induction hypothesis, and the final element f is justified by applying the rule of composition with f_{N_1} and f'_{N_2} as premises.)

(iii) $S \equiv$ <u>if</u> b <u>then</u> S_1 <u>else</u> S_2 <u>fi</u>. By lemma 2.28b, from $\models$ {p} <u>if</u> b <u>then</u> S_1 <u>else</u> S_2 <u>fi</u> {q}, it follows that $\models \{p \wedge b\}S_1\{q\}$ and $\models \{p \wedge \neg b\}S_2\{q\}$. The result now follows by an application of the induction hypothesis, together with the rule of conditionals.

END 2.40.

For later reference, we draw attention to an important step in the proof, viz. the place where we used lemma 2.31.

Remark. Part b of theorem 2.40 is the announced completeness result. Here (as in the corresponding sections in later chapters) we should actually speak of *relative* completeness, i.e. completeness relative to arithmetical truth, since all valid (arithmetically true) assertions are axioms. (See also the remark after definition 2.12.)

Exercises

2.1. Prove $\models S_1;(S_2;S_3) = (S_1;S_2);S_3$.

2.2. Prove that, if $x \notin$ *ivar*(p_2), then $\models \forall x[p_1 \supset p_2] = \exists x[p_1] \supset p_2$.

2.3. Prove

a. (i) $S[x/x] \equiv S$

(ii) $S[y/x][u/z] \equiv S[u/z][y/x]$, provided that $x \not\equiv z$, $x \not\equiv u$, $z \not\equiv y$

(iii) $S[y/x][z/y] \equiv S[z/x]$, provided that $y \notin ivar(S)$

b. (i) $s[x/x] \equiv s$

(ii) $s[t_1/x][t_2/y] \equiv s[t_2/y][t_1[t_2/y]/x]$, provided that $x \not\equiv y$ and $x \notin ivar(t_2)$

(iii) $s[y/x][t/y] \equiv s[t/x]$, provided that $y \notin ivar(s)$

c. As part b, with s replaced by b

d. (i) $p[x/x] \equiv p$

(ii) $\models p[t_1/x][t_2/y] = p[t_2/y][t_1[t_2/y]/x]$, provided that $x \not\equiv y$ and $x \notin ivar(t_2)$

(iii) $\models p[y/x][t/y] = p[t/x]$, provided that $y \notin ivar(p)$

e. $\models \exists x[p] = \exists y[p[y/x]]$, provided that $y \notin ivar(p)$

f. Explain the difference between parts a, b and c, and part d. E.g., why is it not true, in general, that, if $y \notin ivar(p)$, then $p[y/x][t/y] \equiv p[t/x]$?

2.4. Assume $x \not\equiv y$, $x \not\equiv z$ and $y \not\equiv z$, and let $S_1 \equiv z{:=}x;x{:=}y;y{:=}z$, $S_2 \equiv x{:=}x+y;y{:=}x-y;x{:=}x-y$.

a. Is it true that $\models S_1 = S_2$?

b. Let $q \equiv (x=m) \wedge (y=n)$. Show that $\models S_1 \rightarrow q = S_2 \rightarrow q$.

2.5. Find suitable restrictions on x, y, s and t such that $\models x{:=}s;y{:=}t = y{:=}t;x{:=}s$.

2.6. Prove that

a. $\models S \rightarrow (p \vee q) = (S \rightarrow p) \vee (S \rightarrow q)$

b. $\models S \rightarrow (p \wedge q) = (S \rightarrow p) \wedge (S \rightarrow q)$

c. $\models S \rightarrow \underline{false} = \underline{false}$, $\models S \rightarrow \underline{true} = \underline{true}$

d. If $\models p \supset q$, then $\models (S \rightarrow p) \supset (S \rightarrow q)$.

2.7. Find examples of s_1 (s_2) such that $\underline{true} \leftarrow (x{:=}s_1)$ is valid ($\underline{true} \leftarrow (x{:=}s_2)$ is invalid).

2.8. Prove the equivalence of

a. $\models S_1 = S_2$

b. For all $p,q \in \mathcal{Assn}$, $\models \{p\}S_1\{q\}$ iff $\models \{p\}S_2\{q\}$

2.9. Prove $\boxed{\dfrac{p}{\forall x[p]}}$

2.10. Prove $\boxed{\dfrac{\{p\}S\{q_1\},\{p\}S\{q_2\}}{\{p\}S\{q_1 \wedge q_2\}}}$, $\boxed{\dfrac{\{p_1\}S\{q\},\{p_2\}S\{q\}}{\{p_1 \vee p_2\}S\{q\}}}$

2.11. Prove $\boxed{\dfrac{\{p\}S\{q\}}{\{p[s/x]\}S\{q\}} \text{, provided that } x \notin \mathit{ivar}(S,q)}$

2.12. Give an example showing that condition $y \not\equiv x$ in theorem 2.21b may not be omitted.

2.13. Assume that the syntax of *Form* is extended with the clause $f ::= \ldots | f_1 \supset f_2$, with as corresponding semantic extension $F(f_1 \supset f_2)(\sigma) = (F(f_1)(\sigma) \Rightarrow F(f_2)(\sigma))$.

a. Is it true that

$\models \{p \wedge b\}S_1\{q\} \wedge \{p \wedge \neg b\}S_2\{q\} \supset \{p\}$ <u>if</u> b <u>then</u> S_1 <u>else</u> S_2 <u>fi</u> $\{q\}$?

b. Same question for

$\models (p \supset p_1) \wedge \{p_1\}S\{q_1\} \wedge (q_1 \supset q) \supset \{p\}S\{q\}$.

2.14. Consider the following attempt at generalizing substitution to conditions. Let us consider only conditions involving "$\rightarrow$", and let us put, for $p \equiv (S \rightarrow p')$, $p[y/x] \equiv S[y/x] \rightarrow p'[y/x]$. Use the example $p \equiv (S \rightarrow p')$, with $S \equiv x:=z$, $p' \equiv y=m$, to show that theorem 2.21a, in the form $\models ((x:=y) \rightarrow p) = p[y/x]$, becomes incorrect.

2.15. Show that the restriction in lemma 2.34 may be weakened to: $x \notin \mathit{ivar}(S) \wedge (\mathit{ivar}(s) \cap \mathit{lhs}(S) = \emptyset)$, where $\mathit{lhs}(S)$ in the set of all integer variables which occur on the left-hand side of an assignment statement in S.

2.16. Let, for $\phi: \Sigma \rightarrow \Sigma$ and $\Sigma' \subseteq \Sigma$, ϕ^{-1} denote the inverse of the function ϕ, and let $\phi(\Sigma') \overset{\text{df.}}{=} \bigcup_{\sigma \in \Sigma'} \phi(\sigma)$. Let moreover, for $S \in \mathit{Stat}$ and $p \in \mathit{Cond}$, $\phi_S \overset{\text{df.}}{=} M(S)$ and $\Sigma_p \overset{\text{df.}}{=} \{\sigma | T(p)(\sigma) = tt\}$.

Prove

a. $\models$ {p}S{q} iff $\phi_S(\Sigma_p) \subseteq \Sigma_q$ iff $\Sigma_p \subseteq \phi_S^{-1}(\Sigma_q)$

b. $\Sigma_{S\to p} = \phi_S^{-1}(\Sigma_p)$

c. $\Sigma_{p\leftarrow S} = \phi_S(\Sigma_p)$.

2.17. a. Prove lemma 2.24.

b. Show that, for all p,

(i) $\models$ (x:=s) → (p ← (x:=s)) = p iff, for all σ, the function :V →V which maps α to $\mathcal{V}$(s)(σ{α/x}) is injective

(ii) $\models$ ((x:=s) → p) ← (x:=s) = p iff, for all σ, the function :V → V which maps α to $\mathcal{V}$(s)(σ{α/x}) is surjective.

2.18. a. Prove that, for all S and q ∈ *Assn*, if there exists p ∈ *Assn* such that

(i) $\models$ {p}S{q}

(ii) For all r ∈ *Cond*, if $\models$ {r}S{q} then $\models$ r ⊃ p

then $\models$ p = S → q

b. Same as part a, with (ii) replaced by

(ii') For all r ∈ *Assn*, if $\models$ {r}S{q} then $\models$ r ⊃ p

(Hint: this needs application of lemma 2.31.)

2.19. a. Disprove $\mathcal{M}$(S[y/x])(σ) = $\mathcal{M}$(S)(σ{σ(y)/x})

b. Prove that, for y ∉ *svar*(S) and all z,

$$\mathcal{M}(S[y/x])(\sigma)(z) = \begin{cases} \mathcal{M}(S)(\sigma\{\sigma(y)/x\})(x), & \text{if } z \equiv y \\ \mathcal{M}(S)(\sigma\{\sigma(y)/x\})(z), & \text{if } z \not\equiv y \end{cases}$$

2.20. Let $Stat_0$, with typical elements S,..., be defined by

S::= x:=y|S_1;S_2

Let Ax_0 consist of the axioms

(i) x:=y;y:=x = x:=y

(ii) x:=y;x:=z = x:=z, where x ≢ z

(iii) x:=y;z:=x = x:=y;z:=y

(iv) x:=y;z:=y = z:=y;x:=y

and let Pr_0 consist of the proof rules

(i) $\dfrac{S_1=S_2}{S;S_1=S;S_2}$, $\dfrac{S_1=S_2}{S_1;S=S_2;S}$

(ii) $\dfrac{S_1=S_2}{S_2=S_1}$, $\dfrac{S_1=S_2, S_2=S_3}{S_1=S_3}$

(iii) $\dfrac{(S_1;x:=y)=(S_2;x:=y), (S_1;z:=u)=(S_2;z:=u)}{S_1=S_2}$, where $x \not\equiv z$

Prove that, for all $S_1, S_2 \in \mathit{Stat}_0$,

$\vdash_{\mathit{Ax}_0, \mathit{Pr}_0} S_1=S_2$ iff $\models S_1=S_2$.

Chapter 3

WHILE STATEMENTS

3.1. Introduction

In this chapter we extend our simple language *Stat* with the while statement <u>while</u> b <u>do</u> S <u>od</u>. An important new issue is encountered when we try to apply the ideas from the previous chapter to attribute meaning to such statements. Consider, for example, the statement <u>while</u> x≥0 <u>do</u> x:=x+1 <u>od</u>, and suppose we want to determine the outcome of M(<u>while</u> x≥0 <u>do</u> x:=x+1 <u>od</u>)$(\sigma\{\alpha/x\})$, where α is any integer ≥ 0. Clearly, execution of <u>while</u> x≥0 <u>do</u> x:=x+1 <u>od</u>, when started in a state where x has the value α, does not terminate, or, in other words, there exists no state σ' such that M(<u>while</u> x≥0 <u>do</u> x:=x+1 <u>od</u>)$(\sigma\{\alpha/x\}) = \sigma'$. This may also be expressed by saying that, in general, the function $M(S)$ is not everywhere defined, i.e. it is a *partial* function from Σ to Σ (and not a *total*, i.e. everywhere defined, function, as was the case in chapter 2). For reasons which will become clearer as we go along, we prefer to replace partial functions $M(S): \Sigma \xrightarrow[part]{} \Sigma$ by total functions $M(S): \Sigma \cup \{\bot\} \to \Sigma \cup \{\bot\}$, where " $\bot$ " is some new state, not belonging to Σ, and serving the role of the undefined element. (It has become customary to pronounce " $\bot$ " as "bottom".) Thus, for the example just mentioned we shall obtain that M(<u>while</u> x≥0 <u>do</u> x:=x+1 <u>od</u>) $(\sigma\{\alpha/x\}) = \bot$. In general, we organize the definitions in such a way that $M(S): \Sigma \cup \{\bot\} \to \Sigma \cup \{\bot\}$ delivers $\bot$ whenever $M(S): \Sigma \xrightarrow[part]{} \Sigma$ would be undefined. Moreover, we shall ensure that always $M(S)(\bot) = \bot$: no well-defined state can result from an execution starting with the undefined state.

Letting ϕ stand for a typical element of the set of functions

$\Sigma \cup \{\perp\} \to \Sigma \cup \{\perp\}$, we are now faced with the problem: how do we determine ϕ such that M(while b do S od) = ϕ? The so-called *operational* meaning of while b do S od is clear: repeat execution of S (zero or more times) as long as the test b is satisfied. It turns out that the function ϕ which embodies this description is obtained as the limit of a sequence of *approximations* ϕ_i, i = 0,1,..., where (roughly speaking, a precise characterization follows), for each i ≥ 1, ϕ_i corresponds to executing S at most i-1 times.

The notions of approximation and limit require some mathematical setting which we develop in section 3.2. Besides being preparatory for the definition of the semantics of the while statement (which follows in section 3.3), this also serves as the first part of a more extensive mathematical development needed for the treatment of recursive procedures (chapter 5). In section 3.3 we give a precise definition of both the operational semantics and the denotational semantics of the while statement, and prove their equivalence. Furthermore, we show that the function ϕ can be characterized as *least fixed point* of a certain operator. Again, besides being of interest for its own sake, this result foreshadows a fundamental property of recursive procedures.

Section 3.4 is devoted to correctness questions. We adapt the definition of formulae {p}S{q} to cover the case that S may not terminate. Two possibilities arise for the meaning of {p}S{q} in a state σ ($\neq \perp$):

- whenever p is satisfied in σ and execution of S terminates, q is satisfied in the resulting state;
- whenever p is satisfied in σ, execution of S terminates and q is satisfied in the resulting state.

The first possibility leads to the notion of *partial* correctness of S with respect to precondition p and postcondition q. This is the one which will be used primarily in this chapter and also in the sequel. The notion corresponding to the alternative is that of *total* correctness. The issues encountered there which center around formalizing methods for proving program termination are much harder to deal with.

(Chapter 8 provides some more information on these questions.) The main result of section 3.4 is the proof of the soundness of an inference used in proving partial correctness of the while statement. In section 3.5 we investigate weakest preconditions and strongest postconditions. We show that the weakest precondition can be characterized as the *greatest fixed point* of a suitable operator. An analogous result for strongest postconditions is not available, and we have to be satisfied with a less elegant result. Finally, in section 3.6 we consider the question of *completeness*. The system obtained by extending that of section 2.6 with the just-mentioned proof rule for the while statement is shown to be (sound and) complete for partial correctness.

3.2. Complete partially ordered sets

As announced in the introduction, we shall define the meaning of a while statement as a function which is obtained as the limit of a sequence of approximations. The present section introduces a mathematical framework for such definitions, centering around the notion of a *complete partially ordered set* (cpo, for short). Moreover, we shall define the concept of (least or greatest) fixed point of a function from a cpo to itself. As will become abundantly clear in the sequel, both notions are of fundamental importance in all of denotational semantics.

In this section we deviate from the notation as used elsewhere in this book. C,D,... will stand for arbitrary sets, usually with a cpo structure; typical elements of such sets are denoted by x,y,z,..., and f,g,... denote functions: $C \to D$.

We begin our definitions by recalling that of a partially ordered set.

DEFINITION 3.1 (partially ordered set).
Let C be an arbitrary set. A partial order " $\sqsubseteq$ " on C is a subset of $C \times C$ (we write $x \sqsubseteq y$ instead of $\langle x,y \rangle \in \sqsubseteq$) which satisfies

a. $x \sqsubseteq x$ (reflexivity)

b. If $x \sqsubseteq y$ and $y \sqsubseteq x$ then $x = y$ (antisymmetry)

c. If $x \sqsubseteq y$ and $y \sqsubseteq z$ then $x \sqsubseteq z$ (transitivity)

END 3.1.

In a partially ordered set we have the notions of *greatest lower bound* and *least upper bound*:

DEFINITION 3.2 (greatest lower bound and least upper bound).

Let $X \subseteq C$.

a. $y \in C$ is called the greatest lower bound (glb) of X if

   (i) $y \sqsubseteq x$ for all $x \in X$

   (ii) For all $z \in C$, if $z \sqsubseteq x$ for all $x \in X$, then $z \sqsubseteq y$.

   The glb of a set X will be denoted by $\sqcap X$.

b. $z \in C$ is called the least upper bound (lub) of X if

   (i) $x \sqsubseteq z$ for all $x \in X$

   (ii) For all $y \in C$, if $x \sqsubseteq y$ for all $x \in X$, then $z \sqsubseteq y$.

   The lub of a set X will be denoted by $\sqcup X$.

c. glb and lub of a sequence $\langle x_0, x_1, \ldots \rangle$ are denoted by $\prod_{i=0}^{\infty} x_i$ and $\bigsqcup_{i=0}^{\infty} x_i$.

END 3.2.

Apart from some rare exceptional cases, we shall be concerned only with the glb and lub of *chains*:

DEFINITION 3.3 (chains).

An ascending (descending) chain on $(C, \sqsubseteq)$ is a sequence $x_0, x_1, \ldots$, such that $x_i \sqsubseteq x_{i+1}$ ($x_i \sqsupseteq x_{i+1}$), for $i = 0, 1, \ldots$.

END 3.3.

Since we shall deal almost exclusively with ascending chains, we adopt the convention of omitting the qualification "ascending". From now on, a chain $\langle x_i \rangle_{i=0}^{\infty}$ is an ascending chain, unless specifically stated otherwise.

We are now ready for

DEFINITION 3.4 (complete partially ordered sets).
A *complete partially ordered set* (cpo, for short) is a set C together with a partial order " $\sqsubseteq$ " which satisfies the following two requirements:

(i) There is a *least* element with respect to " $\sqsubseteq$ ", i.e. an element " $\bot$ " such that $\bot \sqsubseteq x$ for all $x \in C$.

(ii) Each chain $\langle x_i \rangle_{i=0}^{\infty}$ has a lub $\bigsqcup_{i=0}^{\infty} x_i$.

END 3.4.

Remark. It should be noted that the notion of completeness of a partially ordered set has nothing to do with that of completeness of a proof system.

By way of first - and not yet very interesting - example of a cpo we indicate how each set C may be provided with a cpo structure. First we enlarge C with some element $\bot_C$ not contained in it, and then we define " $\sqsubseteq$ " on $C \cup \{\bot_C\}$ by putting: for all $x_1, x_2 \in C \cup \{\bot_C\}$, $x_1 \sqsubseteq x_2$ iff $x_1 = \bot_C$ or $x_1 = x_2$. The structure obtained in this way is a so-called *discrete cpo* and may be represented pictorially by the following figure:

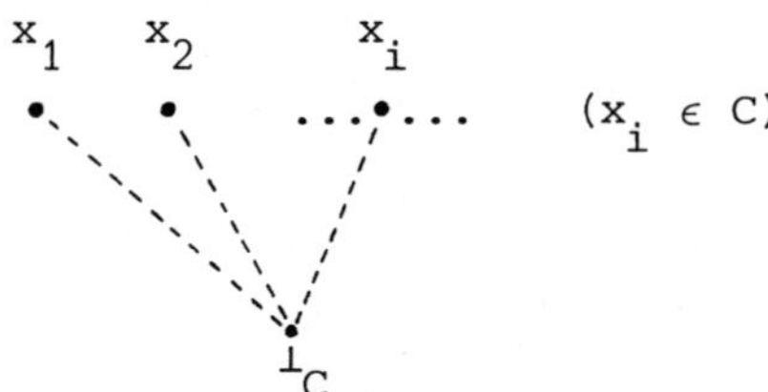

It is left to the reader to verify that this structure satisfies definition 3.4. (Observe that all chains are trivial in that each of them consists of at most two different elements.) We shall apply the above construction to turn the sets V, W and Σ from chapter 2 into cpo's. We add elements $\bot_V$, $\bot_W$ and $\bot_\Sigma$ to them, respectively, and use the following ordering: for each $\alpha_1, \alpha_2 \in V \cup \{\bot_V\}$, $\alpha_1 \sqsubseteq \alpha_2$ iff $\alpha_1 = \bot_V$ or $\alpha_1 = \alpha_2$, and similarly for the other two cases.

We shall often be interested in the *direct product* of partially ordered sets and cpo's.

LEMMA 3.5. Let $(C_1, \sqsubseteq_1)$ and $(C_2, \sqsubseteq_2)$ be partially ordered sets.

a. $(C_1 \times C_2, \sqsubseteq)$ is a partially ordered set with respect to the ordering $\langle x,y \rangle \sqsubseteq \langle x',y' \rangle$ whenever $x \sqsubseteq_1 x'$ and $y \sqsubseteq_2 y'$.
b. If $(C_1, \sqsubseteq_1)$ and $(C_2, \sqsubseteq_2)$ are cpo's, then $(C_1 \times C_2, \sqsubseteq)$ is a cpo.

PROOF.

a. Exercise.
b. $\bot_{C_1 \times C_2} = \langle \bot_{C_1}, \bot_{C_2} \rangle$. Also, it is easily seen that, for $\langle x_i, y_i \rangle_{i=0}^{\infty}$ a chain in $C_1 \times C_2$, $\bigsqcup_{i=0}^{\infty} \langle x_i, y_i \rangle = \langle \bigsqcup_{i=0}^{\infty} x_i, \bigsqcup_{i=0}^{\infty} y_i \rangle$, where the last two lubs are in C_1 and C_2, respectively.

END 3.5.

Remark. Note that, for $(C_1, \sqsubseteq_1)$ and $(C_2, \sqsubseteq_2)$ discrete cpo's, $(C_1 \times C_2, \sqsubseteq)$ need not be discrete.

As soon as we bring functions (from cpo's to cpo's) into the picture, the situation becomes more interesting. First we define the notion of a *monotonic* function. (All through this book, monotonic is short for monotonically *increasing*.)

DEFINITION 3.6 (monotonic functions).

a. Let $(C_1, \sqsubseteq_1)$ and $(C_2, \sqsubseteq_2)$ be partially ordered sets. A function $f\colon C_1 \to C_2$ is called monotonic if, for each $x, y \in C_1$, if $x \sqsubseteq_1 y$, then $f(x) \sqsubseteq_2 f(y)$.
b. The set of monotonic functions: $C_1 \to C_2$ is denoted by $C_1 \to_m C_2$.

END 3.6.

Next, we define a partial ordering on functions $f, g\colon C_1 \to C_2$.

DEFINITION 3.7 (partial ordering on functions).

Let $(C_1,\sqsubseteq_1)$ and $(C_2,\sqsubseteq_2)$ be two partially ordered sets. We define an ordering " $\sqsubseteq$ " on $C_1 \to C_2$ by putting: for each $f,g \in C_1 \to C_2$, $f \sqsubseteq g$ iff $f(x) \sqsubseteq_2 g(x)$ for all $x \in C_1$.

END 3.7.

LEMMA 3.8. The ordering " $\sqsubseteq$ " from definition 3.7 is a partial ordering.

PROOF. Immediate from definitions 3.1 and 3.7.

END 3.8.

The next lemma states an important property of cpo's:

LEMMA 3.9.

a. Let $(C_1,\sqsubseteq_1)$ and $(C_2,\sqsubseteq_2)$ be cpo's. Then $(C_1 \to C_2,\sqsubseteq)$, with " $\sqsubseteq$ " as in definition 3.7, is a cpo.

b. Let $(C_1,\sqsubseteq_1)$ and $(C_2,\sqsubseteq_2)$ be cpo's. Then $(C_1 \to_m C_2,\sqsubseteq)$, with " $\sqsubseteq$ " as in definition 3.7, is a cpo.

PROOF.

a. We have to show that $(C_1 \to C_2,\sqsubseteq)$ has a least element and that each chain in $(C_1 \to C_2,\sqsubseteq)$ has a lub.

(i) As least element $\perp_{C_1 \to C_2}$ we take the function: $C_1 \to C_2$, which maps each element $x_1 \in C_1$ to $\perp_{C_2}$. As notation for this function we employ $\lambda x_1 \cdot \perp_{C_2}$. This is a special case of the so-called λ-notation for functions - often to be used in the sequel - which uses $\lambda x \cdot \ldots x \ldots$ to denote the function f defined by $f(x) = \ldots x \ldots$. We verify that $\lambda x_1 \cdot \perp_{C_2} \sqsubseteq f$ for each $f \in C_1 \to C_2$. By definition 3.7, this amounts to showing that, for each $y_1 \in C_1$, $(\lambda x_1 \cdot \perp_{C_2})(y_1) \sqsubseteq_2 f(y_1)$, or, by the definition of $\lambda x_1 \cdot \perp_{C_2}$, that $\perp_{C_2} \sqsubseteq_2 f(y_1)$ for all $y_1 \in C_1$.

Since $(C_2,\sqsubseteq_2)$ is a cpo with $\bot_{C_2}$ as least element, the result follows.

(ii) Let $\langle f_i \rangle_{i=0}^{\infty}$ be a chain of functions in $C_1 \to C_2$. We define a function f by putting: for each $x_1 \in C_1$, $f(x_1) = \bigsqcup_{i=0}^{\infty} f_i(x_1)$ (lub in C_2!). Observe that, since $\langle f_i \rangle_{i=0}^{\infty}$ is a chain in $(C_1 \to C_2,\sqsubseteq)$, $\langle f_i(x_1) \rangle_{i=0}^{\infty}$ is a chain in $(C_2,\sqsubseteq_2)$ and the lub $\bigsqcup_{i=0}^{\infty} f_i(x_1)$ indeed exists. (Using the λ-notation, we may also write $\lambda x_1 \cdot \bigsqcup_{i=0}^{\infty} f_i(x_1)$ for f.) We prove that f is the desired lub of $\langle f_i \rangle_{i=0}^{\infty}$.

(α) Since, for each i and $x_1 \in C_1$, $f_i(x_1) \sqsubseteq_2 \bigsqcup_{i=0}^{\infty} f_i(x_1)$, we infer that, for each i, $f_i \sqsubseteq f$.

(β) Assume that (*): $f_i \sqsubseteq g$, $i = 0,1,\ldots$. To show that $f \sqsubseteq g$. Choose some $x_1 \in C_1$. We prove that $f(x_1) \sqsubseteq_2 g(x_1)$, i.e. that $\bigsqcup_{i=0}^{\infty} f_i(x_1) \sqsubseteq_2 g(x_1)$. By (*), for $i = 0,1,\ldots,$ $f_i(x_1) \sqsubseteq_2 g(x_1)$, and the result follows by the lub definition in $(C_2,\sqsubseteq_2)$.

b. It is sufficient to show that $\lambda x_1 \cdot \bot_{C_2}$ is a monotonic function, which clearly holds and, moreover, that, for f_i, $i = 0,1,\ldots,$ monotonic, $f = \bigsqcup_{i=0}^{\infty} f_i$ is monotonic. Take any $x_1', x_1'' \in C_1$ such that $x_1' \sqsubseteq x_1''$. Then, for all i, $f_i(x_1') \sqsubseteq_2 f_i(x_1'')$, and we infer that $\bigsqcup_{i=0}^{\infty} f_i(x_1') \sqsubseteq_2 \bigsqcup_{i=0}^{\infty} f_i(x_1'')$, i.e. that $f(x_1') \sqsubseteq_2 f(x_1'')$.

END 3.9.

<u>COROLLARY 3.10</u>. If $\langle f_i \rangle_{i=0}^{\infty}$ is a chain of functions in $(C_1 \to C_2,\sqsubseteq)$ then $(\bigsqcup_{i=0}^{\infty} f_i)(x_1) = \bigsqcup_{i=0}^{\infty} f_i(x_1)$, for all $x_1 \in C_1$.

PROOF. Direct from the definition $\bigsqcup_{i=0}^{\infty} f_i = \lambda x_1 \cdot \bigsqcup_{i=0}^{\infty} f_i(x_1)$.
END 3.10.

Remark. This corollary is the basic property of lubs of function chains. We shall employ it quite frequently below, without explicitly referring to it.

In the sequel, we usually omit indication of the partial ordering " $\sqsubseteq$ " in a cpo $(C,\sqsubseteq)$, and simply write "the cpo C", etc. Also, in case the ordering does occur in an argument, we omit subscripts on it, and always use " $\sqsubseteq$ " instead of " $\sqsubseteq_1$ ", " $\sqsubseteq_2$ ", etc. Moreover, we often omit subscripts on $\bot$.

It is convenient to identify the cpo's $C_1 \times C_2 \to_m C$ and $C_1 \to_m (C_2 \to_m C)$, which is allowed according to

LEMMA 3.11. Let C_1, C_2 and C be cpo's.

a. The following two statements are equivalent

 (i) $f \in C_1 \times C_2 \to_m C$

 (ii) For all $x \in C_1$, $\lambda y \cdot f(x,y) \in C_2 \to_m C$, and, for all $y \in C_2$, $\lambda x \cdot f(x,y) \in C_1 \to_m C$.

b. The mapping $'$: $(C_1 \times C_2 \to C) \to (C_1 \to (C_2 \to C))$ defined by: $f' = \lambda x \cdot \lambda y \cdot f(x,y)$, is a one-one mapping from $C_1 \times C_2 \to_m C$ onto $C_1 \to_m (C_2 \to_m C)$, such that, if $f_1 \sqsubseteq f_2$, then $f_1' \sqsubseteq f_2'$.

PROOF. Exercise.
END 3.11.

Two more definitions conclude this section. The first one is of importance since the condition stated in it turns out to be satisfied by each function which occurs as meaning of a program:

DEFINITION 3.12 (strict functions).
A function f from cpo C_1 to cpo C_2 is called *strict* if $f(\bot) = \bot$.
The set of all strict functions $f\colon C_1 \to C_2$ is denoted by $C_1 \to_s C_2$.
END 3.12.

Strict functions satisfy

LEMMA 3.13. Let C_1 and C_2 be cpo's.

a. $C_1 \to_s C_2$ is a cpo.

b. If C_1 is discrete, then $C_1 \to_s C_2 \subseteq C_1 \to_m C_2$.

PROOF.

a. $\lambda x_1 \cdot \bot$ is strict. Also, for each chain $\langle f_i \rangle_{i=0}^{\infty}$ of strict functions, its lub $\lambda x_1 \cdot \bigsqcup_{i=0}^{\infty} f_i(x_1)$ is strict.

b. Let $x_1', x_1'' \in C_1$ satisfy $x_1' \sqsubseteq x_1''$, and let $f \in C_1 \to_s C_2$. We show that $f(x_1') \sqsubseteq f(x_1'')$. Either $x_1' = \bot$, in which case $f(x_1') = f(\bot) = \bot \sqsubseteq f(x_1'')$, or $x_1' = x_1''$, in which case $f(x_1') \sqsubseteq f(x_1'')$ holds a fortiori.

END 3.13.

Finally, we come to the important definition

DEFINITION 3.14 (fixed points).
Let C be a cpo, $f \in C \to C$, and $x \in C$.

a. x is called a fixed point of f if $f(x) = x$

b. x is called the least (greatest) fixed point of f if x is a fixed point of f and, moreover, for each fixed point y of f, $x \sqsubseteq y$ ($x \sqsupseteq y$). If f has a least (greatest) fixed point, it is denoted by μf (νf).

END 3.14.

Least and (to a much lesser extent) greatest fixed points play an essential role in the sequel. Since many examples of their use will follow, we restrict ourselves here to a few very simple ones.

Examples

1. Let C be any cpo, and let $f_1 = \lambda x \cdot x$. (Thus, f_1 is the identity function which maps each element of C to itself.) Each element of C is a fixed point of f_1, $\bot$ is its least fixed point, and f_1 has a greatest fixed point y if C has y as its greatest element. (The property of having a greatest element is not implied by the cpo definition. However, below we shall encounter a few cpo's which *do* happen to have a greatest element.)
2. Let C be any cpo and let $f_2 = \lambda x \cdot y$, for some $y \in C$. f_2 has y as its only fixed point. Thus, $\mu f_2 = \nu f_2 = y$.
3. Let $D = C_1 \to C_2$ for some cpo's C_1 and C_2. Let x_1 and f denote typical elements of C_1 and D, respectively. Then $\lambda x_1 \cdot \bot$ is the least fixed point of the operator (i.e. mapping from functions to functions) $\lambda f \cdot f \in D \to D$.

3.3. Semantics

In this section we add the while statement to the class of statements *Stat*, provide an operational and denotational definition for the elements of *Stat*, prove their equivalence and, finally, show that the meaning of the while statement may be obtained as least fixed point of a suitable operator.

DEFINITION 3.15 (syntax of *Stat* extended with the while statement). Let $x \in$ *Ivar*, $s \in$ *Iexp* and $b \in$ *Bexp* be as in definition 2.1. The class *Stat*, with typical elements S,..., is defined by

$$S ::= x := s \mid S_1 ; S_2 \mid \underline{\text{if}}\ b\ \underline{\text{then}}\ S_1\ \underline{\text{else}}\ S_2\ \underline{\text{fi}} \mid \underline{\text{while}}\ b\ \underline{\text{do}}\ S\ \underline{\text{od}}$$

END 3.15.

It is convenient to have a special symbol for the so-called dummy statement:

DEFINITION 3.16 (dummy statement).

The symbol D stands for the dummy statement, defined by

$$D \equiv x{:=}x$$

END 3.16.

Remark. There is a slight abuse of language here in that x:=x stands for a *class* of statements (depending on which element of *Ivar* x stands for). The reader who does not like this should incorporate D in definition 3.15 (S::= ...|D), and appropriately extend various treatments by cases below with a fifth clause.

We proceed with the semantic definitions. As we saw above, the first step is the extension of the set of states Σ with an undefined state $\perp_\Sigma$. Clearly, this necessitates a refinement of the definition of $\mathcal{V}$ and $\mathcal{W}$, since we may have to evaluate an expression in an undefined state. The natural solution for this is to deliver an undefined value, as is made precise in the following definitions. First we introduce a discrete cpo structure on the sets V, W and Σ (cf. the example following definition 3.4).

DEFINITION 3.17 (V, W and Σ as cpo's).

Let V_0, W_0 and Σ_0 be the set of integers, the set of truth-values {tt,ff} and the set *Ivar* $\rightarrow V_0$, respectively. Let $\perp_V$, $\perp_W$ and $\perp_\Sigma$ be elements not contained in V_0, W_0 and Σ_0. Let $V = V_0 \cup \{\perp_V\}$, $W = W_0 \cup \{\perp_W\}$, $\Sigma = \Sigma_0 \cup \{\perp_\Sigma\}$, with typical elements α, β and σ. We put $\alpha_1 \sqsubseteq \alpha_2$ iff $\alpha_1 = \perp_V$ or $\alpha_1 = \alpha_2$, and similarly for $\beta_1 \sqsubseteq \beta_2$ and $\sigma_1 \sqsubseteq \sigma_2$.

END 3.17.

Observe the difference with chapter 2. The sets denoted there by V, W and Σ are now denoted by V_0, W_0 and Σ_0, respectively. It should also be noted that a different definition of Σ might have been adopted: Σ = *Ivar* $\rightarrow$ V, with $\perp_\Sigma = \lambda x \cdot \perp_V$. This definition allows functions σ such that, for some arguments $x \in \mathit{Ivar}$, $\sigma(x) \in V_0$, whereas at the same time for some $y \in \mathit{Ivar}$, $\sigma(y) = \bot_V$. Since our semantic definitions nowhere require this additional structure on the states, we prefer definition 3.17, according to which each state σ is either everywhere defined (always yielding an element of V_0), or nowhere defined.

Some adaptations of the notations in chapter 2 are now in order:

DEFINITION 3.18 ($\bot$ in variants and <u>if</u>-<u>then</u>-<u>else</u>-<u>fi</u>).

a. $\bot_\Sigma\{\alpha/x\} = \bot_\Sigma$

b. Let C be any cpo. We put

$$\underline{\text{if}}\ \beta\ \underline{\text{then}}\ c_1\ \underline{\text{else}}\ c_2\ \underline{\text{fi}} = \begin{cases} c_1, & \text{if } \beta = tt \\ c_2, & \text{if } \beta = ff \\ \bot_C, & \text{if } \beta = \bot_W \end{cases}$$

END 3.18.

Note that clause a of this definition preserves lemma 2.5. However, $\sigma\{\alpha/x\}(x) = \alpha$ now only holds for $\sigma \in \Sigma_0$.

Since the cpo Σ is by far the most frequently used in this treatise, we shall resort to the convention of dropping the index Σ from its least element $\bot_\Sigma$. From now on, $\bot$ always means $\bot_\Sigma$, whereas the least elements of V, W and other cpo's will remain to be denoted by $\bot_V$, $\bot_W$ or whatever applies.

Next, we come to the definition of $\mathcal{V}$: $\mathit{Iexp} \to (\Sigma \to_s V)$ and $\mathcal{W}$: $\mathit{Bexp} \to (\Sigma \to_s W)$, with Σ, V and W as in definition 3.17.

DEFINITION 3.19 ($\mathcal{V}$ and $\mathcal{W}$ extended for $\bot$).

a. For each $\sigma \in \Sigma_0$, $\mathcal{V}(s)(\sigma)$ is defined as in definition 2.3.
   Moreover, $\mathcal{V}(s)(\bot) = \bot_V$.

b. For each $\sigma \in \Sigma_0$, $\mathcal{W}(b)(\sigma)$ is defined as in definition 2.3.
   Moreover, $\mathcal{W}(b)(\bot) = \bot_W$.

END 3.19.

In other words, we have, for each $s \in Iexp$, extended the function $V(s)$ from Σ_0 to V_0 in a unique way to a strict function from Σ to V, and similarly for $W(b)$.

Our next definition gives the operational semantics for statements S in *Stat*. We introduce a function O: $Stat \to (\Sigma \to_s \Sigma)$, which coincides with the function M from definition 2.6 for assignment, sequential composition and the conditional statement (apart from its treatment of $\perp$) and in addition reflects the usual operational meaning of the while statement.

DEFINITION 3.20 (operational semantics of $S \in Stat$).

a. $O(x{:=}s)(\sigma) = \sigma\{V(s)(\sigma)/x\}$

b. $O(S_1;S_2)(\sigma) = O(S_2)(O(S_1)(\sigma))$

c. $O(\underline{\text{if}}\ b\ \underline{\text{then}}\ S_1\ \underline{\text{else}}\ S_2\ \underline{\text{fi}})(\sigma) =$
$\underline{\text{if}}\ W(b)(\sigma)\ \underline{\text{then}}\ O(S_1)(\sigma)\ \underline{\text{else}}\ O(S_2)(\sigma)\ \underline{\text{fi}}$

d. $O(\underline{\text{while}}\ b\ \underline{\text{do}}\ S\ \underline{\text{od}})(\sigma) =$

- $\sigma' \in \Sigma_0$, if there exist $n \geq 0$ and $\sigma_0,\ldots,\sigma_n$ (all elements of Σ_0), such that $\sigma = \sigma_0$, $\sigma' = \sigma_n$, $\sigma_i = O(S)(\sigma_{i-1})$, $i = 1,2,\ldots,n$, $W(b)(\sigma_i) = tt$, $i = 0,1,\ldots,n-1$, and $W(b)(\sigma_n) = ff$
- $\perp$, otherwise.

END 3.20.

The following remarks may help in understanding this definition. For S not a while statement, we make no distinction between operational (O) and denotational (M) semantics. It is felt that in these cases it is reasonably clear that the definition of $O(S)$ agrees with the usual operational understanding of how to execute S. A refinement which takes into account not only initial and final states in the definition of $O(S)$, but also keeps a trace of the intermediate states in the so-called computation sequence determined by the execution of S is also possible (and in fact incorporated in the definition of O to be developed in subsequent chapters). However, the present treatment concentrates on the definition of the while statement and we feel that further articulation of $\mathcal{O}$ for S not a while statement would detract from the understanding of the central questions. Secondly, let us have a closer look at clause d of the definition. Clearly, the case that $\mathcal{O}$(while b do S od)(σ) delivers $\sigma' \in \Sigma_0$ is in accordance with the usual meaning of the while statement. Now in which circumstances does this case not apply? Either $\mathcal{W}(b)(\sigma),\mathcal{W}(b)(\mathcal{M}(S)(\sigma)),\mathcal{W}(b)(\mathcal{M}(S;S)(\sigma)),\ldots$, all yield tt as an answer, in which case execution of the while statement does not terminate (take, for example, while true do S od) and $\bot$ is delivered, or one of σ_i, with $\sigma_0 = \sigma$, $\sigma_1 = \mathcal{M}(S)(\sigma)$, $\sigma_2 = \mathcal{M}(S;S)(\sigma),\ldots$, equals $\bot$, in which case the corresponding $\mathcal{W}(b)(\sigma_i)$ delivers $\bot_W$, and it is again appropriate to deliver $\bot$ as final result.

The next lemma first of all states that $\mathcal{O}(S)$ is strict for each $S \in \mathit{Stat}$, and secondly slightly reformulates the definition of $\mathcal{O}$(while b do S od), in order to facilitate the equivalence proof to be given presently (theorem 3.25).

LEMMA 3.21.

a. $\mathcal{O}(S)(\bot) = \bot$

b. Let S^i be short for D, if i = 0, for S, if i = 1, and for S^{i-1};S if i > 1.

$\mathcal{O}$(while b do S od)(σ) =

- $\sigma' \in \Sigma_0$, if there exists $n \geq 0$, such that $\sigma' = \mathcal{O}(S^n)(\sigma)$, $\mathcal{W}(b)(\mathcal{O}(S^m)(\sigma)) = tt$, for $m = 0,1,\ldots,n-1$, and $\mathcal{W}(b)(\mathcal{O}(S^n)(\sigma)) = ff$
- $\bot$, otherwise.

PROOF.

a. The proof is by induction on the complexity of S. If $S \equiv x{:=}s$, $\mathcal{O}(S)(\bot) = \bot\{\mathcal{V}(s)(\bot)/x\} = \bot$, by definition 3.18. If $S \equiv S_1;S_2$, $\mathcal{O}(S_1;S_2)(\bot) = \mathcal{O}(S_2)(\mathcal{O}(S_1)(\bot)) = \mathcal{O}(S_2)(\bot) = \bot$, by two applications of the induction hypothesis. If $S \equiv$ if b then S_1 else S_2 fi, $\mathcal{O}(S)(\bot) =$ if $\bot_W$ then $\mathcal{O}(S_1)(\bot)$ else $\mathcal{O}(S_2)(\bot)$ fi $= \bot$, by definition

3.18. If S $\equiv$ <u>while</u> b <u>do</u> S_1 <u>od</u>, the result follows from the discussion preceding this lemma.

b. Clear from definition 3.20.

END 3.21.

The denotational semantics of S is given by means of the function M: *Stat* $\to (\Sigma \to_s \Sigma)$, defined in

<u>DEFINITION 3.22</u> (denotational semantics of S $\in$ *Stat*).

a. $M(x:=s) = \lambda\sigma\cdot\sigma\{V(s)(\sigma)/x\}$

b. $M(S_1;S_2) = \lambda\sigma\cdot M(S_2)(M(S_1)(\sigma))$

c. $M($<u>if</u> b <u>then</u> S_1 <u>else</u> S_2 <u>fi</u>$)$ =

$\lambda\sigma\cdot$<u>if</u> $W(b)(\sigma)$ <u>then</u> $M(S_1)(\sigma)$ <u>else</u> $M(S_2)(\sigma)$ <u>fi</u>

d. $M($<u>while</u> b <u>do</u> S <u>od</u>$) = \bigsqcup_{i=0}^{\infty} \phi_i$, where

$$\begin{cases} \phi_0 = \lambda\sigma\cdot\bot \\ \phi_{i+1} = \lambda\sigma\cdot \underline{\text{if}}\ W(b)(\sigma)\ \underline{\text{then}}\ \phi_i(M(S)(\sigma))\ \underline{\text{else}}\ \sigma\ \underline{\text{fi}},\ i = 0,1,\ldots \end{cases}$$

END 3.22.

This definition needs justification in two respects. We have to show that it is well-formed in the sense that the lub $\bigsqcup_i \phi_i$ in clause d exists and that, indeed, $M(S) \in \Sigma \to_s \Sigma$. Moreover, we shall prove that it coincides with the operational definition for all S $\in$ *Stat*. In between, a number of examples of $M($<u>while</u> b <u>do</u> S <u>od</u>$)$ will be worked out.

<u>LEMMA 3.23</u>.

a. $\langle\phi_i\rangle_{i=0}^{\infty}$ has a lub in $\Sigma \to_s \Sigma$

b. $M(S) \in \Sigma \to_s \Sigma$.

PROOF.

a. By lemma 3.13, $\Sigma \rightarrow_s \Sigma$ is a cpo. Clearly, for i = 0,1,..., ϕ_i is strict. We now show that $\langle\phi_i\rangle_{i=0}^{\infty}$ is a chain. Firstly, $\phi_0 = \lambda\sigma\cdot\bot \sqsubseteq \phi_1$. Next, assume that $\phi_i \sqsubseteq \phi_{i+1}$ for some i. To show that $\phi_{i+1} \sqsubseteq \phi_{i+2}$, i.e. $\lambda\sigma\cdot\underline{\text{if}}\ \mathcal{W}(b)(\sigma)\ \underline{\text{then}}\ \phi_i(\mathcal{M}(S)(\sigma))$ $\underline{\text{else}}\ \sigma\ \underline{\text{fi}} \sqsubseteq \lambda\sigma\cdot\underline{\text{if}}\ \mathcal{W}(b)(\sigma)\ \underline{\text{then}}\ \phi_{i+1}(\mathcal{M}(S)(\sigma))\ \underline{\text{else}}\ \sigma\ \underline{\text{fi}}$. Take any σ'. Three subcases arise: $\mathcal{W}(b)(\sigma') = \bot_W$, $\mathcal{W}(b)(\sigma') = tt$, and $\mathcal{W}(b)(\sigma') = ff$. In the first and third subcase, both sides of the inclusion reduce to ⊥ or σ', respectively. In the second subcase we have to show that $\phi_i(\mathcal{M}(S)(\sigma')) \sqsubseteq \phi_{i+1}(\mathcal{M}(S)(\sigma'))$, and this follows by the induction hypothesis. Finally, since each ϕ_i, i = 0,1,..., is strict, $\bigsqcup_{i=0}^{\infty} \phi_i$ is strict.

b. Follows by definition 3.22 and part a.

END 3.23.

Examples of definition 3.22.

1. $\mathcal{M}(\underline{\text{while}}\ \underline{\text{true}}\ \underline{\text{do}}\ S\ \underline{\text{od}}) = \bigsqcup_{i=0}^{\infty} \phi'_i$, where $\phi'_0 = \lambda\sigma\cdot\bot$,

   $\phi'_{i+1} = \lambda\sigma\cdot\underline{\text{if}}\ \mathcal{W}(\underline{\text{true}})(\sigma)\ \underline{\text{then}}\ \phi'_i(\mathcal{M}(S)(\sigma))\ \underline{\text{else}}\ \sigma\ \underline{\text{fi}}$, i = 0,1,...,

   i.e. $\phi'_{i+1} = \lambda\sigma\cdot\ \underline{\text{if}}\ \sigma = \bot\ \underline{\text{then}}\ \bot\ \underline{\text{else}}\ \phi'_i(\mathcal{M}(S)(\sigma))\ \underline{\text{fi}}$, i = 0,1,....

   From this, it is easily shown by induction on i that $\phi'_i = \lambda\sigma\cdot\bot$ for each i, and we obtain that $\mathcal{M}(\underline{\text{while}}\ \underline{\text{true}}\ \underline{\text{do}}\ S\ \underline{\text{od}}) = \lambda\sigma\cdot\bot$, as was to be expected.

2. $\mathcal{M}(\underline{\text{while}}\ \underline{\text{false}}\ \underline{\text{do}}\ S\ \underline{\text{od}}) = \bigsqcup_{i=0}^{\infty} \phi''_i$, where $\phi''_0 = \lambda\sigma\cdot\bot$ and $\phi''_{i+1} =$ $\lambda\sigma\cdot\ \underline{\text{if}}\ \mathcal{W}(\underline{\text{false}})(\sigma)\ \underline{\text{then}}\ \phi''_i(\mathcal{M}(S)(\sigma))\ \underline{\text{else}}\ \sigma\ \underline{\text{fi}}$, i = 0,1,.... From this, $\phi''_{i+1} = \lambda\sigma\cdot\sigma$, i = 0,1,..., and we obtain that

$\mathcal{M}$(<u>while</u> <u>false</u> <u>do</u> S <u>od</u>) = $\lambda\sigma\cdot\sigma$.

3. Let $\sigma \in \Sigma_0$.

$\mathcal{M}$(<u>while</u> x>0 <u>do</u> x:=x-1 <u>od</u>)($\sigma\{2/x\}$) = $(\bigsqcup_{i=0}^{\infty} \phi_i)(\sigma\{2/x\}) = \sigma\{0/x\}$,

since

$$\phi_0(\sigma\{2/x\}) = \bot$$

$$\phi_1(\sigma\{2/x\}) = \phi_0(\sigma\{1/x\}) = \bot$$

$$\phi_2(\sigma\{2/x\}) = \phi_1(\sigma\{1/x\}) = \phi_0(\sigma\{0/x\}) = \bot$$

$$\phi_3(\sigma\{2/x\}) = \phi_2(\sigma\{1/x\}) = \phi_1(\sigma\{0/x\}) = \sigma\{0/x\}$$

$$\phi_i(\sigma\{2/x\}) = \sigma\{0/x\}, \quad i > 3$$

whence $(\bigsqcup_{i=0}^{\infty} \phi_i)(\sigma\{2/x\}) = \bigsqcup_{i=0}^{\infty} \phi_i(\sigma\{2/x\}) = \bigsqcup_{i=0}^{\infty} \sigma\{0/x\} = \sigma\{0/x\}$.

By way of preparation for the equivalence theorem stating that $\mathcal{O}(S) = \mathcal{M}(S)$, we need

<u>LEMMA 3.24</u>. Let ϕ_i, i = 0,1,..., be as in definition 3.22. For each $\sigma \in \Sigma$, $\sigma' \in \Sigma_0$ and $i \geq 0$ we have that $\sigma' = \phi_i(\sigma)$ iff there exists j, $0 \leq j < i$, such that

(i) $\sigma' = \mathcal{M}(S^j)(\sigma)$

(ii) $\mathcal{W}(b)(\mathcal{M}(S^k)(\sigma)) = tt$, for k = 0,1,...,j-1

$\mathcal{W}(b)(\mathcal{M}(S^j)(\sigma)) = ff$.

<u>PROOF</u>.

(If) We use induction on i. If i = 0, we have nothing to prove. Now assume the proposition for some $i \geq 0$ and suppose that conditions (i) and (ii) are satisfied with i+1 replacing i. We have to show that then $\sigma' = \phi_{i+1}(\sigma)$, i.e. σ' = <u>if</u> $\mathcal{W}(b)(\sigma)$ <u>then</u> $\phi_i(\mathcal{M}(S)(\sigma))$ <u>else</u> σ <u>fi</u>. First consider the case that $\mathcal{W}(b)(\sigma) = tt$. We have to verify whether $\sigma' = \phi_i(\mathcal{M}(S)(\sigma)) = \phi_i(\sigma'')$, say. Since $\mathcal{W}(b)(\sigma) = tt$, we have for the integer j in conditions (i) and (ii) that j > 0. Thus, they imply conditions (i') $\sigma' = \mathcal{M}(S^{j-1})(\sigma'')$ and (ii') $\mathcal{W}(b)(\mathcal{M}(S^{k-1})(\sigma'')) = tt$, $k-1 = 0,1,\ldots,j-2$ and $\mathcal{W}(b)(\mathcal{M}(S^{j-1})(\sigma'')) = ff$. Hence, by the induction hypothesis, $\sigma' = \phi_i(\sigma'')$ follows. The easier case that $\mathcal{W}(b)(\sigma) = ff$ is left to the reader.

(Only if) Again by induction on i. If $i = 0$, $\phi_0(\sigma) \notin \Sigma_0$, and we have nothing to prove. Otherwise, assume the proposition for some i and let $\sigma' = \phi_{i+1}(\sigma) = \underline{\text{if}}\ \mathcal{W}(b)(\sigma)\ \underline{\text{then}}\ \phi_i(\mathcal{M}(S)(\sigma))\ \underline{\text{else}}\ \sigma\ \underline{\text{fi}}$. We have to show that conditions (i) and (ii) are satisfied with i+1 replacing i. First suppose that $\mathcal{W}(b)(\sigma) = tt$, i.e. that $\sigma' = \phi_i(\mathcal{M}(S)(\sigma)) = \phi_i(\sigma'')$, say. By the induction hypothesis, there exists some j' satisfying (i) and (ii) with σ'' replacing σ. Clearly, it suffices to take $j = j'+1$ to obtain conditions (i) and (ii) for i+1. The case that $\mathcal{W}(b)(\sigma) = ff$ is again left as an exercise.

END 3.24.

This brings us to the basic equivalence theorem on $\mathcal{O}$ and $\mathcal{M}$, the proof of which is based on lemmas 3.21 and 3.24.

THEOREM 3.25. For each $S \in \mathit{Stat}$, $\mathcal{O}(S) = \mathcal{M}(S)$.

PROOF. Induction on the complexity of S. If S is not a while statement, the result is immediate by definitions 3.20 and 3.22. Now let $S \equiv \underline{\text{while}}\ b\ \underline{\text{do}}\ S_1\ \underline{\text{od}}$. First assume that $\mathcal{O}(S)(\sigma) = \sigma'$. By lemma 3.21, either $\sigma' \in \Sigma_0$ and there exists $n \geq 0$ such that $\sigma' = \mathcal{O}(S_1^n)(\sigma)$, $\mathcal{W}(b)(\mathcal{O}(S_1^m)(\sigma)) = tt$, $m = 0,1,\ldots,n-1$, and $\mathcal{W}(b)(\mathcal{O}(S_1^n)(\sigma)) = ff$, or $\sigma' = \perp$. As first subcase, let $\sigma' \in \Sigma_0$. By the induction hypothesis, $\mathcal{O}(S_1) = \mathcal{M}(S_1)$. Thus there exists $n \geq 0$ such that $\sigma' = \mathcal{M}(S_1^n)(\sigma)$, $\mathcal{W}(b)(\mathcal{M}(S_1^m)(\sigma)) = tt$, $m = 0,1,\ldots,n-1$, and $\mathcal{W}(b)(\mathcal{M}(S_1^n)(\sigma)) = ff$. Let $\phi'_0 = \lambda\sigma\cdot\perp$, $\phi'_{i+1} = \lambda\sigma\cdot\underline{\text{if}}\ \mathcal{W}(b)(\sigma)\ \underline{\text{then}}\ \phi'_i(\mathcal{M}(S_1)(\sigma))\ \underline{\text{else}}\ \sigma\ \underline{\text{fi}}$, $i = 0,1,\ldots$. By definition 3.22, $\mathcal{M}(S) = \bigsqcup_{i=0}^{\infty} \phi'_i$. By lemma 3.24,

$\sigma' = \phi_i'(\sigma)$ for each $i \geq n+1$. Thus $\sigma' = \bigsqcup_{i=0}^{\infty} \phi_i'(\sigma) = (\bigsqcup_{i=0}^{\infty} \phi_i')(\sigma) = \mathcal{M}(S)(\sigma)$, as was to be shown. As second subcase, let $\sigma' = \bot$. We assert that then $\phi_k'(\sigma) = \bot$, for $k = 0,1,\ldots$. In fact, if, for some $i \geq 0$, $\phi_i'(\sigma) = \sigma'' \in \Sigma_0$, another application of lemma 3.24, together with the induction hypothesis, would result in some j, $0 \leq j < i$, such that $\sigma'' = \mathcal{O}(S_1^j)(\sigma)$, $\mathcal{W}(b)(\mathcal{O}(S_1^k)(\sigma)) = tt$, $k = 0,1,\ldots,j-1$, and $\mathcal{W}(b)(\mathcal{O}(S_1^j)(\sigma)) = ff$. Thus, we would have obtained that both $\mathcal{O}(S)(\sigma) = \sigma'' \in \Sigma_0$, and $\mathcal{O}(S)(\sigma) = \bot$, which is impossible. Therefore, $\phi_k'(\sigma) = \bot$ for all k, and $\mathcal{M}(S)(\sigma) = \bot$ immediately follows. We now prove the reverse, viz. if $\sigma' = \mathcal{M}(S)(\sigma)$ then $\sigma' = \mathcal{O}(S)(\sigma)$. Assume $\sigma' = \mathcal{M}(S)(\sigma)$, and $\mathcal{O}(S)(\sigma) = \sigma'' \neq \sigma'$. Then, by the above argument, $\mathcal{M}(S)(\sigma) = \sigma''$, and we have obtained a contradiction.

END 3.25.

The last part of this section is devoted to the least-fixed-point characterization of the while statement. Let ϕ_i, $i = 0,1,\ldots$, be as in definition 3.22, and let $\phi = \bigsqcup_{i=0}^{\infty} \phi_i$. We shall exhibit an operator Φ: $(\Sigma \to_s \Sigma) \to (\Sigma \to_s \Sigma)$, such that

(i) $\Phi(\phi) = \phi$ (ϕ is a fixed point of Φ)

(ii) If, for some $\psi \in \Sigma \to_s \Sigma$, $\Phi(\psi) = \psi$, then $\phi \sqsubseteq \psi$ (ϕ is included in each fixed point of Φ).

Together, (i) and (ii) establish that ϕ is the least fixed point of Φ.

<u>THEOREM 3.26</u>. Let $\mathcal{M}$(<u>while</u> b <u>do</u> S <u>od</u>) $= \bigsqcup_{i=0}^{\infty} \phi_i$, with ϕ_i as in definition 3.22. Let ϕ be short for $\bigsqcup_{i=0}^{\infty} \phi_i$, and let

$$\Phi = \lambda\psi\cdot\lambda\sigma\cdot\underline{\text{if}}\ \mathcal{W}(b)(\sigma)\ \underline{\text{then}}\ \psi(\mathcal{M}(S)(\sigma))\ \underline{\text{else}}\ \sigma\ \underline{\text{fi}}$$

(i.e. Φ is that operator from $\Sigma \to_s \Sigma$ to $\Sigma \to_s \Sigma$ which maps each

$\psi_0 \in \Sigma \rightarrow_s \Sigma$ to the function $\lambda\sigma\cdot\underline{\text{if}}\ \mathcal{W}(b)(\sigma)\ \underline{\text{then}}\ \psi_0(\mathcal{M}(S)(\sigma))\ \underline{\text{else}}\ \sigma\ \underline{\text{fi}}$, i.e. to the function which maps each $\sigma_0 \in \Sigma$ to the element $\underline{\text{if}}\ \mathcal{W}(b)(\sigma_0)\ \underline{\text{then}}\ \psi_0(\mathcal{M}(S)(\sigma_0))\ \underline{\text{else}}\ \sigma_0\ \underline{\text{fi}}$). Then $\phi = \mu\Phi$.

PROOF.

a. First we show that $\Phi(\phi) = \phi$, i.e. that for each σ, $\bigsqcup_{i=0}^{\infty} \phi_i(\sigma) = \underline{\text{if}}\ \mathcal{W}(b)(\sigma)\ \underline{\text{then}}\ (\bigsqcup_{i=0}^{\infty} \phi_i)(\mathcal{M}(S)(\sigma))\ \underline{\text{else}}\ \sigma\ \underline{\text{fi}}$. If $\mathcal{W}(b)(\sigma) = \bot_W$, then $\sigma = \bot$ and both sides of the equality reduce to $\bot$. If $\mathcal{W}(b)(\sigma) = tt$, the righthand side of the equality yields $(\bigsqcup_{i=0}^{\infty} \phi_i)(\mathcal{M}(S)(\sigma))$, which reduces to $\bigsqcup_{i=0}^{\infty} \phi_i(\mathcal{M}(S)(\sigma)) = \bigsqcup_{i=0}^{\infty} \phi_{i+1}(\sigma) = \bigsqcup_{i=0}^{\infty} \phi_i(\sigma)$. If $\mathcal{W}(b)(\sigma) = ff$, then, for all $i > 0$, $\phi_i(\sigma) = \sigma$; hence, $\bigsqcup_{i=0}^{\infty} \phi_i(\sigma) = \sigma$ follows.

b. Next, let $\Phi(\psi) = \psi$ for some ψ. We show that then $\phi \sqsubseteq \psi$. Since $\phi = \bigsqcup_{i=0}^{\infty} \phi_i$, it is sufficient to show that $\phi_i \sqsubseteq \psi$, $i = 0,1,\ldots$. Clearly, $\lambda\sigma\cdot\bot \sqsubseteq \psi$. Now assume that $\phi_i \sqsubseteq \psi$ for some i. Then $\phi_{i+1} = \lambda\sigma\cdot\underline{\text{if}}\ \mathcal{W}(b)(\sigma)\ \underline{\text{then}}\ \phi_i(\mathcal{M}(S)(\sigma))\ \underline{\text{else}}\ \sigma\ \underline{\text{fi}} \sqsubseteq$ (ind.) $\lambda\sigma\cdot\underline{\text{if}}\ \mathcal{W}(b)(\sigma)\ \underline{\text{then}}\ \psi(\mathcal{M}(S)(\sigma))\ \underline{\text{else}}\ \sigma\ \underline{\text{fi}} = \Phi(\psi) = \psi$, as was to be shown.

END 3.26.

It should be observed that an operator such as Φ may very well have more than one fixed point. Consider, for example, the special case that $\mathcal{M}(S) = \lambda\sigma\cdot\sigma$. Φ then simplifies to $\lambda\psi\cdot\lambda\sigma\cdot\underline{\text{if}}\ \mathcal{W}(b)(\sigma)\ \underline{\text{then}}\ \psi(\sigma)\ \underline{\text{else}}\ \sigma\ \underline{\text{fi}}$. It is easy to verify that, for each (arbitrary) $\psi_0 \in \Sigma \rightarrow_s \Sigma$, the function $\lambda\sigma\cdot\underline{\text{if}}\ \mathcal{W}(b)(\sigma)\ \underline{\text{then}}\ \psi_0(\sigma)\ \underline{\text{else}}\ \sigma\ \underline{\text{fi}}$ is a fixed point of this Φ. As *least* fixed point it has $\lambda\sigma\cdot\underline{\text{if}}\ \mathcal{W}(b)(\sigma)\ \underline{\text{then}}\ \bot\ \underline{\text{else}}\ \sigma\ \underline{\text{fi}}$, which is in accordance with the fact that $\mathcal{M}(\underline{\text{while}}\ b\ \underline{\text{do}}\ D\ \underline{\text{od}}) = \lambda\sigma\cdot\underline{\text{if}}\ \mathcal{W}(b)(\sigma)\ \underline{\text{then}}\ \bot\ \underline{\text{else}}\ \sigma\ \underline{\text{fi}}$. For each σ, execution of $\underline{\text{while}}$ b $\underline{\text{do}}$ D $\underline{\text{od}}$ does not terminate if $\mathcal{W}(b)(\sigma) = tt$, and yields σ if $\mathcal{W}(b)(\sigma) = ff$.

3.4. Correctness

The approach developed in chapter 2 to various questions concerning correctness of programs will now be extended to deal with the while statement. First, we investigate the consequences of the introduction of the undefined state $\perp$ for the general framework, in particular for the definition of the meaning of {p}S{q}. Secondly, we shall introduce an inference which may be used to prove partial correctness of the while statement (with respect to some pre- and postcondition) and show its soundness.

We start with a discussion of the class of assertions *Assn*. Its syntax is taken over without modification from chapter 2, but its semantics needs extension to cover treatment of the undefined state. First we turn the set T = {tt,ff}, with typical elements $\delta,\ldots$, into the following cpo: $\perp_T$ = ff, and we put $\delta_1 \sqsubseteq \delta_2$ iff $\delta_1 \Rightarrow \delta_2$. In fact, all this amounts to nothing more than the introduction of a cpo structure on T as indicated by figure 3a. Note the difference with W, as given in figure 3b!

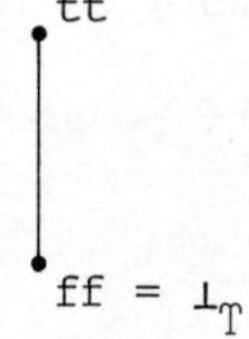

fig.3a: T as cpo

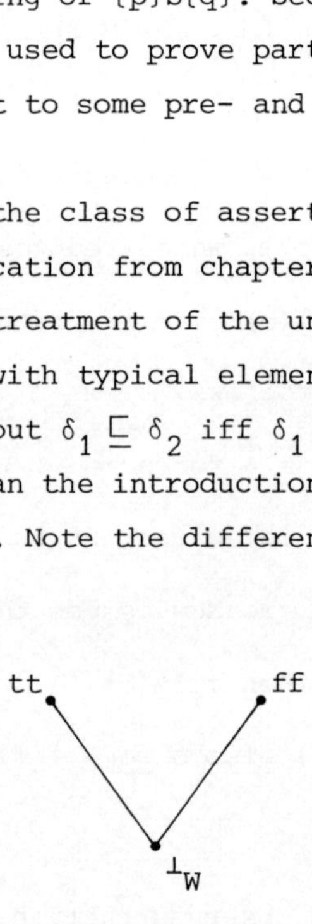

tt ff

$\perp_W$

fig.3b: W as cpo

DEFINITION 3.27 (semantics of assertions).

a. $\Pi \overset{df.}{=} \Sigma \to_s T$ has typical elements $\pi,\ldots$, which are called *predicates*.

b. T: *Assn* $\to \Pi$ is defined by

   (i) For each $\sigma \in \Sigma_0$, $T(p)(\sigma)$ is as in definition 2.9

   (ii) $T(p)(\perp)$ = ff.

END 3.27.

Note that $\Sigma \to_s T$ is a cpo according to lemma 3.13; moreover, the definition of $T(p)$ is such that it is indeed a strict function from Σ to T. The reasons for adopting the structure on T as just defined will become clearer with the further development of the theory. For the moment, we restrict ourselves to the remark that there is an essential difference between the role of a boolean expression b and an assertion p. Each b is part of a program, and it makes no sense, when evaluating it in an undefined state, to yield anything but an undefined value ($\perp_W$). However, assertions p are used to state properties *about* programs and it may well be meaningful to deliver a defined value (ff) in a situation where the program finds itself in an undefined state. Let us point out already one particular consequence of the definition. For $p \in Bexp$, $W(p)$ and $T(p)$ coincide only on Σ_0, since $W(b)(\perp) = \perp_W$, and $T(b)(\perp) = ff$.

The class of correctness formulae *Form* undergoes a slight syntactic extension:

DEFINITION 3.28 (syntax of correctness formulae).
The class *Form*, with typical elements f,..., is given by

$$f ::= p \mid \{p\}S\{q\} \mid S_1 \sqsubseteq S_2 \mid f_1 \wedge f_2$$

END 3.28.

Thus, the only difference with definition 2.10 lies in the clause $S_1 \sqsubseteq S_2$, which will obtain the natural meaning of $M(S_1) \sqsubseteq M(S_2)$. From now on, $S_1 = S_2$ will be short for $S_1 \sqsubseteq S_2 \wedge S_2 \sqsubseteq S_1$. (Of course, there is also the implicit difference that S may now be or contain a while statement.) Again, we shall use the function F: $Form \to (\Sigma \to_s T)$ to define the meaning of correctness formulae. It should be clear how $F(f)$ is to be defined in all cases, but for the one where $f \equiv \{p\}S\{q\}$. As remarked already in the introduction to this chapter, we have the choice between two possibilities:

$$- \mathcal{F}(\{p\}S\{q\})(\sigma) = \begin{cases} tt, & \text{if } \sigma \neq \bot \text{ and} \\ & [\mathcal{T}(p)(\sigma) \wedge \mathcal{M}(S)(\sigma) \neq \bot] \Rightarrow \mathcal{T}(q)(\mathcal{M}(S)(\sigma)) \\ ff, & \text{otherwise} \end{cases}$$

$$- \mathcal{F}(\{p\}S\{q\})(\sigma) = \begin{cases} tt, & \text{if } \sigma \neq \bot \text{ and} \\ & \mathcal{T}(p)(\sigma) \Rightarrow [\mathcal{M}(S)(\sigma) \neq \bot \wedge \mathcal{T}(q)(\mathcal{M}(S)(\sigma))] \\ ff, & \text{otherwise.} \end{cases}$$

We choose the first alternative and postpone a discussion of the second one till a later stage (see chapter 8). If $\mathcal{F}(\{p\}S\{q\})(\sigma) = tt$ for all $\sigma \neq \bot$ (according to the first definition of $\mathcal{F}$) we call S *partially correct* with respect to precondition p and postcondition q. This terminology emphasizes that termination of S for states σ such that $\mathcal{T}(p)(\sigma)$ is satisfied, is not implied. *Only* if execution of S happens to terminate (expressed by the fact that $\mathcal{M}(S)(\sigma) \neq \bot$) do we require that $\mathcal{T}(q)(\mathcal{M}(S)(\sigma))$ holds. This should be contrasted with the second interpretation (S is then called *totally correct* with respect to p and q) where, for each state $\sigma \neq \bot$, if $\mathcal{T}(p)(\sigma)$ holds then S *is* required to terminate with resulting state $\sigma' = \mathcal{M}(S)(\sigma)$ $(\neq \bot)$ such that $\mathcal{T}(q)(\sigma')$ holds. (Observe that it would have been sufficient to formulate the second alternative, for $\sigma \neq \bot$, as $\mathcal{T}(p)(\sigma) \Rightarrow \mathcal{T}(q)(\mathcal{M}(S)(\sigma))$, since, by definition, $\mathcal{T}(q)(\bot) = ff$.)

Altogether, we have

DEFINITION 3.29 (semantics of correctness formulae).
$\mathcal{F}$: *Form* $\to (\Sigma \to_s T)$ is defined as follows: $\mathcal{F}(f)(\bot) = ff$ and, for each $\sigma \neq \bot$,

a. $\mathcal{F}(p)(\sigma) = \mathcal{T}(p)(\sigma)$

b. $\mathcal{F}(\{p\}S\{q\})(\sigma) = \begin{cases} tt, & \text{if } [\mathcal{T}(p)(\sigma) \wedge \mathcal{M}(S)(\sigma) \neq \bot] \Rightarrow \mathcal{T}(q)(\mathcal{M}(S)(\sigma)) \\ ff, & \text{otherwise} \end{cases}$

c. $\mathcal{F}(S_1 \sqsubseteq S_2)(\sigma) = (\mathcal{M}(S_1)(\sigma) \sqsubseteq \mathcal{M}(S_2)(\sigma))$

d. $\mathcal{F}(f_1 \wedge f_2)(\sigma) = \mathcal{F}(f_1)(\sigma) \wedge \mathcal{F}(f_2)(\sigma)$.

END 3.29.

DEFINITION 3.30 (validity and soundness).

a. If $\mathcal{F}(f)(\sigma)$ = tt for all $\sigma \neq \bot$, we call f *valid* and express this by writing

$$\models f$$

b. An inference is a construct of the form $\frac{f_1,\ldots,f_n}{f}$, with f_i, $i = 1,\ldots,n$, and $f \in \mathit{Form}$.

An inference $\frac{f_1,\ldots,f_n}{f}$ is called *sound*, written as

$$\boxed{\frac{f_1,\ldots,f_n}{f}}$$

whenever validity of f_i, $i = 1,\ldots,n$, implies validity of f.

END 3.30.

Examples

1. $\models$ <u>while</u> b <u>do</u> S <u>od</u> = <u>if</u> b <u>then</u> S; <u>while</u> b <u>do</u> S <u>od</u> <u>else</u> D <u>fi</u>.
   Note that this is nothing but a syntactic reformulation of the fixed point property of theorem 3.26.

2. $$\boxed{\frac{S = \underline{\text{if}}\ b\ \underline{\text{then}}\ S_1;S\ \underline{\text{else}}\ D\ \underline{\text{fi}}}{\underline{\text{while}}\ b\ \underline{\text{do}}\ S_1\ \underline{\text{od}} \sqsubseteq S}}$$

   (theorem 3.26 again).

3. $\models$ <u>while</u> <u>true</u> <u>do</u> S_1 <u>od</u> $\sqsubseteq S_2$
   ($\lambda\sigma\cdot\bot \sqsubseteq \phi$ for each $\phi \in \Sigma \rightarrow_s \Sigma$)

4. $\models$ <u>while</u> <u>false</u> <u>do</u> S <u>od</u> = D

5. $\models$ {p} <u>while</u> <u>true</u> <u>do</u> S <u>od</u> {q}
   (Since there is no σ such that $\mathcal{M}$(<u>while</u> <u>true</u> <u>do</u> S <u>od</u>)(σ) $\neq \bot$, we have that, whatever p and q are, $\mathcal{T}(p)(\sigma) \wedge \mathcal{M}$(<u>while</u> <u>true</u> <u>do</u> S <u>od</u>)(σ) $\neq \bot$ $\Rightarrow \mathcal{T}(q)(\mathcal{M}$(<u>while</u> <u>true</u> <u>do</u> S <u>od</u>)(σ)) is vacuously satisfied for all σ.)

6. $\models$ <u>while</u> b <u>do</u> <u>while</u> b <u>do</u> S <u>od</u> <u>od</u> = <u>while</u> b <u>do</u> S <u>od</u>,
   $\models$ <u>while</u> $b_1 \vee b_2$ <u>do</u> S <u>od</u> =
   <u>while</u> b_1 <u>do</u> S <u>od</u>; <u>while</u> b_2 <u>do</u> S; <u>while</u> b_1 <u>do</u> S <u>od</u> <u>od</u>

(The proofs of these two equivalences are rather tedious with the tools available up to now. They become easier in a formalism to be developed later, see chapters 5 and 7.)

7. Is <u>while</u> $b_1 \wedge b_2$ <u>do</u> S <u>od</u> = <u>while</u> b_1 <u>do</u> <u>while</u> b_2 <u>do</u> S <u>od</u> <u>od</u> valid? And <u>while</u> b <u>do</u> S <u>od</u> = <u>if</u> b <u>then</u> <u>while</u> b <u>do</u> S <u>od</u> <u>else</u> D <u>fi</u>?
8. Theorem 2.15 and lemmas 2.27, 2.28 and 2.29 may be taken over without any modification.
9. ⊨ {x=5} <u>while</u> x>0 <u>do</u> x:=x-1 <u>od</u> {x=0}.

For the proof of validity results such as example 9, the following powerful inference is quite useful:

<u>THEOREM 3.31.</u>

$$\frac{\{p \wedge b\} S \{p\}}{\{p\}\ \underline{\text{while}}\ b\ \underline{\text{do}}\ S\ \underline{\text{od}}\ \{p \wedge \neg b\}}$$

In words, if p is an *invariant* of the statement S under the assumption that b is satisfied, then p is also an invariant of the while statement <u>while</u> b <u>do</u> S <u>od</u>. Moreover, as postcondition of the while statement, ¬b always holds.

Before presenting the proof of this theorem, we show how it may be applied in the proof of example 9.

(i) ⊨ {x≥0 ∧ x>0} x:=x-1 {x≥0}

p b p

This follows since, by theorem 2.15 ⊨ {x-1 ≥ 0} x:=x-1 {x≥0}

(ii) From (i) and theorem 3.31,

⊨ {x≥0} <u>while</u> x>0 <u>do</u> x:=x-1 <u>od</u> {x≥0 ∧¬ (x>0)}

p p ¬b

(iii) Since ⊨ (x=5) ⊃ (x≥0) and ⊨ (x≥0) ∧¬ (x>0) = (x=0), the desired result ⊨{x=5} <u>while</u> x>0 <u>do</u> x:=x-1 <u>od</u> {x=0} follows by an application of the rule of consequence (lemma 2.29).

PROOF of theorem 3.31.

a. First we show that $\models$ {true} while b do S od {$\neg$b}. By the definitions it is sufficient to show that, for all $\sigma \neq \bot$, if $\sigma' = (\bigsqcup_{i=0}^{\infty} \phi_i)(\sigma) \wedge \sigma' \neq \bot$ then $T(\neg b)(\sigma')$. So assume $\sigma' = \bigsqcup_{i=0}^{\infty} \phi_i(\sigma)$ and $\sigma' \neq \bot$. Clearly, by discreteness of Σ, $\sigma' = \phi_i(\sigma)$ for some i. Since $\sigma' \neq \bot$, by lemma 3.24 there exists some j such that $\sigma' = M(S^j)(\sigma)$ and $W(b)(M(S^j)(\sigma)) = ff$. From this it follows that $T(\neg b)(\sigma') = tt$, as was to be shown.

b. Next, we show that, if $\models$ {p$\wedge$b}S{p}, then $\models$ {p} while b do S od {p}. So assume (*): $\models$ {p$\wedge$b}S{p}. We have to prove that, for all $\sigma \neq \bot$ and all σ', and all i, if $T(p)(\sigma)$ and $\sigma' = \phi_i(\sigma)$ and $\sigma' \neq \bot$, then $T(p)(\sigma')$. We use induction on i:

(i) i = 0. Clear

(ii) i $\rightarrow$ i+1. Assume the proposition for some i. We verify that then, for all $\sigma \neq \bot$ and σ', if $T(p)(\sigma)$ and $\sigma' = \phi_{i+1}(\sigma)$ and $\sigma' \neq \bot$, then $T(p)(\sigma')$. Since $\sigma \neq \bot$, $W(b)(\sigma) \neq \bot_W$.

(α) Assume $W(b)(\sigma) = tt$. Then $\sigma' = \phi_i(\sigma'')$, with $\sigma'' = M(S)(\sigma)$. Since $\sigma' \neq \bot$, also $\sigma'' \neq \bot$. Since $W(b)(\sigma) = tt$, $\sigma'' \neq \bot$ and $T(p)(\sigma) = tt$, from (*) it follows that $T(p)(\sigma'') = tt$. Since $\sigma'' \neq \bot$, $T(p)(\sigma'') = tt$, $\sigma' = \phi_i(\sigma'')$ and $\sigma' \neq \bot$, application of the induction hypothesis yields that $T(p)(\sigma') = tt$.

(β) Assume that $W(b)(\sigma) = ff$. Then $\sigma' = \sigma$ and $T(p)(\sigma')$ follows from $T(p)(\sigma)$.

c. From part a and the rule of consequence, $\models$ {p} while b do S od {$\neg$b}. From this and part b we infer that if $\models$ {p$\wedge$b}S{p}, then $\models$ {p} while b do S od {$\neg$b} $\wedge$ {p} while b do S od {p}. By exercise 2.10, we therefore obtain that, if $\models$ {p$\wedge$b}S{p}, then $\models$ {p} while b do S od {p$\wedge\neg$b}, as was to be shown.

END 3.31.

3.5. Weakest preconditions and strongest postconditions

The notions of weakest precondition and strongest postcondition are taken over exactly as they are given in definition 2.17. Moreover, the syntactic definition of the class *Cond* is unchanged as well. As to its semantics, we have to take into account the refinement in the definition of $F(\{p\}S\{q\})$ as discussed above. Thus, we arrive at

DEFINITION 3.32 (semantics of conditions).
Let *Cond* be as in definition 2.18, with typical elements p,q,r,....
The function T: $Cond \to (\Sigma \to_S T)$ is defined by

a. For p not of the form $S \to p$ or $p \leftarrow S$, $T(p)$ is as in definition 3.27

$$\text{b. } T(S{\to}p)(\sigma) = \begin{cases} tt, & \text{if } \sigma \neq \bot, \text{ and } M(S)(\sigma) \neq \bot \Rightarrow T(p)(M(S)(\sigma)) \\ ff, & \text{otherwise} \end{cases}$$

$$\text{c. } T(p{\leftarrow}S)(\sigma) = \begin{cases} tt, & \text{if } \sigma \neq \bot, \text{ and there exists } \sigma' \text{ such that } T(p)(\sigma') \\ & \qquad\qquad \text{and } \sigma = M(S)(\sigma') \\ ff, & \text{otherwise.} \end{cases}$$

END 3.32.

It is straightforward from this definition that $S \to p$ and $p \leftarrow S$ are indeed the weakest precondition and strongest postcondition, i.e. that $\models \{p\}S\{q\}$ iff $\models p \supset (S{\to}q)$ iff $\models (p{\leftarrow}S) \supset q$. Inspired by theorems 2.21 and 2.22, we now might look for results of the form

$\models$ <u>while</u> b <u>do</u> S <u>od</u> $\to$ p = ?, and
$\models$ p $\leftarrow$ <u>while</u> b <u>do</u> S <u>od</u> = ??

where at the place of the ? and ?? one would expect constructs from *Cond* involving $S \to p'$ and $p'' \leftarrow S$, for suitable p' and p". However, the language *Cond* is not rich enough to express the desired conditions in a *direct* manner. (See, however, the proposition in section 3.6. Also, in chapter 8, we introduce an extension of *Cond* which does allow us to formulate ? and ?? syntactically.) Instead, we resort to a semantic characterization of the two conditions, i.e. a description of them which stays fully within the realm of the cpo's $\Sigma \to_s \Sigma$, $\Sigma \to_s T$, etc. By way of preparation, we state the following easy lemma:

LEMMA 3.33.

a. Each subset of T has a glb and lub

b. Each subset of Π ($= \Sigma \to_s T$) has a glb and lub

c. T and Π have tt and $\lambda\sigma\cdot(\sigma\neq\bot)$ as greatest elements, respectively.

PROOF. Immediate.

END 3.33.

We also need the semantic counterparts of $S \to p$ and $p \leftarrow S$, in the sense as given in

DEFINITION 3.34 (semantic counterparts of " $\to$ " and " $\leftarrow$ ").

Let $\phi \in \Sigma \to_s \Sigma$, $\pi \in \Pi$. We define the predicates $\phi \to \pi$ and $\pi \leftarrow \phi$ by

$$\text{a. } (\phi{\to}\pi)(\sigma) = \begin{cases} \text{tt, if } \sigma \neq \bot \text{ and } \phi(\sigma) \neq \bot \Rightarrow \pi(\phi(\sigma)) \\ \text{ff, otherwise} \end{cases}$$

$$\text{b. } (\pi{\leftarrow}\phi)(\sigma) = \begin{cases} \text{tt, if } \sigma \neq \bot \text{ and there exists } \sigma' \text{ such that } \pi(\sigma') \text{ and} \\ \qquad\qquad \sigma = \phi(\sigma') \\ \text{ff, otherwise.} \end{cases}$$

END 3.34.

Remark. In the sequel, it is often convenient to replace the definition of $(\phi{\to}\pi)(\sigma)$ by the equivalent formulation:

$$(\phi{\to}\pi)(\sigma) = \begin{cases} \text{tt, if } \sigma \neq \bot \text{ and, for all } \sigma', \text{ if } \sigma' = \phi(\sigma) \text{ and } \sigma' \neq \bot \\ \qquad\qquad \text{then } \pi(\sigma') \\ \text{ff, otherwise.} \end{cases}$$

The next theorem shows how the meaning of <u>while</u> b <u>do</u> S <u>od</u> $\to$ p can be characterized as *greatest fixed point* of a suitable operator.

THEOREM 3.35. Let T(while b do S od $\rightarrow$ p) $= \pi \in \Pi$.

a. $\pi = \bigsqcap_{i=0}^{\infty} \pi_i$, where

$\pi_0 = \lambda\sigma\cdot(\sigma\neq\bot)$,

$\pi_{i+1} = \lambda\sigma\cdot$if $W(b)(\sigma)$ then $(M(S)\rightarrow\pi_i)(\sigma)$ else $T(p)(\sigma)$ fi

b. Let Ψ: $(\Sigma \rightarrow_s T) \rightarrow (\Sigma \rightarrow_s T)$ be given by

$$\Psi = \lambda\pi'\cdot\lambda\sigma\cdot\text{if } W(b)(\sigma) \text{ then } (M(S)\rightarrow\pi')(\sigma) \text{ else } T(p)(\sigma) \text{ fi}$$

Then $\pi = \nu\Psi$.

Notation. In the proof below (as in many cases in the sequel) we shall use a quantifier notation to abbreviate sentences such as "For all σ and σ', if $T(p)(\sigma)$ and $\sigma' = M(S)(\sigma)$ and $\sigma' \neq \bot$ then $T(q)(\sigma')$" to "$\forall\sigma,\sigma'[T(p)(\sigma) \wedge \sigma' = M(S)(\sigma) \wedge \sigma' \neq \bot \Rightarrow T(q)(\sigma')]$", etc.

PROOF.

a. T(while b do S od $\rightarrow$ p) $=$ M(while b do S od) $\rightarrow T(p) =$

$(\bigsqcup_i \phi_i) \rightarrow \pi'$, by the definitions and using π' as an abbreviation for $T(p)$. First we show that $(\bigsqcup_i \phi_i) \rightarrow \pi_i = \bigsqcap_i(\phi_i \rightarrow \pi')$. Take any σ.

$((\bigsqcup_i \phi_i)\rightarrow\pi')(\sigma) = tt$ iff

$(\sigma\neq\bot) \wedge \forall\sigma'[\sigma' = \bigsqcup_i \phi_i(\sigma) \wedge \sigma' \neq \bot \Rightarrow \pi'(\sigma')]$ iff

$(\sigma\neq\bot) \wedge \forall\sigma'[\exists i[\sigma' = \phi_i(\sigma) \wedge \sigma' \neq \bot] \Rightarrow \pi'(\sigma')]$ iff (cf. exercise 2.2)

$(\sigma\neq\bot) \wedge \forall i[\forall\sigma'[\sigma' = \phi_i(\sigma) \wedge \sigma' \neq \bot \Rightarrow \pi'(\sigma')]]$ iff

$\forall i[(\sigma\neq\bot) \wedge \forall\sigma'[\sigma' = \phi_i(\sigma) \wedge \sigma' \neq \bot \Rightarrow \pi'(\sigma')]]$ iff

$\bigsqcap_i(\phi_i \rightarrow \pi')(\sigma)$. Next, we show that, for all i, $\phi_i \rightarrow \pi' = \pi_i$.

i = 0. If $\sigma \in \Sigma_0$, $(\phi_0 \rightarrow \pi')(\sigma) = (\lambda\sigma\cdot\bot \rightarrow \pi')(\sigma) = tt = \pi_0(\sigma)$.

If $\sigma = \bot$, $(\phi_0 \rightarrow \pi')(\sigma) = ff = \pi_0(\sigma)$.

i $\rightarrow$ i+1. Assume (*): $\phi_i \rightarrow \pi' = \pi_i$. To show that $\phi_{i+1} \rightarrow \pi' = \pi_{i+1}$.

Take any σ. If $\sigma = \bot$, clearly $(\phi_{i+1} \rightarrow \pi')(\sigma) = \pi_{i+1}(\sigma) = ff$. Next,

(i) Assume (**): $\mathcal{W}(b)(\sigma) = tt$. Then $(\phi_{i+1} \to \pi')(\sigma)$ iff

$(\sigma \neq \bot) \wedge \forall \sigma'[\sigma' = \phi_{i+1}(\sigma) \wedge \sigma' \neq \bot \Rightarrow \pi'(\sigma')]$ iff (using (**))

$(\sigma \neq \bot) \wedge \forall \sigma'[\sigma' = \phi_i(\mathcal{M}(S)(\sigma)) \wedge \sigma' \neq \bot \Rightarrow \pi'(\sigma')]$ iff

$(\sigma \neq \bot) \wedge \forall \sigma'[\exists \sigma''[\sigma' = \phi_i(\sigma'') \wedge \sigma'' = \mathcal{M}(S)(\sigma) \wedge \sigma' \neq \bot \Rightarrow \pi'(\sigma')]$ iff

$(\sigma \neq \bot) \wedge \forall \sigma', \sigma''[\sigma' = \phi_i(\sigma'') \wedge \sigma'' = \mathcal{M}(S)(\sigma) \wedge \sigma' \neq \bot \Rightarrow \pi'(\sigma')]$ iff

(since $\sigma' \neq \bot$, also $\sigma'' \neq \bot$)

$(\sigma \neq \bot) \wedge \forall \sigma', \sigma''[\sigma'' = \mathcal{M}(S)(\sigma) \wedge \sigma'' \neq \bot \wedge \sigma' = \phi_i(\sigma'') \wedge \sigma' \neq \bot \Rightarrow \pi'(\sigma')]$ iff

$(\sigma \neq \bot) \wedge \forall \sigma''[\sigma'' = \mathcal{M}(S)(\sigma) \wedge \sigma'' \neq \bot \Rightarrow \forall \sigma'[\sigma' = \phi_i(\sigma'') \wedge \sigma' \neq \bot \Rightarrow \pi'(\sigma')]]$ iff (using (*))

$(\sigma \neq \bot) \wedge \forall \sigma''[\sigma'' = \mathcal{M}(S)(\sigma) \wedge \sigma'' \neq \bot \Rightarrow \pi_i(\sigma'')]$ iff

$(\mathcal{M}(S) \to \pi_i)(\sigma)$ iff ((**) and def. of π_{i+1})

$\pi_{i+1}(\sigma)$

(ii) Assume (***): $\mathcal{W}(b)(\sigma) = ff$. Exercise.

b. That $\Psi(\pi) = \pi$ can be seen as follows: From theorem 3.26,

$\models$ <u>while</u> b <u>do</u> S <u>od</u> = <u>if</u> b <u>then</u> S; <u>while</u> b <u>do</u> S <u>od</u> <u>else</u> D <u>fi</u>. Thus

$\models$ <u>while</u> b <u>do</u> S <u>od</u> $\to$ p = <u>if</u> b <u>then</u> S; <u>while</u> b <u>do</u> S <u>od</u> <u>else</u> D <u>fi</u> $\to$ p.

Applying lemma 2.22, and the fact that $\models D \to p = p$, we obtain

$\models$ <u>while</u> b <u>do</u> S <u>od</u> $\to$ p = <u>if</u> b <u>then</u> S $\to$ (<u>while</u> b <u>do</u> S <u>od</u> $\to$ p) <u>else</u> p <u>fi</u>,

and the desired result follows from the definitions of Ψ and π.

Now assume that $\Psi(\pi'') = \pi''$. We show that $\pi'' \sqsubseteq \pi$. It is sufficient to show that $\pi'' \sqsubseteq \pi_i$, for each i = 0,1,.... Clearly, $\pi'' \sqsubseteq \pi_0$. Also the induction step: if $\pi'' \sqsubseteq \pi_i$ then $\pi'' \sqsubseteq \pi_{i+1}$, follows directly from the definitions of π_{i+1} and Ψ, and the fact that $\Psi(\pi'') = \pi''$.

END 3.35.

Remarks.

1. An operator such as Ψ may very well have more than one fixed point. Choosing for example $b \equiv \underline{\text{true}}$ and $S \equiv D$, Ψ reduces to $\lambda\pi'\cdot\lambda\sigma\cdot\underline{\text{if}}\ \sigma=\bot\ \underline{\text{then}}\ ff\ \underline{\text{else}}\ (\lambda\sigma\cdot\sigma \to \pi')(\sigma)\ \underline{\text{fi}} = \lambda\pi'\cdot\lambda\sigma\cdot\underline{\text{if}}\ \sigma\neq\bot$ $\underline{\text{then}}\ ff\ \underline{\text{else}}\ \pi'(\sigma)\ \underline{\text{fi}} = (\pi'\ \text{strict})\ \lambda\pi'\cdot\pi'$. Thus, ψ has as greatest fixed point the predicate $\lambda\sigma\cdot\sigma\neq\bot$ (and many other fixed points (in fact, all elements of Π), with $\lambda\sigma\cdot ff$ as least one). Since $\underline{\text{while}}$ $\underline{\text{true}}$ $\underline{\text{do}}$ D $\underline{\text{od}}$ terminates nowhere, we have indeed $\underline{\text{true}}$ as weakest precondition for every postcondition p, i.e. we have that

$$\models \underline{\text{while}}\ \underline{\text{true}}\ \underline{\text{do}}\ D\ \underline{\text{od}} \to p = \underline{\text{true}}$$

which is in accordance with our greatest fixed point result.

2. The rather tedious proof of this theorem will be replaced in chapter 8 by an argument using more powerful means (see corollary 8.30).

We conclude this section with a semantic characterization of the strongest postcondition $p \leftarrow \underline{\text{while}}\ b\ \underline{\text{do}}\ S\ \underline{\text{od}}$. No fixed point characterization is available. Instead we have

<u>THEOREM 3.36</u>. Let $\pi = \mathcal{T}(b)$, $\pi' = \mathcal{T}(p)$, $\phi = \bigsqcup_i \phi_i$, with ϕ_i as in definition 3.22, $\pi_0 = \lambda\sigma\cdot ff$, $\pi_{i+1} = \pi' \vee \{(\pi\wedge\pi_i) \leftarrow \mathcal{M}(S)\}$. Then

$$\pi' \leftarrow \phi \ = \ \neg\pi \wedge \bigsqcup_{i=0}^{\infty} \pi_i.$$

<u>PROOF</u>. By way of explanation we remark that the intended meaning of π_i, $i \geq 1$, is: For each $\sigma\neq\bot$, $\pi_i(\sigma) = \exists k\ (0 \leq k < i)\ \exists\sigma'[\pi'(\sigma') \wedge \sigma = \mathcal{M}(S^k)(\sigma') \wedge \forall j\ (0 \leq j < k)\ [\pi(\mathcal{M}(S^j)(\sigma'))]]$. We prove only that $\pi' \leftarrow \phi \sqsubseteq \neg\pi \wedge \bigsqcup_{i=0}^{\infty} \pi_i$, leaving the reverse inclusion as an exercise. $\pi' \leftarrow \phi \sqsubseteq \neg\pi$ follows as in the proof of theorem 3.31. There remains the proof of $\pi' \leftarrow \phi \sqsubseteq \bigsqcup_{i=0}^{\infty} \pi_i$. It is sufficient to show that

$\pi' \leftarrow \phi_i \sqsubseteq \bigsqcup_{i=0}^{\infty} \pi_i$, $i = 0,1,\ldots$. Take any σ. We show that $(\pi' \leftarrow \phi_i)(\sigma) \sqsubseteq (\bigsqcup_i \pi_i)(\sigma)$. If $\sigma = \bot$, the result is clear. Otherwise, assume that $\exists\sigma'[\pi'(\sigma') \wedge \sigma = \phi_i(\sigma')]$ holds. From lemma 3.24 we obtain that there exists some j, $0 \le j < i$, such that $\sigma = \mathcal{M}(S^j)(\sigma')$, $\mathcal{W}(b)(\mathcal{M}(S^k)(\sigma')) = tt$, $k = 0,1,\ldots,j-1$, and $\mathcal{W}(b)(\mathcal{M}(S^j)(\sigma)) = ff$. We prove that $\exists\sigma'[\pi'(\sigma') \wedge \sigma = \phi_i(\sigma')] \sqsubseteq \pi_{j+1}(\sigma)$. Let $\sigma_k = \mathcal{M}(S^k)(\sigma')$, $k = 0,\ldots,j$. (Thus, $\sigma_0 = \sigma'$, $\sigma_j = \sigma$.) Then, for $k = 0,\ldots,j$, $\pi_{k+1}(\sigma_k)$ holds. In fact, $\pi_1(\sigma_0)$ holds since $\pi'(\sigma_0)$ holds. Next, we show that, for $k = 1,\ldots,j$, $\pi_{k+1}(\sigma_k)$ follows from $\pi_k(\sigma_{k-1})$. Since $k \le j$, $k-1 \le j-1$. Hence $\pi(\sigma_{k-1}) = \mathcal{W}(b)(\mathcal{M}(S^{k-1})(\sigma'))$ holds. From $\pi_k(\sigma_{k-1})$, $\pi(\sigma_{k-1})$, $\sigma_k = \mathcal{M}(S)(\sigma_{k-1})$ and the definition of π_{k+1}, the desired result $\pi_{k+1}(\sigma_k)$ follows. Taking $k = j$, we obtain $\pi_{j+1}(\sigma_j)$, or $\pi_{j+1}(\sigma)$, as was to be shown.

END 3.36.

Remarks

1. Though $\pi' \rightarrow \phi$ itself is not characterized as a fixed point, $\bigsqcup_i \pi_i$ *is* least fixed point of the operator $\Psi': \Pi \rightarrow \Pi$ defined by

   $$\Psi' = \lambda\pi''\cdot[\pi' \vee \{(\pi \wedge \pi'') \leftarrow \mathcal{M}(S)\}].$$

2. Of this theorem as well, a more concise proof using somewhat more advanced tools will be discussed in chapter 8 (see corollary 8.33).

3.6. Completeness

Just as in section 2.6, now that we have a number of validity and soundness results at our disposal, we may ask whether we have sufficient material for a completeness theorem. We show that this is in fact the case, provided we are willing to accept one important proposition which we cannot prove without recourse to tools not developed at the present stage of our theory.

PROPOSITION. Let $p \in \mathit{Assn}$ and $S \in \mathit{Stat}$. There exist *assertions* q_1 and q_2 such that

$$\models q_1 = S \to p \quad \text{and} \quad \models q_2 = p \leftarrow S$$

END.

Remarks.

1. The proposition states an *expressibility* result: weakest preconditions and strongest postconditions are expressible by means of assertions. The reader should compare this with lemma 2.31, where a similar result was obtained for the language of chapter 2. The addition of the while statement introduces an essential complication in the proof, in that we now need the tools of recursive function theory to prove the proposition. In chapter 5, we shall encounter a generalization of the same result for a language with recursive procedures; a full proof of the proposition for this general case will be provided in the appendix. While statements being a special case of recursive procedures - see chapter 5 for details -, we conclude that the above proposition can be obtained as a corollary from the results of the appendix.
2. For our present purposes, we do not need any properties about variables occurring in q_1 and q_2 (cf. lemma 2.31).

The notion of formal proof is defined exactly as in definition 2.38. We now define a system of axioms and proof rules which enables us to prove a natural extension of theorem 2.40.

DEFINITION 3.37 (formal proof system for formulae {p}S{q}).

a. Let $\mathcal{Ax}$ be as in definition 2.39a

b. Let $\mathcal{Pr}$ consist of

(i) The rules of composition, conditionals and consequence (just as in definition 2.39b)

(ii) $$\frac{\{p\wedge b\}S\{p\}}{\{p\}\ \underline{\text{while}}\ b\ \underline{\text{do}}\ S\ \underline{\text{od}}\ \{p\wedge\neg b\}}$$ (while rule)

END 3.37.

THEOREM 3.38 (soundness and completeness theorem). Let p,q $\in$ $\mathcal{Assn}$ and S $\in$ $\mathcal{Stat}$. Then

$$\vdash_{\mathcal{Ax},\mathcal{Pr}} \{p\}S\{q\} \quad \text{iff} \quad \models \{p\}S\{q\}$$

PROOF.

a. ($\Rightarrow$). The validity of the axioms and the soundness of the rules as mentioned in definition 3.37b(i) are clear. Furthermore, rule 3.37b(ii) is sound by theorem 3.31. The result now follows by an argument exactly similar to the one used in the proof of part a of theorem 2.40.

b. ($\Leftarrow$). Induction on the complexity of S. If S is an assignment statement or a conditional statement, the argument is the same as in part b of the proof of theorem 2.40. If S $\equiv$ S_1;S_1, the argument is also the same, but for replacing an appeal to lemma 2.31 by an appeal to the proposition. Finally, let S $\equiv$ while b do S_1 od, and let r be an assertion (which exists by the proposition), such that $\models$ r = S $\rightarrow$ q. We show that

(i) $\models \{r\wedge b\}S_1\{r\}$

(ii) $\models p \supset r$

(iii) $\models r \wedge \neg b \supset q$.

Once this has been established, we have finished. In fact, since S_1 has less complexity than S, by the induction hypothesis from (i) we obtain that

$\vdash_{\mathcal{Ax},\mathcal{Pr}}\{r \wedge b\}S_1\{r\}$

From this and the while rule we infer

$\vdash_{\mathcal{Ax},\mathcal{Pr}}\{r\}\ \underline{\text{while}}\ b\ \underline{\text{do}}\ S_1\ \underline{\text{od}}\ \{r \wedge \neg b\}$

From (ii), (iii) and the definition of $\mathcal{Ax}$ we obtain

$\vdash_{\mathcal{Ax},\mathcal{Pr}}\ p \supset r,\quad \vdash_{\mathcal{Ax},\mathcal{Pr}}\ r \wedge \neg b \supset q$

The desired result then follows from these three facts and the rule of consequence. There remains the proof of (i), (ii) and (iii).

(i) We have $\models\ r = S \rightarrow q = \underline{\text{while}}\ b\ \underline{\text{do}}\ S_1\ \underline{\text{od}} \rightarrow q$

$= \underline{\text{if}}\ b\ \underline{\text{then}}\ S_1;\ \underline{\text{while}}\ b\ \underline{\text{do}}\ S_1\ \underline{\text{od}}\ \underline{\text{else}}\ D\ \underline{\text{fi}} \rightarrow q.$

Hence, clearly,

$\models\ r \wedge b \supset (S_1;\ \underline{\text{while}}\ b\ \underline{\text{do}}\ S_1\ \underline{\text{od}} \rightarrow q)$

$\supset (S_1 \rightarrow (\underline{\text{while}}\ b\ \underline{\text{do}}\ S_1\ \underline{\text{od}} \rightarrow q))$

$\supset S_1 \rightarrow r$

which is equivalent to $\models \{r \wedge b\}S_1\{r\}$

(ii) Immediate from $\models\ \{p\}S\{q\}$ and the definition of r

(iii) Similar to the argument in part (i), we have that

$\models\ r \wedge \neg b \supset (D \rightarrow q) = q.$

END 3.38.

Exercises

3.1. a. Prove that definition 3.2 is correct in the sense that each set X has at most one glb and lub.

b. Prove that each function: $C \rightarrow C$ has at most one least (greatest) fixed point.

3.2. Prove that each finite partially ordered set which has a least element is a cpo.

3.3. Give an example of a function which has a discrete cpo as its domain, and which is monotonic but not strict.

3.4. Let C, C_1,..., D,... be cpo's with typical elements x, x_1,..., y,.... Prove

a. $\lambda x \cdot x \in C \to_s C$

b. $\lambda x \cdot y \in C \to_m D$

c. If $f \in C_2 \to_m C_3$, $g \in C_1 \to_m C_2$, and $f \circ g \overset{df.}{=} \lambda x_1 \cdot f(g(x_1))$, then $f \circ g \in C_1 \to_m C_3$

d. If $f_1, f_2 \in C \to_m D$, then <u>if</u> β <u>then</u> f_1 <u>else</u> f_2 <u>fi</u> $\in C \to_m D$.

3.5. Let $i \in \mathbb{N}$, and let $f_i : V \to V$ be defined by:
$f_i(\bot_V) = \bot_V$ and for $\alpha \neq \bot_V$, $f_i(\alpha) =$ <u>if</u> $\alpha \le i$ <u>then</u> α <u>else</u> $\bot_V$ <u>fi</u>.
Determine $\bigsqcup_{i=0}^{\infty} f_i$.

3.6. Is $([0,1],\le)$ a cpo? And $([0,1),\le)$?
(Here " ≤ " denotes the standard ordering on real numbers.)

3.7. Let D be the set $\{[a,b] \mid a,b \in \mathbb{R} \cup \{-\infty,+\infty\},\ a \le b\}$.
Let $[a,b] \sqsubseteq [c,d]$ iff $a \le c$ and $d \le b$. Determine $\bot_D$, and show that D is a cpo.

3.8. Prove that σ' in definition 3.20 is uniquely determined (and infer that $\mathcal{O}(S)$ is indeed a function, i.e. that for all σ, σ', σ", if $\mathcal{O}(S)(\sigma) = \sigma'$ and $\mathcal{O}(S)(\sigma) = \sigma''$, then $\sigma' = \sigma''$).

3.9. Let $\mathcal{M}'$ be as $\mathcal{M}$, but for the clause $\mathcal{M}'$(<u>while</u> b <u>do</u> S <u>od</u>) $= \bigsqcup_{i=0}^{\infty} \psi_i$, with

$\psi_0 = \lambda\sigma \cdot \bot$

$\psi_{i+1} = \lambda\sigma \cdot$ <u>if</u> $\mathcal{W}(b)(\sigma)$ <u>then</u> $\mathcal{M}'(S)(\psi_i(\sigma))$ <u>else</u> σ <u>fi</u>, i = 0,1,...

Is $\mathcal{M}' = \mathcal{M}$?

3.10. Prove that

$\models$ <u>while</u> b <u>do</u> S <u>od</u>; <u>if</u> b <u>then</u> S_1 <u>else</u> S_2 <u>fi</u> = <u>while</u> b <u>do</u> S <u>od</u>; S_2.

3.11. Let us extend *Stat* with the syntactic clause

$S ::= \ldots | \underline{\text{while}}\ b\ \underline{\text{do}}\ S_1\ \underline{\text{od}}\ \underline{\text{else}}\ S_2\ \underline{\text{fi}}$,

with as corresponding semantic definition:

$\mathcal{M}(\underline{\text{while}}\ b\ \underline{\text{do}}\ S_1\ \underline{\text{od}}\ \underline{\text{else}}\ S_2\ \underline{\text{fi}}) = \bigsqcup_{i=0}^{\infty} \psi_i$, with

$\psi_0 = \lambda\sigma\cdot\bot$

$\psi_{i+1} = \lambda\sigma\cdot\underline{\text{if}}\ \mathcal{W}(b)(\sigma)\ \underline{\text{then}}\ \psi_i(\mathcal{M}(S_1)(\sigma))\ \underline{\text{else}}\ \mathcal{M}(S_2)(\sigma)\ \underline{\text{fi}}$,

$i = 0,1,\ldots$

Prove that

$\models \underline{\text{while}}\ b\ \underline{\text{do}}\ S_1\ \underline{\text{od}}\ \underline{\text{else}}\ S_2\ \underline{\text{fi}} = \underline{\text{while}}\ b\ \underline{\text{do}}\ S_1\ \underline{\text{od}};\ S_2$.

3.12. Prove that

a. $\models \{(x=m) \wedge (m\geq 0) \wedge (y=1) \wedge (z\neq 0)\}$

$\underline{\text{while}}\ x>0\ \underline{\text{do}}\ y:=y\times z;\ x:=x-1\ \underline{\text{od}}$

$\{(x=0) \wedge (m\geq 0) \wedge (y=z^m) \wedge (z\neq 0)\}$

(Hint: use the invariant $(x\geq 0) \wedge (m\geq 0) \wedge (y=z^{m-x}) \wedge (z\neq 0)$.)

b. $\models \{(x=m) \wedge (m\geq 0) \wedge (y=1)\}$

$\underline{\text{while}}\ x>0\ \underline{\text{do}}\ y:=x\times y;\ x:=x-1\ \underline{\text{od}}$

$\{(x=0) \wedge (m\geq 0) \wedge (y=m!)\}$

(Hint: use the invariant $(x\geq 0) \wedge (m\geq 0) \wedge (y=m!/x!)$.)

3.13. a. Prove $\mathcal{M}(\underline{\text{while}}\ x>0\ \underline{\text{do}}\ y:=y+y;\ x:=x-1\ \underline{\text{od}})(\sigma\{\alpha/x\}\{1/y\}) = \sigma\{0/x\}\{2^\alpha/y\}$, provided that $\alpha \geq 0$

(Hint: show that, for $\alpha_1,\alpha_2 \geq 0$, $i > \alpha_1$, $\phi_i(\sigma\{\alpha_1/x\}\{2^{\alpha_2}/y\}) = \sigma\{0/x\}\{2^{\alpha_1+\alpha_2}/y\}$.)

b. Prove with the aid of theorem 3.31

$\models \{(x=m) \wedge (m\geq 0) \wedge (y=1)\}$

$\underline{\text{while}}\ x>0\ \underline{\text{do}}\ y:=y+y;\ x:=x-1\ \underline{\text{od}}$

$\{(x=0) \wedge (m\geq 0) \wedge (y=2^m)\}$.

3.14. Which of the following inferences are sound?

a. $$\frac{\{p\wedge b\}S\{p\},\ p\wedge\neg b \supset q}{\{p\}\ \underline{\text{while}}\ b\ \underline{\text{do}}\ S\ \underline{\text{od}}\ \{q\}}$$

b. $$\frac{\{p\}S\{q\},\ q \supset \underline{\text{if}}\ b\ \underline{\text{then}}\ p\ \underline{\text{else}}\ r\ \underline{\text{fi}}}{\{q\}\ \underline{\text{while}}\ b\ \underline{\text{do}}\ S\ \underline{\text{od}}\ \{r\}}$$

c. $$\frac{\{q\}S\{p\},\ p \supset \underline{\text{if}}\ b\ \underline{\text{then}}\ q\ \underline{\text{else}}\ r\ \underline{\text{fi}}}{\{q\}\ \underline{\text{while}}\ b\ \underline{\text{do}}\ S\ \underline{\text{od}}\ \{r\}}$$

3.15. Let $\underline{\text{repeat}}\ S\ \underline{\text{until}}\ b \equiv S;\ \underline{\text{while}}\ \neg b\ \underline{\text{do}}\ S\ \underline{\text{od}}$

a. Prove the soundness of the following inferences:

(i) $$\frac{\{p \vee (q \wedge \neg b)\}S\{q\}}{\{p\}\ \underline{\text{repeat}}\ S\ \underline{\text{until}}\ b\ \{q \wedge b\}}$$

(ii) $$\frac{\{p\}S\{q\},\ (q \wedge \neg b) \supset p}{\{p\}\ \underline{\text{repeat}}\ S\ \underline{\text{until}}\ b\ \{q \wedge b\}}$$

(iii) $$\frac{\{p\}S\{q\},\ q \supset \underline{\text{if}}\ b\ \underline{\text{then}}\ r\ \underline{\text{else}}\ p\ \underline{\text{fi}}}{\{p\}\ \underline{\text{repeat}}\ S\ \underline{\text{until}}\ b\ \{r \wedge b\}}$$

b. Prove that

$\models \underline{\text{repeat}}\ S\ \underline{\text{until}}\ b_1 \wedge b_2 = \underline{\text{repeat}}\ \underline{\text{repeat}}\ S\ \underline{\text{until}}\ b_1\ \underline{\text{until}}\ b_2.$

3.16. Determine p and q such that, for all S, $\models \{p\}S\{q\}$ iff S terminates for no input state.

3.17. Prove that, for p,q $\in$ *Assn*,

$$\boxed{\frac{\{p\}S\{q\}}{\{p[s/x]\}S\{q[s/x]\}},\ \text{provided that } ivar(x{:=}s) \cap ivar(S) = \emptyset}$$

3.18. Let Φ be the function from theorem 3.26. Prove that, in general, Φ has no *greatest* fixed point.

3.19. a. Prove that

$\models \underline{\text{while}}\ b\ \underline{\text{do}}\ S\ \underline{\text{od}} = \underline{\text{if}}\ b\ \underline{\text{then}}\ \underline{\text{while}}\ b\ \underline{\text{do}}\ S\ \underline{\text{od}}\ \underline{\text{else}}\ D\ \underline{\text{fi}}$

(Cf. example 7 after definition 3.30.)

b. Determine S such that

(i) $\models S = \underline{\text{if}}\ b\ \underline{\text{then}}\ S\ \underline{\text{else}}\ D\ \underline{\text{fi}}$

(ii) $$\boxed{\frac{S' = \underline{\text{if}}\ b\ \underline{\text{then}}\ S'\ \underline{\text{else}}\ D\ \underline{\text{fi}}}{S \sqsubseteq S'}}$$

3.20. Extend exercise 2.17 to the framework of chapter 3.

3.21. Extend exercise 2.18 to the framework of chapter 3.

(Hint: part b now needs application of the proposition of section 3.6.)

Chapter 4

SUBSCRIPTED VARIABLES

4.1. Introduction

This chapter constitutes a very modest venture into the realm of data structures. We introduce the notion of array with the corresponding construct of *subscripted variable*, and investigate the consequences of this extension for the theory as developed up to now. However, we shall not deal with all ramifications of the array concept. First, we omit all treatment of the effect of array *bounds* in a declaration. This is motivated not so much by the fact that denotational semantics would not know how to deal with array bounds - which it does -, but rather by our general preference to concentrate on issues in proof methodology, where the role of bounds in arrays is not too clear. We suspect that a fundamental study of the notion of an *error* in a program would be required for this, and this is a problem we avoid altogether in the present treatise (let alone the implementation-oriented questions about storage allocation). Secondly, we restrict ourselves to one-dimensional arrays. We expect that no serious problems will be encountered in extending the theory of the present chapter to more-dimensional arrays (except, again, for a satisfactory treatment of errors such as a[1,2] := a[3]).

Even in the case of one-dimensional arrays without bounds, we are confronted with some interesting complications. To give a first impression of them, we compare the assignments x:=1 and a[s]:=1, where, as usual, s is some integer expression (which now may contain subscripted variables). Clearly, we have that

$\models$ {$\underline{\text{true}}$} x:=1 {x=1},

and one might expect that, analogously,

$$\models \{\underline{\text{true}}\}\ a[s]:=1\ \{a[s]=1\} \qquad (?)$$

However, this is not true in general. Choose for example $s \equiv a[2]$, and let us consider the precondition $a[1] = 2 \wedge a[2] = 2$. It may be verified that

$$\models \{a[1]=2 \wedge a[2]=2\}\ a[a[2]]:=1\ \{a[a[2]]=2\} \qquad (4.1)$$

In fact, since $a[2] = 2$, the assignment $a[a[2]]:=1$ sets $a[2]$ to 1. Hence, after its execution we have that $a[a[2]] = a[1]$ (the value of which is unchanged) $= 2$! On the other hand, if (?) would indeed hold, then, taking $s \equiv a[2]$ in it, and applying the rule of consequence, we would obtain that

$$\models \{a[1]=2 \wedge a[2]=2\}\ a[a[2]]:=1\ \{a[a[2]]=1\} \qquad (4.2)$$

thus contradicting (4.1). We therefore conclude that (?) cannot be true. We see that assignment to subscripted variables indeed necessitates additional analysis, in particular insofar as correctness questions are concerned. A complete answer to these will be given in section 4.3, which we precede by a section (4.2) which deals with the consequences of subscripted variables for the (syntax and) semantics of our language.

4.2. Semantics

We begin with some syntactic preparations. The previously introduced class of *simple* integer variables, with typical elements x,y,z,u,..., is renamed as *Svar*, and a class *Avar* of *array variables*, with typical elements a,..., is introduced. Next, we give

DEFINITION 4.1 (*Stat* extended with subscripted variables).

a. The class *Ivar* (of *integer variables*), with typical elements v,w,..., is defined by

v::= x|a[s]

b. The class *Iexp*, with typical elements s,t,..., is defined by

s::= v|m|s_1+s_2|...|<u>if</u> b <u>then</u> s_1 <u>else</u> s_2 <u>fi</u>

c. The class *Bexp*, with typical elements b,..., is defined by

b::= <u>true</u>|<u>false</u>|s_1=s_2|...|¬b|b_1⊃b_2

d. The class *Stat*, with typical elements S,..., is defined by

S::= v:=s|S_1;S_2|<u>if</u> b <u>then</u> S_1 <u>else</u> S_2 <u>fi</u>|<u>while</u> b <u>do</u> S <u>od</u>

END 4.1.

Examples

1. a[a[1]] := a[a[2]]+3
2. <u>if</u> a[1] = a[2] <u>then</u> x:=a_1[x] <u>else</u> y:=a_2[y] <u>fi</u>
3. <u>while</u> a[1] > 0 <u>do</u> a[1] := a[a[1]] <u>od</u>.

As difference with definition 3.15, we note the introduction of the class of simple or subscripted integer variables *Ivar*, with typical elements v,w,..., and the replacement of x by v in the definitions of s and S.

The semantic framework needs more substantial adjustment. To begin with, we have to adapt our notion of state. Up to now, a state was simply a function from variables x to integers α. For a subscripted variable a[s], the situation is more complex. It is not feasible to simply extend the domain of states σ to the new class *Ivar*. Instead, we introduce a new class of *intermediate variables* *Intv*, defined

- apart from a few refinements to be dealt with below - as

$$\mathit{Intv} = \mathit{Svar} \cup (\mathit{Avar} \times V) \tag{4.3}$$

with corresponding modification of Σ to

$$\Sigma = \mathit{Intv} \rightarrow V \tag{4.4}$$

These definitions are used as follows: in order to determine the value of a subscripted variable a[s], it is first - through a function to be defined presently - mapped onto some element $<a,\alpha>$ in *Intv*, where α is the current value of the subscript s, and, next, σ is applied to the result $<a,\alpha>$ yielding some integer α' as value of a[s]. Moreover, there is the following point to consider here. Let us employ the statement a[s] := a[t] as an example. In order to find the change of state determined by this assignment, we have to

(i) evaluate s in state σ (with result α, say), and deliver the result $<a,\alpha>$ (which is an element of *Intv*) for a[s];

(ii) evaluate t in state σ (with result α', say), leading to the intermediate result $<a,\alpha'> \in \mathit{Intv}$ for a[t];

(iii) apply σ to $<a,\alpha'>$, yielding the value $\alpha'' = \sigma(<a,\alpha'>)$ as final result for a[t];

(iv) change the state σ to a new state σ' which is like σ, but for the fact that now $\sigma'(<a,\alpha>) = \alpha''$ is satisfied.

Thus, we see that during our calculations a subscripted variable on the left-hand side of an assignment statement is treated differently (only step (i)) from one on the right-hand side (step (ii) *and* step (iii)). Step (i) delivers the so-called left-hand value of a[s] in state σ, i.e. the element $L(a[s])(\sigma)$ in *Intv*, whereas (ii) and (iii) together yield the right-hand value of a[t] in state σ, i.e. the element $R(a[t])(\sigma)$ in V. (For *simple* variables, the result of $L(x)(\sigma)$ is nothing but x itself, whereas $R(x)(\sigma)$ coincides with $V(x)(\sigma)$ - i.e. with $\sigma(x)$ - as before.) There is one further complication in the definitions of *Intv* and Σ, stemming from the possible presence of undefined states. Instead of (4.3) and (4.4) we use in fact

$$\begin{aligned} \mathit{Intv} &= \mathit{Intv}_0 \cup \{\bot_{\mathit{Intv}}\} \\ \mathit{Intv}_0 &= \mathit{Svar} \cup (\mathit{Avar} \times V_0) \end{aligned} \tag{4.5}$$

and

$$\begin{aligned} \Sigma &= \Sigma_0 \cup \{\bot\} \\ \Sigma_0 &= \mathit{Intv}_0 \to V_0 \end{aligned} \tag{4.6}$$

which definitions are motivated on the one hand by the wish to turn *Intv* into a discrete cpo, and, on the other hand, by the fact that we organize the definitions so that $\bot_V$ is delivered as right-hand value for some s *only* in the state $\bot$. In this way, we can completely separate the case where an undefined result occurs from the cases where everything is well-defined.

DEFINITION 4.2 (semantics of *Stat* with subscripted variables).
Let *Intv*, with typical elements $\xi,\ldots$, and Σ (with typical elements σ) be as in (4.5) and (4.6).

a. For $\xi_1,\xi_2 \in \mathit{Intv}$ we put $\xi_1 = \xi_2$ if either ξ_1 and ξ_2 are both equal to $\bot_{\mathit{Intv}}$, or $\xi_1 = x \in \mathit{Ivar}$, $\xi_2 = y \in \mathit{Ivar}$, and $x \equiv y$, or $\xi_1 = \langle a_1,\alpha_1\rangle \in \mathit{Avar} \times V_0$, $\xi_2 = \langle a_2,\alpha_2\rangle \in \mathit{Avar} \times V_0$, with $a_1 \equiv a_2$ and $\alpha_1 = \alpha_2$.

   Also, $\xi_1 \sqsubseteq \xi_2$ iff $\xi_1 = \bot_{\mathit{Intv}}$ or $\xi_1 = \xi_2$.

b. $\bot\{\alpha/\xi\} = \bot$ and, for $\sigma \in \Sigma_0$, $\sigma\{\alpha/\xi\}$ is defined (as usual) by

$$\sigma\{\alpha/\xi\}(\xi') = \begin{cases} \alpha, & \text{if } \xi = \xi' \\ \sigma(\xi'), & \text{if } \xi \neq \xi'. \end{cases}$$

c. The functions L, R and W are of type

   $L\colon \mathit{Ivar} \to (\Sigma \to_s \mathit{Intv})$

   $R\colon \mathit{Iexp} \to (\Sigma \to_s V)$

   $W\colon \mathit{Bexp} \to (\Sigma \to_s W)$

and are defined by

(i) $L(v)(\perp) = \perp_{Intv}$ and, for $\sigma \in \Sigma_0$

$L(x)(\sigma) = x$, $L(a[s])(\sigma) = \langle a, R(s)(\sigma)\rangle$

(ii) $R(s)(\perp) = \perp_V$ and, for $\sigma \in \Sigma_0$,

$R(v)(\sigma) = \sigma(L(v)(\sigma))$, $R(m)(\sigma) = \alpha$,

where α is the integer denoted by the integer constant m,

$R(s_1+s_2)(\sigma) = R(s_1)(\sigma) + R(s_2)(\sigma)$,

$R(\underline{if}\ b\ \underline{then}\ s_1\ \underline{else}\ s_2\ \underline{fi})(\sigma) = \underline{if}\ W(b)(\sigma)\ \underline{then}\ R(s_1)(\sigma)$

$\underline{else}\ R(s_2)(\sigma)\ \underline{fi}$

(iii) $W(b)(\sigma)$: just as in definition 3.19, but for the clause

$W(s_1=s_2)(\sigma) = (R(s_1)(\sigma) = R(s_2)(\sigma))$.

d. The function M is of the type: $Stat \to (\Sigma \to_s \Sigma)$ and is defined by

(i) $M(v{:=}s)(\sigma) = \sigma\{R(s)(\sigma)/L(v)(\sigma)\}$

(ii) For S not an assignment statement, definition 3.22 is taken over.

END 4.2.

Examples (we write $\sigma(a,\alpha)$ for $\sigma(\langle a,\alpha\rangle)$).

1. $M(x{:=}x+1)(\sigma\{0/x\}) = \sigma\{0/x\}\{R(x+1)(\sigma\{0/x\})/L(x)(\sigma\{0/x\})\} =$
$\sigma\{0/x\}\{R(x)(\sigma\{0/x\}) + 1/x\} = \sigma\{0/x\}\{1/x\} = \sigma\{1/x\}$.
(For simple variables everything has remained as it was.)
2. Assume that $\sigma(a,1) = 2$, $\sigma(a,2) = 1$. Then $R(a[a[1]])(\sigma) =$
$\sigma(L(a[a[1]])(\sigma)) = \sigma(a,R(a[1])(\sigma)) = \sigma(a,\sigma(L(a[1])(\sigma))) =$
$\sigma(a,\sigma(a,R(1)(\sigma))) = \sigma(a,\sigma(a,1)) = \sigma(a,2) = 1$.
3. Assume that $\sigma(a,1) = \sigma(a,2) = 2$. Then $M(a[a[2]]{:=}1)(\sigma) =$
$\sigma\{R(1)(\sigma)/L(a[a[2]])(\sigma)\} = \sigma\{1/\langle a,R(a[2])(\sigma)\rangle\} =$
$\sigma\{1/\langle a,\sigma(L(a[2])(\sigma))\rangle\} = \sigma\{1/\langle a,\sigma(a,2)\rangle\} = \sigma\{1/\langle a,2\rangle\}$.
Furthermore, we have that

$\mathcal{W}(a[a[2]]=1)(\sigma\{1/\langle a,2\rangle\}) = (\mathcal{R}(a[a[2]])(\sigma\{1/\langle a,2\rangle\}) = 1) = \ldots =$
$(\sigma\{1/\langle a,2\rangle\}(a,1) = 1) = (\sigma(a,1) = 1) = (2=1) = ff.$

We conclude that, for a state which satisfies the precondition $a[1] = 2 \wedge a[2] = 2$, after the assignment $a[a[2]] := 1$ the post-condition $a[a[2]] = 1$ indeed does not hold.

As is readily seen, the consequences of the introduction of subscripted variables are limited to the treatment of states, variables and expressions, and of assignment, whereas there are no (visible) effects on the other kinds of statements. Accordingly, as we shall see in the next section, correctness questions are wholly devoted to the assignment statement.

4.3. Correctness

As starting point of this section we agree that the definitions of both syntax and semantics of *Assn*, *Cond*, and *Form* undergo no explicit changes. (Implicitly, they of course inherit the changes just introduced in the definitions of the syntax and of Σ, $\mathcal{L}$, $\mathcal{R}$, $\mathcal{W}$ and $\mathcal{M}$. For example, we now have assertions such as $a[1] > a[2]$, or $\exists x[a[x]=y]$ (but *not* of the form $\exists a[\ldots]$, let alone $\exists v[\ldots]$ for v subscripted).) Also, almost all results of the preceding chapters can be taken over - either literally or with a few appropriate modifications - but for theorem 2.21. In fact, this section is solely concerned with the question as to how to obtain weakest preconditions and strongest postconditions for the assignment statement v:=t.

We begin with the weakest-precondition-case. Let us consider the example concerning the (non-)validity of (?): {<u>true</u>} a[s]:=1 {a[s]=1} somewhat more closely. It seems natural to argue by analogy with theorem 2.15 and to expect the validity of (!): {p[t/v]} v:=t {p}. More specifically, let us investigate which result is obtained by substituting the expression 1 for the variable a[s] in the postcondition $p \equiv (a[s]=1)$. Replacement of all occurrences of a[s] in p by 1 results in the precondition $(1=1)$ and - by the equivalence $\models (1=1) = \underline{\text{true}}$ - we would have derived the validity of (?) from that of (!). The contradiction obtained in this way may be remedied in two ways. Either we have to modify the rule (!), or we have to refine the notion of substitution. It appears that the second possibility leads to a solution. We shall present a careful definition of p[t/v] and, using this new definition, we shall prove the validity of {p[t/v]} v:=t {p}, even for v ≡ a[s].

Before stating the new definition, we introduce the notation for the classes of (free) variables occurring in our various constructs:

DEFINITION 4.3 (*svar, avar, intv*).

a. The set of all simple variables occurring in S, s or b, or occurring *free* in p is denoted by *svar*(S), *svar*(s), *svar*(b), or *svar*(p), respectively.

b. The set of all array variables occurring in S,...,p is denoted by *avar*(S),...,*avar*(p).

c. *intv*(S) = *svar*(S) ∪ $\{\langle a,\alpha\rangle \mid a \in$ *avar*(S), $\alpha \in V_0\}$, and similarly for *intv*(s), *intv*(b), *intv*(p).

END 4.3.

Remarks

1. Note that *svar*(S) ⊆ *Svar*, *avar*(S) ⊆ *Avar*, *intv*(S) ⊆ *Intv*, and similarly for s, b and p.
2. *svar* replaces *ivar* of chapters 2, 3 (just as *Svar* replaces *Ivar*). From now on, sets *ivar*(S),..., no longer appear in our considerations.
3. Again, we use *svar*(t,p) for *svar*(t) ∪ *svar*(p), etc.
4. *intv*(S),..., is not used in the present chapter, but introduced here only for subsequent use in later chapters.

Examples

1. *svar*(∃x[x > y − z]) = {y,z}
2. *svar*(a_1[x] := y+a_2[z+a_3[u]]) = {x,y,z,u}
   avar(a_1[x] := y+a_2[z+a_3[u]]) = {a_1,a_2,a_3}
   intv(a_1[x] := y+a_2[z+a_3[u]]) = {x,y,z,u} ∪ $\{\langle a_i,\alpha\rangle \mid i=1,2,3,\ \alpha\in V_0\}$.

From now on we shall use (in this chapter only) a different pair of brackets for substitution. Instead of s[t/v] and p[t/v] we write s<t/v> and p<t/v>. (Without this modification we would be forced to consider hardly readable expressions such as a[a[1]][a[2]/a[a[1]]].)

DEFINITION 4.4 (substitution for subscripted variables).

a. s<t/v> and b<t/v>. The only interesting case is s ≡ w (see clause c below), the other cases being either immediate, or easily taken care of by induction on the complexity of s or b.

b. p<t/v>. All cases are again either immediate, or easy by induction on the complexity of p, except, possibly, for the case ∃x[p']<t/v>, with v ≡ a[s]. For this we put

$$\exists x[p']\langle t/a[s]\rangle \equiv \begin{cases} \exists x[p'\langle t/a[s]\rangle], & \text{if } x \notin \textit{svar}(t,s), \\ \exists x'[p'\langle x'/x\rangle\langle t/a[s]\rangle], & \text{if } x \in \textit{svar}(t,s), \\ \quad \text{where } x' \text{ is the first simple variable} & \\ \quad \notin \textit{svar}(p',t,s). & \end{cases}$$

c. w<t/v>. We distinguish two subcases:
   (i) v ≡ x ∈ *Svar*. Then
       x<t/x> ≡ t, y<t/x> ≡ y (x ≢ y), and a[s]<t/x> ≡ a[s<t/x>]
   (ii) v ≡ a[s]. Then
       x<t/a[s]> ≡ x,
       a'[s']<t/a[s]> ≡ a'[s'<t/a[s]>], a ≢ a',
       a[s']<t/a[s]> ≡ <u>if</u> s'<t/a[s]> = s <u>then</u> t <u>else</u> a[s'<t/a[s]>] <u>fi</u>.

END 4.4.

Remarks

1. The very last clause of this definition is the most interesting one. The reader might care to verify that adopting a more naive definition: a[s']<t/a[s]> ≡ if s' = s then t else a[s'<t/a[s]>] fi, would again allow us to infer the validity of (?) from that of (!).
2. As we saw in chapter 2, S[t/x] is not, in general, well-defined and we therefore restricted ourselves to the substitution S[y/x]. Now that we have subscripted variables available, one might consider extending this to S[w/v]. However, this gives slight complications for S an assignment statement, and will not be introduced. Instead, we restrict ourselves to S[v/x] - which we *do* need in later chapters -, the straightforward definition of which we leave to the reader.

Examples

1. Let a' ≢ a.
   a'[a[2]]<1/a[2]> ≡ a'[a[2]<1/a[2]>] ≡
   a'[if 2<1/a[2]> = 2 then 1 else a[2<1/a[2]>] fi] ≡
   a'[if 2 = 2 then 1 else a[2] fi]
   Semantically (but not syntactically), this expression may be simplified to a'[1].
2. a[a[2]]<1/a[a[2]]> ≡
   if a[2]<1/a[a[2]]> = a[2] then 1 else a[a[2]<1/a[a[2]]>] fi ≡
   if if 2 = a[2] then 1 else a[2] fi = a[2]
   then 1 else a[if 2 = a[2] then 1 else a[2] fi] fi.
   Semantically, this expression may be simplified to
   if a[2] = 2 then a[1] else 1 fi.

Remark. We may use the second example to see what the new definition of substitution yields for the following instance of (!):

{(a[a[2]]=1)<1/a[a[2]]>} a[a[2]]:=1 {a[a[2]]=1}.

We obtain

$\{$<u>if</u> a[2]=2 <u>then</u> a[1]=1 <u>else</u> <u>true</u> <u>fi</u>$\}$ a[a[2]]:=1 $\{$a[a[2]]=1$\}$

and we can easily verify that, contrary to (?), this correctness formula *is* valid.

Before applying definition 4.4 in the announced new version of theorem 2.21a, we first prove the following simple lemma:

<u>LEMMA 4.5</u>.

a. $\models$ s<v/v> = s

b. $\models$ p<v/v> = p.

<u>PROOF</u>. We treat only part a, leaving part b as exercise. The proof is by induction on the complexity of s. All cases are straightforward, but for the subcase that s $\equiv$ a[s_1] and v $\equiv$ a[s_2]. Thus, let us consider a[s_1]<a[s_2]/a[s_2]>. By definition 4.4, this is identical with <u>if</u> s_1<a[s_2]/a[s_2]> = s_2 <u>then</u> a[s_2] <u>else</u> a[s_1<a[s_2]/a[s_2]>] <u>fi</u>. By the induction hypothesis, $\models$ s_1<a[s_2]/a[s_2]> = s_1. Together, we obtain

$\models$ a[s_1]<a[s_2]/a[s_2]> = <u>if</u> s_1 = s_2 <u>then</u> a[s_2] <u>else</u> a[s_1] <u>fi</u>

Since it is easily seen that

$\models$ <u>if</u> s_1 = s_2 <u>then</u> a[s_2] <u>else</u> a[s_1] <u>fi</u> = a[s_1]

we have obtained the desired result in the subcase, thus completing the proof.

END 4.5.

We now come to the first main theorem of this chapter, expressing the analog of theorem 2.21a for the new definition of substitution.

<u>THEOREM 4.6</u>. Let p $\in$ *Assn*.

$\models$ (v:=t) $\rightarrow$ p = p<t/v>.

PROOF. The proof follows the same lines as that of theorem 2.21a, in that we easily see that it is sufficient to prove that, for all σ,

$$\mathcal{R}(s<t/v>)(\sigma) = \mathcal{R}(s)(\sigma\{\mathcal{R}(t)(\sigma)/\mathcal{L}(v)(\sigma)\})$$
$$\mathcal{W}(b<t/v>)(\sigma) = \mathcal{W}(b)(\sigma\{\mathcal{R}(t)(\sigma)/\mathcal{L}(v)(\sigma)\})$$
$$\mathcal{T}(p<t/v>)(\sigma) = \mathcal{T}(p)(\sigma\{\mathcal{R}(t)(\sigma)/\mathcal{L}(v)(\sigma)\}).$$

Again, the proof proceeds by (simultaneous) induction on the complexity of the expressions s and b, and of p, assuming the relevant analogs of lemma 2.16b (exercise). We restrict ourselves to part of the treatment of the two most interesting subcases.

(i) $\mathcal{T}(\exists x[p']<t/v>)(\sigma) = \mathcal{T}(\exists x[p'])(\sigma\{\mathcal{R}(t)(\sigma)/\mathcal{L}(v)(\sigma)\})$

(α) $x \notin svar(t,v)$. Then

$\mathcal{T}(\exists x[p']<t/v>)(\sigma) = \mathcal{T}(\exists x[p'<t/v>])(\sigma) =$

$\exists\alpha[\mathcal{T}(p'<t/v>)(\sigma\{\alpha/x\})] =$ (ind.)

$\exists\alpha[\mathcal{T}(p')(\sigma\{\alpha/x\}\{\mathcal{R}(t)(\sigma\{\alpha/x\})/\mathcal{L}(v)(\sigma\{\alpha/x\})\})] =$ (lemma 2.16b)

$\exists\alpha[\mathcal{T}(p')(\sigma\{\mathcal{R}(t)(\sigma)/\mathcal{L}(v)(\sigma)\}\{\alpha/x\})] =$

$\mathcal{T}(\exists x[p'])(\sigma\{\mathcal{R}(t)(\sigma)/\mathcal{L}(v)(\sigma)\})$

(β) $x \in svar(t,v)$. Very similar to the proof of lemma 2.16c, case (iii)(γ)

(ii) $\mathcal{R}(a[s_1]<t/a[s_2]>)(\sigma) = \mathcal{R}(a[s_1])(\sigma\{\mathcal{R}(t)(\sigma)/\mathcal{L}(a[s_2])(\sigma)\})$

Let $\mathcal{R}(t)(\sigma) = \alpha$, $\mathcal{R}(s_2)(\sigma) = \alpha'$ and (hence) $\mathcal{L}(a[s_2])(\sigma) = <a,\alpha'>$

From the definitions it follows that we have to prove that

$$\mathcal{R}(\underline{\text{if}}\ s_1<t/a[s_2]> = s_2\ \underline{\text{then}}\ t\ \underline{\text{else}}\ a[s_1<t/a[s_2]>]\ \underline{\text{fi}})(\sigma) \\ = \\ \mathcal{R}(a[s_1])(\sigma\{\alpha/<a,\alpha'>\}) \qquad (4.7)$$

i.e. that both

$$(\mathcal{R}(s_1<t/a[s_2]>)(\sigma) = \sigma') \Rightarrow (\alpha = \mathcal{R}(a[s_1])(\sigma\{\alpha/<a,\alpha'>\})) \qquad (4.8)$$

and

$$(\mathcal{R}(s_1<t/a[s_2]>)(\sigma) \neq \alpha') \Rightarrow (\mathcal{R}(a[s_1<t/a[s_2]>])(\sigma) = \\ \mathcal{R}(a[s_1])(\sigma\{\alpha/<a,\alpha'>\})). \qquad (4.9)$$

(α) Proof of (4.8). By the induction hypothesis, it is sufficient to show

$$(\mathcal{R}(s_1)(\sigma\{\alpha/\langle a,\alpha'\rangle\}) = \alpha') \Rightarrow (\alpha = \mathcal{R}(a[s_1])(\sigma\{\alpha/\langle a,\alpha'\rangle\}))$$

or

$$(\mathcal{R}(s_1)(\sigma\{\alpha/\langle a,\alpha'\rangle\}) = \alpha') \Rightarrow (\alpha = \sigma\{\alpha/\langle a,\alpha'\rangle\}(a,\mathcal{R}(s_1)(\sigma\{\alpha/\langle a,\alpha'\rangle\})))$$

which indeed holds, since $\sigma\{\alpha/\langle a,\alpha'\rangle\}(a,\alpha') = \alpha$.

(β) Proof of (4.9). Let $\alpha'' = \mathcal{R}(s_1)(\sigma\{\alpha/\langle a,\alpha'\rangle\})$. On the one hand we have

$$\begin{aligned}
&\mathcal{R}(a[s_1\langle t/a[s_2]\rangle])(\sigma) = \\
&\sigma(a,\mathcal{R}(s_1\langle t/a[s_2]\rangle)(\sigma)) = \text{(induction hypothesis)} \\
&\sigma(a,\mathcal{R}(s_1)(\sigma\{\alpha/\langle a,\alpha'\rangle\})) = \\
&\sigma(a,\alpha'')
\end{aligned}$$

and on the other hand

$$\begin{aligned}
&\mathcal{R}(a[s_1])(\sigma\{\alpha/\langle a,\alpha'\rangle\}) = \\
&\sigma\{\alpha/\langle a,\alpha'\rangle\}(a,\alpha'') = (\alpha' \neq \alpha'') \\
&\sigma(a,\alpha'')
\end{aligned}$$

together establishing (4.9).

END 4.6.

After having settled the weakest-precondition-case, we turn to a treatment of strongest postconditions for the assignment statement $v := t$. A treatment which unifies both the cases that $v \in \mathit{Svar}$ and that $v \equiv a[s]$, for some $a \in \mathit{Avar}$ and $s \in \mathit{Iexp}$, seems impossible. Instead, we use theorem 2.21b for the first case and provide a separate theorem, with a new construct for the postcondition, for the second case. We shall first state the theorem, then provide some explanation and examples, and finally give its proof.

THEOREM 4.7. Let $p \in \mathit{Assn}$.

$$\models (p \leftarrow (a[s]:=t)) =$$

$$\exists y,z[p<y/a[z]> \wedge (z = s<y/a[z]>) \wedge (a[z] = t<y/a[z]>)]$$

where y and z are variables not in *svar*(p,s,t).

By way of explanation, let us consider the following special case: p ≡ <u>true</u> and t ≡ m. We then obtain

$$\models (\underline{true} \leftarrow (a[s]:=m)) = \exists y,z[(z = s<y/a[z]>) \wedge (a[z]=m)]$$

where y and z are not in *svar*(s).

This result may be interpreted as follows: After the assignment a[s]:=m (for precondition <u>true</u>), there exists some z (with as its right-hand value the old right-hand value of s, say α) such that a[z]=m, and such that, moreover, there exists some y (with as its right-hand value the old right-hand value of a[s]) such that z = s<y/a[z]>.

(Our interpretation of the role of y might suggest that we could as well simply replace it by a[z]. However, this would not do, since in the state σ' after the assignment, a[z] has a *new* right-hand value $\sigma'(a,\alpha)$, which may well be different from $\sigma(a,\alpha)$, the intended value of y.)

Examples

1. Let $p \equiv a[1]=2 \wedge a[2]= 2$, $s \equiv a[2]$ and $t \equiv 1$.

   As strongest postcondition we obtain

$$\exists y,z[(a[1]=2 \wedge a[2]=2)<y/a[z]> \wedge z=a[2]<y/a[z]> \wedge a[z]=1<y/a[z]>].$$

   An application of definition 4.4 yields

$\exists y,z[\underline{if}\ 1 = z\ \underline{then}\ y\ \underline{else}\ a[1]\ \underline{fi} = 2 \wedge$
$\quad \underline{if}\ 2 = z\ \underline{then}\ y\ \underline{else}\ a[2]\ \underline{fi} = 2 \wedge$
$\quad z = \underline{if}\ 2 = z\ \underline{then}\ y\ \underline{else}\ a[2]\ \underline{fi} \wedge$
$\quad a[z] = 1].$

A comparison of the second and third term of the conjunction yields that z = 2, and the assertion reduces to $\exists y[a[1]= 2 \wedge y=2 \wedge a[2]= 1]$, i.e. to $a[1]= 2 \wedge a[2]= 1$ (implying, among others, that a[a[2]]= 2).

2. Let $p \equiv \underline{true}$, $t \equiv 1$ and $s \equiv a[2]$.
We leave it as an exercise to verify that theorem 4.7 in this case yields

$$\models (\underline{true} \leftarrow (a[a[2]]:=1)) = (a[a[2]]=1 \vee a[2]= 1).$$

Note that, combining the various examples, we have obtained that the invalid formula

$$\{\underline{true}\}\ a[a[2]]:=1\ \{a[a[2]]=1\}$$

may be repaired by either (on the basis of theorem 4.6) strengthening the precondition, resulting in

$$\models \{\underline{if}\ a[2]=2\ \underline{then}\ a[1]=1\ \underline{else}\ \underline{true}\ \underline{fi}\}\ a[a[2]]:=1\ \{a[a[2]]=1\}$$

or (on the basis of theorem 4.7) weakening the postcondition yielding

$$\models \{\underline{true}\}\ a[a[2]]:=1\ \{a[a[2]]=1 \vee a[2]=1\}.$$

PROOF of theorem 4.7. By the various definitions we have to show, for all σ, the equivalence of (i) and (ii):

(i) $\exists\sigma'[T(p)(\sigma') \wedge \sigma = \sigma'\{R(t)(\sigma')/\langle a,R(s)(\sigma')\rangle\}]$

(ii) $\exists\alpha,\alpha'$ such that

(α) $T(p)(\sigma\{\alpha/y,\alpha'/z\}\{\alpha/\langle a,\alpha'\rangle\})$

(β) $\alpha' = R(s)(\sigma\{\alpha/y,\alpha'/z\}\{\alpha/\langle a,\alpha'\rangle\})$

(γ) $\sigma(a,\alpha') = R(t)(\sigma\{\alpha/y,\alpha'/z\}\{\alpha/\langle a,\alpha'\rangle\})$.

(i) ⇒ (ii). Let us take $\alpha' \overset{\text{df.}}{=} R(s)(\sigma')$ and $\alpha \overset{\text{df.}}{=} \sigma'(a,\alpha')$. We show that (α), (β) and (γ) hold for this choice of α and α'.

(α) $T(p)(\sigma\{\alpha/y,\alpha'/z\}\{\alpha/<a,\alpha'>\})$ = (y and z not free in p)

$T(p)(\sigma\{\alpha/<a,\alpha'>\})$ = (assumption on σ)

$T(p)(\sigma'\{R(t)(\sigma')/<a,R(s)(\sigma')>\}\{\alpha/<a,\alpha'>\})$ =

$T(p)(\sigma'\{R(t)(\sigma')/<a,\alpha'>\}\{\alpha/<a,\alpha'>\}$ =

$T(p)(\sigma'\{\sigma'(a,\alpha')/<a,\alpha'>\})$ =

$T(p)(\sigma')$, which holds by assumption

(β) $R(s)(\sigma\{\alpha/y,\alpha'/z\}\{\alpha/<a,\alpha'>\})$ = (y and z not free in s)

$R(s)(\sigma\{\alpha/<a,\alpha'>\})$ = (similar to part (α))

$R(s)(\sigma')$ = (definition α')

α'

(γ) $R(t)(\sigma\{\alpha/y,\alpha'/z\}\{\alpha/<a,\alpha'>\}) = \ldots = R(t)(\sigma')$ =

$\sigma'\{R(t)(\sigma')/<a,\alpha'>\}(a,\alpha') = \sigma(a,\alpha')$.

(ii) ⇒ (i). Take $\sigma' \overset{df.}{=} \sigma\{\alpha/<a,\alpha'>\}$. Then $T(p)(\sigma')$ =

$T(p)(\sigma\{\alpha/<a,\alpha'>\})$ = (y and z not free in p)

$T(p)(\sigma\{\alpha/y,\alpha'/z\}\{\alpha/<a,\alpha'>\})$ = (ass. (α)) tt.

We show that, also, $\sigma = \sigma'\{R(t)(\sigma')/<a,R(s)(\sigma')>\}$.

By the definition of σ', $\sigma'\{R(t)(\sigma')/<a,R(s)(\sigma')>\}$ =

$\sigma\{\alpha/<a,\alpha'>\}\{R(t)(\sigma\{\alpha/<a,\alpha'>\})/<a,R(s)(\sigma\{\alpha/<a,\alpha'>\})>\}$ =

(ass. (β) and (γ)) $\sigma\{\alpha/<a,\alpha'>\}\{\sigma(a,\alpha')/<a,\alpha'>\}$ =

$\sigma\{\sigma(a,\alpha')/<a,\alpha'>\} = \sigma$.

END 4.7.

With theorems 4.6 and 4.7 we have accomplished our intended generalization of theorem 2.21 to assignment to subscripted variables.

Exercises

4.1. a. Prove lemma 4.5b

b. Prove that neither $s<v/v> \equiv s$, nor $\models v<t/v> = t$.

4.2. Prove that

⊨ a[a[a[2]]]<1/a[2]> = if a[1] = 2 then 1 else a[a[1]] fi.

4.3. Prove that the formula

{v=m ∧ w=n} z:=v;v:=w;w:=x {v=n ∧ w=m}

is invalid.

4.4. Determine

a. (a[a[1]] := a[a[2]]) → (a[a[1]] = a[a[2]])

b. (a[a[1] + a[2] + a[3]] := 4) → (a[a[1] + a[2] + a[3]] = 4).

4.5. Prove

⊨ {p} x:=s {∃y[p<y/x>]}, provided that y ≢ x and y ∉ *svar*(p).

Disprove

⊨ {p} v:=s {∃y[p<y/v>]}, provided that y ∉ *svar*(v,p).

4.6. Prove

{a[0] = 0}

⊨ while a[0] ≤ 100 do a[a[0]] := a[0]; a[0] := a[0] + 1 od

{∀x[(0<x) ∧ (x≤100) ⊃ (a[x]=x)]}

(Hint: Use the invariant a[0] ≤ 101 ∧ ∀x[(0<x) ∧

∧ (x<a[0]) ⊃ (a[x]=x)].)

4.7. Assume the natural definitions of the substitutions v<a'/a>, s<a'/a>, b<a'/a> and p<a'/a>, and of the variant notation $\sigma\{\sigma(a',\alpha)/<a,\alpha>\}_{\alpha\in V_0}$.

Prove that $L(v<a'/a>)(\sigma) = L(v)(\sigma\{\sigma(a',\alpha)/<a,\alpha>\}_{\alpha\in V_0})$,

and similarly for R, W and T.

4.8. Prove

a. $$\frac{\{p\}S\{q\}}{\{p<a'/a>\}S<a'/a>\{q<a'/a>\}},\quad \text{provided } a' \notin \mathit{avar}(S,q)$$

b. $$\frac{\{p\}S\{q\}}{\{p<a'/a>\}S\{q<a'/a>\}},\quad \text{provided } \{a,a'\} \cap \mathit{avar}(S) = \emptyset$$

c. $\dfrac{\{p\}S\{q\}}{\{p<a'/a>\}S\{q\}}$, provided $a \notin \mathit{avar}(S,q)$

4.9. Investigate the consequences of replacing x by v in the inference of lemma 2.34. (Hint: This may need definition of a (free) occurrence of a variable in an expression, statement and assertion.)

4.10. Let us introduce the new syntactic construct (a,s,t), for arbitrary $a \in \mathit{Avar}$, $s,t \in \mathit{Iexp}$, which may appear wherever an array variable may appear. Moreover, we put (a,s,t)[s'] ≡ <u>if</u> s=s' <u>then</u> t <u>else</u> a[s'] <u>fi</u>. Assuming the natural definition of substitution for array variables, prove that

⊨ {p<(a,s,t)/a>} a[s]:=t {p}

(As instance of this result we have, for example,
⊨ {(a,a[2],1)[(a,a[2],1)[2]] = 1} a[a[2]] := 1 {a[a[2]] = 1}.)

4.11. Consider the following language which does not allow nested subscription: S,b,p,q are as before; furthermore, we have *Ivar*, with typical elements v, *Sexp*, with typical elements r, and *Iexp*, with typical elements s,t, defined by

v::= x|a[r]
$r ::= x|m|r_1+r_2|\ldots|$<u>if</u> b <u>then</u> r_1 <u>else</u> r_2 <u>fi</u>
$s ::= v|m|s_1+s_2|\ldots|$<u>if</u> b <u>then</u> s_1 <u>else</u> s_2 <u>fi</u>

Let (the central clause in) the definition of substitution be given by

a[r]<t/a[r']> ≡ <u>if</u> r=r' <u>then</u> t <u>else</u> a[r] <u>fi</u>

a. Prove ⊨ (v:=t) → p = p<t/v>
b. Prove ⊨ p ← (v:=t) = ∃y[p<y/v> ∧ v=t<y/v>], provided that $y \notin \mathit{svar}(p,v,t)$.

4.12. Discuss the extension of the theory of chapter 4 to two-dimensional arrays.
(Hint: Introduce, besides *Svar*, *A1va* and *A2va*, and put $Ivar = Svar \cup A1va \times V_0 \cup A2va \times V_0 \times V_0$, etc.)

Chapter 5

RECURSIVE PROCEDURES

5.1. Introduction

Recursion is a key concept in programming practice and theory. As usual in this book, we shall not dwell on the pragmatics of the concept, but concentrate on theoretical issues. In this chapter, we shall restrict ourselves to recursive procedures *without parameters*, leaving a treatment of some of the various parameter mechanisms one encounters in programming languages to chapter 9. Also, we consider only procedures which change the state, rather than procedures which deliver some value (function designators, in ALGOL 60 terminology). Thus, we shall not so much be concerned with recursion as illustrated by (in an ALGOL-like language)

$\underline{\text{integer}}$ $\underline{\text{procedure}}$ fac(n); fac := $\underline{\text{if}}$ n=0 $\underline{\text{then}}$ 1 $\underline{\text{else}}$ n×fac(n−1) $\underline{\text{fi}}$

but rather with examples such as

$\underline{\text{procedure}}$ P_1; $\underline{\text{if}}$ x>0 $\underline{\text{then}}$ x:=x−1; P_1 $\underline{\text{else}}$ D $\underline{\text{fi}}$

or

$\underline{\text{procedure}}$ P_2; $\underline{\text{if}}$ x>0 $\underline{\text{then}}$ x:=x−1; P_2; x:=x+1 $\underline{\text{else}}$ D $\underline{\text{fi}}$.

We assume that the reader is familiar with the usual meaning of procedures such as P_1 or P_2. No doubt, he will then notice that execution of P_1 has the same effect as that of the while statement $\underline{\text{while}}$ x>0 $\underline{\text{do}}$ x:=x−1 $\underline{\text{od}}$. In fact, it is not difficult to show that for each while statement an equivalent recursive procedure may be found (see exercise 5.19); accordingly, it will appear that the theory of recursion subsumes that of chapter 3.

First a word about the *syntax*. The general form of a program with recursion in an ALGOL-like language is something like

$$\underline{\text{begin}}\ \underline{\text{procedure}}\ P_1;S_1;\ldots;\ \underline{\text{procedure}}\ P_n;S_n;\quad S\quad \underline{\text{end}} \tag{5.1}$$

i.e. a *system* of declarations of, in general, mutually dependent recursive procedures $P_1,\ldots,P_n$, together with a statement S as main program. For brevity, we shall write $P_i \Leftarrow S_i$ for the declaration $\underline{\text{procedure}}\ P_i;S_i$. Adopting as well a different delimiter structure, program (5.1) is written in our syntax as $\langle\langle P_i \Leftarrow S_i\rangle_{i=1}^n | S\rangle$. Note that we do not allow the *procedure bodies* S_i themselves to contain procedure declarations. (A limited treatment of this feature will be given in chapter 7.)

Section 5.2 continues the development of the mathematical framework as started in section 3.2. We shall see that, besides the notion of monotonicity of a function as introduced there, we have the fundamental concept of *continuity*. A monotonic function f is called continuous if the value f(x) of the function, applied to the limit $x = \bigsqcup_i x_i$ of a chain of approximations x_i to x, is equal to the limit of the approximations $f(x_i)$ to f(x), i.e. if $f(\bigsqcup_i x_i) = \bigsqcup_i f(x_i)$. We show that each continuous function has a least fixed point, and present a number of their basic properties. It will turn out in this and subsequent chapters that *each* function which occurs as the meaning of a program is in fact continuous. However, this is not at all a deep result, since it is an immediate corollary from the discreteness of the domain Σ. Much more interesting is the notion of continuity on the next-higher level, i.e. when applied not to functions $\Sigma \rightarrow_s \Sigma$, but to *operators* $(\Sigma \rightarrow_s \Sigma) \rightarrow (\Sigma \rightarrow_s \Sigma)$. We shall obtain as one of the central results of denotational semantics that the meaning of a recursive procedure P_i is given as the i-th component of the simultaneous least fixed point of the system of continuous operators $<\Phi_1,\ldots,\Phi_n>$, where, for $j = 1,\ldots,n$, Φ_j is derived in some canonical fashion from the procedure body S_j associated with P_j through its declaration. The actual development of this result goes as follows:

(i) First we define the *operational* semantics $\mathcal{O}(S)$ of a statement S involving recursive procedures on the basis of the usual understanding of the effect of a procedure call. By this we mean nothing but the rule that execution of a procedure call P_i consists in execution of the associated procedure body S_i. (Note that this so-called body replacement rule may be applied repeatedly whenever S_i contains (recursive) occurrences of some P_j, $1 \le j \le n$.)

(ii) Next, we give the *denotational* meaning $\mathcal{M}(S)$, using, for $S \equiv P_i$, the least fixed point definition just mentioned.

(iii) Finally, we prove the equivalence of the two definitions, essentially stating that, for each S, $\mathcal{O}(S) = \mathcal{M}(S)$.

Section 5.2 is partly preparatory for the definition of $\mathcal{M}$ and the equivalence result just mentioned. Besides this, it contains material for section 5.4 and some results used in later chapters. As an example we mention theorem 5.14 which compares *simultaneous* least fixed points with *iterated* ones. One way to understand this theorem is by interpreting it as stating the equivalence of the following two programs (extending our syntax for a moment).

```
begin procedure P1;S1;
      procedure P2;S2;
      P1
end
```

and

```
begin procedure P1;
      begin procedure P2;S2;
            S1
      end;
      P1
end
```

Thus, denotational semantics has its surprises; who would have thought that a non-trivial property of least fixed points would be needed to prove the intuitively quite natural equivalence of these two programs?

In section 5.4 we study methods for proving correctness properties of recursive procedures. Again, we extend the framework as presented in section 3.4. Correctness formulae such as $S_1 \sqsubseteq S_2$ or $\{p\}S\{q\}$ are now always accompanied by declarations, and validity results of the form $\models f$ are replaced by $\models \langle\langle P_i \Leftarrow S_i\rangle_{i=1}^n | f\rangle$. Inferences are extended in a similar way. The great majority of the correctness results of the previous chapters can be taken over either immediately, or through the translation of while statements to recursive procedures. In addition, there is one fundamental new proof rule - called Scott's induction rule - which serves to derive properties of recursive procedures. The general version of the rule is probably rather hard to comprehend, which is why we present it in a number of stages. Basically, the rule may be viewed as a means to perform induction on the recursion depth of a given call P_i, i.e. on the depth of the tree which reflects the structure of the (inner) recursive calls P_j resulting from the (outer) call P_i.

In section 5.5 we present a sound and complete proof system for partial correctness. It turns out that the various correctness results collected in section 5.4 are not yet sufficient to obtain a complete system, and that some further rules are needed. E.g., certain substitution formulae which are extensions of results from chapter 2 are necessary. However, these formulae turn out to be *invalid* with respect to the validity definition of section 5.4. Therefore, we have to refine this definition; the notion of a function not using a simple (or array) variable reappears here. Furthermore, the completeness proof requires an analog of the proposition of section 3.6, establishing the existence of assertions expressing weakest preconditions and strongest postconditions. Finally, we give the completeness proof. As the reader will no doubt notice, this proof is quite complicated; its difficulty exceeds that of all previously encountered arguments.

5.2. Continuous functions and their least fixed points

(The notational conventions of section 3.2 also apply to this section.)

From definition 3.4 we recall that a cpo is defined as a pair $(C,\sqsubseteq)$, with C a non-empty set and " $\sqsubseteq$ " a partial ordering on C such that

(i) C contains a least element $\perp$

(ii) Each chain $\langle x_i \rangle_{i=0}^{\infty}$ of elements in C has a lub $\bigsqcup_{i=0}^{\infty} x_i$ in C.

Moreover, we introduced the notion of a monotonic function from cpo C to cpo C' (where confusion is unlikely, we again omit in the sequel explicit indication of the partial orderings) and showed that the collection of all monotonic functions: $C \to_m C'$ forms a cpo.

We now introduce the notion of *continuous* function.

DEFINITION 5.1 (continuous functions).

Let C, C' be cpo's. A monotonic function f: C → C' is called continuous if, for each chain $\langle x_i \rangle_{i=0}^{\infty}$ of elements in C,

$$f(\bigsqcup_{i=0}^{\infty} x_i) \sqsubseteq \bigsqcup_{i=0}^{\infty} f(x_i)$$

END 5.1.

Observe that the lub of the sequence $<f(x_i)>_{i=0}^{\infty}$ (of elements in C') exists, since from the monotonicity of f and the fact that $<x_i>_{i=0}^{\infty}$ is a chain, it follows that $<f(x_i)>_{i=0}^{\infty}$ is also a chain. As first simple property of continuous functions we have

LEMMA 5.2. Let $f \in C \to_m C'$. f is continuous iff, for each chain $<x_i>_{i=0}^{\infty}$ in C,

$$f(\bigsqcup_{i=0}^{\infty} x_i) = \bigsqcup_{i=0}^{\infty} f(x_i).$$

PROOF. (If) is trivial. In order to prove the (Only if) part, it is sufficient to show that, for each $f \in C \to_m C'$, $\bigsqcup_{i=0}^{\infty} f(x_i) \sqsubseteq f(\bigsqcup_{i=0}^{\infty} x_i)$. Clearly, $x_i \sqsubseteq \bigsqcup_{i=0}^{\infty} x_i$, i = 0,1,.... Thus, by the monotonicity of f, $f(x_i) \sqsubseteq f(\bigsqcup_{i=0}^{\infty} x_i)$, i = 0,1,.... We see that $f(\bigsqcup_{i=0}^{\infty} x_i)$ is an upper bound for each element of the chain $<f(x_i)>_{i=0}^{\infty}$, thus implying that $\bigsqcup_{i=0}^{\infty} f(x_i) \sqsubseteq f(\bigsqcup_{i=0}^{\infty} x_i)$.

END 5.2.

Examples

1. If C is a discrete cpo and D is an arbitrary cpo, then each $f: C \to_s D$ is continuous: Consider a chain $<x_i>_{i=0}^{\infty}$ in C. By discreteness, there is some i_0 such that $\bigsqcup_{i=0}^{\infty} x_i = x_{i_0}$. Hence, $f(\bigsqcup_{i=0}^{\infty} x_i) = f(x_{i_0}) \sqsubseteq \bigsqcup_{i=0}^{\infty} f(x_i)$.
2. Recall that V and W stand for the discrete cpo's of the integers and truth-values extended with $\bot_V$ and $\bot_W$, respectively. We agree that the well-known arithmetic operations on V_0 are extended to V by the convention that $\bot_V$ is delivered as a result whenever one of

the arguments is $\bot_V$. (E.g., $\bot_V+0 = \bot_V$, $\bot_V-1 = \bot_V$, $\alpha\times\bot_V = \bot_V$, etc.) Let f,... and F,... be typical elements of $V \rightarrow_m V$ and $(V \rightarrow_m V) \rightarrow (V \rightarrow_m V)$, respectively. Consider the operator F defined by

$$F = \lambda f \cdot \lambda\alpha \cdot \underline{\text{if}}\ \alpha=0\ \underline{\text{then}}\ 1\ \underline{\text{else}}\ \alpha\times f(\alpha-1)\ \underline{\text{fi}}$$

We shall show that this F is (monotonic and) continuous.

a. F is monotonic. Let $f_1 \sqsubseteq f_1$. To show that $F(f_1) \sqsubseteq F(f_2)$, i.e. that, for all α, $\underline{\text{if}}\ \alpha=0\ \underline{\text{then}}\ 1\ \underline{\text{else}}\ \alpha\times f_1(\alpha-1)\ \underline{\text{fi}} \sqsubseteq \underline{\text{if}}\ \alpha=0\ \underline{\text{then}}\ 1\ \underline{\text{else}}\ \alpha\times f_2(\alpha-1)\ \underline{\text{fi}}$. If $\alpha=\bot_V$ or $\alpha=0$, both sides of the inequality yield $\bot_V$ or 1, respectively. Otherwise, we have to show that $\alpha\times f_1(\alpha-1) \sqsubseteq \alpha\times f_2(\alpha-1)$. Since $f_1 \sqsubseteq f_2$, $f_1(\alpha-1) \sqsubseteq f_2(\alpha-1)$. Thus, it is sufficient to show that if $\alpha_1 \sqsubseteq \alpha_2$, then $\alpha\times\alpha_1 \sqsubseteq \alpha\times\alpha_2$. (Note that, by lemma 3.11 and commutativity of $\times$, this implies that $\times \in V\times V \rightarrow_m V$.) If $\alpha_1=\bot_V$, then $\alpha\times\alpha_1 = \alpha\times\bot_V = \bot_V \sqsubseteq \alpha\times\alpha_2$. If $\alpha_1=\alpha_2$, clearly $\alpha\times\alpha_1 \sqsubseteq \alpha\times\alpha_2$.

b. F is continuous. Let $\langle f_i\rangle_{i=0}^{\infty}$ be a chain of elements in $V \rightarrow_m V$. We prove that $F(\bigsqcup_{i=0}^{\infty} f_i) \sqsubseteq \bigsqcup_{i=0}^{\infty} F(f_i)$. Choose some α. We have to show that $\underline{\text{if}}\ \alpha=0\ \underline{\text{then}}\ 1\ \underline{\text{else}}\ \alpha \times (\bigsqcup_{i=0}^{\infty} f_i)(\alpha-1)\ \underline{\text{fi}} \sqsubseteq \bigsqcup_{i=0}^{\infty}$ $(\underline{\text{if}}\ \alpha=0\ \underline{\text{then}}\ 1\ \underline{\text{else}}\ \alpha\times f_i(\alpha-1)\ \underline{\text{fi}})$. If $\alpha=\bot_V$ or $\alpha=0$ this is clear. There remains the proof of $\alpha \times (\bigsqcup_{i=0}^{\infty} f_i)(\alpha-1) \sqsubseteq \bigsqcup_{i=0}^{\infty} (\alpha \times f_i(\alpha-1))$. Now $\alpha \times (\bigsqcup_{i=0}^{\infty} f_i)(\alpha-1) = \alpha \times \bigsqcup_{i=0}^{\infty} f_i(\alpha-1) = \bigsqcup_{i=0}^{\infty}(\alpha \times f_i(\alpha-1))$, where the last equality follows from

(i) $\langle f_i\rangle_{i=0}^{\infty}$ is a chain in $V \rightarrow_m V$; hence, $\langle f_i(\alpha-1)\rangle_{i=0}^{\infty}$ is a chain in V

(ii) $\times$ is a monotonic function: $V \times V \to V$, and therefore (by an argument analogous to example 1) also a continuous function.

(iii) By (ii), for each chain $\langle \alpha_i \rangle_{i=0}^{\infty}$ in V, we have that $\alpha \times \bigsqcup_{i=0}^{\infty} \alpha_i$ $= \times(\langle \alpha, \bigsqcup_{i=0}^{\infty} \alpha_i \rangle) = \times(\bigsqcup_{i=0}^{\infty} \langle \alpha, \alpha_i \rangle) = \bigsqcup_{i=0}^{\infty} \times(\langle \alpha, \alpha_i \rangle) = \bigsqcup_{i=0}^{\infty} (\alpha \times \alpha_i)$ (where we have changed the notation from $\alpha' \times \alpha''$ to $\times(\langle \alpha', \alpha'' \rangle)$ in order to make explicit how the continuity definition was applied).

3. (A non-continuous function). Let $F: (V \to_m V) \to (V \to_m V)$ be defined as follows: for each $f \in V \to_m V$, let $F(f) = \bot_{V \to_m V}$ if $f(\alpha) = \bot_V$ for some $\alpha \neq \bot_V$, and $F(f) = f$, otherwise. (Note that F may be viewed as testing whether f is total. If yes, then f, if no, then $\bot_{V \to_m V}$ is delivered.) F is monotonic (exercise) but not continuous. Consider for example the following chain of functions $\langle f_i \rangle_{i=0}^{\infty}$ in $V \to_m V$: For each $i = 0,1,\ldots$, $f_i(\alpha) =$ <u>if</u> $\alpha \leq i$ <u>then</u> α <u>else</u> $\bot_V$ <u>fi</u>. Clearly, $\langle f_i \rangle_{i=0}^{\infty}$ is a chain such that $\bigsqcup_{i=0}^{\infty} f_i = \lambda\alpha \cdot \alpha$. Thus, $F(\bigsqcup_{i=0}^{\infty} f_i) =$ $F(\lambda\alpha \cdot \alpha) = \lambda\alpha \cdot \alpha$. On the other hand, we have that, for each i, $F(f_i) = \bot_{V \to_m V}$, whence $\bigsqcup_{i=0}^{\infty} F(f_i) = \bot_{V \to_m V}$ (which is thus different from $F(\bigsqcup_{i=0}^{\infty} f_i)$).

After these examples we state the first important property of continuous functions. From now on, we shall use $[C \to C']$ to denote the set of all continuous functions from cpo C to cpo C'.

<u>LEMMA 5.3</u>. $[C \to C']$ is a cpo.

Before giving the proof of this lemma, we first prove a useful auxiliary proposition.

LEMMA 5.4. Let, for $i = 0,1,\ldots$, $j = 0,1,\ldots$, x_{ij} be elements of cpo C. Suppose that, for all i,j,k,ℓ with $i \le k$ and $j \le \ell$ we have that $x_{ij} \sqsubseteq x_{k\ell}$. Then

$$\bigsqcup_{i=0}^{\infty} \bigsqcup_{j=0}^{\infty} x_{ij} = \bigsqcup_{j=0}^{\infty} \bigsqcup_{i=0}^{\infty} x_{ij} = \bigsqcup_{k=0}^{\infty} x_{kk}.$$

PROOF.

a. For each i we have that $x_{i0} \sqsubseteq x_{i1} \sqsubseteq \ldots$; hence $\bigsqcup_{j=0}^{\infty} x_{ij}$ exists for each i. Moreover, since, for each i and j, $x_{i,j} \sqsubseteq x_{i+1,j}$, for each i we have that $\bigsqcup_{j=0}^{\infty} x_{ij} \sqsubseteq \bigsqcup_{j=0}^{\infty} x_{i+1,j}$, whence $\bigsqcup_{i=0}^{\infty} \bigsqcup_{j=0}^{\infty} x_{ij}$ exists. By symmetry, so does $\bigsqcup_{j=0}^{\infty} \bigsqcup_{i=0}^{\infty} x_{ij}$; the existence of $\bigsqcup_{k=0}^{\infty} x_{kk}$ should be clear.

b. For all i and j we have that $x_{ij} \sqsubseteq \bigsqcup_{i=0}^{\infty} x_{ij} \sqsubseteq \bigsqcup_{j=0}^{\infty} \bigsqcup_{i=0}^{\infty} x_{ij}$; hence $\bigsqcup_{j=0}^{\infty} x_{ij} \sqsubseteq \bigsqcup_{j=0}^{\infty} \bigsqcup_{i=0}^{\infty} x_{ij}$ holds for all i. From this we obtain that $\bigsqcup_{i=0}^{\infty} \bigsqcup_{j=0}^{\infty} x_{ij} \sqsubseteq \bigsqcup_{j=0}^{\infty} \bigsqcup_{i=0}^{\infty} x_{ij}$. By symmetry, the reverse inclusion also holds, thus proving that $\bigsqcup_{i=0}^{\infty} \bigsqcup_{j=0}^{\infty} x_{ij} = \bigsqcup_{j=0}^{\infty} \bigsqcup_{i=0}^{\infty} x_{ij}$.

c. $\bigsqcup_{i=0}^{\infty} \bigsqcup_{j=0}^{\infty} x_{ij} = \bigsqcup_{k=0}^{\infty} x_{kk}$. Exercise.

END 5.4.

We now give the

PROOF of lemma 5.3. Since $\lambda x \cdot \bot_{C'}$ is clearly continuous, it is sufficient to show that each chain $\langle f_i \rangle_{i=0}^{\infty}$ in $[C \to C']$ has a lub $\bigsqcup_{i=0}^{\infty} f_i$ in $[C \to C']$. As in the proof of lemma 3.9, we take $\bigsqcup_{i=0}^{\infty} f_i = \lambda x \cdot \bigsqcup_{i=0}^{\infty} f_i(x)$. We have to prove that $\bigsqcup_{i=0}^{\infty} f_i$ is continuous, i.e. that for each chain $\langle x_j \rangle_{j=0}^{\infty}$, $(\bigsqcup_{i=0}^{\infty} f_i)(\bigsqcup_{j=0}^{\infty} x_j) = \bigsqcup_{j=0}^{\infty}\{(\bigsqcup_{i=0}^{\infty} f_i)(x_j)\}$. Now $(\bigsqcup_{i=0}^{\infty} f_i)(\bigsqcup_{j=0}^{\infty} x_j) = \bigsqcup_{i=0}^{\infty}\{f_i(\bigsqcup_{j=0}^{\infty} x_j)\}$ = (all f_i continuous) $\bigsqcup_{i=0}^{\infty} \bigsqcup_{j=0}^{\infty} f_i(x_j)$ = (lemma 5.4)

$\bigsqcup_{j=0}^{\infty} \bigsqcup_{i=0}^{\infty} f_i(x_j) = \bigsqcup_{j=0}^{\infty}\{(\bigsqcup_{i=0}^{\infty} f_i)(x_j)\}$.

END 5.3.

The next lemma generalizes lemma 3.11 for continuous functions:

LEMMA 5.5. Let C_1, C_2 and C be cpo's.

a. The following two statements are equivalent

(i) $f \in [C_1 \times C_2 \to C]$

(ii) For all $x \in C_1$, $\lambda y \cdot f(x,y) \in [C_2 \to C]$, and, for all $y \in C_2$, $\lambda x \cdot f(x,y) \in [C_1 \to C]$

b. The mapping $'$: $(C_1 \times C_2 \to C) \to (C_1 \to (C_2 \to C))$ defined by $f' = \lambda x \cdot \lambda y \cdot f(x,y)$, induces a one-one mapping from $[C_1 \times C_2 \to C]$ onto $[C_1 \to [C_2 \to C]]$.

PROOF. Exercise.

END 5.5.

Remark. This lemma allows us to identify the cpo's $[C_1 \times C_2 \to C]$ and $[C_1 \to [C_2 \to C]]$, which will be of some convenience in the sequel. Its generalization to arbitrary $n > 2$ should be clear.

Various simple classes of functions are continuous, and continuity is preserved by composition and if-then-else-fi. These results are brought together in lemmas 5.6 and 5.7.

LEMMA 5.6. Let $C, C_1, \ldots, D, \ldots$ be arbitrary cpo's with typical elements $x, x_1, \ldots, y, \ldots$.

a. $\lambda x \cdot x \in [C \to C]$

b. $\lambda x \cdot y \in [C \to D]$

c. If $f \in [C_2 \to C_3]$ and $g \in [C_1 \to C_2]$, then $f \circ g \ (\overset{\text{df.}}{=} \lambda x_1 \cdot f(g(x_1))) \in [C_1 \to C_3]$.

d. If $f_1, f_2 \in [C \to D]$, then <u>if</u> β <u>then</u> f_1 <u>else</u> f_2 <u>fi</u> $\in [C \to D]$.

PROOF. We prove only cases a and c. Let $\langle x_i\rangle_{i=0}^{\infty}$ be a chain.

a. $(\lambda x\cdot x)(\bigsqcup_i x_i) = \bigsqcup_i x_i = \bigsqcup_i(\lambda x\cdot x)(x_i)$

b. $(f\circ g)(\bigsqcup_i x_i) = f(g(\bigsqcup_i x_i)) =$ (cont. g) $f(\bigsqcup_i g(x_i)) =$ (cont. f) $\bigsqcup_i f(g(x_i)) = \bigsqcup_i (f\circ g)(x_i)$.

END 5.6.

For subsequent use (in section 5.3) we need a somewhat generalized version of lemma 5.6.

LEMMA 5.7. Under similar assumptions as in lemma 5.6:

a. $\lambda x_1\cdot\ldots\cdot\lambda x_n\cdot x_i \in [C_1 \to [C_2 \to \ldots [C_n \to C_i] \ldots]]$

b. $\lambda x_1\cdot\ldots\cdot\lambda x_n\cdot x \in [C_1 \to [C_2 \to \ldots [C_n \to C] \ldots]]$

c. If $f_1 \in [C_1 \to [C_2 \to \ldots [C_n \to [D_2 \to D_3]] \ldots]]$ and $f_2 \in [C_1 \to [C_2 \to \ldots [C_n \to [D_1 \to D_2]] \ldots]]$, then $\lambda x_1\cdot\ldots\cdot\lambda x_n\cdot f_1(x_1)\ldots(x_n)\circ f_2(x_1)\ldots(x_n) \in [C_1 \to [C_2 \to \ldots [C_n \to [D_1 \to D_3]] \ldots]]$

d. If $f_1, f_2 \in [C_1 \to [C_2 \to \ldots [C_n \to [C \to D]] \ldots]]$ and $g \in [C \to W]$, then $\lambda x_1\cdot\ldots\cdot\lambda x_n\cdot\lambda x\cdot$ <u>if</u> $g(x)$ <u>then</u> $f_1(x_1)\ldots(x_n)(x)$ <u>else</u> $f_2(x_1)\ldots(x_n)(x)$ <u>fi</u> $\in [C_1 \to [C_2 \to \ldots [C_n \to [C \to D]] \ldots]]$.

PROOF. We prove only case c. For simplicity's sake, take n = 1. Let $\langle x_i\rangle_{i=0}^{\infty}$ be a chain in C. $(\lambda x\cdot f_1(x)\circ f_2(x))(\bigsqcup_i x_i) = f_1(\bigsqcup_i x_i)\circ f_2(\bigsqcup_i x_i) =$ $\lambda y_1\cdot f_1(\bigsqcup_i x_i)(f_2(\bigsqcup_j x_j)(y_1)) = \lambda y_1\cdot f_1(\bigsqcup_i x_i)(\bigsqcup_j f_2(x_j)(y_1)) =$ $\lambda y_1\cdot\bigsqcup_i\bigsqcup_j f_1(x_i)(f_2(x_j)(y_1)) = \lambda y_1\cdot\bigsqcup_k f_1(x_k)(f_2(x_k)(y_1)) =$ $\bigsqcup_k \lambda y_1\cdot f_1(x_k)(f_2(x_k)(y_1)) = \bigsqcup_k f_1(x_k)\circ f_2(x_k)$. Thus we have established that $\lambda x\cdot f_1(x)\circ f_2(x) \in [C_1 \to (D_1 \to D_3)]$. Since, moreover, for each x, $f_1(x)\circ f_2(x) \in [D_1 \to D_3]$, we obtain that

$\lambda x \cdot f_1(x) \circ f_2(x) \in [C_1 \rightarrow [D_1 \rightarrow D_3]]$, as was to be shown.

END 5.7.

As we have seen already, least fixed points form a central theme of denotational semantics. Now one of the attractive features of a continuous function is that it always possesses a least fixed point:

<u>THEOREM 5.8</u>. Let C be a cpo and $f \in [C \rightarrow C]$. f has a least fixed point μf satisfying

$$\mu f = \bigsqcup_{i=0}^{\infty} f^i(\perp),$$

where $f^0 = \lambda x \cdot x$, and $f^{i+1} = f \circ f^i$, $i = 0,1,\ldots$.

<u>PROOF</u>. First we observe that by the continuity (and, hence, monotonicity) of f, and since $\perp \sqsubseteq f(\perp)$, we have that $f^i(\perp) \sqsubseteq f^{i+1}(\perp)$, and we conclude that $\bigsqcup_{i=0}^{\infty} f^i(\perp)$ indeed exists. Moreover, we have that

(i) $f(\bigsqcup_{i=0}^{\infty} f^i(\perp)) = \text{(cont. f)} \bigsqcup_{i=0}^{\infty} f(f^i(\perp)) = \bigsqcup_{i=0}^{\infty} f^{i+1}(\perp) = \bigsqcup_{i=0}^{\infty} f^i(\perp)$,

and we see that $\bigsqcup_{i=0}^{\infty} f^i(\perp)$ is indeed a fixed point of f.

(ii) Let $f(x) = x$. We show that, for all i, $f^i(\perp) \sqsubseteq x$.

$i = 0$. $\perp \sqsubseteq x$ is clear.

$i \rightarrow i+1$. Let $f^i(\perp) \sqsubseteq x$.

By monotonicity $f^{i+1}(\perp) = f(f^i(\perp)) \sqsubseteq f(x) = x$.

By the lub definition we therefore conclude that $\bigsqcup_{i=0}^{\infty} f^i(\perp) \sqsubseteq x$.

Taking (i) and (ii) together, we have established that $\bigsqcup_{i=0}^{\infty} f^i(\perp)$ is a fixed point of f which is included in each fixed point of f, i.e. that $\mu f = \bigsqcup_{i=0}^{\infty} f^i(\perp)$.

END 5.8.

LEMMA 5.9. Let C be a cpo and let $f \in [C \to C]$.
If $f(y) \sqsubseteq y$, then $\mu f \sqsubseteq y$.

PROOF. In part (ii) of the proof of theorem 5.8, it is sufficient to assume that $f(x) \sqsubseteq x$.
END 5.9.

We now discuss how to introduce a generalization of theorem 5.8 to what might be called the n-dimensional case. Let $C_1,\ldots,C_n$ be cpo's, and let $f_i \in [C_1\times\ldots\times C_n \to C_i]$, $i = 1,\ldots,n$. We combine the n-tuple of functions $f_1,\ldots,f_n$ to one function $\langle f_1,\ldots,f_n\rangle: C_1\times\ldots\times C_n \to C_1\times\ldots\times C_n$, by putting $\langle f_1,\ldots,f_n\rangle(x_1,\ldots,x_n) = \langle f_1(x_1,\ldots,x_n),\ldots,f_n(x_1,\ldots,x_n)\rangle$. It is straightforward to verify that $\langle f_1,\ldots,f_n\rangle$ is continuous, i.e. that $\langle f_1,\ldots,f_n\rangle \in [C_1\times\ldots\times C_n \to C_1\times\ldots\times C_n]$. Thus, it has a least fixed point $\mu[\langle f_1,\ldots,f_n\rangle]$ (or $\mu[f_1,\ldots,f_n]$, for short), for which we have the following corollary of theorem 5.8:

COROLLARY 5.10. Let, for $k = 1,\ldots,n$,

$$x_k^0 = \bot_{C_k}$$

$$x_k^{i+1} = f_k(x_1^i,\ldots,x_n^i), \qquad i = 0,1,\ldots$$

Then $\mu[f_1,\ldots,f_n] = \bigsqcup_{i=0}^{\infty} \langle x_1^i,\ldots,x_n^i\rangle$.

PROOF. Follows from theorem 5.8.
END 5.10.

In the sequel we shall indicate an appeal to the fixed point property of μf (property (i) of theorem 5.8) by *fpp*, whereas use of the least fixed point property (property (ii) of theorem 5.8, possibly in the stronger version of lemma 5.9) will be indicated by *lfp*.

It is of some interest to observe that the least-fixed point operator μ, which maps each $f \in [C \to C]$ to $\mu f \in C$, is itself continuous:

LEMMA 5.11. Let C be a cpo, $f \in [C \to C]$ and $\mu = \lambda f \cdot \bigsqcup_{i=0}^{\infty} f^i(\bot)$. Then $\mu \in [[C \to C] \to C]$.

PROOF. First we show that μ is monotonic. Let $f,g \in [C \to C]$ such that $f \sqsubseteq g$. It is easily shown by induction on i that, for each i, $f^i(\bot) \sqsubseteq g^i(\bot)$, and from this it follows that $\bigsqcup_{i=0}^{\infty} f^i(\bot) \sqsubseteq \bigsqcup_{i=0}^{\infty} g^i(\bot)$, i.e. that $\mu f \sqsubseteq \mu g$. Next, we prove that μ is continuous. Let $\langle f_i \rangle_{i=0}^{\infty}$ be a chain in $[C \to C]$. We must show that $\mu(\bigsqcup_i f_i) \sqsubseteq \bigsqcup_i \mu f_i$. By *lfp* it is sufficient to prove that

$$(\bigsqcup_i f_i)(\bigsqcup_j \mu f_j) = \bigsqcup_j \mu f_j$$

which is established as follows: $(\bigsqcup_i f_i)(\bigsqcup_j \mu f_j) = \bigsqcup_i f_i(\bigsqcup_j \mu f_j) =$ (cont. f_i) $\bigsqcup_i \bigsqcup_j f_i(\mu f_j) = \bigsqcup_k f_k(\mu f_k) =$ (*fpp*) $\bigsqcup_k \mu f_k$.

END 5.11.

We now interrupt our sequence of basic properties of continuous functions and their least fixed points with the presentation of a few examples, intended to further familiarize the reader with calculations with least fixed points. Later, it will turn out that some of these examples were inspired by questions of program correctness.

Examples

1. Let $f,g \in [C \to C]$. By lemma 5.6, $f \circ g \in [C \to C]$. Thus, $f \circ g$ has a least fixed point $\mu[f \circ g]$. We show that this satisfies

   $$\mu[f \circ g] = f(\mu[g \circ f]).$$

   In fact, $f(\mu[g \circ f]) =$ (by *fpp*) $f((g \circ f)(\mu[g \circ f])) = (f \circ g)(f(\mu[g \circ f]))$, whence, by *lfp*, $\mu[f \circ g] \sqsubseteq f(\mu[g \circ f])$. By symmetry, also $\mu[g \circ f] \sqsubseteq g(\mu[f \circ g])$. Applying f on both sides we obtain $f(\mu[g \circ f]) \sqsubseteq f(g(\mu[f \circ g])) =$ (*fpp*) $\mu[f \circ g]$. Together, we have established the desired result.

2. Let $f \in [C \times C \to C]$. It is left to the reader to verify that $\lambda x \cdot f(x,x) \in [C \to C]$. Thus, $\lambda x \cdot f(x,x)$ has a least fixed point, say $x_0 = \mu[\lambda x \cdot f(x,x)]$. We show that this satisfies

$$x_0 = \mu[\lambda x \cdot f(x,x_0)].$$

Let us write x_1 for $\mu[\lambda x \cdot f(x,x_0)]$. By *fpp* and the definition of x_0, we have that $f(x_0,x_0) = x_0$. By *lfp* and the definition of x_1 we obtain that $x_1 \sqsubseteq x_0$. From this and the monotonicity of f it follows that $f(x_1,x_1) \sqsubseteq f(x_1,x_0) =$ (def. x_1 and *fpp*) x_1. By the definition of x_0 and *lfp* we conclude that $x_0 \sqsubseteq x_1$. Thus, $x_1 = x_0$ follows.
3. Let $f,g \in [C \to C]$. If $f(\perp) = g(\perp)$ and, for some $i \geq 1$, $f^i \circ g = g \circ f$, then $\mu f = \mu g$. This is shown as follows: first we prove, by induction on k that, for all $k \geq 1$, $g^k(\perp) = f^{1+i+\ldots+i^{k-1}}(\perp)$.

$k=1$. $g(\perp) = f(\perp)$ holds by assumption.

$k \to k+1$. Assume $g^k(\perp) = f^{1+i+\ldots+i^{k-1}}(\perp)$. Then

$$g^{k+1}(\perp) = g(f^{i+1+\ldots+i^{k-1}}(\perp)) = f^{i\times(1+i+\ldots+i^{k-1})}(g(\perp)) =$$
$$f^{i\times(1+i+\ldots+i^{k-1})}(f(\perp)) = f^{1+i+\ldots+i^k}(\perp).$$

Furthermore, we have that

$$\mu g = \bigsqcup_{k=0}^{\infty} g^k(\perp) = \bigsqcup_{k=0}^{\infty} f^{1+i+\ldots+i^{k-1}}(\perp) = \bigsqcup_{k=0}^{\infty} f^k(\perp) = \mu f$$

where the one but last equality holds since, for each chain $\langle x_i \rangle_{i=0}^{\infty}$ and each strictly monotonically increasing (with respect to the standard ordering on natural numbers) function ψ: $\mathbb{N} \to \mathbb{N}$, we have that $\bigsqcup_i x_i = \bigsqcup_i x_{\psi(i)}$.

Further examples of a similar nature are contained in the section on exercises. We continue our discussion on fixed point theory with the presentation of some further important properties of the μ-operator. The first result establishes that μ preserves continuity:

THEOREM 5.12. Let C be a cpo and let $f \in [C \to [C \to C]]$. Then $\lambda x \cdot \mu[f(x)] \in [C \to C]$.

PROOF. First we show that $\lambda x \cdot \mu[f(x)]$ is monotonic and next that it is continuous.

1. $x_1 \sqsubseteq x_2 \Rightarrow$ (mon. f) $f(x_1) \sqsubseteq f(x_2) \Rightarrow$ (by theorem 5.11, μ is monotonic) $\mu[f(x_1)] \sqsubseteq \mu[f(x_2)]$.
2. Let $\langle x_i \rangle_{i=0}^{\infty}$ be a chain in C. $\mu[f(\bigsqcup_i x_i)] =$ (cont. f) $\mu[\bigsqcup_i f(x_i)] =$ (by theorem 5.11, μ is continuous) $\bigsqcup_i \mu[f(x_i)]$.

END 5.12.

The final theorem of this section (theorem 5.14) deals with the connection between simultaneous and iterated least fixed points of a system of functions. Remember that, for $f_i \in [C_1 \times \ldots \times C_n \to C_i]$, $i = 1,\ldots,n$, we encountered the least fixed point of $\langle f_1,\ldots,f_n \rangle$ in the discussion following theorem 5.8. For reasons which will become clear in a moment, we call $\mu[f_1,\ldots,f_n]$ the *simultaneous* least fixed point of the system $\langle f_1,\ldots,f_n \rangle$. We shall contrast this with another technique of obtaining least fixed points, viz. that of *iterating* the μ-operator in a certain way, and show how in both ways the same result is obtained. Theorem 5.14 not only holds for continuous functions, but, more generally, for monotonic functions provided the existence of their least fixed points is guaranteed. The next theorem describes such a situation, which has some interest for future applications in which we have to deal with least fixed points of functions which are monotonic but not continuous.

THEOREM 5.13. Let $(C,\sqsubseteq)$ be a partially ordered set with the property that *each* subset $X \subseteq C$ has a least upper bound. (Such a set is called a *complete lattice*.)

a. Each subset $X \subseteq C$ has a greatest lower bound
b. Each monotonic function $f\colon C \to C$ has a least fixed point μf,

satisfying

$$\mu f = \sqcap \{x \mid f(x) = x\} = \sqcap \{x \mid f(x) \sqsubseteq x\}.$$

Remark. Clearly, any complete lattice is a cpo (with $\perp = \sqcap C$). Hence, we can use the relevant results of section 3.2.

PROOF.

a. Choose some $X \subseteq C$. Let $X_0 \overset{\text{df.}}{=} \{y \mid y \in C \text{ and } y \sqsubseteq x \text{ for all } x \in X\}$, and let $x_0 \overset{\text{df.}}{=} \sqcup X_0$. We show that $x_0 = \sqcap X$.

(i) $x_0 \sqsubseteq x$ for all $x \in X$. Choose some $x_1 \in X$. We have $y \sqsubseteq x_1$ for all $y \in X_0$, whence $\sqcup X_0 \sqsubseteq x_1$, i.e. $x_0 \sqsubseteq x_1$.

(ii) Assume that, for some z, $z \sqsubseteq x$ for all $x \in X$. To show $z \sqsubseteq x_0$. From the assumption on z we have that $z \in X_0$; hence $z \sqsubseteq \sqcup X_0 = x_0$.

b. Let $x_0 \overset{\text{df.}}{=} \sqcap \{x \mid f(x) = x\}$. It is sufficient to show that $f(x_0) = x_0$. In fact, then x_0 is a fixed point of f which is included in each fixed point of f, and we may take $\mu f = x_0$. Let $x_1 \overset{\text{df.}}{=} \sqcap \{x \mid f(x) \sqsubseteq x\}$. Clearly, $x_1 \sqsubseteq x_0$. If we can show that $f(x_1) = x_1$, then (from the glb property) $x_0 \sqsubseteq x_1$ and, hence, $x_0 = x_1$, which in turn implies $f(x_0) = x_0$. There remains the proof of $f(x_1) = x_1$.

(i) $f(x_1) \sqsubseteq x_1$. It is sufficient to show that, for all x such that $f(x) \sqsubseteq x$, we have that $f(x_1) \sqsubseteq x$. So assume that $f(x) \sqsubseteq x$. By the definition of x_1, $x_1 \sqsubseteq x$ and, by the monotonicity of f, therefore $f(x_1) \sqsubseteq f(x)$. Since we assumed that $f(x) \sqsubseteq x$, $f(x_1) \sqsubseteq x$ follows.

(ii) $x_1 \sqsubseteq f(x_1)$. By part (i), $f(f(x_1)) \sqsubseteq f(x_1)$. By the glb property of x_1, this implies that $x_1 \sqsubseteq f(x_1)$.

END 5.13.

In the next theorem, we restrict ourselves to the case $n = 2$, leaving its generalization to the reader.

THEOREM 5.14. Let C,D be complete lattices.

a. $C \times D$, ordered as defined in lemma 3.5, is a complete lattice. Let $f: C\times D \to_m C$ and $g: C\times D \to_m D$, and let $\langle f,g\rangle: C\times D \to C\times D$ be defined by $\langle f,g\rangle(x,y) = \langle f(x,y),g(x,y)\rangle$

b. $\langle f,g\rangle \in C\times D \to_m C\times D$

c. $\langle f,g\rangle$ has a (simultaneous) least fixed point $\mu[f,g]$ satisfying

$$\begin{aligned}\mu[f,g] &= \sqcap \{\langle x,y\rangle \mid \langle f,g\rangle(x,y) = \langle x,y\rangle\}\\ &= \sqcap \{\langle x,y\rangle \mid \langle f,g\rangle(x,y) \sqsubseteq \langle x,y\rangle\}\end{aligned}$$

d. (i) For each $x \in C$, $\lambda y\cdot g(x,y) \in D \to_m D$

(ii) $\lambda x\cdot\mu[\lambda y\cdot g(x,y)] \in C \to_m D$

(iii) If $f: C\times D \to_m C$ and $h: C \to_m D$, then $\lambda x\cdot f(x,h(x)): C \to_m C$

(iv) $\lambda x\cdot f(x,\mu[\lambda y\cdot g(x,y)]) \in C \to_m C$

e. Let $x_0 = \mu[\lambda x\cdot f(x,\mu[\lambda y\cdot g(x,y)])]$

$y_0 = \mu[\lambda y\cdot g(x_0,y)]$

Then $\mu[f,g] = \langle x_0,y_0\rangle$

(The fact that x_0 and y_0 involve nested application of the μ-operator justifies our terminology of iterated least fixed points.)

PROOF. Parts a, b, d(i) and d(iii) are clear from the definitions and previous results, and d(iv) is immediate from d(ii) and d(iii). Part c is the two-dimensional version of theorem 5.13. We therefore exhibit only the proofs of parts d(ii) and e.

d(ii). By d(i), $\lambda y\cdot g(x,y) \in D \to_m D$, for each $x \in C$. Hence $\mu[\lambda y\cdot g(x,y)]$ exists (and belongs to D) for each $x \in C$. We now prove that $\lambda x\cdot\mu[\lambda y\cdot g(x,y)]$ is monotonic. Assume that $x_1 \sqsubseteq x_2$. We show that

$\mu[\lambda y \cdot g(x_1,y)] \sqsubseteq \mu[\lambda y \cdot g(x_2,y)]$, or, by theorem 5.13, that $y_1 \stackrel{df.}{=} \sqcap \{y \mid g(x_1,y) \sqsubseteq y\} \sqsubseteq y_2 \stackrel{df.}{=} \sqcap \{y \mid g(x_2,y) \sqsubseteq y\}$. It is sufficient to prove that, for each y' such that $g(x_2,y') \sqsubseteq y'$, we have that $y_1 \sqsubseteq y'$. So assume that $g(x_2,y') \sqsubseteq y'$. Then $g(x_1,y') \sqsubseteq$ (mon. g) $g(x_2,y') \sqsubseteq y'$, and $y_1 \sqsubseteq y'$ follows from the glb property.

e. Observe that from d(iii) and d(ii) we have that both x_0 and y_0 exist. From the definitions of x_0 and y_0 we derive that

$$x_0 = f(x_0,\mu[\lambda y \cdot g(x_0,y)]) = f(x_0,y_0)$$
$$y_0 = g(x_0,y_0)$$

and this implies (by *lfp* for $\mu[f,g]$) that $\mu[f,g] \sqsubseteq \langle x_0,y_0\rangle$. There remains the proof of the reverse inclusion. Let $\mu[f,g] \stackrel{df.}{=} \langle x_1,y_1\rangle$, and let $y_2 \stackrel{df.}{=} \mu[\lambda y \cdot g(x_1,y)]$. Since $g(x_1,y_1) = y_1$, we obtain by the definition of y_2 and *lfp* (based on theorem 5.13!), that $y_2 \sqsubseteq y_1$ and, therefore, that $f(x_1,y_2) \sqsubseteq f(x_1,y_1) = x_1$. Replacing, in this inclusion, y_2 by its definition we obtain $f(x_1,\mu[\lambda y \cdot g(x_1,y)] \sqsubseteq x_1$, from which, by the definition of x_0 and *lfp*, it follows that $x_0 \sqsubseteq x_1$. Then $g(x_0,y_1) \sqsubseteq g(x_1,y_1) = y_1$ also follows and, by the definition of y_0 and *lfp*, we finally obtain that $y_0 \sqsubseteq y_1$.

END 5.14.

Remarks

1. For *continuous* f: C×D → C and g: C×D → D we do not need the complete lattice structure on C and D to guarantee existence of the various least fixed points. Thus, theorem 5.14e holds a fortiori for such continuous f,g even on arbitrary cpo's and not just on complete lattices (note that the complete lattice structure is not

used in the proof of theorem 5.14e).

2. As a word of caution, let us emphasize that various results presented in this section do not hold on cpo's for functions which are monotonic but not continuous, not even in a situation where the *existence* of their least fixed points is ensured in some way. Often it is, in addition, necessary to have the lub-characterization of μf available (see for example exercise 5.6).

5.3. Semantics

In this section we extend the class of statements with (parameterless) recursive procedures, assign meaning to them as least fixed points of suitably chosen operators, and justify this definition by means of a comparison with their operational semantics where execution of a procedure call amounts to the execution of the procedure body associated with the procedure name through its declaration.

We begin with the syntax. For simplicity's sake, we omit the while statement as introduced in chapter 3, since later it will appear that the while statement is nothing but a simple special case of a recursive procedure anyway. We start our extension with the introduction of the class *Pvar* of *procedure variables*, with typical elements P,Q,.... We then define the syntactic classes of *statements, declarations* and *programs*, where a program is made up from a pair consisting of a system of declarations and a statement.

DEFINITION 5.15 (syntax of programs with recursive procedures).

a. The class *Stat*, with typical elements S,..., is given by

$$S::= v:=t \mid S_1;S_2 \mid \underline{\text{if}}\ b\ \underline{\text{then}}\ S_1\ \underline{\text{else}}\ S_2\ \underline{\text{fi}} \mid P$$

b. The class *Decl*, with typical elements E,..., is given by

$$E::= P_1 \Leftarrow S_1,\ldots,P_n \Leftarrow S_n, \quad n \geq 0,$$

where $P_i \not\equiv P_j$, $1 \leq i < j \leq n$.

c. The class *Prog*, with typical elements R,..., is given by

R::= <E:S>

END 5.15.

Remarks

1. A sequence $E \equiv P_1 \Leftarrow S_1,\ldots,P_n \Leftarrow S_n$ is usually written as $<P_i \Leftarrow S_i>_{i=1}^n$. Note that the definition of E allows an empty sequence of declarations.
2. In the sequel we shall use the somewhat more readable notation $<E|S>$ instead of $<E:S>$. (Observe that BNF does not allow us to define this directly.)
3. A program $R \equiv <E|S>$, with $E \equiv <P_i \Leftarrow S_i>_{i=1}^n$, is called *closed* whenever all procedure variables occurring in it are *declared*, i.e. whenever for each P occurring in S or any of the S_i, $i = 1,\ldots,n$, we have that $P \equiv P_j$, for some j, $1 \le j \le n$.
4. The classes *Ivar*, *Iexp* and *Bexp*, together with the functions *L*, *R* and *W* remain unchanged with respect to the previous definitions.
5. As before, $D \equiv x:=x$ denotes the dummy statement.
6. For $E \equiv <P_i \Leftarrow S_i>_{i=1}^n$, *svar*(E) is defined as $\bigcup_{i=1}^n$ *svar*(S_i), and similarly for *avar*(E) and *intv*(E). (This notation is used in section 5.5; for *svar*(S), *avar*(S) and *intv*(S) see definition 4.3.)

Examples

1. <P ⇐ <u>if</u> x>0 <u>then</u> x:=x-1; y:=y+1; P <u>else</u> D <u>fi</u>|y:=0; x:=10;P>
   (After execution, x has the value 0 and y has the value 10.)
2. <P ⇐ <u>if</u> x>0 <u>then</u> x:=x-1; P; x:=x+1 <u>else</u> D <u>fi</u>|x:=10; P>
   (After execution, x has the value 10.)
3. <P⇐P|P>, <P⇐Q,Q⇐P|<u>if</u> x>y <u>then</u> P <u>else</u> Q <u>fi</u>>
   (Neither of these two programs terminates.)
4. <P_1 ⇐ <u>if</u> x>0 <u>then</u> P_2;P_1 <u>else</u> D <u>fi</u>,
   P_2 ⇐ <u>if</u> x>0 <u>then</u> x:=x-1; y:=y+1; P_2 <u>else</u> D <u>fi</u>|y:=0; x:=10; P_1>
   (After execution, x has the value 0 and y has the value 10.)

We proceed with the definition of the operational semantics of the elements of *Prog*. As opposed to the approach taken in denotational semantics - where the meaning of a program is found directly as a (strict) function from states to states - in the operational view adopted here wè take into account the, finite or infinite, sequence of *intermediate* states encountered during execution of the program. We denote the class of such finite or infinite sequences (which we shall call *computation sequences*) by $\Sigma^+ \cup \Sigma^\omega$ (Σ^+ is the class of all finite, non-empty sequences of states, Σ^ω the class of all infinite sequences), and define the computation sequence determined by program R for input state σ using the partial function *Comp* of type

$$Comp\colon Prog \xrightarrow[\text{part}]{} (\Sigma \to (\Sigma^+ \cup \Sigma^\omega)).$$

As we shall see, *Comp* may be undefined for programs which are not closed.

In the definition of *Comp* we use two additional operations:

(i) The function $\kappa\colon \Sigma^+ \cup \Sigma^\omega \to \Sigma$, which, when applied to a computation sequence, yields
- the last element of the sequence, provided it is finite
- $\perp$ otherwise

Therefore, $\kappa(\langle\sigma_1,\ldots,\sigma_n\rangle) = \sigma_n$, $\kappa(\langle\sigma_1,\ldots\rangle) = \perp$.

(ii) The operation of *concatenation* of two sequences, denoted by $^\frown$ and defined by

$$\langle\sigma_1,\ldots,\sigma_m\rangle^\frown\langle\sigma_{m+1},\ldots,\sigma_n\rangle = \langle\sigma_1,\ldots,\sigma_m,\sigma_{m+1},\ldots,\sigma_n\rangle$$

$$\langle\sigma_1,\ldots,\sigma_m\rangle^\frown\langle\sigma_{m+1},\ldots\rangle = \langle\sigma_1,\ldots,\sigma_m,\sigma_{m+1},\ldots\rangle$$

$$\langle\sigma_1,\ldots\rangle^\frown\langle\sigma_1',\ldots,\sigma_n'\rangle = \langle\sigma_1,\ldots\rangle$$

$$\langle\sigma_1,\ldots\rangle^\frown\langle\sigma_1',\ldots\rangle = \langle\sigma_1,\ldots\rangle$$

Thus, concatenation on the right-hand side of an infinite sequence has no effect.

In the next definition, the non-procedure-cases should be clear on the basis of the usual understanding of the programming concepts concerned, except possibly for the addition of an extra σ in case c. This is motivated by the wish to make a certain argument by induction on the length of the computation sequence go through. (Idem for a similar addition in case d.) In the case that the statement is a procedure call, the body replacement rule as customary in ALGOL-like languages is used.

DEFINITION 5.16 (computation sequences).

$Comp\colon \mathit{Prog} \xrightarrow[\text{part}]{} (\Sigma \to (\Sigma^{+} \cup \Sigma^{\omega}))$ is defined by: $Comp(R)(\bot) = \langle\bot\rangle$

and for $\sigma \neq \bot$

a. $Comp(\langle E|v:=t\rangle)(\sigma) = \langle\sigma\{\mathcal{R}(t)(\sigma)/\mathcal{L}(v)(\sigma)\}\rangle$

b. $Comp(\langle E|S_1;S_2\rangle)(\sigma) =$

$Comp(\langle E|S_1\rangle)(\sigma)^{\frown}\, Comp(\langle E|S_2\rangle)(\kappa(Comp(\langle E|S_1\rangle)(\sigma)))$

c. $Comp(\langle E|\underline{\text{if}}\ b\ \underline{\text{then}}\ S_1\ \underline{\text{else}}\ S_2\ \underline{\text{fi}}\rangle)(\sigma) =$

$\underline{\text{if}}\ \mathcal{W}(b)(\sigma)\ \underline{\text{then}}\ \langle\sigma\rangle^{\frown}\, Comp(\langle E|S_1\rangle)(\sigma)\ \underline{\text{else}}\ \langle\sigma\rangle^{\frown}\, Comp(\langle E|S_2\rangle)(\sigma)\ \underline{\text{fi}}$

(Note that, since $\sigma \neq \bot$, $\mathcal{W}(b)(\sigma) \neq \bot_W$.)

d. $Comp(\langle E|P\rangle)(\sigma) = \begin{cases} \langle\sigma\rangle^{\frown}\, Comp(\langle E|S\rangle)(\sigma), & \text{if } P \Leftarrow S \text{ occurs in } E \\ \text{undefined,} & \text{otherwise} \end{cases}$

END 5.16.

Clearly, $Comp(R)$ is undefined only when R contains some undeclared procedure variable.

Examples

1. $Comp(\langle E|x:=1;y:=2\rangle)(\sigma) = \langle\sigma\{1/x\},\sigma\{1/x\}\{2/y\}\rangle$

2. $Comp(\langle P\Leftarrow P|P\rangle)(\sigma) = \langle\sigma\rangle^{\frown}\, Comp(\langle P\Leftarrow P|P\rangle)(\sigma) =$

$\langle\sigma,\sigma\rangle^{\frown}\, Comp(\langle P\Leftarrow P|P\rangle)(\sigma) = \ldots = \langle\sigma,\sigma,\ldots\rangle$

3. $Comp(\langle P\Leftarrow P|Q\rangle)(\sigma)$ is undefined for $Q \not\equiv P$.

Note that, strictly speaking, the definition of $\mathcal{Comp}(\langle E|P\rangle)$ is not fully rigorous, in that - as we saw in example 2 - it may be that on the right-hand side of the equation defining $\mathcal{Comp}(\langle E|P\rangle)$, $\mathcal{Comp}(\langle E|P\rangle)$ itself occurs. The intended interpretation of the definition is that it serves as a mechanism for generating (possibly infinite) sequences. This generation process may be made more precise (cf. the remark following theorem A.27 of the appendix). However, at the present stage of the development we feel that such elaboration would somewhat obscure the discussion, which is why we prefer the definition in its more intuitive form.

As operational meaning $\mathcal{O}$ of programs in $\mathcal{Prog}$ we now define

<u>DEFINITION 5.17</u> (operational semantics of programs with recursive procedures).

$\mathcal{O}$ is of type: $\mathcal{Prog} \xrightarrow[\text{part}]{} (\Sigma \to_s \Sigma)$ and is given by

$$\mathcal{O}(R) = \lambda\sigma\cdot\kappa(\mathcal{Comp}(R)(\sigma))$$

END 5.17.

In words, the operational meaning of program R for input σ is obtained by taking the last element of the computation sequence determined by R and σ, if this exists, and ⊥, otherwise.

Examples

1. $\mathcal{O}(\langle E|x:=1;y:=2\rangle)(\sigma) = \kappa(\langle\sigma\{1/x\},\sigma\{1/x\}\{2/y\}\rangle) = \sigma\{1/x\}\{2/y\}$
2. $\mathcal{O}(\langle P\Leftarrow P|P\rangle)(\sigma) = \kappa(\langle\sigma,\sigma,\ldots\rangle) = \bot$
3. $\mathcal{O}(\langle P\Leftarrow S|Q\rangle)(\sigma)$ is undefined for $Q \not\equiv P$.

$\mathcal{O}$ satisfies various natural properties as stated in

<u>LEMMA 5.18</u>.

a. $\mathcal{O}(\langle E|S_1;S_2\rangle)(\sigma) = \mathcal{O}(\langle E|S_2\rangle)(\mathcal{O}(\langle E|S_1\rangle)(\sigma))$

b. $\mathcal{O}(\langle E|\underline{\text{if}}\ b\ \underline{\text{then}}\ S_1\ \underline{\text{else}}\ S_2\ \underline{\text{fi}}\rangle)(\sigma) =$
$\underline{\text{if}}\ \mathcal{W}(b)(\sigma)\ \underline{\text{then}}\ \mathcal{O}(\langle E|S_1\rangle)(\sigma)\ \underline{\text{else}}\ \mathcal{O}(\langle E|S_2\rangle)(\sigma)\ \underline{\text{fi}}$

c. $\mathcal{O}(\langle P \Leftarrow S | P \rangle)(\sigma) = \mathcal{O}(\langle P \Leftarrow S | S \rangle)(\sigma)$.

PROOF.

a. We distinguish two cases (leaving the undefined cases as an exercise).

(i) $Comp(\langle E | S_1 \rangle)(\sigma)$ is infinite. Then $\mathcal{O}(\langle E | S_1 \rangle)(\sigma) = \bot$ and
$\mathcal{O}(\langle E | S_1 ; S_2 \rangle)(\sigma) = \kappa(Comp(\langle E | S_1 ; S_2 \rangle)(\sigma)) =$
$\kappa(Comp(\langle E | S_1 \rangle)(\sigma)^{\frown} \ldots) = \bot = \mathcal{O}(\langle E | S_2 \rangle)(\bot) =$
$\mathcal{O}(\langle E | S_2 \rangle)(\mathcal{O}(\langle E | S_1 \rangle)(\sigma))$

(ii) $Comp(\langle E | S_1 \rangle)(\sigma)$ is finite. Then $\mathcal{O}(\langle E | S_1 ; S_2 \rangle)(\sigma) =$
$\kappa(Comp(\langle E | S_1 ; S_2 \rangle)(\sigma)) =$
$\kappa(Comp(\langle E | S_1 \rangle)(\sigma)^{\frown}\ Comp(\langle E | S_2 \rangle)(\kappa(Comp(\langle E | S_1 \rangle)(\sigma)))) =$
$\kappa(Comp(\langle E | S_2 \rangle)(\kappa(Comp(\langle E | S_1 \rangle)(\sigma)))) =$
$\mathcal{O}(\langle E | S_2 \rangle)(\mathcal{O}(\langle E | S_1 \rangle)(\sigma))$

b. Exercise

c. If $\sigma = \bot$, the result is clear. Otherwise, $\mathcal{O}(\langle P \Leftarrow S | P \rangle)(\sigma) =$
$\kappa(Comp(\langle P \Leftarrow S | P \rangle)(\sigma)) = \kappa(\langle \sigma \rangle^{\frown}\ Comp(\langle P \Leftarrow S | S \rangle)(\sigma)) =$
$\kappa(Comp(\langle P \Leftarrow S | S \rangle)(\sigma)) = \mathcal{O}(\langle P \Leftarrow S | S \rangle)(\sigma)$.

END 5.18.

After thus having defined the operational meaning $\mathcal{O}(R)$ for $R \in \mathit{Prog}$, we turn to its denotational meaning. Somewhat unexpectedly, we do not introduce for this purpose a function $\mathcal{M}: \mathit{Prog} \to (\Sigma \to_s \Sigma)$ but, instead, use

$$\mathcal{M}: \mathit{Prog} \to (\Gamma \to (\Sigma \to_s \Sigma))$$

where Γ, with typical elements $\gamma, \ldots$ is defined by: $\Gamma = \mathit{Pvar} \to (\Sigma \to_s \Sigma)$. Thus, it is meaningful to write equations of the form $\mathcal{M}(R)(\gamma)(\sigma) = \sigma'$.

The role of the additional argument γ - note that this gives meaning to procedure *variables* - is similar to the role of the state for integer variables, namely, in that it serves to store and retrieve their meanings. For procedure variables, their meaning is stored upon declaration and retrieved upon call of the variable (where the retrieved value is arbitrary in the case of an undeclared procedure variable). As notational convention, we from now on write M, with typical elements $\phi,\psi,\ldots$, for $\Sigma \to_s \Sigma$, M^n $(n \geq 1)$ for $M\times\ldots\times M$ (n factors M), and $[M^n \to M]$, with typical elements $\Phi,\Psi,\ldots$, for the cpo which we identify (lemma 5.5) with

$$\underbrace{[M \to [M \to \ldots \to}_{n\times} [M \to M]\ldots]]$$

Moreover, we introduce the simultaneous variant notation $\gamma\{\phi_i/P_i\}_{i=1}^n$ for that function: $Pvar \to M$ which delivers, when applied to some $P \in Pvar$, ϕ_i in case $P \equiv P_i$ for some i, $1 \leq i \leq n$, and $\gamma(P)$, otherwise. (The notation will be used only in situations where $P_i \not\equiv P_j$ for $i \neq j$, $1 \leq i, j \leq n$.)

The definition of M: $Prog \to (\Gamma \to M)$ will use an auxiliary function N: $Stat \to (\Gamma \to M)$. For non-recursive procedures it is fairly straightforward what to do. Consider, for example, $R \equiv \langle P \Leftarrow x:=x+1 \mid x:=0;P\rangle$. Take any γ. We put $M(R)(\gamma) = N(x:=0;P)(\gamma\{N(x:=x+1)(\gamma)/P\})$. Thus, the meaning of P is stored in γ. Next, we evaluate
$N(x:=0;P)(\gamma\{N(x:=x+1)(\gamma)/P\}) =$
$N(P)(\gamma\{N(x:=x+1)(\gamma)/P\}) \circ N(x:=0)(\gamma\{N(x:=x+1)(\gamma)/P\}) =$
$N(x:=x+1)(\gamma) \circ N(x:=0)(\gamma\{N(x:=x+1)(\gamma)/P\})$,
where, for any γ', $N(P)(\gamma')$ is nothing but $\gamma'(P)$, explaining why $N(P)(\gamma\{N(x:=x+1)(\gamma)/P\}) = N(x:=x+1)(\gamma)$. Cf. the equation $R(x)(\sigma\{\alpha/x\}) = \alpha$. Also, for S without procedure variables, $N(S)(\gamma)$ is the same as $M(S)$ as defined in chapter 2; thus, collecting all results, we obtain $M(x:=x+1) \circ M(x:=0)$ as the meaning of the program $R \equiv \langle P \Leftarrow x:=x+1 \mid x:=0;P\rangle$.

For *recursive* P, the situation is less easy. In order to prepare the way for their treatment, we recall the least fixed point characterization for the while statement. Remember that, according to theorem 3.26,

$$M(\underline{\text{while}}\ b\ \underline{\text{do}}\ S\ \underline{\text{od}}) = \phi = \mu\Phi =$$
$$\mu[\lambda\phi'\cdot\lambda\sigma\cdot\underline{\text{if}}\ W(b)(\sigma)\ \underline{\text{then}}\ \phi'(M(S)(\sigma))\ \underline{\text{else}}\ \sigma\ \underline{\text{fi}}].$$

We shall illustrate the approach we take for recursive procedures in general by a discussion of the following special case:
Let $R \equiv \langle P \Leftarrow \underline{\text{if}}\ b\ \underline{\text{then}}\ S;P\ \underline{\text{else}}\ D\ \underline{\text{fi}} \mid P\rangle$, where S is some statement without occurrences of procedure variables. We expect the meaning of this R to be the same as that of the while statement just given. Now let us try out the following definition:

$$M(\langle P \Leftarrow \underline{\text{if}}\ b\ \underline{\text{then}}\ S;P\ \underline{\text{else}}\ D\ \underline{\text{fi}} \mid P\rangle)(\gamma) =$$
$$N(P)(\gamma\{\psi/P\}) = \psi = \mu\Psi \qquad (*)$$

where $\Psi = \lambda\phi'\cdot N(\underline{\text{if}}\ b\ \underline{\text{then}}\ S;P\ \underline{\text{else}}\ D\ \underline{\text{fi}})(\gamma\{\phi'/P\}) =$
$\lambda\phi'\cdot\lambda\sigma\cdot\underline{\text{if}}\ W(b)(\sigma)\ \underline{\text{then}}\ N(S;P)(\gamma\{\phi'/P\})(\sigma)\ \underline{\text{else}}\ N(D)(\gamma\{\phi'/P\})(\sigma)\ \underline{\text{fi}} =$
$\lambda\phi'\cdot\lambda\sigma\cdot\underline{\text{if}}\ W(b)(\sigma)\ \underline{\text{then}}\ (N(P)(\gamma\{\phi'/P\})\circ N(S)(\gamma\{\phi'/P\}))(\sigma)\ \underline{\text{else}}\ \sigma\ \underline{\text{fi}} =$
$\lambda\phi'\cdot\lambda\sigma\cdot\underline{\text{if}}\ W(b)(\sigma)\ \underline{\text{then}}\ \phi'(N(S)(\gamma\{\phi'/P\})(\sigma))\ \underline{\text{else}}\ \sigma\ \underline{\text{fi}}.$
(In this definition we have anticipated some of the more straightforward parts of the definition of N.) Since S was supposed to contain no procedure variables, it is clear that $N(S)(\gamma\{\phi'/P\}) = M(S)$ (with M as in chapter 2), and we have obtained

$$\psi = \mu[\lambda\phi'\cdot\lambda\sigma\cdot\underline{\text{if}}\ W(b)(\sigma)\ \underline{\text{then}}\ \phi'(M(S)(\sigma))\ \underline{\text{else}}\ \sigma\ \underline{\text{fi}}]$$

i.e. $\psi = \phi$. Altogether, we see that the least fixed point definition (*) delivers the desired result for R equivalent to the while statement. This may yield some confidence in our using the same idea in the definition of M for *arbitrary* R. Full justification follows later when we prove, for any R, that its denotational meaning $M(R)$ coincides with its operational meaning $O(R)$.

So how do we treat the general case? Consider a program $R \equiv \langle\langle P_i \Leftarrow S_i\rangle_{i=1}^n \mid S\rangle$. In determining $M(R)(\gamma)$, we store in γ as meaning of $P_1,\ldots,P_n$, the functions $\phi_1,\ldots,\phi_n$, respectively, where the n-tuple $\langle\phi_1,\ldots,\phi_n\rangle$ (each $\phi_i \in M$) is the simultaneous least fixed point of the n-tuple of operators $\langle\Phi_1,\ldots,\Phi_n\rangle$ (each $\Phi_j \in [M^n \to M]$, so $\langle\Phi_1,\ldots,\Phi_n\rangle \in [M^n \to M^n]$). Here each Φ_j, $1 \le j \le n$, is defined by

$$\Phi_j = \lambda\phi_1'\cdot\ldots\cdot\lambda\phi_n'\cdot N(S_j)(\gamma\{\phi_i'/P_i\}_{i=1}^n)$$

i.e. Φ_j - the definition of which uses the j-th procedure body S_j - is given by requiring that for arbitrary elements $\langle\phi_1',\ldots,\phi_n'\rangle \in M^n$, it delivers the meaning of S_j in that variant of γ which assigns ϕ_i' to P_i, $i = 1,\ldots,n$.

Definition 5.19 summarizes the preceding discussion. We shall illustrate it with various examples and, after that, justify the definition insofar as it concerns the existence of the least fixed point of the system $\langle\Phi_1,\ldots,\Phi_n\rangle$. This will follow from the continuity of the Φ_j, $j = 1,\ldots,n$. Finally, we shall give the justification proper of M, which will be based on a comparison with the intuitively clear(er) definition of O.

DEFINITION 5.19 (denotational semantics of programs with recursive procedures).

The functions N: *Stat* $\to (\Gamma \to M)$ and M: *Prog* $\to (\Gamma \to M)$ are defined as follows:

a. (i) $N(v{:=}t)(\gamma) = \lambda\sigma\cdot\sigma\{R(t)(\sigma)/L(v)(\sigma)\}$

(ii) $N(S_1;S_2)(\gamma) = N(S_2)(\gamma)\circ N(S_1)(\gamma)$

(iii) $N(\underline{\text{if}}\ b\ \underline{\text{then}}\ S_1\ \underline{\text{else}}\ S_2\ \underline{\text{fi}})(\gamma) =$
$\lambda\sigma\cdot\underline{\text{if}}\ W(b)(\sigma)\ \underline{\text{then}}\ N(S_1)(\gamma)(\sigma)\ \underline{\text{else}}\ N(S_2)(\gamma)(\sigma)\ \underline{\text{fi}}$

(iv) $N(P)(\gamma) = \gamma(P)$

b. $M(\langle\langle P_i \Leftarrow S_i\rangle_{i=1}^n \mid S\rangle)(\gamma) = N(S)(\gamma\{\phi_i/P_i\}_{i=1}^n)$, where

$$\langle\phi_1,\ldots,\phi_n\rangle = \mu[\Phi_1,\ldots,\Phi_n]$$

and, for j = 1,...,n,

$$\Phi_j = \lambda\phi'_1\cdot\ldots\cdot\lambda\phi'_n\cdot N(S_j)(\gamma\{\phi'_i/P_i\}_{i=1}^n).$$

END 5.19.

Examples

1. $M(\langle P \Leftarrow P | P\rangle)(\gamma) = N(P)(\gamma\{\phi/P\}) = \phi$, where $\phi = \mu\Phi$, and $\Phi = \lambda\phi'\cdot N(P)(\gamma\{\phi'/P\}) = \lambda\phi'\cdot\gamma\{\phi'/P\}(P) = \lambda\phi'\cdot\phi'$. Clearly, $\mu\Phi = \lambda\sigma\cdot\bot$. We conclude therefore that $M(\langle P \Leftarrow P | P\rangle)(\gamma) = \lambda\sigma\cdot\bot$, which agrees with the result obtained above that $O(\langle P \Leftarrow P | P\rangle) = \lambda\sigma\cdot\bot$.
2. $M(\langle P \Leftarrow \underline{\text{if}}\ b\ \underline{\text{then}}\ S;P\ \underline{\text{else}}\ D\ \underline{\text{fi}} \mid P\rangle)(\gamma) = N(P)(\gamma\{\phi/P\}) = \phi$, where $\phi = \mu\Phi$ and (*): $\Phi = \lambda\phi'\cdot N(\underline{\text{if}}\ b\ \underline{\text{then}}\ S;P\ \underline{\text{else}}\ D\ \underline{\text{fi}})(\gamma\{\phi'/P\})$. By theorem 5.8 we have, for continuous Φ - we here anticipate the proof of Φ's continuity to be given presently - that $\mu\Phi = \bigsqcup_{i=0}^{\infty} \Phi^i(\bot_M)$. Applying this to (*), we obtain that $\phi = \bigsqcup_i \phi_i$, with $\phi_0 = \Phi^0(\bot_M) = \lambda\sigma\cdot\bot$, and, for i = 0,1,...,

$$\begin{aligned}\phi_{i+1} &= \Phi(\phi_i)\\ &= [\lambda\phi'\cdot N(\underline{\text{if}}\ b\ \underline{\text{then}}\ S;P\ \underline{\text{else}}\ D\ \underline{\text{fi}})(\gamma\{\phi'/P\})](\phi_i)\\ &= N(\underline{\text{if}}\ b\ \underline{\text{then}}\ S;P\ \underline{\text{else}}\ D\ \underline{\text{fi}})(\gamma\{\phi_i/P\})\\ &= \lambda\sigma\cdot\underline{\text{if}}\ W(b)(\sigma)\ \underline{\text{then}}\ N(S;P)(\gamma\{\phi_i/P\})(\sigma)\ \underline{\text{else}}\\ &\qquad N(D)(\gamma\{\phi_i/P\})(\sigma)\ \underline{\text{fi}}\\ &= \lambda\sigma\cdot\underline{\text{if}}\ W(b)(\sigma)\ \underline{\text{then}}\ \phi_i(N(S)(\gamma\{\phi_i/P\})(\sigma))\ \underline{\text{else}}\ \sigma\ \underline{\text{fi}}.\end{aligned}$$

Again assuming for simplicity that S contains no occurrences of a procedure variable, so that the equality $N(S)(\gamma\{\phi_i/P\}) = M(S)$ - with M as in chapter 2 - is satisfied, we finally obtain that

$$\phi_{i+1} = \lambda\sigma\cdot\underline{\text{if}}\ W(b)(\sigma)\ \underline{\text{then}}\ \phi_i(M(S)(\sigma))\ \underline{\text{else}}\ \sigma\ \underline{\text{fi}}$$

and we have once more obtained the result that the meaning of the present example as based on definition 5.19 is the same as the meaning of <u>while</u> b <u>do</u> S <u>od</u>.

3. $M(\langle P \Leftarrow \underline{if}\ x>0\ \underline{then}\ x:=x-1;P;x:=x+1\ \underline{else}\ D\ \underline{fi} \mid P\rangle)(\gamma) =$ $N(P)(\gamma\{\phi/P\}) = \phi$, with $\phi = \mu\Phi$ and $\Phi = \lambda\phi'\cdot N(\underline{if}\ x>0$ $\underline{then}\ x:=x-1;P;x:=x+1\ \underline{else}\ D\ \underline{fi})(\gamma\{\phi'/P\})$. We have that $\mu\Phi = \bigsqcup_{i=0}^{\infty} \phi_i$, with $\phi_0 = \lambda\sigma\cdot\bot$ and, for $i = 0,1,\ldots$, $\phi_{i+1} = \lambda\sigma\cdot\underline{if}\ W(x>0)(\sigma)$ $\underline{then}\ \phi_i(\sigma\{R(x-1)(\sigma)/x\})\{R(x+1)(\phi_i(\sigma\{R(x-1)(\sigma)/x\}))/x\}\ \underline{else}\ \sigma\ \underline{fi}$. By way of example we evaluate $\phi(\sigma\{2/x\})$.

$\phi_0(\sigma\{2/x\}) = \bot$

$\phi_1(\sigma\{2/x\}) = \phi_0(\ldots)\{\ldots\} = \bot\{\ldots\} = \bot$

$\phi_2(\sigma\{2/x\}) = \phi_1(\sigma\{1/x\})\{R(x+1)(\phi_1(\sigma\{1/x\}))/x\} = \phi_0(\ldots)\{\ldots\}\{\ldots\}=\bot$

$\phi_3(\sigma\{2/x\}) = \phi_2(\sigma\{1/x\})\{R(x+1)(\phi_2(\sigma\{1/x\}))/x\}$.

We first calculate

$$\begin{aligned}\phi_2(\sigma\{1/x\}) &= \phi_1(\sigma\{0/x\})\{R(x+1)(\phi_1(\sigma\{0/x\}))/x\}\\ &= \sigma\{0/x\}\{R(x+1)(\sigma\{0/x\})/x\} = \sigma\{0/x\}\{1/x\} = \sigma\{1/x\}.\end{aligned}$$

Using this, we obtain

$\phi_3(\sigma\{2/x\}) = \sigma\{1/x\}\{R(x+1)(\sigma\{1/x\})/x\} = \sigma\{1/x\}\{2/x\} = \sigma\{2/x\}$.

In the same way it follows, that $\phi_i(\sigma\{2/x\}) = \sigma\{2/x\}$ for all $i \geq 3$; hence $\phi(\sigma\{2/x\}) = (\bigsqcup_i \phi_i)(\sigma\{2/x\}) = \bigsqcup_i \phi_i(\sigma\{2/x\}) = \bigsqcup_i \sigma\{2/x\} =$ $\sigma\{2/x\}$.

4. $M(\langle P \Leftarrow Q, Q \Leftarrow P \mid Q\rangle)(\gamma) = N(Q)(\gamma\{\phi_1/P,\phi_2/Q\})$, where $\langle\phi_1,\phi_2\rangle =$ $\mu[\Phi_1,\Phi_2]$, and

$\Phi_1 = \lambda\phi_1'\cdot\lambda\phi_2'\cdot N(Q)(\gamma\{\phi_1'/P,\phi_2'/Q\}) = \lambda\phi_1'\cdot\lambda\phi_2'\cdot\phi_2'$

$\Phi_2 = \lambda\phi_1'\cdot\lambda\phi_2'\cdot N(P)(\gamma\{\phi_1'/P,\phi_2'/Q\}) = \lambda\phi_1'\cdot\lambda\phi_2'\cdot\phi_1'$

From this, it easily follows that $<\phi_1,\phi_2> = <\lambda\sigma\cdot\bot,\lambda\sigma\cdot\bot>$ and we have obtained the result that $M(<P\Leftarrow Q, Q\Leftarrow P \mid Q>)(\gamma) = \lambda\sigma\cdot\bot$.

As an immediate consequence of definition 5.19, we obtain the following natural equivalence result for recursive procedures:

<u>LEMMA 5.20</u>. Let $E \equiv <P_i \Leftarrow S_i>_{i=1}^n$. Then, for $j = 1,\ldots,n$,

$$M(<E|P_j>) = M(<E|S_j>).$$

<u>PROOF</u>. Take any γ. By definition 5.19, $M(<E|P_j>)(\gamma) = N(P_j)(\gamma\{\phi_i/P_i\}_{i=1}^n) = \phi_j$, where

$$<\phi_1,\ldots,\phi_n> = \mu[\Phi_1,\ldots,\Phi_n],$$

$$\Phi_k = \lambda\phi_1'\cdot\ldots\cdot\lambda\phi_n'\cdot N(S_k)(\gamma\{\phi_i'/P_i\}_{i=1}^n), \quad k = 1,\ldots,n.$$

Moreover, we have that $M(<E|S_j>)(\gamma) = N(S_j)(\gamma\{\phi_i/P_i\}_{j=1}^n)$. From the fixed point property it follows that $\Phi_j(\phi_1,\ldots,\phi_n) = \phi_j$, or $N(S_j)(\gamma\{\phi_i/P_i\}_{i=1}^n) = \phi_j = N(P_j)(\gamma\{\phi_i/P_i\}_{i=1}^n)$, and we conclude that, indeed, $M(<E|P_j>)(\gamma) = M(<E|S_j>)(\gamma)$.

END 5.20.

Our next theorem establishes that the operators Φ_j, as used in definition 5.19, *are* continuous functions: $M^n \to M$, thus implying both the existence of the least fixed point $\mu[\Phi_1,\ldots,\Phi_n]$ and the applicability of corollary 5.10.

<u>THEOREM 5.21</u>.

$$\lambda\phi_1\cdot\ldots\cdot\lambda\phi_n\cdot N(S)(\gamma\{\phi_i/P_i\}_{i=1}^n) \in [M^n \to M].$$

<u>PROOF</u>. The proof of the monotonicity of the function is left as exercise. In the proof of its continuity we use induction on the complexity of S.

a. $\lambda\phi_1\cdot\ldots\cdot\lambda\phi_n\cdot N(v{:=}t)(\gamma\{\phi_i/P_i\}_{i=1}^n) =$

$\lambda\phi_1\cdot\ldots\cdot\lambda\phi_n\cdot\lambda\sigma\cdot\sigma\{R(t)(\sigma)/L(v)(\sigma)\} = \lambda\phi_1\cdot\ldots\cdot\lambda\phi_n\cdot\bar{\phi}$, say.

Now apply lemma 5.7b.

b. $$\lambda\phi_1\cdot\ldots\cdot\lambda\phi_n\cdot N(P)(\gamma\{\phi_i/P_i\}_{i=1}^n) = \begin{cases} \lambda\phi_1\cdot\ldots\cdot\lambda\phi_n\cdot\gamma(P), & \text{if } P \not\equiv P_i,\ i = 1,\ldots,n \\ \lambda\phi_1\cdot\ldots\cdot\lambda\phi_n\cdot\phi_i, & \text{if } P \equiv P_i, \text{ for some } i. \end{cases}$$

In the first subcase apply lemma 5.7b, and in the latter lemma 5.7a.

c. $\lambda\phi_1\cdot\ldots\cdot\lambda\phi_n\cdot N(S_1;S_2)(\gamma\{\phi_i/P_i\}_{i=1}^n) =$

$\lambda\phi_1\cdot\ldots\cdot\lambda\phi_n\cdot N(S_2)(\gamma\{\phi_i/P_i\}_{i=1}^n)\circ N(S_1)(\gamma\{\phi_i/P_i\}_{i=1}^n)$.

By the induction hypothesis, the functions

$\Phi_j \overset{\text{df.}}{=} \lambda\phi_1\cdot\ldots\cdot\lambda\phi_n\cdot N(S_j)(\gamma\{\phi_i/P_i\}_{i=1}^n)$, $j = 1,2$, are continuous,

from which it follows, by lemma 5.7c, that

$\lambda\phi_1\cdot\ldots\cdot\lambda\phi_n\cdot\Phi_2(\phi_1)\ldots(\phi_n)\circ\Phi_1(\phi_1)\ldots(\phi_n)$ is also continuous.

d. The <u>if</u>-<u>then</u>-<u>else</u>-<u>fi</u> case is immediate by induction and lemma 5.7d.

END 5.21.

We conclude this section with the proof of the equivalence of the operational and denotational semantics of any $R \in Prog$.

<u>THEOREM 5.22</u>. Let $R \in Prog$ be a closed program. Then, for all $\gamma \in \Gamma$,

$$O(R) = M(R)(\gamma).$$

<u>PROOF</u>. Let $R \equiv \langle E|S\rangle$, with $E \equiv \langle P_i \Leftarrow S_i\rangle_{i=1}^n$.

a. $O(\langle E|S\rangle) \sqsubseteq M(\langle E|S\rangle)(\gamma)$.

We show that, for all σ, $O(\langle E|S\rangle)(\sigma) \sqsubseteq M(\langle E|S\rangle)(\gamma)(\sigma)$, or

$\kappa(Comp(\langle E|S\rangle)(\sigma)) \sqsubseteq M(\langle E|S\rangle)(\gamma)(\sigma)$. If $Comp(\langle E|S\rangle)(\sigma)$ is infinite, then $\kappa(Comp(\langle E|S\rangle)(\sigma)) = \bot$, and the proposition is clear. For a finite computation sequence $\mathit{Comp}(\langle E|S\rangle)(\sigma)$, we apply induction on its length. If $\sigma = \bot$, the result is immediate. Otherwise, we distinguish the cases

(i) $S \equiv v{:=}t$. $\mathcal{O}(\langle E|v{:=}t\rangle)(\sigma) = \kappa(\mathit{Comp}(\langle E|v{:=}t\rangle)(\sigma)) =$
$\kappa(\langle\sigma\{\mathcal{R}(t)(\sigma)/\mathcal{L}(v)(\sigma)\}\rangle) = \sigma\{\mathcal{R}(t)(\sigma)/\mathcal{L}(v)(\sigma)\} =$
$\mathcal{M}(\langle E|v{:=}t\rangle)(\gamma)(\sigma)$.

(ii) $S \equiv S';S''$. Clearly, the length of the sequences $\mathit{Comp}(\langle E|S'\rangle)(\sigma)$ and $\mathit{Comp}(\langle E|S''\rangle)(\kappa(\mathit{Comp}(\langle E|S'\rangle)(\sigma)))$ is less than that of $\mathit{Comp}(\langle E|S';S''\rangle)(\sigma)$. Thus, by the induction hypothesis, $\mathcal{O}(\langle E|S'\rangle)(\sigma) \sqsubseteq \mathcal{M}(\langle E|S'\rangle)(\gamma)(\sigma)$, and
$\mathcal{O}(\langle E|S''\rangle)(\mathcal{O}(\langle E|S'\rangle)(\sigma)) \sqsubseteq \mathcal{M}(\langle E|S''\rangle)(\gamma)(\mathcal{O}(\langle E|S'\rangle)(\sigma))$.
Combining these two facts, the desired result follows from lemma 5.18a, the definition of $\mathcal{M}(\langle E|S';S''\rangle)(\gamma)(\sigma)$, and the monotonicity of $\lambda\sigma\cdot\mathcal{M}(R)(\gamma)(\sigma)$.

(iii) $S \equiv \underline{\text{if}}\ b\ \underline{\text{then}}\ S'\ \underline{\text{else}}\ S''\ \underline{\text{fi}}$. Similar to (ii). (Note that $\mathit{Comp}(\langle E|S\rangle)(\sigma)$ has one more element (viz. σ) than $\mathit{Comp}(\langle E|S'\rangle)(\sigma)$ or $\mathit{Comp}(\langle E|S''\rangle)(\sigma)$.)

(iv) $S \equiv P$. Since P is declared in E, $P \equiv P_i$, for some i, $1 \le i \le n$. By lemma 5.18c, $\mathcal{O}(\langle E|P_i\rangle)(\sigma) = \mathcal{O}(\langle E|S_i\rangle)(\sigma)$. Since the sequence $\mathit{Comp}(\langle E|S_i\rangle)(\sigma)$ is shorter than the sequence $\mathit{Comp}(\langle E|P_i\rangle)(\sigma)$, we have by induction that $\mathcal{O}(\langle E|S_i\rangle)(\sigma) \sqsubseteq$ $\mathcal{M}(\langle E|S_i\rangle)(\gamma)(\sigma)$. Since, by lemma 5.20, $\mathcal{M}(\langle E|S_i\rangle)(\gamma)(\sigma) =$ $\mathcal{M}(\langle E|P_i\rangle)(\gamma)(\sigma)$, the desired result follows.

b. $\mathcal{M}(\langle E|S\rangle)(\gamma) \sqsubseteq \mathcal{O}(\langle E|S\rangle)$.

By the definition of $\mathcal{M}$ we have to show that

$$N(S)(\gamma\{\phi_i/P_i\}_{i=1}^{n}) \sqsubseteq O(<E|S>) \qquad (*)$$

with ϕ_i, $i = 1,\ldots,n$, as usual. Putting

$$<\phi_1^0,\ldots,\phi_n^0> = <\lambda\sigma\cdot\bot,\ldots,\lambda\sigma\cdot\bot>$$

$$<\phi_1^{k+1},\ldots,\phi_n^{k+1}> = <\Phi_1(\phi_1^k,\ldots,\phi_n^k),\ldots,\Phi_n(\phi_1^k,\ldots,\phi_n^k)>,\ k = 0,1,\ldots$$

we have, by corollary 5.10, that $\phi_i = \bigsqcup_{k=0}^{\infty} \phi_i^k$, $i = 1,\ldots,n$. By the continuity of $\lambda\phi_1'\cdot\ldots\cdot\lambda\phi_n'\cdot N(S)(\gamma\{\phi_i'/P_i\}_{i=1}^{n})$, we have that

$$N(S)(\gamma\{\bigsqcup_k \phi_i^k/P_i\}_{i=1}^{n}) = \bigsqcup_k N(S)(\gamma\{\phi_i^k/P_i\}_{i=1}^{n}).$$

In order to prove (*) it is therefore sufficient to show that for all S and all k

$$N(S)(\gamma\{\phi_i^k/P_i\}_{i=1}^{n}) \sqsubseteq O(<E|S>).$$

For this purpose we use induction on the entity $<k,\ell(S)>$ - here $\ell(S)$ denotes the length of S, and we use the ordering $<k_1,\ell_1> \prec <k_2,\ell_2>$ iff either $k_1 < k_2$, or $k_1 = k_2$ and $\ell_1 < \ell_2$ - in the following way:

(i) $S \equiv v{:=}t$. Direct from the definitions.

(ii) $S \equiv S';S''$. Clearly, $\ell(S') < \ell(S)$ and $\ell(S'') < \ell(S)$; hence, $<k,\ell(S')> \prec <k,\ell(S)>$ and $<k,\ell(S'')> \prec <k,\ell(S)>$. By the induction hypothesis, $N(S')(\gamma\{\phi_i^k/P_i\}_{i=1}^{n}) \sqsubseteq O(<E|S'>)$, and $N(S'')(\gamma\{\phi_i^k/P_i\}_{i=1}^{n}) \sqsubseteq O(<E|S''>)$. Together, we have that $N(S';S'')(\gamma\{\phi_i^k/P_i\}_{i=1}^{n}) \sqsubseteq O(<E|S';S''>)$.

(iii) $S \equiv$ <u>if</u> b <u>then</u> S_1 <u>else</u> S_2 <u>fi</u>. Similar to (ii).

(iv) $S \equiv P$, with $P \equiv P_j$, for some j, $1 \le j \le n$. If $k = 0$, we have nothing to prove. Otherwise, we have that

$N(P_j)(\gamma\{\phi_i^k/P_i\}_{i=1}^n) = \phi_j^k = \Phi_j(\phi_1^{k-1},\ldots,\phi_n^{k-1}) =$ (df. Φ_j)

$N(S_j)(\gamma\{\phi_i^{k-1}/P_i\}_{i=1}^n) \sqsubseteq$ (ind., since $<k-1,\ell(S_j)> \langle <k,\ell(P_j)>$)

$O(<E|S_j>) =$ (lemma 5.18) $O(<E|P_j>)$.

END 5.22.

Thus, we have accomplished the main goal of this section, i.e. we have established that the denotational meaning of S using least fixed points coincides with the operational meaning using the rule of body replacement.

5.4. Correctness

This section is devoted to a study of methods for proving correctness of programs involving recursive procedures. We introduce an extension of our previous formalism of correctness formulae and their validity, and inferences and their soundness. Furthermore, we present as central proof rule an induction rule due to Scott, illustrated by various examples.

As before, we are interested both in proving validity of partial correctness formulae of the form {p}S{q}, and of inclusion and equivalences of the form $S_1 \sqsubseteq S_2$ and $S_1 = S_2$, respectively. Typical examples of validity results we expect to be able to derive are:

$\models <P \Leftarrow S|P=S>$, $\models <P \Leftarrow P|P \sqsubseteq S>$, $\models <P \Leftarrow P|\{p\}P\{q\}>$,

$\models <P \Leftarrow x:=x+1|\{x=0\}P\{x=1\}>$,

$\models <P \Leftarrow \underline{if}\ x>0\ \underline{then}\ x:=x-1;P\ \underline{else}\ D\ \underline{fi}|\{x=5\}P\{x=0\}>$,

$\models <P_1 \Leftarrow \underline{if}\ b\ \underline{then}\ P_2;P_1\ \underline{else}\ D\ \underline{fi},\ P_2 \Leftarrow \underline{if}\ b\ \underline{then}\ S;P_2\ \underline{else}\ D\ \underline{fi}|P_1=P_2>$,

$\models <P_1 \Leftarrow \underline{if}\ b\ \underline{then}\ S_1;P_1\ \underline{else}\ S_2\ \underline{fi},\ P_2 \Leftarrow \underline{if}\ b\ \underline{then}\ S_1;P_2\ \underline{else}\ D\ \underline{fi}|$

$P_1 = P_2;S_2>$

etc.

We observe a natural extension of the correctness formalism of the previous chapters. Since statements have meaning only with respect to a system of declarations, there is a corresponding extension of correctness formulae f to constructs $<E|f>$. However, this is not yet the most general form of correctness formulae we need. Instead, we shall introduce constructs of the form $<E|f_1 \Rightarrow f_2>$, of which, as we shall see, formulae $<E|f>$ are a special case. As will appear below, the additional structure on correctness formulae is necessary for the formulation of Scott's induction rule.

DEFINITION 5.23 (syntax of generalized correctness formulae).

a. The syntactic classes Assn, with typical elements p,q,r,..., and Form, with typical elements f,..., are taken over without changes from the previous chapters.

b. (i) The syntactic class Gfor of *generalized correctness formulae*, with typical elements g,..., is defined by

$$g ::= \ <E:f_1 \Rightarrow f_2>$$

(ii) $<E:f>$ is short for $<E : \underline{true} \Rightarrow f>$

END 5.23.

Remarks

1. Again, we shall use $<E|f_1 \Rightarrow f_2>$ instead of $<E : f_1 \Rightarrow f_2>$.
2. We shall often drop the qualification "generalized" on a correctness formula g.
3. Note that the symbol " $\Rightarrow$ " from now on serves two purposes:
   a. As before, it denotes the semantic operation of implication between truth values
   b. It also occurs in the syntactic construct $<E|f_1 \Rightarrow f_2>$, to which meaning will be attributed shortly.

(This is one of the occasions where, for lack of a sufficient number of available symbols, we have to admit defeat in our struggle to maintain a one-one correspondence between symbols and their uses.)

Examples of generalized correctness formulae

1. $<P \Leftarrow S \mid P = S>$, $<P \Leftarrow P \mid P \sqsubseteq S>$,

   $<P_1 \Leftarrow \underline{\text{if}}\ b\ \underline{\text{then}}\ S_1;P_1\ \underline{\text{else}}\ S_2\ \underline{\text{fi}},$

   $P_2 \Leftarrow \underline{\text{if}}\ b\ \underline{\text{then}}\ S_1;P_2\ \underline{\text{else}}\ D\ \underline{\text{fi}} \mid P_1 = P_2;S_2>.$

2. $<P \Leftarrow P \mid \{p\}P\{q\}>$,

   $<P \Leftarrow \underline{\text{if}}\ x>0\ \underline{\text{then}}\ x:=x-1;P\ \underline{\text{else}}\ D\ \underline{\text{fi}} \mid \{x=5\}P\{x=0\}>.$

3. $<P \Leftarrow \underline{\text{if}}\ b\ \underline{\text{then}}\ S;P\ \underline{\text{else}}\ D\ \underline{\text{fi}} \mid \{p \wedge b\}S\{p\} \Rightarrow \{p\}P\{p \wedge \neg b\}>$,

   $<E \mid S_1 \sqsubseteq S_2 \Rightarrow S;S_1 \sqsubseteq S;S_2>.$

We now turn to the definition of the meaning of the elements $p \in \mathit{Assn}$, $f \in \mathit{Form}$ and $g \in \mathit{Gfor}$. No changes are needed in type and definition of $\mathcal{T}$: $\mathit{Assn} \to \Pi$. For the class Form, the situation is different. Since correctness formulae contain, in general, occurrences of statements S, the meaning of which involves the additional argument $\gamma \in \Gamma$, a corresponding extension is needed for the definition of $\mathcal{F}$.

DEFINITION 5.24 (semantics of correctness formulae).
The function $\mathcal{F}$ of type: $\mathit{Form} \to (\Gamma \to \Pi)$ is defined by: $\mathcal{F}(f)(\gamma)(\bot) = ff$, and, for $\sigma \neq \bot$,

a. $\mathcal{F}(p)(\gamma)(\sigma) = \mathcal{T}(p)(\sigma)$

b. $\mathcal{F}(\{p\}S\{q\})(\gamma)(\sigma) =$

$$\begin{cases} tt, & \text{if } \forall\sigma'[\mathcal{T}(p)(\sigma) \wedge \sigma' = \mathcal{N}(S)(\gamma)(\sigma) \wedge \sigma' \neq \bot \Rightarrow \mathcal{T}(q)(\sigma')], \\ ff, & \text{otherwise} \end{cases}$$

c. $\mathcal{F}(S_1 \sqsubseteq S_2)(\gamma)(\sigma) = \mathcal{N}(S_1)(\gamma)(\sigma) \sqsubseteq \mathcal{N}(S_2)(\gamma)(\sigma)$

d. $\mathcal{F}(f_1 \wedge f_2)(\gamma)(\sigma) = \mathcal{F}(f_1)(\gamma)(\sigma) \wedge \mathcal{F}(f_2)(\gamma)(\sigma)$

END 5.24.

A comparison with definition 3.29 will show that the introduction of the extra γ is indeed the only change. In particular, the interpretation of $\{p\}S\{q\}$ as expressing partial correctness (i.e. nothing is required in the case that the computation specified by S does not terminate) is again adopted.

Next, we come to the treatment of $\mathcal{Gfor}$. The function G which attributes meaning to elements $g \in \mathcal{Gfor}$ is of type: $\mathcal{Gfor} \to (\Gamma \to T)$. Thus, we have as important difference with the functions T and F that the state σ is *not* an argument of G. The reason for this - and, in general, the motivation for the " ⇒ " construct - will be discussed after we have provided the definitions of validity of generalized correctness formulae, and of inferences and their soundness. Right now, we only comment on the treatment of E. Just as in section 5.3, we use the argument γ to store the meaning of the procedure variables declared in E.

DEFINITION 5.25 (semantics of generalized correctness formulae).
The function G is of the type: $\mathcal{Gfor} \to (\Gamma \to T)$ and is given by:

$$G(\langle\langle P_i \Leftarrow S_i\rangle_{i=1}^n \mid f_1 \Rightarrow f_2\rangle)(\gamma) = \begin{cases} tt, \text{ if } \forall\sigma\neq\bot[F(f_1)(\gamma\{\phi_i/P_i\}_{i=1}^n)(\sigma)] \Rightarrow \\ \qquad \forall\sigma\neq\bot[F(f_2)(\gamma\{\phi_i/P_i\}_{i=1}^n)(\sigma)] \\ ff, \text{ otherwise} \end{cases}$$

where ϕ_i, $i = 1,\dots,n$, are as in definition 5.19.
END 5.25.

DEFINITION 5.26 (validity of generalized correctness formulae).
A generalized correctness formula g is called valid, written as

$$\models g$$

whenever $G(g)(\gamma) = tt$ for all $\gamma \in \Gamma$.
END 5.26.

DEFINITION 5.27 (inferences and their soundness).
An *inference* is a construct of the form $\frac{g_1,\dots,g_n}{g}$, with $n \geq 1$, $g \in \mathcal{Gfor}$, and, for $i = 1,\dots,n$, $g_i \in \mathcal{Gfor}$. An *inference* is called *sound*, written as

$$\boxed{\frac{g_1,\ldots,g_n}{g}}$$

whenever validity of each of g_i, i = 1,...,n, implies validity of g. END 5.27.

Examples

1. Valid correctness formulae

   $<P \Leftarrow S \mid P = S>$, $<P \Leftarrow P \mid \{p\}P\{q\}>$, etc.

   (The examples presented before in this section are in fact all valid.)

2. a. $$\frac{<E \mid \{p\}S_1\{q\} \wedge \{q\}S_2\{r\}>}{<E \mid \{p\}S_1;S_2\{r\}>}$$

   b. $$\frac{< \mid \{p\}P\{q\} \Rightarrow \{p\}S\{q\}>}{<P \Leftarrow S \mid \{p\}P\{q\}>}$$

   (More about this example, the soundness of which may not be obvious at the present stage, after theorem 5.37.)

We pause a moment to survey the various constructs and their meanings we have introduced up to now. In particular, we shall compare the validity of the generalized correctness formula $<E \mid f_1 \Rightarrow f_2>$ with the soundness of the inference $\frac{<E \mid f_1>}{<E \mid f_2>}$. Let $E \equiv <P_i \Leftarrow S_i>_{i=1}^n$.

(i) $<E \mid f_1 \Rightarrow f_2>$ is valid iff, for all γ, $G(<E \mid f_1 \Rightarrow f_2>)(\gamma)$ = tt. By definition 5.25, this means that

$$\forall\gamma[\forall\sigma\neq\perp[F(f_1)(\gamma\{\phi_i/P_i\}_{i=1}^n)(\sigma)] \Rightarrow \forall\sigma\neq\perp[F(f_2)(\gamma\{\phi_i/P_i\}_{i=1}^n)(\sigma)]]$$

with ϕ_i, i = 1,...,n, as usual.

(ii) $\frac{<E \mid f_1>}{<E \mid f_2>}$ is sound iff validity of $<E \mid f_1>$ implies validity of $<E \mid f_2>$. Now $<E \mid f_1>$ is valid iff, for all γ, $G(<E \mid f_1>)(\gamma)$ = tt. Since, by definition 5.23, $<E \mid f_1>$ is short for $<E \mid \underline{true} \Rightarrow f_1>$, we obtain that $\langle E|f_1\rangle$ is valid iff

$$\forall\gamma[\forall\sigma\neq\bot[\mathcal{F}(\underline{\text{true}})(\gamma\{\phi_i/P_i\}_{i=1}^n)(\sigma)] \Rightarrow \forall\sigma\neq\bot[\mathcal{F}(f_1)(\gamma\{\phi_i/P_i\}_{i=1}^n)(\sigma)]].$$

Since, for all γ', $\mathcal{F}(\underline{\text{true}})(\gamma')(\sigma) = \mathcal{T}(\underline{\text{true}})(\sigma) = tt$, this simplifies to

$$\forall\gamma\forall\sigma\neq\bot[\mathcal{F}(f_1)(\gamma\{\phi_i/P_i\}_{i=1}^n)(\sigma)].$$

Similarly, $\langle E|f_2\rangle$ is valid iff

$$\forall\gamma\forall\sigma\neq\bot[\mathcal{F}(f_2)(\gamma\{\phi_i/P_i\}_{i=1}^n)(\sigma)]$$

Combining these two results, we see that $\dfrac{\langle E|f_1\rangle}{\langle E|f_2\rangle}$ is sound iff

$$\forall\gamma\forall\sigma\neq\bot[\mathcal{F}(f_1)(\gamma\{\phi_i/P_i\}_{i=1}^n)(\sigma)] \Rightarrow \forall\gamma\forall\sigma\neq\bot[\mathcal{F}(f_2)(\gamma\{\phi_i/P_i\}_{i=1}^n)(\sigma)].$$

The differences between cases (i) and (ii) is therefore determined by the quantification pattern of the γ's, and not of the σ's. In case (i), the pattern is of the form

$$\forall\gamma[\forall\sigma\neq\bot[(1)] \Rightarrow \forall\sigma\neq\bot[(2)]] \qquad (*)$$

whereas in case (ii) it is of the form

$$\forall\gamma\forall\sigma\neq\bot[(1)] \Rightarrow \forall\gamma\forall\sigma\neq\bot[(2)] \qquad (**)$$

From predicate logic (cf. the discussion following definition 2.26) we recall that a formula of type (*) is stronger than one of type (**). We therefore see that the validity of $\langle E|f_1 \Rightarrow f_2\rangle$ is a stronger fact than the soundness of $\dfrac{\langle E|f_1\rangle}{\langle E|f_2\rangle}$. Thus, the reader may now understand at least the difference in meaning between the two notions. Note that in the special case that $f_i \in \mathcal{Assn}$, $i = 1,2$, the difference vanishes, since assertions contain no occurrences of procedure variables, whence difference in use of the γ-argument has no effect. In other words,

$\models$ $<E|p_1 \Rightarrow p_2>$ and $\dfrac{<E|p_1>}{<E|p_2>}$ express the same fact which, according to the discussion following definition 2.26, is, in general, weaker than $\models$ $<E|p_1 \supset p_2>$! Of course, there remains the question as to which use we are going to put the $<E|f_1 \Rightarrow f_2>$ construct. As announced already, it will serve in the formulation of Scott's induction rule, which we shall present soon after a few more preparations.

Before doing this, we first list some general validity and soundness results of the $<E|f_1 \Rightarrow f_2>$ formalism, partly stating basic properties of " $\Rightarrow$ ", and partly extending the results on partial correctness used in 2.6 and 3.6.

LEMMA 5.28.

a. $\dfrac{<E|f>}{<E|f_0 \Rightarrow f>}$

b. $\dfrac{<E|f_1 \Rightarrow f_2>, <E|f_2 \Rightarrow f_3>}{<E|f_1 \Rightarrow f_3>}$

c. $\dfrac{<E|f \Rightarrow f_1>, <E|f \Rightarrow f_2>}{<E|f \Rightarrow f_1 \wedge f_2>}$

d. $\models <E|f_1 \wedge \ldots \wedge f_n \Rightarrow f_i>$, $n \geq 1$, $1 \leq i \leq n$

e. $\models <E|\{p[t/v]\}v{:=}t\{p\}>$

f. $\models <E|\{p\}S_1\{q\} \wedge \{q\}S_2\{r\} \Rightarrow \{p\}S_1;S_2\{r\}>$

g. $\models <E|\{p \wedge b\}S_1\{q\} \wedge \{p \wedge \neg b\}S_2\{q\} \Rightarrow \{p\}$ if b then S_1 else S_2 fi $\{q\}>$

h. $\models <E|(p \supset p_1) \wedge \{p_1\}S\{q_1\} \wedge (q_1 \supset q) \Rightarrow \{p\}S\{q\}>$.

PROOF. The proofs are all straightforward from the definitions, as we shall illustrate by giving those of cases c and f.

c. Let $E \equiv \langle P_i \Leftarrow S_i \rangle_{i=1}^n$, $\gamma \in \Gamma$, ϕ_i, $i = 1,\ldots,n$, as usual, and $\bar{\gamma} = \gamma\{\phi_i/P_i\}_{i=1}^n$. We have to show that from the two assumptions

$$\forall\gamma[\forall\sigma\neq\bot[F(f)(\bar{\gamma})(\sigma)] \Rightarrow \forall\sigma\neq\bot[F(f_1)(\bar{\gamma})(\sigma)]]$$

$$\forall\gamma[\forall\sigma\neq\bot[F(f)(\bar{\gamma})(\sigma)] \Rightarrow \forall\sigma\neq\bot[F(f_2)(\bar{\gamma})(\sigma)]]$$

it follows that

$$\forall\gamma[\forall\sigma\neq\bot[F(f)(\bar{\gamma})(\sigma)] \Rightarrow \forall\sigma\neq\bot[F(f_1 \wedge f_2)(\bar{\gamma})(\sigma)]].$$

Choose some γ and suppose that $\forall\sigma\neq\bot[F(f)(\bar{\gamma})(\sigma)]$. By the two assumptions, we infer that $\forall\sigma\neq\bot[F(f_1)(\bar{\gamma})(\sigma)]$ and $\forall\sigma\neq\bot[F(f_2)(\bar{\gamma})(\sigma)]$, from which we conclude that $\forall\sigma\neq\bot[F(f_1 \wedge f_2)(\bar{\gamma})(\sigma)]$, as was to be shown.

f. Let E, γ, ϕ_i and $\bar{\gamma}$ be as in part c. We have to show

$$\forall\gamma[\forall\sigma\neq\bot[F(\{p\}S_1\{q\} \wedge \{q\}S_2\{r\})(\bar{\gamma})(\sigma)] \Rightarrow$$
$$\forall\sigma\neq\bot[F(\{p\}S_1;S_2\{r\})(\bar{\gamma})(\sigma)]].$$

Choose some γ and assume the antecedent of the implication. Take any $\sigma \neq \bot$. We show that $\forall\sigma'[T(p)(\sigma) \wedge \sigma' = N(S_1;S_2)(\bar{\gamma})(\sigma) \wedge \sigma'\neq\bot \Rightarrow T(r)(\sigma')]$, or, equivalently, that $\forall\sigma',\sigma''[T(p)(\sigma) \wedge \sigma'' = N(S_1)(\bar{\gamma})(\sigma) \wedge \sigma''\neq\bot \wedge \sigma' = N(S_2)(\bar{\gamma})(\sigma'') \wedge \sigma'\neq\bot \Rightarrow T(r)(\sigma')]$. (Since $\sigma'\neq\bot$, $\sigma''\neq\bot$.) Take any σ',σ''. By the first part of the assumption, $T(p)(\sigma) \wedge \sigma'' = N(S_1)(\bar{\gamma})(\sigma) \wedge \sigma''\neq\bot \Rightarrow T(q)(\sigma'')$. By the second part of the assumption, $T(q)(\sigma'') \wedge \sigma' = N(S_2)(\bar{\gamma})(\sigma'') \wedge \sigma' \neq \bot \Rightarrow T(r)(\sigma')$. This establishes the desired result.

END 5.28.

We now start our preparations for Scott's rule. First, we extend our syntax with a special symbol for the statement the meaning of which is the nowhere defined function.

DEFINITION 5.29 (the nowhere defined statement).
The syntax of *Stat* is extended with the clause

$S ::= \ \ldots \mid \Omega$

with as its semantics $N(\Omega)(\gamma) = \lambda\sigma\cdot\perp$, for all γ.
END 5.29.

We should adapt the considerations of section 5.3 to this extension. However, since it is quite obvious how this is to be done (e.g. we put $Comp(\langle E \mid \Omega\rangle)(\sigma) = \langle\perp\rangle$, and extend various of the proofs in section 5.3 with an additional clause dealing with $S \equiv \Omega$), we will not bother with the details of this.

Secondly, we introduce the notion of *substitution* of statements S_i for procedure variables P_i, $i = 1,\ldots,n$, in a statement S. It is also possible to define, more generally, substitution in a program R, but we shall not need this. Observe that we define *simultaneous* substitution - at the same time for $P_1,\ldots,P_n$ - instead of simple substitution. (As always, we shall assume that all the P_i, $i = 1,\ldots,n$, are different.)

DEFINITION 5.30 (substitution for procedure variables).
$S[S_i/P_i]_{i=1}^n$ is defined by induction on the complexity of S.

a. $(v:=t)[S_i/P_i]_{i=1}^n \equiv v:=t$

b. $\Omega[S_i/P_i]_{i=1}^n \equiv \Omega$

c. $(S';S'')[S_i/P_i]_{i=1}^n \equiv (S'[S_i/P_i]_{i=1}^n;S''[S_i/P_i]_{i=1}^n)$

d. <u>if</u> b <u>then</u> S' <u>else</u> S" <u>fi</u> $[S_i/P_i]_{i=1}^n \equiv$

<u>if</u> b <u>then</u> $S'[S_i/P_i]_{i=1}^n$ <u>else</u> $S''[S_i/P_i]_{i=1}^n$ <u>fi</u>

e. $P[S_i/P_i]_{i=1}^n \equiv \begin{cases} S_j, & \text{if } P \equiv P_j, \text{ for some } j,\ 1 \le j \le n \\ P, & \text{otherwise.} \end{cases}$

END 5.30.

As key property of this substitution we have the following analog of lemma 2.16c:

<u>LEMMA 5.31</u>.

$$N(S[S_i/P_i]_{i=1}^n)(\gamma) = N(S)(\gamma\{N(S_i)(\gamma)/P_i\}_{i=1}^n).$$

<u>PROOF</u>. We use induction on the complexity of S. We only treat case e (of definition 5.30), leaving the other, even easier, cases to the reader.

$$N(P[S_i/P_i]_{i=1}^n)(\gamma) = \begin{cases} N(S_j)(\gamma), & \text{if } P \equiv P_j, \text{ for some } j,\ 1 \le j \le n \\ N(P)(\gamma), & \text{otherwise} \end{cases}$$

$$N(P)(\gamma\{N(S_i)(\gamma)/P_i\}_{i=1}^n) = \begin{cases} N(S_j)(\gamma), & \text{if } P \equiv P_j, \text{ for some } j,\ 1 \le j \le n \\ N(P)(\gamma), & \text{otherwise.} \end{cases}$$

END 5.31.

We discuss two examples where lemma 5.31 is combined with previous results to obtain syntactic formulations of semantic facts from section 5.3:

1. $\models \langle E \mid S_1 \sqsubseteq S_2 \Rightarrow S[S_1/P] \sqsubseteq S[S_2/P]\rangle$

   By definition 5.26, we must show that

   $G(\langle E \mid S_1 \sqsubseteq S_2 \Rightarrow S[S_1/P] \sqsubseteq S[S_2/P]\rangle)(\gamma) = tt$, for all γ.

   Choose some γ. We have to prove that (ϕ_i, i = 1,...,n, as usual)

$$\forall\sigma\neq\perp[\mathcal{F}(S_1 \sqsubseteq S_2)(\gamma\{\phi_i/P_i\}_{i=1}^n)(\sigma)] \Rightarrow$$
$$\forall\sigma\neq\perp[\mathcal{F}(S[S_1/P] \sqsubseteq S[S_2/P])(\gamma\{\phi_i/P_i\}_{i=1}^n)(\sigma)] \qquad (*)$$

Let $\gamma' = \gamma\{\phi_i/P_i\}_{i=1}^n$. By definition 5.24, we may rewrite (*) as

$$\mathcal{N}(S_1)(\gamma') \sqsubseteq \mathcal{N}(S_2)(\gamma') \Rightarrow$$
$$\mathcal{N}(S[S_1/P])(\gamma') \sqsubseteq \mathcal{N}(S[S_2/P])(\gamma')$$

(Since, for any S and γ, $\mathcal{N}(S)(\gamma)(\perp) = \perp$, we have that $\mathcal{N}(S_1)(\gamma) \sqsubseteq \mathcal{N}(S_2)(\gamma)$ and $\forall\sigma\neq\perp[\mathcal{N}(S_1)(\gamma)(\sigma) \sqsubseteq \mathcal{N}(S_2)(\gamma)(\sigma)]$ are equivalent. This remark will often be used tacitly below.)

Thus, using lemma 5.31,

$$\mathcal{N}(S_1)(\gamma') \sqsubseteq \mathcal{N}(S_2)(\gamma') \Rightarrow$$
$$\mathcal{N}(S)(\gamma'\{\mathcal{N}(S_1)(\gamma')/P\}) \sqsubseteq \mathcal{N}(S)(\gamma'\{\mathcal{N}(S_2)(\gamma')/P\})$$

Let $\phi'_i \overset{\text{df.}}{=} \mathcal{N}(S_i)(\gamma')$, $i = 1,2$. What we have to prove may then be formulated as: $\phi'_1 \sqsubseteq \phi'_2 \Rightarrow \mathcal{N}(S)(\gamma'\{\phi'_1/P\}) \sqsubseteq \mathcal{N}(S)(\gamma'\{\phi'_2/P\})$, and this implication follows from the monotonicity of the function $\lambda\phi'\cdot\mathcal{N}(S)(\gamma'\{\phi'/P\})$ (cf. theorem 5.21).

2. $\models \langle P \Leftarrow S | S[\bar{S}/P] \sqsubseteq \bar{S} \Rightarrow P \sqsubseteq \bar{S}\rangle$

(This is, for $n = 1$, the least fixed point property of recursive procedures as suggested by lemma 5.9.) We verify whether, for all γ, $\mathcal{G}(\langle P \Leftarrow S | S[\bar{S}/P] \sqsubseteq \bar{S} \Rightarrow P \sqsubseteq \bar{S}\rangle)(\gamma)$. Choose some γ. We must prove that $\forall\sigma\neq\perp[\mathcal{F}(S[\bar{S}/P] \sqsubseteq \bar{S})(\gamma\{\phi/P\})(\sigma)] \Rightarrow \forall\sigma\neq\perp[\mathcal{F}(P \sqsubseteq \bar{S})(\gamma\{\phi/P\})(\sigma)]$, with $\phi = \mu\Phi = \mu[\lambda\phi'\cdot\mathcal{N}(S)(\gamma\{\phi'/P\})]$. Thus, we show that

$$\mathcal{N}(S[\bar{S}/P])(\gamma\{\phi/P\}) \sqsubseteq \mathcal{N}(\bar{S})(\gamma\{\phi/P\})$$

$$\Rightarrow$$

$$\mathcal{N}(P)(\gamma\{\phi/P\}) \sqsubseteq \mathcal{N}(\bar{S})(\gamma\{\phi/P\}),$$

or, using lemma 5.31,

$$\mathcal{N}(S)(\gamma\{\phi/P\}\{\mathcal{N}(\bar{S})(\gamma\{\phi/P\})/P\}) \sqsubseteq \mathcal{N}(\bar{S})(\gamma\{\phi/P\})$$

$$\Rightarrow$$

$$\phi \sqsubseteq \mathcal{N}(\bar{S})(\gamma\{\phi/P\})$$

or, using the analog of lemma 2.5, that

$$\mathcal{N}(S)(\gamma\{\mathcal{N}(\bar{S})(\gamma\{\phi/P\})/P\}) \sqsubseteq \mathcal{N}(\bar{S})(\gamma\{\phi/P\})$$

$$\Rightarrow$$

$$\phi \sqsubseteq \mathcal{N}(\bar{S})(\gamma\{\phi/P\}).$$

Now let $\bar{\phi} \overset{\text{df.}}{=} \mathcal{N}(\bar{S})(\gamma\{\phi/P\})$. What we have to show then takes the following form: If

a. $\phi = \mu\Phi$

b. $\Phi(\bar{\phi}) \sqsubseteq \bar{\phi}$, then

c. $\phi \sqsubseteq \bar{\phi}$,

and this is immediate by lemma 5.9.

Besides substitution in statements we also define substitution in correctness formulae $f \in \mathcal{Form}$:

<u>DEFINITION 5.32</u> (substitution in correctness formulae).

$f[S_i/P_i]_{i=1}^n$ is defined by induction on the complexity of f.

a. $p[S_i/P_i]_{i=1}^n \equiv p$

b. $(\{p\}S\{q\})[S_i/P_i]_{i=1}^n \equiv \{p\}S[S_i/P_i]_{i=1}^n\{q\}$

c. $(S' \sqsubseteq S'')[S_i/P_i]_{i=1}^n \equiv (S'[S_i/P_i]_{i=1}^n \sqsubseteq S''[S_i/P_i]_{i=1}^n)$

d. $(f_1 \wedge f_2)[S_i/P_i]_{i=1}^n \equiv f_1[S_i/P_i]_{i=1}^n \wedge f_2[S_i/P_i]_{i=1}^n$

END 5.32.

As analog of lemma 5.31 we have

LEMMA 5.33.

$$F(f[S_i/P_i]_{i=1}^n)(\gamma) = F(f)(\gamma\{N(S_i)(\gamma)/P_i\}_{i=1}^n).$$

PROOF. By the definitions and lemma 5.31.

END 5.33.

At last, we arrive at

THEOREM 5.34 (Scott's induction rule).

$$\frac{<\ |f[\Omega/P_i]_{i=1}^n>,\ <\ |f \Rightarrow f[S_i/P_i]_{i=1}^n>}{<<P_i \Leftarrow S_i>_{i=1}^n\ |\ f>}$$

We precede the proof of the soundness of this inference with some comments. In words, the rule amounts to the following (taking n = 1 for simplicity). Assume we want to prove the validity of a correctness formula f in the presence of the declaration $P \Leftarrow S$. It then suffices to prove the validity of the following two formulae without the declaration $P \Leftarrow S$ being available. (Note that, as a consequence of the γ-formalism, this amounts to the freedom to assign to occurrences of the procedure variable P some *arbitrary meaning*; see also the discussion preceding definition 5.18.)

a. $<\ |f[\Omega/P]>$ (basis step)

b. $<\ |f \Rightarrow f[S/P]>$ (induction step)

We see that the rule uses the " $\Rightarrow$ " construct in an essential manner. In fact, an alternative formulation which leaves the first assumption unchanged but replaces the requirement that b be valid by the weaker one that

$$\text{b}'.\ \frac{<\ |\ f>}{<\ |\ f[S/P]>}$$

be sound, would *not*, in general, allow us to infer the desired conclusion. (The reader should inspect the proof of theorem 5.34 to see why this is the case.)

The following example shows us how the soundness of the inference in example 2b following definition 5.27 may be obtained as a special case of Scott's rule. Choose n = 1 and $f \equiv \{p\}P\{q\}$, and note that $<\ |\{p\}\Omega\{q\}>$ is always valid, which is why it may be omitted in the antecedent of the inference. There remains

$$\boxed{\frac{<\ |\{p\}P\{q\} \Rightarrow \{p\}S\{q\}>}{<P \Leftarrow S\ |\ \{p\}P\{q\}>}}$$

It will appear that the soundness proof to be given now relies heavily on the continuity of the function

$$\lambda\phi_1'\cdot\ldots\cdot\lambda\phi_n'\cdot\mathcal{N}(S)(\gamma\{\phi_i'/P_i\}_{i=1}^n)$$

and, in particular, on the possibility, for continuous Φ, to obtain $\mu\Phi$ as $\bigsqcup_{i=0}^{\infty} \Phi^i(\bot_M)$.

PROOF of theorem 5.34. We show that from

a. $\models\ <\ |f[\Omega/P_i]_{i=1}^n>$, and

b. $\models\ <\ |f \Rightarrow f[S_i/P_i]_{i=1}^n>$

it follows that

c. $\models\ <<P_i \Leftarrow S_i>_{i=1}^n|f>$.

Using the various definitions we can rewrite this as: From

a'. $\forall\gamma\forall\sigma\neq\bot[\mathcal{F}(f[\Omega/P_i]_{i=1}^n)(\gamma)(\sigma)]$

b'. $\forall\gamma[\forall\sigma\neq\bot[\mathcal{F}(f)(\gamma)(\sigma)] \Rightarrow \forall\sigma\neq\bot[\mathcal{F}(f[S_i/P_i]_{i=1}^n)(\gamma)(\sigma)]]$

it follows that

c'. $\forall\gamma\forall\sigma\neq\bot[F(f)(\gamma\{\phi_i/P_i\}_{i=1}^n)(\sigma)]$,

with ϕ_i, i = 1,...,n, as usual.

An application of lemma 5.33 yields the equivalent formulation: From

a". $\forall\gamma\forall\sigma\neq\bot[F(f)(\gamma\{\lambda\sigma\cdot\bot/P_i\}_{i=1}^n)(\sigma)]$, and

b". $\forall\gamma[\forall\sigma\neq\bot[F(f)(\gamma)(\sigma)] \Rightarrow \forall\sigma\neq\bot[F(f)(\gamma\{N(S_i)(\gamma)/P_i\}_{i=1}^n)(\sigma)]]$

it follows that

c". $\forall\gamma\forall\sigma\neq\bot[F(f)(\gamma\{\phi_i/P_i\}_{i=1}^n)(\sigma)]$.

Choose some $\bar{\gamma}$. We show that a" and b" imply that $\forall\sigma\neq\bot[F(f)(\bar{\gamma}\{\phi_i/P_i\}_{i=1}^n)(\sigma)]$, using the following auxiliary proposition to be proved below: Let ϕ_i^k, i = 1,...,n, k = 0,1,..., be as in the proof of theorem 5.22, with $\bar{\gamma}$ replacing γ. Then we have

$$\forall k\forall\sigma\neq\bot[F(f)(\bar{\gamma}\{\phi_i^k/P_i\}_{i=1}^n)(\sigma)] \Rightarrow \forall\sigma\neq\bot[F(f)(\bar{\gamma}\{\phi_i/P_i\}_{i=1}^n)(\sigma)]. \qquad (*)$$

Using (*), it is sufficient to show that a" and b" imply that, for all k, $\forall\sigma\neq\bot[F(f)(\bar{\gamma}\{\phi_i^k/P_i\}_{i=1}^n)(\sigma)]$. This we show by induction on k.

<u>k = 0</u>. Use that $\phi_i^0 = \lambda\sigma\cdot\bot$, i = 1,...,n, and choose $\bar{\gamma}$ for γ in a".

<u>k → k+1</u>. Assume $\forall\sigma\neq\bot[F(f)(\bar{\gamma}\{\phi_i^k/P_i\}_{i=1}^n)(\sigma)]$. Now apply b" with

$\bar{\gamma}\{\phi_i^k/P_i\}_{i=1}^n$ as choice for γ. We obtain that

$\forall\sigma\neq\bot[F(f)(\bar{\gamma}\{\phi_j^k/P_j\}_{j=1}^n\{N(S_i)(\bar{\gamma}\{\phi_j^k/P_j\}_{j=1}^n)/P_i\}_{i=1}^n)(\sigma)]$

or, by an analog of lemma 2.5, that

$\forall\sigma\neq\bot[F(f)(\bar{\gamma}\{N(S_i)(\bar{\gamma}\{\phi_j^k/P_j\}_{j=1}^n)/P_i\}_{i=1}^n)(\sigma)]$

or, by the definition of ϕ_i^{k+1}, that

$\forall\sigma\neq\bot[F(f)(\bar{\gamma}\{\phi_i^{k+1}/P_i\}_{i=1}^n)(\sigma)]$.

There remains the proof of (*). We apply induction on the complexity of f.

a. $f \equiv p \in \mathit{Assn}$. Clear, since $F(p)$ does not depend on γ.

b. $f \equiv \{p\}S\{q\}$. Assume that

$\forall k \forall \sigma \neq \bot [F(\{p\}S\{q\})(\bar{\gamma}\{\phi_i^k/P_i\}_{i=1}^n)(\sigma)]$, or

$\forall k \forall \sigma \neq \bot, \sigma' [T(p)(\sigma) \wedge \sigma' = N(S)(\bar{\gamma}\{\phi_i^k/P_i\}_{i=1}^n)(\sigma) \wedge \sigma' \neq \bot \Rightarrow T(q)(\sigma')]$, or

$\forall \sigma \neq \bot, \sigma' [T(p)(\sigma) \wedge \sigma' = \bigsqcup_k N(S)(\bar{\gamma}\{\phi_i^k/P_i\}_{i=1}^n)(\sigma) \wedge \sigma' \neq \bot \Rightarrow T(q)(\sigma')]$, or

by theorem 5.21,

$\forall \sigma \neq \bot, \sigma' [T(p)(\sigma) \wedge \sigma' = N(S)(\bar{\gamma}\{\bigsqcup_k \phi_i^k/P_i\}_{i=1}^n)(\sigma) \wedge \sigma' \neq \bot \Rightarrow T(q)(\sigma')]$,

which amounts to the desired conclusion

$\forall \sigma \neq \bot [F(\{p\}S\{q\})(\bar{\gamma}\{\bigsqcup_k \phi_i^k/P_i\}_{i=1}^n)(\sigma)]$.

c. $f \equiv S_1 \sqsubseteq S_2$. Assume that

$\forall k \forall \sigma \neq \bot [F(S_1 \sqsubseteq S_2)(\bar{\gamma}\{\phi_i^k/P_i\}_{i=1}^n)(\sigma)]$

From the definition of F it follows that

$\forall k [N(S_1)(\bar{\gamma}\{\phi_i^k/P_i\}_{i=1}^n) \sqsubseteq N(S_2)(\bar{\gamma}\{\phi_i^k/P_i\}_{i=1}^n)]$,

or by the lub property,

$\bigsqcup_k N(S_1)(\bar{\gamma}\{\phi_i^k/P_i\}_{i=1}^n) \sqsubseteq \bigsqcup_k N(S_2)(\bar{\gamma}\{\phi_i^k/P_i\}_{i=1}^n)$.

By theorem 5.21, this implies that

$N(S_1)(\bar{\gamma}\{\bigsqcup_k \phi_i^k/P_i\}_{i=1}^n) \sqsubseteq N(S_2)(\bar{\gamma}\{\bigsqcup_k \phi_i^k/P_i\}_{i=1}^n)$,

thus yielding the desired result

$\forall \sigma \neq \bot [F(S_1 \sqsubseteq S_2)(\bar{\gamma}\{\bigsqcup_k \phi_i^k/P_i\}_{i=1}^n)(\sigma)]$.

d. $f \equiv f_1 \wedge f_2$. Direct by induction.

END 5.34.

Examples. We begin with three very simple examples which are not so much included to show the power of the rule (a direct treatment of them without Scott's rule being quite feasible), but rather to illustrate the pattern one follows in applying it.

1. $\models \langle P \Leftarrow P \mid P \sqsubseteq S\rangle$

Apply Scott's rule with n = 1, $P_1 \equiv S_1 \equiv P$, and $f \equiv P \sqsubseteq S$. We have to verify whether

a. $\models \langle \mid \Omega \sqsubseteq S[\Omega/P]\rangle$, which is clear

b. $\models \langle \mid P \sqsubseteq S \Rightarrow P \sqsubseteq S\rangle$, which is also very clear.

2. $\models \langle P \Leftarrow S,\ Q \Leftarrow S[Q/P] \mid P = Q\rangle$.

Take $f \equiv (P = Q)$. We have to verify whether

a. $\models \langle \mid \Omega = \Omega\rangle$

b. $\models \langle \mid P = Q \Rightarrow S = S[Q/P]\rangle$, and this follows easily as a variation on the examples following lemma 5.31.

3. $\models \langle P \Leftarrow P \mid \{p\}P\{q\}\rangle$.

Take $f \equiv \{p\}P\{q\}$. Both $\models \langle \mid \{p\}\Omega\{q\}\rangle$ and $\models \langle \mid \{p\}P\{q\} \Rightarrow \{p\}P\{q\}\rangle$ are obvious.

We now treat three somewhat more interesting examples.

4. $\models \langle P_1 \Leftarrow \underline{\text{if}}\ b\ \underline{\text{then}}\ S_1;P_1\ \underline{\text{else}}\ D\ \underline{\text{fi}},$

$P_2 \Leftarrow \underline{\text{if}}\ b\ \underline{\text{then}}\ S_1;P_2\ \underline{\text{else}}\ S_2\ \underline{\text{fi}} \mid P_1;S_2 = P_2\rangle$.

Let $f \equiv P_1;S_2 = P_2$.

a. $\models \langle \mid \Omega;S_2 = \Omega\rangle$ is clear.

b. $\models \langle \mid P_1;S_2 = P_2 \Rightarrow \underline{\text{if}}\ b\ \underline{\text{then}}\ S_1;P_1\ \underline{\text{else}}\ D\ \underline{\text{fi}};S_2 =$

$$\underline{\text{if}}\ b\ \underline{\text{then}}\ S_1;P_2\ \underline{\text{else}}\ S_2\ \underline{\text{fi}}\rangle$$

is also easy, using example 3c after definition 2.12.

Caution. We have apparently used the restriction that S_2 contain no occurrences of either P_1 or P_2. Our result also holds without this restriction, but we then need a generalized version of Scott's rule as given in theorem 5.37.

5. $\models$ <$P \Leftarrow$ <u>if</u> b <u>then</u> S;P <u>else</u> D <u>fi</u> | P; <u>if</u> b <u>then</u> S_1 <u>else</u> S_2 <u>fi</u> = P;S_2>.

This example will not be worked out; a similar remark as the one in example 4 applies.

6. $\models$ <$P_1 \Leftarrow$ <u>if</u> b <u>then</u> $P_2;P_1$ <u>else</u> D <u>fi</u>,

$P_2 \Leftarrow$ <u>if</u> b <u>then</u> S;P_2 <u>else</u> D <u>fi</u> | $P_1 = P_2$>.

By *fpp* and the previous example, $\models$ <$P_1 \Leftarrow$ <u>if</u> b <u>then</u> $P_2;P_1$ <u>else</u> D <u>fi</u>, $P_2 \Leftarrow$ <u>if</u> b <u>then</u> S;P_2 <u>else</u> D <u>fi</u> | $P_2;P_1 = P_2$; <u>if</u> b <u>then</u> $P_2;P_1$ <u>else</u> D <u>fi</u> = P_2;D = P_2>. Next we obtain

$\models$ <$P_1 \Leftarrow$ <u>if</u> b <u>then</u> $P_2;P_1$ <u>else</u> D <u>fi</u>,

$P_2 \Leftarrow$ <u>if</u> b <u>then</u> S;P_2 <u>else</u> D <u>fi</u> | P_1 = (*fpp* for P_1)

<u>if</u> b <u>then</u> $P_2;P_1$ <u>else</u> D <u>fi</u> =

<u>if</u> b <u>then</u> P_2 <u>else</u> D <u>fi</u> = (*fpp* for P_2)

<u>if</u> b <u>then</u> <u>if</u> b <u>then</u> S;P_2 <u>else</u> D <u>fi</u> <u>else</u> D <u>fi</u> =

<u>if</u> b <u>then</u> S;P_2 <u>else</u> D <u>fi</u> = (*fpp* for P_2) P_2>.

(Observe that the equivalence just derived amounts to the simple fact that $\models$ <u>while</u> b <u>do</u> S <u>od</u> = <u>while</u> b <u>do</u> <u>while</u> b <u>do</u> S <u>od</u> <u>od</u>.)

For our next example, we need Scott's induction rule in a somewhat more general form, as stated in

<u>THEOREM 5.35</u> (Scott's induction rule, first generalization).

$$\frac{<\ | f_0 \Rightarrow f[\Omega/P_i]_{i=1}^n>, <\ | f_0 \wedge f \Rightarrow f[S_i/P_i]_{i=1}^n>}{<<P_i \Leftarrow S_i>_{i=1}^n \mid f_0 \Rightarrow f>}$$

provided that f_0 contains no occurrences of any of the P_i, i = 1,...,n

PROOF. According to the various definitions we have to show that from

a. $\forall\gamma[\forall\sigma\neq\bot[F(f_0)(\gamma)(\sigma)] \Rightarrow \forall\sigma\neq\bot[F(f[\Omega/P_i]_{i=1}^n)(\gamma)(\sigma)]]$

b. $\forall\gamma[\forall\sigma\neq\bot[F(f_0)(\gamma)(\sigma)] \wedge \forall\sigma\neq\bot[F(f)(\gamma)(\sigma)] \Rightarrow$

$\quad\forall\sigma\neq\bot[F(f[S_i/P_i]_{i=1}^n)(\gamma)(\sigma)]]$

it follows that

c. $\forall\gamma[\forall\sigma\neq\bot[F(f_0)(\gamma\{\phi_i/P_i\}_{i=1}^n)(\sigma)] \Rightarrow \forall\sigma\neq\bot[F(f)(\gamma\{\phi_i/P_i\}_{i=1}^n)(\sigma)]]$.

Take any $\bar{\gamma}$. Since none of the P_i, i = 1,...,n, occurs free in f_0, we have that $\forall\sigma\neq\bot[F(f_0)(\bar{\gamma}\{\phi_i/P_i\}_{i=1}^n)(\sigma)]$ iff $\forall\sigma\neq\bot[F(f_0)(\bar{\gamma})(\sigma)]$. Now let us assume that $\forall\sigma\neq\bot[F(f_0)(\bar{\gamma})(\sigma)]$ holds. By an argument exactly similar to that of the proof of theorem 5.34, we can show that then $\forall k\forall\sigma\neq\bot[F(f)(\bar{\gamma}\{\phi_i^k/P_i\}_{i=1}^n)(\sigma)]$ also holds. Thus, as in the proof of theorem 5.34, we obtain that $\forall\sigma\neq\bot[F(f)(\bar{\gamma}\{\phi_i/P_i\}_{i=1}^n)(\sigma)]$, as was to be shown.

END 5.35.

Example 7. Let S be without any occurrences of P. Then ⊨ <P ⇐ <u>if</u> b <u>then</u> S;P <u>else</u> D <u>fi</u> | {p∧b}S{p} ⇒ {p}P{p∧¬b}>. (Observe that, if we identify the P from this example with the while statement <u>while</u> b <u>do</u> S <u>od</u> (assuming S without any procedure variables), we obtain that ⊨ < | {p∧b}S{p} ⇒ {p} <u>while</u> b <u>do</u> S <u>od</u> {p∧¬b}>, which in turn implies the soundness of the inference in theorem 3.31.) We apply theorem 5.35 with $f_0 \equiv$ {p∧b}S{p} and f ≡ {p}P{p∧¬b}. We have to verify whether

a. ⊨ < |{p∧b}S{p} ⇒ {p}Ω{p∧¬b}>, which is evident, and

b. ⊨ < |{p∧b}S{p} ∧ {p}P{p∧¬b} ⇒ {p} <u>if</u> b <u>then</u> S;P <u>else</u> D <u>fi</u> {p∧¬b}>, which easily follows using lemma 5.28.

The form of Scott's rule as given in theorem 5.35 is not yet general enough for convenient application in a number of cases. To be more specific, note that the inductive argument proceeds simultaneously for all procedures in the system $<P_i \Leftarrow S_i>_{i=1}^{n}$. Occasionally, it is desirable to single out a subset of the system to perform the induction on, whereas the other procedures of the system are left untouched. We shall provide a version of the rule which allows this. Though its formulation is intuitively rather clear, its proof is complicated since the technique of theorem 5.14 (simultaneous vs iterated least fixed points) has to be added to the argument used in the proof of theorem 5.34.

LEMMA 5.36.

$$<<P_i \Leftarrow S_i>_{i=1}^{n} \mid f_0 \Rightarrow f[\Omega/Q_j]_{j=1}^{m}>,$$

$$<<P_i \Leftarrow S_i>_{i=1}^{n} \mid f_0 \wedge f \Rightarrow f[S_j'/Q_j]_{j=1}^{m}>$$

$$<<P_i \Leftarrow S_i>_{i=1}^{n}, <Q_j \Leftarrow S_j'>_{j=1}^{m} \mid f_0 \Rightarrow f>$$

provided that the Q_j, $j = 1,\ldots,m$, are different from the P_i, $i = 1,\ldots,n$, and do not occur in f_0 or any of the S_i, $i = 1,\ldots,n$

PROOF. We have to show that from the validity of the two premises it follows that

$$\forall\gamma[\forall\sigma\neq\bot[\mathcal{F}(f_0)(\bar{\gamma})(\sigma)] \Rightarrow \forall\sigma\neq\bot[\mathcal{F}(f)(\bar{\gamma})(\sigma)]]$$

where $\bar{\gamma} = \gamma\{\phi_i/P_i\}_{i=1}^{n}\{\psi_j/Q_j\}_{j=1}^{m}$, and

$$<\phi_1,\ldots,\phi_n,\psi_1,\ldots,\psi_m> =$$

$$\mu[\lambda\phi_1'\cdot\ldots\cdot\lambda\phi_n'\cdot\lambda\psi_1'\cdot\ldots\cdot\lambda\psi_m'\cdot<\mathcal{N}(S_i)(\gamma\{\phi_i'/P_i\}_{i=1}^{n}\{\psi_j'/Q_j\}_{j=1}^{m})>_{i=1}^{n},$$
$$<\mathcal{N}(S_j')(\gamma\{\phi_i'/P_i\}_{i=1}^{n}\{\psi_j'/Q_j\}_{j=1}^{m})>_{j=1}^{m}].$$

Choose γ, assume (*): $\forall\sigma\neq\bot[F(f_0)(\bar{\gamma})(\sigma)]$, to show $\forall\sigma\neq\bot[F(f)(\bar{\gamma})(\sigma)]$. Let

$$\Phi \overset{df.}{=} \lambda\phi_1'\cdot\ldots\cdot\lambda\psi_m'\cdot\langle N(S_i)(\gamma\{\phi_i'/P_i\}_{i=1}^n\{\psi_j'/Q_j\}_{j=1}^m)\rangle_{i=1}^n$$

$$\Psi \overset{df.}{=} \lambda\phi_1'\cdot\ldots\cdot\lambda\psi_m'\cdot\langle N(S_j')(\gamma\{\phi_i'/P_i\}_{i=1}^n\{\psi_j'/Q_j\}_{j=1}^m)\rangle_{j=1}^m.$$

Then $\langle\phi_1,\ldots,\phi_n,\psi_1,\ldots,\psi_m\rangle = \mu[\langle\Phi,\Psi\rangle]$. By theorem 5.14e we obtain

$$\langle\phi_1,\ldots,\phi_n\rangle =$$

$$\mu[\lambda\phi_1'\cdot\ldots\cdot\lambda\phi_n'\cdot\Phi(\phi_1',\ldots,\phi_n',\mu[\lambda\psi_1'\cdot\ldots\cdot\lambda\psi_m'\cdot\Psi(\phi_1',\ldots,\psi_m')])] = \qquad (5.2)$$

$$\mu[\lambda\phi_1'\cdot\ldots\cdot\lambda\phi_n'\cdot\langle N(S_i)(\gamma\{\phi_i'/P_i\}_{i=1}^n\{\mu_j[\ldots]/Q_j\}_{j=1}^m)\rangle_{i=1}^n]$$

(where, for $\mu[f_1,\ldots,f_n] = \langle x_1,\ldots,x_n\rangle$, we write $\mu_j[f_1,\ldots,f_n]$ for x_j), and, furthermore,

$$\langle\psi_1,\ldots,\psi_m\rangle =$$

$$\mu[\lambda\psi_1'\cdot\ldots\cdot\lambda\psi_m'\cdot\Psi(\phi_1,\ldots,\phi_n,\psi_1',\ldots,\psi_m')] = \qquad (5.3)$$

$$\mu[\lambda\psi_1'\cdot\ldots\cdot\lambda\psi_m'\cdot\langle N(S_j')(\gamma\{\phi_i/P_i\}_{i=1}^n\{\psi_j'/Q_j\}_{j=1}^m)\rangle_{j=1}^m].$$

Since the Q_j, $j = 1,\ldots,m$ do not occur in the S_i, $i = 1,\ldots,n$, we have, for $i = 1,\ldots,n$,

$$N(S_i)(\gamma\{\phi_i/P_i\}_{i=1}^n\{\ldots/Q_j\}_{j=1}^m) = N(S_i)(\gamma\{\phi_i/P_i\}_{i=1}^n)$$

which implies that (5.2) may be simplified to

$$\langle\phi_1,\ldots,\phi_n\rangle = \mu[\lambda\phi_1'\cdot\ldots\cdot\lambda\phi_n'\cdot\langle N(S_i)(\gamma\{\phi_i'/P_i\}_{i=1}^n)\rangle_{i=1}^n] \qquad (5.4)$$

Now by corollary 5.10 and (5.3) we have that $\langle\psi_1,\ldots,\psi_m\rangle =$ $\bigsqcup_k \langle\psi_1^k,\ldots,\psi_m^k\rangle$, where, for $j = 1,\ldots,m$

$$\psi_j^0 = \lambda\sigma\cdot\bot$$

$$\psi_j^{k+1} = N(S_j')(\gamma\{\phi_i/P_i\}_{i=1}^n\{\psi_j^k/Q_j\}_{j=1}^m), \quad k = 0,1,\ldots$$

Since the Q_j, $j = 1,\dots,m$, do not occur in f_0 we have, by (*)

$$\forall\bar{\psi}_1,\dots,\bar{\psi}_m\ \forall\sigma\neq\bot[\mathcal{F}(f_0)(\gamma\{\phi_i/P_i\}_{i=1}^n\{\bar{\psi}_j/Q_j\}_{j=1}^m)(\sigma)] \qquad (5.5)$$

We next show by induction on k that

$$\forall k\forall\sigma\neq\bot[\mathcal{F}(f)(\gamma\{\phi_i/P_i\}_{i=1}^n\{\psi_j^k/Q_j\}_{j=1}^m)(\sigma)]$$

<u>k = 0</u>. By the first premise of the inference we have that $\models \langle\langle P_i \Leftarrow S_i\rangle_{i=1}^n \mid f_0 \Rightarrow f[\Omega/Q_j]_{j=1}^m\rangle$. Thus, we obtain (**): $\forall\sigma\neq\bot[\mathcal{F}(f_0)(\gamma\{\tilde{\phi}_i/P_i\}_{i=1}^n(\sigma)] \Rightarrow \forall\sigma\neq\bot[\mathcal{F}(f[\Omega/Q_j]_{j=1}^m)(\gamma\{\tilde{\phi}_i/P_i\}_{i=1}^n)(\sigma)]$, where $\langle\tilde{\phi}_1,\dots,\tilde{\phi}_n\rangle = \mu[\lambda\phi_1'\cdot\dots\cdot\lambda\phi_n'\cdot\langle\mathcal{N}(S_i)(\gamma\{\phi_i'/P_i\}_{i=1}^n)\rangle_{i=1}^n]$, from which, by (5.4), $\tilde{\phi}_i = \phi_i$, $i = 1,\dots,n$. By (5.5), $\forall\sigma\neq\bot[\mathcal{F}(f_0)(\gamma\{\phi_i/P_i\}_{i=1}^n)(\sigma)]$, from which, by (**), $\forall\sigma\neq\bot[\mathcal{F}(f[\Omega/Q_j]_{j=1}^m)(\gamma\{\phi_i/P_i\}_{i=1}^n)(\sigma)]$, implying that $\forall\sigma\neq\bot[\mathcal{F}(f)(\gamma\{\phi_i/P_i\}_{i=1}^n\{\lambda\sigma\cdot\bot/Q_j\}_{j=1}^m)(\sigma)]$.

<u>k → k+1</u>. By the second premise of the inference, $\models \langle\langle P_i \Leftarrow S_i\rangle_{i=1}^n \mid f_0\wedge f \Rightarrow f[S_j'/Q_j]_{j=1}^m\rangle$, from which we obtain $\forall\sigma\neq\bot[\mathcal{F}(f_0\wedge f)(\gamma\{\phi_i/P_i\}_{i=1}^n\{\psi_j^k/Q_j\}_{j=1}^m)(\sigma)] \Rightarrow$ $\forall\sigma\neq\bot[\mathcal{F}(f[S_j'/Q_j]_{j=1}^m)(\gamma\{\phi_i/P_i\}_{i=1}^n\{\psi_j^k/Q_j\}_{j=1}^m)(\sigma)]$. By (5.5) and the induction hypothesis, $\forall\sigma\neq\bot[\mathcal{F}(f_0\wedge f)(\gamma\{\phi_i/P_i\}_{i=1}^n\{\psi_j^k/Q_j\}_{j=1}^m)(\sigma)]$, and we infer that $\forall\sigma\neq\bot[\mathcal{F}(f[S_j'/Q_j]_{j=1}^m)(\gamma\{\phi_i/P_i\}_{i=1}^n\{\psi_j^k/Q_j\}_{j=1}^m)(\sigma)]$ holds, which implies that we also have $\forall\sigma\neq\bot[\mathcal{F}(f)(\gamma\{\phi_i/P_i\}_{i=1}^n\{\mathcal{N}(S_j')(\gamma\{\phi_i/P_i\}_{i=1}^n\{\psi_j^k/Q_j\}_{j=1}^m)/Q_j\}_{j=1}^m)(\sigma)]$, i.e. that $\forall\sigma\neq\bot(\mathcal{F}(f)(\gamma\{\phi_i/P_i\}_{i=1}^n\{\psi_j^{k+1}/Q_j\}_{j=1}^m)(\sigma)]$, thus concluding the induction step.

Now by an argument similar to the one used in the proof of theorem 5.34, we obtain that $\forall\sigma\neq\bot[\mathcal{F}(f)(\gamma\{\phi_i/P_i\}_{i=1}^n\{\bigsqcup_k \psi_j^k/Q_j\}_{j=1}^m)(\sigma)]$, from which we can conclude that $\forall\sigma\neq\bot[F(f)(\gamma\{\phi_i/P_i\}_{i=1}^{n}\{\psi_j/Q_j\}_{j=1}^{m})(\sigma)]$, as was to be shown.

END 5.36.

Example 8. Using Scott's induction rule as given in the above lemma, we can easily derive that $\models$ <$P_0 \Leftarrow x:=x-1$, $P \Leftarrow$ <u>if</u> x>0 <u>then</u> P_0;P <u>else</u> D <u>fi</u> | {x≥0}P{x=0}> from $\models$ <$P_0 \Leftarrow x:=x-1$ | {x≥0}Ω{x=0}> and $\models$ <$P_0 \Leftarrow x:=x-1$ | {x≥0}P{x=0} ⇒ {x≥0} <u>if</u> x>0 <u>then</u> P_0;P <u>else</u> D <u>fi</u> {x=0}>. Note that the format of the rule as in theorem 5.34 would not allow this derivation.

We now arrive at the formulation of Scott's rule in its final form, which extends the previous version in that we allow induction on *some* (and not necessarily all) occurrences of a procedure variable in a formula. We first state and prove the rule, and then illustrate it by two further examples.

<u>THEOREM 5.37</u> (Scott's induction rule, final form).

$$\frac{\begin{array}{l}\langle\langle P_i \Leftarrow S_i\rangle_{i=1}^{n} \mid f_0 \Rightarrow f[\Omega/Q_i]_{i=1}^{n}\rangle,\\ \langle\langle P_i \Leftarrow S_i\rangle_{i=1}^{n} \mid f_0 \wedge f \Rightarrow f[S_i'/Q_i]_{i=1}^{n}\rangle\end{array}}{\langle\langle P_i \Leftarrow S_i\rangle_{i=1}^{n} \mid f_0 \Rightarrow f[P_i/Q_i]_{i=1}^{n}\rangle}$$

provided that, for i = 1,...,n

(i) $Q_i \not\equiv P_j$, j = 1,...,n

(ii) Q_i does not occur in f_0 or any of the S_j, j = 1,...,n

(iii) $S_i \equiv S_i'[P_j/Q_j]_{j=1}^{n}$

<u>PROOF</u>. By lemma 5.36, from the validity of the two premises of the inference we obtain that

$$\models \langle\langle P_i \Leftarrow S_i\rangle_{i=1}^{n}, \langle Q_i \Leftarrow S_i'\rangle_{i=1}^{n} \mid f_0 \Rightarrow f\rangle.$$

We also have, by the requirement on the S_i', that

$$\models \langle\langle P_i \Leftarrow S_i\rangle_{i=1}^n, \langle Q_i \Leftarrow S_i'\rangle_{i=1}^n \mid (P_1 = Q_1)\wedge\ldots\wedge(P_n = Q_n)\rangle$$

(Exercise.) Combining the two results we obtain

$$\models \langle\langle P_i \Leftarrow S_i\rangle_{i=1}^n, \langle Q_i \Leftarrow S_i'\rangle_{i=1}^n \mid f_0 \Rightarrow f[P_i/Q_i]_{i=1}^n\rangle$$

Now since S_i, $i = 1,\ldots,n$, and $f_0 \Rightarrow f[P_i/Q_i]_{i=1}^n$ have no occurrences of any Q_j, $j = 1,\ldots,n$, we finally infer (again using theorem 5.14e, details are left as exercise) that

$$\models \langle\langle P_i \Leftarrow S_i\rangle_{i=1}^n \mid f_0 \Rightarrow f[P_i/Q_i]_{i=1}^n\rangle$$

as was to be shown.

END 5.37.

Example 9. We prove that $\langle P \Leftarrow S \mid P;P = P\rangle$, where $S \equiv$ <u>if</u> b <u>then</u> $\bar{S}$;P;P <u>else</u> D <u>fi</u>. Let $f_0 \equiv$ <u>true</u>, $f \equiv (Q;P = Q)$, and let $S' \equiv$ <u>if</u> b <u>then</u> $\bar{S}$;Q;Q <u>else</u> D <u>fi</u>, where Q is some procedure variable not occurring in $\bar{S}$. (Note that $S \equiv S'[P/Q]$.) The Ω-case of the induction is clear. Next, we verify whether

$\models \langle P \Leftarrow S \mid Q;P = Q \Rightarrow$

<u>if</u> b <u>then</u> $\bar{S}$;Q;Q <u>else</u> D <u>fi</u>; P = <u>if</u> b <u>then</u> $\bar{S}$;Q;Q <u>else</u> D <u>fi</u>$\rangle$.

By *fpp* applied to P this is equivalent with

$\models \langle P \Leftarrow S \mid Q;P = Q \Rightarrow$

<u>if</u> b <u>then</u> $\bar{S}$;Q;Q;P <u>else</u> <u>if</u> b <u>then</u> $\bar{S}$;P;P <u>else</u> D <u>fi</u> <u>fi</u> =

<u>if</u> b <u>then</u> $\bar{S}$;Q;Q <u>else</u> D <u>fi</u>$\rangle$

which is clearly satisfied.

Example 10. $\models \langle P \Leftarrow$ <u>if</u> b <u>then</u> $\bar{S}$;P <u>else</u> D <u>fi</u> $\mid \{p\wedge b\}\bar{S}\{p\} \Rightarrow \{p\}P\{p\wedge\neg b\}\rangle$. (This is example 7, but without the restriction that P does not occur in $\bar{S}$.) Take

S $\equiv$ <u>if</u> b <u>then</u> $\bar{S}$;P <u>else</u> D <u>fi</u>,

S' $\equiv$ <u>if</u> b <u>then</u> $\bar{S}$;Q <u>else</u> D <u>fi</u>, (note that $S \equiv S'[P/Q]$)

$f_0 \equiv \{p \wedge b\}\bar{S}\{p\}$,

$f \equiv \{p\}Q\{p \wedge \neg b\}$,

where Q is some procedure variable $\not\equiv$ P, which does not occur in $\bar{S}$. Then apply the above theorem (and an argument similar to that of example 7).

5.5. Completeness

In this section we address the usual question: "Do we have enough validity and soundness results available to establish a completeness theorem?" The answer is "Not yet". Only after addition of a number of further rules which, as we shall see, necessitate a refinement of the notion of validity as developed up to now, are we able to provide a theorem which continues the results from sections 2.6 and 3.6. (From now on, we shall often use "rule" loosely to refer to either a correctness formula or an inference. Also, when we say that a proof system is sound we actually mean that all axioms of the system are valid and that all its proof rules are sound.) Before starting on this, let us first survey the results from section 5.4 which play a role in this. We shall need the validity and soundness of the following formulae and inferences:

1. $\dfrac{\langle E \mid f\rangle}{\langle E \mid f_0 \Rightarrow f\rangle}$ (weakening)

2. $\dfrac{\langle E \mid f_1 \Rightarrow f_2\rangle, \langle E \mid f_2 \Rightarrow f_3\rangle}{\langle E \mid f_1 \Rightarrow f_3\rangle}$ (transitivity)

3. $\dfrac{\langle E \mid f \Rightarrow f_1\rangle, \langle E \mid f \Rightarrow f_2\rangle}{\langle E \mid f \Rightarrow f_1 \wedge f_2\rangle}$ (collection)

4. $\langle E \mid f_1 \wedge f_2 \wedge \ldots \wedge f_n \Rightarrow f_i\rangle$, $n \geq 1$, $1 \leq i \leq n$ (selection)

5. $\langle E \mid \{p[t/v]\}\ v:=t\ \{p\}\rangle$ (assignment)

6. $\langle E \mid \{p\}S_1\{q\} \wedge \{q\}S_2\{r\} \Rightarrow \{p\}S_1;S_2\{r\}\rangle$ (composition)

7. $\langle E \mid \{p\wedge b\}S_1\{q\} \wedge \{p\wedge\neg b\}S_2\{q\} \Rightarrow \{p\}$ $\underline{\text{if}}$ b $\underline{\text{then}}$ S_1 $\underline{\text{else}}$ S_2 $\underline{\text{fi}}$ $\{q\}\rangle$ (conditionals)

8. $\langle E \mid (p\supset p_1) \wedge \{p_1\}S\{q_1\} \wedge (q_1\supset q) \Rightarrow \{p\}S\{q\}\rangle$ (consequence)

9.
$$\frac{\langle\langle P_i \Leftarrow S_i\rangle_{i=1}^n \mid \{p_1\}Q_1\{q_1\}\wedge\ldots\wedge\{p_n\}Q_n\{q_n\} \Rightarrow \{p_1\}S_1[Q_j/P_j]_{j=1}^n\{q_1\}\wedge\ldots\wedge \{p_n\}S_n[Q_j/P_j]_{j=1}^n\{q_n\}\rangle}{\langle\langle P_i \Leftarrow S_i\rangle_{i=1}^n \mid \{p_1\}P_1\{q_1\}\wedge\ldots\wedge\{p_n\}P_n\{q_n\}\rangle}$$
(induction)

where the Q_i, $i = 1,\ldots,n$, are all different from the P_j, $j = 1,\ldots,n$, and do not occur in the S_k, $k = 1,\ldots,n$.

The first eight rules were considered in lemma 5.28. Rule 9 is a special case of Scott's induction rule (theorem 5.37). It will turn out that we need five additional results, before a completeness theorem becomes possible. Two of these do not yet require elaboration of the validity definition. One of them is in fact quite simple, and the proof of its validity is left as an easy exercise:

10. $\langle E \mid \{p\}S\{q_1\} \wedge \{p\}S\{q_2\} \Rightarrow \{p\}S\{q_1\wedge q_2\}\rangle$ (conjunction)

The second additional rule is slightly ad hoc; we have not aimed at a version which is as general as possible, but restrict ourselves to a formulation which just serves its purpose in the completeness proof

11.
$$\frac{\langle\langle P_i \Leftarrow S_i\rangle_{i=1}^n \mid (f_1 \Rightarrow f_2)[Q_i/P_i]_{i=1}^n\rangle}{\langle\langle P_i \Leftarrow S_i\rangle_{i=1}^n \mid f_1 \Rightarrow f_2\rangle}$$
(instantiation)

where the Q_i, $i = 1,\ldots,n$, are all different from the P_j, $j = 1,\ldots,n$, and do not occur in f_1 or f_2.

In words, the soundness of this inference amounts to the rather obvious fact that, if a correctness formula mentioning procedure variables Q_i, i = 1,...,n, is valid in the presence of a system of declarations $<P_i \Leftarrow S_i>_{i=1}^n$ - so that these Q_i have arbitrary meanings (the Q_i are not declared) - then it remains valid when the Q_i are instantiated to (the meanings of) the P_i.

Example. The inference

$$\frac{<P \Leftarrow S \mid \{p\}Q\{q\} \Rightarrow \{p\}\bar{S}[Q/P]\{q\}>}{<P \Leftarrow S \mid \{p\}P\{q\} \Rightarrow \{p\}\bar{S}\{q\}>}$$

is sound, provided ($Q \not\equiv P$ and) Q does not occur in $\bar{S}$. The soundness of rule 11 is the content of

LEMMA 5.38.

$$\frac{<<P_i \Leftarrow S_i>_{i=1}^n \mid (f_1 \Rightarrow f_2)[Q_i/P_i]_{i=1}^n>}{<<P_i \Leftarrow S_i>_{i=1}^n \mid f_1 \Rightarrow f_2>}$$

where the Q_i, i = 1,...,n, are all different from the P_j, j = 1,...,n, and do not occur in f_1 or f_2

PROOF. For each γ, let ϕ_i^γ, i = 1,...,n, be defined in the usual way by

$$<\phi_1^\gamma,\ldots,\phi_n^\gamma> = \mu[\Phi_1^\gamma,\ldots,\Phi_n^\gamma]$$

$$\Phi_j^\gamma = \lambda\psi_1\cdot\ldots\cdot\lambda\psi_n\cdot N(S_j)(\gamma\{\psi_i/P_i\}_{i=1}^n), \quad j = 1,\ldots,n.$$

We have to show that

$$\forall\gamma[\forall\sigma\neq\bot[F(f_1[Q_i/P_i]_{i=1}^n)(\gamma\{\phi_i^\gamma/P_i\}_{i=1}^n)(\sigma)] \Rightarrow$$
$$\forall\sigma\neq\bot[F(f_2[Q_i/P_i]_{i=1}^n)(\gamma\{\phi_i^\gamma/P_i\}_{i=1}^n)(\sigma)]] \qquad (5.6)$$

$\Rightarrow$

$$\forall\gamma[\forall\sigma\neq\perp[\mathcal{F}(f_1)(\gamma\{\phi_i^{\gamma}/P_i\}_{i=1}^{n})(\sigma)] \Rightarrow \forall\sigma\neq\perp[\mathcal{F}(f_2)(\gamma\{\phi_i^{\gamma}/P_i\}_{i=1}^{n})(\sigma)]] \qquad (5.7)$$

In order to prove that (5.6) $\Rightarrow$ (5.7), we assume (5.6), choose some $\bar{\gamma}$ and show that $\forall\sigma\neq\perp[\mathcal{F}(f_1)(\bar{\gamma}\{\phi_i^{\bar{\gamma}}/P_i\}_{i=1}^{n})(\sigma)]\Rightarrow\forall\sigma\neq\perp[\mathcal{F}(f_2)(\bar{\gamma}\{\phi_i^{\bar{\gamma}}/P_i\}_{i=1}^{n})(\sigma)]$. Clearly, it suffices to show that we can find some $\bar{\bar{\gamma}}$ such that, for all f without occurrences of Q_i, $i = 1,\dots,n$, $\mathcal{F}(f[Q_i/P_i]_{i=1}^{n})(\bar{\bar{\gamma}}\{\phi_i^{\bar{\bar{\gamma}}}/P_i\}_{i=1}^{n}) = \mathcal{F}(f)(\bar{\gamma}\{\phi_i^{\bar{\gamma}}/P_i\}_{i=1}^{n})$. We show that the choice $\bar{\bar{\gamma}} = \bar{\gamma}\{\phi_i^{\bar{\gamma}}/Q_i\}_{i=1}^{n}$ satisfies this requirement. We have

$$\mathcal{F}(f[Q_i/P_i]_{i=1}^{n})(\bar{\bar{\gamma}}\{\phi_i^{\bar{\bar{\gamma}}}/P_i\}_{i=1}^{n}) = \text{(def. } \bar{\bar{\gamma}})$$

$$\mathcal{F}(f[Q_i/P_i]_{i=1}^{n})(\bar{\gamma}\{\phi_j^{\bar{\gamma}}/Q_j\}_{j=1}^{n}\{\phi_k^{\bar{\gamma}\{\phi_i^{\bar{\gamma}}/Q_i\}_{i=1}^{n}}/P_k\}_{k=1}^{n}) = \text{(lemma 5.33)}$$

$$\mathcal{F}(f)(\bar{\gamma}\{\phi_j^{\bar{\gamma}}/Q_j\}_{j=1}^{n}\{\phi_k^{\bar{\gamma}\{\cdot\}}/P_k\}_{k=1}^{n}\{\bar{\gamma}\{\cdot\}\{\cdot\}(Q_i)/P_i\}_{i=1}^{n}) =$$

$$\mathcal{F}(f)(\bar{\gamma}\{\phi_j^{\bar{\gamma}}/Q_j\}_{j=1}^{n}\{\phi_k^{\bar{\gamma}\{\cdot\}}/P_k\}_{k=1}^{n}\{\phi_i^{\bar{\gamma}}/P_i\}_{i=1}^{n}) = \text{(properties \{ \}-notation)}$$

$$\mathcal{F}(f)(\bar{\gamma}\{\phi_j^{\bar{\gamma}}/Q_j\}_{j=1}^{n}\{\phi_i^{\bar{\gamma}}/P_i\}_{i=1}^{n}) = (Q_j \text{ not in } f)$$

$$\mathcal{F}(f)(\bar{\gamma}\{\phi_i^{\bar{\gamma}}/P_i\}_{i=1}^{n})$$

END 5.38.

We now come to the last three rules of our system:

12. $\langle E|\{p\}S\{p\}\rangle$ (invariance)

provided that *intv*(p) ∩ *intv*(E,S) = ∅ (for *intv*, cf. definition 4.3 and remark 6 after definition 5.15).

13. $\langle E|\{p\}S\{q\} \Rightarrow \{p[y/x][a'/a]\}S\{q\}\rangle$ (substitution, I)

provided that $x \notin$ *svar*(E,S,q) and $a \notin$ *avar*(E,S,q).

14. $\langle E|\{p\}S\{q\} \Rightarrow \{p[y/x][a'/a]\}S[y/x][a'/a]\{q[y/x][a'/a]\}\rangle$ (substitution, II)

provided that

. either $x \equiv y$, or $x \notin$ *svar*(E), $y \notin$ *svar*(E,S,q)

. either $a \equiv a'$, or $a \notin$ *avar*(E), $a' \notin$ *avar*(E,S,q).

Rule 12 expresses an *invariance* property: Assertions p, such that none of their free simple or array variables occur in either the statement S or the system of declarations E, remain invariant throughout execution of S. As to rules 13 and 14, the first is a combination of (a special case of) exercise 2.11 and 4.8c, and the second of lemma 2.30 and exercise 4.8a. As we shall see presently, the invariance and substitution rules are indispensable for the completeness theorem. *However, with the definitions as used up to now, formulae* 12 *to* 14 *are invalid!* Consider, for example, rule 12 with E empty, $S \equiv P$, and $p \equiv (x=0)$. Its validity would amount to the truth of

$$\forall\gamma\forall\sigma\neq\bot,\sigma'[\mathcal{T}(x=0)(\sigma) \wedge \sigma' = \gamma(P)(\sigma) \wedge \sigma'\neq\bot \Rightarrow \mathcal{T}(x=0)(\sigma')] \qquad (5.8)$$

It is easily seen, however, that this is not true in general. E.g. let γ, σ and σ' be such that

1. $\gamma(P)(\bar{\sigma}) = \bar{\sigma}\{1/x\}$, for all $\bar{\sigma}$
2. $\sigma(x) = 0$
3. $\sigma' = \gamma(P)(\sigma)$.

Then, by 1, $\sigma' = \sigma\{1/x\}$ $(\neq \bot)$, and we see that $\mathcal{T}(x=0)(\sigma')$ is not satisfied. The explanation of this somewhat surprising phenomenon is that, for P undeclared, $\gamma(P)$ is a completely arbitrary function, and there is no reason for it to satisfy the same properties as functions $\gamma(P')$ which are obtained as meanings of *declared* P'. (Due to the restrictions on *intv*(p), for declared P', (5.8) is indeed true (as will be shown below).) The construction of analogous counterexamples to the validity of rules 13 and 14 is left to the reader. A way out of the problem of the invalidity of 12 to 14 might seem to require that the pair $<E|S>$ occurring in them be closed. This would indeed turn them into valid formulae, but would, on the other hand, not serve the purpose of the completeness theorem. The structure of the induction rule (rule 9) is responsible for this. As its premise we have the formula

$$<<P_i \Leftarrow S_i>_{i=1}^n | \{p_1\}Q_1\{q_1\} \wedge \ldots \wedge \{p_n\}Q_n\{q_n\} \Rightarrow$$
$$\{p_1\}S_1[Q_j/P_j]_{j=1}^n\{q_1\} \wedge \ldots \wedge \{p_n\}S_n[Q_j/P_j]_{j=1}^n\{q_n\}>,$$

which, clearly, contains undeclared procedure variables (viz. the Q_i, $i = 1,\ldots,n$). Thus, even if we start out with a closed formula and try to construct a formal proof for it, at intermediate stages we are going to encounter formulae which *do* have undeclared procedure variables. Moreover, we shall want to apply rules 12 to 14 exactly to formulae of this sort. Altogether, we see that we cannot restrict these rules as indicated: we do want to have them available for non-closed formulae. Therefore, we have to resort to a different solution. We modify the definition of validity of a generalized correctness formula $g \equiv <E|f_1 \Rightarrow f_2>$. Instead of requiring that $\mathcal{G}(g)(\gamma)$ holds for all $\gamma \in \Gamma$, we shall require this only for a class of suitably restricted γ's, say all $\gamma \in \Gamma^E \subsetneq \Gamma$. Here the class Γ^E consists of mappings γ which depend upon the set of declarations E in the sense that *all* functions $\gamma(P)$ are postulated to have certain properties which are satisfied by those functions which are obtained as meanings of procedures declared in E. In other words, for $E \equiv <P_i \Leftarrow S_i>_{i=1}^n$, for *all* P we shall impose certain restrictions on $\gamma(P)$ - for $\gamma \in \Gamma^E$ - which are provable for $P \in \{P_1,\ldots,P_n\}$, but have to be postulated for $P \notin \{P_1,\ldots,P_n\}$.

Now which properties are we thinking of? We recall from chapter 2 the notions of a function (not) *setting* or *using* a variable. Due to the subsequent introduction of the ι-state and of subscripted variables, the definitions need some updating (and will be phrased only in the negative sense, the positive formulation playing no role anyway):

DEFINITION 5.39 (a function or setting or using a variable).
Let $\phi \in M$.

a. ϕ *does not set* $x \in \mathit{Svar}$ or $a \in \mathit{Avar}$ whenever, for all σ, if $\phi(\sigma) \neq \bot$ then $\phi(\sigma)(x) = \sigma(x)$, or, for all $\alpha \in V_0$, $\phi(\sigma)(a,\alpha) = \sigma(a,\alpha)$, respectively. (Note that, if $\phi(\sigma) \neq \bot$ then $\sigma \neq \bot$.)
b. ϕ *does not use* $x \in \mathit{Svar}$ or $a \in \mathit{Avar}$ whenever, for all σ and $\alpha \in V_0$, $\phi(\sigma\{\alpha/x\}) = \phi(\sigma)\{\alpha/x\}$, or, for all $\alpha' \in V_0$, $\phi(\sigma\{\alpha/\langle a,\alpha'\rangle\}) = \phi(\sigma)\{\alpha/\langle a,\alpha'\rangle\}$, respectively.

END 5.39.

As before, we have as immediate consequences of the definition:

LEMMA 5.40.

a. If ϕ does not use x, then ϕ does not set x
b. If ϕ does not use a, then ϕ does not set a
c. If ϕ sets none of the elements of *svar*(v) or *avar*(v), then, for all σ, if $\phi(\sigma) \neq \bot$ then $L(v)(\sigma) = L(v)(\phi(\sigma))$, and similarly for t, b and p.

PROOF. Similar to the proofs of lemmas 2.37a and 2.36.
END 5.40.

The following lemma generalizes lemmas 2.36a and 2.37b.

LEMMA 5.41. Let $E \equiv \langle P_i \Leftarrow S_i\rangle_{i=1}^n$, and let $S \in \mathit{Stat}$.

a. If x (a[s], for any s) does not occur as the left-hand side of any assignment statement in S or any of the S_i, $i = 1,\dots,n$, and, moreover, for all P, $\gamma(P)$ does not set x(a), then $M(\langle E|S\rangle)(\gamma)$ does not set x(a)
b. If x(a) does not occur in S or any of the S_i, $i = 1,\dots,n$, and,

moreover, for all P, $\gamma(P)$ does not use x(a), then $M(\langle E|S\rangle)(\gamma)$ does not use x(a).

PROOF.

a. We only consider the case $x \in Svar$, leaving $a \in Avar$ as an exercise. Let ϕ_i^k, $i = 1,\dots,n$, $k = 0,1,\dots$, be as usual. Clearly, it is sufficient to prove that, under the stated assumptions on S_i and γ, for all $\bar{S}$ such that x does not occur as left-hand side of any assignment statement in $\bar{S}$, $N(\bar{S})(\gamma\{\phi_i^k/P_i\}_{i=1}^n)$ does not set x. We use induction on the entity $\langle k,\ell(\bar{S})\rangle$ as defined in the proof of theorem 5.22. If $\bar{S}$ is not a procedure variable, the proof is easy by induction (and in fact similar to the proof of lemma 2.36a). If $\bar{S} \equiv P$, then either $P \notin \{P_1,\dots,P_n\}$ and the result follows by the assumption on γ, or $P \equiv P_j$, for some j, $1 \le j \le n$, and $N(P_j)(\gamma\{\phi_i^k/P_i\}_{i=1}^n) = \phi_j^k$. If $k = 0$, ϕ_j^k does not set x by definition. Otherwise, $\phi_j^k = N(S_j)(\gamma\{\phi_i^{k-1}/P_i\}_{i=1}^n)$, and the result follows by the assumption on S_j and the fact that $\langle k-1,\ell(S_j)\rangle < \langle k,\ell(P_j)\rangle$.

b. Exercise.

END 5.41.

Next, we come to the definition of the class Γ^E:

DEFINITION 5.42 (restricted meaning functions).

Γ^E is the class of all functions: $Pvar \to M$, which satisfy: for all $P \in Pvar$, $\gamma(P)$ does not use any of the simple or array variables which are not in *svar*(E) or *avar*(E), respectively.

END 5.42.

The class Γ^E is used in the modified validity definition:

DEFINITION 5.43 (validity, revised version).

A generalized correctness formula $g \equiv \langle E|f_1 \Rightarrow f_2\rangle$ is called valid ($\models g$)

whenever, for all $\gamma \in \Gamma^E$, $G(g)(\gamma)$ holds.

END 5.43.

Remarks

1. In this definition, G is the function as defined in definition 5.25.
2. The definition of soundness of an inference remains unchanged (but, of course, it now refers to the revised notion of validity).

Rules 1 to 14 are all valid or sound with respect to the new definition of validity. For rules 1 to 11 this should be clear, since the problems arising in connection with rules 12 to 14 do not occur with these rules. In fact, all proofs as given before immediately carry over with $\gamma \in \Gamma$ replaced by $\gamma \in \Gamma^E$, as a result of the following lemma:

LEMMA 5.44. Let $E \equiv \langle P_i \Leftarrow S_i \rangle_{i=1}^n$, and let ϕ_i, $i = 1,\ldots,n$, be as usual. If $\gamma \in \Gamma^E$, then $\gamma\{\phi_i/P_i\}_{i=1}^n \in \Gamma^E$.

PROOF. Let $\gamma \in \Gamma^E$ and let $\bar{\gamma} = \gamma\{\phi_i/P_i\}_{i=1}^n$. We have to show that, for all $P \in Pvar$, $\bar{\gamma}(P)$ does not use any of the simple or array variables not in *svar*(E) or *avar*(E), respectively. If $P \notin \{P_1,\ldots,P_n\}$, this is true since $\gamma \in \Gamma^E$. Otherwise, $\bar{\gamma}(P) = \bar{\gamma}(P_j) = \phi_j$, for some j, $1 \le j \le n$, and we must show that $\phi_j = N(S_j)(\gamma\{\phi_i/P_i\}_{i=1}^n)$ does not use any of the simple or array variables not occurring in (S_j or any of the) S_i, $i = 1,\ldots,n$. Now this follows by lemma 5.41b.

END 5.44.

Caution. It should be noted that all inferences in our proof system have the property that the declarations appearing above and below the $\frac{\ldots}{\ldots}$ are identical. There is no reason to consider possible inferences $\dfrac{\ldots,\langle E_1|\ldots\rangle,\ldots}{\langle E_2|\ldots\rangle}$, with $E_1 \not\equiv E_2$, except, possibly, for rule 9. Taking n = 1 for simplicity, why have we not used as alternative the already encountered rule $\frac{<\ |\{p\}P\{q\} \Rightarrow \{p\}S\{q\}>}{<P \Leftarrow S|\{p\}P\{q\}>}$ (i.e. the special case of theorem 5.34 discussed in section 5.4)? The explanation for this is that Scott's induction in the form of rule 9 is sound with respect to the new definition of validity, but in the form as given in theorem 5.34 it is unsound! Observe that, according to definition 5.43 - and writing, for the moment, ε for the empty declaration (so that $svar(\varepsilon) = avar(\varepsilon) = \emptyset$) - we would have to show (cf. formulae a', b' and c' in the proof of theorem 5.34) that (*): $\forall\gamma \in \Gamma^{\varepsilon}[\ldots] \wedge \forall\gamma \in \Gamma^{\varepsilon}[\ldots] \Rightarrow \forall\gamma \in \Gamma^{E}[\ldots]$. Since, clearly, $\Gamma^{\varepsilon} \subsetneq \Gamma^{E}$, we cannot apply the argument as given in the proof of theorem 5.34 to establish (*). (It is left to the reader to construct a specific counterexample to theorem 5.34 with respect to the new validity definition.) Also observe that the proof of theorem 5.37 uses the inference of lemma 5.36 which, for given S_i, $i = 1,\ldots,n$, and *arbitrary* S'_j, $j = 1,\ldots,m$, is not sound (with respect to the new validity definition), but, for $n = m$ and S'_j satisfying $S_j \equiv S'_j[P_i/Q_i]_{i=1}^{n}$, $j = 1,\ldots,n$, *is* sound (since then $svar(S'_i) = svar(S_i)$ and $avar(S'_i) = avar(S_i)$, $i = 1,\ldots,n$).

The proof of the validity of rules 12 to 14 runs as follows:

<u>LEMMA 5.45.</u>

a. $\models <E|\{p\}S\{p\}>$,
   provided $intv(p) \cap intv(E,S) = \emptyset$
b. $\models <E|\{p\}S\{q\} \Rightarrow \{p[y/x][a'/a]\}S\{q\}>$,
   provided $x \notin svar(E,S,q)$ and $a \notin avar(E,S,q)$
c. $\models <E|\{p\}S\{q\} \Rightarrow \{p[y/x][a'/a]\}S[y/x][a'/a]\{q[y/x][a'/a]\}>$,
   provided
   . either $x \equiv y$, or $x \notin svar(E)$ and $y \notin svar(E,S,q)$
   . either $a \equiv a'$, or $a \notin avar(E)$ and $a' \notin avar(E,S,q)$.

<u>PROOF</u>. Let $E \equiv <P_i \Leftarrow S_i>_{i=1}^{n}$.

a. We have to show that, under the given assumptions, for all $\gamma \in \Gamma^{E}$:

$\forall\sigma\neq\bot,\sigma'[T(p)(\sigma) \wedge \sigma' = N(S)(\gamma\{\phi_i/P_i\}_{i=1}^n)(\sigma) \wedge \sigma'\neq\bot \Rightarrow T(p)(\sigma')]$,

where ϕ_i, i = 1,...,n, are as usual. Let $\phi \overset{df.}{=} N(S)(\gamma\{\phi_i/P_i\}_{i=1}^n)$. By lemma 5.44, $\gamma\{\phi_i/P_i\}_{i=1}^n \in \Gamma^E$; hence, by lemma 5.41b, ϕ does not use any of the simple or array variables not occurring in E or S. By the assumptions on p, it follows that ϕ does not use any of the free simple or array variables of p and, therefore, a fortiori does not set any of these variables. Now let σ,σ' be such that $T(p)(\sigma)$, $\sigma' = \phi(\sigma)$, and $\sigma' \neq \bot$. By lemma 5.40c, since $\phi(\sigma) \neq \bot$, $T(p)(\sigma') = T(p)(\phi(\sigma)) = T(p)(\sigma)$, as was to be shown.

b. We show that, under the given assumptions, for all $\gamma \in \Gamma^E$, and ϕ_i, i = 1,...,n, as usual,

$$\begin{aligned}&\forall\sigma\neq\bot,\sigma'[T(p)(\sigma) \wedge \sigma' = \\ &\qquad N(S)(\gamma\{\phi_i/P_i\}_{i=1}^n)(\sigma) \wedge \sigma'\neq\bot \Rightarrow T(q)(\sigma')]\end{aligned} \tag{5.9}$$

$\Rightarrow$

$$\begin{aligned}&\forall\sigma\neq\bot,\sigma'[T(p[y/x][a'/a])(\sigma) \wedge \sigma' = \\ &\qquad N(S)(\gamma\{\phi_i/P_i\}_{i=1}^n)(\sigma) \wedge \sigma'\neq\bot \Rightarrow T(q)(\sigma')]\end{aligned} \tag{5.10}$$

Choose some $\gamma \in \Gamma^E$ and assume (5.9), to show (5.10). Let $\phi = N(S)(\gamma\{\phi_i/P_i\}_{i=1}^n)$. By the assumptions, ϕ does not use x or a. Now let σ,σ' be such that $T(p[y/x][a'/a])(\sigma)$, $\sigma' = \phi(\sigma)$ and $\sigma' \neq \bot$. To show that $T(q)(\sigma')$. Since $\sigma' = \phi(\sigma)$, $\sigma'\{\sigma(y)/x\}\{\sigma(a',\alpha)/\langle a,\alpha\rangle\}_{\alpha\in V_0} = \phi(\sigma)\{\sigma(y)/x\}\{\sigma(a',\alpha)/\langle a,\alpha\rangle\}_{\alpha\in V_0}$ = (since ϕ does not use x or a) $\phi(\sigma\{\sigma(y)/x\}\{\sigma(a',\alpha)/\langle a,\alpha\rangle\}_{\alpha\in V_0})$. Moreover, since x and a do not occur (free) in q, $T(q)(\sigma') = T(q)(\sigma'\{\sigma(y)/x\}\{\sigma(a',\alpha)/\langle a,\alpha\rangle\}_{\alpha\in V_0})$. The desired result then follows from (5.9), with σ and σ' replaced by $\sigma\{\sigma(y)/x\}\{\sigma(a',\alpha)/<a,\alpha>\}_{\alpha\in V_0}$ and $\sigma'\{\sigma(y)/x\}\{\sigma(a',\alpha)/<a,\alpha>\}_{\alpha\in V_0}$, also using the fact (cf. exercise 4.7) that $T(p[y/x][a'/a])(\sigma) = T(p)(\sigma\{\sigma(y)/x\}\{\sigma(a',\alpha)/<a,\alpha>\}_{\alpha\in V_0})$.

c. (This proof follows the lines of the second proof of lemma 2.30. Cf. also exercise 4.8a.) Throughout, we treat only the simple-variable case, leaving the treatment of the array case as an easy variation to the reader. First we prove the following claim (cf. lemma 2.32). For each E and S, each $y,z \notin svar(E,S)$, $\gamma \in \Gamma^E$, $\bar{\gamma} = \gamma\{\phi_i/P_i\}_{i=1}^n$, σ and α, there exists $\bar{\sigma}$ and $\bar{\alpha}$ such that

$$N(S[y/x])(\bar{\gamma})(\sigma\{\alpha/y\}) = \bar{\sigma}\{\bar{\alpha}/y\}$$
$$N(S[z/x])(\bar{\gamma})(\sigma\{\alpha/z\}) = \bar{\sigma}\{\bar{\alpha}/z\}$$

It is sufficient to show the claim with $\bar{\gamma}$ replaced by $\bar{\gamma}^k = \gamma\{\phi_i^k/P_i\}_{i=1}^n$, with ϕ_i^k, $i = 1,\ldots,n$, $k = 0,1,\ldots$, as usual. The usual induction on $<k,\ell(S)>$ applies; if S is not a procedure variable, the argument of lemma 2.32 may be followed. If $S \equiv P_j$, $1 \le j \le n$, the claim is reduced to the case $<k-1,\ell(S_j)>$. So the only case which remains is $S \equiv P$, for some $P \notin \{P_1,\ldots,P_n\}$. We then have to prove the claim in the form

$$N(P)(\bar{\gamma}^k)(\sigma\{\alpha/y\}) = \bar{\sigma}\{\bar{\alpha}/y\}$$
$$N(P)(\bar{\gamma}^k)(\sigma\{\alpha/z\}) = \bar{\sigma}\{\bar{\alpha}/z\}$$

or, since $P \notin \{P_1,\ldots,P_n\}$, that

$$\gamma(P)(\sigma\{\alpha/y\}) = \bar{\sigma}\{\bar{\alpha}/y\}$$
$$\gamma(P)(\sigma\{\alpha/z\}) = \bar{\sigma}\{\bar{\alpha}/z\}.$$

Now since $y,z \notin svar(E)$, $\gamma(P)$ does not use y and z; hence, $\gamma(P)(\sigma\{\alpha/y\}) = \gamma(P)(\sigma)\{\alpha/y\}$, and similarly for z. Thus, we see that we can take $\bar{\sigma} = \gamma(P)(\sigma)$ and $\bar{\alpha} = \alpha$. Next, we need the analog of corollary 2.33. For each $x \notin svar(E)$, $y \notin svar(E,S)$, $\gamma \in \Gamma^E$, $\bar{\gamma} = \gamma\{\phi_i/P_i\}_{i=1}^n$, σ and α there exist $\bar{\sigma}$ and $\bar{\alpha}$ such that

$$\begin{aligned} &N(S)(\bar{\gamma})(\sigma\{\alpha/x\}) = \bar{\sigma}\{\bar{\alpha}/x\} \\ &N(S[y/x])(\bar{\gamma})(\sigma\{\alpha/y\}) = \bar{\sigma}\{\bar{\alpha}/y\} \end{aligned} \tag{5.11}$$

In fact, this is immediate from the claim just proved, by the same argument as used in corollary 2.33. (The reader who checks the details will observe the need for the restriction $x \notin svar(E)$.) Finally, the proof of the validity of rule 14 now follows as in the second proof of lemma 2.30 (with an appeal to the corollary replaced by an appeal to (5.11)).

END 5.45.

After thus having concluded our proof that the system with rules 1 to 14 is satisfactory insofar as it concerns the validity and soundness of the respective rules, we show that it is indeed a complete system for partial correctness. Before embarking upon this, we first discuss an example illustrating a few of the complications encountered in the completeness proof. We shall show that for E ⇐ <u>if</u> x>0 <u>then</u> x:=x-1;P;x:=x+1 <u>else</u> D <u>fi</u>,

$$\vdash \langle E \mid \{x=z\}P\{x=z\}\rangle$$

By the induction rule, it is sufficient to prove that

$$\vdash \langle E \mid \{x=z\}Q\{x=z\} \Rightarrow \{x=z\}\ \underline{\text{if}}\ x>0\ \underline{\text{then}}\ x:=x-1;Q;x:=x+1\ \underline{\text{else}}\ D\ \underline{\text{fi}}\ \{x=z\}\rangle \tag{5.12}$$

Now once we have derived that (*): $\vdash \langle E \mid \{x=z\}Q\{x=z\} \Rightarrow \{x=z-1\}Q\{x=z-1\}\rangle$, (5.12) is easily obtained by the rules for assignment, composition and conditionals. However, it takes a rather inordinate amount of work to establish (*). Below, we give all details of the initial part of the proof of (*), and then omit some of the trivial steps in the remainder of the proof of (5.12).

1. $\vdash \langle E \mid (x=z) \wedge (z=z'-1) \supset (z=z'-1) \rangle$

   (all valid assertions are axioms)

2. $\vdash \langle E \mid \{z=z'-1\}Q\{z=z'-1\} \rangle$

   (invariance)

3. $\vdash \langle E \mid (z=z'-1) \supset (z=z'-1) \rangle$

   (see 1)

4. $\vdash \langle E \mid ((x=z) \wedge (z=z'-1) \supset (z=z'-1)) \wedge \{z=z'-1\}Q\{z=z'-1\} \wedge$
   $((z=z'-1) \supset (z=z'-1)) \rangle$

   (1,2,3, collection (2×))

5. $\vdash \langle E \mid \{(x=z) \wedge (z=z'-1)\}Q\{z=z'-1\} \rangle$

   (4, consequence)

6. $\vdash \langle E \mid (x=z) \wedge (z=z'-1) \supset (x=z) \rangle$

   (see 1)

7. $\vdash \langle E \mid \{x=z\}Q\{x=z\} \Rightarrow ((x=z) \wedge (z=z'-1) \supset (x=z)) \rangle$

   (6, weakening)

8. $\vdash \langle E \mid \{x=z\}Q\{x=z\} \Rightarrow \{x=z\}Q\{x=z\} \rangle$

   (selection)

9. $\vdash \langle E \mid (x=z) \supset (x=z) \rangle$

   (see 1)

10. $\vdash \langle E \mid \{x=z\}Q\{x=z\} \Rightarrow ((x=z) \supset (x=z)) \rangle$

    (9, weakening)

11. $\vdash \langle E \mid \{x=z\}Q\{x=z\} \Rightarrow ((x=z) \wedge (z=z'-1) \supset (x=z)) \wedge \{x=z\}Q\{x=z\} \wedge$
    $((x=z) \supset (x=z)) \rangle$

    (7,8,10, collection (2×))

12. $\vdash \langle E \mid ((x=z) \wedge (z=z'-1) \supset (x=z)) \wedge \{x=z\}Q\{x=z\} \wedge ((x=z) \supset (x=z)) \Rightarrow$
    $\{(x=z) \wedge (z=z'-1)\}Q\{x=z\} \rangle$

    (consequence)

13. $\vdash \langle E \mid \{x=z\}Q\{x=z\} \Rightarrow \{(x=z) \wedge (z=z'-1)\}Q\{x=z\} \rangle$

    (11,12, transitivity)

14. $\vdash \langle E \mid \{x=z\}Q\{x=z\} \Rightarrow \{(x=z) \wedge (z=z'-1)\}Q\{z=z'-1\}\rangle$

(5, weakening)

15. $\vdash \langle E \mid \{x=z\}Q\{x=z\} \Rightarrow \{(x=z) \wedge (z=z'-1)\}Q\{x=z\} \wedge$
$\{(x=z) \wedge (z=z'-1)\}Q\{z=z'-1\}\rangle$

(13,14, collection)

16. $\vdash \langle E \mid \{(x=z) \wedge (z=z'-1)\}Q\{x=z\} \wedge \{(x=z) \wedge (z=z'-1)\}Q\{z=z'-1\} \Rightarrow$
$\{(x=z) \wedge (z=z'-1)\}Q\{(x=z) \wedge (z=z'-1)\}\rangle$

(conjunction)

17. $\vdash \langle E \mid \{x=z\}Q\{x=z\} \Rightarrow \{(x=z) \wedge (z=z'-1)\}Q\{(x=z) \wedge (z=z'-1)\}\rangle$

(15,16, transitivity)

18. $\vdash \langle E \mid \{x=z\}Q\{x=z\} \Rightarrow \{(x=z) \wedge (z=z'-1)\}Q\{x=z'-1\}\rangle$

(17, consequence)

(Some details in the derivation of 18 from 17 have been omitted. Similarly, trivial steps in the remaining part of the proof will be omitted.)

19. $\vdash \langle E \mid \{(x=z) \wedge (z=z'-1)\}Q\{x=z'-1\} \Rightarrow \{(x=x) \wedge (x=z'-1)\}Q\{x=z'-1\}\rangle$

(substitution, I)

20. $\vdash \langle E \mid \{x=z\}Q\{x=z\} \Rightarrow \{(x=x) \wedge (x=z'-1)\}Q\{x=z'-1\}\rangle$

(18,19, transitivity)

21. $\vdash \langle E \mid \{x=z\}Q\{x=z\} \Rightarrow \{x=z'-1\}Q\{x=z'-1\}\rangle$

(20, consequence)

22. $\vdash \langle E \mid \{x=z'-1\}Q\{x=z'-1\} \Rightarrow \{x=z-1\}Q\{x=z-1\}\rangle$

(substitution, II)

23. $\vdash \langle E \mid \{x=z\}Q\{x=z\} \Rightarrow \{x=z-1\}Q\{x=z-1\}\rangle$

(21,22, transitivity)

(Note that (23) coincides with (*) above.)

24. $\vdash \langle E \mid \{x=z\}Q\{x=z\} \Rightarrow \{x=z\}\ x:=x-1\ \{x=z-1\}\rangle$

(assignment)

25. $\vdash \langle E \mid \{x=z\}Q\{x=z\} \Rightarrow \{x=z-1\}\ x:=x+1\ \{x=z\}\rangle$

(assignment)

26. $\vdash$ <E|{x=z}Q{x=z} ⇒ {x=z} x:=x-1;Q;x:=x+1 {x=z}>
(23,24,25, composition)

27. $\vdash$ <E|{x=z}Q{x=z} ⇒ {x=z}D{x=z}>
(assignment, def. of D)

28. $\vdash$ <E|{x=z}Q{x=z} ⇒ {x=z} _if_ x>0 _then_ x:=x-1;Q;x:=x+1 _else_ D _fi_ {x=z}>
(26,27, conditionals)

29. $\vdash$ <E|{x=z}P{x=z}> (28, induction).

Let us draw attention to some of the interesting steps in this proof, viz. steps 2, 19 and 22, requiring application of rules 12 to 14. As we shall see below in the completeness proof, these steps are special cases of general ideas in the proof (cf. formulae (5.13), (5.17) and (5.18)).

We now start the preparations for the completeness proof. First, we need an important expressibility result which is the analog of the proposition in section 3.6:

PROPOSITION. Let <E|S> be a closed program.

a. For all q ∈ *Assn* there exists r_1 ∈ *Assn* such that *intv*(r_1) ⊆ *intv*(E,S,q) and, for all p ∈ *Assn*,

$$\models \text{<E|\{p\}S\{q\}>} \quad \text{iff} \quad \models \text{<E|}p \supset r_1\text{>}$$

b. For all p ∈ *Assn* there exists r_2 ∈ *Assn* such that *intv*(r_1) ⊆ *intv*(p,E,S) and, for all q ∈ *Assn*,

$$\models \text{<E|\{p\}S\{q\}>} \quad \text{iff} \quad \models \text{<E|}r_2 \supset q\text{>}$$

END.

Remarks

1. Observe that r_1 and r_2 play the role of weakest precondition and strongest postcondition, respectively. Exceeding the limits of our syntax - only for the duration of this remark - we might rephrase

the proposition as establishing the existence of assertions r_1, r_2 such that $\models \langle E|r_1 = \langle E|S\rangle \rightarrow q\rangle$, and $\models \langle E|r_2 = p \leftarrow \langle E|S\rangle\rangle$.

2. A proof of this proposition using tools from recursive function theory is given in the appendix.
3. We emphasize the restriction to closed $\langle E|S\rangle$. Clearly, it is not possible, in general, to provide a syntactic characterization (through r_1 and r_2) of $\{p\}S\{q\}$ when E or S contain undeclared procedure variables (determining functions which are not necessarily obtainable as the result of a computation).

We shall need the following lemma, the proof of which is based on the proposition:

<u>LEMMA 5.46</u>. Let $\langle E|S';S''\rangle$ be a closed program. If $\models \langle E|\{p\}S';S''\{q\}\rangle$, then there exists an assertion r such that $\models \langle E|\{p\}S'\{r\}\rangle$ and $\models \langle E|\{r\}S''\{q\}\rangle$.

<u>PROOF</u>. Let $E \equiv \langle P_i \Leftarrow S_i\rangle_{i=1}^n$ and let ϕ_i, i = 1,...,n, be as usual. Assume $\models \langle E|\{p\}S';S''\{q\}\rangle$. By the proposition (part b, a similar proof could be based on part a), there exists some r such that, for all $\bar{q}$, $\models \langle E|\{p\}S'\{\bar{q}\}\rangle$ iff $\models \langle E|r \supset \bar{q}\rangle$. Taking $\bar{q} \equiv r$, we immediately obtain that $\models \langle E|\{p\}S'\{r\}\rangle$. Furthermore, from the proposition it is easily seen that, for all σ, $T(r)(\sigma) = (\sigma \neq \bot) \wedge \exists\gamma \in \Gamma^E, \exists\sigma'[T(p)(\sigma') \wedge \sigma = N(S')(\gamma\{\phi_i/P_i\}_{i=1}^n)(\sigma')]$. Since $\langle E|S'\rangle$ is closed, $N(S')(\gamma\{\phi_i/P_i\}_{i=1}^n)$ does not depend on γ, which we express by writing $N(S')(\{\phi_i/P_i\}_{i=1}^n)$ for it. The result for r now simplifies to: $T(r)(\sigma) = (\sigma \neq \bot) \wedge \exists\sigma'[T(p)(\sigma') \wedge \sigma = N(S')(\{\phi_i/P_i\}_{i=1}^n)(\sigma')]$. We show that $\models \langle E|\{r\}S''\{q\}\rangle$. Using the various definitions and the fact that $N(S'')$ does not depend on γ either, we must prove that $\forall\sigma \neq \bot, \sigma'[T(r)(\sigma) \wedge \sigma' = N(S'')(\{\phi_i/P_i\}_{i=1}^n)(\sigma) \wedge \sigma' \neq \bot \Rightarrow T(q)(\sigma')]$. Now by the result for r, this

may be rewritten as

$$\forall\sigma\neq\bot,\sigma'[\exists\bar{\sigma}[\mathcal{T}(p)(\bar{\sigma}) \wedge \sigma =$$

$$\mathcal{N}(S')(\{\phi_i/P_i\}_{i=1}^{n})(\bar{\sigma})] \wedge \sigma' = \mathcal{N}(S'')(\{\phi_i/P_i\}_{i=1}^{n})(\sigma) \wedge \sigma'\neq\bot \Rightarrow \mathcal{T}(q)(\sigma')]$$

By some manipulations with the quantifiers (also using the fact that $\exists\bar{\sigma}[\mathcal{T}(p)(\bar{\sigma})] = \exists\bar{\sigma}\neq\bot[\mathcal{T}(p)(\bar{\sigma})]$) we obtain from this

$$\forall\bar{\sigma}\neq\bot,\sigma'[\mathcal{T}(p)(\bar{\sigma}) \wedge \exists\sigma[\sigma' =$$

$$\mathcal{N}(S'')(\{\phi_i/P_i\}_{i=1}^{n})(\sigma) \wedge \sigma = \mathcal{N}(S')(\{\phi_i/P_i\}_{i=1}^{n})(\bar{\sigma})] \wedge \sigma'\neq\bot \Rightarrow \mathcal{T}(q)(\sigma')]$$

or, equivalently,

$$\forall\bar{\sigma}\neq\bot,\sigma'[\mathcal{T}(p)(\bar{\sigma}) \wedge \sigma' = \mathcal{N}(S';S'')(\{\phi_i/P_i\}_{i=1}^{n})(\bar{\sigma}) \wedge \sigma'\neq\bot \Rightarrow \mathcal{T}(q)(\sigma')].$$

Using the fact that <E|S';S"> is closed, we see that this amounts to the validity of <E|{p}S';S"{q}>, which holds by assumption.

END 5.46.

We are now sufficiently prepared for our main (soundness and) completeness theorem. Let Ax consist of all valid assertions (i.e. all formulae <E|p> such that $\models$ <E|p>; note that, though E is syntactically required, the meaning of p does not depend upon E), together with the set {4,5,6,7,8,10,12,13,14} and let $Pr \overset{df.}{=} \{1,2,3,9,11\}$ (where the numbers refer to the rules listed above). Let the notion of *formal proof* be adapted to the present situation in that we replace everywhere in its definition correctness formulae f,..., by generalized correctness formulae g,... . Then

THEOREM 5.47 (soundness and completeness theorem).
Let <E|S> be closed.

$$\vdash_{Ax,Pr} \langle E|\{p\}S\{q\}\rangle \quad \text{iff} \quad \models \langle E|\{p\}S\{q\}\rangle.$$

PROOF. Throughout the proof (and the accompanying lemmas) we write $\vdash$ for $\vdash_{Ax,Pr}$.

a. ($\Rightarrow$). This follows in the usual manner by the validity and soundness of the axioms and proof rules in the system Ax, Pr as established above.

b. ($\Leftarrow$). The proof of this part depends upon a key lemma which we first state and prove:

LEMMA 5.48. Let $E \equiv \langle P_i \Leftarrow S_i \rangle_{i=1}^n$, and let $R \equiv \langle E|S \rangle$ be a closed program. Let $x_1,\ldots,x_k$, $a_1,\ldots,a_\ell$ be the simple and array variables occurring in E. Let $Q_1,\ldots,Q_n$ be procedure variables different from $P_1,\ldots,P_n$, and let $z_1,\ldots,z_k$, $a_1',\ldots,a_\ell'$ be simple and array variables not occurring in R. Let $p_0 \equiv (x_1=z_1) \wedge \ldots \wedge (x_k=z_k) \wedge (a_1=a_1') \wedge \ldots \wedge (a_\ell=a_\ell')$, where, for any a',a", a' = a" is short for $\forall x[a'[x] = a''[x]]$. Let, moreover, for $i = 1,\ldots,n$, $r^{(i)}$ be an assertion determined by

$$\text{For all } q,\ \models \langle E|\{p_0\}P_i\{q\}\rangle \quad \text{iff} \quad \models \langle E|r^{(i)} \supset q\rangle$$

(The existence of these $r^{(i)}$ is ensured by the proposition.) Then we have: For any $p,q \in Assn$, if

$$\models \langle E|\{p\}S\{q\}\rangle$$

then

$$\vdash \langle E|\{p_0\}Q_1\{r^{(1)}\}\wedge\ldots\wedge\{p_0\}Q_n\{r^{(n)}\} \Rightarrow \{p\}S[Q_i/P_i]_{i=1}^n\{q\}\rangle$$

PROOF. We use induction on the complexity of S. Let f_0 be an abbreviation for the formula $\{p_0\}Q_1\{r^{(1)}\}\wedge\ldots\wedge\{p_0\}Q_n\{r^{(n)}\}$.

a. $S \equiv v:=t$. The argument is a simple variation on that of section 2.6. Specifically, assume that $\models \langle E|\{p\}v:=t\{q\}\rangle$. Clearly, $\models \langle E|p \supset q[t/v]\rangle$, from which it follows that $\vdash \langle E|p \supset q[t/v]\rangle$. By the assignment rule, $\vdash \langle E|\{q[t/v]\}v:=t\{q\}\rangle$. Also, $\vdash \langle E|q \supset q\rangle$ is clear. Two applications of the collection rule yield that $\vdash \langle E|(p \supset q[t/v]) \wedge \{q[t/v]\}v:=t\{q\} \wedge (q \supset q)\rangle$. By the rules of transitivity and consequence, it follows that $\vdash \langle E|\{p\}v:=t\{q\}\rangle$ and, finally, $\vdash \langle E|f_0 \Rightarrow \{p\}v:=t\{q\}\rangle$ follows by the weakening rule.

b. $S \equiv S';S''$. Again, the argument is similar to that in sections 2.6 and 3.6. Assume that $\models \langle E|\{p\}S';S''\{q\}\rangle$. By lemma 5.46, there exists $r \in \mathit{Assn}$ such that $\models \langle E|\{p\}S'\{r\}\rangle$ and $\models \langle E|\{r\}S''\{q\}\rangle$. By the induction hypothesis, $\vdash \langle E|f_0 \Rightarrow \{p\}S'[Q_i/P_i]_{i=1}^n\{r\}\rangle$ and $\vdash \langle E|f_0 \Rightarrow \{r\}S''[Q_i/P_i]_{i=1}^n\{q\}\rangle$. The desired result now follows by the collection and composition rules (and by transitivity, which will be used tacitly in the sequel), also using the fact that $(S';S'')[Q_i/P_i]_{i=1}^n \equiv S'[Q_i/P_i]_{i=1}^n;S''[Q_i/P_i]_{i=1}^n$.

c. $S \equiv$ <u>if</u> b <u>then</u> S' <u>else</u> S'' <u>fi</u>. This is easy by induction, using the fact that if $\models \langle E|\{p\}$ <u>if</u> b <u>then</u> S' <u>else</u> S'' <u>fi</u> $\{q\}\rangle$, then $\models \langle E|\{p\wedge b\}S'\{q\}\rangle$ and $\models \langle E|\{p\wedge\neg b\}S''\{q\}\rangle$, and the rule of conditionals.

d. $S \equiv P_i$, for some i, $1 \le i \le n$. (Since $\langle E|S\rangle$ is closed, $S \equiv P \notin \{P_1,\ldots,P_n\}$ is not possible.) Assume that $\models \langle E|\{p\}P_i\{q\}\rangle$, to show that $\vdash \langle E|f_0 \Rightarrow \{p\}Q_i\{q\}\rangle$. Let z_h', $h = 1,\ldots,k$ and a_j'', $j=1,\ldots,\ell$, be completely fresh variables (i.e. not occurring in E, p or q). Let $p' \equiv p[z_h'/z_h]_{h=1}^k[a_j''/a_j']_{j=1}^\ell$, $q' \equiv q[z_h'/z_h]_{h=1}^k[a_j''/a_j']_{j=1}^\ell$. By (the soundness of) substitution rule II, from $\models \langle E|\{p\}P_i\{q\}\rangle$ it follows that (*): $\models \langle E|\{p'\}P_i\{q'\}\rangle$. Furthermore, we have

$$\vdash \langle E|\{p'[z_h/x_h]_{h=1}^k[a_j'/a_j]_{j=1}^\ell\}Q_i\{p'[z_h/x_h]_{h=1}^k[a_j'/a_j]_{j=1}^\ell\}\rangle \tag{5.13}$$

(Since $p'[z_h/x_h]_{h=1}^k[a_j'/a_j]_{j=1}^\ell$ contains no occurrence of any simple or array variable in E (or Q_i), we have here an instance of the invariance rule.)

$$\begin{array}{l}\vdash \langle E|f_0 \Rightarrow \{p_0 \wedge p'[z_h/x_h]_{h=1}^k[a_j'/a_j]_{j=1}^\ell\}\\ \qquad Q_i\\ \qquad \{r^{(i)} \wedge p'[z_h/x_h]_{h=1}^k[a_j'/a_j]_{j=1}^\ell\}\rangle\end{array} \tag{5.14}$$

(This follows from (5.13) and the rule of conjunction, as may be seen as follows. Firstly, from the selection rule, $\vdash \langle E \mid f_0 \Rightarrow \{p_0\}Q_i\{r^{(i)}\}\rangle$. The general form of what remains to be shown is: if $\vdash \langle E \mid \{p_1\}S\{q_1\}\rangle$, then $\vdash \langle E \mid \{p_2\}S\{q_2\} \Rightarrow \{p_1 \wedge p_2\}S\{q_1 \wedge q_2\}\rangle$. Clearly, if $\vdash \langle E \mid \{p_1\}S\{q_1\}\rangle$ then $\vdash \langle E \mid \{p_2\}S\{q_2\} \Rightarrow \{p_1\}S\{q_1\}\rangle$ (by weakening). From this we obtain, essentially by the rule of consequence, that $\vdash \langle E \mid \{p_2\}S\{q_2\} \Rightarrow \{p_1 \wedge p_2\}S\{q_1\}\rangle$. Moreover, we always have (again by the consequence rule) that $\vdash \langle E \mid \{p_2\}S\{q_2\} \Rightarrow \{p_1 \wedge p_2\}S\{q_2\}\rangle$. By the collection rule, $\vdash \langle E \mid \{p_2\}S\{q_2\} \Rightarrow \{p_1 \wedge p_2\}S\{q_1\} \wedge \{p_1 \wedge p_2\}S\{q_2\}\rangle$. The desired result now follows by the conjunction rule.)

As next step we have:

$$\begin{array}{l}\models \langle E \mid \{p'\}P_i\{q'\} \\ \Rightarrow \\ \models \langle E \mid r^{(i)} \wedge p'[z_h/x_h]_{h=1}^{k}[a'_j/a_j]_{j=1}^{\ell} \supset q'\rangle\end{array} \tag{5.15}$$

(This is the content of the auxiliary lemma 5.49, to be proved below.) From (*), (5.14) and (5.15), the fact that all valid assertions are included in $\mathcal{A}x$, and the rule of consequence we obtain

$$\vdash \langle E \mid f_0 \Rightarrow \{p_0 \wedge p'[z_h/x_h]_{h=1}^{k}[a'_j/a_j]_{j=1}^{\ell}\}Q_i\{q'\}\rangle \tag{5.16}$$

Furthermore, by repeated use of the substitution rule I:

$$\begin{array}{l}\vdash \langle E \mid \{p_0 \wedge p'[z_h/x_h]_{h=1}^{k}[a'_j/a_j]_{j=1}^{\ell}\}Q_i\{q'\}\rangle \\ \qquad \Rightarrow \\ \qquad \{(p_0 \wedge p'[z_h/x_h]_{h=1}^{k}[a'_j/a_j]_{j=1}^{\ell})[x_h/z_h]_{h=1}^{k}[a_j/a'_j]_{j=1}^{\ell}\}Q_i\{q'\}\rangle\end{array} \tag{5.17}$$

(In fact, we may apply this rule since, for $h = 1,\ldots,\ell$, $z_h \notin$ *svar*(E,Q_i,q'), and, for $j = 1,\ldots,\ell$, $a'_j \notin$ *avar*(E,Q_i,q').) Now it is easily seen that

(i) $\models \langle E \mid ((x_1=z_1) \wedge \ldots \wedge (x_k=z_k) \wedge (a_1=a'_1) \wedge \ldots$

$\wedge\ (a_\ell=a'_\ell))[x_h/z_h]_{h=1}^{k}[a_j/a'_j]_{j=1}^{\ell}\rangle$, hence, by the definition of p_0,

$\models \langle E \mid p_0[x_h/z_h]_{h=1}^{k}[a_j/a'_j]_{j=1}^{\ell}\rangle$

(ii) $\models \langle E \mid p'[z_h/x_h]_{h=1}^{k}[a'_j/a_j]_{j=1}^{\ell}[x_h/z_h]_{h=1}^{k}[a_j/a'_j]_{j=1}^{\ell} = p'\rangle$

(since, for $h = 1,\dots,k$, $j = 1,\dots,\ell$, $z_h \notin svar(p')$, $a'_j \notin avar(p')$, we can apply exercise 2.3 (and its analog)).

From this, (5.16), (5.17) and the rule of consequence we next obtain that

$$\vdash \langle E \mid f_0 \Rightarrow \{p'\}Q_i\{q'\}\rangle.$$

As a final step, from this and substitution rule II we infer

$$\vdash \langle E \mid f_0 \Rightarrow \{p'[z_h/z'_h]_{h=1}^{k}[a'_j/a''_j]_{j=1}^{\ell}\}Q_i\{q'[z_h/z'_h]_{h=1}^{k}[a'_j/a''_j]_{j=1}^{\ell}\}\rangle \tag{5.18}$$

from which the desired result

$$\vdash \langle E \mid f_0 \Rightarrow \{p\}Q_i\{q\}\rangle$$

follows by the equivalence $\models \langle E \mid p'[z_h/z'_h]_{h=1}^{k}[a'_j/a''_j]_{j=1}^{\ell} = p\rangle$ and similarly for q, and the rule of consequence.
END 5.48.

<u>LEMMA 5.49</u>. Under the above definitions

$$\models \langle E \mid \{p'\}P_i\{q'\}\rangle$$

$$\Rightarrow$$

$$\models \langle E \mid r^{(i)} \wedge p'[z_h/x_h]_{h=1}^{k}[a'_j/a_j]_{j=1}^{\ell} \supset q'\rangle.$$

<u>PROOF</u>. Assume $\models \langle E \mid \{p'\}P_i\{q'\}\rangle$. Choose some γ and let ϕ_i be as usual. We have to show that

$$\forall\sigma\neq\bot,\sigma'[T(p')(\sigma) \wedge \sigma' = \phi_i(\sigma) \wedge \sigma'\neq\bot \Rightarrow T(q')(\sigma')]$$

$$\Rightarrow \tag{5.19}$$

$$\forall\sigma''\neq\bot[T(r^{(i)} \wedge p'[z_h/x_h]_{h=1}^{k}[a_j'/a_j]_{j=1}^{\ell})(\sigma'') \Rightarrow T(q')(\sigma'')]$$

Let σ'' be such that $\sigma''\neq\bot, T(r^{(i)})(\sigma'')$ and $T(p'[z_h/x_h]_{h=1}^{k}[a_j'/a_j]_{j=1}^{\ell})(\sigma'')$. To show that $T(q')(\sigma'')$. By an argument as used in the proof of lemma 5.46, we have that $T(r^{(i)})(\sigma'') = (\sigma''\neq\bot) \wedge \exists\bar{\sigma}[T(p_0)(\bar{\sigma}) \wedge \sigma'' = \phi_i(\bar{\sigma})]$, or, by the definition of p_0, that $T(r^{(i)})(\sigma'') = (\sigma''\neq\bot) \wedge$ $\exists\bar{\sigma}[\bigwedge_{h=1}^{k} (\bar{\sigma}(x_h) = \bar{\sigma}(z_h)) \wedge \bigwedge_{j=1}^{\ell} \bigwedge_{\alpha\in V_0} (\bar{\sigma}(a_j,\alpha) = \bar{\sigma}(a_j',\alpha)) \wedge (\sigma'' = \phi_i(\bar{\sigma}))]$. From the antecedent of the implication (5.19), with $\bar{\sigma}$ and σ'' replacing σ and σ', respectively, it follows that, in order to establish our desired result (i.e. that $T(q')(\sigma'')$), all we have to show is that $T(p')(\bar{\sigma})$ holds. This may be seen as follows. We know that $T(p'[z_h/x_h]_{h=1}^{k}[a_j'/a_j]_{j=1}^{\ell})(\sigma'')$ holds. Now

$$T(p'[z_h/x_h]_{h=1}^{k}[a_j'/a_j]_{j=1}^{\ell})(\sigma'') = \text{(cf. the proof of lemma 5.45a)}$$

$$T(p'[z_h/x_h]_{h=1}^{k}[a_j'/a_j]_{j=1}^{\ell})(\bar{\sigma}) = \text{(properties of substitution)}$$

$$T(p')(\bar{\sigma}\{\bar{\sigma}(z_h)/x_h\}_{h=1}^{k}\{\bar{\sigma}(a_j',\alpha)/\langle a_j,\alpha\rangle\}_{j=1,\alpha\in V_0}^{\ell})$$

$$= \text{(assumption on } \bar{\sigma})$$

$$T(p')(\bar{\sigma}\{\bar{\sigma}(x_h)/x_h\}_{h=1}^{k}\{\bar{\sigma}(a_j,\alpha\rangle/\langle a_j,\alpha\rangle\}_{j=1,\alpha\in V_0}^{\ell}) =$$

$$T(p')(\bar{\sigma})$$

and we conclude that $T(p')(\bar{\sigma})$ also holds.

END 5.49.

We now continue with the proof of theorem 5.47. By the definition of $r^{(i)}$ we have, for $i = 1,\dots,n$, $\models \langle E|\{p_0\}P_i\{r^{(i)}\}\rangle$. By *fpp*, this implies that

$$\models \langle E \,|\, \{p_0\}S_i\{r^{(i)}\}\rangle$$

Thus, by lemma 5.48, we infer that, for i = 1,...,n,

$$\vdash \langle E \,|\, \{p_0\}Q_1\{r^{(1)}\} \wedge \ldots \wedge \{p_0\}Q_n\{r^{(n)}\} \Rightarrow \{p_0\}S_i[Q_j/P_j]_{j=1}^{n}\{r^{(i)}\}\rangle$$

By the collection rule we obtain from this

$$\vdash \langle E \,|\, \{p_0\}Q_1\{r^{(1)}\} \wedge \ldots \wedge \{p_0\}Q_n\{r^{(n)}\} \Rightarrow \{p_0\}S_1[Q_j/P_j]_{j=1}^{n}\{r^{(1)}\} \wedge \ldots \wedge \{p_0\}S_n[Q_j/P_j]_{j=1}^{n}\{r^{(n)}\}\rangle$$

By the induction rule this implies that

$$\vdash \langle E \,|\, \{p_0\}P_1\{r^{(1)}\} \wedge \ldots \wedge \{p_0\}P_n\{r^{(n)}\}\rangle \tag{5.20}$$

Now assume that, for some p, q, and closed $\langle E|S\rangle$:

$$\models \langle E \,|\, \{p\}S\{q\}\rangle$$

By lemma 5.48 we obtain from this

$$\vdash \langle E \,|\, \{p_0\}Q_1\{r^{(1)}\} \wedge \ldots \wedge \{p_0\}Q_n\{r^{(n)}\} \Rightarrow \{p\}S[Q_j/P_j]_{j=1}^{n}\{q\}\rangle$$

By the instantiation rule we infer

$$\vdash \langle E \,|\, \{p_0\}P_1\{r^{(1)}\} \wedge \ldots \wedge \{p_0\}P_n\{r^{(n)}\} \Rightarrow \{p\}S\{q\}\rangle \tag{5.21}$$

Finally, from (5.20) and (5.21) we obtain

$$\vdash \langle E \,|\, \{p\}S\{q\}\rangle$$

as was to be shown.

END 5.47.

Exercises

5.1. Prove that each monotonic function on a finite domain is continuous.

5.2. Let C be a complete lattice, and let $x \sqcap y$ be short for $\sqcap\{x,y\}$. Let $f: C \to_m C$. Prove that, for all y, if

(i) for all x, $f(x \sqcap y) \sqsubseteq f(x) \sqcap y$, then

(ii) $\mu f \sqsubseteq y$.

5.3. Prove the following least-fixed properties:

a. If $f,g,h \in [C \to C]$, $f \circ g = g \circ f$, $f \circ h = h \circ f$, and $g(\bot) \sqsubseteq h(\bot)$, then $g(\mu f) \sqsubseteq h(\mu f)$

b. If $f,g \in [C \to C]$ and $f \circ g = f \circ g \circ f$, then $f(\mu g) = \mu[f \circ g]$

c. If $f,f_1,f_2 \in [C \to C]$, $f(\bot) = \bot$, $f \circ f_1 = f_2 \circ f$, then $f(\mu f_1) = \mu f_2$

d. If $f,g \in [C \to C]$ and $f \circ g = g \circ f$, then f and g have a least *common* fixed point x, i.e. x satisfies

(i) $f(x) = g(x) = x$

(ii) For all $y \in C$, if $f(y) = g(y) = y$, then $x \sqsubseteq y$

Is x necessarily equal to μf or μg?

5.4. Let C_i, $i = 1,\dots,n$, be complete lattices. Let $f_i: C_1 \times \dots \times C_n \to_m C_i$, $i = 1,\dots,n$. Let

(i) $g \overset{\text{df.}}{=} \lambda x_1 \cdot \dots \cdot \lambda x_{n-1} \cdot \mu[\lambda x_n \cdot f_n(x_1,\dots,x_n)]$

(ii) $\bar{f}_i \overset{\text{df.}}{=} \lambda x_1 \cdot \dots \cdot \lambda x_{n-1} \cdot f_i(x_1,\dots,x_{n-1},g(x_1,\dots,x_{n-1}))$, $i = 1,\dots,n-1$

Prove that

$\mu[f_1,\dots,f_n] = \langle \mu[\bar{f}_1,\dots,\bar{f}_{n-1}], g(\mu[\bar{f}_1,\dots,\bar{f}_{n-1}]) \rangle$.

5.5. Let $f \in [C \times D \to C]$, $g \in [C \times D \to D]$.

Prove that $\mu[f,g] = \bigsqcup_{k=0}^{\infty} \langle x^k, y^k \rangle$, where

$x^0 = \bot_C$, $\qquad y^0 = \bot_D$,

$x^{k+1} = f(x^k, y^{k+1})$, $k = 0,1,\dots$, $\qquad y^{k+1} = \mu[\lambda y \cdot g(x^k, y)]$, $k = 0,1,\dots$

5.6.

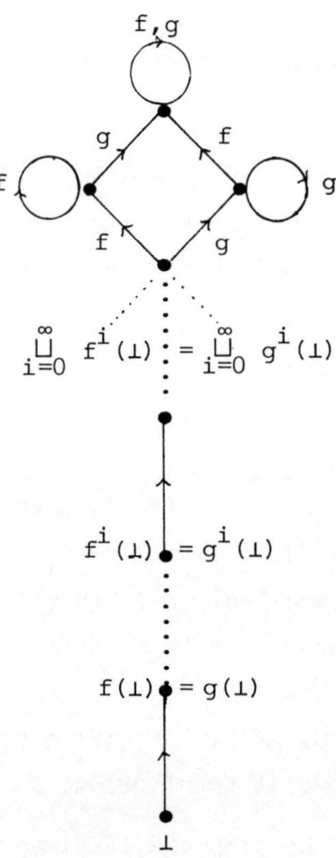

Consider the partially ordered set with corresponding definitions of f and g as suggested by the above picture. Verify that f and g are monotonic functions such that $f(\bot) = g(\bot)$ and $f \circ g = g \circ f$, but $\mu f \neq \mu g$.

5.7. Let $R \equiv \langle E|S\rangle$ be a closed program. The *recursion depth rd* of a finite computation sequence $\mathit{Comp}(\langle E|S\rangle)(\sigma)$ (with $\sigma \neq \bot$ and $E \equiv \langle P_i \Leftarrow S_i\rangle_{i=1}^{n}$) is defined informally as the depth of the tree of body replacement steps executed in the computation sequence. Formally, the definition is given by

(i) $rd(\mathit{Comp}(\langle E|v:=t\rangle)(\sigma)) = 0$

(ii) $rd(\mathit{Comp}(\langle E|S';S''\rangle)(\sigma)) =$

$\max(rd(\mathit{Comp}\ \langle E|S'\rangle)(\sigma)),\ rd(\mathit{Comp}(\langle E|S''\rangle)(\mathcal{O}(\langle E|S'\rangle)(\sigma))))$

(iii) $rd(\mathit{Comp}(<E|\underline{if}\ b\ \underline{then}\ S'\ \underline{else}\ S''\ \underline{fi}>)(\sigma)) =$

$\underline{if}\ \mathcal{W}(b)(\sigma)\ \underline{then}\ rd(\mathit{Comp}(<E|S'>)(\sigma))$

$\underline{else}\ rd(\mathit{Comp}(<E|S''>)(\sigma))\ \underline{fi}$

(iv) $rd(\mathit{Comp}(<E|P_j>)(\sigma)) = rd(\mathit{Comp}(<E|S_j>)(\sigma)) + 1$

Let γ, ϕ_i, $i = 1,\ldots,n$, ϕ_i^k, $i = 1,\ldots,n$, $k = 0,1,\ldots$ be as usual.

Prove

a. For all S and $k \geq 0$, $\mathcal{N}(S)(\gamma\{\phi_i^k/P_i\}_{i=1}^n)(\sigma) =$

$$\begin{cases} \sigma', & \text{if } \mathcal{O}(<E|S>)(\sigma) = \sigma' \text{ and } rd(\mathit{Comp}(<E|S>)(\sigma)) < k \\ \bot, & \text{otherwise} \end{cases}$$

b. $\phi_i = \mathcal{O}(<E|S_i>)$, $i = 1,\ldots,n$

c. For all γ, $\mathcal{M}(R)(\gamma) = \mathcal{O}(R)$.

5.8. Prove the equivalence of the following two programs mentioned in section 5.1:

```
begin procedure P1;S1;
      procedure P2;S2;
      P1
end
```

and

```
begin procedure P1;
      begin procedure P2;S2;
            S1
      end;
      P1
end
```

(Hint: this needs introduction of a syntax allowing nested declarations, and theorem 5.14.)

5.9. Prove $\models <P \Leftarrow \underline{if}\ b\ \underline{then}\ S;P\ \underline{else}\ D\ \underline{fi}\ |\ \{\underline{true}\}P\{\neg b\}>$.

5.10. Prove directly (i.e. without using operational semantics) that, for closed R and any γ_1, γ_2,

$$M(R)(\gamma_1) = M(R)(\gamma_2).$$

5.11. Prove that, if S_1 and S_2 are without occurrences of P_1 or P_2, then

$\models \langle P_1 \Leftarrow S[P_1/P, S_1/Q], P_2 \Leftarrow S[P_2/P, S_2/Q] \mid S_1 \sqsubseteq S_2 \Rightarrow P_1 \sqsubseteq P_2\rangle$.

5.12. Prove that, if S_1 has no occurrences of P_1 or P_2, then

$\models \langle P_1 \Leftarrow S_1;S_2, P_2 \Leftarrow S_2[S_1;P_2/P_1] \mid P_1 = S_1;P_2\rangle$.

5.13. Show by means of an example that the restriction in theorem 5.35 that f_0 be without occurrences of any of the P_i, $i = 1,\dots,n$, is necessary.

5.14. Prove that

$\models \langle P_1 \Leftarrow \underline{\text{if}}\ b_1\ \underline{\text{then}}\ S_1;P_1\ \underline{\text{else}}\ D\ \underline{\text{fi}},$
$\quad P_2 \Leftarrow \underline{\text{if}}\ b_2\ \underline{\text{then}}\ S_2;P_1;P_2\ \underline{\text{else}}\ D\ \underline{\text{fi}},$
$\quad P_3 \Leftarrow \underline{\text{if}}\ b_1\ \underline{\text{then}}\ S_1;P_3\ \underline{\text{else}}$
$\quad\quad \underline{\text{if}}\ b_2\ \underline{\text{then}}\ S_2;P_3\ \underline{\text{else}}\ D\ \underline{\text{fi}}\ \underline{\text{fi}} \mid P_1;P_2 = P_3\rangle$.

5.15. a. Prove

$$\frac{\langle E \mid S_1 \sqsubseteq S_2\rangle}{\langle E \mid S_1[S/P] \sqsubseteq S_2[S/P]\rangle}$$

b. Disprove

$\models \langle E \mid S_1 \sqsubseteq S_2 \Rightarrow S_1[S/P] \sqsubseteq S_2[S/P]\rangle$.

5.16. Prove that the inference $\dfrac{\langle E \mid f\rangle}{\langle E,E' \mid f\rangle}$ is sound with respect to the validity definition of section 5.4, but unsound with respect to the validity definition of section 5.5.

5.17. Prove

$\models \langle E \mid \{p\}S\{q\} \Rightarrow \{p[s/x][a'/a]\}S\{q[s/x][a'/a]\}\rangle$,

provided that $x \notin \mathit{svar}(E,S)$ $a \notin \mathit{avar}(E,S)$, $\mathit{intv}(s) \cap \mathit{intv}(E,S) = \emptyset$.

5.18. Let the property of a statement S being *regular in a procedure variable* P be defined inductively as follows:

(i) If S contains no occurrences of P, then S is regular in P

(ii) P is regular in P

(iii) If S_1 contains no occurrences of P and S_2 is regular in P, then $S_1;S_2$ is regular in P

(iv) If S_1 and S_2 are regular in P, then <u>if</u> b <u>then</u> S_1 <u>else</u> S_2 <u>fi</u> is regular in P.

Moreover, we call a statement *regular* if it is regular in all procedure variables occurring in it.

Prove

a. Let $n \geq 1$, and let $S_1,\ldots,S_n$, S be regular statements. For each i, $1 \leq i \leq n$, there exist $m \geq n$, regular $S_{n+1},\ldots,S_m$, and k, $1 \leq k \leq m$, such that $\models\ \langle\langle P_j \Leftarrow S_j\rangle_{j=1}^{m} | P_i;S = P_k\rangle$.

(Hint: cf. example 4 after theorem 5.34).

b. Let $n \geq 1$, and let $S_1,\ldots,S_n$ be regular statements. For each S there exist $m \geq n$, regular $S_{n+1},\ldots,S_m$, and k, $1 \leq k \leq m$, such that $\models \langle\langle P_j \Leftarrow S_j\rangle_{j=1}^{m} | S = P_k\rangle$.

5.19. Let $Stat_3$ ($Stat_5$) be the class of statements as introduced in chapter 3 (chapter 5). Prove that, for each $S \in Stat_3$, there exist $n \geq 1$, regular $S_1,\ldots,S_n \in Stat_5$, and j, $1 \leq j \leq n$, such that $\langle\langle P_i \Leftarrow S_i\rangle_{i=1}^{n} | S = P_j\rangle$.

5.20. Let $R \equiv \langle\langle P_i \Leftarrow S_i\rangle_{i=1}^{n} | S\rangle$. We define the substitution $R[\bar{S}/P]$ as follows: $\langle\langle P_i \Leftarrow S_i\rangle_{i=1}^{n} | S\rangle[\bar{S}/P]$

$\equiv \langle\langle P_i \Leftarrow S_i\rangle_{i=1}^{n} | S\rangle$, if $P \in \{P_1,\ldots,P_n\}$

$\equiv \langle\langle P_i \Leftarrow S_i[\bar{S}/P]\rangle_{i=1}^{n} | S[\bar{S}/P]\rangle$, if $P \notin \{P_1,\ldots,P_n\}$ and none of the P_i, $i = 1,\ldots,n$, occurs in $\bar{S}$

$\equiv \langle\langle P_i' \Leftarrow S_i[P_j'/P_j]_{j=1}^{n}[\bar{S}/P]\rangle_{i=1}^{n} | S[P_j'/P_j]_{j=1}^{n}[\bar{S}/P]\rangle$, if $P \notin \{P_1,\ldots,P_n\}$ and some of the P_i, $i = 1,\ldots,n$, occur in $\bar{S}$, where $P'_1,\ldots,P'_n$ are (the first) procedure variables different from $P_1,\ldots,P_n$, and not occurring in S_i, $i = 1,\ldots,n$, S, or $\bar{S}$.

Investigate whether the usual properties of substitution are preserved by this definition. For example, is $\mathcal{M}(R[\bar{S}/P])(\gamma) = \mathcal{M}(R)(\gamma\{\mathcal{M}(\bar{S})(\gamma)/P\}$, etc.

5.21. Let $E \equiv P \Leftarrow$ <u>if</u> b <u>then</u> $\bar{S}$;P <u>else</u> D <u>fi</u>, where P does not occur in $\bar{S}$. Let S be any statement. Assume that, for each p and q, the following two facts are equivalent

(i) $\models \langle E|\{p\}S\{q\}\rangle$

(ii) There exists r such that

$\models \langle E|(p\supset r) \wedge \{r\wedge b\}S\{r\} \wedge (r\wedge\neg b \supset q)\rangle$

Prove that

$\models \langle E|P = S\rangle$.

5.22. Let A_1,A_2,A_3 be statements without occurrences of P, and let $E \equiv P \Leftarrow$ <u>if</u> b <u>then</u> A_1;P;A_2 <u>else</u> A_3 <u>fi</u>. Prove that, for all p,q, $\models \langle E|\{p\}P\{q\}\rangle$ iff there exist p_i,q_i, $i = 0,1,\ldots$, such that, for $i = 0,1,\ldots$,

$\models \langle E|\{p_i\wedge b\}A_1\{p_{i+1}\} \wedge \{q_{i+1}\}A_2\{q_i\} \wedge$
$\{p_i\wedge\neg b\}A_3\{q_i\} \wedge (p\supset p_0) \wedge (q_0\supset q)\rangle$

(Hint: in order to prove "only if", take (using the proposition of section 5.5) $p_i = p \leftarrow \langle E|(b;A_1)^i\rangle$, $i = 0,1,\ldots$

$q_i = \langle E|A_2^i\rangle \rightarrow q$

where, for each A, $(b;A)^0 \equiv D$

$(b;A)^{i+1} \equiv$ <u>if</u> b <u>then</u> A; $(b;A)^i$ <u>else</u> D <u>fi</u>, $i = 0,1,\ldots$)

5.23. Prove

$\vdash \langle P \Leftarrow$ <u>if</u> x>0 <u>then</u> x:=x-1;P;y:=y+1;P;x:=x+1 <u>else</u> D <u>fi</u>|
$\{(x=n) \wedge (y=m)\}P\{(x=n) \wedge (y=m+2^n-1)\}\rangle$.

5.24. Prove that the rule of instantiation (rule 11) is not necessary for the completeness proof, i.e. that for each formal proof of a formula <E|{p}S{q}> there exists another formal proof of the same formula which does not use the rule of instantiation.

5.25. Design a (sound and) complete proof system for formulae <E|{p}S{q}>, where (<E|S> is closed and) all procedure bodies in E are regular.

Chapter 6

BLOCKS

6.1. Introduction

A *block* is a construct of the form begin new x;S end, introducing the *local* simple variable x by means of the *simple variable declaration* new x. Local variables of statements are like bound variables of assertions as introduced in chapter 2. In particular, blocks satisfy the property that begin new x;S end is equivalent to begin new y;S[y/x] end, provided that y does not occur free in S: systematic replacement of the local x by some fresh y preserves the meaning of the block. As a consequence, in a program containing nested blocks such as begin new x;x:=0; begin new x;x:=1 end; x:=x+1 end, the local x of the inner block has nothing to do with the x of the outer block; thus, after the assignment x:=x+1, x has the value 1 (and not 2).

In this chapter we define the semantics of statements involving blocks, discuss the correctness of such statements, and present a sound and complete proof system for correctness formulae {p}S{q}.

In order not to distract from the main issues relating to locality, we omit for the moment from our considerations programs involving iteration or recursion. In chapter 9 we shall encounter a synthesis of the ideas from chapter 5 about recursion with those developed below to deal with blocks.

It is not easy to define the semantics of a block in a satisfactory way, i.e. such that

a. its intuitive meaning, as prescribed e.g. in the ALGOL 60 report, is captured exactly;

b. the associated notion of correctness allows both a smooth mathematical theory and a proof system which can be shown to be sound and complete without undue effort.

As a first attempt at defining M(begin new x;S end)(σ), we might try to follow the definition of $T(\exists x[p])(\sigma)$, in that we put (*): $M(\underline{\text{begin}}\ \underline{\text{new}}\ x;S\ \underline{\text{end}})(\sigma) = \bigcup_{\alpha \in V_0} M(S)(\sigma\{\alpha/x\})$. That is, for each state σ we deliver as outcome a set of states, consisting of all possible outcomes of executing S for arbitrary initial values of x. The defects of this definition are twofold. First of all it does not deal satisfactorily with the nested block case just mentioned (though this could be remedied by some mechanism of choosing a *fresh* simple variable upon entry of a block). Secondly (and more importantly), it introduces an element of *nondeterminacy* into our language which we want to avoid, if only because we do not know of a treatment of this satisfying requirement b in a situation where blocks are combined with recursion. (The nondeterminacy we deal with in chapter 7 is very different, since this only concerns *programmer-prescribed* non-determinacy. Technically, the nondeterminacy of (*) is unbounded, whereas that of chapter 7 is bounded.) We therefore reject definition (*), and resort to another technique, viz. that of introducing *addresses* (e,...) together with (i) a new class of mappings, called *environments* (ε,...), from simple variables to addresses, and (ii) a change in the definition of states: a state now has the set of addresses instead of that of simple variables as its domain. (For simplicity's sake, we temporarily forget about subscripted variables.) Thus, instead of

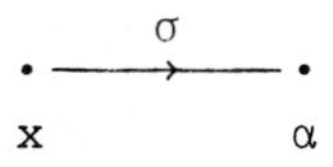

$$\underset{x}{\bullet} \xrightarrow{\ \sigma\ } \underset{\alpha}{\bullet}$$

we introduce

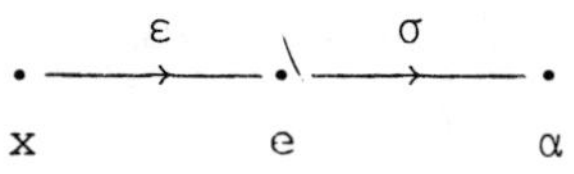

$$\underset{x}{\bullet} \xrightarrow{\ \varepsilon\ } \underset{e}{\bullet} \xrightarrow{\ \sigma\ } \underset{\alpha}{\bullet}$$

Furthermore, environments are *partial* functions, whereas states are total. Each address is associated with an integer, but not all simple variables are associated with addresses. The effect of a block begin new x;S end is now that the current environment is *extended*. A fresh variable y is chosen and linked to a fresh address e, and, through the technique of substituting y for x in S, we obtain the effect that the local x of the block begin new x;S end is addressed through e, thus achieving that this x has nothing to do with some simple variable x occurring in surrounding blocks.

However, we still have not solved our problem. In the choice of <y,e> indicated above, we have to be specific which y,e to choose (otherwise, we are back at nondeterminacy). Now the choice of y,e to be the *first* simple variable and *first* address available seems plausible, but this has undesirable consequences. For example - anticipating that the validity of a correctness formula is defined as a natural extension of that of previous chapters - we obtain

$$\models \{\underline{\text{true}}\}\ \underline{\text{begin}}\ \underline{\text{new}}\ x;x:=0\ \underline{\text{end}};\ \underline{\text{begin}}\ \underline{\text{new}}\ z;y:=z\ \underline{\text{end}}\ \{y=0\} \qquad (6.1)$$

Upon entry of the first block, we find the first free address and store 0 in it. Upon exit from this block, the address is free again; hence, it is chosen once more as the first free address upon entry of the second block, and 0 is then assigned to y. (In fact, (6.1) might well be true in many implementations of ALGOL-like languages.) Apart from the fact that (6.1) indicates an overspecification in our semantics (what we really want after execution of the two blocks is that y=0 *may* be true, but does not *have* to be true), it also leads to an *incomplete* proof theory. There is no intermediate assertion p such that $\models$ {true} begin new x;x:=0 end {p} and $\models$ {p} begin new z;y:=z end {y=0}, and the familiar arguments of the preceding chapters break down.

There are at least two ways out of the new problem. The first is to make sure that phenomenon (6.1) cannot occur, by arranging the definitions in such a way that an address is never chosen twice as first free address. The second solution consists in *restricting* the class of statements considered by requiring that they contain only blocks in which all local simple variables are initialized in the program text (z is not initialized in this sense in <u>begin</u> <u>new</u> z;y:=z <u>end</u>). Though from a purely semantic point of view the first solution is to be preferred, we have decided to adopt the second one. Our reasons for this are twofold:

a. The mathematical theory of correctness for programs with only initialized local simple variables is substantially simpler than a theory which does not impose this requirement.
b. Writing programs which contain uninitialized local variables is bad programming style, and their correctness is probably not a very interesting topic anyway.

(The reader who wants to pursue the first solution is referred to exercises 6.11, 6.12, where some hints are provided on how to develop a theory incorporating the idea of "no address ever used twice as first free address".)

The chapter is organized in the usual way. Section 6.2 brings the semantic definitions, in particular introducing environments. Next the initialization requirement is made precise, and various consequences of this requirement for the mathematical properties of our constructs are derived. Section 6.3 introduces the definition of correctness, and presents a proof system for which soundness is proved in that section and completeness in the next. Once the foundations laid in section 6.2 are understood, the results of 6.3 and 6.4 are not too difficult extensions of the ideas of chapters 2 and 4. In particular, weakest preconditions and strongest postconditions reappear with rather elegant formulae dealing with blocks. Some surprises remain, however. For example, for the strongest postconditions we shall observe a difference between the *syntactic* characterization of that notion and its *semantic* definition.

6.2. Semantics

We begin with the new syntax:

DEFINITION 6.1 (statements with blocks).
The class of statements *Stat*, with typical elements S,..., is defined by

$$S ::= v:=s \mid S_1;S_2 \mid \underline{\text{if}}\ b\ \underline{\text{then}}\ S_1\ \underline{\text{else}}\ S_2\ \underline{\text{fi}} \mid \underline{\text{begin}}\ \underline{\text{new}}\ x;S\ \underline{\text{end}}$$

END 6.1.

Remarks

1. $x \in Svar$, $v \in Ivar$, $s \in Iexp$, $b \in Bexp$ are as usual.
2. For simplicity's sake, we do not introduce array declarations (of the form begin new a;S end).
3. As we saw above, the prefix new x binds occurrences of x in begin new x;S end in the same way as $\exists x$ binds occurrences of x in $\exists x[p]$. *svar*(S) now denotes the class of all *free* simple variables of S; thus, *svar*(begin new x;S end) = *svar*(S)\{x}. *avar*(S) and *intv*(S) are defined as before (cf. definition 4.3). For example, *intv*(begin new x; $x:=a_1[y+a_2[z]]$ end) = $\{y,z\} \cup \{\langle a_i,\alpha\rangle \mid i = 1,2, \alpha \in V_0\}$.
4. Substitution S[v/x] is defined analogously to p[s/x]. We give only the definition for S a block:
   begin new y;S end [v/x]
   ≡ begin new y;S end, if x ≡ y
   ≡ begin new y;S[v/x] end, if x ≢ y and y ∉ *svar*(v)
   ≡ begin new y';S[y'/y][v/x] end, if x ≢ y and y ∈ *svar*(v),
   where y' is the first simple variable ∉ *svar*(x,S,v).

Next, we introduce the syntactic notion of *congruence* between statements, a concept which will play a part in certain of the technical manipulations below. Roughly, two statements are congruent if they differ at most in their bound simple variables. The precise definition is given in

DEFINITION 6.2 (congruence).
Two statements S,S' may be congruent, denoted by $S \cong S'$, and defined by

a. $v:=s \cong v:=s$

b. If $S[y/x] \cong S'$ and $y \notin svar(S)$, then
   begin **new** x;S **end** $\cong$ **begin** **new** y;S' **end**

c. If $S_1 \cong S_1'$, $S_2 \cong S_2'$, then $S_1;S_2 \cong S_1';S_2'$, **if** b **then** S_1 **else** S_2 **fi** $\cong$ **if** b **then** S_1' **else** S_2' **fi**, and **begin** **new** x;S_1 **end** $\cong$ **begin** **new** x;S_1' **end**

END 6.2.

Remarks

1. Clearly, if $S \cong S'$ then $intv(S) = intv(S')$.
2. We omit the proofs of
   a. " $\cong$ " is an equivalence relation
   b. $S[v/x][w/y] \cong S[w/y][v[w/y]/x]$, provided that $x \not\equiv y$ and $x \notin svar(w)$. In particular, $S[z/x][u/y] \cong S[u/y][z/x]$, provided that $x \not\equiv y$, $x \not\equiv u$, $y \not\equiv z$
   c. $S[y/x][v/y] \cong S[v/x]$, provided that $y \notin svar(S)$
   d. $S \cong S[v/x]$, provided that $x \notin svar(S)$
   e. If $S \cong S'$, then $S[v/x] \cong S'[v/x]$.

We now proceed with the development of the semantic framework. The main new tool consists in the introduction of a class of *addresses* Addr, with typical elements e,..., together with (restricting ourselves for the moment to simple variables, the general case following soon):

- A class of funtions (satisfying certain restrictions to be specified below) Env, with typical elements ε,..., from Svar to Addr. Elements of Env are called environments.
- A change in the definition of Σ: it now consists of the functions

from $Addr_0$ to V_0 (instead of *Svar* to V_0 as was the case before), united with the undefined state $\perp$.

Thus, the picture

$$\begin{array}{ccc} & \Sigma_0 & \\ & \in & \\ & \sigma & \\ \bullet & \longrightarrow & \bullet \\ x & & \alpha \\ \in & & \in \\ Svar & & V_0 \end{array}$$

is replaced by

$$\begin{array}{ccccc} & Env & & \Sigma_0 & \\ & \in & & \in & \\ & \varepsilon & & \sigma & \\ \bullet & \longrightarrow & \bullet & \longrightarrow & \bullet \\ x & & e & & \alpha \\ \in & & \in & & \in \\ Svar & & Addr_0 & & V_0 \end{array}$$

More specifically, *Addr* is a discrete cpo, given as $Addr_0 \cup \{\perp_A\}$, where $Addr_0$ is some infinite well-ordered set and $\perp_A$ is not an element of $Addr_0$, together with the usual definition: $e_1 \sqsubseteq e_2$ iff $e_1 = \perp_A$ or $e_1 = e_2$. Environments are employed in our treatment of simple variable declarations in the following way. First, for each v,s,b,S, the functions L,R,W,M (which from now on have ε as additional argument) will always deliver the $\perp$-element of the appropriate domain in case ε is not defined (i.e. applying ε yields $\perp_A$) for some element of *intv*(v),...,*intv*(S), respectively. Secondly, the effect of the declaration <u>new</u> x in the block <u>begin</u> <u>new</u> x;S <u>end</u> is to extend the current environment with the first available fresh pair <y,e>, and to replace evaluation of S in the current environment by that of S[y/x] in the extended environment. In this way, we achieve that ε keeps a trace in its domain of all simple variables which have been declared locally, whereas global variables either are already included in the domain of ε (in which case the semantic definitions run parallel to those of chapters 2, 4), or, if not, result in the delivery of the appropriate

$\perp$-element. Some examples may help. Let us use the notation $\varepsilon = \langle x_1,e_1\rangle,\ldots,\langle x_n,e_n\rangle$ for the environment which yields, for $i=1,\ldots,n$, $e_i \in \mathit{Addr}_0$ as the result of $\varepsilon(x_i)$, and $\perp_A$ for all other simple variables. Moreover, the variant notation $\sigma\{\alpha/x\}$ of the preceding chapters is now replaced by $\sigma\{\alpha/e\}$ (which satisfies the obvious analogs of lemma 2.5).

1. $R(x+y)(\langle x,e_1\rangle,\langle y,e_2\rangle)(\sigma) = \sigma(e_1)+\sigma(e_2)$. Compare the picture

$$x \xrightarrow{\ \varepsilon\ } e_1 \xrightarrow{\ \sigma\ } \sigma(e_1)$$

$$y \xrightarrow{\ \varepsilon\ } e_2 \xrightarrow{\ \sigma\ } \sigma(e_2)$$

   $R(x+y)(\langle x,e\rangle)(\sigma) = \perp_V$ (ε is undefined on y)

2. $M(x{:=}0;$ <u>begin</u> <u>new</u> $x;x{:=}1;y{:=}x$ <u>end</u>$)(\langle y,e\rangle)(\varepsilon)(\sigma) = \perp$

   (ε is undefined on the global x)

   $M(x{:=}0;$ <u>begin</u> <u>new</u> $x;x{:=}1;y{:=}x$ <u>end</u>$)(\langle x,e\rangle,\langle y,\bar{e}\rangle)(\sigma) =$

   $M($<u>begin</u> <u>new</u> $x;x{:=}1;y{:=}x$ <u>end</u>$)(\langle x,e\rangle,\langle y,\bar{e}\rangle)(\sigma\{0/e\}) =$

   $M(z{:=}1;y{:=}z)(\langle x,e\rangle,\langle y,\bar{e}\rangle,\langle z,\bar{\bar{e}}\rangle)(\sigma\{0/e\})$

   (where z is the first simple variable $\not\equiv x,y$,

   $\bar{\bar{e}}$ the first address $\neq e,\bar{e}$) =

   $M(y{:=}z)(\langle x,e\rangle,\langle y,\bar{e}\rangle,\langle z,\bar{\bar{e}}\rangle)(\sigma\{0/e\}\{1/\bar{\bar{e}}\}) =$

   $\sigma\{0/e\}\{1/\bar{\bar{e}}\}\{1/\bar{e}\}$.

<u>DEFINITION 6.3</u> (environments).

(For easier reference, we include in this definition some of the previously given ones, even if they remain unchanged.)

a. Let $V = V_0 \cup \{\perp_V\}$, $W = W_0 \cup \{\perp_W\}$, $\mathit{Addr} = \mathit{Addr}_0 \cup \{\perp_A\}$ be discrete cpo's, with typical elements α,β,e. Addr_0 is assumed to be an infinite, well-ordered set.

b. Let $\Sigma = \Sigma_0 \cup \{\perp\}$, where $\Sigma_0 = \mathit{Addr}_0 \to V_0$

c. Let $\mathit{Intv} = \mathit{Svar} \cup (\mathit{Avar} \times V_0)$, with typical elements $\xi,\ldots$

   Let Env be the class of those functions $\varepsilon\colon \mathit{Intv} \to \mathit{Addr}$ which satisfy restrictions (i) to (iii) below. Let $\mathrm{dom}(\varepsilon) = \{\xi \mid \varepsilon(\xi) \neq \perp_A\}$, range($\varepsilon$) = {e | e = $\varepsilon(\xi)$ for some $\xi \in$ dom(ε)}

(i) For all ξ_1, ξ_2, if $\varepsilon(\xi_1) = \varepsilon(\xi_2)$ and $\varepsilon(\xi_1) \neq \perp_A$, then $\xi_1 = \xi_2$. (I.e. ε is 1-1 on its domain.)

(ii) For all a $\in$ *Avar*, $\varepsilon(a,\alpha) \neq \perp_A$ for some $\alpha \in V_0 \Longleftrightarrow \varepsilon(a,\alpha) \neq \perp_A$ for all $\alpha \in V_0$

(iii) *Svar*\dom(ε) is infinite, $Addr_0$\range(ε) is infinite.

END 6.3.

Remarks

1. Our system of definitions is organized in such a way that we never need to evaluate $\varepsilon(a,\perp_V)$; hence, only V_0 features in the definition of *Intv*.
2. (restrictions on ε)
   (i) The requirement that ε be 1-1 corresponds to the customary stack implementation of simple variable declarations, where different variables correspond to different addresses. Technically, the requirement is used in the proof of lemma 6.9 which generalizes lemma 2.16c and similar results in chapter 4
   (ii) $\varepsilon(a,\alpha) \neq \perp_A$ for some $\alpha \in V_0 \Longleftrightarrow \varepsilon(a,\alpha) \neq \perp_A$ for all $\alpha \in V_0$. This is a consequence of "no array bounds"
   (iii) As the effect of a simple variable declaration, we extend the environment with a new pair <y,e>, such that y $\notin$ dom(ε) and (to preserve ε as a 1-1 function) e $\notin$ range(ε). (Here we adopt the convention that e $\notin$ range(ε) is short for e $\in Addr_0$\range(ε) and, therefore, implies that e $\neq \perp_A$.) Since we have to be sure that such a pair always exists, we require *Svar*\dom(ε) and $Addr_0$\range(ε) to be infinite.

We now first give the definitions of *L*, *R* and *W*, which are easy variations on those of chapter 4.

<u>DEFINITION 6.4</u> (semantics of *Ivar*, *Iexp* and *Bexp*).

a. The function *L*: *Ivar* $\rightarrow$ (*Env* $\rightarrow$ ($\Sigma \rightarrow_s$ *Addr*)) is defined by:

$L(v)(\varepsilon)(\sigma) = \bot_A$ if $intv(v) \not\subseteq dom(\varepsilon)$ or $\sigma = \bot$. Otherwise

(i) $L(x)(\varepsilon)(\sigma) = \varepsilon(x)$

(ii) $L(a[s])(\varepsilon)(\sigma) = \varepsilon(a, R(s)(\varepsilon)(\sigma))$

b. The function R: *Iexp* $\to$ (*Env* $\to (\Sigma \to_s V)$) is defined by:

$R(s)(\varepsilon)(\sigma) = \bot_V$ if $intv(s) \not\subseteq dom(\varepsilon)$ or $\sigma = \bot$. Otherwise

(i) $R(v)(\varepsilon)(\sigma) = \sigma(L(v)(\varepsilon)(\sigma))$

(ii) $R(m)(\varepsilon)(\sigma) = \alpha$, where α is the integer denoted by the integer constant m

(iii) $R(s_1+s_2)(\varepsilon)(\sigma) = R(s_1)(\varepsilon)(\sigma) + R(s_2)(\varepsilon)(\sigma)$

(iv) $R(\underline{\text{if}}\ b\ \underline{\text{then}}\ s_1\ \underline{\text{else}}\ s_2\ \underline{\text{fi}})(\varepsilon)(\sigma) =$
$\underline{\text{if}}\ W(b)(\varepsilon)(\sigma)\ \underline{\text{then}}\ R(s_1)(\varepsilon)(\sigma)\ \underline{\text{else}}\ R(s_2)(\varepsilon)(\sigma)\ \underline{\text{fi}}$

c. The function W: *Bexp* $\to$ (*Env* $\to (\Sigma \to_s W)$) is defined by:

$W(b)(\varepsilon)(\sigma) = \bot_W$ if $intv(b) \not\subseteq dom(\varepsilon)$ or $\sigma = \bot$. Otherwise,

(i) $W(\underline{\text{true}})(\varepsilon)(\sigma) = tt, \ldots,$

(v) $W(b_1 \supset b_2)(\varepsilon)(\sigma) = (W(b_1)(\varepsilon)(\sigma) \Rightarrow W(b_2)(\varepsilon)(\sigma))$

END 6.4.

Remark. Observe that part a of the definition implies that, for $e \notin range(\varepsilon)$, if $L(v)(\varepsilon)(\sigma) = \bar{e}$, $\bar{e} \neq \bot_A$, then $e \neq \bar{e}$.

Before giving the definition of M, we introduce the following notation: for each ε, $x \notin dom(\varepsilon)$, $e \notin range(\varepsilon)$, we write $\varepsilon \cup \langle x,e\rangle$ for the extension of ε yielding e when applied to x (and yielding $\varepsilon(\xi)$ for all $\xi \neq x$). We shall also employ, for $n \geq 0$, constructs $\varepsilon \cup \langle x_i, e_i\rangle_{i=1}^{n}$. By using this notation we imply that $x_i \notin dom(\varepsilon)$, $e_i \notin range(\varepsilon)$, $(x_i \equiv x_j) \Rightarrow (i=j)$, $(e_i = e_j) \Rightarrow (i=j)$, $1 \leq i, j \leq n$.

<u>DEFINITION 6.5</u> (semantics of statements).

The function M: *Stat* $\to$ (*Env* $\to (\Sigma \to_s \Sigma)$) is defined by:

$M(S)(\varepsilon)(\sigma) = \bot$, if $intv(S) \not\subseteq dom(\varepsilon)$ or $\sigma = \bot$. Otherwise,

a. $M(v{:=}s)(\varepsilon)(\sigma) = \sigma\{R(s)(\varepsilon)(\sigma)/L(v)(\varepsilon)(\sigma)\}$

b. $M(S_1;S_2)(\varepsilon)(\sigma) = M(S_2)(\varepsilon)(M(S_1)(\varepsilon)(\sigma))$

c. $M(\underline{\text{if}}\ b\ \underline{\text{then}}\ S_1\ \underline{\text{else}}\ S_2\ \underline{\text{fi}})(\varepsilon)(\sigma) =$
$\underline{\text{if}}\ W(b)(\varepsilon)(\sigma)\ \underline{\text{then}}\ M(S_1)(\varepsilon)(\sigma)\ \underline{\text{else}}\ M(S_2)(\varepsilon)(\sigma)\ \underline{\text{fi}}$

d. M(<u>begin</u> <u>new</u> x;S <u>end</u>)(ε)(σ) = M(S[y/x])(ε∪<y,e>)(σ),
where y is the first simple variable ∉ dom(ε),
and e the first address ∉ range(ε).

END 6.5.

Clauses a to c of this definition should be clear. As to clause d, we observe (i) the introduction of the first fresh (i.e. not in dom(ε)) simple variable y, and the first fresh (not in range(ε)) address e, (ii) extension of ε with <y,e>, and (iii) substitution of y for x in S (see also the examples preceding definition 6.3).

Remarks

1. We leave it to the reader to verify that M(S)(ε)(σ) = ⊥ *only* if *intv*(S) ⊈ dom(ε) or σ = ⊥.
2. Our use of substitution in the definition of blocks has two reasons. Firstly, we like to stay close to the intuition of the programmer, who understands (we think) the meaning of a program such as <u>begin</u> <u>new</u> x;S_1; <u>begin</u> <u>new</u> x;S_2 <u>end</u>; S_3 <u>end</u> through that of $S_1[x_1/x];S_2[x_2/x];S_3[x_1/x]$, for some fresh x_1,x_2. Secondly, the proof rule for blocks (see section 6.3) uses substitution, and its justification is facilitated by our semantics. It should be noted, however, that a definition which avoids substitution is also possible (and, in fact, preferred by many authors in denotational semantics). We then replace clause d by M(<u>begin</u> <u>new</u> x;S <u>end</u>)(ε)(σ) = M(S)(ε[e/x])(σ), where e is the first address ∉ range(ε), and ε[e/x] an (ad-hoc) notation for (i) ε ∪ <x,e>, if x ∉ dom(ε) (ii) ε{e/x}, if x ∈ dom(ε). Adopting this definition would require various changes in the theory to follow; for example, lemma 6.6 no longer holds. Also, certain definitions of chapter 9 would require modification, so as to preserve "static scope" for procedures (cf. remarks 3 and 4 following definition 9.3).

After thus having completed the syntactic and semantic definitions proper, we continue with a number of lemmas expressing various properties of our constructs implied by these definitions.

The first lemma states that congruent statements are equivalent.

LEMMA 6.6. $S \cong S' \Rightarrow M(S) = M(S')$.

PROOF. We show that, if $S \cong S'$, then, for all ε,σ, $M(S)(\varepsilon)(\sigma) = M(S')(\varepsilon)(\sigma)$. Since $intv(S) = intv(S')$, we only have to consider the case that $intv(S) \subseteq dom(\varepsilon)$, $\sigma \neq \bot$. We use induction on the complexity of S, and the definition of " $\cong$ ". If S is not a block, the result is clear. Otherwise, if $S \equiv$ begin new $x;S_1$ end, then either $S' \equiv$ begin new $x;S_1'$ end, with $S_1 \cong S_1'$, and the result is again clear by induction and remark 2e after definition 6.2, or $S' \equiv$ begin new $y;S_1'$ end, with $y \notin svar(S_1)$ and $S_1[y/x] \cong S_1'$. Choose ε such that $intv(S_1)\backslash\{x\} \subseteq dom(\varepsilon)$. Then $M(S)(\varepsilon)(\sigma) = M(S_1[z/x])(\varepsilon \cup \langle z,e\rangle)(\sigma)$, with $\langle z,e\rangle$ as usual, and $M($begin new $y;S_1'$ end$)(\varepsilon)(\sigma) = M(S_1'[z/y])(\varepsilon \cup \langle z,e\rangle)(\sigma)$ = (by the induction hypothesis and remark 2e after definition 6.2) $M(S_1[y/x][z/y])(\varepsilon \cup \langle z,e\rangle)(\sigma)$ = (by induction and remark 2c after definition 6.2) $M(S_1[z/x])(\varepsilon \cup \langle z,e\rangle)(\sigma)$, thus establishing the desired result.
END 6.6.

In the next lemma we combine two ideas:

a. Let us call pairs $\langle\varepsilon,\sigma\rangle$, $\langle\bar{\varepsilon},\bar{\sigma}\rangle$ *matching* over some $\delta \subseteq Intv$ satisfying $\delta \subseteq dom(\varepsilon) \cap dom(\bar{\varepsilon})$, if either $\sigma = \bot$, $\bar{\sigma} = \bot$, or $\sigma \neq \bot$, $\bar{\sigma} \neq \bot$, and (*) $(\sigma \circ \varepsilon)|\delta = (\bar{\sigma} \circ \bar{\varepsilon})|\delta$, where the notation $(\sigma \circ \varepsilon)|\delta$ denotes the function composed of σ and ε, restricted to δ. We expect that evaluating an expression in matching pairs leads to the same result (it makes no difference whether the same value is associated with a simple variable through different addresses) and, indeed, we shall see that, assuming $intv(s) \subseteq \delta$ and (*), $R(s)(\varepsilon)(\sigma) = R(s)(\bar{\varepsilon})(\bar{\sigma})$, and similarly for $b \in Bexp$.

b. Furthermore, we shall need the fact that it makes no difference in the outcome to substitute different fresh simple variables y,z for some simple variable x, as long as these simple variables are associated with the same address. I.e. we have that, for

$y,z \notin dom(\varepsilon)$, $e \notin range(\varepsilon)$, $\mathcal{R}(s[y/x])(\varepsilon \cup \langle y,e\rangle)(\sigma) =$
$\mathcal{R}(s[z/x])(\varepsilon \cup \langle z,e\rangle)(\sigma)$.

The actual formulation of the lemma combines and slightly extends these two ideas and, moreover, includes simultaneous substitution, since this is the form we shall need in subsequent applications (i.e. in the proof of theorem 6.12). Results a,b above then follow as simple corollaries.

LEMMA 6.7. Let $n \geq 0$.

a. If

(i) $intv(s)\backslash\{x_i\}_{i=1}^n \subseteq \delta \subseteq dom(\varepsilon) \cap dom(\bar{\varepsilon})$, $\sigma \neq \bot$, $\bar{\sigma} \neq \bot$

(ii) $(\sigma \circ \varepsilon)|\delta = (\bar{\sigma} \circ \bar{\varepsilon})|\delta$

(iii) For $i = 1,\ldots,n$, either $\sigma(e_i) = \bar{\sigma}(\bar{e}_i)$, or $x_i \notin svar(s)$

then

(iv) $\mathcal{R}(s[y_i/x_i]_{i=1}^n)(\varepsilon \cup \langle y_i,e_i\rangle_{i=1}^n)(\sigma) =$

$\mathcal{R}(s[z_i/x_i]_{i=1}^n)(\bar{\varepsilon} \cup \langle z_i,\bar{e}_i\rangle_{i=1}^n)(\bar{\sigma})$.

b. Similarly for $b \in \mathcal{B}exp$.

PROOF. We first observe that - by our definition of the notation $\varepsilon \cup \langle y_i,e_i\rangle_i$ - we have that $y_i \notin dom(\varepsilon)$ (whence, a fortiori, $y_i \notin svar(s)$), $e_i \notin range(\varepsilon)$, $(y_i \equiv y_j) \Rightarrow (i = j)$, $(e_i = e_j) \Rightarrow (i = j)$, $1 \leq i, j \leq n$, and similarly for $\bar{\varepsilon} \cup \langle z_i,\bar{e}_i\rangle_i$. (Observations to this effect will not be repeated below in comparable situations.) The lemma is proved by simultaneous induction on the complexity of s and b. We discuss only the various possibilities for s a variable:

(α) $s \equiv x_j$, for some j, $1 \leq j \leq n$. We have to show that $\mathcal{R}(y_j)(\varepsilon \cup \langle y_i,e_i\rangle_i)(\sigma) = \mathcal{R}(z_j)(\bar{\varepsilon} \cup \langle z_i,\bar{e}_i\rangle_i)(\bar{\sigma})$, i.e. that $\sigma(e_j) = \bar{\sigma}(\bar{e}_j)$, which is clear by assumption (iii)

(β) $s \equiv u$, $u \not\equiv x_i$, $1 \leq i \leq n$. Then the desired result amounts to $\sigma((\varepsilon \cup \langle y_i,e_i\rangle_i)(u)) = \bar{\sigma}((\bar{\varepsilon} \cup \langle z_i,\bar{e}_i\rangle_i)(u))$. Since $u \in intv(s)\backslash\{x_i\}$, we have that $u \not\equiv y_i,z_i$, $i = 1,\ldots,n$. Hence, we have to show that $\sigma(\varepsilon(u)) = \bar{\sigma}(\bar{\varepsilon}(u))$, which is clear by assumption (ii)

(γ) $s \equiv a[s_0]$. By the induction hypothesis,

$R(s_0[y_i/x_i]_i)(\varepsilon\cup\langle y_i,e_i\rangle_i)(\sigma) = R(s_0[z_i/x_i]_i)(\bar{\varepsilon}\cup\langle z_i,\bar{e}_i\rangle_i)(\bar{\sigma})$

(= α, say). We have to show that

$\sigma((\varepsilon\cup\langle y_i,e_i\rangle_i)(a,\alpha)) = \bar{\sigma}((\bar{\varepsilon}\cup\langle z_i,\bar{e}_i\rangle_i)(a,\alpha))$, i.e. that

$\sigma(\varepsilon(a,\alpha)) = \bar{\sigma}(\bar{\varepsilon}(a,\alpha))$, which again follows from (ii).

END 6.7.

COROLLARY 6.8.

a. If

(i) $intv(s) \subseteq \delta \subseteq dom(\varepsilon) \cap dom(\bar{\varepsilon})$, $\sigma \neq \perp$, $\bar{\sigma} \neq \perp$

(ii) $(\sigma\circ\varepsilon)|\delta = (\bar{\sigma}\circ\bar{\varepsilon})|\delta$

then

(iii) $R(s)(\varepsilon)(\sigma) = R(s)(\bar{\varepsilon})(\bar{\sigma})$

b. If

(i) $intv(s)\backslash\{x\} \subseteq dom(\varepsilon)$, $\sigma \neq \perp$

then

(ii) $R(s[y/x])(\varepsilon\cup\langle y,e\rangle)(\sigma) = R(s[z/x])(\varepsilon\cup\langle z,e\rangle)(\sigma)$

c. Similarly for $b \in \mathcal{B}exp$.

PROOF.

a. Take n = 0 in lemma 6.7

b. Take n = 1, $\varepsilon = \bar{\varepsilon}$, $\sigma = \bar{\sigma}$, $e = \bar{e}$, $\delta = dom(\varepsilon)$ in lemma 6.7

c. Clear.

END 6.8.

Lemma 6.9 generalizes (part of) lemma 2.16c and similar results from chapter 4.

LEMMA 6.9.

a. If $intv(s,t,v) \subseteq dom(\varepsilon)$ then

$R(s[t/v])(\varepsilon)(\sigma) = R(s)(\varepsilon)(\sigma\{R(t)(\varepsilon)(\sigma)/L(v)(\varepsilon)(\sigma)\})$

b. Similarly for $b \in \mathcal{B}exp$.

PROOF. Apart from one detail, the proof runs completely parallel to those of chapters 2, 4. In order to pinpoint the difference, let us consider the special case that $s \equiv y$, $v \equiv x$, with $x \not\equiv y$. Let $R(t)(\varepsilon)(\sigma) = \alpha$. We have to show that $R(y)(\varepsilon)(\sigma) = R(y)(\varepsilon)(\sigma\{\alpha/L(x)(\varepsilon)(\sigma)\})$, i.e. that $\sigma(\varepsilon(y)) = \sigma\{\alpha/\varepsilon(x)\}(\varepsilon(y))$. Now since $x \not\equiv y$, $\varepsilon(x) \neq \varepsilon(y)$ (here we use that ε restricted to its domain is 1-1), and the desired result follows.

END 6.9.

The following corollary of this lemma is needed in section 6.4:

COROLLARY 6.10. Let $intv(s)\backslash\{x\} \subseteq dom(\varepsilon)$. Then

$$R(s[y/x])(\varepsilon \cup \langle x,e\rangle \cup \langle y,\bar{e}\rangle)(\sigma\{\alpha/\bar{e}\}) =$$
$$R(s)(\varepsilon \cup \langle x,e\rangle)(\sigma\{\alpha/e\}).$$

PROOF. $R(s[y/x])(\varepsilon \cup \langle x,e\rangle \cup \langle y,\bar{e}\rangle)(\sigma\{\alpha/\bar{e}\})$ = (lemma 6.9) $R(s)(\varepsilon \cup \langle x,e\rangle \cup \langle y,\bar{e}\rangle)(\sigma\{\alpha/\bar{e}\}\{\alpha/e\})$ = (corollary 6.8a) $R(s)(\varepsilon \cup \langle x,e\rangle)(\sigma\{\alpha/e\})$.

END 6.10.

Remark. A proof of this lemma using only corollary 6.8 is also possible (exercise).

We now introduce another important notion, viz. that of initialization (of a local simple variable). By way of example, we have that the local x is initialized in (*): begin new x;x:=0 end, but not in (**): begin new x;y:=x end. A crucial technical difference between statements such as (*) and (**) is that statements of the first type preserve the property of matching, whereas those of the second type do not. The former claim is a special case of theorem 6.12 to be proved below. As to the latter, take $\varepsilon = \langle y,e\rangle$, $\bar{\varepsilon} = \langle y,\bar{e}\rangle$, choose $\sigma \neq \bot$ such that $\sigma(e) = \sigma(\bar{e})$, and observe that, for $\delta = \{y\}$, we have that $(\sigma\circ\varepsilon)|\delta = (\sigma\circ\bar{\varepsilon})|\delta$. However, for $\sigma' = M(\text{begin new } x;y:=x \text{ end})(\langle y,e\rangle)(\sigma)$, $\bar{\sigma}' = M(\text{begin new } x;y:=x \text{ end})(\langle y,\bar{e}\rangle)(\sigma)$, we have that $\sigma' = \sigma\{\sigma(e_1)/e\}$, e_1 the first address $\neq e$, $\bar{\sigma}' = \sigma\{\sigma(\bar{e}_1)/\bar{e}\}$, $\bar{e}_1$ the first address $\neq \bar{e}$, and we infer that $(\sigma'\circ\varepsilon)|\delta = (\bar{\sigma}'\circ\bar{\varepsilon})|\delta$ holds *only* if $\sigma(e_1) = \sigma(\bar{e}_1)$.

The next definition makes the notion of initialization of local variables precise:

DEFINITION 6.11 (initialization).

a. For each $S \in \mathit{Stat}$, *init*(S) is the smallest subset of Svar satisfying
   (i) If $x \notin$ *svar*(s) then $x \in$ *init*(x:=s)
   (ii) If $x \in$ *init*(S_1), or $x \notin$ *svar*(S_1) and $x \in$ *init*(S_2), then $x \in$ *init*(S_1;S_2)
   (iii) If $x \notin$ *svar*(b) and $x \in$ *init*(S_i), i = 1,2, then $x \in$ *init*(if b then S_1 else S_2 fi)
   (iv) If $x \not\equiv y$, $x \in$ *init*(S), then $x \in$ *init*(begin new y;S end)
b. We say that all local simple variables of a statement S are initialized whenever, for each substatement of S which has the form of a block begin new x;S_0 end, we have that $x \in$ *init*(S_0) or $x \notin$ *svar*(S_0).

END 6.11.

Examples. $x \in$ *init*(x:=0), $x \notin$ *init*(x:=x+1), $x \in$ *init*(y:=0;x:=y), $x \notin$ *init*(if x=0 then x:=1 else x:=2 fi), $x \notin$ *init*(begin new z; z:=x end).

From now on - till the end of this chapter - we assume that all our statements satisfy the requirement that all their local simple variables are initialized.

The main theorem which we obtain as result of this requirement should not offer too many difficulties to the reader who has understood lemma 6.7. We want to establish two properties which are of importance for application in sections 6.3, 6.4.

a. If $<\varepsilon,\sigma>$ matches $<\bar{\varepsilon},\bar{\sigma}>$ over $\delta \subseteq dom(\varepsilon) \cap dom(\bar{\varepsilon})$, $\sigma' = M(S)(\varepsilon)(\sigma)$, $\bar{\sigma}' = M(S)(\bar{\varepsilon})(\bar{\sigma})$, then $<\varepsilon,\sigma'>$ also matches $<\bar{\varepsilon},\bar{\sigma}'>$ over δ
b. For $intv(S)\backslash\{x\} \subseteq \delta = dom(\varepsilon)$, $\sigma \neq \bot$, $\sigma' = M(S[y/x])(\varepsilon \cup <y,e>)(\sigma)$, $\sigma'' = M(S[z/x])(\varepsilon \cup <z,e>)(\sigma)$, we have that $<\varepsilon,\sigma'>$ matches $<\varepsilon,\sigma''>$ over δ.

The actual formulation of the theorem is somewhat more complicated; it has properties a,b as corollaries. It may be helpful to approach the theorem through the following argument. Let us compare the statements S[y/x], S[z/x] for some simple variables y,z which do not occur free in S. We assert that executing these two statements has the same effect upon the elements of *intv*(S), provided either y,z have the same initial value, or x is initialized in S, or x does not occur free in S. As a result of our treatment of simple variable declarations - which add additional substitutions to our constructs - it is convenient to consider the more general case of substitutions

$$S[y_i/x_i]_{i=1}^n, \quad S[z_i/x_i]_{i=1}^n, \qquad \text{for } n \geq 0.$$

This idea we moreover combine with the already mentioned property that our statements preserve the property of matching. Finally, we remark that result (vi) of the theorem is not used in its applications, but serves only to make the induction argument - on the complexity of S - go through for $S \equiv S_1;S_2$.

<u>THEOREM 6.12</u>. Let $n \geq 0$.

If

(i) $intv(S)\setminus\{x_i\}_{i=1}^n \subseteq \delta \subseteq dom(\varepsilon) \cap dom(\bar{\varepsilon})$, $\sigma \neq \bot$, $\bar{\sigma} \neq \bot$

(ii) $(\sigma\circ\varepsilon)|\delta = (\bar{\sigma}\circ\bar{\varepsilon})|\delta$

(iii) For all $i = 1,\ldots,n$, $\sigma(e_i) = \bar{\sigma}(\bar{e}_i)$, or $x_i \in init(S)$, or $x_i \notin svar(S)$

(iv) $\sigma' = M(S[y_i/x_i]_{i=1}^n)(\varepsilon\cup\langle y_i,e_i\rangle_{i=1}^n)(\sigma)$

$\bar{\sigma}' = M(S[z_i/x_i]_{i=1}^n)(\bar{\varepsilon}\cup\langle z_i,\bar{e}_i\rangle_{i=1}^n)(\bar{\sigma})$

then

(v) $(\sigma'\circ\varepsilon)|\delta = (\bar{\sigma}'\circ\bar{\varepsilon})|\delta$

(vi) For all $i = 1,\ldots,n$, if $\sigma(e_i) = \bar{\sigma}(\bar{e}_i)$ or $x_i \in init(S)$, then $\sigma'(e_i) = \bar{\sigma}'(\bar{e}_i)$.

<u>PROOF</u>. We first note that, from (i) and the remark following definition 6.5, we have that $\sigma' \neq \bot$, $\bar{\sigma}' \neq \bot$, whence (v), (vi) are well-defined.

We use induction on the complexity of S to prove that (i),...,(iv) imply (v), (vi).

1. $S \equiv x_j := s$, for some j, $1 \le j \le n$. Clearly, then $x_i \notin init(S)$ for $i \ne j$; hence, for $i \ne j$, either $\sigma(e_i) = \bar{\sigma}(\bar{e}_i)$, or $x_i \notin svar(S)$.

   a. $x_j \in init(S)$. Then $x_j \notin svar(s)$. We have

   $$\sigma' = \sigma\{R(s[y_i/x_i]_i)(\varepsilon \cup \langle y_i, e_i\rangle_i)(\sigma)/e_j\}$$

   $$\bar{\sigma}' = \bar{\sigma}\{R(s[z_i/x_i]_i)(\bar{\varepsilon} \cup \langle z_i, \bar{e}_i\rangle_i)(\bar{\sigma})/\bar{e}_j\}.$$

   Since $(\sigma \circ \varepsilon)|\delta = (\bar{\sigma} \circ \bar{\varepsilon})|\delta$, and $e_j \notin range(\varepsilon)$, $\bar{e}_j \notin range(\bar{\varepsilon})$, it is clear that $(\sigma' \circ \varepsilon)|\delta = (\bar{\sigma}' \circ \bar{\varepsilon})|\delta$. Also, for $i \ne j$, if $\sigma(e_i) = \bar{\sigma}(\bar{e}_i)$ then $\sigma'(e_i) = \bar{\sigma}'(\bar{e}_i)$. Finally, since, by lemma 6.7,

   $$R(s[y_i/x_i]_i)(\varepsilon \cup \langle y_i, e_i\rangle_i)(\sigma) = R(s[z_i/x_i]_i)(\bar{\varepsilon} \cup \langle z_i, \bar{e}_i\rangle_i)(\bar{\sigma}),$$

   we also have that $\sigma'(e_j) = \bar{\sigma}'(\bar{e}_j)$.

   b. $\sigma(e_j) = \bar{\sigma}(\bar{e}_j)$. Again, the desired result is immediate from the assumptions and lemma 6.7.

2. $S \equiv v := s$, $v \not\equiv x_i$, $1 \le i \le n$. Then $x_i \notin init(S)$, $i = 1,...,n$, and, hence, for $i = 1,...,n$, $\sigma(e_i) = \bar{\sigma}(\bar{e}_i)$, or $x_i \notin svar(S)$ (and, hence, $x_i \notin svar(s)$). Now

   $$\sigma' = \sigma\{R(s[\,]_i)(\varepsilon \cup \langle y_i, e_i\rangle_i)(\sigma)/L(v[\,]_i)(\varepsilon \cup \langle y_i, e_i\rangle_i)(\sigma)\}$$

   $$\bar{\sigma}' = \bar{\sigma}\{R(s[\,]_i)(\bar{\varepsilon} \cup \langle z_i, \bar{e}_i\rangle_i)(\bar{\sigma})/L(v[\,]_i)(\bar{\varepsilon} \cup \langle z_i, \bar{e}_i\rangle_i)(\bar{\sigma})\}.$$

   a. $v \equiv u$, $u \not\equiv x_i$, $1 \le i \le n$. Then, using lemma 6.7 again, $\sigma' = \sigma\{\alpha/\varepsilon(u)\}$, $\bar{\sigma}' = \bar{\sigma}\{\alpha/\bar{\varepsilon}(u)\}$, where $\alpha = R(s[\,]_i)(\varepsilon \cup \langle y_i, e_i\rangle_i)(\sigma) = R(s[\,]_i)(\bar{\varepsilon} \cup \langle z_i, \bar{e}_i\rangle_i)(\bar{\sigma})$. The desired result is then immediate from the assumptions.

   b. $v \equiv a[t]$. Then $\sigma' = \sigma\{\alpha/\varepsilon(a,\alpha')\}$, $\bar{\sigma}' = \bar{\sigma}\{\alpha/\bar{\varepsilon}(a,\alpha')\}$, with α as in part a, and $\alpha' = R(t[\,]_i)(\varepsilon \cup \langle y_i, e_i\rangle_i)(\sigma) = R(t[\,]_i)(\bar{\varepsilon} \cup \langle z_i, \bar{e}_i\rangle_i)(\bar{\sigma})$. Again, this directly leads to the desired result.

3. $S \equiv S_1; S_2$. Let

$$\sigma'' = M(S_1[\,]_i)(\varepsilon \cup \langle y_i, e_i\rangle_i)(\sigma)$$

$$\bar{\sigma}'' = M(S_1[\,]_i)(\bar{\varepsilon} \cup \langle z_i, \bar{e}_i\rangle_i)(\bar{\sigma})$$

$$\sigma' = M(S_2[\,]_i)(\varepsilon \cup \langle y_i, e_i\rangle_i)(\sigma'')$$

$$\bar{\sigma}' = M(S_2[\,]_i)(\bar{\varepsilon} \cup \langle z_i, \bar{e}_i\rangle_i)(\bar{\sigma}'').$$

We have, for $i = 1,\ldots,n$, either $\sigma(e_i) = \bar{\sigma}(\bar{e}_i)$, or $x_i \in \mathit{init}(S_1;S_2)$, or $x_i \notin \mathit{svar}(S_1;S_2)$. Thus, we have that, for $i = 1,\ldots,n$, either
(α) $\sigma(e_i) = \bar{\sigma}(\bar{e}_i)$, or
(β) $x_i \in \mathit{init}(S_1)$, or
(γ) $x_i \notin \mathit{svar}(S_1)$ and $x_i \in \mathit{init}(S_2)$, or
(δ) $x_i \notin \mathit{svar}(S_1)$ and $x_i \notin \mathit{svar}(S_2)$.
By induction we obtain that $(\sigma''\circ\varepsilon)|\delta = (\bar{\sigma}''\circ\bar{\varepsilon})|\delta$ and
(ε) For $i = 1,\ldots,n$, if $\sigma(e_i) = \bar{\sigma}(\bar{e}_i)$ or $x_i \in \mathit{init}(S_1)$ then
$\sigma''(e_i) = \bar{\sigma}''(\bar{e}_i)$
Taking these results together we get, for $i = 1,\ldots,n$, either
(ξ) $\sigma''(e_i) = \bar{\sigma}''(\bar{e}_i)$, or
(η) $x_i \in \mathit{init}(S_2)$, or
(θ) $x_i \notin \mathit{svar}(S_2)$.
Another application of the induction hypothesis then yields that
$(\sigma'\circ\varepsilon)|\delta = (\bar{\sigma}'\circ\bar{\varepsilon})|\delta$ and
(ι) For $i = 1,\ldots,n$, if $\sigma''(e_i) = \bar{\sigma}''(\bar{e}_i)$ or $x_i \in \mathit{init}(S_2)$ then
$\sigma'(e_i) = \bar{\sigma}(\bar{e}_i)$.
Finally, combining (ε),(ι) we obtain that, for $i = 1,\ldots,n$,
if $\sigma(e_i) = \bar{\sigma}(\bar{e}_i)$ or $x_i \in \mathit{init}(S_1;S_2)$ then $\sigma'(e_i) = \bar{\sigma}'(\bar{e}_i)$.

4. $S \equiv$ <u>if</u> b <u>then</u> S_1 <u>else</u> S_2 <u>fi</u>. Exercise.
5. $S \equiv$ <u>begin</u> <u>new</u> x;S_1 <u>end</u>. By our general initialization requirement, $x \in \mathit{init}(S_1)$ or $x \notin \mathit{svar}(S_1)$. By properties of " $\cong$ " (cf. lemma 6.6) without lack of generality we may assume that $x \not\equiv x_i, y_i, z_i$, $i = 1,\ldots,n$. Let

$$\sigma' = M(S_1[y_i/x_i]_i[y/x])(\varepsilon \cup \langle y_i, e_i\rangle_i \cup \langle y, e\rangle)(\sigma)$$

where y is the first simple variable $\notin \mathrm{dom}(\varepsilon) \cup \{y_i\}_i$ and e is the first address $\notin$ range(ε) $\cup$ $\{e_i\}_i$, and

$$\bar{\sigma}' = M(S_1[z_i/x_i]_i[z/x])(\bar{\varepsilon} \cup \langle z_i, \bar{e}_i \rangle_i \cup \langle z, \bar{e} \rangle)(\bar{\sigma})$$

with $\langle z, \bar{e} \rangle$ defined similarly. Since

(i) $x \in init(S_1)$ or $x \notin svar(S_1)$

and, for $i = 1, \ldots, n$, either

(ii) $\sigma(e_i) = \bar{\sigma}(\bar{e}_i)$, or

(iii) $x_i \in init(S)$ and, hence, $x_i \in init(S_1)$, or

(iv) $x_i \notin svar(S)$ and, hence, $x_i \notin svar(S_1)$,

the desired result is immediate by the induction hypothesis.

END 6.12.

We now state the corollaries of this theorem which play a part in sections 6.3, 6.4:

COROLLARY 6.13.

a. If

(i) $intv(S) \subseteq \delta \subseteq dom(\varepsilon) \cap dom(\bar{\varepsilon})$, $\sigma \neq \bot$, $\bar{\sigma} \neq \bot$

(ii) $(\sigma \circ \varepsilon) | \delta = (\bar{\sigma} \circ \bar{\varepsilon}) | \delta$

(iii) $\sigma' = M(S)(\varepsilon)(\sigma)$, $\bar{\sigma}' = M(S)(\bar{\varepsilon})(\bar{\sigma})$

then

(iv) $(\sigma' \circ \varepsilon) | \delta = (\bar{\sigma}' \circ \bar{\varepsilon}) | \delta$.

b. If

(i) $intv(S) \backslash \{x\} \subseteq \delta = dom(\varepsilon)$, $\sigma \neq \bot$

(ii) $\sigma' = M(S[y/x])(\varepsilon \cup \langle y, e \rangle)(\sigma)$

$\sigma'' = M(S[z/x])(\varepsilon \cup \langle z, e \rangle)(\sigma)$

then

(iii) $(\sigma' \circ \varepsilon) | \delta = (\sigma'' \circ \varepsilon) | \delta$.

PROOF. Immediate from theorem 6.12.

END 6.13.

Remark. Part b of this corollary is not the strongest possible result. We even have that from conditions (i), (ii) it follows that $\sigma' = \sigma''$

(see exercise 6.10). However, the above form is sufficient for our purposes, and it has the advantage of being immediately obtainable from theorem 6.12.

6.3. Correctness

In this section we introduce syntax and semantics of assertions and correctness formulae, derive the analogs of lemmas 6.7 and 6.9, and give definitions of validity and soundness adapted to the presence of environments. Moreover, we present a proof system including a new rule to deal with blocks for which we prove soundness in this section and completeness in the next.

DEFINITION 6.14 (assertions).

a. The syntax of the class of assertions Assn remains unchanged.

b. The function T: $\mathit{Assn} \to (\mathit{Env} \to (\Sigma \to_s T))$ is defined by:

$T(p)(\varepsilon)(\sigma)$ = ff if $\mathit{intv}(p) \not\subseteq \mathrm{dom}(\varepsilon)$ or $\sigma = \bot$. Otherwise

(i) $T(\underline{\text{true}})(\varepsilon)(\sigma) = tt, \ldots,$

(v) $T(p_1 \supset p_2)(\varepsilon)(\sigma) = (T(p_1)(\varepsilon)(\sigma) \Rightarrow T(p_2)(\varepsilon)(\sigma))$

(vi) $T(\exists x[p])(\varepsilon)(\sigma) = \exists\alpha[T(p[y/x])(\varepsilon \cup \langle y,e\rangle)(\sigma\{\alpha/e\})]$

where y is the first simple variable $\notin \mathrm{dom}(\varepsilon)$ and e the first address $\notin \mathrm{range}(\varepsilon)$.

END 6.14.

We see that, apart from clause b(vi), the definition of T is the natural extension of the one used before. In clause b(vi), we combine the previous treatment of $T(\exists x[p])$ (existential quantification $\exists\alpha[\ldots\sigma\{\alpha/\ldots\}]$) with the idea of extending the environment with a new pair <y,e> exactly as used in definition 6.5d. (Note that putting $T(\exists x[p])(\varepsilon)(\sigma) = \exists\alpha[T(p)(\varepsilon)(\sigma\{\alpha/\varepsilon(x)\})]$ may fail if (the bound simple variable) $x \notin \mathrm{dom}(\varepsilon)$.)

We assume that the congruence relation is also defined for assertions (cf. definition 6.2). The central clause in the definition is:

if $p[y/x] \cong p'$ and $y \notin svar(p)$ then $\exists x[p] \cong \exists y[p']$, and the remaining clauses should be clear. Moreover, we shall use the equivalents of the remarks following definition 6.2 (e.g. $p[y/x][s/y] \cong p[s/x]$, provided $y \notin svar(p)$, etc.).

Analogously to lemma 6.7 we have

LEMMA 6.15. Let $n \geq 0$.

If

(i) $intv(p) \setminus \{x_i\}_i \subseteq \delta \subseteq dom(\varepsilon) \cap dom(\bar{\varepsilon})$, $\sigma \neq \bot$, $\bar{\sigma} \neq \bot$

(ii) $(\sigma \circ \varepsilon)|\delta = (\bar{\sigma} \circ \bar{\varepsilon})|\delta$

(iii) For $i = 1,\ldots,n$, $\sigma(e_i) = \bar{\sigma}(\bar{e}_i)$, or $x_i \notin svar(p)$

then

(iv) $T(p[y_i/x_i]_{i=1}^{n})(\varepsilon \cup \langle y_i,e_i\rangle_{i=1}^{n})(\sigma) =$

$T(p[z_i/x_i]_{i=1}^{n})(\bar{\varepsilon} \cup \langle z_i,\bar{e}_i\rangle_{i=1}^{n})(\bar{\sigma})$.

PROOF. Induction on the complexity of p, using lemma 6.7 for the case $p \equiv (s_1=s_2)$. We give some details of the case $p \equiv \exists x[p_1]$. By properties of " $\cong$ " we may assume that $x \not\equiv x_i,y_i,z_i$, $i = 1,\ldots,n$. We have to show that, assuming (i) to (iii), and applying definition 6.14b(vi)

$$\exists \alpha[T(p_1[y_i/x_i]_i[y/x])(\varepsilon \cup \langle y_i,e_i\rangle_i \cup \langle y,e\rangle)(\sigma\{\alpha/e\})] =$$

$$\exists \bar{\alpha}[T(p_1[z_i/x_i]_i[z/x])(\bar{\varepsilon} \cup \langle z_i,\bar{e}_i\rangle_i \cup \langle z,\bar{e}\rangle)(\bar{\sigma}\{\bar{\alpha}/\bar{e}\})],$$

where $\langle y,e\rangle$ is the first pair not in $\langle dom(\varepsilon) \cup \{y_i\}_i, range(\varepsilon) \cup \{e_i\}_i\rangle$, and $\langle z,\bar{e}\rangle$ is defined similarly. The desired result is now immediate from the induction hypothesis, with $n' = n+1$, $\sigma' = \sigma\{\alpha/e\}$, $\bar{\sigma}' = \bar{\sigma}\{\bar{\alpha}/\bar{e}\}$, and taking $\alpha = \bar{\alpha}$.

END 6.15.

COROLLARY 6.16.

a. If

(i) $intv(p) \subseteq \delta \subseteq dom(\varepsilon) \cap dom(\bar{\varepsilon})$, $\sigma \neq \bot$, $\bar{\sigma} \neq \bot$

(ii) $(\sigma \circ \varepsilon)|\delta = (\bar{\sigma} \circ \bar{\varepsilon})|\delta$

then

(iii) $\mathcal{T}(p)(\varepsilon)(\sigma) = \mathcal{T}(p)(\bar{\varepsilon})(\bar{\sigma})$

b. If

(i) $intv(p)\backslash\{x\} \subseteq dom(\varepsilon)$, $\sigma \neq \perp$

then

(ii) $\mathcal{T}(p[y/x])(\varepsilon \cup \langle y,e\rangle)(\sigma) = \mathcal{T}(p[z/x])(\varepsilon \cup \langle z,e\rangle)(\sigma)$.

PROOF. Clear from lemma 6.15.

END 6.16.

Preparatory to lemma 6.18, which is the counterpart of lemma 6.9 for assertions, we need a lemma about interchanging substitutions, where one of the substitutions is for a possibly subscripted variable. In formulation and proof of this lemma we temporarily return to the <t/v> notation for a possibly subscripted variable v.

LEMMA 6.17.

a. Assume $y \notin svar(s,v)$. Then $s\langle t/v\rangle[y/x] \cong s[y/x]\langle t[y/x]/v[y/x]\rangle$

b. Similarly for $b \in \mathcal{Bexp}$

c. Similarly for $p \in \mathcal{Assn}$.

PROOF. a and b are proved by simultaneous induction on the complexity of s,b and, next, c is proved by induction on the complexity of p. We only treat one special case of a, viz. $s \equiv a[s_1]$, $v \equiv a[s_2]$. We have to show that, if $y \notin svar(s_1,s_2)$

$$a[s_1]\langle t/a[s_2]\rangle[y/x] \cong$$
$$a[s_1][y/x]\langle t[y/x]/a[s_2][y/x]\rangle.$$

Applying definition 4.4 to the left-hand side (lhs) and right-hand side (rhs), we obtain

$$\text{lhs} \equiv \underline{\text{if}}\ s_1\langle t/a[s_2]\rangle = s_2\ \underline{\text{then}}\ t\ \underline{\text{else}}\ a[s_1\langle t/a[s_2]\rangle]\ \underline{\text{fi}}\ [y/x] \equiv$$
$$\underline{\text{if}}\ s_1\langle t/a[s_2]\rangle[y/x] = s_2[y/x]\ \underline{\text{then}}\ t[y/x]$$
$$\underline{\text{else}}\ a[s_1\langle t/a[s_2]\rangle][y/x]\ \underline{\text{fi}} \cong$$

(by the induction hypothesis)

$$\underline{if}\ s_1[y/x]<t[y/x]/a[s_2[y/x]]> = s_2[y/x]\ \underline{then}\ t[y/x]$$
$$\underline{else}\ a[s_1[y/x]<t[y/x]/a[s_2[y/x]]>]\ \underline{fi} \equiv$$
$$a[s_1[y/x]]<t[y/x]/a[s_2[y/x]]> \equiv$$
$$a[s_1][y/x]<t[y/x]/a[s_2][y/x]> \equiv$$

rhs.

END 6.17.

We can now prove

LEMMA 6.18. If $intv(p,s,v) \subseteq \mathrm{dom}(\varepsilon)$ then

$$T(p[s/v])(\varepsilon)(\sigma) = T(p)(\varepsilon)(\sigma\{R(s)(\varepsilon)(\sigma)/L(v)(\varepsilon)(\sigma)\}).$$

PROOF. Induction on the complexity of p, using lemma 6.9 for the case $p \equiv (s_1=s_2)$. We only give some details for the case $p \equiv \exists x[p_1]$. Without loss of generality, we may assume $x \notin svar(s,v)$, $x \not\equiv y$, where y is the first simple variable $\notin \mathrm{dom}(\varepsilon)$. We have to show that

$$\exists\alpha[T(p_1[s/v][y/x])(\varepsilon\cup<y,e>)(\sigma\{\alpha/e\})] =$$
$$\exists\alpha'[T(p_1[y/x])(\varepsilon\cup<y,e>)(\sigma\{R(s)(\varepsilon)(\sigma)/L(v)(\varepsilon)(\sigma)\}\{\alpha'/e\})].$$

By lemma 6.17, the induction hypothesis, and corollary 6.8a,

$$\exists\alpha[T(p_1[s/v][y/x])(\varepsilon\cup<y,e>)(\sigma\{\alpha/e\})] =$$
$$\exists\alpha[T(p_1[y/x][s/v])(\varepsilon\cup<y,e>)(\sigma\{\alpha/e\})] =$$
$$\exists\alpha[T(p_1[y/x])(\varepsilon\cup<y,e>)$$
$$(\sigma\{\alpha/e\}\{R(s)(\varepsilon\cup<y,e>)(\sigma\{\alpha/e\})/L(v)(\varepsilon\cup<y,e>)(\sigma\{\alpha/e\})\})] =$$
$$\exists\alpha[T(p_1[y/x])(\varepsilon\cup<y,e>)(\sigma\{\alpha/e\}\{R(s)(\varepsilon)(\sigma)/L(v)(\varepsilon)(\sigma)\})].$$

Since $e \neq L(v)(\varepsilon)(\sigma)$ $(\overset{\mathrm{df.}}{=} \bar{e})$, the desired result follows taking $\alpha = \alpha'$ and using $\sigma\{R(s)(\varepsilon)(\sigma)/\bar{e}\}\{\alpha/e\} = \sigma\{\alpha/e\}\{R(s)(\varepsilon)(\sigma)/\bar{e}\}$.

END 6.18.

COROLLARY 6.19. Let $intv(p)\backslash\{x\} \subseteq \mathrm{dom}(\varepsilon)$. Then

$$T(p[y/x])(\varepsilon\cup<x,e> \cup <y,\bar{e}>)(\sigma\{\alpha/\bar{e}\}) = T(p)(\varepsilon\cup<x,e>)(\sigma\{\alpha/e\}).$$

PROOF. As for corollary 6.10.
END 6.19.

We continue with the discussion of correctness formulae. We restrict our attention to formulae not involving inclusions $S_1 \sqsubseteq S_2$ (having nothing particularly interesting to report about them) and, accordingly, drop this clause from our syntax. In the semantics of correctness formulae, ε is added as argument in the by now usual way.

DEFINITION 6.20 (correctness formulae).

a. The class of correctness formulae *Form*, with typical elements f,..., is defined by

$$f ::= p \mid \{p\}S\{q\} \mid f_1 \wedge f_2$$

b. The function F: $Form \to (Env \to (\Sigma \to_s T))$ is defined by

$F(f)(\varepsilon)(\sigma)$ = ff if $intv(f) \not\subseteq dom(\varepsilon)$ or $\sigma \neq \bot$. Otherwise,

(i) $F(p)(\varepsilon)(\sigma) = T(p)(\varepsilon)(\sigma)$

(ii) $F(\{p\}S\{q\})(\varepsilon)(\sigma) = \forall\sigma'[T(p)(\varepsilon)(\sigma) \wedge \sigma' = M(S)(\varepsilon)(\sigma) \Rightarrow T(q)(\varepsilon)(\sigma')]$

(iii) $F(f_1 \wedge f_2)(\varepsilon)(\sigma) = F(f_1)(\varepsilon)(\sigma) \wedge F(f_2)(\varepsilon)(\sigma)$.

END 6.20.

Remark. Note that, in clause b(ii), we do not have to require that $\sigma' \neq \bot$, since this is a result of the conditions $\sigma \neq \bot$ and $intv(f) \subseteq dom(\varepsilon)$, whence $intv(S) \subseteq dom(\varepsilon)$.

An important consequence of corollaries 6.16a and 6.13a is that correctness formulae yield the same result for matching argument pairs:

LEMMA 6.21. If

(i) $intv(f) \subseteq \delta \subseteq dom(\varepsilon) \cap dom(\bar{\varepsilon}), \sigma \neq \bot, \bar{\sigma} \neq \bot$

(ii) $(\sigma \circ \varepsilon) \mid \delta = (\bar{\sigma} \circ \bar{\varepsilon}) \mid \delta$

then

(iii) $F(f)(\varepsilon)(\sigma) = F(f)(\bar{\varepsilon})(\bar{\sigma})$.

PROOF. Induction on the complexity of f. If $f \equiv p$ or $f \equiv f_1 \wedge f_2$, the result is clear by corollary 6.16a and induction, respectively. Now let $f \equiv \{p\}S\{q\}$, and let ε, $\bar{\varepsilon}$, δ, σ, $\bar{\sigma}$ satisfy (i), (ii). We have to show that

$$\forall\sigma'[T(p)(\varepsilon)(\sigma) \wedge \sigma' = M(S)(\varepsilon)(\sigma) \Rightarrow T(q)(\varepsilon)(\sigma')] \quad (6.2)$$

$$\Longleftrightarrow$$

$$\forall\bar{\sigma}'[T(p)(\bar{\varepsilon})(\bar{\sigma}) \wedge \bar{\sigma}' = M(S)(\bar{\varepsilon})(\bar{\sigma}) \Rightarrow T(q)(\bar{\varepsilon})(\bar{\sigma}')] \quad (6.3)$$

We prove only " $\Rightarrow$ ", " $\Leftarrow$ " then follows by symmetry. Assume (6.2), and let $\bar{\varepsilon}$, $\bar{\sigma}$, $\bar{\sigma}'$ be such that

1. $T(p)(\bar{\varepsilon})(\bar{\sigma})$
2. $\bar{\sigma}' = M(S)(\bar{\varepsilon})(\bar{\sigma})$.

To show

3. $T(q)(\bar{\varepsilon})(\bar{\sigma}')$.

By 1, (i), (ii) and corollary 6.16a we have

4. $T(p)(\varepsilon)(\sigma)$. Now let
5. $\sigma' = M(S)(\varepsilon)(\sigma)$. Then, by (6.2),
6. $T(q)(\varepsilon)(\sigma')$.

By 2, 5, (i), (ii) and corollary 6.13a, we have

7. $(\bar{\sigma}'\circ\bar{\varepsilon})|\delta = (\sigma'\circ\varepsilon)|\delta$.

The desired result 3 now follows from 6, 7 and corollary 6.16a.
END 6.21.

Lemma 6.21 enables us to give smooth proofs of the soundness of a proof system for correctness of statements involving blocks, which we shall present in a moment. First we still have to define validity and soundness; these definitions are without surprises.

DEFINITION 6.22 (validity and soundness).

a. A correctness formula f is called *valid* ($\models$ f) if $F(f)(\varepsilon)(\sigma)$ holds for all ε such that $intv(f) \subseteq dom(\varepsilon)$ and all $\sigma \neq \bot$

b. An inference $\frac{f_1,\ldots,f_n}{f}$ is called *sound* $\left(\boxed{\frac{f_1,\ldots,f_n}{f}}\right)$, if validity of f_i, $i = 1,\ldots,n$, implies validity of f.

END 6.22.

Examples

1. $\models$ {true} begin new x;x:=0;y:=x end {y=0}.

2. $\boxed{\dfrac{\{p \wedge (x=x)\}S\{q\}}{\{p\}S\{q\}}}$

As to example 2, this may seem an immediate result from the rule of consequence. However, this is not as obvious as it appears at first sight. Consider the case that $x \notin$ *svar*(p,S,q). The validity of the premise of the rule is then of the form (*): for all ε such that *intv*(x,p,S,q) $\subseteq$ dom(ε), all $\sigma \neq \bot[\ldots]$, whereas that of the conclusion of the rule is of the form (**): for all ε such that *intv*(p,S,q) $\subseteq$ dom(ε), all $\sigma \neq \bot[\ldots]$. Since *intv*(p,S,q) $\subsetneq$ *intv*(x,p,S,q), the class of ε over which we quantify in (*) is properly contained in the class of ε over which we quantify in (**), and the implication (*) $\Rightarrow$ (**) is no longer as straightforward as it was before the introduction of environments. (Let us assure the reader who might feel somewhat worried about this, that we shall soon prove that the rule of consequence does hold, so that he can rely again on the intuition built up previously.)

We now present the proof system which is sound and complete for correctness formulae {p}S{q}:

1. {p[t/v]} v:=t {p} (assignment)

2. $\dfrac{\{p\}S_1\{q\},\{q\}S_2\{r\}}{\{p\}S_1;S_2\{r\}}$ (composition)

3. $\dfrac{\{p \wedge b\}S_1\{q\},\{p \wedge \neg b\}S_2\{q\}}{\{p\}\ \underline{\text{if}}\ b\ \underline{\text{then}}\ S_1\ \underline{\text{else}}\ S_2\ \underline{\text{fi}}\ \{q\}}$ (conditionals)

4. $$\frac{\{p\}S[y/x]\{q\}}{\{p\}\ \underline{\text{begin}}\ \underline{\text{new}}\ x;S\ \underline{\text{end}}\ \{q\}},\ \text{where } y \notin \mathit{svar}(p,S,q) \qquad \text{(blocks)}$$

I.e., if $\models \{p\}S[y/x]\{q\}$ holds for some fresh y, then $\models \{p\}$ begin new x;S end $\{q\}$ holds, and this is just what we expect as the effect of the simple variable declaration new x.

5. $$\frac{p \supset p_1, \{p_1\}S\{q_1\},\ q_1 \supset q}{\{p\}S\{q\}} \qquad \text{(consequence)}$$

In the remainder of this section, we prove that the system of rules 1 to 5 is sound.

LEMMA 6.23. $\models \{p[t/v]\}\ v{:=}t\ \{p\}$.

PROOF. We have to show that, for all ε such that $\mathit{intv}(p[t/v],v,t,p) \subseteq \mathrm{dom}(\varepsilon)$, and all $\sigma \neq \bot$

$$\forall\sigma'[T(p[t/v])(\varepsilon)(\sigma) \wedge \sigma' = M(v{:=}t)(\varepsilon)(\sigma) \Rightarrow T(p)(\varepsilon)(\sigma')].$$

By lemma 6.18 and definition 6.5 this is equivalent to

$$\forall\sigma'[T(p)(\varepsilon)(\sigma\{R(t)(\varepsilon)(\sigma)/L(v)(\varepsilon)(\sigma)\}) \wedge \sigma' =$$
$$\sigma\{R(t)(\varepsilon)(\sigma)/L(v)(\varepsilon)(\sigma)\} \Rightarrow T(p)(\varepsilon)(\sigma')]$$

which is clearly satisfied.
END 6.23.

LEMMA 6.24. $$\boxed{\frac{\{p\}S_1\{q\},\{q\}S_2\{r\}}{\{p\}S_1;S_2\{r\}}}$$

PROOF. By the various definitions, we have to show that from

1. For all ε such that $\mathit{intv}(p,S_1,q) \subseteq \mathrm{dom}(\varepsilon)$, all $\sigma \neq \bot$, $F(\{p\}S_1\{q\})(\varepsilon)(\sigma)$
2. For all ε such that $\mathit{intv}(q,S_2,r) \subseteq \mathrm{dom}(\varepsilon)$, all $\sigma \neq \bot$, $F(\{q\}S_2\{r\})(\varepsilon)(\sigma)$

it follows that

3. For all ε such that $intv(p,S_1,S_2,r) \subseteq dom(\varepsilon)$, all $\sigma \neq \bot$, $F(\{p\}S_1;S_2\{r\})(\varepsilon)(\sigma)$.

Assume 1, 2, and choose ε_0 such that $intv(p,S_1,S_2,r) \subseteq dom(\varepsilon_0)$. To show $\forall\sigma\neq\bot[F(\{p\}S_1;S_2\{r\})(\varepsilon_0)(\sigma)]$. Let ε_1 be an extension of ε_0 such that $intv(p,S_1,q,S_2,r) \subseteq dom(\varepsilon_1)$. By 1 and 2, we obtain that $\forall\sigma\neq\bot[F(\{p\}S_1\{q\})(\varepsilon_1)(\sigma)]$ and $\forall\sigma\neq\bot[F(\{q\}S_2\{r\})(\varepsilon_1)(\sigma)]$. By an argument exactly as in chapter 2, we infer that $\forall\sigma\neq\bot[F(\{p\}S_1;S_2\{r\})(\varepsilon_1)(\sigma)]$. The desired result now follows from this and lemma 6.21.

END 6.24.

<u>LEMMA 6.25</u>.
$$\frac{\{p\wedge b\}S_1\{q\},\{p\wedge\neg b\}S_2\{q\}}{\{p\}\ \underline{if}\ b\ \underline{then}\ S_1\ \underline{else}\ S_2\ \underline{fi}\ \{q\}}$$

<u>PROOF</u>. Exercise.

END 6.25.

<u>LEMMA 6.26</u>.
$$\frac{\{p\}S[y/x]\{q\}}{\{p\}\ \underline{begin}\ \underline{new}\ x;S\ \underline{end}\ \{q\}},\ \text{where } y \notin svar(p,S,q)$$

<u>PROOF</u>. We have to show that

$$\begin{array}{l}\text{For all } \varepsilon \text{ such that } intv(p,S[y/x],q) \subseteq dom(\varepsilon), \text{ all } \sigma \neq \bot \\ \forall\sigma'[T(p)(\varepsilon)(\sigma) \wedge \sigma' = M(S[y/x])(\varepsilon)(\sigma) \Rightarrow T(q)(\varepsilon)(\sigma')]\end{array} \qquad (6.4)$$

$$\Rightarrow$$

$$\begin{array}{l}\text{For all } \varepsilon \text{ such that } intv(p,\underline{begin}\ \underline{new}\ x;S\ \underline{end},q) \subseteq dom(\varepsilon), \text{ all } \sigma \neq \bot \\ \forall\sigma''[T(p)(\varepsilon)(\sigma) \wedge \sigma'' = M(\underline{begin}\ \underline{new}\ x;S\ \underline{end})(\varepsilon)(\sigma) \Rightarrow T(q)(\varepsilon)(\sigma'')].\end{array} \qquad (6.5)$$

So assume (6.4), and let ε, σ, σ'' be such that

1. $intv(p,\underline{begin}\ \underline{new}\ x;S\ \underline{end},q) \subseteq dom(\varepsilon)$, $\sigma \neq \bot$
2. $T(p)(\varepsilon)(\sigma)$
3. $\sigma'' = M(\underline{begin}\ \underline{new}\ x;S\ \underline{end})(\varepsilon)(\sigma)$

To show

4. $T(q)(\varepsilon)(\sigma'')$

Since $y \notin svar(p,S,q)$, we may, without lack of generality, assume

$y \notin dom(\varepsilon)$. (If, contrariwise, $\varepsilon = \varepsilon_0 \cup \langle y,e_0\rangle$ for some ε_0, e_0, replace ε everywhere by ε_0 and apply lemma 6.21.) By 3 and definition 6.5

5. $\sigma'' = M(S[z/x])(\varepsilon\cup\langle z,e\rangle)(\sigma)$, with $\langle z,e\rangle$ as usual.

By 2 and corollary 6.16a

6. $T(p)(\varepsilon\cup\langle y,e\rangle)(\sigma)$. Now let

7. $\sigma' = M(S[y/x])(\varepsilon\cup\langle y,e\rangle)(\sigma)$ (Note that, since $intv(S)\backslash\{x\} \subseteq dom(\varepsilon)$, we have that $intv(S[y/x]) \subseteq dom(\varepsilon\cup\langle y,e\rangle)$.)

Then, by 6,7 and (6.4) we obtain

8. $T(q)(\varepsilon\cup\langle y,e\rangle)(\sigma')$, from which, since $y \notin svar(q)$,

9. $T(q)(\varepsilon)(\sigma')$.

By 5, 7 and corollary 6.13b, for $\delta = dom(\varepsilon)$,

10. $(\sigma''\circ\varepsilon)|\delta = (\sigma'\circ\varepsilon)|\delta$.

The desired result 4 now follows from 9, 10 and corollary 6.16a.

END 6.26.

<u>LEMMA 6.27.</u>

$$\frac{p \supset p_1, \{p_1\}S\{q_1\}, q_1 \supset q}{\{p\}S\{q\}}$$

<u>PROOF</u>. Combine the argument to show soundness of the consequence rule as used in the previous chapters with the idea of extending the environments used in the definition of $\models \{p\}S\{q\}$ to include $intv(p_1,q_1)$ in their domain (cf. the proof of lemma 6.24). Details are left to the reader.

END 6.27.

Altogether, we have established

<u>THEOREM 6.28</u> (soundness theorem).

The proof system consisting of rules 1 to 5 is sound.

<u>PROOF</u>. Lemmas 6.23 - 6.27.

END 6.28.

6.4. Completeness

The system of rules 1 to 5 as presented in section 6.3, extended in the usual way with all valid assertions, is complete. More precisely, we shall prove the following fact: let us define Ax, Pr as

1. Ax consists of
   a. The assignment rule
   b. All assertions p such that $\models p$.
2. Pr consists of the rules of composition, conditionals, blocks and consequence.

Then, for all $p,q \in \mathit{Assn}$, $S \in \mathit{Stat}$ (Stat as in definition 6.1, but obeying the initialization requirement), if $\models \{p\}S\{q\}$ then $\vdash_{\mathit{Ax},\mathit{Pr}} \{p\}S\{q\}$. For the proof of this we need some preparations. The first one consists in showing that the rules of conditionals and blocks may be reversed, as formulated in

LEMMA 6.29.

a. $$\frac{\{p\}\ \underline{\text{if}}\ b\ \underline{\text{then}}\ S_1\ \underline{\text{else}}\ S_2\ \underline{\text{fi}}\ \{q\}}{\{p\wedge b\}S_1\{q\} \wedge \{p\wedge\neg b\}S_2\{q\}}$$

b. $$\frac{\{p\}\ \underline{\text{begin}}\ \underline{\text{new}}\ x;S\ \underline{\text{end}}\ \{q\}}{\{p\}S[y/x]\{q\}}, \text{ where } y \notin \mathit{svar}(p,S,q)$$

PROOF.

a. Exercise.

b. Let $y \notin \mathit{svar}(p,S,q)$. We show that (6.5) $\Rightarrow$ (6.4) (cf. the proof of lemma 6.26). Assume (6.5), and let ε, σ, σ' be such that
   1. $\mathit{intv}(p,S[y/x],q) \subseteq \mathrm{dom}(\varepsilon)$, $\sigma \neq \bot$
   2. $\mathcal{T}(p)(\varepsilon)(\sigma)$
   3. $\sigma' = \mathcal{M}(S[y/x])(\varepsilon)(\sigma)$

   To show

   4. $\mathcal{T}(q)(\varepsilon)(\sigma')$.

Without lack of generality (lemma 6.21 again) we may assume that $y \in dom(\varepsilon)$. (Note that, if $x \notin svar(S)$, then $y \in dom(\varepsilon)$ is not a consequence of $intv(S[y/x]) \subseteq dom(\varepsilon)$.) Thus, $\varepsilon = \varepsilon_0 \cup \langle y,e_0\rangle$, say.

By 2 and corollary 6.16a

5. $\mathcal{T}(p)(\varepsilon_0)(\sigma)$.

Now let

6. $\sigma'' = \mathcal{M}($<u>begin</u> <u>new</u> x;S <u>end</u>$)(\varepsilon_0)(\sigma)$.

By definition 6.5, we have

7. $\sigma'' = \mathcal{M}(S[z/x])(\varepsilon_0 \cup \langle z,\bar{e}\rangle)(\sigma)$, with z the first simple variable not in $dom(\varepsilon_0)$ and $\bar{e}$ the first address not in $range(\varepsilon_0)$.

By 5, 6 and (6.5) we obtain

8. $\mathcal{T}(q)(\varepsilon_0)(\sigma'')$.

Also, by 3,

9. $\sigma' = \mathcal{M}(S[y/x])(\varepsilon_0 \cup \langle y,e_0\rangle)(\sigma)$.

Since (by our general requirement on local variables) $x \in init(S)$ or $x \notin svar(S)$, from 7, 9 and theorem 6.12 we obtain, for $\delta = dom(\varepsilon_0)$,

10. $(\sigma'' \circ \varepsilon_0)|\delta = (\sigma' \circ \varepsilon_0)|\delta$.

Thus, from 8, 10 and corollary 6.16a

11. $\mathcal{T}(q)(\varepsilon_0)(\sigma')$.

The desired result 4 is now immediate from 11 and corollary 6.16a.

END 6.29.

Secondly, we investigate what happens with weakest preconditions and strongest postconditions in the presence of blocks. Contrary to the situation in previous chapters, there is a certain asymmetry between the results for weakest preconditions and strongest postconditions. Therefore, we first treat the former notion and then devote a separate discussion to the latter. Let us recall that we call an assertion r a weakest precondition with respect to a statement S and an assertion q if the following requirement is satisfied:

$$\text{For all } p\ [\models \{p\}S\{q\} \iff \models p \supset r] \tag{6.6}$$

Clearly, by the definition of $\models \{p\}S\{q\}$, if we can find an assertion r such that (i) $intv(r) \subseteq intv(S,q)$, and (ii) for all ε such that $intv(S,q) \subseteq dom(\varepsilon)$, and all $\sigma \neq \bot$ we have

$$\mathcal{T}(r)(\varepsilon)(\sigma) = \forall\sigma'[\sigma' = \mathcal{M}(S)(\varepsilon)(\sigma) \Rightarrow \mathcal{T}(q)(\varepsilon)(\sigma')] \qquad (6.7)$$

then we have established that an assertion r satisfying (6.6) always exists, i.e. weakest preconditions are *expressible*, cf. lemma 2.31 and the propositions of sections 3.6 and 5.5. The next definition introduces, for each S and q, an assertion r for which we shall prove in lemma 6.32 that it indeed satisfies (6.7).

DEFINITION 6.30 (assertions for weakest preconditions).
For each S,q we define an assertion, denoted by S{q}, by induction on the complexity of S:

a. $(v{:=}t)\{q\} \equiv q[t/v]$
b. $(S_1;S_2)\{q\} \equiv S_1\{S_2\{q\}\}$
c. <u>if</u> b <u>then</u> S_1 <u>else</u> S_2 <u>fi</u> $\{q\} \equiv (b \wedge S_1\{q\}) \vee (\neg b \wedge S_2\{q\})$
d. <u>begin</u> <u>new</u> x;S <u>end</u> $\{q\} \equiv \forall y[S[y/x]\{q\}]$, where y is the first simple variable $\notin svar(S,q)$.

END 6.30.

Remarks

1. Contrary to the approach taken in other chapters, we find it convenient to avoid the introduction of *conditions* $S \rightarrow q$, and restrict ourselves completely to assertions.
2. Clearly, we have that $intv(S\{q\}) \subseteq intv(S,q)$.
3. Clauses a to c of this definition are reformulations of ideas from chapters 2,4; clause d is new. As we shall see, its simple formulation is a consequence of the initialization requirement.

In the next lemma we state some desirable properties of S{q}, viz.

- it preserves congruence
- definition 6.30d is invariant - up to congruence - under a change of

bound variable; thus, the choice of y as *first* simple variable $\notin$ *svar*(S,q), made for definiteness, is justified

- S{q} is preserved by substitution of a fresh simple variable.

LEMMA 6.31.

a. If $S \cong S'$ then $S\{q\} \cong S'\{q\}$

b. $\forall y[S[y/x]\{q\}] \cong \forall z[S[z/x]\{q\}]$, where $y,z \notin svar(S,q)$

c. $S\{q\}[y/x] \cong S[y/x]\{q[y/x]\}$, where $y \notin svar(S,q)$.

PROOF. Parts a and b are proved simultaneously by induction on the complexity of S. Part c is also by induction on the complexity of S. If $S \equiv v{:=}t$, use lemma 6.17. If S is a block, use parts a,b.
END 6.31.

We now prove

LEMMA 6.32. For all ε such that $intv(S,q) \subseteq dom(\varepsilon)$, and all $\sigma \neq \bot$

$$T(S\{q\})(\varepsilon)(\sigma) = \forall\sigma'[\sigma' = M(S)(\varepsilon)(\sigma) \Rightarrow T(q)(\varepsilon)(\sigma')]$$

PROOF. Induction on the complexity of S.

a. $S \equiv v{:=}s$. Use lemma 6.18

b. $S \equiv S_1;S_2$. Apart from the presence of the ε-arguments, this is a reformulation of the result $\models (S_1;S_2) \rightarrow q = S_1 \rightarrow (S_2 \rightarrow q)$ from chapter 2

c. $S \equiv$ <u>if</u> b <u>then</u> S_1 <u>else</u> S_2 <u>fi</u>. Exercise.

d. $S \equiv$ <u>begin</u> <u>new</u> $x;S_1$ <u>end</u>. We have to show that, for all ε such that *intv*(<u>begin</u> <u>new</u> $x;S_1$ <u>end</u>,q) $\subseteq dom(\varepsilon)$, all $\sigma \neq \bot$ (and $\langle z,e\rangle$ as usual)

$$\forall\sigma'[\sigma' = M(\underline{\text{begin}}\ \underline{\text{new}}\ x;S_1\ \underline{\text{end}})(\varepsilon)(\sigma) \Rightarrow T(q)(\varepsilon)(\sigma')]$$

$$\Longleftrightarrow$$

$$\forall\alpha[T((S_1[y/x]\{q\})[z/y])(\varepsilon\cup\langle z,e\rangle)(\sigma\{\alpha/e\})]$$

By definition 6.5, the induction hypothesis, lemma 6.31c, the fact that $S_1[y/x][z/y] \cong S_1[z/x]$, $y,z \notin svar(q)$, and corollary 6.16a, the above equivalence amounts to

$$\forall\sigma'[\sigma' = \mathcal{M}(S_1[z/x])(\varepsilon\cup\langle z,e\rangle)(\sigma) \Rightarrow \mathcal{T}(q)(\varepsilon)(\sigma')]$$

$$\Leftrightarrow$$

$$\forall\alpha,\sigma''[\sigma'' = \mathcal{M}(S_1[z/x])(\varepsilon\cup\langle z,e\rangle)(\sigma\{\alpha/e\}) \Rightarrow \mathcal{T}(q)(\varepsilon)(\sigma'')]$$

By theorem 6.12, since $x \in$ *init*(S_1) or $x \notin$ *svar*(S_1), if $\sigma' = \mathcal{M}(S_1[z/x])(\varepsilon\cup\langle z,e\rangle)(\sigma)$, $\sigma'' = \mathcal{M}(S_1[z/x])(\varepsilon\cup\langle z,e\rangle)(\sigma\{\alpha/e\})$, then $(\sigma'\circ\varepsilon)|\delta = (\sigma''\circ\varepsilon)|\delta$, where $\delta = \mathrm{dom}(\varepsilon)$.

Hence, the desired result is immediate by corollary 6.16a.

END 6.32.

This concludes our discussion of weakest preconditions. As we shall soon see, lemma 6.32 allows us to give a completeness proof which is a fairly straightforward combination of the methods of section 2.6 with lemma 6.29b. Before doing this, we first analyze the strongest postcondition problem. (The outcome of this analysis is not necessary for the completeness proof of this section. However, we shall employ the results in chapter 9.)

The expressibility problem for strongest postconditions exhibits a phenomenon not present for weakest preconditions. For the purpose of the present discussion only, we introduce *two* notions of strongest postcondition:

a. An assertion r is called a *syntactic* strongest postcondition with respect to p and S if it satisfies

$$\text{For all } q\ [\models \{p\}S\{q\} \Leftrightarrow\ \models r \supset q] \tag{6.8}$$

b. An assertion r is called a *semantic* strongest postcondition with respect to p and S if it satisfies (i) *intv*(r) $\subseteq$ *intv*(p,S), and (ii) for all ε such that *intv*(p,S) $\subseteq \mathrm{dom}(\varepsilon)$, all $\sigma \neq \bot$

$$\mathcal{T}(r)(\varepsilon)(\sigma) = \exists\sigma'[\mathcal{T}(p)(\varepsilon)(\sigma') \wedge \sigma = \mathcal{M}(S)(\varepsilon)(\sigma')] \tag{6.9}$$

Contrary to the results for weakest preconditions, these two notions do not coincide. More specifically, we have the following results:

1. For each p,S,r, if r satisfies (6.9) then r satisfies (6.8): each semantic strongest postcondition for p,S is a syntactic strongest postcondition for p,S. This an immediate consequence of the definition of $\models \{p\}S\{q\}$.
2. For all p and S, the syntactic strongest postcondition is always expressible (i.e. there exists some r satisfying (6.8)). This is the content of lemma 6.37.
3. There exist p and S such that the semantic strongest postcondition is not expressible (no r satisfying (6.9)). This is shown by the following example: take p $\equiv$ <u>true</u>, S $\equiv$ <u>begin</u> <u>new</u> x;x:=0 <u>end</u>, $\varepsilon = \emptyset$, end e the first address (not in range($\emptyset$)). The right-hand side of (6.9) then simplifies to $\exists\sigma'[\sigma = \sigma'\{0/e\}]$. It is easily seen that there exists no assertion r such that, for all σ, $T(r)(\emptyset)(\sigma) = \exists\sigma'[\sigma = \sigma'\{0/e\}]$. In fact, r would then have to express the property "$\sigma(e) = 0$", which is clearly impossible.

Our proof that the syntactic strongest postcondition is expressible uses an auxiliary result involving a variant on the semantic characterization of strongest postconditions as given in (6.9).

<u>LEMMA 6.33</u>. For each p,S,q we have

$$\text{For all } \varepsilon \text{ such that } intv(p,S,q) \subseteq dom(\varepsilon), \text{ all } \sigma \neq \bot \qquad (6.10)$$
$$\exists\sigma'[T(p)(\varepsilon)(\sigma') \wedge \sigma = M(S)(\varepsilon)(\sigma')] \Rightarrow T(q)(\varepsilon)(\sigma)$$
$$\Longleftrightarrow$$
$$\text{For all } \varepsilon \text{ such that } intv(p,S,q) \subseteq \delta = dom(\varepsilon), \text{ all } \sigma \neq \bot \qquad (6.11)$$
$$\exists\sigma''[T(p)(\varepsilon)(\sigma'') \wedge (\sigma\circ\varepsilon)|\delta = (M(S)(\varepsilon)(\sigma'')\circ\varepsilon)|\delta] \Rightarrow T(q)(\varepsilon)(\sigma)$$

<u>PROOF</u>. " $\Leftarrow$ " is obvious. In order to prove " $\Rightarrow$ ", assume (6.10), and let ε, σ, σ'' be such that $intv(p,S,q) \subseteq \delta = dom(\varepsilon)$, $T(p)(\varepsilon)(\sigma'')$, and $(\sigma\circ\varepsilon)|\delta = (M(S)(\varepsilon)(\sigma'')\circ\varepsilon)|\delta$. To show $T(q)(\varepsilon)(\sigma)$, let $\bar{\sigma} = M(S)(\varepsilon)(\sigma'')$, whence (*): $(\sigma\circ\varepsilon)|\delta = (\bar{\sigma}\circ\varepsilon)|\delta$. By (6.10) we infer that $T(q)(\varepsilon)(\bar{\sigma})$,

and the desired result follows from (*) and corollary 6.16a.
END 6.33.

We now give, for each p and S, the definition of an assertion {p}S for which we show in lemma 6.36 that it expresses the condition used in (6.11).

DEFINITION 6.34 (assertions for syntactic strongest postconditions). For each p,S, we define an assertion, denoted by {p}S, by induction on the complexity of S

a. $\{p\}x:=s \equiv \exists y[p[y/x] \wedge x = s[y/x]]$, y the first simple variable $\notin$ *svar*(p,x,s)
b. $\{p\}a[s]:=t \equiv \exists y,z[p[y/a[z]] \wedge z = s[y/a[z]] \wedge a[z] = t[y/a[z]]]$, y(z) the first (second) simple variable $\notin$ *svar*(p,s,t)
c. $\{p\}S_1;S_2 \equiv \{\{p\}S_1\}S_2$
d. {p} <u>if</u> b <u>then</u> S_1 <u>else</u> S_2 <u>fi</u> $\equiv \{p \wedge b\}S_1 \vee \{p \wedge \neg b\}S_2$
e. {p} <u>begin</u> <u>new</u> x;S <u>end</u> $\equiv \exists y[\{p\}S[y/x]]$, y the first simple variable $\notin$ *svar*(p,S)

END 6.34.

Remarks

1. Observe that *intv*({p}S) $\subseteq$ *intv*(p,S).
2. Again, only clause e contains a new idea, the remaining ones being taken from chapters 2,4.

Similarly to lemma 6.31, we have

LEMMA 6.35.

a. If S $\cong$ S', then {p}S $\cong$ {p}S'
b. $\exists y[\{p\}S[y/x]] \cong \exists z[\{p\}S[z/x]]$, where y,z $\notin$ *svar*(p,S)
c. $(\{p\}S)[y/x] \cong \{p[y/x]\}S[y/x]$, where y $\notin$ *svar*(p,S).

PROOF. Exercise.
END 6.35.

Next we show that {p}S satisfies the announced property:

LEMMA 6.36. For each p,S, each ε such that $intv(p,S) \subseteq \delta = dom(\varepsilon)$, $\sigma \neq \bot$

$$\mathcal{T}(\{p\}S)(\varepsilon)(\sigma) = \exists\sigma'[\mathcal{T}(p)(\varepsilon)(\sigma') \wedge (\sigma\circ\varepsilon)|\delta = (\mathcal{M}(S)(\varepsilon)(\sigma')\circ\varepsilon)|\delta]$$

PROOF. Induction on the complexity of S

a. $S \equiv x:=s$. We have to show that, for all ε such that $intv(p,x,s) \subseteq dom(\varepsilon)$, all $\sigma \neq \bot$ (using properties of substitution; cf. also theorem 2.21)

$$\exists\alpha[\mathcal{T}(p[z/x] \wedge x{=}s[z/x])(\varepsilon\cup\langle z,e\rangle)(\sigma\{\alpha/e\})] \quad (\langle z,e\rangle \text{ as usual})$$
$$\Longleftrightarrow$$
$$\exists\sigma'[\mathcal{T}(p)(\varepsilon)(\sigma') \wedge (\sigma\circ\varepsilon)|\delta = (\sigma'\{\bar{\alpha}/\bar{e}\}\circ\varepsilon)|\delta]$$
where $\bar{\alpha} = \mathcal{R}(s)(\varepsilon)(\sigma')$, $\bar{e} = \varepsilon(x)$

" $\Rightarrow$ ". Take $\sigma' = \sigma\{\alpha/\bar{e}\}$. Since $\mathcal{T}(p[z/x])(\varepsilon\cup\langle z,e\rangle)(\sigma\{\alpha/e\})$, by corollary 6.19 also $\mathcal{T}(p)(\varepsilon)(\sigma\{\alpha/\bar{e}\}$, i.e. $\mathcal{T}(p)(\varepsilon)(\sigma')$. Moreover, since $\sigma(\bar{e}) = \sigma\{\alpha/e\}(\varepsilon(x)) = \mathcal{R}(s[z/x])(\varepsilon\cup\langle z,e\rangle)(\sigma\{\alpha/e\})$, by corollary 6.10 we have that $\sigma(\bar{e}) = \mathcal{R}(s)(\varepsilon)(\sigma\{\alpha/\bar{e}\}) = \mathcal{R}(s)(\varepsilon)(\sigma') = \bar{\alpha}$, and $(\sigma\circ\varepsilon)|\delta = (\sigma'\{\bar{\alpha}/\bar{e}\}\circ\varepsilon)|\delta$ follows.

" $\Leftarrow$ ". Take $\alpha = \sigma'(\bar{e})$.

b. $S \equiv a[s]:=t$. Follows by adapting the proof of theorem 4.7 to the present framework.

c. $S \equiv S_1;S_2$. By the various definitions and the induction hypothesis, it suffices to show that, for ε, δ, σ as usual

$$\exists\sigma',\sigma''[\mathcal{T}(p)(\varepsilon)(\sigma') \wedge \sigma'' = \mathcal{M}(S_1)(\varepsilon)(\sigma') \wedge (\sigma\circ\varepsilon)|\delta = (\mathcal{M}(S_2)(\varepsilon)(\sigma'')\circ\varepsilon)|\delta]$$
$$\Longleftrightarrow$$
$$\exists\sigma_2[\exists\sigma_1[\mathcal{T}(p)(\varepsilon)(\sigma_1) \wedge (\sigma_2\circ\varepsilon)|\delta = (\mathcal{M}(S_1)(\varepsilon)(\sigma_1)\circ\varepsilon)|\delta] \wedge (\sigma\circ\varepsilon)|\delta = (\mathcal{M}(S_2)(\varepsilon)(\sigma_2)\circ\varepsilon)|\delta]$$

Take $\sigma' = \sigma_1$. Then $(\sigma''\circ\varepsilon)|\delta = (\sigma_2\circ\varepsilon)|\delta$, from which we obtain, by corollary 6.13a, that $(M(S_2)(\varepsilon)(\sigma'')\circ\varepsilon)|\delta = (M(S_2)(\varepsilon)(\sigma_2)\circ\varepsilon)|\delta$, thus implying the desired equivalence result.

d. $S \equiv$ <u>if</u> b <u>then</u> S_1 <u>else</u> S_2 <u>fi</u>. Exercise.

e. $S \equiv$ <u>begin</u> <u>new</u> x;S_1 <u>end</u>. Using the induction hypothesis, properties of substitution, and y,z $\notin$ *svar*(p), what we have to show amounts to ($\varepsilon,\delta,\sigma,\langle z,e\rangle$ as usual)

$$\exists\sigma'[T(p)(\varepsilon)(\sigma') \wedge (\sigma\circ\varepsilon)|\delta = (M(S[z/x])(\varepsilon\cup\langle z,e\rangle)(\sigma')\circ\varepsilon)|\delta]$$

$$\Longleftrightarrow$$

$$\exists\alpha,\sigma''[T(p)(\varepsilon\cup\langle z,e\rangle)(\sigma'') \wedge (\sigma\{\alpha/e\}\circ(\varepsilon\cup\langle z,e\rangle))|(\delta\cup\{z\}) = (M(S[z/x])(\varepsilon\cup\langle z,e\rangle)(\sigma'')\circ(\varepsilon\cup\langle z,e\rangle))|(\delta\cup\{z\})]$$

" $\Leftarrow$ " is clear. For " $\Rightarrow$ ", take $\sigma'' = \sigma'$, and $\alpha = M(S[z/x])(\varepsilon\cup\langle z,e\rangle)(\sigma'')(e)$.

END 6.36.

We finally conclude our treatment of strongest postconditions with

<u>LEMMA 6.37</u>. For each p,S there exists an assertion r such that

$$\text{for all } q\ [\models \{p\}S\{q\} \Longleftrightarrow \models r\supset q].$$

<u>PROOF</u>. Follows from the definition of $\models\{p\}S\{q\}$, lemma 6.33, and lemma 6.36.

END 6.37.

Having thus completed our analysis of weakest preconditions and strongest postconditions, we now turn to the proof of the completeness theorem:

<u>THEOREM 6.38</u> (completeness theorem).

Let Ax, Pr be as stated in the beginning of this section. Then

$$\models\{p\}S\{q\} \Rightarrow\ \vdash_{Ax,Pr} \{p\}S\{q\}$$

PROOF. Induction on the complexity of S.

a. $S \equiv v{:=}s$. As before, $\models \{p\}\ v{:=}s\ \{q\}$ implies $\models p \supset q[s/v]$. Now argue as in the proof of theorem 2.40.

b. $S \equiv S_1;S_2$. We have that from $\models \{p\}S_1;S_2\{q\}$ it follows that $\models \{p\}S_1\{S_2\{q\}\}$, and $\models \{S_2\{q\}\}S_2\{q\}$, with the assertion $S_2\{q\}$ as given in definition 6.30. Now use the induction hypothesis and the composition rule.

c. $S \equiv$ if b then S_1 else S_2 fi. Exercise.

d. $S \equiv$ begin new x;S_1 end. By lemma 6.29b, for $y \notin$ *svar*(p,S_1,q), we have that $\models \{p\}S_1[y/x]\{q\}$. By induction, this implies that $\vdash_{Ax,Pr} \{p\}S_1[y/x]\{q\}$, and the desired result follows by the rule of blocks.

END 6.38.

Exercises

6.1. Is *Env*, with the (usual) ordering $\varepsilon_1 \sqsubseteq \varepsilon_2$ iff, for all ξ, $\varepsilon_1(\xi) \sqsubseteq \varepsilon_2(\xi)$, a cpo?

6.2. Extend lemma 6.17 to constructs of the form $s<t_1/v_1><t_2/v_2>$, etc.

6.3. Prove

a. $$\frac{p}{p[s/x]}$$

b. $$\frac{p \supset q}{p \supset \forall z[q]}, \text{ provided that } z \notin svar(p)$$

6.4. Prove

$\models \{p\}S\{p\}$, provided that $intv(p) \cap intv(S) = \emptyset$.

6.5. Prove that lemmas 6.31, 6.32 remain true if we replace definition 6.30d by begin new x;S end $\{q\} \equiv \exists y[S[y/x]\{q\}]$, where y is the first simple variable $\notin$ *svar*(S,q).

6.6. Prove

$$\frac{\{p[y/x]\}S\{q[y/x]\}}{\{p\}\ \underline{\text{begin}}\ \underline{\text{new}}\ x;S\ \underline{\text{end}}\ \{q\}},\ \text{where } y \notin \mathit{svar}(p,S,q)$$

6.7. Prove

a. $$\frac{\{p\}S\{q\}}{\{p[s/x]\}S\{q\}},\ \text{where } x \notin \mathit{svar}(S,q)$$

b. $$\frac{\{p\}S\{q\}}{\{p[y/x]\}S[y/x]\{q[y/x]\}},\ \text{where } y \notin \mathit{svar}(S,q)$$

(Hint: use $\models \{p\}S\{q\}$ iff $\models p \supset S\{q\}$, exercise 6.3a, and lemma 6.31.)

6.8. Prove that in lemmas 6.26, 6.29b and definition 6.30d, lemma 6.31, the restriction on y may be weakened to, respectively

- $y \notin \mathit{svar}(p,q) \cup (\mathit{svar}(S)\backslash\{x\})$
- idem
- $y \notin (\mathit{svar}(S)\backslash\{x\}) \cup \mathit{svar}(q)$
- $y \notin \mathit{svar}(S,q)\backslash\{x\}$,

and analogously for definition 6.34e, lemma 6.35.

In the remaining exercises, we do not assume that all local simple variables of a statement are initialized.

6.9. Prove

a. $\models$ {<u>true</u>} <u>begin</u> <u>new</u> x;x:=0 <u>end</u>; <u>begin</u> <u>new</u> z;y:=z <u>end</u> {y=0}

b. $\models$ {<u>true</u>} <u>begin</u> <u>new</u> x;y:=x <u>end</u>; <u>begin</u> <u>new</u> z;u:=z <u>end</u> {y=u}.

6.10. Prove that, for all ε such that $\mathit{intv}(S)\backslash\{x\} \subseteq \mathrm{dom}(\varepsilon)$,

$M(S[y/x])(\varepsilon\cup\langle y,e\rangle) = M(S[z/x])(\varepsilon\cup\langle z,e\rangle)$.

6.11. (redefinition of matching) Let us call two pairs $\langle\varepsilon,\sigma\rangle,\langle\bar{\varepsilon},\bar{\sigma}\rangle$ matching over $\delta \subseteq \mathit{Intv}$ if either $\sigma = \bot$, $\bar{\sigma} = \bot$, or

(i) $\sigma \neq \bot$, $\bar{\sigma} \neq \bot$

(ii) $(\sigma \circ \varepsilon)|\delta = (\bar{\sigma} \circ \bar{\varepsilon})|\delta$

(iii) For k = 1,2,..., if e_k is the k-th address $\notin$ range(ε), $\bar{e}_k$ is the k-th address $\notin$ range($\bar{\varepsilon}$), then $\sigma(e_k) = \bar{\sigma}(\bar{e}_k)$.

Prove that theorem 6.28 also holds for statements which do not obey the initialization requirement.

(Hint: such statements preserve the property of matching in its redefined form, a result necessary for the proof of soundness of the composition and consequence rules. For the block rule use exercise 6.10.)

6.12. (redefinition of semantics) Let $\Sigma \stackrel{\text{df.}}{=} (Addr_0 \to (V_0 \times \{+,-\})) \cup \{\bot\}$ and let us put, for $\sigma(e) = \langle\alpha,\pm\rangle$, $\sigma(e)_1 = \alpha$, $\sigma(e)_2 = \pm$. (+(-) is a flag indicating (by $\sigma(e)_2 = +(-)$) that address e has not (has) been used before as first free address.) We define

M(<u>begin</u> <u>new</u> x;S <u>end</u>)(ε)(σ) =
$M(S[y/x])(\varepsilon \cup \langle y,e\rangle)(\sigma\{\langle\sigma(e)_1,-\rangle/e\})$

where y is the first simple variable $\notin$ dom(ε) and e the first address $\notin$ range(ε) such that $\sigma(e)_2 = +$.

Investigate the consequences of this definition for the theory of chapter 6.

Chapter 7

NONDETERMINISTIC STATEMENTS

7.1. Introduction

This chapter is mainly devoted to a study of the programming concept of nondeterminacy. We introduce the syntactic construct $S_1 \cup S_2$, with as intended meaning: $S_1 \cup S_2$ is executed by choosing in some unspecified manner either S_1 or S_2, and executing it. Though this construct may be somewhat less common in current programming languages than the ones encountered before, we have at least three reasons for wanting to study it:

- We consider it to be the first step on the way to an analysis of *parallelism*. Since the present status of the research on semantics and proof theory of parallelism is, in our opinion, not yet such that it justifies a treatment on the textbook-level, we refrain from a discussion of the next steps in this analysis. All we do here is to give one small example which may give a first idea of the connections between the two notions. Consider the two statements $A_1;A_2$ and $A_3;A_4$, where each of the A_i, $i = 1,\ldots,4$, is an *atomic* statement, i.e., its execution is not interruptible by that of any other statement. According to the usual meaning of the parallel execution of two statements - let us syntactically write $S_1 \| S_2$ for this - we have that $A_1;A_2 \| A_3;A_4$ is equivalent with $A_1;A_2;A_3;A_4 \cup A_1;A_3;A_2;A_4 \cup A_1;A_3;A_4;A_2 \cup A_3;A_1;A_2;A_4 \cup A_3;A_1;A_4;A_2 \cup A_3;A_4;A_1;A_2$. (The general idea is to arbitrarily merge the atomic statements which constitute S_1 and S_2, but such that the order in which they occur in S_1 and S_2 is preserved.)
- There is at least one programming concept which clearly involves

nondeterminacy in our sense in a direct way, viz. Dijkstra's *guarded commands*. We shall see that both his constructs <u>if</u> $b_1 \to S_1$ □ ... □ $b_n \to S_n$ <u>fi</u> and <u>do</u> $b_1 \to S_1$ □ ... □ $b_n \to S_n$ <u>od</u> can be expressed immediately in our syntax, and, accordingly, obtain as it were for free a rigorous treatment of their semantics and correctness.

- Nondeterminacy is a central notion in abstract machine theory. Therefore, it is of some independent interest to investigate the consequences for our semantic framework of its incorporation in a programming language. As we shall see, the necessary extensions are non-trivial and rely on a recently proposed ordering-definition on an appropriate domain.

Besides the introduction of nondeterministic statements, this chapter also presents a new syntactic formalism to deal with parameterless recursive procedures. Its appearance at the present stage of the development is not so much a matter of principle, but is rather motivated by reasons of convenience. The new formalism differs from the one used in chapter 5 in that it avoids the notion of procedure declaration, and replaces it by the so-called μ-notation. Statement variables X,Y,... take the place of the previously used procedure variables P,Q,..., and a statement-variable-binding prefix μX[...] is introduced which on the one hand is similar to the ∃x[...] construct encountered before (insofar as the notions of free and bound occurrence, substitution, etc., are concerned) and on the other hand is used to replace a program which according to the syntax of chapter 5 would be written as $\langle P \Leftarrow \ldots P \ldots P \ldots \mid P \rangle$ by the statement μX[...X...X...]. If one so wishes, one may view this as a means to do away with declarations by explicitly providing the procedure body at each call (with the exception, of course, of inner recursive calls). The introduction of the μ-formalism is motivated mainly by its advantages for studying problems concerning flow of control, allowing a concise formulation of various results which would be cumbersome to express in the syntax of chapter 5.

Section 2 of this chapter introduces the necessary extensions to the semantic framework. Statements are no longer assigned meanings as functions from states to states, but from states to sets of states of a certain kind. These sets are ordered with a new ordering, and it is necessary to verify that the relevant material of sections 5.2 and 5.3 may be carried over. We do not give an operational semantics of our new language. This is a rather difficult topic, necessitating the development of a formalism to deal with possibly infinite computation trees. In particular, a rigorous proof of the equivalence of operational and denotational semantics is far from easy. Therefore, we have decided not to include a treatment of these issues in this book. All we do is to provide an occasional reference to the operational view in order to support the intuition in understanding the mathematical definitions. Once the appropriate mathematical foundations have been laid, the semantic definitions proper of our language constructs turn out to be a straightforward variation on the definitions from chapter 5.

Section 7.3 discusses correctness questions. The absence of declarations simplifies the correctness formalism, which is essentially an adaptation of section 5.4 to the new syntax. No essentially new notions are provided; instead, the main interest of this section lies in its examples. Some of these are reformulations of previous results, but we also deal with a few problems which would have been somewhat awkward to tackle in the old formalism. Observe that there is no section on completeness. We expect that the techniques of section 5.5 can be modified appropriately to deal with the μ-calculus, but we have not explored this possibility at the moment of writing this. (For completeness results on the correctness of nondeterministic statements in the framework of dynamic logic see the bibliographical remarks concerning this chapter at the end of our book.)

7.2. Semantics

As usual, we start with the new syntax. This is going to look somewhat unfamiliar, since we shall introduce at the same time three new ideas:

- The new semantic concept of nondeterministic choice between two statements S_1 and S_2, written as $S_1 \cup S_2$.
- A new syntactic treatment of recursion through the so-called μ-formalism.
- Boolean expressions are incorporated as a subclass of the class of statements. As we shall see, on the one hand this allows us to *define* conditional statements and guarded commands in terms of the given constructs, and, on the other hand, facilitates various correctness considerations.

Let *Stmv*, with typical elements X,Y,... be a new syntactic class the elements of which are called ***statement variables***. (Its role will be similar, though not identical, to that of *Pvar*.) Just as *Svar*, the set *Stmv* is assumed to be well-ordered (cf. definition 7.13).

DEFINITION 7.1 (nondeterministic statements and the μ-formalism). The class of statements *Stat*, with typical elements S,..., is defined by

$$S::= v:=t \mid b \mid S_1;S_2 \mid S_1 \cup S_2 \mid X \mid \mu X[S] \ .$$

The classes *Ivar*, with typical elements v,w,..., *Iexp*, with typical elements s,t,..., and *Bexp*, with typical elements b,..., are left unchanged with respect to the previous definitions.
END 7.1.

We adopt the convention that ";" has priority over "∪", i.e. that a statement $S_1;S_2 \cup S_3$ is parsed as $((S_1;S_2) \cup S_3)$ and not as $(S_1;(S_2 \cup S_3))$, and similarly for $S_1 \cup S_2;S_3$. For the conditional statement, in previous chapters written as <u>if</u> b <u>then</u> S_1 <u>else</u> S_2 <u>fi</u>, we now write $b;S_1 \cup \neg b;S_2$. According to the semantics of our new class *Stat*, to be given presently, this definition preserves the usual meaning of the conditional statement. A discussion of how we express the guarded commands is postponed for a little while. As we saw in the introduction, the construct $\mu X[S]$ corresponds to parameterless recursive procedures as introduced in chapter 5 in the following way: suppose we have, in the syntax of chapter 5, a program $<P \Leftarrow S | P>$, where $S \equiv ...P...P...$ is a statement which, in general, contains occurrences of P (i.e., recursive calls). In the new formalism this program is written as $\mu X[...X...X...]$. Next we explain what happens for *systems* of recursive procedures. Consider the program $<P_1 \Leftarrow S_1, P_2 \Leftarrow S_2 | P_1>$, or, rather, in an informal notation, $<P_1 \Leftarrow S_1(P_1,P_2), P_2 \Leftarrow S_2(P_1,P_2) | P_1>$, where, for any S, writing $S(P_1,P_2)$ instead of S indicates that we are interested in the (free) occurrences of P_1 and P_2 in S. In the μ-formalism we have as corresponding statement $\mu X[S_1(X,\mu Y[S_2(X,Y)])]$, where we use, for arbitrary S,S',S", the (also informal) notation S(S',S") for the result of substituting in S, S' for P_1 and S" for P_2. We observe here an approach which reminds us of theorem 5.14: The simultaneous recursion $<P_1 \Leftarrow S_1, P_2 \Leftarrow S_2 | P_1>$ is replaced by an equivalent iterated recursion in the μ-formalism. Of course, for the moment these considerations are only about syntax; the claim that the same meaning is attributed to recursive procedures in both formalisms will have to be substantiated later.

The introduction of nondeterminacy requires an extension of our semantic framework. As first step we note that the meaning of a statement is no longer a function from states to states, but from states to *sets of states*. As an example we have that execution of $x:=x+1 \cup x:=x+2$ for input state $\sigma\{0/x\}$ yields the set of output states $\{\sigma\{1/x\},\sigma\{2/x\}\}$. It will be clear that, owing to the possibility of repeated use of the choice operation "$\cup$", we have to admit *finite* sets of states as outcomes of a state transformation determined by some $S \in$ *Stat*. However, infinite resulting sets are just as well possible. Consider the recursive procedure $\mu X[x:=x+1;X \cup D]$.

(As usual, D stands for the dummy statement, say x:=x.) The intended meaning of this construct is the following: either perform the dummy statement, or increase x by 1 and call the procedure again, i.e. again, either perform the dummy statement, or increase x by 1 and call the procedure again, i.e. etc. Observe that a sequence of choices which *always* selects the first term is possible, thus leading to a nonterminating computation. Accordingly, when we apply this procedure to the state $\sigma\{0/x\}$, say, we expect as resulting output the set of states $\{\sigma\{0/x\}\ \sigma\{1/x\},\ldots,\bot\}$. The phenomenon that an infinite output set has $\bot$ as one of its members is in fact a general property, which may be explained by viewing the execution of a statement as a *tree* of computations, and then using König's lemma which tells us that a finitely-branching tree with infinitely many nodes has at least one infinite path.

This brief sketch of the operational meaning of nondeterminacy in combination with recursion will have to suffice here. As remarked above, we shall not introduce a formal definition of the operational semantics of $S \in \mathit{Stat}$. In the present chapter we only give the precise definition of its mathematical semantics. Partly, this follows the lines as developed already in chapter 5, but as an important new feature we have, as we just saw, the fact that we are now dealing with functions, not from states to states, but from states to either finite sets of states, or infinite sets containing $\bot$. Therefore, as first step in the semantic definitions we give

DEFINITION 7.2 (range of state transformations).
The set T, with typical elements $\tau,\ldots$, consists of
a. All finite subsets of Σ
b. All infinite subsets of Σ which contain $\bot$
END 7.2.

(Do not confuse this set T with the set $\mathrm{T} = \{tt,ff\}$!)

As all our semantic domains, T has to be provided with some ordering.

This is given in

DEFINITION 7.3 (T as cpo).
Let $\tau_1,\tau_2 \in T$. $\tau_1 \sqsubseteq \tau_2$ holds iff either $\perp \in \tau_1$ and $\tau_1\backslash\{\perp\} \subseteq \tau_2$, or $\perp \notin \tau_1$ and $\tau_1 = \tau_2$.
END 7.3.

The ordering in this definition is the so-called Egli-Milner ordering. The motivation for it is the following: Let τ_1,τ_2 be two approximations to the set of output states for a given statement S and input state σ. When shall we consider τ_2 as a better approximation to the final result than τ_1? We see whether τ_1 contains $\perp$. If so, then this indicates a path in the computation tree which may not yet be completed. (Here we have a process in mind which obtains the meaning of a (statement involving a) recursive procedure through successive approximations, starting with $\lambda\sigma\cdot\perp$ as zero-th step. Correspondingly, we construct a sequence of computation trees, each of which has the input state σ as its root, while the set of leaves constitutes the current approximation τ_i to the final result τ. Compare also the figures below.) A better approximation may contain more real (i.e. well-defined) outcomes; hence the clause $\tau_1\backslash\{\perp\} \subseteq \tau_2$. Observe that this means that we leave open the question whether $\perp \in \tau_2$: both the answers yes and no are possible. If $\perp \notin \tau_1$, then there are no computation paths needing completion, and $\tau_1 \sqsubseteq \tau_2$ holds only if $\tau_1 = \tau_2$. It should be stressed that this interpretation of "$\sqsubseteq$" is solely determined by our view of how to obtain the result of a recursive procedure through successive approximations, and is completely different from the normal set-inclusion ordering between sets. For example, there is no reason to view $\{\sigma\{1/x\}\}$ as an approximation to $\{\sigma\{1/x\},\sigma\{2/x\}\}$. Accordingly, our definitions will be such that $x{:=}1 \sqsubseteq x{:=}1 \cup x{:=}2$ is not valid. Let us now support our explanation of the Egli-Milner ordering in terms of computation trees with a few pictures. First we consider the trees accompanying the execution of $\mu X[x{:=}x+1;X \cup D]$, for input state $\sigma\{0/x\}$. At each moment, the set of leaves of the i-th tree constitutes the i-th approximation τ_i to the final result $\tau = \{\sigma\{0/x\}, \sigma\{1/x\},\ldots,\perp\}$.

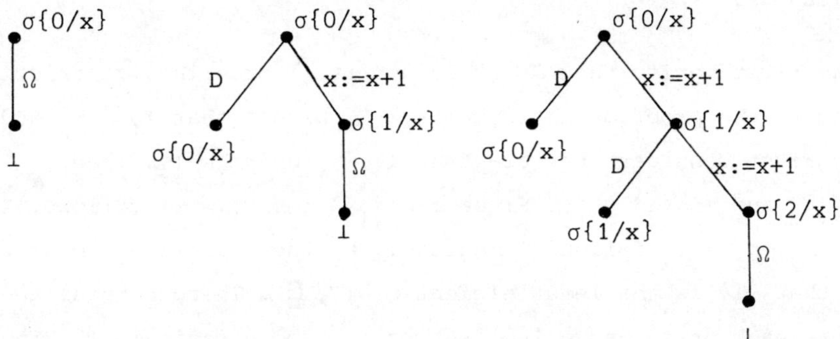

Thus, $\tau_0 = \{\perp\}$, $\tau_1 = \{\sigma\{0/x\},\perp\}$, $\tau_2 = \{\sigma\{0/x\}, \sigma\{1/x\},\perp\}$, etc. Clearly, $\tau_0 \sqsubseteq \tau_1 \sqsubseteq \tau_2 \sqsubseteq \ldots$, by definition 7.3, and, moreover (cf. lemma 7.4 below), $\bigsqcup_i \tau_i = \{\sigma\{0/x\},\sigma\{1/x\},\sigma\{2/x\},\ldots,\perp\}$. Next we treat the statement $\mu X[x>0;x:=x-1;X \cup x\leq 0;(x:=x-1 \cup x:=x-2)]$, for input state $\sigma\{1/x\}$. The computation trees in this case are (we use the convention that branches terminating in $\emptyset$ are omitted; the omitted part has been dotted in the second tree)

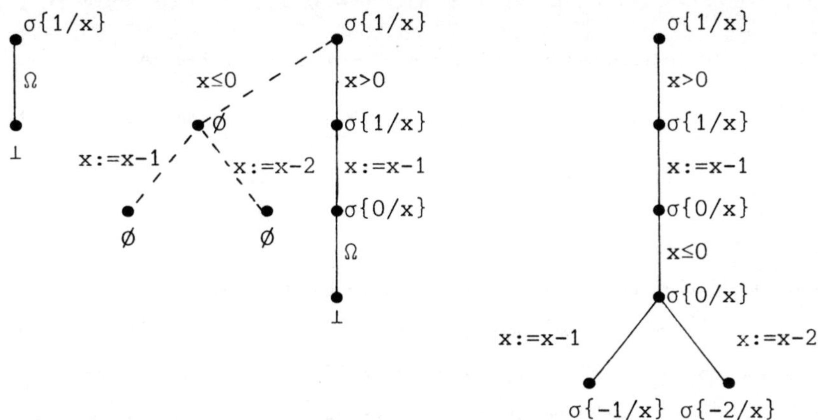

and the corresponding chain of approximations $\tau_0 \sqsubseteq \tau_1 \sqsubseteq \ldots$ is: $\{\perp\} \sqsubseteq \{\perp\} \sqsubseteq \{\sigma\{-1/x\},\sigma\{-2/x\}\} \sqsubseteq \{\sigma\{-1/x\},\sigma\{-2/x\}\} \sqsubseteq \ldots$. (Note that $\tau_2 = \tau_3 = \ldots = \bigsqcup_i \tau_i$.)

The next lemma states that T is indeed a cpo:

LEMMA 7.4. T is a cpo with respect to the ordering "$\sqsubseteq$" of definition 7.3.

PROOF. We first verify that " $\sqsubseteq$ " is a partial ordering, restricting ourselves to the proof of antisymmetry. So assume that $\tau_1 \sqsubseteq \tau_2$ and $\tau_2 \sqsubseteq \tau_1$. First consider the case that $\bot \in \tau_1$ and $\bot \in \tau_2$. Then $\tau_1\backslash\{\bot\} \subseteq \tau_2$ and $\tau_2\backslash\{\bot\} \subseteq \tau_1$. Since $\bot \in \tau_1 \cap \tau_2$, $\tau_1 = \tau_2$ follows. If $\bot \notin \tau_1 \cap \tau_2$, $\tau_1 = \tau_2$ follows immediately by the definition. Next we observe that $\{\bot\}$ is the least element of $(T, \sqsubseteq)$. There remains the proof that each chain has a lub. Let $\langle\tau_i\rangle_{i=0}^{\infty}$ be a chain in T. Either $\bot \in \tau_i$, for all i = 0,1,..., in which case we put $\bigsqcup_{i=0}^{\infty} \tau_i = \bigcup_{i=0}^{\infty} \tau_i$, or $\bot \notin \tau_{i_0}$ for some i_0. Then $\tau_i = \tau_{i_0}$ for all $i \geq i_0$, and we may take $\bigsqcup_{i=0}^{\infty} \tau_i = \tau_{i_0}$. We show that, in the case that $\bot \in \tau_i$ for all i = 0,1,..., our definition satisfies the requirements. First we prove that $\tau_i \sqsubseteq \bigcup_{i=0}^{\infty} \tau_i$, for all i = 0,1,... . Choose some i. Since $\bot \in \tau_i$, it suffices to show that $\tau_i\backslash\{\bot\} \subseteq \bigcup_i \tau_i$, which is evident. Next, let, for some τ, $\tau_i \sqsubseteq \tau$, for all i = 0,1,... . To show that $\bigcup_i \tau_i \sqsubseteq \tau$. By the assumption, $\tau_i\backslash\{\bot\} \subseteq \tau$ for all i, hence $\bigcup_i(\tau_i\backslash\{\bot\}) \subseteq \tau$, i.e. $(\bigcup_i \tau_i)\backslash\{\bot\} \subseteq \tau$. Since $\bot \in \bigcup_i \tau_i$, we conclude that $\bigcup_i \tau_i \sqsubseteq \tau$.

END 7.4.

As range of the function M (with respect to some $\gamma \in \Gamma$ as to be introduced in a moment), we now take the collection of all functions $\Sigma \to_s T$ instead of $\Sigma \to_s \Sigma$. I.e., we put $M \stackrel{df.}{=} \Sigma \to_s T$. Also, we attribute meaning to statement variables using elements γ in the set $\Gamma = Stmv \to M$ (this follows the same pattern as in chapter 5, with *Pvar* replaced by *Stmv*), and altogether we have again

$$M\colon \mathit{Stat} \to (\Gamma \to M).$$

(We assume that our using the same letters as in chapter 5 will not lead to confusion.)

There is a complication which arises in this approach when we want to deal with composition of functions. Consider a composed statement $S_1;S_2$ and assume, for some γ, $M(S_1)(\gamma) = \phi_1 \in \Sigma \to_s T$ and $M(S_2)(\gamma) = \phi_2 \in \Sigma \to_s T$. We cannot now simply form $\phi_2 \circ \phi_1$ as $\lambda\sigma\cdot\phi_2(\phi_1(\sigma))$, since ϕ_2 has Σ and not T as its domain. Hence the following definition:

<u>DEFINITION 7.5</u> (extension of $\phi\colon \Sigma \to_s T$ to $\hat{\phi}\colon T \to_s T$)
For each $\phi\colon \Sigma \to_s T$ we define $\hat{\phi}\colon T \to_s T$ by putting

$$\hat{\phi} = \lambda\tau\cdot \bigcup_{\sigma\in\tau} \phi(\sigma).$$

END 7.5.

The following properties of the ^-operation are of importance:

<u>LEMMA 7.6.</u>
a. $\phi \in M \Rightarrow \hat{\phi} \in T \to_m T$
b. $\phi \in M \Rightarrow \hat{\phi} \in [T \to T]$
c. $\hat{} \in M \to_m [T \to T]$
d. $\hat{} \in [M \to [T \to T]]$

<u>PROOF.</u>
a. Let $\phi \in M$ and $\tau_1, \tau_2 \in T$ such that $\tau_1 \sqsubseteq \tau_2$. To show that $\hat{\phi}(\tau_1) \sqsubseteq \hat{\phi}(\tau_2)$. If $\bot \notin \tau_1$, then $\tau_1 = \tau_2$ and the result is immediate. If $\bot \in \tau_1$, then $\tau_1\backslash\{\bot\} \subseteq \tau_2$, and $\bot \in \hat{\phi}(\tau_1) = \bigcup_{\sigma\in\tau_1} \phi(\sigma)$. In order to prove that $\hat{\phi}(\tau_1) \sqsubseteq \hat{\phi}(\tau_2)$, we have to prove that $\{\bigcup_{\sigma\in\tau_1} \phi(\sigma)\}\backslash\{\bot\} \subseteq \hat{\phi}(\tau_2)$. Since $\bigcup_{\sigma\in\tau_1} \phi(\sigma) = \{\bigcup_{\sigma\in\tau_1\backslash\{\bot\}} \phi(\sigma)\} \cup \{\bot\}$ we have $\{\bigcup_{\sigma\in\tau_1} \phi(\sigma)\}\backslash\{\bot\} \subseteq \bigcup_{\sigma\in\tau_1\backslash\{\bot\}} \phi(\sigma) \subseteq \bigcup_{\sigma\in\tau_2} \phi(\sigma) = \hat{\phi}(\tau_2)$.

b. Let $\phi \in M$, and let $\langle\tau_i\rangle_{i=0}^{\infty}$ be a chain in T. To show $\hat{\phi}(\bigsqcup_i \tau_i) \sqsubseteq \bigsqcup_i \hat{\phi}(\tau_i)$. If $\bot \notin \tau_{i_0}$ for some i_0, then $\bigsqcup_i \tau_i = \tau_{i_0}$, and the result is clear. Otherwise, $\bot \in \tau_i$ for all $i = 0,1,\ldots$, $\bigsqcup_i \tau_i = \bigcup_i \tau_i$ and, by strictness of ϕ, $\bot \in \hat{\phi}(\tau_i)$, for all $i = 0,1,\ldots$, so that $\bigsqcup_i \hat{\phi}(\tau_i) = \bigcup_i \hat{\phi}(\tau_i)$. What we have to prove can then be written as

$$\left\{\bigcup_{\sigma\in\bigcup_i\tau_i} \phi(\sigma)\right\} \setminus \{\bot\} \subseteq \bigcup_i \bigcup_{\sigma\in\tau_i} \phi(\sigma),$$

which is clearly satisfied.

c. Exercise.

d. Let $\langle\phi_i\rangle_{i=0}^{\infty}$ be a chain in M. To show $(\bigsqcup_i \phi_i)\hat{} \sqsubseteq \bigsqcup_i \hat{\phi}_i$. Take some $\tau \in T$. We distinguish two cases.

(i) τ is finite, say $\tau = \{\sigma_1,\ldots,\sigma_n\}$. We consider only the case that $n = 2$, leaving the obvious generalization to $n \neq 2$ as exercise. We have that $(\bigsqcup_i \phi_i)\hat{}(\tau) = \bigsqcup_i \phi_i(\sigma_1) \cup \bigsqcup_i \phi_i(\sigma_2)$, and $(\bigsqcup_i \hat{\phi}_i)(\tau) = \bigsqcup_i \{\phi_i(\sigma_1) \cup \phi_i(\sigma_2)\}$. The desired result immediately follows from the following fact: let $\langle\tau_i\rangle_{i=0}^{\infty}$ and $\langle\tau'_i\rangle_{i=0}^{\infty}$ be two chains. Then $\bigsqcup_i \tau_i \cup \bigsqcup_i \tau'_i = \bigsqcup_i(\tau_i \cup \tau'_i)$. This is seen as follows: We distinguish four subcases.

(α) $\bot \in \tau_i \cap \tau'_i$, for all $i = 0,1,\ldots$. Then $\bot \in \tau_i \cup \tau'_i$, for all $i = 0,1,\ldots$, and the result follows since $\bigcup_i \tau_i \cup \bigcup_i \tau'_i = \bigcup_i(\tau_i \cup \tau'_i)$.

(β) $\bot \in \tau_i$, for all $i = 0,1,\ldots$, and $\bot \notin \tau'_{i'_0}$. Then $\bigsqcup_i \tau_i \cup \bigsqcup_i \tau'_i = (\bigcup_i \tau_i) \cup \tau'_{i'_0} = \bigcup_i(\tau_i \cup \tau'_{i'_0}) = \bigcup_{i\geq i'_0}(\tau_i \cup \tau'_i) =$

$\bigcup_i(\tau_i \cup \tau_i') = \bigsqcup_i(\tau_i \cup \tau_i')$.

(γ) Symmetric to case (β).

(δ) $\bot \notin \tau_{i_0}$ and $\bot \notin \tau'_{i'_0}$, for some i_0 and i'_0. Let $j = \max\{i_0, i'_0\}$. Then $\bigsqcup_i \tau_i \cup \bigsqcup_i \tau'_i = \tau_{i_0} \cup \tau'_{i'_0} = \tau_j \cup \tau'_j = \bigsqcup_i(\tau_i \cup \tau'_i)$.

(ii) τ is infinite and, hence, contains $\bot$. We show that $(\bigsqcup_i \phi_i)\hat{}(\tau) = (\bigsqcup_i \hat{\phi}_i)(\tau)$, i.e., that $\bigcup_{\sigma\in\tau}(\bigsqcup_i \phi_i)(\sigma) = \bigsqcup_i \bigcup_{\sigma\in\tau} \phi_i(\sigma)$. Since $\bot \in \tau$, $\bot \in \bigcup_{\sigma\in\tau} \phi_i(\sigma)$, for all $i = 0,1,\ldots$. Hence, $\bigsqcup_i \bigcup_{\sigma\in\tau} \phi_i(\sigma) = \bigcup_i \bigcup_{\sigma\in\tau} \phi_i(\sigma) = \bigcup_{\sigma\in\tau} \bigcup_i \phi_i(\sigma)$. Thus, we have to show that $\bigcup_{\sigma\in\tau} \bigsqcup_i \phi_i(\sigma) = \bigcup_{\sigma\in\tau} \bigcup_i \phi_i(\sigma)$. By the definition of $\bigsqcup$ we have that, for all σ, either $\bigsqcup_i \phi_i(\sigma) = \bigcup_i \phi_i(\sigma)$, or $\bigsqcup_i \phi_i(\sigma) = \bigcup_i \phi_i(\sigma)\backslash\{\bot\}$. Since, moreover, $\bot \in \bigcup_{\sigma\in\tau} \bigsqcup_i \phi_i(\sigma)$ and $\bot \in \bigcup_{\sigma\in\tau} \bigcup_i \phi_i(\sigma)$, the desired result follows.

END 7.6.

We show by means of a counter example that lemma 7.6d does not hold if the condition that $\bot$ be an element of each infinite set τ is omitted. Consider the set $\tau = \{\sigma\{0/x\}, \sigma\{1/x\}, \ldots\}$ and let ϕ_i, $i = 0,1,\ldots$, be defined by $\phi_i = \lambda\sigma\cdot\{$<u>if</u> $\sigma=\bot$ <u>then</u> $\bot$ <u>else</u> <u>if</u> $\sigma(x)\geq i$ <u>then</u> $\bot$ <u>else</u> σ <u>fi</u> <u>fi</u>$\}$. Clearly, $\langle\phi_i\rangle_{i=0}^{\infty}$ is a chain and every ϕ_i, $i = 0,1,\ldots$, is strict. We have that $\hat{\phi}_0(\tau) = \bigcup_{\sigma\in\tau} \phi_0(\sigma) = \{\bot\}$, $\hat{\phi}_1(\tau) = \{\bot, \sigma\{0/x\}\}$, $\hat{\phi}_2(\tau) = \{\bot, \sigma\{0/x\}, \sigma\{1/x\}\}, \ldots$, and $\bigsqcup_i \hat{\phi}_i(\tau) = \{\bot, \sigma\{0/x\}, \sigma\{1/x\}, \ldots\}$ follows. On the other hand, it can be verified that $(\bigsqcup_i \phi_i)(\sigma\{j/x\}) = \{\sigma\{j/x\}\}$, for $j = 0,1,\ldots$, and therefore $(\bigsqcup_i \phi_i)^\wedge(\tau) = \bigcup_{\sigma\in\tau} (\bigsqcup_i \phi_i)(\sigma) = \{\sigma\{0/x\},\sigma\{1/x\},\ldots\}$ follows. We conclude that, indeed, $(\bigsqcup_i \phi_i)^\wedge \neq \bigsqcup_i \hat{\phi}_i$.

Lemma 7.6 shows us that we can safely define composition of functions using ^, as is done in

<u>DEFINITION 7.7</u> (composition and union of functions).

Let $\phi_1,\phi_2 \in M$.

a. $\phi_1 \circ \phi_2 \stackrel{\text{df.}}{=} \lambda\sigma\cdot\hat{\phi}_1(\phi_2(\sigma))$

b. $\phi_1 \cup \phi_2 \stackrel{\text{df.}}{=} \lambda\sigma\cdot\phi_1(\sigma) \cup \phi_2(\sigma)$

(Here the second "∪" is nothing but the set-theoretic union of two elements in T.)

END 7.7.

Remark. We leave it to the reader to verify, using lemma 7.6, that both "∘" and "∪" are continuous in both their arguments.

We finally arrive at the main semantic definition of this section. As we did with definition 5.19, we follow its presentation with a justification as to the continuity of the operators involved.

<u>DEFINITION 7.8</u> (semantics of statements with nondeterminacy and the μ-formalism). M: *Stat* $\to (\Gamma \to M)$ is defined by

a. $M(v{:=}t)(\gamma) = \lambda\sigma\cdot\{\sigma\{R(t)(\sigma)/L(v)(\sigma)\}\}$

b. $M(b)(\gamma) = \lambda\sigma\cdot$<u>if</u> $W(b)(\sigma)$ <u>then</u> $\{\sigma\}$ <u>else</u> $\emptyset$ <u>fi</u>

c. $M(S_1;S_2)(\gamma) = M(S_2)(\gamma) \circ M(S_1)(\gamma)$

d. $M(S_1 \cup S_2)(\gamma) = M(S_1)(\gamma) \cup M(S_2)(\gamma)$

e. $M(X)(\gamma) = \gamma(X)$

f. $M(\mu X[S])(\gamma) = \mu[\lambda\phi\cdot M(S)(\gamma\{\phi/X\})]$

END 7.8.

Clause b deserves a little elucidation, which we give through an analysis of the meaning of $b;S_1 \cup \neg b;S_2$. Let us assume that we have already established that, for some γ and σ, $M(S_1)(\gamma)(\sigma) = \tau_1$ and $M(S_2)(\gamma)(\sigma) = \tau_2$. We have that $M(b;S_1 \cup \neg b;S_2)(\gamma)(\sigma) = M(b;S_1)(\gamma)(\sigma) \cup M(\neg b;S_2)(\gamma)(\sigma) = M(S_1)(\gamma)\hat{}(M(b)(\gamma)(\sigma)) \cup M(S_2)(\gamma)\hat{}(M(\neg b)(\gamma)(\sigma))$. First we consider the case that $W(b)(\sigma) = tt$. Then $M(b)(\gamma)(\sigma) = \{\sigma\}$ and $M(\neg b)(\gamma)(\sigma) = \emptyset$, so that $M(b;S_1 \cup \neg b;S_2)(\gamma)(\sigma) = M(S_1)(\gamma)\hat{}(\{\sigma\}) \cup M(S_2)(\gamma)\hat{}(\emptyset) = \tau_1 \cup \emptyset = \tau_1$. If $W(b)(\sigma) = ff$, we find in a similar way that $M(b;S_1 \cup \neg b;S_2)(\gamma)(\sigma) = \tau_2$. Finally, if $W(b)(\sigma) = \bot_W$, then $\sigma = \bot$, and we obtain that $M(b;S_1 \cup \neg b;S_2)(\gamma)(\sigma) = \{\bot\}$. Taking these results together, we obtain that $b;S_1 \cup \neg b;S_2$ acquires the same meaning as we would have attributed to <u>if</u> b <u>then</u> S_1 <u>else</u> S_2 <u>fi</u>, supposing this were included in our syntax.

<u>THEOREM 7.9</u>.

$$\lambda\phi_1 \cdot \ldots \cdot \lambda\phi_n \cdot M(S)(\gamma\{\phi_1/X_1,\ldots,\phi_n/X_n\}) \in [M^n \to M].$$

<u>PROOF</u>. The proof of the monotonicity of the function is left as exercise. We prove its continuity by induction on the complexity of S. For simplicity's sake we consider only the case that n = 1.

a. $S \equiv (v:=t)$ or $S \equiv b$. Then $M(S)(\gamma\{\phi/X\})$ does not depend on ϕ and we have nothing to prove.

b. $S \equiv S_1;S_2$. As in theorem 5.21, it suffices to prove that, for $\Phi_1,\Phi_2 \in [M \to M]$, $\lambda\phi\cdot\Phi_1(\phi) \circ \Phi_2(\phi) \in [M\to M]$. The proof is very similar to that of lemma 5.7c, but we give the details here because we have to be careful about the role of the ^-operation. So let $\langle\phi_i\rangle_{i=0}^{\infty}$ be a chain in M. $\Phi_1(\bigsqcup_i \phi_i) \circ \Phi_2(\bigsqcup_i \phi_i) =$

$\lambda\sigma\cdot\Phi_1(\bigsqcup_i \phi_i)\hat{}(\Phi_2(\bigsqcup_i \phi_i)(\sigma)) =$ (cont. Φ_1,Φ_2)

$\lambda\sigma\cdot(\bigsqcup_i \Phi_1(\phi_i))\hat{}(\bigsqcup_j \Phi_2(\phi_j)(\sigma)) =$ (lemma 7.6d)

$\lambda\sigma\cdot \bigsqcup_i(\Phi_1(\phi_i)\hat{\ })(\bigsqcup_j \Phi_2(\phi_j)(\sigma))$ = (lemma 7.6b and similar to lemma 5.7c)

$\lambda\sigma\cdot \bigsqcup_k(\Phi_1(\phi_k)\hat{\ })(\Phi_2(\phi_k)(\sigma)) =$

$\bigsqcup_k \Phi_1(\phi_k) \circ \Phi_2(\phi_k)$.

c. $S \equiv S_1 \cup S_2$. This case follows easily from the fact (noted in the proof of lemma 7.6d) that, for chains $<\tau_i>_{i=0}^{\infty}$ and $<\tau'_i>_{i=0}^{\infty}$, we have that $\bigsqcup_i \tau_i \cup \bigsqcup_i \tau'_i = \bigsqcup_i(\tau_i \cup \tau'_i)$.

d. $S \equiv X$. Clear.

e. $S \equiv \mu Y[S_1]$. Then $\lambda\phi\cdot M(S)(\gamma\{\phi/X\}) = \lambda\phi\cdot\mu[\lambda\psi\cdot M(S_1)(\gamma\{\phi/X,\psi/Y\})]$. Defining Φ: $M \to (M \to M)$ by

$$\Phi = \lambda\psi_1\cdot\lambda\psi_2\cdot M(S_1)(\gamma\{\psi_1/X,\psi_2/Y\})$$

we have that $\Phi \in [M^2 \to M]$, by induction. Thus, there remains the proof that, for this Φ, $\lambda\phi\cdot\mu[\lambda\psi\cdot\Phi(\phi)(\psi)] \in [M \to M]$, or, that $\lambda\phi\cdot\mu[\Phi(\phi)] \in [M \to M]$. Now this follows immediately by theorem 5.12.

END 7.9.

We provide two further illustrations of the consequences of definition 7.8.

1. *Guarded commands*. Consider the statement $S \equiv b_1;S_1 \cup b_2;S_2 \cup \ldots \cup b_n;S_n$. The reader will have no difficulty in convincing himself that the meaning of S for arbitrary σ may be described by
   - either one or more of the b_i, $i = 1,\ldots,n$, is true for σ. Then nondeterministically select some j such that $\mathcal{W}(b_j)(\sigma) = tt$, and execute S_j for input state σ;
   - or none of the b_i, $i = 1,\ldots,n$, is true for σ. In that case, since $M(S)(\gamma)(\sigma) = \emptyset$, no state can be delivered.

Altogether we find that the construct just given has the same meaning as the if-command $\underline{if}\ b_1 \to S_1 \square \ldots \square\ b_n \to S_n\ \underline{fi}$. Next, we consider $\mu X[(b_1;S_1 \cup \ldots \cup b_n;S_n);X \cup (\neg b_1 \wedge \ldots \wedge \neg b_n)]$, where X occurs in none of the S_i, $i = 1,\ldots,n$. The meaning of this is the same as that of $\underline{while}\ b_1 \vee \ldots \vee b_n\ \underline{do}\ b_1;S_1 \cup \ldots \cup b_n;S_n\ \underline{od}$, i.e., it coincides with that of the do-command $\underline{do}\ b_1 \to S_1 \square \ldots \square\ b_n \to S_n\ \underline{od}$.

2. With a slight abuse of language - mixing in one formal construct programs and statements as introduced in chapters 5 and 7, and assuming γ defined on $\mathit{Pvar} \cup \mathit{Stmv}$ - and anticipating the definition of validity to be given in Section 7.3, we prove that

$$\langle P_1 \Leftarrow S_1, P_2 \Leftarrow S_2 | P_1 \rangle$$
$$\models =$$
$$\mu X[S_1[X/P_1, \mu Y[S_2[X/P_1, Y/P_2]]/P_2]].$$

This is done as follows: From theorem 5.14 we obtain: If

$$\langle \phi_1, \phi_2 \rangle = \mu[\lambda\phi_1'\cdot\lambda\phi_2'\cdot \mathcal{M}(S_1)(\gamma\{\phi_1'/P_1, \phi_2'/P_2\}), \lambda\phi_1'\cdot\lambda\phi_2'\cdot \mathcal{M}(S_2)(\gamma\{\phi_1'/P_1, \phi_2'/P_2\})]$$

then

$$\phi_1 = \mu[\lambda\phi_1'\cdot \mathcal{M}(S_1)(\gamma\{\phi_1'/P_1, \mu[\lambda\phi_2'\cdot \mathcal{M}(S_2)(\gamma\{\phi_1'/P_1, \phi_2'/P_2\})]/P_2\})]. \qquad (7.1)$$

Moreover, we have that

$$\mathcal{M}(\mu X[S_1[X/P_1, \mu Y[S_2[X/P_1, Y/P_2]]/P_2]])(\gamma) =$$
$$\mu[\lambda\phi'\cdot \mathcal{M}(S_1[X/P_1, \mu Y[S_2[X/P_1, Y/P_2]]/P_2])(\gamma\{\phi'/X\})] = \text{(cf. lemma 5.31)}$$
$$\mu[\lambda\phi'\cdot \mathcal{M}(S_1)(\gamma\{\phi'/X\}\{\mathcal{M}(X)(\gamma\{\phi'/X\})/P_1, \mathcal{M}(\mu Y[\ldots])(\gamma\{\phi'/X\})/P_2\})] =$$
$$\mu[\lambda\phi'\cdot \mathcal{M}(S_1)(\gamma\{\phi'/X\}\{\phi'/P_1, \mu[\lambda\phi''\cdot \mathcal{M}(S_2[X/P_1, Y/P_2])(\gamma\{\phi'/X\}\{\phi''/Y\})]/P_2\})] =$$
$$\mu[\lambda\phi'\cdot \mathcal{M}(S_1)(\gamma\{\phi'/X\}\{\phi'/P_1, \mu[\lambda\phi''\cdot \mathcal{M}(S_2)(\gamma\{\phi'/X\}\{\phi''/Y\}\{\mathcal{M}(X)(\gamma\{\phi'/X\}\{\phi''/Y\})/P_1, \mathcal{M}(Y)(\gamma\{\phi'/X\}\{\phi''/Y\})/P_2\})]/P_2\})] =$$

(X and Y not free in S_1 or S_2)

$\mu[\lambda\phi'\cdot M(S_1)(\gamma\{\phi'/P_1,\mu[\lambda\phi''\cdot M(S_2)(\gamma\{\phi'/P_1,\phi''/P_2\})]/P_2\})]$.

The desired result now follows from (7.1) and definition 5.19.

It is sometimes convenient to also have available a formalism which shares with the approach of chapter 5 the possibility of having a *system* of procedures expressed directly (and not indirectly through iterating the μ-operator), but which maintains the declaration-free treatment of recursion as introduced in this chapter. Therefore, we introduce the following variants of definitions 7.1 and 7.8 (without bothering to introduce a separate name for the new class of statements; the context should make clear to which language we refer at a given moment):

DEFINITION 7.10 (nondeterminacy with simultaneous μ-statements).

a. The class *Stat*, with typical elements S,..., is defined by

$$S::= v:=t\,|\,b\,|\,S_1;S_2\,|\,S_1\cup S_2\,|\,X\,|\,\mu_i X_1\ldots X_n[S_1,\ldots,S_n]$$

where in the last clause we have $n \geq 1$, $1 \leq i \leq n$, $X_i \not\equiv X_j$ for $i \neq j$, $1 \leq i, j \leq n$.

b. M: *Stat* → (Γ → M) is defined by

(i) No changes in definition 7.8 as to the first five clauses

(ii) $M(\mu_i X_1\ldots X_n[S_1,\ldots,S_n])(\gamma) =$

$\mu_i[\lambda\phi_1\cdot\ldots\cdot\lambda\phi_n\cdot M(S_1)(\gamma\{\phi_j/X_j\}_{j=1}^n),\ldots,$

$\lambda\phi_1\cdot\ldots\cdot\lambda\phi_n\cdot M(S_n)(\gamma\{\phi_j/X_j\}_{j=1}^n)]$

where, in general, for $f_1,\ldots,f_n$ as in corollary 5.10,

$\mu_i[f_1,\ldots,f_n] = x_i$, for $i = 1,\ldots,n$, iff $\mu[f_1,\ldots,f_n] = \langle x_1,\ldots,x_n\rangle$.

END 7.10.

It should be obvious how to justify this definition by a theorem analogous to theorem 7.9.

7.3. Correctness

The major definitions of the sections on correctness of chapters 3 and 5 are taken over without essential changes. In particular this holds for the syntax and semantics of assertions $p \in \mathit{Assn}$ and correctness formulae $f \in \mathit{Form}$. There are two slight changes in the definition of F as given in definition 5.24. First, M replaces N, and, secondly, in the case $f \equiv \{p\}S\{q\}$, we put: $F(\{p\}S\{q\})(\gamma)(\sigma) = \forall\sigma'[T(p)(\sigma) \wedge \sigma' \in M(S)(\gamma)(\sigma) \wedge \sigma' \neq \bot \Rightarrow T(q)(\sigma')]$. (Thus, we have replaced $\sigma' = N(S)(\gamma)(\sigma)$ by $\sigma' \in M(S)(\gamma)(\sigma)$.) Observe also that we have a small syntactic ambiguity in that $b_1 = b_2$ now is short for both $(b_1 \supset b_2) \wedge (b_2 \supset b_1)$ and for $(b_1 \sqsubseteq b_2) \wedge (b_2 \sqsubseteq b_1)$. No semantic ambiguity arises from this, however. Since we do not have to carry with us explicitly the set of procedure declarations any more, our treatment of the class of generalized correctness formulae may be simplified:

DEFINITION 7.11 (generalized correctness formulae).

a. The syntactic class Gfor, with typical elements g,...,is given by

$$g ::= f_1 \Rightarrow f_2$$

b. G: $\mathit{Gfor} \rightarrow (\Gamma \rightarrow T)$ is defined by

$$G(f_1 \Rightarrow f_2)(\gamma) = \begin{cases} tt, & \text{if } \forall\sigma\neq\bot[F(f_1)(\gamma)(\sigma)] \Rightarrow \forall\sigma\neq\bot[F(f_2)(\gamma)(\sigma)] \\ ff, & \text{otherwise} \end{cases}$$

END 7.11.

Again, the generalized correctness formula <u>true</u> ⇒ f is abbreviated to f. Validity of generalized correctness formulae g and soundness of inferences $\frac{g_1,\ldots,g_n}{g}$ are defined exactly as in section 5.4 (i.e.

without the refinements of section 5.5).

Examples

7.1. $\models S;(S_1 \cup S_2) = S;S_1 \cup S;S_2$, $\models (S_1 \cup S_2);S = S_1;S \cup S_2;S$

7.2. $\models b_1 \vee b_2 = b_1 \cup b_2$, $\models b_1 \wedge b_2 = b_1;b_2$, $\models b \wedge \neg b = \underline{\text{false}}$,

$\models S \cup \underline{\text{false}} = S$, $\models D = \underline{\text{true}}$, $\models \underline{\text{false}} \cup S = S$,

$\models \underline{\text{true}};S = S$, $\models \underline{\text{false}};\ S = \underline{\text{false}}$, $\models \Omega;S = \Omega$. (We do *not* have that $\models S \cup \Omega = S$, or $\models S;\Omega = \Omega$, or $\models S;\underline{\text{false}} = \underline{\text{false}}$.

For example, $\models S;\Omega = \Omega$ does not hold since

$(\lambda\sigma\cdot\{\bot\})\hat{\ }(\emptyset) = \emptyset \neq \{\bot\}$.)

7.3. $\models b;(b;S_1 \cup \neg b;S_2) \cup \neg b;S_3 = b;S_1 \cup \neg b;S_3$

(Compare the result from chapter 2: $\models$ <u>if</u> b <u>then</u> <u>if</u> b <u>then</u> S_1 <u>else</u> S_2 <u>fi</u> <u>else</u> S_3 <u>fi</u> = <u>if</u> b <u>then</u> S_1 <u>else</u> S_3 <u>fi</u>.)

7.4. a. $\models (S_1 \sqsubseteq S_1') \wedge (S_2 \sqsubseteq S_2') \Rightarrow (S_1;S_2 \sqsubseteq S_1';S_2') \wedge (S_1 \cup S_2 \sqsubseteq S_1' \cup S_2')$

b. $\models S \cup \Omega \sqsubseteq S \cup S'$ (but not, in general, $\models S \sqsubseteq S \cup S'$).

7.5. a. $\models (S_1 \sqsubseteq S_3) \wedge (S_2 \sqsubseteq S_3) \Rightarrow (S_1 \cup S_2 \sqsubseteq S_3)$

b. $S_1 \cup S_2 \sqsubseteq S_3 \Rightarrow (S_1 \sqsubseteq S_3) \wedge (S_2 \sqsubseteq S_3)$ is not valid.

7.6. Let X not occur in S.

a. $\models \mu X[b;S;X \cup \neg b] = b;S;\mu X[b;S;X \cup \neg b] \cup \neg b$

b. $\models b;S;S_0 \cup \neg b \sqsubseteq S_0 \Rightarrow \mu X[b;S;X \cup \neg b] \sqsubseteq S_0$

(a and b together constitute a reformulation of theorem 3.26.)

Caution. It is not true that $\models b_1 \supset b_2$ and $\models b_1 \sqsubseteq b_2$ are equivalent. In fact, since execution of b_1 considered as a statement terminates for all states $\sigma \neq \bot$, we have that $\models b_1 \sqsubseteq b_2$ iff $\models b_1 = b_2$. Observe that this is an immediate consequence of our definition that, for $\bot \notin \tau_1$, $\tau_1 \sqsubseteq \tau_2$ iff $\tau_1 = \tau_2$.

The rules for dealing with partial correctness of statements which are not recursive procedures are collected in lemma 7.12. Most of it is a repetition of previous results (lemma 5.28), but the cases that $S \equiv b$ or $S \equiv S_1 \cup S_2$ are new.

LEMMA 7.12.

a. $\dfrac{f}{f_0 \Rightarrow f}$

b. $\dfrac{f_1 \Rightarrow f_2,\ f_2 \Rightarrow f_3}{f_1 \Rightarrow f_3}$

c. $\dfrac{f \Rightarrow f_1,\ f \Rightarrow f_2}{f \Rightarrow f_1 \wedge f_2}$

d. $\models f_1 \wedge \ldots \wedge f_n \Rightarrow f_i,\ n \geq 1,\ 1 \leq i \leq n$

e. $\models \{p[t/v]\}\ v := t\{p\}$

f. $\models p \supset (b \supset q) \Rightarrow \{p\}b\{q\}$

g. $\models \{p\}S_1\{q\} \wedge \{q\}S_2\{r\} \Rightarrow \{p\}S_1;S_2\{r\}$

h. $\models \{p\}S_1\{q\} \wedge \{p\}S_2\{q\} \Rightarrow \{p\}S_1 \cup S_2\{q\}$

i. $\models (p \supset p_1) \wedge \{p_1\}S\{q_1\} \wedge (q_1 \supset q) \Rightarrow \{p\}S\{q\}$.

PROOF. We only give the proof of clauses f and h.

f. We have to show that, for all γ, if $\forall\sigma\neq\bot[\mathcal{T}(p)(\sigma) \wedge \mathcal{T}(b)(\sigma) \Rightarrow \mathcal{T}(q)(\sigma)]$ then $\forall\sigma\neq\bot,\sigma'[\mathcal{T}(p)(\sigma) \wedge \sigma' \in \mathcal{M}(b)(\gamma)(\sigma) \wedge \sigma'\neq\bot \Rightarrow \mathcal{T}(q)(\sigma')]$. Choose some γ, $\sigma \neq \bot$ and σ', and assume that $\mathcal{T}(p)(\sigma) \wedge \sigma' \in \mathcal{M}(b)(\gamma)(\sigma) \wedge \sigma' \neq \bot$. Clearly, $\mathcal{W}(b)(\sigma) = tt$ or $\mathcal{W}(b)(\sigma) = ff$. In the first case, $\sigma' \in \mathcal{M}(b)(\gamma)(\sigma)$ reduces to $\sigma' \in \{\sigma\}$, and the result is clear. In the second case, $\sigma' \in M(b)(\gamma)(\sigma)$ amounts to $\sigma' \in \emptyset$, and we have nothing to prove.

h. Choose some γ, and assume that $\forall\sigma\neq\bot,\sigma'[T(p)(\sigma) \wedge \sigma' \in M(S_1)(\gamma)(\sigma) \wedge \sigma'\neq\bot \Rightarrow T(q)(\sigma')]$, and $\forall\sigma\neq\bot,\sigma'[T(p)(\sigma) \wedge \sigma' \in M(S_2)(\gamma)(\sigma) \wedge \sigma'\neq\bot \Rightarrow T(q)(\sigma')]$. To show that $\forall\sigma\neq\bot,\sigma'[T(p)(\sigma) \wedge \sigma' \in M(S_1 \cup S_2)(\gamma)(\sigma) \wedge \sigma'\neq\bot \Rightarrow T(q)(\sigma')]$. Choose some $\sigma \neq \bot$, and let $\sigma' \in M(S_1 \cup S_2)(\gamma)(\sigma)$. Clearly, either $\sigma' \in M(S_1)(\gamma)(\sigma)$, or $\sigma' \in M(S_2)(\gamma)(\sigma)$. In the first case we apply the first assumption, in the second case the second assumption, and the desired result is immediate.

END 7.12.

We now turn to the formulation of Scott's rule. Again, our first step is a precise definition of substitution. The notions of free and bound occurrences of a statement variable in a statement are defined similarly to definition 2.13. ($\mu X[\ldots]$ binds occurrences of X just as $\exists x[\ldots]$ binds occurrences of x.) *stmv*(S) denotes the set of all statement variables which occur free in S.

DEFINITION 7.13 (substitution).

$S_0[S/X]$ is defined by induction on the complexity of S_0. If S_0 is not a μ-statement, the definition is analogous to definition 5.30. Otherwise, let $S_0 \equiv \mu Y[S_1]$. We put (compare definition 2.14):

$\mu Y[S_1][S/X]$

$\equiv \mu Y[S_1]$, if $X \equiv Y$

$\equiv \mu Y[S_1[S/X]]$, if $X \not\equiv Y$, and $Y \notin stmv(S)$

$\equiv \mu Y'[S_1[Y'/Y][S/X]]$, if $X \not\equiv Y$, and $Y \in stmv(S)$,

where Y' is the first statement variable different from X, such that $Y' \notin stmv(S,S_1)$.

END 7.13.

The next lemma restates a number of familiar properties, partly dealing with substitution:

LEMMA 7.14.

a. If $X \notin stmv(S)$, then $M(S)(\gamma\{\phi/X\}) = M(S)(\gamma)$

b. $M(S_0[S/X])(\gamma) = M(S_0)(\gamma\{M(S)(\gamma)/X\})$

c. $\models \mu X[S] = \mu Y[S[Y/X]]$, provided $Y \notin stmv(S)$

d. $\models S[S_1/X][S_2/X] = S[S_1[S_2/X]/X]$

e. $\models S[S_1/X][S_2/Y] = S[S_2/Y][S_1[S_2/Y]/X]$, provided that $X \not\equiv Y$, and that $X \notin stmv(S_2)$

f. $\models S_1 \sqsubseteq S_2 \Rightarrow S[S_1/X] \sqsubseteq S[S_2/X]$

g. $\models \mu X[S] = S[\mu X[S]/X]$

h. $\models S_0[S/X] \sqsubseteq S \Rightarrow \mu X[S_0] \sqsubseteq S$.

i. $$\frac{S_1 \sqsubseteq S_2}{S_1[S/X] \sqsubseteq S_2[S/X]} \qquad \frac{S_1 \sqsubseteq S_2}{\mu X[S_1] \sqsubseteq \mu X[S_2]}$$

PROOF. Most clauses are essentially variants on previously encountered facts. By way of example, we give part of the proofs of clauses b and i.

b. We use induction on the complexity of S_0. All cases are straightforward, except maybe for the case that $S_0 \equiv \mu Y[S_1]$.

(i) $X \equiv Y$. $M(\mu Y[S_1][S/X])(\gamma) = M(\mu Y[S_1])(\gamma) = M(\mu Y[S_1])(\gamma\{M(S)(\gamma)/X\})$,
by part a and the fact that $X \notin stmv(\mu Y[S_1])$.

(ii) $X \not\equiv Y$ and $Y \notin stmv(S)$. $M(\mu Y[S_1][S/X])(\gamma) =$
$M(\mu Y[S_1[S/X]])(\gamma) = \mu[\lambda\phi \cdot M(S_1[S/X])(\gamma\{\phi/Y\})] =$ (ind.)
$\mu[\lambda\phi \cdot M(S_1)(\gamma\{\phi/Y, M(S)(\gamma\{\phi/Y\})/X\})] =$ ($Y \notin stmv(S)$ and part a)
$\mu[\lambda\phi \cdot M(S_1)(\gamma\{\phi/Y, M(S)(\gamma)/X\})] = M(\mu Y[S_1])(\gamma\{M(S)(\gamma)/X\})$

(iii) $X \not\equiv Y$ and $Y \in stmv(S)$. Follows from an appropriate combination of the arguments of part (ii) and of lemma 2.16, part c(iii)(γ).

i. Assume (*): $\models S_1 \sqsubseteq S_2$; we show that then $\models \mu X[S_1] \sqsubseteq \mu X[S_2]$. *By lfp* it is sufficient to show that $\models S_1[\mu X[S_2]/X] \sqsubseteq \mu X[S_2]$, or, by *fpp*, that $\models S_1[\mu X[S_2]/X] \sqsubseteq S_2[\mu X[S_2]/X]$. Now this follows from (*) and the first part of i.

END 7.14.

Various of the semantic results of section 5.2 can also be formulated syntactically:

Examples

7.6. a. $\models \mu X[S_1[S_2/X]] = S_1[\mu X[S_2[S_1/X]]/X]$

(See also example 1 after lemma 5.11.)

b. If X does not occur free in S_0, then

$\models \mu X[S_0;S_1] = S_0;\mu X[S_1[S_0;X/X]]$

(Consequence of part a; see also exercise 5.12.)

7.7. $\models \mu X[S[X/Y]] = \mu X[S[\mu X[S[X/Y]]/Y]]$

(See also example 2 after lemma 5.11.)

Definition 7.13 and lemma 7.14 may be extended to simultaneous substitutions $S[S_i/X_i]_{i=1}^n$ (provided that all X_i, $i = 1,\ldots,n$, are different), and also to the case that S and S_i, $i = 1,\ldots,n$, are as in definition 7.10. We leave this as a somewhat laborious exercise to the reader, but shall freely use the definitions and results, where necessary.

Our next lemma shows how a syntactic version of theorem 5.14 may be formulated and proved using the simultaneous μ-notation.

LEMMA 7.15. Let $n,m \geq 1$. For each $i = 1,\ldots,n$,

$$\mu_i\, X_1 \ldots X_{n+m}[S_1,\ldots,S_{n+m}]$$

$\models =$

$$\mu_i\ X_1 \ldots X_n [S_1[\mu_j\ X_{n+1} \ldots X_{n+m} [S_{n+1}, \ldots, S_{n+m}]/X_j]_{j=n+1}^{n+m}, \ldots,$$

$$S_n[\mu_j\ X_{n+1} \ldots X_{n+m} [S_{n+1}, \ldots, S_{n+m}]/X_j]_{j=n+1}^{n+m}].$$

PROOF. We restrict ourselves to the case that n = m = 1. Its extension to the general case should be clear. We use the informal notation for substitution, intended to make the structure of the proof more perspicuous. Let $\mu_i \overset{\text{df.}}{\equiv} \mu_i X_1 X_2 [S_1(X_1,X_2),\ S_2(X_1,X_2)]$, $i = 1,2$, $\mu \overset{\text{df.}}{\equiv} \mu X_1[S_1(X_1,\mu X_2[S_2(X_1,X_2)])]$, and $\mu_2'(X_1) \overset{\text{df.}}{\equiv}$ $\mu X_2[S_2(X_1,X_2)]$. We show that $\models \mu = \mu_1$.

(i) $\models \mu \sqsubseteq \mu_1$.

By the definition of $\mu_2'(X_1)$, we have that $\mu_2'(\mu_1) \equiv$ $\mu X_2[S_2(\mu_1,X_2)]$. By the definition of μ_2 and *fpp*, $\models S_2(\mu_1,\mu_2) =$ μ_2. Thus, by the definition of $\mu_2'(\mu_1)$ and *lfp*, $\models \mu_2'(\mu_1) \sqsubseteq \mu_2$. From this, using monotonicity and *fpp*, we obtain $\models S_1(\mu_1,\mu_2'(\mu_1)) \sqsubseteq S_1(\mu_1,\mu_2) = \mu_1$. By the definition of μ and *lfp*, we finally infer that $\models \mu \sqsubseteq \mu_1$.

(ii) $\models \mu_1 \sqsubseteq \mu$.

By the definitions of μ and $\mu_2'(\mu)$, and *fpp*, $\models S_1(\mu,\mu_2'(\mu)) = \mu$. By the definition of $\mu_2'(\mu)$ and *fpp*, $\models S_2(\mu,\mu_2'(\mu)) = \mu_2'(\mu)$. Thus, by the definition of μ_1 and *lfp*, $\models \mu_1 \sqsubseteq \mu$.

END 7.15.

Remark. A version of this lemma which does not partition the set of indices {1,...,n+m} into the disjoint subsets {1,...,n} and {n+1,...,n+m}, but into two arbitrary disjoint subsets, is also possible, but slightly tedious to formulate, and therefore omitted.

Two little steps are still to be made before we formulate Scott's induction in the present setting.

1. As before, we put $\Omega \equiv \mu X[X]$, so that $\mathcal{M}(\Omega)(\gamma) = \lambda\sigma\cdot\{\bot\}$.
2. We assume $f[S/X]$ and $f[S_i/X_i]_{i=1}^{n}$ defined. (See also definition 5.32.)

THEOREM 7.16.

a. (Scott's induction for simple μ-constructs)

$$\frac{f_0 \Rightarrow f[\Omega/X],\; f_0 \wedge f \Rightarrow f[S/X]}{f_0 \Rightarrow f[\mu X[S]/X]}\text{, provided that } X \notin \mathit{stmv}\ (f_0)$$

b. (Scott's induction for simultaneous μ-constructs)

$$\frac{f_0 \Rightarrow f[\Omega/X_i]_{i=1}^{n},\; f_0 \wedge f \Rightarrow f[S_i/X_i]_{i=1}^{n}}{f_0 \Rightarrow f[\mu_i X_1 \ldots X_n[S_1,\ldots,S_n]/X_i]_{i=1}^{n}}\text{, provided that } X_i \notin \mathit{stmv}\ (f_0),\ i = 1,\ldots,n$$

PROOF. The proof may be given through a straightforward adaptation of the arguments in section 5.4.

END 7.16.

Examples

7.8.

$$\frac{\{p\}X\{q\} \Rightarrow \{p\}S\{q\}}{\{p\}\ \mu X[S]\ \{q\}}$$

(This is a special case of theorem 7.16a.)

7.9. $\models \mu X[\mu Y[S]] = \mu X[S[X/Y]]$

We give a proof of $\models \mu X[\mu Y[S]] \sqsubseteq \mu X[S[X/Y]]$, leaving the reverse inclusion as an exercise. If $X \equiv Y$, the result is clear. Now assume $X \not\equiv Y$. We first use theorem 7.16a with $f_0 \equiv \underline{true}$ and $f \equiv X \sqsubseteq \mu X[S[X/Y]]$. It is sufficient to show that $\models X \sqsubseteq \mu X[S[X/Y]] \Rightarrow \mu Y[S] \sqsubseteq \mu X[S[X/Y]]$. In order to prove this, we use Scott's induction again, this time with $f_0 \equiv X \sqsubseteq \mu X[S[X/Y]]$, $f \equiv Y \sqsubseteq \mu X[S[X/Y]]$. Thus, it suffices to prove that $\models (X \sqsubseteq \mu X[\ldots]) \wedge (Y \sqsubseteq \mu X[\ldots]) \Rightarrow S \sqsubseteq \mu X[\ldots]$, or, using *fpp*, that $\models (X \sqsubseteq \mu X[\ldots]) \wedge (Y \sqsubseteq \mu X[\ldots]) \Rightarrow S \sqsubseteq S[X/Y][\mu X[\ldots]/X]$. By lemma 7.14e, we may rewrite this as

$\models (X \sqsubseteq \mu X[\ldots]) \wedge (Y \sqsubseteq \mu X[\ldots]) \Rightarrow S \sqsubseteq S[\mu X[\ldots]/X][\mu X[\ldots]/Y]$,

and the desired result now follows from (a special case of) the two-dimensional version of lemma 7.14f:

$\models (X \sqsubseteq S_1) \wedge (Y \sqsubseteq S_2) \Rightarrow S \sqsubseteq S[S_1/X][S_2/Y]$.

(A proof of $\models \mu X[\mu Y[S]] \sqsubseteq \mu X[S[X/Y]]$ which avoids Scott's induction (and only uses *lfp* and *fpp*) is also possible (exercise). The proof exhibited here is given to illustrate nested application of Scott's induction.)

In some of the following examples we use the convention that statements without occurrences of the relevant statement variable(s) are denoted by $A,\ldots,A_1,\ldots,A',\ldots$

7.10. $\models \mu X[A_1;X \cup A_2;A_3] = \mu X[A_1;X \cup A_2];A_3$

This is an extension of example 4 after theorem 5.34 (and in fact a key property of procedures of this type).

7.11. Let, for X not free in S, $b{*}S \overset{df.}{\equiv} \mu X[b;S;X \cup \neg b]$

(i.e., b*S denotes the former <u>while</u> b <u>do</u> S <u>od</u>).

We prove that $\models (b_1 \vee b_2)*S = b_1*S;b_2*(S;b_1*S)$. We have that

$\models (b_1 \vee b_2)*S =$ (def.)

$\mu X[(b_1 \vee b_2);S;X \cup \neg(b_1 \vee b_2)] =$ (examples 7.1 and 7.2, and since $\models b_1 \vee b_2 = b_1 \vee (\neg b_1 \wedge b_2)$)

$\mu X[b_1;S;X \cup \neg b_1;b_2;S;X \cup \neg b_1;\neg b_2] =$ (for some new Y, by example 7.9)

$\mu X[\mu Y[b_1;S;Y; \cup \neg b_1;b_2;S;X \cup \neg b_1;\neg b_2]] =$ (example 7.10)

$\mu X[\mu Y[b_1;S;Y \cup \neg b_1];(b_2;S;X \cup \neg b_2)] =$ (def. b*S)

$\mu X[b_1*S;(b_2;S;X \cup \neg b_2)] =$ (example 7.6b)

$b_1*S;\mu X[b_2;S;b_1*S;X \cup \neg b_2] =$ (def. b*S)

$b_1*S;b_2*(S;b_1*S)$.

7.12. $\models (b_1 \wedge b_2)*S;b_1*S = b_1*S$. We prove only "$\sqsubseteq$". By Scott's induction, it suffices to show that $\models X;b_1*S \sqsubseteq b_1*S \Rightarrow (b_1;b_2;S;X \cup \neg b_1 \cup \neg b_2);b_1*S \sqsubseteq b_1*S$. Using the assumption and the fact that $\models \neg b_1;b_1*S = \neg b_1$, it suffices to prove that $\models b_1;b_2;S;b_1*S \cup \neg b_1 \cup \neg b_2;b_1*S \sqsubseteq b_1*S$, or, using the facts that $\models \neg b_2;b_1*S = \neg b_2;b_1;S;b_1*S \cup \neg b_2;\neg b_1$ and $\models \neg b_1 \cup \neg b_1;\neg b_2 = \neg b_1$, that $\models b_1;b_2;S;b_1*S \cup \neg b_1 \cup b_1;\neg b_2;S;b_1*S \sqsubseteq b_1*S$, or, using that, for each S_0, $\models b_1;b_2;S_0 \cup b_1;\neg b_2;S_0 = b_1;S_0$, that $\models b_1;S;b_1*S \cup \neg b_1 \sqsubseteq b_1*S$, which is immediate by *fpp*.

7.13. This example illustrates how partial correctness of recursive procedures may be derived choosing suitable intermediate assertions. Consider for instance the procedure

$\mu X[A_1;X;A_2;X;A_3 \cup A_4]$, and assume we want to prove $\models \{p_0\}\ \mu X[A_1;X;A_2;X;A_3 \cup A_4]\ \{q_0\}$. Using Scott's induction, we see that it suffices to find p_1,p_2,q_1,q_2 such that

$$\models \{p_0\}A_1\{p_1\} \wedge \{q_1\}A_2\{p_2\} \wedge \{q_2\}A_3\{q_0\} \wedge \{p_0\}A_4\{q_0\} \wedge$$
$$(p_1 \supset p_0) \wedge (q_0 \supset p_1) \wedge (p_2 \supset p_0) \wedge (q_0 \supset q_2)$$

Calling this correctness formula f_0, all we have to prove is that $\models f_0 \wedge \{p_0\}X\{q_0\} \Rightarrow \{p_0\}(A_1;X;A_2;X;A_3 \cup A_4)\ \{q_0\}$, which is immediate by lemma 7.12, parts g, h and i. (The structure of the intermediate assertions is suggested by the construct $\{p_0\}A_1\{p_1\}\ X\ \{q_1\}A_2\{p_2\}\ X\ \{q_2\}A_3\{q_0\} \cup \{p_0\}A_4\{q_0\}$.)

7.14. Our final example uses a number of concepts we do not introduce formally since they only serve to provide some background to a certain equivalence result which we will formulate completely within our language. Let us consider the problem of traversing a forest (finite collection of trees) while performing in each node of each tree a certain action A which does not interfere with the traversal process. We employ a family-oriented terminology for trees: A_s, A_b and A_f denote the actions of visiting the eldest son, next-younger brother and father of a given node, while b_s and b_b denote the questions "has this node a son?", and "has this node a (next-) younger brother?", respectively.

We compare the two programs

$$\mu' \overset{df.}{\equiv} \mu X[A;(b_s;A_s;X;A_f \cup \neg b_s);(b_b;A_b;X \cup \neg b_b)], \text{ and}$$
$$\mu'' \overset{df.}{\equiv} \mu X[A;(b_s;A_s;X;b_b*(A_b;X);A_f \cup \neg b_s)].$$

After some contemplation of these definitions, the reader might be tempted to conjecture that $\models \mu' = \mu''; b_b*(A_b;\mu'')$. This is indeed true, but rather than being dependent on the tree traversal model, it is an immediate corollary of the following general equivalence between μ-constructs: Let (again using our informal notation)

$$\mu_0 \overset{\text{df.}}{\equiv} \mu X[S_0(S_1(X), S_2(X))] \tag{7.2}$$

$$\mu_1(Y) \overset{\text{df.}}{\equiv} \mu X[S_1(S_0(X,Y))] \tag{7.3}$$

$$\mu_2 \overset{\text{df.}}{\equiv} \mu X[S_2(S_0(\mu_1(X),X))]. \tag{7.4}$$

Then

$$\models \mu_0 = S_0(\mu_1(\mu_2),\mu_2). \tag{7.5}$$

We first show how this result may be specialized to the above mentioned tree-traversal equivalence. Choose $S_0(X_1,X_2) \overset{\text{df.}}{\equiv} X_2;X_1$, $S_1(X) \overset{\text{df.}}{\equiv} b_b;A_b;X \cup \neg b_b$, $S_2(X) \overset{\text{df.}}{\equiv} A;(b_s;A_s;X;A_f \cup \neg b_s)$. We then obtain $\mu_0 \equiv \mu X[S_2(X);S_1(X)] \equiv \mu'$, $\mu_1(Y) \equiv \mu X[b_b;A_b;Y;X \cup \neg b_b] = b_b*(A_b;Y)$, and $\mu_2 \equiv \mu X[A;(b_s;A_s;X;b_b*(A_b;X);A_f \cup \neg b_s)] \equiv \mu''$, from which we infer the desired result

$\models \mu' = S_0(\mu_1(\mu_2),\mu_2) = \mu_2;\mu_1(\mu_2) = \mu'';b_b*(A_b;\mu'')$.

Next, we prove (7.5).

$\sqsubseteq$: By (7.3) and (7.4) we have that $\models \mu_1(\mu_2) = S_1(S_0(\mu_1(\mu_2),\mu_2))$ and $\models \mu_2 = S_2(S_0(\mu_1(\mu_2),\mu_2))$. It follows that $\models S_0(S_1(S_0(\mu_1(\mu_2),\mu_2)), S_2(S_0(\mu_1(\mu_2),\mu_2))) = S_0(\mu_1(\mu_2),\mu_2)$, and we obtain $\models \mu_0 \sqsubseteq S_0(\mu_1(\mu_2),\mu_2)$, by (7.2) and *lfp*.

$\sqsupseteq$: By (7.2) we have that $\models S_1(\mu_0) = S_1(S_0(S_1(\mu_0),S_2(\mu_0)))$;

thus, by (7.3) and *lfp*:

$$\models \mu_1(S_2(\mu_0)) \sqsubseteq S_1(\mu_0). \tag{7.6}$$

Using (7.6), and applying Scott's induction with $f_0 \equiv$ true, $f \equiv S_0(\mu_1(X),X) \sqsubseteq \mu_0$, we show that $\models f[\mu_2/X]$:

(i) Ω-step: Left to the reader. (Hint: this needs inner application of Scott's induction.)

(ii) Induction step: We prove that

$\models f \Rightarrow S_0(\mu_1(S_2(S_0(\mu_1(X),X))), S_2(S_0(\mu_1(X),X))) \sqsubseteq \mu_0$.

Using the induction hypothesis, we find that it is sufficient to show that $\models S_0(\mu_1(S_2(\mu_0)), S_2(\mu_0)) \sqsubseteq \mu_0$, or, by *fpp*, that $\models S_0(\mu_1(S_2(\mu_0)), S_2(\mu_0)) \sqsubseteq S_0(S_1(\mu_0),S_2(\mu_0))$, which follows by (7.6) and monotonicity.

Exercises

7.1. Prove that, for $\phi_1,\phi_2,\phi_3 \in M$,

a. $(\phi_1 \circ \phi_2) \circ \phi_3 = \phi_1 \circ (\phi_2 \circ \phi_3)$

b. $\phi_1 \circ (\phi_2 \cup \phi_3) = (\phi_1 \circ \phi_2) \cup (\phi_1 \circ \phi_3)$, $(\phi_1 \cup \phi_2) \circ \phi_3 = (\phi_1 \circ \phi_3) \cup (\phi_2 \circ \phi_3)$.

7.2. Let, for $i,j = 0,1,\ldots$, τ_{ij} be such that

(i) $i \leq j \Rightarrow \tau_{ik} \sqsubseteq \tau_{jk}$, $k = 0,1,\ldots$

(ii) $\overset{\infty}{\underset{j=0}{\cup}} \tau_{ij} \in T$

a. Show that $\langle \overset{\infty}{\underset{j=0}{\cup}} \tau_{ij} \rangle_{i=0}^{\infty}$ is a chain in T

b. Show that, in general

(*) $\overset{\infty}{\underset{j=0}{\cup}} \overset{\infty}{\underset{i=0}{\sqcup}} \tau_{ij} \in T$

does not hold

c. Assume that τ_{ij}, i,j = 0,1,..., are such that (*) *does* hold.

Prove

(i) $\bigcup_{j=0}^{\infty} \bigsqcup_{i=0}^{\infty} \tau_{ij} \subseteq \bigsqcup_{i=0}^{\infty} \bigcup_{j=0}^{\infty} \tau_{ij}$

(ii) $\bigsqcup_{i=0}^{\infty} \bigcup_{j=0}^{\infty} \tau_{ij} \sqsubseteq \bigcup_{j=0}^{\infty} \bigsqcup_{i=0}^{\infty} \tau_{ij}$

(iii) In general, $\bigsqcup_{i=0}^{\infty} \bigcup_{j=0}^{\infty} \tau_{ij} \neq \bigcup_{j=0}^{\infty} \bigsqcup_{i=0}^{\infty} \tau_{ij}$

7.3. Justify the remark on ambiguity just preceding definition 7.11.

7.4. Let us define

(i) $\phi: \Sigma \rightarrow_s T$ is deterministic if, for all σ, $\phi(\sigma)$ consists of precisely one state

(ii) $\gamma \in \Gamma$ is deterministic if, for all X, $\gamma(X)$ is deterministic

(iii) $S \in$ *Stat* is deterministic if, for all deterministic γ, $M(S)(\gamma)$ is deterministic.

Prove

a. v := t is deterministic

b. If S_1 and S_2 are deterministic, then $S_1;S_2$ and, for all b, $b;S_1 \cup \neg b;S_2$ are deterministic

c. If S is deterministic then $\mu X[S]$ is deterministic.

7.5. Consider the following program written in the syntax of chapter 5: $<P_1 \Leftarrow S_1, P_2 \Leftarrow S_2, P_3 \Leftarrow S_3 \mid P_1>$. Give an equivalent statement in the syntax of chapter 7.

7.6. a. Prove

$$\frac{f \Rightarrow (S_1 \sqsubseteq S_2)}{f \Rightarrow ((S_1[S/X] \sqsubseteq S_2[S/X]) \wedge (\mu X[S_1] \sqsubseteq \mu X[S_2]))}$$

provided that $X \notin stmv(f)$

b. Show that, in general, it is not true that

$\models (S_1 \sqsubseteq S_2) \Rightarrow (S_1[S/X] \sqsubseteq S_2[S/X])$, or

$\models (S_1 \sqsubseteq S_2) \Rightarrow (\mu X[S_1] \sqsubseteq \mu X[S_2])$.

7.7. a. $\models b*S = b*S; \neg b$

b. $\models b*(b*S) = b*S$

c. $\models b_1*S;(b_1 \vee b_2)*S = (b_1 \vee b_2)*S$

d. $\models b_1*(b_2*S) = b_1*((b_1 \wedge b_2)*S;(\neg b_1 \wedge b_2)*S)$.

7.8. Prove that

$\models (b_2;S_1 = S_1;b_2) \wedge (b_2;S_2 = S_2;b_2) \Rightarrow$

$b_1*(b_2;S_1 \cup \neg b_2;S_2) = b_2;(b_1*S_1) \cup \neg b_2;(b_1*S_2)$.

7.9. Prove that, if X is not free in A_1 or A_2, and Y_1 and Y_2 are not free in A_1, A_2, S_1 or S_2, then

$\mu X[A_1;S_1 \cup A_2;S_2]$

$\models =$

$A_1;\mu Y_1[S_1[A_1;Y_1 \cup A_2;\ \mu Y_2[S_2[A_1;Y_1 \cup A_2;Y_2/X]]/X]] \cup$

$A_2;\mu Y_2[S_2[A_1;\mu Y_1[S_1[A_1;Y_1 \cup A_2;Y_2/X]] \cup A_2;Y_2/X]]$.

7.10. Let $S_0 \equiv D$, $S_i \equiv S_{i-1};b_i*(A_i;S_{i-1})$, $i = 1,\ldots,n$.

Assume $X \notin$ *stmv* $(A_1,\ldots,A_n)$.

Prove

$\models S_n = \mu X[b_1;A_1;X \cup \neg b_1;b_2;A_2;X \cup \ldots \cup \neg b_1;\ldots;\neg b_{n-1};b_n;A_n;X \cup$
$\neg b_1;\ldots;\neg b_{n-1};\neg b_n]$.

7.11. Let us call a statement S *total*, if for all γ and $\sigma \neq \perp$, $\perp \notin M(S)(\gamma)(\sigma)$. Let $\mu_1 \stackrel{\text{df.}}{\equiv} \mu X[S_1]$, $\mu_2 \stackrel{\text{df.}}{\equiv} \mu X[S_2]$,

$\mu_3 \overset{\text{df.}}{\equiv} \mu X[S_1[S_2/X]]$, $\mu_4 \overset{\text{df.}}{\equiv} \mu X[S_2[S_1/X]]$. Prove that, if μ_1, μ_2, μ_3 and μ_4 are all total, then $\models \mu_1 = \mu_2$ iff $\models \mu_3 = \mu_4$.

7.12. a. Prove that, for $i = 1,\ldots,n$,

$$\mu_i X_1 \ldots X_n [S_1(S_{11}(X_1,\ldots,X_n),\ldots,S_{1m}(X_1,\ldots,X_n)),\ldots, S_n(S_{n1}(X_1,\ldots,X_n),\ldots,S_{nm}(X_1,\ldots,X_n))]$$

$$\models =$$

$$S_i(\mu_{i1} X_1 \ldots X_{nm}[S_{11}(S_1(X_{11},\ldots,X_{1m}),\ldots,S_n(X_{n1},\ldots,X_{nm})),\ldots, S_{nm}(S_1(X_{11},\ldots,X_{1m}),\ldots,S_n(X_{n1},\ldots,S_{nm}))],\ldots, \mu_{im} X_1 \ldots X_{nm}[S_{11}(S_1(\ldots),\ldots,S_n(\ldots)),\ldots,S_{nm}(S_1(\ldots),\ldots, S_n(\ldots))])$$

b. Derive example 7.14 as a consequence of part a.

7.13. Let the property of a statement X being *regular in a set of statement variables* $\mathcal{X}$ be defined inductively as follows:

(i) $v:=t$, b, and $X \in \mathcal{X}$ are regular in $\mathcal{X}$

(ii) If S_1 is regular in $\emptyset$ and S_2 is regular in $\mathcal{X}$, then $S_1;S_2$ is regular in $\mathcal{X}$

(iii) If S_1 and S_2 are regular in $\mathcal{X}$, then $S_1 \cup S_2$ is regular in $\mathcal{X}$

(iv) If S is regular in $\mathcal{X} \cup \{Y\}$, then $\mu Y[S]$ is regular in $\mathcal{X}$.

S is called *regular* if it is regular in $\emptyset$. (Note that a regular statement contains no free statement variables.)

Prove that if S is regular in $\{X_1,\ldots,X_n\}$, then there exist regular $S_1,\ldots,S_{n+1}$ such that

$\models S = S_1;X_1 \cup \ldots \cup S_n;X_n \cup S_{n+1}$.

7.14. Prove using Scott's induction that

$$\frac{S_1[S_1[S_2/X]/X] = S_2[S_1/X],\ S_1[\Omega/X] = S_2[\Omega/X]}{\mu X[S_1] = \mu X[S_2]}$$

(Hint: (i) Proof of $\models \mu X[S_1] \sqsubseteq \mu X[S_2]$. Use theorem 7.16, with

$f_0 \equiv \underline{\text{true}}$, $f \equiv ((X \sqsubseteq S_1) \wedge (S_1 \sqsubseteq S_2) \wedge (X \sqsubseteq \mu X[S_2]))$,

and $S \equiv S_1$

(ii) Proof of $\models \mu X[S_2] \sqsubseteq \mu X[S_1]$. Use theorem 7.16, with

$f_0 \equiv \underline{\text{true}}$, $f \equiv (S_2 \sqsubseteq \mu X[S_1])$ and $S \equiv S_1$.

Cf. also example 3 after lemma 5.11.)

7.15. Prove that

$\{(x=n) \wedge (y=m) \wedge (n\geq 0)\}$

$\models \mu X[(x>0);x:=x-1;X;y:=y+1;X;x:=x+1 \cup (x\leq 0)]$

$\{(x=n) \wedge (y=m+2^n-1)\}$.

7.16. Let $\mathit{Assg} = \{v:=t \mid v \in \mathit{Ivar} \wedge t \in \mathit{Iexp}\}$. Let Alph be the (infinite) alphabet defined by

$\mathit{Alph} = \mathit{Assg} \cup \mathit{Bexp}$.

Let Statc be the class of all statements (as introduced in chapter 7) without free statement variables. Let Lang: $\mathit{Statc} \to 2^{\mathit{Alph}^*}$ be the following mapping:

(i) $\mathit{Lang}(\Omega) = \emptyset$, $\mathit{Lang}(v:=t) = \{v:=t\}$, $\mathit{Lang}(b) = \{b\}$

(ii) $\mathit{Lang}(S_1;S_2) = \mathit{Lang}(S_1)\mathit{Lang}(S_2)$

(iii) $Lang(S_1 \cup S_2) = Lang(S_1) \cup Lang(S_2)$

(iv) $Lang(\mu X[S]) = \bigcup_{i=0}^{\infty} Lang(S_X^{(i)})$, where

$$S_X^{(0)} \equiv \Omega$$

$$S_X^{(i+1)} \equiv S[S_X^{(i)}/X], \quad i = 0,1,\ldots .$$

a. Show that for each $S \in$ *Statc*, *Lang*(S) is a context free language over *Alph*.

b. Show that for each regular S, *Lang*(S) is a regular language over *Alph*.

7.17. Let *Statd* be defined by

$$S ::= v:=t \mid S_1;S_2 \mid \underline{\text{if}}\ b_1 \rightarrow S_1 \square \ldots \square b_n \rightarrow S_n\ \underline{\text{fi}} \mid \underline{\text{do}}\ b_1 \rightarrow S_1 \square \ldots \square b_n \rightarrow S_n\ \underline{\text{od}}$$

and let *Ax*, *Pr* be defined by

(i) *Ax* consists of

(α) all valid assertions

(β) $\{p[t/v]\}\ v:=t\ \{p\}$

(ii) *Pr* consists of

(α) $$\frac{\{p\}S_1\{q\},\{q\}S_2\{r\}}{\{p\}S_1;S_2\{r\}}$$

(β) $$\frac{p \supset p_1, \{p_1\}S\{q_1\}, q_1 \supset q}{\{p\}S\{q\}}$$

(γ) $$\frac{\{p \wedge b_1\}S_1\{q\},\ldots,\{p \wedge b_n\}S_n\{q\}}{\{p\}\ \underline{\text{if}}\ b_1 \rightarrow S_1 \square \ldots \square b_n \rightarrow S_n\ \underline{\text{fi}}\ \{q\}}$$

(δ) $$\frac{\{p \wedge b_1\}S_1\{p\},\ldots,\{p \wedge b_n\}S_n\{p\}}{\{p\}\ \underline{\text{do}}\ b_1 \rightarrow S_1 \square \ldots \square b_n \rightarrow S_n\ \underline{\text{od}}\ \{p \wedge \neg b_1 \wedge \ldots \wedge \neg b_n\}}$$

Prove that, for all $p,q \in$ *Assn*, and all $S \in$ *Statd*,

$\vdash_{Ax,\,Pr}$ {p}S{q} iff $\models$ {p}S{q}

(Hint: cf. section 3.6.)

Chapter 8

WEAKEST PRECONDITIONS, STRONGEST POSTCONDITIONS AND TERMINATION

8.1. Introduction

In this chapter we study weakest preconditions and strongest postconditions, in particular - insofar as weakest preconditions are concerned - as an aid to investigate formal properties of termination.

Remember that in chapter 2 we introduced the constructs $S \to p$ and $p \leftarrow S$, which were provided with meaning such that $\models \{p\}S\{q\}$ iff $\models p \supset (S \to q)$ iff $\models (p \leftarrow S) \supset q$, i.e. such that $S \to p$ is the *weakest precondition* (for partial correctness) of S with respect to p, and $p \leftarrow S$ the *strongest postcondition*. We now introduce a new type of correctness formula: [p]S[q], which has as intended meaning that it holds in a given state σ whenever, if p holds in σ, then S terminates and all output states satisfy q. Also, if [p]S[q] is satisfied in all states, we call S *totally* correct with respect to p and q. Moreover, we define a construct $S \triangleright p$ which plays the same role with respect to total correctness as $S \to p$ does for partial correctness, i.e. which satisfies $\models [p]S[q]$ iff $\models p \supset (S \triangleright q)$. (We shall not introduce a syntactic construct for the strongest postcondition with respect to total correctness.) Clearly, $S \triangleright$ <u>true</u> is satisfied in a state σ precisely when $\perp$ is not a possible outcome of the execution of S for this σ, i.e. when S terminates in σ. Thus, the study of $S \triangleright$ <u>true</u> is a means of analyzing termination properties of the statement S. Finally, we also pay some attention to the construct $S \leftarrow p \overset{df.}{\equiv} \neg(S \to \neg p)$. Summarizing, we have

a. Three weakest-precondition-type constructs

(i) $S \to p$ (with as intended meaning in a given state $\neq \perp$):

all convergent computations (i.e. computations which do not deliver ⊥) yield output satisfying p

(ii) S ⊳ p (idem): all computations converge with output states satisfying p

(iii) S ↞ p (idem): there is at least one convergent computation with output satisfying p (since, by the definition of S ↞ p and (i), it is not true that all convergent computations yield output satisfying ¬p)

b. One strongest-postcondition-type construct: p ← S.

In chapters 2 and 4 we have shown how to determine (v:=s) → p and p ← (v:=s), and how to express $(S_1;S_2)$ → p, p ← $(S_1;S_2)$, <u>if</u> b <u>then</u> S_1 <u>else</u> S_2 <u>fi</u> → p, and p ← <u>if</u> b <u>then</u> S_1 <u>else</u> S_2 <u>fi</u>, in terms of constructs involving S_1 → ... and S_2 → ..., and ... ← S_1 and ... ← S_2, respectively. Two questions which arise naturally at this stage are whether there are analogous results for S ⊳ p and whether these results may be extended for the while statement, recursive procedures, and nondeterminacy. The first question, and the S ≡ $S_1 \cup S_2$ case of the second, are easy; the simple formulae taking care of them may be found in section 8.2. As to the while statement, a *semantic* reduction of <u>while</u> b <u>do</u> S <u>od</u> → p and p ← <u>while</u> b <u>do</u> S <u>od</u> was presented in section 3.5. There remain the questions of a *syntactic* treatment of these cases (and of <u>while</u> b <u>do</u> S <u>od</u> ⊳ p) and of an analysis of μX[S] → p, p ← μX[S], and μX[S] ⊳ p, in general. No completely satisfactory solution to these problems is available. Rather, we discuss various approaches which may be considered as providing some partial insight, without, however, settling the question in full.

In section 8.2 we present the basic definitions for S → p, p ← S, S ⊳ p (and S ↞ p), with S as in chapter 7, and list the fundamental properties of these constructs. Section 8.3 gives a full *semantic* analysis of S ⊳ p. More specifically, after having observed that the meaning of S ⊳ p is nothing but the composition $\mathcal{T}(p) \circ \mathcal{M}(S)$ - details are supplied below - we explore the idea of assigning meaning to statements not as functions from states to (sets of) states, but from predicates to predicates, in the following manner. We define a mapping P: *Stat* $\to [\Pi \to \Pi]$ - forgetting for the moment about the analogs of the γ-arguments - satisfying the relationship $P(S)(\pi) = \pi \circ M(S)$. In view of the preceding remark on the meaning of S $\rhd$ p, we may also say that we consider statements as mappings from postconditions to weakest preconditions (with respect to total correctness).

In section 8.4 we propose an extension to the syntax of conditions, viz. by introducing *recursive* conditions $\mu Z[p]$, where Z is a *condition variable* which, in general, will occur in p. This allows us to reduce $\mu X[S] \to p$, $p \leftarrow \mu X[S]$ and $\mu X[S] \rhd p$, for the case that S is *regular* in X, i.e. S has the form $S_1;X \cup S_2$, where S_1 and S_2 are without free occurrences of X. The results obtained in this section (for conditions with respect to partial correctness) provide a syntactic counterpart for the semantic results of section 3.5. We draw attention, in particular, to the greatest-fixed-point result for $\mu X[S_1;X \cup S_2] \to p$, which uses a quite elegant relationship between least and greatest fixed points.

Finally, section 8.5 is devoted to a study of S $\rhd$ <u>true</u>. Contrary to the general case S $\rhd$ p, it *is* known how to syntactically decompose S $\rhd$ <u>true</u>, albeit that the formula for $\mu X[S] \rhd$ <u>true</u> may be rather difficult to appreciate. Moreover, this section introduces the (syntactic) notion of (upper - and lower -) derivative of a statement (with respect to a statement variable or set of statement variables, respectively). They play a part in the analysis of the reasons why a recursive procedure may fail to terminate. As further tool we introduce the (semantic) notion of well-foundedness of a function $\phi: \Sigma \to_s T$ with respect to some predicate π, and we combine these two notions to prove a central theorem which expresses $\mu X[S] \rhd$ <u>true</u> in terms of the well-foundedness of a certain construct involving the derivatives of S with respect to X. The reader should be prepared that the proofs in this section are considerably more complicated than the previously encountered ones.

8.2. Conditions and total correctness

In this section we present various elementary properties of $S \to p$ and $p \leftarrow S$, and, moreover, introduce the construct $[p]S[q]$, with the intended meaning that $\models [p]S[q]$ holds whenever S is totally correct with respect to p and q, i.e. whenever for each input state satisfying p, execution of S terminates and all output states (remember that S may be nondeterministic) satisfy q. Furthermore, we introduce, for each statement S and postcondition p, the syntactic notion of weakest precondition *with respect to total correctness* $S \triangleright p$.

A number of semantic preparations, partly extending the material of section 7.2, are necessary. We recall our introduction of the two cpo's $T = \{tt, ff\}$ and $\Pi = \Sigma \to_s T$, with typical elements δ and π, respectively, and ordered by $\delta_1 \sqsubseteq \delta_2$ iff $\delta_1 \Rightarrow \delta_2$, $\pi_1 \sqsubseteq \pi_2$ iff $\pi_1(\sigma) \sqsubseteq \pi_2(\sigma)$, for all σ. As noted before, each subset Δ of T has a glb and lub, $\sqcap \Delta$ and $\sqcup \Delta$ respectively, satisfying the obvious properties

$$\sqcap \Delta = \begin{cases} tt, & \text{if } ff \notin \Delta \\ ff, & \text{if } ff \in \Delta \end{cases}$$

$$\sqcup \Delta = \begin{cases} tt, & \text{if } tt \in \Delta \\ ff, & \text{if } tt \notin \Delta \end{cases}$$

Furthermore, each subset Π' of Π has a glb and lub, satisfying $\sqcap \Pi' = \lambda\sigma\cdot\sqcap\{\pi'(\sigma) \mid \pi' \in \Pi'\}$, $\sqcup \Pi' = \lambda\sigma\cdot\sqcup\{\pi'(\sigma) \mid \pi' \in \Pi'\}$. In other words, both T and Π are complete lattices (cf. theorem 5.13).

Similar to definition 7.5, we now extend each function $\pi: \Sigma \to_s T$ to a function $\hat{\pi}: T \to_s T$, in

DEFINITION 8.1 (" $\hat{}$ " for $\pi \in \Pi$).

Let $\pi: \Sigma \to_s T$. $\hat{\pi}: T \to_s T$ is defined by

$$\hat{\pi} = \lambda\tau \cdot \bigsqcap_{\sigma\in\tau} \pi(\sigma)$$

END 8.1.

Remarks

1. Observe that this definition implies that $\hat{\pi}(\emptyset) = tt$.
2. Since, by strictness, $\pi(\bot) = ff$, we clearly have that $\hat{\pi}(\tau) = tt$ iff τ is finite and $\pi(\sigma) = tt$ for all $\sigma \in \tau$.

Analogously to lemma 7.6 we have

LEMMA 8.2.

a. $\pi \in \Pi \Rightarrow \hat{\pi} \in T \to_m T$

b. $\pi \in \Pi \Rightarrow \hat{\pi} \in [T \to T]$

c. $\hat{} \in \Pi \to_m [T \to T]$

d. $\hat{} \in [\Pi \to [T \to T]]$.

PROOF.

a. Let $\pi \in \Pi$, $\tau_1 \sqsubseteq \tau_2$. To show $\hat{\pi}(\tau_1) \sqsubseteq \hat{\pi}(\tau_2)$. Either $\bot \in \tau_1$, in which case $\hat{\pi}(\tau_1) = ff$, and the result is clear. Or $\tau_1 = \tau_2$, and the result is again obvious.

b. Let $\pi \in \Pi$ and let $\langle\tau_i\rangle_{i=0}^{\infty}$ be a chain in T. To show $\hat{\pi}(\bigsqcup_i \tau_i) \sqsubseteq \bigsqcup_i \hat{\pi}(\tau_i)$. If $\bot \in \tau_i$ for all i, then $\bot \in \bigsqcup_i \tau_i$, and $\hat{\pi}(\bigsqcup_i \tau_i) = ff$. Otherwise, let $\bot \notin \tau_{i_0}$ for some i_0, so that $\bigsqcup_i \tau_i = \tau_{i_0}$. Then $\hat{\pi}(\bigsqcup_i \tau_i) = \hat{\pi}(\tau_{i_0}) \sqsubseteq \bigsqcup_i \hat{\pi}(\tau_i)$.

c. Exercise.

d. Let $\langle\pi_i\rangle_{i=0}^{\infty}$ be a chain in Π. To show $(\bigsqcup_i \pi_i)\hat{} \sqsubseteq \bigsqcup_i \hat{\pi}_i$. Choose some τ. We prove that $(\bigsqcup_i \hat{\pi}_i)(\tau) = (\bigsqcup_i \pi_i)\hat{}(\tau)$.

(i) τ is finite. We consider only the case that $\tau = \{\sigma_1,\sigma_2\}$. The desired result follows directly from the fact that, for chains

$<\delta_i>_{i=0}^{\infty}$ and $<\delta_i'>_{i=0}^{\infty}$, $(\bigsqcup_i \delta_i) \wedge (\bigsqcup_i \delta_i') = \bigsqcup_i (\delta_i \wedge \delta_i')$

(ii) If τ is infinite, then $\perp \in \tau$, and $(\bigsqcup_i \hat{\pi}_i)(\tau) = ff = (\bigsqcup_i \pi_i)\hat{}(\tau)$.

END 8.2.

Lemma 8.2 shows us that it is safe (with respect to continuity requirements, see corollary 8.4) to define " $\circ$ " as in

DEFINITION 8.3 (" $\circ$ " for π and ϕ).
For each $\pi \in \Pi$ and $\phi \in M$, $\pi \circ \phi$ ($\in \Pi$) is defined by

$$\pi \circ \phi = \lambda\sigma \cdot \hat{\pi}(\phi(\sigma))$$

END 8.3.

COROLLARY 8.4. " $\circ$ " is continuous in both its arguments, i.e.

a. For $<\phi_i>_{i=0}^{\infty}$ a chain in M, $\pi \circ \bigsqcup_i \phi_i = \bigsqcup_i (\pi \circ \phi_i)$

b. For $<\pi_i>_{i=0}^{\infty}$ a chain in Π, $(\bigsqcup_i \pi_i) \circ \phi = \bigsqcup_i (\pi_i \circ \phi)$.

PROOF. Immediate from lemma 8.2b and 8.2d, respectively.
END 8.4.

After thus having concluded our semantic preparations, we present syntax and semantics of our various constructs. First, we agree that the syntactic classes *Stat* and *Assn* are as in chapter 7. Next, we (re-)introduce the class of conditions *Cond*, as studied before in chapters 2, 3 and 4, but now extended with the weakest precondition construct for total correctness $S \triangleright p$, and, as to its semantics, adapted to the framework as developed in chapter 7.

DEFINITION 8.5 (syntax of conditions).

a. The class of conditions *Cond*, with typical elements p,q,r,..., is defined by

$$p ::= \underline{true} \mid \ldots \mid \exists x[p] \mid S \rightarrow p \mid p \leftarrow S \mid S \triangleright p$$

b. $S \leftarrow p \overset{df.}{\equiv} \neg(S \rightarrow \neg p)$

END 8.5.

Remark. According to definition 8.5, $b_1 \leftarrow b_2$ is now syntactically ambiguous. However, as we leave to the reader to verify, it is not semantically ambiguous according to the definition to be given presently.

Examples. $b \rightarrow \underline{false}$, $(x=0) \leftarrow (x:=y+z)$, $\mu X[(x>0);x:=x-1;X \cup (x\leq 0)] \triangleright \underline{true}$.

In accordance with what we have said already about these constructs (and with previous definitions), we define the meaning of $S \rightarrow p$, $p \leftarrow S$, $S \triangleright p$, $\{p\}S\{q\}$ and $[p]S[q]$ (to be introduced presently) in such a way that $\models \{p\}S\{q\}$ iff $\models p \supset (S \rightarrow q)$ iff $\models (p \leftarrow S) \supset q$, and $\models [p]S[q]$ iff $\models p \supset (S \triangleright q)$. In our definition of the semantics of conditions, we have to take into account the possibility that they contain occurrences of free statement variables (such as, e.g. in $X \rightarrow \underline{true}$), whence the necessity to supply an additional argument $\gamma \in \Gamma$. Thus, T is now of type

$$T\colon Cond \rightarrow (\Gamma \rightarrow \Pi)$$

and we define it in

<u>DEFINITION 8.6</u> (semantics of conditions).

Let $p \in Cond$ and $\gamma \in \Gamma$. $T(p)(\gamma)(\bot) = ff$, and, for $\sigma \neq \bot$,

a. $T(\underline{true})(\gamma)(\sigma) = tt, \ldots, T(\exists x[p])(\gamma)(\sigma) = \exists\alpha[T(p)(\gamma)(\sigma\{\alpha/x\})]$ (cf. definition 2.9)

b. $T(S\rightarrow p)(\gamma)(\sigma) = \forall\sigma'[\sigma' \in M(S)(\gamma)(\sigma) \wedge \sigma' \neq \bot \Rightarrow T(p)(\gamma)(\sigma')]$

c. $T(p\leftarrow S)(\gamma)(\sigma) = \exists\sigma'[T(p)(\gamma)(\sigma') \wedge \sigma \in M(S)(\gamma)(\sigma')]$

d. $T(S \triangleright p)(\gamma)(\sigma) = T(p)(\gamma)\hat{}(M(S)(\gamma)(\sigma))$

END 8.6.

We see that clause a is as usual, clauses b and c are as in

chapter 3 (apart from the role of the γ-argument), whereas clause d is new. Note that, since $T(p)(\gamma) \in \Pi$, it is meaningful to apply the $\hat{}$-operator to it. Moreover, we have that $T(S \triangleright p)(\gamma)(\sigma) = tt$ whenever $\bot$ is not a possible output state of S for input state σ (S terminates for σ) and, furthermore, p is satisfied for all output states. (This should be contrasted with clause b, where p is only required to hold in output states $\neq \bot$.) Clause d may also be written as $T(S \triangleright p)(\gamma) = T(p)(\gamma) \circ M(S)(\gamma)$. From this we see that the syntactic operator " $\triangleright$ " has a very natural interpretation through the semantic composition operator " $\circ$ ", thus underlining the importance of the notion of weakest precondition with respect to total correctness. Finally, it should be clear that $S \leftarrow p$ holds in some given γ and σ iff there is at least one σ' ($\neq \bot$) such that $\sigma' \in M(S)(\gamma)(\sigma)$ and $T(p)(\gamma)(\sigma')$ holds.

From chapter 3 we recall the semantic definitions of " $\rightarrow$ " and " $\leftarrow$ ":

<u>DEFINITION 8.7</u> (semantic definitions of " $\rightarrow$ " and " $\leftarrow$ ").

a. $(\phi\rightarrow\pi)(\sigma) = (\sigma\neq\bot) \wedge \forall\sigma'[\sigma' \in \phi(\sigma) \wedge \sigma'\neq\bot \Rightarrow \pi(\sigma')]$

b. $(\pi\leftarrow\phi)(\sigma) = (\sigma\neq\bot) \wedge \exists\sigma'[\pi(\sigma') \wedge \sigma \in \phi(\sigma')]$

END 8.7.

In the next lemma we collect the monotonicity and continuity properties of the operators " $\rightarrow$ ", " $\leftarrow$ ", and " $\circ$ ".

<u>LEMMA 8.8</u>.

a. (i) $\pi_1 \sqsubseteq \pi_2 \Rightarrow (\phi\rightarrow\pi_1) \sqsubseteq (\phi\rightarrow\pi_2)$

(ii) $\phi_1 \sqsubseteq \phi_2 \Rightarrow (\phi_2\rightarrow\pi) \sqsubseteq (\phi_1\rightarrow\pi)$ (i.e. $\phi\rightarrow\pi$ is antimonotonic in ϕ)

(iii) $\phi \rightarrow \pi$ is not continuous in π

(iv) $\phi \rightarrow \bigsqcap_i \pi_i = \bigsqcap_i (\phi \rightarrow \pi_i)$

(v) For $\langle\phi_i\rangle_{i=0}^{\infty}$ a chain in M, $(\bigsqcup_i \phi_i) \rightarrow \pi = \bigsqcap_i (\phi_i \rightarrow \pi)$

b. $\pi \leftarrow \phi$ is continuous in both π and ϕ

c. $\pi \circ \phi$ is continuous in both π and ϕ.

PROOF.

a. We consider only part (iii). The result is obtained from the fact that the following two formulae are not equivalent in general:

(α) $\forall\sigma'\exists i[\sigma' \in \phi(\sigma) \wedge \sigma'\neq\bot \Rightarrow \pi_i(\sigma')]$

(β) $\exists i\forall\sigma'[\sigma' \in \phi(\sigma) \wedge \sigma'\neq\bot \Rightarrow \pi_i(\sigma')]$

b. We consider only continuity in ϕ and show that, for $<\phi_i>_{i=0}^{\infty}$ a chain, $\pi \leftarrow \bigsqcup_i \phi_i = \bigsqcup_i (\pi\leftarrow\phi_i)$. Take some $\sigma \neq \bot$.

$(\pi \leftarrow \bigsqcup_i \phi_i)(\sigma) = \exists\sigma'[\pi(\sigma') \wedge \sigma \in \bigsqcup_i \phi_i(\sigma')] =$

$\exists\sigma'[\pi(\sigma') \wedge \exists i[\sigma \in \phi_i(\sigma')]] = \exists\sigma'\exists i[\pi(\sigma') \wedge \sigma \in \phi_i(\sigma')] =$

$\exists i\exists\sigma'[\pi(\sigma') \wedge \sigma \in \phi_i(\sigma')] = \bigsqcup_i (\pi\leftarrow\phi_i)(\sigma)$

c. Corollary 8.4.

END 8.8.

Next, we come to syntax and semantics of correctness formulae. We introduce two extensions:

- the [p]S[q] construct for total correctness
- we allow the p,..., occurring in correctness formulae to be conditions and not just assertions (as was the case in chapters 5, 6 and 7).

DEFINITION 8.9 (syntax and semantics of correctness formulae).

a. The class of correctness formulae *Form*, with typical elements f,..., is defined by

$$f ::= p \mid \{p\}S\{q\} \mid [p]S[q] \mid S_1 \sqsubseteq S_2 \mid f_1 \wedge f_2$$

where p,q,... $\in$ *Cond* and S $\in$ *Stat*

b. The function F: *Form* $\to (\Gamma \to \Pi)$ is defined by:

For each f and γ, $F(\gamma)(\bot) = ff$, and for $\sigma \neq \bot$,

(i) $F(p)(\gamma)(\sigma) = T(p)(\gamma)(\sigma)$

(ii) $F(\{p\}S\{q\})(\gamma)(\sigma) =$

$\forall\sigma'[T(p)(\gamma)(\sigma) \wedge \sigma' \in M(S)(\gamma)(\sigma) \wedge \sigma'\neq\bot \Rightarrow T(q)(\gamma)(\sigma')]$

(iii) $F([p]S[q])(\gamma)(\sigma) = T(p)(\gamma)(\sigma) \Rightarrow T(q)(\gamma)\hat{}(M(S)(\gamma)(\sigma))$

(iv) $F(S_1 \sqsubseteq S_2)(\gamma)(\sigma) = M(S_1)(\gamma)(\sigma) \sqsubseteq M(S_2)(\gamma)(\sigma)$

(v) $F(f_1 \wedge f_2)(\gamma)(\sigma) = F(f_1)(\gamma)(\sigma) \wedge F(f_2)(\gamma)(\sigma)$

END 8.9.

The definitions of generalized correctness formulae and their validity, and of inferences and their soundness, are exactly as in chapter 7.

The following lemma states that our definitions satisfy the intended relationships:

LEMMA 8.10.

a. $\models \{p\}S\{q\}$ iff $\models p \supset (S \rightarrow q)$ iff $\models (p \leftarrow S) \supset q$

b. $\models [p]S[q]$ iff $\models p \supset (S \triangleright q)$.

PROOF. Part a is as in chapter 3, part b is immediate by definitions 8.6 and 8.9.

END 8.10.

It is not difficult to determine the various conditions, either directly or through an induction on the complexity of the statement involved, except for the case that this statement is a recursive procedure. In fact, as announced already in its introduction, a good deal of the remainder of this chapter is devoted to an analysis of this case.

The simple cases are brought together in

THEOREM 8.11.

a. (i) $\models (v:=t) \rightarrow p = p[t/v]$, provided $p \in \mathit{Assn}$

(ii) $\models b \rightarrow p = b \supset p$

(iii) $\models (S_1;S_2) \rightarrow p = S_1 \rightarrow (S_2 \rightarrow p)$

(iv) $\models (S_1 \cup S_2) \rightarrow p = (S_1 \rightarrow p) \wedge (S_2 \rightarrow p)$

b. (i) Let $p \in \mathit{Assn}$. $\models p \leftarrow (x:=t) = \ldots$, $\models p \leftarrow (a[s] := t)$ $= \ldots$ (these cases are exactly as in chapter 4)

(ii) $\models p \leftarrow b = p \wedge b$

(iii) $\models p \leftarrow (S_1;S_2) = (p \leftarrow S_1) \leftarrow S_2$

(iv) $\models p \leftarrow (S_1 \cup S_2) = (p \leftarrow S_1) \vee (p \leftarrow S_2)$

c. (i) $\models (v:=t) \rhd p = p[t/v]$, provided $p \in \mathit{Assn}$

(ii) $\models b \rhd p = b \supset p$

(iii) $\models (S_1;S_2) \rhd p = S_1 \rhd (S_2 \rhd p)$

(iv) $\models (S_1 \cup S_2) \rhd p = (S_1 \rhd p) \wedge (S_2 \rhd p)$.

PROOF. The proofs of parts a and b are left as exercises (most of it being a repetition of previously obtained results anyway). As to part c(i), since, for all γ and $\sigma \neq \perp$, $\perp \notin M(v:=t)(\gamma)(\sigma)$, $\models (v:=t) \rhd p = (v:=t) \rightarrow p$, and the result follows by part a. Next, we consider case c(ii). We have that $\models b \rhd p$ iff, for all γ and $\sigma \neq \perp$, $T(p)(\gamma)\hat{\ }(M(b)(\gamma)(\sigma)) = tt$. Choose some γ and $\sigma \neq \perp$. Either $T(b)(\gamma)(\sigma) = ff$ and, hence, $M(b)(\gamma)(\sigma) = \emptyset$, in which case $T(p)(\gamma)\hat{\ }(M(b)(\gamma)(\sigma)) = tt$ holds by definition, or $T(b)(\gamma)(\sigma) = tt$ and, hence, $M(b)(\gamma)(\sigma) = \{\sigma\}$, in which case $T(p)(\gamma)\hat{\ }(M(b)(\gamma)(\sigma)) = tt$ iff $T(p)(\gamma)(\sigma) = tt$. Altogether we see that $T(p)(\gamma)\hat{\ }(M(b)(\gamma)(\sigma)) = tt$ precisely when $T(b \supset p)(\gamma)(\sigma) = tt$, and we have proved that $\models b \rhd p = b \supset p$. Cases (iii) and (iv) are consequences of the easily proven facts that, for each $\pi \in \Pi$, $\phi_1, \phi_2 \in M$, $\pi \circ (\phi_1 \circ \phi_2) = (\pi \circ \phi_1) \circ \phi_2$, and $\pi \circ (\phi_1 \cup \phi_2) = (\pi \circ \phi_1) \wedge (\pi \circ \phi_2)$.
END 8.11.

Lemma 8.12 lists a number of results on special cases for S and p in the conditions.

LEMMA 8.12.

a. $\models S \rightarrow \underline{true}$, $\models \neg(\underline{false} \leftarrow S)$

b. (i) $T(S \rightarrow \underline{false})(\gamma)(\sigma) = tt$ whenever γ and σ are such that $\sigma \neq \perp$ and $M(S)(\gamma)(\sigma)$ contains no states $\neq \perp$

(ii) $T(\underline{true} \leftarrow S)(\gamma)(\sigma) = tt$ whenever γ and σ are such that $\sigma \neq \perp$ and σ belongs to the range of the function $M(S)(\gamma)$

(iii) $T(S \rhd \underline{true})(\gamma)(\sigma) = tt$ whenever γ and σ are such that ($\sigma \neq \perp$ and) $M(S)(\gamma)(\sigma)$ does not contain $\perp$

(iv) $T(S \rhd \underline{false})(\gamma)(\sigma) = ff$ whenever γ and σ are such that $M(S)(\gamma)(\sigma) \neq \emptyset$

c. $\models \Omega \rightarrow p$, $\models \neg(p \leftarrow \Omega)$, $\models \neg(\Omega \rhd p)$

d. $\models D \rightarrow p = p$, $\models p \leftarrow D = p$, $\models D \rhd p = p$

e. $\models \underline{false} \rightarrow p$, $\models \neg(p \leftarrow \underline{false})$, $\models \underline{false} \rhd p$.

PROOF. Exercise. (Note that parts d and e in fact follow from theorem 8.11, parts a(ii), b(ii) and c(ii).)
END 8.12.

As immediate corollary of the monotonicity results of lemma 8.8, we moreover have

LEMMA 8.13.

a. $\models (p_1 \supset p_2) \quad \Rightarrow$
$((S \rightarrow p_1) \supset (S \rightarrow p_2)) \wedge ((p_1 \leftarrow S) \supset (p_2 \leftarrow S)) \wedge ((S \rhd p_1) \supset (S \rhd p_2))$

b. $\models (S_1 \sqsubseteq S_2) \Rightarrow$
$((S_2 \rightarrow p) \supset (S_1 \rightarrow p)) \wedge ((p \leftarrow S_1) \supset (p \leftarrow S_2)) \wedge ((S_1 \rhd p) \supset (S_2 \rhd p))$

PROOF. Lemma 8.8.
END 8.13.

We close this section with a version of Scott's induction rule intended to facilitate proofs of the validity of conditions containing occurrences of recursive procedures. Contrary to the situation in chapter 7, the appropriate continuity condition is not automatically satisfied, which is why an explicit additional requirement is added to the rule. By way of preparation, we introduce the following

DEFINITION 8.14 (semantic and syntactic (anti-)continuity).

a. Let C be a cpo, D a complete lattice and $f: C \rightarrow D$. We call f *continuous* (*anti-continuous*) whenever, for each chain $\langle x_i \rangle_{i=0}^{\infty}$, $f(\bigsqcup_i x_i) = \bigsqcup_i f(x_i)$ $(f(\bigsqcup_i x_i) = \bigsqcap_i f(x_i))$.

b. Let $X \in Stmv$ and $p \in Cond$. We call p *semantically continuous* (*semantically anti-continuous*) in X whenever, for all γ, the function $\lambda\phi\cdot T(p)(\gamma\{\phi/X\})$ is a continuous (anti-continuous) function: $M \to \Pi$.

c. A condition p may be *syntactically continuous* (*syntactically anti-continuous*) in a statement variable X, written as $p \in sc(X)$ ($p \in sac(X)$). The classes $sc(X)$ and $sac(X)$ are defined by

(i) $X \notin stmv(p) \Rightarrow p \in sc(X) \cap sac(X)$

(ii) $p \in sc(X) \Rightarrow \neg p \in sac(X)$

$p \in sac(X) \Rightarrow \neg p \in sc(X)$

(iii) $p \in sac(X),\ q \in sc(X) \Rightarrow p \supset q \in sc(X)$

$p \in sc(X),\ q \in sac(X) \Rightarrow p \supset q \in sac(X)$

(iv) $p \in sc(X) \Rightarrow \{\exists x[p],\ p \leftarrow S,\ S \triangleright p\} \subseteq sc(X)$

(v) $p \in sac(X) \Rightarrow S \to p \in sac(X)$

END 8.14.

Remark. Note that, in part a, the fact that D is a complete lattice implies that a continuous (anti-continuous) function is a fortiori monotonic (anti-monotonic).

The requirement that $p \in sc(X)$ ($p \in sac(X)$) is a sufficient (but not a necessary!) condition that p be semantically continuous (anti-continuous) in X:

LEMMA 8.15.

a. If $p \in sc(X)$, then p is continuous in X

b. If $p \in sac(X)$, then p is anti-continuous in X

PROOF. We do not give the full proof, but consider a representative case. Consider the clause $p \in sac(X) \Rightarrow (S \to p) \in sac(X)$. Corresponding to this, we show that, if, for all γ, $\lambda\phi\cdot T(p)(\gamma\{\phi/X\})$ is anti-continuous, then, for all γ, $\lambda\phi\cdot T(S \to p)(\gamma\{\phi/X\})$ is anti-continuous. Choose some γ, and let $\langle\phi_i\rangle_{i=0}^{\infty}$ be a chain in M. Then $\lambda\phi\cdot T(S\to p)(\gamma\{\phi/X\})(\bigsqcup_i \phi_i)$ $= T(S\to p)(\gamma\{\bigsqcup_i \phi_i/X\}) = M(S)(\gamma\{\bigsqcup_i \phi_i/X\}) \to T(p)(\gamma\{\bigsqcup_i \phi_i/X\}) =$

= ($\lambda\phi\cdot M(S)(\gamma\{\phi/X\})$ is (always) continuous, $\lambda\phi\cdot T(p)(\gamma\{\phi/X\})$ is anti-continuous by assumption) $\bigsqcup_i M(S)(\gamma\{\phi_i/X\}) \rightarrow \bigsqcap_j T(p)(\gamma\{\phi_j/X\})$ = (lemma 8.8a, parts (iv), (v)) $\bigsqcap_i \bigsqcap_j (M(S)(\gamma\{\phi_i/X\}) \rightarrow T(p)(\gamma\{\phi_j/X\}))$ = $\bigsqcap_k (M(S)(\gamma\{\phi_k/X\}) \rightarrow T(p)(\gamma\{\phi_k/X\})) = \bigsqcap_k T(S\rightarrow p)(\gamma\{\phi_k/X\})$.

END 8.15.

We leave it to the reader to give the (usual) definition of the substitution p[S/X] and to prove that, for each γ, $T(p[S/X])(\gamma) = T(p)(\gamma\{M(S)(\gamma)/X\})$.

<u>LEMMA 8.16</u> (Scott's induction for conditions).

$$\frac{p[\Omega/X],\ p \Rightarrow p[S/X]}{p[\mu X[S]/X]}\ ,\quad \text{provided that p is semantically anti-continuous in X}$$

<u>PROOF</u>. Choose some γ. By applying the first and (repeatedly) the second assumption, we obtain that, for all i = 0,1,...,

$$\forall\sigma\neq\bot[T(p)(\gamma\{\phi_i/X\})(\sigma)]$$

where $\phi_0 = \lambda\sigma\cdot\bot$, $\phi_{i+1} = M(S)(\gamma\{\phi_i/X\})$, i = 0,1,... . Thus, $\bigsqcap_{i=0}^{\infty} \forall\sigma\neq\bot[T(p)(\gamma\{\phi_i/X\})(\sigma)]$ holds, or, equivalently, $\forall\sigma\neq\bot[\bigsqcap_{i=0}^{\infty} T(p)(\gamma\{\phi_i/X\})(\sigma)]$ holds. By anti-continuity of p in X, this implies that $\forall\sigma\neq\bot[T(p)(\gamma\{\bigsqcup_i \phi_i/X\})(\sigma)]$ which amounts to the validity of p[μX[S]/X].

END 8.16.

We shall encounter examples of applying this version of Scott's rule in section 8.4 and (in a slightly modified version) in section 8.5.

8.3. Statements as predicate transformers

Our inability to provide a general syntactic analysis of the $\mu X[S] \triangleright p$ construct, leads us to the consideration of a *semantic* counterpart of this problem in the following sense: up to now, we have always assigned meanings to statements as functions from states to (sets of) states. We now introduce, by way of alternative to this, as meaning of a statement a function from predicates to predicates. Remember that a *predicate* is an element of the set $\Pi = \Sigma \rightarrow_s T$. The set $[\Pi \rightarrow \Pi]$ is called the set of *predicate transformers*, with typical elements $\eta,\ldots$. Accordingly, we introduce a new mapping $\mathcal{P}$ of type

$$\mathcal{P}: \mathit{Stat} \rightarrow [\Pi \rightarrow \Pi] \tag{8.1}$$

(In order not to obscure our main point, we neglect for a little while the role of the analog of the set Γ.) Thus, it is meaningful to write $\mathcal{P}(S)(\pi) = \pi'$. The relationship of this with the $S \triangleright p$ construct is that we shall define $\mathcal{P}$ in such a way that the following property is satisfied for each S and p:

$$\mathcal{P}(S)(\mathcal{T}(p)) = \mathcal{T}(S \triangleright p) \tag{8.2}$$

(Again, this formula will be refined in a moment.) Thus, we may say that we view, in this section, statements as mappings from postconditions to weakest preconditions (with respect to total correctness), and show how this mapping may be defined for *each* type of statement (thus, in particular, for recursive procedures), such that (8.2) is satisfied. Since statements may contain free statement variables, formula (8.1) is not precisely what we want. Instead, we introduce the set of functions Θ:

$$\Theta = \mathit{Stmv} \rightarrow [\Pi \rightarrow \Pi]$$

with typical elements $\vartheta,\ldots$, and we shall define $\mathcal{P}$ to be of type

$$P\colon \mathit{Stat} \to (\Theta \to [\Pi \to \Pi]).$$

Therefore, after supplying the as yet suppressed γ- and ϑ-arguments, the precise formulation of (8.2) becomes:

$$P(S)(\vartheta)(T(p)(\gamma)) \;=\; T(S \triangleright p)(\gamma) \tag{8.3}$$

Moreover, we observe that we cannot hope to be able to prove (8.3) for some statement which is, or contains, a free statement variable, since, as usual, $\gamma(X)$ and $\vartheta(X)$ are completely arbitrary. Therefore, we have to impose an additional requirement on the $<\gamma,\vartheta>$ pairs, which we formulate in

DEFINITION 8.17 (consistency of a $<\gamma,\vartheta>$-pair).
Let $\gamma \in \mathit{Stmv} \to M$ and $\vartheta \in \mathit{Stmv} \to [\Pi \to \Pi]$. The pair $<\gamma,\vartheta>$ is called *consistent* whenever, for all X and π,

$$\vartheta(X)(\pi) \;=\; \pi \circ \gamma(X)$$

END 8.17.

We now define P in such a way (definition 8.18) that we can prove (theorem 8.19) that (8.3) is satisfied for each consistent pair $<\gamma,\vartheta>$.

DEFINITION 8.18 (semantics of statements as predicate transformers).
$P\colon \mathit{Stat} \to (\Theta \to [\Pi \to \Pi])$ is defined by

a. $P(v{:=}t)(\vartheta) \;=\; \lambda\pi\cdot\lambda\sigma\cdot\pi(\sigma\{R(t)(\sigma)/L(v)(\sigma)\})$

b. $P(b)(\vartheta) \;=\; \lambda\pi\cdot\lambda\sigma\cdot\underline{\text{if}}\ W(b)(\sigma)\ \underline{\text{then}}\ \pi(\sigma)\ \underline{\text{else}}\ tt\ \underline{\text{fi}}$

c. $P(S_1;S_2)(\vartheta) \;=\; \lambda\pi\cdot P(S_1)(\vartheta)(P(S_2)(\vartheta)(\pi))$

d. $P(S_1 \cup S_2)(\vartheta) \;=\; \lambda\pi\cdot(P(S_1)(\vartheta)(\pi) \wedge P(S_2)(\vartheta)(\pi))$

e. $P(X)(\vartheta) \;=\; \vartheta(X)$

f. $P(\mu X[S])(\vartheta) \;=\; \mu[\lambda\eta\cdot P(S)(\vartheta\{\eta/X\})]$

END 8.18.

Remarks

1. Formulation and proof of a theorem which justifies this definition

just as theorem 7.9 justifies definition 7.8, is left to the reader.

2. For parts b, c and d compare our previous results that $\models b \rhd p = b \supset p$, $\models (S_1;S_2) \rhd p = S_1 \rhd (S_2 \rhd p)$, and $\models (S_1 \cup S_2) \rhd p = (S_1 \rhd p) \wedge (S_2 \rhd p)$.

<u>THEOREM 8.19</u>. For each consistent pair $\langle\gamma,\vartheta\rangle$:

$$\mathcal{P}(S)(\vartheta)(\mathcal{T}(p)(\gamma)) = \mathcal{T}(S \rhd p)(\gamma)$$

<u>PROOF</u>. By the definition of $\mathcal{T}(S \rhd p)(\gamma)$, we have to show that $\mathcal{P}(S)(\vartheta)(\mathcal{T}(p)(\gamma)) = \mathcal{T}(p)(\gamma) \circ \mathcal{M}(S)(\gamma)$. Thus, it is sufficient to show that, for arbitrary π (and consistent $\langle\gamma,\vartheta\rangle$), $\mathcal{P}(S)(\vartheta)(\pi) = \pi \circ \mathcal{M}(S)(\gamma)$. We prove this by induction on the complexity of S.

a. $S \equiv v:=t$. Choose some σ. By the definition of $\mathcal{P}$ and $\mathcal{M}$, we have that $\mathcal{P}(v:=t)(\vartheta)(\pi)(\sigma) = \pi(\sigma\{\mathcal{R}(t)(\sigma)/\mathcal{L}(v)(\sigma)\}) = (\pi \circ \mathcal{M}(v:=t)(\gamma))(\sigma)$, as was to be shown.

b. $S \equiv b$. Clearly, for $\sigma \neq \bot$, $\mathcal{P}(b)(\vartheta)(\pi)(\sigma) = tt$ iff $\mathcal{W}(b)(\sigma) \Rightarrow \pi(\sigma)$, and this coincides with the requirement that $(\pi \circ \mathcal{M}(b)(\gamma))(\sigma)$ be satisfied.

c. $S \equiv S_1;S_2$. By induction, $\mathcal{P}(S_2)(\vartheta)(\pi) = \pi \circ \mathcal{M}(S_2)(\gamma)$. Again by induction, $\mathcal{P}(S_1)(\vartheta)(\pi \circ \mathcal{M}(S_2)(\gamma)) = (\pi \circ \mathcal{M}(S_2)(\gamma)) \circ \mathcal{M}(S_1)(\gamma) = \pi \circ (\mathcal{M}(S_2)(\gamma) \circ \mathcal{M}(S_1)(\gamma)) = \pi \circ \mathcal{M}(S_1;S_2)(\gamma)$, as was to be shown.

d. $S \equiv S_1 \cup S_2$. Exercise.

e. $S \equiv X$. Direct by the consistency requirement.

f. $S \equiv \mu X[S_1]$. Let $\phi_0 = \lambda\sigma\cdot\bot$, $\phi_{i+1} = \mathcal{M}(S_1)(\gamma\{\phi_i/X\})$, $i = 0,1,\ldots$, and $\eta_0 = \lambda\pi\cdot\lambda\sigma\cdot ff$, $\eta_{i+1} = \mathcal{P}(S_1)(\vartheta\{\eta_i/X\})$, $i = 0,1,\ldots$. It suffices to show that, for all π, $\bigsqcup_{i=0}^{\infty} \eta_i(\pi) = \pi \circ \bigsqcup_{i=0}^{\infty} \phi_i$, or, by continuity of "$\circ$", that, for all π, $\bigsqcup_{i=0}^{\infty} \eta_i(\pi) = \bigsqcup_{i=0}^{\infty} (\pi \circ \phi_i)$. We show by induction on i that, for all π, $\eta_i(\pi) = \pi \circ \phi_i$. Since, for all π, $\pi(\bot) = ff$, the result is clear for $i = 0$. Now assume (*): for all π, $\eta_i(\pi) = \pi \circ \phi_i$. To show that, for all π, $\eta_{i+1}(\pi) = \pi \circ \phi_{i+1}$, i.e.

that, for all π, $P(S_1)(\vartheta\{\eta_i/X\})(\pi) = \pi \circ M(S_1)(\gamma\{\phi_i/X\})$. By the induction hypothesis on S_1 (which has smaller complexity than $\mu X[S_1]$), it is sufficient to show that the pair $<\gamma\{\phi_i/X\},\vartheta\{\eta_i/X\}>$ is consistent, i.e. that for all $Y \in \mathit{Stmv}$, and all π, $\vartheta\{\eta_i/X\}(Y)(\pi) = \pi \circ \gamma\{\phi_i/X\}(Y)$

(i) $Y \equiv X$. Then what we have to show reduces to:

For all π, $\eta_i(\pi) = \pi \circ \phi_i$, which is nothing but (*)

(ii) $Y \not\equiv X$. Then the desired result simplifies to:

For all π, $\vartheta(Y)(\pi) = \pi \circ \gamma(Y)$, which follows from the consistency of $<\gamma,\vartheta>$.

END 8.19.

8.4. Recursive conditions and regular recursive procedures

This section is devoted to an analysis of $S \rightarrow p$, $p \leftarrow S$ and $S \triangleright p$ for S a *regular* statement. Intuitively, a statement is regular iff it is semantically equivalent to some flow chart (allowing nondeterminacy). Since we do not present a formal discussion of flow charts in our treatise, we shall pursue this correspondence only through some examples, and not go into a rigorous investigation of it. We have in fact encountered the notion of regularity before (in exercises 5.18, 5.19 and 7.13). The definition we give now is somewhat simpler than that of exercise 7.13 (cf. remark 3 following the definition):

DEFINITION 8.20 (regular statements).

a. $v := t$ and b are regular

b. If S_1 and S_2 are regular, then $S_1;S_2$, $S_1 \cup S_2$ and $\mu X[S_1;X \cup S_2]$ are regular.

END 8.20.

Examples

1. $x:=0$, $x>0;x:=x-1 \cup (x\leq 0)$, $\mu X[x>0;x:=x-1;X \cup (x\leq 0)]$ and $\mu X[x>0;\mu Y[y>0;y:=y-1;Y \cup (y\leq 0)];x:=x-1;X \cup (x\leq 0)]$ are all regular.

2. If S_1 and S_2 are regular then $\mu X[b_1;S_1;b_2;S_2;X \cup b_1;S_1;\neg b_2 \cup \neg b_1]$ is regular.
3. X and $\mu X[x>0;x:=x-1;X;x:=x+1 \cup (x\leq 0)]$ are not regular.

Remarks

1. Note that a regular statement contains no free statement variables.
2. Each while statement is regular, or, more precisely, if S is regular then $\mu X[b;S;X \cup \neg b]$ is regular.
3. a. Each S which is regular according to definition 8.20 is regular according to exercise 7.13
   b. If S_1, S_2, S_3 are regular (according to definition 8.20) then $\mu X[\mu Y[S_1;Y \cup S_2;X] \cup S_3]$ is regular according to exercise 7.13 but not according to definition 8.20
   c. For each S which is regular according to exercise 7.13, there exists some S' which is regular according to definition 8.20, and such that $\models S = S'$.
4. a. As flow chart corresponding to the second example above we have

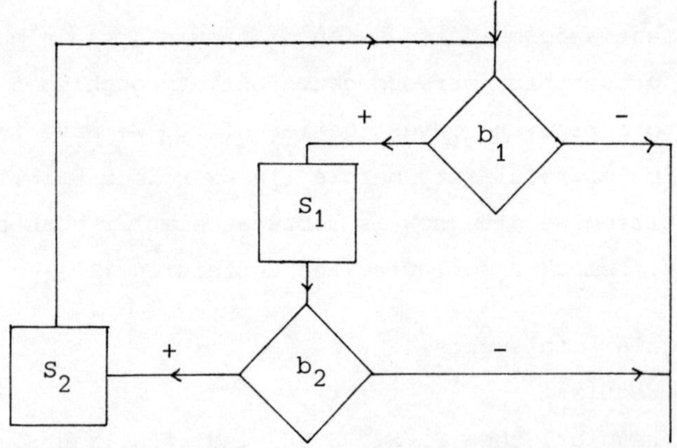

   b. As regular statement corresponding to the flow chart

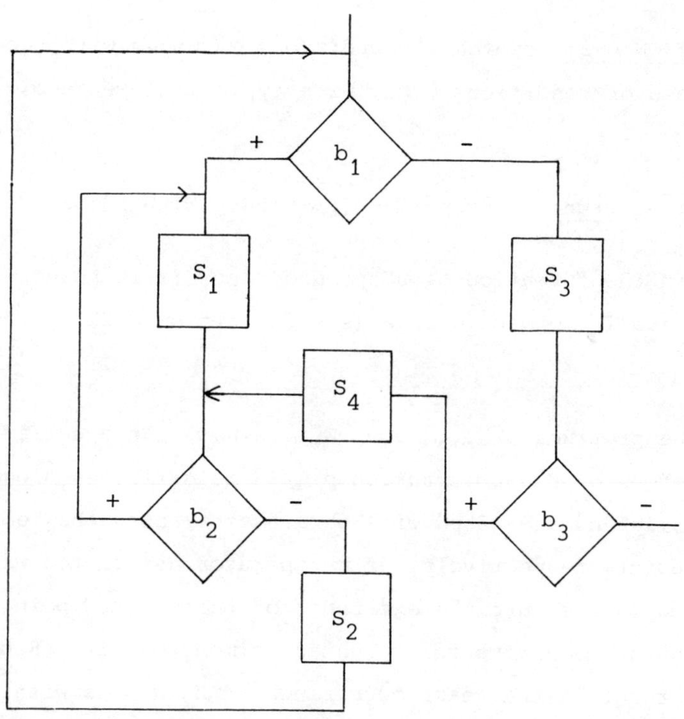

we have

$\mu X[(b_1;S_1 \cup \neg b_1;S_3;b_3;S_4);\mu Y[b_2;S_1;Y \cup \neg b_2;S_2];X \cup \neg b_1;S_3;\neg b_3]$.

If S is regular but not a μ-term, the results for $S \rightarrow p$, $p \leftarrow S$ and $S \triangleright p$ obtained in section 8.2 apply. There remains the treatment of $\mu X[S_1;X \cup S_2] \rightarrow p$, $p \leftarrow \mu X[S_1;X \cup S_2]$, and $\mu X[S_1;X \cup S_2] \triangleright p$. We present an extension of the class of conditions with so-called *recursive* conditions, and show how to reduce the three conditions just given in terms of constructs involving such recursive conditions. (Remember that a purely semantic treatment of this problem, for conditions with respect to partial correctness of the while statement, was already given in section 3.5.)

We now give the definition of the extended class *Cond* (we do not bother to use a separate name for it). Let *Cndv*, with typical elements

Z,..., be a well-ordered set of *condition variables*.

DEFINITION 8.21 (syntax of conditions extended with recursion).
The class of conditions *Cond*, with typical elements p,q,r,..., is given by

$$p ::= \underline{\text{true}} \mid \ldots \mid \exists x[p] \mid S \rightarrow p \mid p \leftarrow S \mid S \triangleright p \mid Z \mid \mu Z[p] \mid \nu Z[p]$$

where in the formation of $\mu Z[p]$ and $\nu Z[p]$ it is required that p be *syntactically monotonic* in Z (see definition 8.22).
END 8.21.

The prefixes $\mu Z[\ldots]$ and $\nu Z[\ldots]$ have the usual effect on binding occurrences of Z. *Substitution* $p[q/Z]$ is defined analogously to $S[S'/X]$. $\mu Z[p]$ and $\nu Z[p]$ will obtain as meaning the least and greatest fixed point, respectively, of an operator associated with p in the usual way. To ensure the *existence* of these fixed points, we have imposed the requirements of syntactic monotonicity. Roughly, this notion requires that each occurrence of Z in p is within the scope of an even number of $\neg$-signs. More precisely, we define it in

DEFINITION 8.22 (syntactic monotonicity).
A condition p may be *syntactically monotonic* in Z, or *syntactically anti-monotonic* in Z. Let sm(Z) and sa(Z) denote the classes of all such conditions, respectively.

a. (i) If p does not contain Z free, then $p \in sm(Z)$

(ii) $p \in sa(Z) \Rightarrow \neg p \in sm(Z)$

(iii) $p_1 \in sa(Z) \wedge p_2 \in sm(Z) \Rightarrow p_1 \supset p_2 \in sm(Z)$

(iv) $p \in sm(Z) \Rightarrow \{\exists x[p], S \rightarrow p, p \leftarrow S, S \triangleright p\} \subseteq sm(Z)$

(v) $Z \in sm(Z)$

(vi) $p \in sm(Z) \cap sm(Z_1) \Rightarrow \{\mu Z_1[p], \nu Z_1[p]\} \subseteq sm(Z)$

b. (i) - (iv) As clauses a(i) - (iv), with sm and sa interchanged

(v) $p \in sa(Z) \cap sm(Z_1) \Rightarrow \{\mu Z_1[p], \nu Z_1[p]\} \subseteq sa(Z)$

END 8.22.

Examples. true $\in$ sm(Z) $\cap$ sa(Z), Z $\in$ sm(Z)\sa(Z), Z $\supset$ Z $\notin$ sm(Z) $\cup$ sa(Z), $\neg\mu Z_1[S \to (Z_1 \wedge \neg Z)] \in$ sm(Z)\sa(Z), p $\in$ sm(Z) $\Rightarrow$ S$\leftarrow$p $\in$ sm(Z).

In the definition of the semantics of, possibly recursive, conditions, we apply the usual technique of introducing a set of functions giving meaning to condition variables:

$$\Xi = Cndv \to \Pi$$

where Ξ has typical elements ξ,... . (We again adopt the customary variant notation $\xi\{\pi/Z\}$. Also, we assume that no confusion will arise with our use of ξ as a typical element of the set *Intv* (cf. chapter 4).) As type of the function T we therefore have

$$T\colon Cond \to (\Gamma \to (\Xi \to \Pi))$$

Note that, since conditions may now contain both statement variables and condition variables, we need both γ- and ξ-arguments, and it is meaningful to write $T(p)(\gamma)(\xi)(\sigma) = \delta$.

For our treatment of the $\nu Z[p]$ construct, we need a lemma which ensures the existence of the *greatest* fixed point of a monotonic function in suitable circumstances:

LEMMA 8.23. Let C be a complete lattice, and let $f\colon C \to_m C$. Then νf exists and, moreover,

$$\nu f = \bigsqcup\{x \mid x=f(x)\} = \bigsqcup\{x \mid f(x) \sqsupseteq x\}$$

PROOF. Dual to that of theorem 5.13b (with ν replacing μ, $\bigsqcup$ replacing $\bigsqcap$, and $\sqsupseteq$ replacing $\sqsubseteq$).
END 8.23.

This brings us to the definition of the semantics of the new class *Cond*.

DEFINITION 8.24 (semantics of *Cond* with recursive conditions).
The function $\mathcal{T}$: $\mathit{Cond} \to (\Gamma \to (\Xi \to \Pi))$ is defined by: $\mathcal{T}(p)(\gamma)(\xi)(\bot) = ff$, and, for $\sigma \neq \bot$

a. $\mathcal{T}(\underline{true})(\gamma)(\xi)(\sigma) = tt, \ldots, \mathcal{T}(\exists x[p])(\gamma)(\xi)(\sigma) = \exists\alpha[\mathcal{T}(p)(\gamma)(\xi)(\sigma\{\alpha/x\})]$

b. $\mathcal{T}(S\to p)(\gamma)(\xi)(\sigma) = \forall\sigma'[\sigma' \in \mathcal{M}(S)(\gamma)(\sigma) \wedge \sigma'\neq\bot \Rightarrow \mathcal{T}(p)(\gamma)(\xi)(\sigma')]$

c. $\mathcal{T}(p\leftarrow S)(\gamma)(\xi)(\sigma) = \exists\sigma'[\mathcal{T}(p)(\gamma)(\xi)(\sigma') \wedge \sigma \in \mathcal{M}(S)(\gamma)(\sigma')]$

d. $\mathcal{T}(S \triangleright p)(\gamma)(\xi)(\sigma) = (\mathcal{T}(p)(\gamma)(\xi) \circ \mathcal{M}(S)(\gamma))(\sigma)$

e. $\mathcal{T}(Z)(\gamma)(\xi)(\sigma) = \xi(Z)(\sigma)$

f. $\mathcal{T}(\mu Z[p])(\gamma)(\xi)(\sigma) = \mu[\lambda\pi\cdot\mathcal{T}(p)(\gamma)(\xi\{\pi/Z\})](\sigma)$

g. $\mathcal{T}(\nu Z[p])(\gamma)(\xi)(\sigma) = \nu[\lambda\pi\cdot\mathcal{T}(p)(\gamma)(\xi\{\pi/Z\})](\sigma)$

END 8.24.

It is left to the reader to verify that, for p syntactically monotonic in Z, we have that, for each γ and ξ, $\lambda\pi\cdot\mathcal{T}(p)(\gamma)(\xi\{\pi/Z\})$ is a monotonic function: $\Pi \to \Pi$, thus justifying the existence of the least and greatest fixed points on the right-hand side of clauses f and g (by theorem 5.13, lemma 8.23, and the fact that Π is a complete lattice).

Syntax and semantics of (generalized) correctness formulae $f \in \mathit{Form}$ and $g \in \mathit{Gfor}$ are just as before, but for the fact that the conditions appearing in it may now be recursive, leading to the appearance of an additional ξ-argument at appropriate places. We do not give the full definition, but only an example clause: For $\sigma \neq \bot$, $\mathcal{F}([p]S[q])(\gamma)(\xi)(\sigma) = [\mathcal{T}(p)(\gamma)(\xi)(\sigma) \Rightarrow \mathcal{T}(q)(\gamma)(\xi)^{\wedge}(\mathcal{M}(S)(\gamma)(\sigma))]$.
As definitions of validity and soundness we have

DEFINITION 8.25 (validity and soundness in the presence of recursive conditions).

a. A generalized correctness formula $g \equiv (f_1 \Rightarrow f_2)$ is called *valid* (as always written as $\models g$), whenever
$\forall\gamma\forall\xi[\forall\sigma\neq\bot[\mathcal{F}(f_1)(\gamma)(\xi)(\sigma)] \Rightarrow \forall\sigma\neq\bot[\mathcal{F}(f_2)(\gamma)(\xi)(\sigma)]]$

b. $\boxed{\dfrac{g_1,\ldots,g_n}{g}}$ holds whenever validity of $g_1,\ldots,g_n$ implies validity of g.

END 8.25.

Some simple properties of our new conditions are collected in

LEMMA 8.26.

a. $\models \mu Z[p] = p[\mu Z[p]/Z]$, $\models \nu Z[p] = p[\nu Z[p]/Z]$

b. $\models (p[q/Z] \supset q) \Rightarrow (\mu Z[p] \supset q)$

$\models (q \supset p[q/Z]) \Rightarrow (q \supset \nu Z[p])$

c. $\mathcal{T}(p[q/Z])(\gamma)(\xi) = \mathcal{T}(p)(\gamma)(\xi\{\mathcal{T}(q)(\gamma)(\xi)/Z\})$

d. $p \in sm(Z) \Rightarrow \models (q_1 \supset q_2) \Rightarrow (p[q_1/Z] \supset p[q_2/Z])$

$p \in sa(Z) \Rightarrow \models (q_2 \supset q_1) \Rightarrow (p[q_1/Z] \supset p[q_2/Z])$

e. (i) $\dfrac{f \Rightarrow (p_1 \supset p_2)}{f \Rightarrow (p_1[q/Z] \supset p_2[q/Z])}$, provided that $Z \notin cndv(f)$

(ii) $\dfrac{f \Rightarrow (p_1 \supset p_2)}{f \Rightarrow (\mu Z[p_1] \supset \mu Z[p_2])}$, provided that $Z \notin cndv(f)$

PROOF. Exercise.

END 8.26.

We have now arrived at the main theorem of this section.

THEOREM 8.27. Let $\mu X[S_1;X \cup S_2]$ be a regular recursive procedure and let $Z \notin cndv(p)$.

a. $\models \mu X[S_1;X \cup S_2] \rightarrow p = \nu Z[(S_1 \rightarrow Z) \wedge (S_2 \rightarrow p)]$

b. $\models p \leftarrow \mu X[S_1;X \cup S_2] = \mu Z[(Z \leftarrow S_1) \vee p] \leftarrow S_2$

c. $\models \mu X[S_1;X \cup S_2] \triangleright p = \mu Z[(S_1 \triangleright Z) \wedge (S_2 \triangleright p)]$.

PROOF. The proof of parts a and b requires a number of auxiliary lemmas, some of which are of independent interest as well. Throughout we assume, without lack of generality, that $X \notin stmv(p)$.

LEMMA 8.28.

a. $\models S \to p = \neg(S \leftarrow \neg p)$

b. $\models (S_1;S_2) \leftarrow p = S_1 \leftarrow (S_2 \leftarrow p)$

c. $\models (S_1 \cup S_2) \leftarrow p = (S_1 \leftarrow p) \vee (S_2 \leftarrow p)$

d. $\models \mu X[S_1;X \cup S_2] \leftarrow p = \mu Z[(S_1 \leftarrow Z) \vee (S_2 \leftarrow p)]$.

PROOF. We give only the proof of part d, leaving parts a to c as exercises.

(i) $\models \mu Z[(S_1 \leftarrow Z) \vee (S_2 \leftarrow p)] \supset (\mu X[S_1;X \cup S_2] \leftarrow p)$.

By *fpp* (for $\mu X[\ldots]$),

$\models \mu X[S_1;X \cup S_2] \leftarrow p = (S_1;\mu X[S_1;X \cup S_2] \cup S_2) \leftarrow p$. Thus, by parts b and c, $\models \mu X[S_1;X \cup S_2] \leftarrow p = S_1 \leftarrow (\mu X[S_1;X \cup S_2] \leftarrow p) \vee (S_2 \leftarrow p)$, and by *lfp* (for $\mu Z[\ldots]$), we obtain the desired result.

(ii) $\models \mu X[S_1;X \cup S_2] \leftarrow p \supset \mu Z[(S_1 \leftarrow Z) \vee (S_2 \leftarrow p)]$.

Let $p_0 \overset{\text{df.}}{\equiv} (X \leftarrow p) \supset \mu Z[\ldots]$. By lemma 8.15, p_0 is anti-continuous in X (see also exercise 8.3e). Thus, by lemma 8.16, it is sufficient to verify that

(α) $\models (\Omega \leftarrow p) \supset \mu Z[\ldots]$, which is clear since $\models \neg(\Omega \leftarrow p)$

(β) $\models (X \leftarrow p) \supset \mu Z[\ldots] \Rightarrow ((S_1;X \cup S_2) \leftarrow p) \supset \mu Z[\ldots]$. This easily follows by parts b, c, lemma 8.26d, and *fpp* for $\mu Z[\ldots]$.

END 8.28.

LEMMA 8.29. $\models \nu Z[p] = \neg\mu Z[\neg p[\neg Z/Z]]$. (Note that, if p is syntactically monotonic in Z, then so is $\neg p[\neg Z/Z]$.)

PROOF. Let $\mu Z[\ldots] \overset{\text{df.}}{\equiv} \mu Z[\neg p[\neg Z/Z]]$. We first show that $\neg\mu Z[\ldots]$ is a fixed point of p. By *fpp* we have $\models \mu Z[\ldots] = \neg p[\neg Z/Z][\mu Z[\ldots]/Z] = \neg p[\neg\mu Z[\ldots]/Z]$, from which we infer that $\models \neg\mu Z[\ldots] = p[\neg\mu Z[\ldots]/Z]$. Next, we show that each fixed point of p is contained in $\neg\mu Z[\ldots]$. Assume that, for some q, (*): $\models p[q/Z] = q$. We show that $\models q \supset \neg\mu Z[\ldots]$, or, equivalently, that $\models \mu Z[\ldots] \supset \neg q$. By *lfp*, it is sufficient to show that

$\models \neg p[\neg Z/Z][\neg q/Z] \supset \neg q$, or, that

$\models \neg p[\neg\neg q/Z] \supset \neg q$, or, that

$\models \neg p[q/Z] \supset \neg q$, or, that

$\models q \supset p[q/Z]$, which follows from (*).

END 8.29.

Having lemmas 8.28 and 8.29 available, we can give the

PROOF of theorem 8.27a. We have successively

$\models \mu X[S_1;X \cup S_2] \rightarrow p =$ (lemma 8.28a)

$\neg(\mu X[S_1;X \cup S_2] \leftarrow \neg p) =$ (lemma 8.28d)

$\neg(\mu Z[(S_1 \leftarrow Z) \vee (S_2 \leftarrow \neg p)]) =$ (lemma 8.28a)

$\neg(\mu Z[\neg(S_1 \rightarrow \neg Z) \vee \neg(S_2 \rightarrow p)]) =$

$\neg(\mu Z[\neg((S_1 \rightarrow \neg Z) \wedge (S_2 \rightarrow p))]) =$ (lemma 8.29)

$\nu Z[(S_1 \rightarrow Z) \wedge (S_2 \rightarrow p)]$.

END 8.27a.

COROLLARY 8.30.

$$\models \mu X[b;S;X \cup \neg b] \rightarrow p = \nu Z[(b \supset (S \rightarrow Z)) \wedge (\neg b \supset p)] =$$

$$\nu Z[(b \wedge (S \rightarrow Z)) \vee (\neg b \wedge p)]$$

(This is a syntactic reformulation of theorem 3.35.)

PROOF. Immediate by theorem 8.27a.

END 8.30.

We proceed with the proof of theorem 8.27b. We need the following two lemmas:

LEMMA 8.31. $\models p \leftarrow \mu X[S;X \cup D] = p \leftarrow \mu X[X;S \cup D]$.

PROOF. First, we observe that it is *not* true that $\models \mu X[S;X \cup D] = \mu X[X;S \cup D]$. Take, for example, $S \equiv \underline{false}$. Then $\models \mu X[\underline{false};X \cup D] = \mu X[\underline{false} \cup D] = D$, whereas $\models \mu X[X;\underline{false} \cup D] = \Omega \cup D$. However, it is not difficult to prove the following claim: for each γ and σ, $M(\mu X[S;X \cup D])(\gamma)(\sigma) \subseteq M(\mu X[X;S \cup D])(\gamma)(\sigma) \subseteq M(\mu X[S;X \cup D])(\gamma)(\sigma) \cup \{\bot\}$ (i.e. the two sets $M(\mu X[S;X \cup D])(\gamma)(\sigma)$ and $M(\mu X[X;S \cup D])(\gamma)(\sigma)$ are equal, but for the possible presence of $\bot$ in the second one and absence in the first). The proof of the claim is straightforward from the following fact (the proof of which we leave to the reader): let ϕ be arbitrary (in M) and let $\phi_0 = \phi_0' = \lambda\sigma\cdot\bot$, $\phi_{i+1} = (\phi \circ \phi_i) \cup (\lambda\sigma\cdot\sigma)$, $\phi_{i+1}' = (\phi_i' \circ \phi) \cup (\lambda\sigma\cdot\sigma)$. Then, for each σ, $(\bigsqcup_i \phi_i)(\sigma) \subseteq (\bigsqcup_i \phi_i')(\sigma) \subseteq (\bigsqcup_i \phi_i)(\sigma) \cup \{\bot\}$. The proof of the lemma is now direct from the observation that, if ϕ' and ϕ'' are such that, for all σ, $\phi'(\sigma) \subseteq \phi''(\sigma) \subseteq \phi'(\sigma) \cup \{\bot\}$, then, for each π, $\pi \leftarrow \phi' = \pi \leftarrow \phi''$.

END 8.31.

LEMMA 8.32. $\models p \leftarrow \mu X[X;S \cup D] = \mu Z[(Z \leftarrow S) \vee p]$.

PROOF.

(i) $\models \mu Z[(Z \leftarrow S) \vee p] \supset (p \leftarrow \mu X[X;S \cup D])$

Similar to the proof of lemma 8.28d(i)

(ii) $\models (p \leftarrow \mu X[X;S \cup D]) \supset \mu Z[(Z \leftarrow S) \vee p]$

Apply Scott's induction rule with $p_0 \equiv (p \leftarrow X) \supset \mu Z[\ldots]$.

END 8.32.

PROOF of theorem 8.27b.

$\models\ p \leftarrow \mu X[S_1;X \cup S_2] =$ (cf. example 7.10)

$p \leftarrow \mu X[S_1;X \cup D];S_2) =$ (lemma 8.11b(iii))

$(p \leftarrow \mu X[S_1;X \cup D]) \leftarrow S_2 =$ (lemma 8.31)

$(p \leftarrow \mu X[X;S_1 \cup D]) \leftarrow S_2 =$ (lemma 8.32)

$\mu Z[(Z \leftarrow S_1) \vee p] \leftarrow S_2$.

END 8.27b.

COROLLARY 8.33.

$$\models p \leftarrow \mu X[b;S;X \cup \neg b] = \neg b \wedge \mu Z[p \vee ((Z \wedge b) \leftarrow S)]$$

(This is a syntactic reformulation of theorem 3.36.)

PROOF.

$\models p \leftarrow \mu X[b;S;X \cup \neg b] = \mu Z[(Z \leftarrow b;S) \vee p] \leftarrow \neg b =$

$\mu Z[((Z \leftarrow b) \leftarrow S) \vee p] \leftarrow \neg b =$ (since $\models p \leftarrow b = p \wedge b$)

$\mu Z[((Z \wedge b) \leftarrow S) \vee p] \wedge \neg b$.

END 8.33.

Finally, we give the

PROOF of theorem 8.27c.

(i) $\models \mu Z[(S_1 \triangleright Z) \wedge (S_2 \triangleright p)] \supset \mu X[S_1;X \cup S_2] \triangleright p$

Similar to the proof of lemma 8.28a

(ii) $\models \mu X[S_1;X \cup S_2] \triangleright p \supset \mu Z[(S_1 \triangleright Z) \wedge (S_2 \triangleright p)]$

By Scott's induction rule, applied to $p_0 \equiv (X \triangleright p) \supset \mu Z[\ldots]$.

END 8.27c.

Remark. Note that an attempt at proving $\models (\mu X[S_1;X \cup S_2] \rightarrow p) \supset \mu Z[(S_1 \rightarrow Z) \wedge (S_2 \rightarrow p)]$ by applying Scott's induction rule to $p_0 \equiv (X \rightarrow p) \supset \mu Z[\ldots]$, breaks down since, in general, p_0 is not semantically anti-continuous in X.

8.5. Derivatives and termination

By virtue of our definition of the meaning of the $S \triangleright p$ construct, we have that a statement S terminates (for a certain state σ), whenever the weakest precondition $S \triangleright$ true is satisfied (in σ). Contrary to what is known for the general case $S \triangleright p$, it *is* possible to give a syntactic reduction of $S \triangleright$ true, even for the case that S is a recursive procedure, say $S \equiv \mu X[S_1]$. The first part of this section is devoted to a presentation of this result, the proof of which turns out to be fairly involved. In the second part, we introduce the syntactic notions of *upper and lower derivative* of a statement with respect to a statement variable (set of statement variables), and show how these play a part in the analysis of statement termination. Finally, we relate the property of termination of a recursive procedure $\mu X[S_1]$ to the so-called well-foundedness of (the meaning of) a construct involving the upper and lower derivatives of S_1 with respect to X.

We begin with an analysis of $S \triangleright \underline{true}$. For this purpose we first introduce a slight variant of the syntax of conditions. We omit the $p \leftarrow S$ and $\nu Z[p]$ constructs, which serve no purpose for the present considerations, and add one new construct, viz. for each $X \in \mathit{Stmv}$, the condition $\tilde{X}$.

DEFINITION 8.34 (modified conditions).

a. The class of conditions *Cond*, with typical elements p,q,r,..., is defined by

$$p ::= \underline{true} \mid \ldots \mid \exists x[p] \mid S \rightarrow p \mid S \triangleright p \mid Z \mid \mu Z[p] \mid \tilde{X}$$

where it is required that, in $\mu Z[p]$, p be syntactically monotonic in Z.

b. T: *Cond* $\rightarrow (\Gamma \rightarrow (\Xi \rightarrow \Pi))$ is defined as usual for p not of the form $\tilde{X}$ and, for $p \equiv \tilde{X}$, we put

$$T(\tilde{X})(\gamma)(\xi)(\sigma) = tt \quad \text{iff} \quad \neg[\bot \in \gamma(X)(\sigma)]$$

END 8.34.

Remarks

1. Definition 8.34 will be used only in the present section.
2. Note that $\tilde{X}$ is satisfied in state σ precisely when X terminates in σ, i.e. we have that $\models \tilde{X} = X \triangleright \underline{true}$.

Next, we introduce a syntactic operation " $\sim$ ": *Stat* $\rightarrow$ *Cond*, with as intended meaning: for each S, $\tilde{S}$ is that condition which expresses termination of S. Thus, we aim at the result that

$$\models \tilde{S} = S \triangleright \underline{true} \qquad (8.4)$$

We shall show how to define " $\sim$ " by induction on the complexity of S, such that (8.4) is indeed satisfied. Note that, for $S \equiv X \in$ *Stmv*, there is no possibility of syntactically reducing S; hence, we have simply included $\tilde{X}$ as an element of the class *Cond* and assigned it the appropriate meaning. In what follows, we need the operation of substitution in conditions not only in the form p[q/Z], but also in the form $p[q/\tilde{X}]$. Strictly speaking, this is not yet defined, since $\tilde{X}$ is not an element of *Cndv*. However, it should be clear how to provide a definition of $p[q/\tilde{X}]$ by a direct analogy with the p[q/Z] case. E.g. we have that $\tilde{Y}[q/\tilde{X}] \equiv q$, if $X \equiv Y$, and $\tilde{Y}[q/\tilde{X}] \equiv \tilde{Y}$, if $X \not\equiv Y$.

The following simple lemma about our various substitutions will be needed below:

<u>LEMMA 8.35</u>.

$$\frac{p_1 = p_2}{p_1[S_i/X_i]_{i=1}^{k}[q_i/\tilde{X}_i]_{i=1}^{\ell}[r_i/Z_i]_{i=1}^{m} = p_2[S_i/X_i]_{i=1}^{k}[q_i/\tilde{X}_i]_{i=1}^{\ell}[r_i/Z_i]_{i=1}^{m}}$$

<u>PROOF</u>. Exercise.
END 8.35.

We now come to the definition of $\tilde{S}$:

<u>DEFINITION 8.36</u> (conditions for statement termination).

a. $(v:=t)^{\sim} \equiv \underline{true}$, $\tilde{b} \equiv \underline{true}$

b. $(S_1;S_2)^{\sim} \equiv \tilde{S}_1 \wedge (S_1 \rightarrow \tilde{S}_2)$, $(S_1 \cup S_2)^{\sim} \equiv \tilde{S}_1 \wedge \tilde{S}_2$

c. $\mu X[S]^{\sim} \equiv \mu Z[\tilde{S}[\mu X[S]/X][Z/\tilde{X}]]$, where Z is the first condition variable.

END 8.36.

Remarks

1. In order that the definition be well-formed, we have to verify whether, for each X and S, $\tilde{S} \in sm(\tilde{X})$ (where $sm(\tilde{X})$ is defined analogously to sm(Z), cf. definition 8.22). This is left to the reader. Note that $\tilde{S} \notin sc(X)$ (cf. definition 8.14). However, as we shall see below, it *is* true that $\models S_1 \sqsubseteq S_2 \Rightarrow \tilde{S}[S_1/X] \sqsubseteq \tilde{S}[S_2/X]$.
2. Note that $\tilde{S}$ contains no free condition variables, from which it follows that we can always choose the same Z (first element of *Cndv*) in clause c.

Clauses a and b of this definition should be clear:

a. Since v:=t and b always terminate, both $\models (v{:=}t) \rhd \underline{true}$ and $\models b \rhd \underline{true}$ hold, thus satisfying our goal $\models \tilde{S} = S \rhd \underline{true}$, for these two types of S.
b. We show by induction that $\models \tilde{S} = S \rhd \underline{true}$ is preserved by these definitions. $\models (S_1;S_2) \rhd \underline{true} = S_1 \rhd (S_2 \rhd \underline{true}) =$ (by the general fact that $\models S \rhd p = (S \rhd \underline{true}) \wedge (S \rightarrow p)$) $S_1 \rhd \underline{true} \wedge (S_1 \rightarrow (S_2 \rhd \underline{true})) =$ (ind.) $\tilde{S}_1 \wedge (S_1 \rightarrow \tilde{S}_2) = (S_1;S_2)^{\sim}$.
The case that $S \equiv S_1 \cup S_2$ is even easier.

Clause c deserves some more explanation. We anticipate an auxiliary result to be derived below, viz. that for each S and S_0,

$$\models S[S_0/X]^{\sim} = \tilde{S}[S_0/X][\tilde{S}_0/\tilde{X}] \tag{8.5}$$

which may be understood as follows. We want to express termination of $S[S_0/X]$ (i.e. $S[S_0/X]^{\sim}$) in terms of termination of S (i.e. $\tilde{S}$), and of termination of S_0 (i.e. $\tilde{S}_0$). The first guess might be that (*): $\models S[S_0/X]^{\sim} = \tilde{S}[\tilde{S}_0/\tilde{X}]$. However, this is not good enough.

E.g. consider the case that $S \equiv X;S_1$, where S_1 has no free occurrences of X. According to definition 8.36b, we have that $\tilde{S} \equiv \tilde{X} \wedge (X \rightarrow \tilde{S}_1)$. Applying (*) to this special case would result in $\models (X;S_1)[S_0/X]^{\sim} = \{\tilde{X} \wedge (X \rightarrow \tilde{S}_1)\}[\tilde{S}_0/\tilde{X}] = \tilde{S}_0 \wedge (X \rightarrow \tilde{S}_1)$, whereas what we *do* need is: $(X;S_1)[S_0/X]^{\sim} \equiv (S_0;S_1)^{\sim} \equiv \tilde{S}_0 \wedge (S_0 \rightarrow \tilde{S}_1)$. We see that, in general, $\tilde{S}$ contains free occurrences of both $\tilde{X}$ *and of* X and, in determining $S[S_0/X]^{\sim}$, we have to substitute, in $\tilde{S}$, $\tilde{S}_0$ for $\tilde{X}$ and, *also*, S_0 for X.

We now apply (8.5) to the special case that $S_0 \equiv \mu X[S]$. Using *fpp* for $\mu X[S]$, we obtain that

$$\models \underbrace{\mu X[S]^{\sim}} = S[\mu X[S]/X]^{\sim} = \tilde{S}[\mu X[S]/X][\underbrace{\mu X[S]^{\sim}}/\tilde{X}] \tag{8.6}$$

Thus, we see that $\mu X[S]^{\sim}$ satisfies the fixed point relationship (8.6) and we conclude that, once (8.5) is available, we have as a consequence of it that

$$\models \mu Z[\tilde{S}[\mu X[S]/X][Z/\tilde{X}]] \supset \mu X[S]^{\sim}.$$

This argument at least explains the structure of definition 8.36c. Of course, we still have to establish that defining $\mu X[S]^{\sim}$ as the *least* fixed point $\mu Z[\tilde{S}[\mu X[S]/X][Z/\tilde{X}]]$ satisfies our desired result (8.4). Before proceeding with the proof of this, we first show that "~" preserves *congruence*, where congruence is a syntactic relationship between two statements or two conditions (in general, between two constructs the formation of which involves bound variables, cf. definition 6.2) defined as follows:

DEFINITION 8.37 (congruence).

a. Two statements S_1, S_2 may be *congruent*, denoted by $S_1 \cong S_2$, and defined by
   - (i) $v:=t \cong v:=t$, $b \cong b$, $X \cong X$
   - (ii) If $S[Y/X] \cong S'$, then $\mu X[S] \cong \mu Y[S']$, where $Y \notin stmv(S)$

(iii) If $S_1 \cong S_1'$, $S_2 \cong S_2'$, then $S_1;S_2 \cong S_1';S_2'$, $S_1 \cup S_2 \cong S_1' \cup S_2'$, $\mu X[S_1] \cong \mu X[S_1']$.

(Note that two statements are congruent iff they differ at most in their bound (statement) variables.)

b. Two conditions p_1, p_2 may be *congruent*, denoted by $p_1 \cong p_2$, and defined by

(i) $\underline{true} \cong \underline{true}$, $\underline{false} \cong \underline{false}$, $(s_1 = s_2) \cong (s_1 = s_2)$, $Z \cong Z$, $X \cong X$

(ii) If $p[Z'/Z] \cong p'$, then $\mu Z[p] \cong \mu Z'[p']$, where $Z' \notin$ *cndv*(p)

(iii) If $p_1 \cong p_1'$, $p_2 \cong p_2'$, then $\neg p_1 \cong \neg p_1'$, $(p_1 \supset p_2) \cong (p_1' \supset p_2')$, $\exists x[p_1] \cong \exists x[p_1']$, $\mu Z[p_1] \cong \mu Z[p_1']$

(iv) If $S \cong S'$, $p \cong p'$, then $S \rightarrow p \cong S' \rightarrow p'$, $S \triangleright p \cong S' \triangleright p'$

(Note that two conditions are congruent iff they differ at most in their bound (statement and condition) variables.)

END 8.37.

Remarks

1. We omit the proof that " $\cong$ " is an equivalence relation.
2. Clearly, if $S \cong S'$, then $\models S = S'$, and similarly for conditions.
3. Many of the previous results on substitution have stronger formulations as congruences (cf. exercise 2.3, lemma 7.14). E.g. we have $S[S_1/X][S_2/Y] \cong S[S_2/Y][S_1[S_2/Y]/X]$, provided that $X \not\equiv Y$ and $X \notin$ *stmv*(S_2).
4. Below, we shall need the following facts, the proof of which we omit:

   a. If $S \cong S'$, and $S_0 \cong S_0'$, then $S[S_0/X] \cong S'[S_0'/X]$

   b. If $p \cong p'$, then

      (i) if $p_0 \cong p_0'$ then $p[p_0/Z] \cong p'[p_0'/Z]$, $p[p_0/\widetilde{X}] \cong p'[p_0'/\widetilde{X}]$

      (ii) if $S \cong S'$ then $p[S/X] \cong p'[S'/X]$.

We now show

LEMMA 8.38. If $S \cong S'$, then $\tilde{S} \cong \tilde{S}'$.

PROOF. The proof proceeds by proving simultaneously, by induction on the complexity of S, that

$$S \cong S' \Rightarrow \tilde{S} \cong \tilde{S}' \tag{8.7}$$

$$S[X'/X]^{\sim} \cong \tilde{S}[X'/X][\tilde{X}'/\tilde{X}] \tag{8.8}$$

The interesting case is that $S \equiv \mu Y[S_0]$ and $S' \equiv \mu Y'[S_0']$, where $S_0[Y'/Y] \cong S_0'$, with $Y' \notin stmv(S_0)$ (whence Y' and $\tilde{Y}'$ do not occur free in $\tilde{S}_0$). We first prove (8.7) for this S. We have

$$\begin{aligned} \tilde{S} &\equiv \mu Z[\tilde{S}_0[S/Y][Z/\tilde{Y}]] \\ \tilde{S}' &\equiv \mu Z[\tilde{S}_0'[S'/Y'][Z/\tilde{Y}']]. \end{aligned}$$

Now $\tilde{S}_0' \cong S_0[Y'/Y]^{\sim}$ (by the induction hypothesis for (8.7))

$\cong \tilde{S}_0[Y'/Y][\tilde{Y}'/\tilde{Y}]$ (by the induction hypothesis for (8.8)).

Hence, by remark 4 above,

$\tilde{S}_0'[S'/Y'][Z/\tilde{Y}'] \cong \tilde{S}_0[Y'/Y][\tilde{Y}'/\tilde{Y}][S'/Y'][Z/\tilde{Y}']$ (by properties of substitution) $\cong \tilde{S}_0[S'/Y][Z/\tilde{Y}] \cong \tilde{S}_0[S/Y][Z/\tilde{Y}]$,

and the desired result $\tilde{S} \cong \tilde{S}'$ follows by definition 8.37b(iii).

Next, we prove (8.8) for $S \equiv \mu Y[S_0]$. If $Y \equiv X$, then $X \notin stmv(S)$, whence $X, \tilde{X}$ do not occur free in $\tilde{S}$. It is easily verified that, in that case, $S[X'/X]^{\sim} \cong \tilde{S} \cong S[X'/X][\tilde{X}'/\tilde{X}]$. If $Y \equiv X'$, we replace the proof of $S[Y/X]^{\sim} \cong S[Y/X][\tilde{Y}/\tilde{X}]$ by that of $\mu Y'[S_0[Y'/Y]][Y/X]^{\sim} \cong \mu Y'[S_0[Y'/Y]]^{\sim}[Y/X][\tilde{Y}/\tilde{X}]$ (for some fresh Y') which is allowed by (8.7) and remark 4 above. Now assume $Y \not\equiv X, X'$. Then

$$\begin{aligned} S[X'/X]^{\sim} &\cong \mu Y[S_0][X'/X]^{\sim} \\ &\cong \mu Y[S_0[X'/X]]^{\sim} \cong \end{aligned}$$

$$\cong \mu Z[S_0[X'/X]^{\sim}[\mu Y[S_0[X'/X]]/Y][Z/\tilde{Y}]]$$

$$\text{(ind. hyp.)} \cong \mu Z[\tilde{S}_0[X'/X][\tilde{X}'/\tilde{X}][\mu Y[S_0[X'/X]]/Y][Z/\tilde{Y}]]$$

$$(Y \not\equiv X,X') \cong \mu Z[\tilde{S}_0[\mu Y[S_0]/Y][Z/\tilde{Y}]][X'/X][\tilde{X}'/\tilde{X}]$$

$$\cong \tilde{S}[X'/X][\tilde{X}'/\tilde{X}]$$

END 8.38.

We are now sufficiently prepared for the proof of

THEOREM 8.39. $\models \tilde{S} = S \rhd \underline{\text{true}}$.

PROOF. The proof proceeds in a number of steps.

a. We first show that $(S[S_i/X_i]_{i=1}^n)^{\sim} \cong \tilde{S}[S_i/X_i]_{i=1}^n[\tilde{S}_i/\tilde{X}_i]_{i=1}^n$ (i.e. we generalize (8.8) above). We use induction on the complexity of S, and treat only the case that $S \equiv \mu Y[S_0]$. By lemma 8.38 we may assume that $Y \not\equiv X_i$, $Y \notin stmv(S_i)$, $i = 1,\dots,n$. (Hence, $\tilde{Y} \not\equiv \tilde{X}_i$, $Y,\tilde{Y}$ not free in $\tilde{S}_i$, $i = 1,\dots,n$.) We have

$$(S[S_i/X_i]_i)^{\sim} \cong \mu Y[S_0][S_i/X_i]_i^{\sim}$$

$$\cong \mu Y[S_0[S_i/X_i]_i]^{\sim}$$

$$\cong \mu Z[S_0[S_i/X_i]_i^{\sim}[\mu Y[S_0[S_i/X_i]_i]/Y][Z/\tilde{Y}]]$$

$$\text{(ind. hyp.)} \cong \mu Z[\tilde{S}_0[S_i/X_i]_i[\tilde{S}_i/\tilde{X}_i]_i[\mu Y[S_0[S_i/X_i]_i]/Y][Z/\tilde{Y}]$$

$$\cong \mu Z[\tilde{S}_0[\mu Y[S_0]/Y][Z/\tilde{Y}]][S_i/X_i]_i[\tilde{S}_i/\tilde{X}_i]_i$$

$$\cong \tilde{S}[S_i/X_i]_i[\tilde{S}_i/\tilde{X}_i]_i$$

b. Next, we show that

$$\models \tilde{S}[S_i/X_i]_{i=1}^n[S_i \rhd \underline{\text{true}} / \tilde{X}_i]_{i=1}^n \supset S[S_i/X_i]_{i=1}^n \rhd \underline{\text{true}} \tag{8.9}$$

We use induction on the complexity of S, and consider only the cases that $S \equiv S';S''$, $S \equiv \mu Y[S_0]$.

(i) $S \equiv S';S''$

$\models (S';S'')^{\sim}[S_i/X_i]_i[S_i \triangleright \underline{true}/\tilde{X}_i]_i =$

$\{\tilde{S}' \wedge (S' \to \tilde{S}'')\}[\ ]_i[\ ]_i =$ ($\tilde{X}_i$ does not occur in S')

$\tilde{S}'[\ ]_i[\ ]_i \wedge (S'[S_i/X_i]_i \to S''[\ ]_i[\ ]_i) \supset$ (ind. hyp.)

$(S'[S_i/X_i]_i \triangleright \underline{true}) \wedge (S'[S_i/X_i]_i \to S''[S_i/X_i]_i \triangleright \underline{true}) =$

$S'[S_i/X_i]_i \triangleright (S''[S_i/X_i]_i \triangleright \underline{true}) = (S';S'')[S_i/X_i]_i \triangleright \underline{true}$

(ii) $S \equiv \mu Y[S_0]$. By lemma 8.38 we may assume that $Y \not\equiv X_i$, $Y \notin stmv(S_i)$, $i = 1,\ldots,n$. We show that

$\models \mu Y[S_0]^{\sim}[S_i/X_i]_i[S_i \triangleright \underline{true}/\tilde{X}_i]_i \supset \mu Y[S_0][S_i/X_i]_i \triangleright \underline{true}$,

i.e. that $\models \mu Z[\tilde{S}_0[S/Y][Z/\tilde{Y}]][S_i/X_i]_i[S_i \triangleright \underline{true}/\tilde{X}_i]_i \supset$

$\mu Y[S_0][S_i/X_i]_i \triangleright \underline{true}$.

By *lfp* (for $\mu Z[\ldots]$) and properties of substitution, it is sufficient to show that

$\models \tilde{S}_0[S_i/X_i]_i[S[S_i/X_i]_i/Y][S_i \triangleright \underline{true}/\tilde{X}_i]_i[S[S_i/X_i]_i \triangleright \underline{true}/\tilde{Y}]$

$\supset S[S_i/X_i]_i \triangleright \underline{true} =$ (*fpp* for S)

$S_0[S_i/X_i]_i[S[S_i/X_i]_i/Y] \triangleright \underline{true}$

and this validity result follows by the induction hypothesis (with $n' = n+1$, $S'_i \equiv S_i$, $i = 1,\ldots,n$, $S'_{n+1} \equiv S[S_i/X_i]_i$).

Thus having completed the proof of (8.9) we immediately obtain (taking $n = 0$) that $\models \tilde{S} \supset (S \triangleright \underline{true})$.

c. The following step is the proof of

$$\models (S'_i \sqsubseteq S''_i)_{i=1}^n \wedge (q'_i \supset q''_i)_{i=1}^n \Rightarrow \tilde{S}[S'_i/X_i]_{i=1}^n[q'_i/\tilde{Y}_i]_{i=1}^n \supset \tilde{S}[S''_i/X_i]_{i=1}^n[q''_i/\tilde{Y}_i]_{i=1}^n$$

Again, we use induction on the complexity of S, and consider two cases:

(i) $S \equiv S_1;S_2$. We have $\tilde{S} \equiv \tilde{S}_1 \wedge (S_1 \rightarrow \tilde{S}_2)$. Now, clearly

(α) $\models \tilde{S}_1 \wedge (S_1 \triangleright \tilde{S}_2) \supset \tilde{S}_1 \wedge (S_1 \rightarrow \tilde{S}_2)$.

Also, by part b and the fact that, for each $\bar{S}$,

$\models (\bar{S} \triangleright \underline{true}) \wedge (\bar{S} \rightarrow p) = \bar{S} \triangleright p$, we furthermore have

(β) $\models \tilde{S}_1 \wedge (S_1 \rightarrow \tilde{S}_2) \supset \tilde{S}_1 \wedge (S_1 \triangleright \tilde{S}_2)$.

Together, we have that $\models \tilde{S} = \tilde{S}_1 \wedge (S_1 \triangleright \tilde{S}_2)$.

Now by lemma 8.35 (and writing $[']$ for $[S_i'/X_i]_{i=1}^n$, $['^{\sim}]$ for $[q_i'/\tilde{Y}_i]_{i=1}^n$, etc.) we have

$\models \tilde{S}[']['^{\sim}] = \tilde{S}_1[']['^{\sim}] \wedge (S_1['] \triangleright \tilde{S}_2[']['^{\sim}])$

$\models \tilde{S}['']['''^{\sim}] = \tilde{S}_1['']['''^{\sim}] \wedge (S_1[''] \triangleright \tilde{S}_2['']['''^{\sim}])$.

Furthermore, by the induction hypothesis and lemma 7.14f

$\models (' \sqsubseteq '') \wedge ('\supset'') \Rightarrow \tilde{S}_1[']['^{\sim}] \supset \tilde{S}_1['']['''^{\sim}]$

$\models (' \sqsubseteq '') \wedge ('\supset'') \Rightarrow \tilde{S}_2[']['^{\sim}] \supset \tilde{S}_2['']['''^{\sim}]$

$\models (' \sqsubseteq '') \quad\quad \Rightarrow S_1['] \sqsubseteq S_1['']$.

Hence, since, for each X and Z, $X \triangleright Z$ is monotonic in X and Z,

$\models (' \sqsubseteq '') \wedge ('\supset'') \Rightarrow \tilde{S}[']['^{\sim}] \supset \tilde{S}['']['''^{\sim}]$

(ii) $S \equiv \mu Y[S_0]$. Choose some $Z' \notin$ *cndv*(q_i', q_i''), $i = 1,\ldots,n$. Then $\tilde{S} \cong \mu Z'[S_0[S/Y][Z'/\tilde{Y}]]$. By lemma 8.38, without lack of generality we may assume that $Y \notin$ *stmv*$(X_i, S_i', S_i'', q_i', q_i'')$, $i = 1,\ldots,n$ and that $\tilde{Y} \not\equiv \tilde{Y}_i$, $\tilde{Y}$ not free in q_i', q_i'', $i = 1,\ldots,n$.

Now

$\tilde{S}[']['^{\sim}] \cong \mu Z'[\tilde{S}_0[S/Y][Z'/\tilde{Y}][']['^{\sim}]]$

$\cong \mu Z'[\tilde{S}_0['][S[']/Y]['^{\sim}][Z'/\tilde{Y}]]$

and

$\tilde{S}['']['''^{\sim}] \cong \mu Z'[\tilde{S}_0[''][S['']/Y]['''^{\sim}][Z'/\tilde{Y}]]$.

By lemma 7.14f, $\models$ (' $\sqsubseteq$ '') $\Rightarrow$ S['] $\sqsubseteq$ S['']. Hence, by the induction hypothesis, with n' = n+1,

$$\models (' \sqsubseteq '') \wedge (' \supset '') \Rightarrow \tilde{S}_0['][S[']/Y]['^{\sim}][Z'/\tilde{Y}] \supset \tilde{S}_0[''][S['']/Y][''^{\sim}][Z'/\tilde{Y}]$$

and the desired result follows by lemma 8.26e(ii).

d. Finally, we show that $\models S \rhd \underline{true} \supset \tilde{S}$. We use induction on S and treat only the case that $S \equiv \mu Y[S_0]$. We prove that $\models \mu Y[S_0] \rhd \underline{true} \supset \mu Y[S_0]^{\sim}$, by applying Scott's induction rule to the formula (*): $p \equiv (Y \rhd \underline{true}) \supset \mu Y[S_0]^{\sim}$. We leave it to the reader to verify (cf. exercise 8.12) that we may apply lemma 8.16 in the somewhat modified version

$$\frac{p[\Omega/X],\ ((X \sqsubseteq \mu X[S]) \wedge p) \Rightarrow p[S/X]}{p[\mu X[S]/X]}$$

provided that p is semantically anti-continuous in X

$\models p[\Omega/Y]$ is clear for p as in (*). There remains the induction step $\models (Y \sqsubseteq \mu Y[S_0]) \wedge (Y \rhd \underline{true} \supset \mu Y[S_0]^{\sim}) \Rightarrow ((S_0 \rhd \underline{true}) \supset \mu Y[S_0]^{\sim})$. We know that $\models Y \rhd \underline{true} = \tilde{Y}$. Also, by the induction hypothesis, $\models S_0 \rhd \underline{true} \supset \tilde{S}_0$. Combining this with part b, we have that $\models S_0 \rhd \underline{true} = \tilde{S}_0$. Thus, it is sufficient to prove that $\models (Y \sqsubseteq \mu Y[S_0]) \wedge (\tilde{Y} \supset \mu Y[S_0]^{\sim}) \Rightarrow (\tilde{S}_0 \supset \mu Y[S_0]^{\sim})$, or, by *fpp* applied to $\mu Y[S_0]^{\sim}$, that

$$\models (Y \sqsubseteq \mu Y[S_0]) \wedge (\tilde{Y} \supset \mu Y[S_0]^{\sim}) \Rightarrow (\tilde{S}_0 \supset \tilde{S}_0[\mu Y[S_0]/Y][\mu Y[S_0]^{\sim}/\tilde{Y}])$$

Now this validity result is nothing but a special case of part c.

e. The desired result $\models S \triangleright \underline{true} = \tilde{S}$ is obtained by combining parts b and d.

END 8.39.

After thus having established that definition 8.36 indeed ensures that $\models \tilde{S} = S \triangleright \underline{true}$, i.e. that " $\sim$ " provides an adequate syntactic characterization of termination, we proceed with the introduction of the notion of *derivative* of a statement. As we shall see at a somewhat later stage, this concept plays a part in the analysis of the reason why a statement terminates (or, rather, why it may fail to terminate).

We shall in fact introduce two notions of derivative:

- Firstly, we define the *upper* derivative of a statement S with respect to a statement variable X. The result, denoted by $\frac{dS}{dX}$, is again a statement, and has the following intended meaning: dropping the γ-arguments for a while, we have that $\sigma' \in M(\frac{dS}{dX})(\sigma)$ iff execution of S for input state σ leads to σ' as an intermediate state just before execution of X starts. (Observe that more than one σ' may satisfy this condition.) E.g. if $S \equiv S_1;X;S_2;X;S_3 \cup S_4$ (where X does not occur in S_i, $i = 1,\ldots,4$), then

  $$\sigma' \in M(\frac{dS}{dX})(\sigma) \text{ iff } \sigma' \in M(S_1)(\sigma) \text{ or } \sigma' \in M(S_1;X;S_2)(\sigma).$$

  For statements without recursion, we may also briefly say that $\frac{dS}{dX}$ is the union of all prefixes of X in S.
- Secondly, we have the *lower* derivative of a statement S with respect to a (possibly empty) set of statement variables $\mathcal{X}$. The result, denoted by $\delta_{\mathcal{X}}(S)$, is a *condition*, and has as intended meaning that $\delta_{\mathcal{X}}(S)$ is true in a state σ whenever S terminates in σ *provided* that, for each $X \in \mathcal{X}$, execution of X for the states σ' in $M(\frac{dS}{dX})(\sigma)$ terminates.

From the second part, it should be clear that we expect $\delta_{\emptyset}(S)$ to be identical with $\tilde{S}$. Moreover, combining the two intended meanings of $\frac{dS}{dX}$ and $\delta_{\mathcal{X}}(S)$, we also expect that the following result holds: for each $X \notin \mathcal{X}$,

$$\models \delta_X(S) = (\frac{dS}{dX} \to \tilde{X}) \wedge \delta_{X\cup\{X\}}(S).$$

Let us give the verbal transliteration of this fact in the case that $X = \emptyset$: for each statement S, S terminates in $\sigma \neq \bot$ iff both (i) and (ii) are satisfied:

(i) Execution of X terminates for all σ' ($\neq \bot$) in $M(\frac{dS}{dX})(\sigma)$

(ii) S terminates in σ *provided* that execution of X for states σ' in $M(\frac{dS}{dX})(\sigma)$ terminates.

(Note that a more naive equivalence: $\models \tilde{S} = \tilde{X} \wedge \delta_{\{X\}}(S)$ would not work, since termination of X is required for the wrong states.)

We proceed with the precise definitions of the two types of derivatives:

DEFINITION 8.40 (upper derivative).
For each S and X, $\frac{dS}{dX}$ is an element of *Stat*, defined by induction on the complexity of S:

a. $\frac{d\ v{:=}t}{dX} \equiv \underline{\text{false}}$, $\frac{db}{dX} \equiv \underline{\text{false}}$, $\frac{dY}{dX} \equiv \begin{cases} D & \text{, if } X \equiv Y \\ \underline{\text{false}}, & \text{if } X \not\equiv Y \end{cases}$

b. $\frac{d(S_1;S_2)}{dX} \equiv \frac{dS_1}{dX} \cup S_1;\frac{dS_2}{dX}$, $\frac{d(S_1 \cup S_2)}{dX} \equiv \frac{dS_1}{dX} \cup \frac{dS_2}{dX}$

c. $\frac{d\ \mu Y[S]}{dX} \equiv \begin{cases} \underline{\text{false}} & \text{, if } X \equiv Y \\ \mu X_1[\{\frac{dS}{dX} \cup \frac{dS}{dY}; X_1\}[\mu Y[S]/Y]], & \text{if } X \not\equiv Y \\ \quad \text{where } X_1 \text{ is the first statement variable such that} \\ \quad X_1 \notin \mathit{stmv}(X,Y,S). \end{cases}$

END 8.40.

Remark. Note that $\mathit{stmv}(\frac{dS}{dX}) \subseteq \mathit{stmv}(S)$ and that, if $X \notin \mathit{stmv}(S)$, then $\models \frac{dS}{dX} = \underline{\text{false}}$.

DEFINITION 8.41 (lower derivative).
For each S and $X \subseteq \mathit{Stmv}$, $\delta_X(S)$ is an element of *Cond*, defined by induction on the complexity of S:

a. $\delta_{\mathcal{X}}(v{:=}t) \equiv \underline{\text{true}},\ \delta_{\mathcal{X}}(b) \equiv \underline{\text{true}},\ \delta_{\mathcal{X}}(Y) \equiv \begin{cases} \underline{\text{true}}, & \text{if } Y \in \mathcal{X} \\ \tilde{Y}, & \text{if } Y \notin \mathcal{X} \end{cases}$

b. $\delta_{\mathcal{X}}(S_1;S_2) \equiv \delta_{\mathcal{X}}(S_1) \wedge (S_1 \to \delta_{\mathcal{X}}(S_2))$

$\delta_{\mathcal{X}}(S_1 \cup S_2) \equiv \delta_{\mathcal{X}}(S_1) \wedge \delta_{\mathcal{X}}(S_2)$

c. $\delta_{\mathcal{X}}(\mu Y[S]) \equiv \mu Z[\delta_{\mathcal{X}\setminus\{Y\}}(S)[\mu Y[S]/Y][Z/\tilde{Y}]]$, where Z is the first condition variable.

END 8.41.

Remark. Observe that

a. The definitions of $\delta_{\emptyset}(S)$ and $\tilde{S}$ coincide

b. (i) $\tilde{X}$ free in $\delta_{\mathcal{X}}(S) \Rightarrow \delta_{\mathcal{X}}(S) \in sm(\tilde{X})$

(ii) $stmv(\delta_{\mathcal{X}}(S)) \subseteq stmv(S)$

(iii) $\tilde{X}$ free in $\delta_{\mathcal{X}}(S) \Rightarrow X \in stmv(S),\ X \notin \mathcal{X}$

(iv) $X \notin stmv(S) \Rightarrow \delta_{\mathcal{X}}(S) \equiv \delta_{\mathcal{X}\setminus\{X\}}(S)$

c. $\models \delta_{\mathcal{X}}(S_1;S_2;S_3) = \delta_{\mathcal{X}}(S_1) \wedge (S_1 \to \delta_{\mathcal{X}}(S_2)) \wedge (S_1;S_2 \to \delta_{\mathcal{X}}(S_3))$.

A few words of explanation of these definitions may be helpful. As to definition 8.40, if we view $\frac{dS}{dX}$ as the union of all prefixes of X in S, we easily understand parts a and b. In particular, prefixes of X in $S_1;S_2$ are either prefixes of X in S_1, or constituted from S_1 followed by prefixes of X in S_2. As to clause c, if $X \equiv Y$, then X does not appear free in $\mu Y[S]$, and the definition should be clear. Otherwise we argue (cf. our discussion of the $\sim$-definition above) by using a property which we expect to be satisfied by the $\frac{dS}{dX}$ formalism:

$$\models \frac{d\, S[S_0/Y]}{dX} = (\frac{dS}{dX})[S_0/Y] \cup (\frac{dS}{dY})[S_0/Y] ; \frac{dS_0}{dX} \tag{8.10}$$

In words (first forgetting the substitutions on the right-hand side): prefixes of X in $S[S_0/Y]$ are obtained either as prefixes of X in S, or by composing prefixes of Y in S on the right with prefixes of X in S_0.

Supplementing this description with the indicated substitutions then explains the plausibility of (8.10). Taking $S_0 \equiv \mu Y[S]$ and applying *fpp* for $\mu Y[S]$, we obtain as property of $\frac{d\ \mu Y[S]}{dX}$:

$$\models \underbrace{\frac{d\ \mu Y[S]}{dX}} = \frac{dS}{dX}[\mu Y[S]/Y] \cup \frac{dS}{dY}[\mu Y[S]/Y] ; \underbrace{\frac{d\ \mu Y[S]}{dX}}$$

We again observe a fixed point structure, leading us to expect (by now we know that most fixed points we encounter are least fixed points anyway) that clause c of definition 8.40 is indeed what we need.

As to definition 8.41, clauses a and b should be clear from the intended meaning of the construct, whereas clause c is very similar in structure to clause c of definition 8.36.

THEOREM 8.42. For each $X \notin \mathcal{X}$

$$\models \delta_{\mathcal{X}}(S) = (\frac{dS}{dX} \to \tilde{X}) \wedge \delta_{\mathcal{X}\cup\{X\}}(S).$$

PROOF. Induction on the complexity of S. If S is not of the form $\mu Y[S_1]$, the proof is immediate from the definitions. Now assume $S \equiv \mu Y[S_1]$. For easier readability, we replace use of the first condition variable Z in our formulae by that of different variables Z_1, $Z_2, \ldots$. First we consider the case that $Y \equiv X$. We have to show that

$$\mu Z_1[\delta_{\mathcal{X}\backslash\{Y\}}(S_1)[\mu Y[S_1]/Y][Z_1/\tilde{Y}]]$$

$$\models =$$

$$(\underline{\text{false}} \to \tilde{X}) \wedge \mu Z_2[\delta_{\mathcal{X}\cup\{X\}\backslash\{Y\}}(S_1)[\mu Y[S_1]/Y][Z_2/\tilde{Y}]]$$

Now this is clear, since $\models$ false $\to \tilde{X}$ and, moreover, from $Y \equiv X$ and $X \notin \mathcal{X}$ it follows that $\mathcal{X}\backslash\{Y\} = \mathcal{X} \cup \{X\}\backslash\{Y\}$ $(= \mathcal{X})$.

Next, assume $Y \not\equiv X$. Then we must prove

$$\mu Z_1[\delta_{\mathcal{X}\backslash\{Y\}}(S_1)[\mu Y[S_1]/Y][Z_1/\tilde{Y}]]$$

$$\models = \tag{8.11}$$

$$\left\{\mu X_1\left[\left(\frac{dS_1}{dX} \cup \frac{dS_1}{dY}; X_1\right)[\mu Y[S_1]/Y]\right] \rightarrow \tilde{X}\right\} \wedge$$

$$\mu Z_2[\delta_{\mathcal{X}\cup\{X\}\backslash\{Y\}}(S_1)[\mu Y[S_1]/Y][Z_2/\tilde{Y}]].$$

For shortness' sake, in the remainder of the proof we abbreviate $[\mu Y[S_1]/Y]$ to $[\cdot]$. Call the left-hand side lhs and the right-hand side rhs.

<u>(i) Proof of lhs ⊃ rhs</u>. Firstly we observe that, by *fpp* and properties of " → ", and using that X_1 is a new variable, we have that

$$\mu X_1\left[\left(\frac{dS_1}{dX} \cup \frac{dS_1}{dY}; X_1\right)[\cdot]\right] \rightarrow \tilde{X}$$

$$\models = \tag{8.12a}$$

$$\left(\left(\frac{dS_1}{dX}\right)[\cdot] \rightarrow \tilde{X}\right) \wedge \left(\left(\frac{dS_1}{dY}[\cdot] \rightarrow (\mu X_1[\ldots] \rightarrow \tilde{X}\right)\right)$$

Also, since $Y \notin \mathcal{X} \cup \{X\}\backslash\{Y\}$, we have by the induction hypothesis (S_1 has smaller complexity than $\mu Y[S_1]$):

$$\models \delta_{\mathcal{X}\cup\{X\}\backslash\{Y\}}(S_1) = \left(\frac{dS_1}{dY} \rightarrow \tilde{Y}\right) \wedge \delta_{\mathcal{X}\cup\{X,Y\}}(S_1) \tag{8.12b}$$

from which it follows that ($\tilde{Y}$ not being free in $\delta_{\mathcal{X}\cup\{X,Y\}}(S_1)$):

$$\mu Z_2[\delta_{\mathcal{X}\cup\{X\}\backslash\{Y\}}(S_1)[\cdot][Z_2/\tilde{Y}]]$$

$$\models = \tag{8.12c}$$

$$\mu Z_3\left[\left(\frac{dS_1}{dY}[\cdot] \rightarrow Z_3\right) \wedge \delta_{\mathcal{X}\cup\{X,Y\}}(S_1)[\cdot]\right]$$

or, using *fpp*, that $\models \mu Z_2[\ldots] = (\frac{dS_1}{dY}[\cdot] \rightarrow \mu Z_2[\ldots]) \wedge \delta_{\mathcal{X}\cup\{X,Y\}}(S_1)[\cdot]$. Combining this with (8.12a) we obtain

$$\text{rhs}$$

$$\models = \tag{8.12d}$$

$$\left(\frac{dS_1}{dX}[\cdot] \rightarrow \tilde{X}\right) \wedge \overbrace{\left\{\frac{dS_1}{dY}[\cdot] \rightarrow \overbrace{(\mu X_1[\ldots] \rightarrow \tilde{X})}\right\} \wedge \left\{\frac{dS_1}{dY}[\cdot] \rightarrow \overbrace{\mu Z_2[\ldots]}\right\}}^{\text{rhs}}$$

$$\wedge\ \delta_{\mathcal{X}\cup\{X,Y\}}(S_1)[\cdot]$$

i.e. by properties of " $\rightarrow$ ", that

$$\models \text{rhs} = \left(\frac{dS_1}{dX}[\cdot] \rightarrow \tilde{X}\right) \wedge \left(\frac{dS_1}{dY}[\cdot] \rightarrow \text{rhs}\right) \wedge \delta_{X \cup \{X,Y\}}(S_1)[\cdot] \qquad (8.12e)$$

Also, since $\models \delta_{X\cup\{X,Y\}}(S_1) = \delta_{(X\setminus\{Y\})\cup\{X\}\cup\{Y\}}(S_1)$, two applications of the induction hypothesis yield that

$$\models \delta_{X\setminus\{Y\}}(S_1) = \left(\frac{dS_1}{dX} \rightarrow \tilde{X}\right) \wedge \left(\frac{dS_1}{dY} \rightarrow \tilde{Y}\right) \wedge \delta_{X\cup\{X,Y\}}(S_1) \qquad (8.12f)$$

from which we infer that

$$\delta_{X\setminus\{Y\}}(S_1)[\cdot][\text{rhs}/\tilde{Y}]$$
$$\models = \qquad (8.12g)$$
$$\left(\frac{dS_1}{dX}[\cdot] \rightarrow \tilde{X}\right) \wedge \left(\frac{dS_1}{dY}[\cdot] \rightarrow \text{rhs}\right) \wedge \delta_{X\cup\{X,Y\}}(S_1)[\cdot]$$

Combining (8.12e) and (8.12g) we obtain that

$$\models \text{rhs} = \delta_{X\setminus\{Y\}}(S_1)[\cdot][\text{rhs}/\tilde{Y}]$$

from which the desired result, lhs $\supset$ rhs, is immediate by *lfp*.

(ii) <u>Proof of rhs $\supset$ lhs</u>.

We show that $\models \mu Z_2[\ldots] \supset \{(\mu X_1[\ldots] \rightarrow \tilde{X}) \supset \mu Z_1[\ldots]\}$.

Using (8.12c) and *lfp*, it is sufficient to show that

$$\delta_{X\cup\{X,Y\}}(S_1)[\cdot] \wedge \left[\frac{dS_1}{dY}[\cdot] \rightarrow \{(\mu X_1[\ldots] \rightarrow \tilde{X}) \supset \mu Z_1[\ldots]\}\right]$$
$$\models \supset \qquad (8.12h)$$
$$\{(\mu X_1[\ldots] \rightarrow \tilde{X}) \supset \mu Z_1[\ldots]\}$$

or, by (8.12a), that

$$\delta_{X\cup\{X,Y\}}(S_1)[\cdot] \wedge \left[\frac{dS_1}{dY}[\cdot] \rightarrow \{(\mu X_1[\ldots] \rightarrow \tilde{X}) \supset \mu Z_1[\ldots]\}\right]$$
$$\models \supset$$
$$\left[\left(\frac{dS_1}{dX}[\cdot] \rightarrow \tilde{X}\right) \wedge \left\{\frac{dS_1}{dY}[\cdot] \rightarrow (\mu X_1[\ldots] \rightarrow \tilde{X})\right\} \supset \mu Z_1[\ldots]\right].$$

So let us assume that (in a given state) the following conditions all hold:

$$\delta_{X\cup\{X,Y\}}(S_1)[\cdot] \tag{8.12i}$$

$$\frac{dS_1}{dY}[\cdot] \rightarrow \{(\mu X_1[\ldots] \rightarrow \tilde{X}) \supset \mu Z_1[\ldots]\} \tag{8.12j}$$

$$\frac{dS_1}{dX}[\cdot] \rightarrow \tilde{X} \tag{8.12k}$$

$$\frac{dS_1}{dY}[\cdot] \rightarrow (\mu X_1[\ldots] \rightarrow \tilde{X}) \tag{8.12l}$$

To show that

$$\mu Z_1[\delta_{X\setminus\{Y\}}(S_1)[\cdot][Z_1/\tilde{Y}]] \tag{8.12m}$$

also holds, or, using (8.12f) and *fpp*, that

$$\frac{dS_1}{dX}[\cdot] \rightarrow \tilde{X} \tag{8.12n}$$

$$\frac{dS_1}{dY}[\cdot] \rightarrow \mu Z_1[\ldots] \tag{8.12o}$$

$$\delta_{X\cup\{X,Y\}}(S_1)[\cdot] \tag{8.12p}$$

We see that (8.12n) and (8.12p) coincide with (8.12k) and (8.12i), so there remains the proof of (8.12o). Now this follows easily from (8.12j) and (8.12l), using the general property of " $\rightarrow$ " that, if $S \rightarrow (p \supset q)$ and $S \rightarrow p$ both hold in a given state, then $S \rightarrow q$ holds in that state.

END 8.42.

COROLLARY 8.43. For each $x \notin X$

$$\models \delta_X(S) = (\frac{dS}{dx} \rhd \tilde{x}) \wedge \delta_{X\cup\{x\}}(S).$$

PROOF. Replace " $\rightarrow$ " by " $\rhd$ " in the proof of theorem 8.42.

END 8.43.

As final part of this section, we shall relate the upper and lower derivative of a recursive procedure to its termination using the notion of well-foundedness of a function with respect to a predicate.

DEFINITION 8.44 (well-foundedness).
A function $\phi: \Sigma \to_s T$ is called well-founded in σ with respect to a predicate π if the following two conditions are satisfied:

(i) There exists no infinite sequence $\sigma_0 = \sigma, \sigma_1, \sigma_2, \ldots$, such that $\sigma_{i+1} \in \phi(\sigma_i)$, $i = 0,1,\ldots$

(ii) There exists no finite sequence $\sigma_0 = \sigma, \sigma_1, \ldots, \sigma_k$, such that $\sigma_{i+1} \in \phi(\sigma_i)$, $i = 0,\ldots,k-1$, $\sigma_k \neq \bot$ and $\pi(\sigma_k) = ff$.

END 8.44.

Remarks

1. Note that, by strictness, ϕ is not well-founded in $\bot$ with respect to any π.
2. Note that if, for each $\sigma' \in \phi(\sigma)$, ϕ is well-founded in σ' with respect to π and, moreover, $\pi(\sigma) = tt$, then ϕ is well-founded in σ with respect to π.

The following lemma relates well-foundedness to least fixed points of suitable operators:

LEMMA 8.45. For each ϕ, σ and π:

a. $\mu[\lambda\pi' \cdot ((\pi' \circ \phi) \wedge \pi)](\sigma) = tt \Rightarrow \phi$ is well-founded in σ with respect to π.

b. ϕ is well-founded in σ with respect to $\pi \Rightarrow \mu[\lambda\pi' \cdot ((\phi \to \pi') \wedge \pi)](\sigma) = tt$.

PROOF.

a. Let $\pi_1 \overset{df.}{=} \mu[\lambda\pi' \cdot ((\pi' \circ \phi) \wedge \pi)]$ and let $\pi_{\phi,\pi}$ denote the predicate which, for each σ, expresses that ϕ is well-founded in σ with respect to π. We show that $\pi_1 \sqsubseteq \pi_{\phi,\pi}$ or, by *lfp*, that $(\pi_{\phi,\pi} \circ \phi) \wedge \pi \sqsubseteq \pi_{\phi,\pi}$. Now this is immediate by the second remark after definition 8.44.

b. Let $\pi_2 \stackrel{df.}{=} \mu[\lambda\pi'\cdot((\phi \to \pi') \wedge \pi)]$. Assume that ϕ is well-founded in σ with respect to π, but $\pi_2(\sigma) = ff$. Clearly, $\sigma \neq \bot$. By *fpp*, then $((\phi \to \pi_2) \wedge \pi)(\sigma) = ff$. Thus, either $\pi(\sigma) = ff$, contradicting definition 8.44(ii), or there exists $\sigma' \in \phi(\sigma)$, $\sigma' \neq \bot$, such that $\pi_2(\sigma') = ff$. Thus, again by *fpp*, either $\pi(\sigma') = ff$, contradicting definition 8.44(ii), or we obtain $\sigma'' \neq \bot$ such that $\sigma'' \in \phi(\sigma')$ and $\pi_2(\sigma'') = ff$. Repeating the argument, either we find a finite sequence $\sigma_0 = \sigma,\dots,\sigma_k$ $(k \geq 0)$ such that $\sigma_{i+1} \in \phi(\sigma_i)$, $i = 0,\dots,k-1$, $\sigma_k \neq \bot$, and $\pi(\sigma_k) = ff$, or we obtain an infinite sequence $\sigma_0 = \sigma,\sigma_1,\sigma_2,\dots$, such that $\sigma_{i+1} \in \phi(\sigma_i)$, $i = 0,1,\dots$. In both cases, we have found a contradiction.

END 8.45.

<u>COROLLARY 8.46</u>. Let us call a statement S well-founded with respect to a condition p if, for all γ, ξ and $\sigma \neq \bot$, $\mathcal{M}(S)(\gamma)$ is well-founded in σ with respect to $\mathcal{T}(p)(\gamma)(\xi)$. Then

a. $\models \mu Z[(S \rhd Z) \wedge p] \Rightarrow$ S is well-founded with respect to p

b. S is well-founded with respect to p $\Rightarrow\ \models \mu Z[(S \to Z) \wedge p]$.

<u>PROOF</u>. Direct by lemma 8.45.

END 8.46.

Finally, we come to our main theorem (an intuitive explanation of which we shall provide after its proof). The theorem gives a characterization of termination of a recursive procedure $\mu X[S]$ in terms of the well-foundedness of the statement $\mathring{S}$ with respect to the condition $\underset{\circ}{S}$, where $\mathring{S}$ and $\underset{\circ}{S}$ are defined by

$$\mathring{S} \equiv \left(\frac{dS}{dX}\right)[\mu X[S]/X]$$

$$\underset{\circ}{S} \equiv \delta_{\{X\}}(S)[\mu X[S]/X].$$

<u>THEOREM 8.47</u>. The following two facts are equivalent:

a. $\models \mu X[S] \rhd$ <u>true</u>

b. $\mathring{S}$ is well-founded with respect to $\underset{\circ}{S}$.

PROOF. The proof proceeds in a number of steps.

a. By theorem 8.42

$$\models \tilde{S} = (\frac{dS}{dX} \rightarrow \tilde{X}) \wedge \delta_{\{X\}}(S)$$

b. Substituting $\mu X[S]$ for X on both sides, we obtain

$$\models \tilde{S}[\mu X[S]/X] = (\overset{\circ}{S} \rightarrow \tilde{X}) \wedge \underset{\circ}{S}$$

c. Substituting Z for $\tilde{X}$ (recalling that $\tilde{X}$ does not occur free in $\delta_{\{X\}}(S)$), we obtain

$$\models \tilde{S}[\mu X[S]/X][Z/\tilde{X}] = (\overset{\circ}{S} \rightarrow Z) \wedge \underset{\circ}{S}$$

d. Prefixing both sides by $\mu Z[\ldots]$ we obtain (by lemma 8.26e(ii))

$$\models \mu Z[\tilde{S}[\mu X[S]/X][Z/\tilde{X}]] = \mu Z[(\overset{\circ}{S} \rightarrow Z) \wedge \underset{\circ}{S}]$$

e. By definition 8.36 and theorem 8.39, we obtain

$$\models \mu X[S] \rhd \underline{true} = \mu Z[(\overset{\circ}{S} \rightarrow Z) \wedge \underset{\circ}{S}]$$

f. Repeating a to e, but now starting from corollary 8.43, we obtain

$$\models \mu X[S] \rhd \underline{true} = \mu Z[(\overset{\circ}{S} \rhd Z) \wedge \underset{\circ}{S}]$$

g. The desired result now follows from e, f and corollary 8.46.

END 8.47.

Thus, we have derived the following result: A recursive procedure $\mu X[S]$ terminates for all input states $\neq \bot$ iff $\overset{\circ}{S}$ is well-founded with respect to $\underset{\circ}{S}$. How should one understand this proposition? Let us consider, for example, the procedure $\mu \overset{df.}{\equiv} \mu X[S]$, where $S \equiv A_1;X;A_2;X;A_3 \cup A_4$, with $X \notin stmv(A_i)$, $i = 1,\ldots,4$. Clearly, $\overset{\circ}{S} \equiv A_1 \cup A_1;\mu;A_2$. Also, since $X \notin stmv(A_i)$, $i = 1,\ldots,4$, it is not difficult to verify that $\models \delta_{\{X\}}(S) = \tilde{A}_1 \wedge (A_1;X \rightarrow \tilde{A}_2) \wedge (A_1;X;A_2;X \rightarrow \tilde{A}_3) \wedge \tilde{A}_4$, from which it follows that $\models \underset{\circ}{S} = \tilde{A}_1 \wedge (A_1;\mu \rightarrow \tilde{A}_2) \wedge (A_1;\mu;A_2;\mu \rightarrow \tilde{A}_3) \wedge \tilde{A}_4$. We now interpret the fact that $\mathring{S}$ is well-founded with respect to $\underset{\circ}{S}$. Forgetting about the γ- and ξ-arguments, we obtain that, for each σ,

a. There exists no infinite sequence $\sigma_0 = \sigma, \sigma_1, \sigma_2, \ldots$, such that $\sigma_{i+1} \in M(\mathring{S})(\sigma_i)$, i.e. such that $\sigma_{i+1} \in M(A_1 \cup A_1;\mu;A_2)(\sigma)$. Since $\mathring{S}$ is nothing but the statement executed between a call of μ at a certain level of recursion depth and a call at the next-deeper level, we see that the non-existence of such an infinite sequence amounts to the impossibility of infinite recursion, i.e. it is not possible that the procedure goes on calling itself indefinitely.

b. There exists no finite sequence $\sigma_0 = \sigma, \ldots, \sigma_k$ $(k \geq 0)$ such that $\sigma_{i+1} \in M(\mathring{S})(\sigma_i)$, $i = 0, \ldots, k-1$, $\sigma_k \neq \bot$, and $T(\underset{\circ}{S})(\sigma_k) = ff$. Assume that, contrariwise, such a sequence would exist. This would mean that at a certain level of recursion depth, we would have obtained an intermediate state $\sigma_k \neq \bot$ such that $T(\underset{\circ}{S})(\sigma_k) = ff$. Now from the definition of $\underset{\circ}{S}$ we obtain

$\models \neg\underset{\circ}{S} = \neg\tilde{A}_1 \vee (A_1;\mu \leftarrow \neg\tilde{A}_2) \vee (A_1;\mu;A_2;\mu \leftarrow \neg\tilde{A}_3) \vee \neg\tilde{A}_4$.

(Remember that $S \leftarrow p \equiv \neg(S \rightarrow \neg p)$.) Thus, we see that $\underset{\circ}{S}$ is false in σ_k $(\neq \bot)$ iff either

(i) A_1 does not terminate in σ_k, or

(ii) There exists at least one $\sigma' \neq \bot$ such that $\sigma' \in M(A_1;\mu)(\sigma_k)$ and A_2 does not terminate in σ', or

(iii) There exists at least one $\sigma'' \neq \bot$ such that $\sigma'' \in M(A_1;\mu;A_2;\mu)(\sigma_k)$ and A_3 does not terminate in σ'', or

(iv) A_4 does not terminate in σ_k.

Altogether, we see that $\underset{\circ}{S}$ is false in $\sigma_k \neq \bot$ precisely when there is some instance of *local* non-termination stemming from σ_k, i.e. non-termination which is not due to infinite recursion of μ, but to non-termination of one of the A-components.

Combining results a and b we infer that $\mu X[S]$ terminates everywhere whenever, for all σ, there is neither the possibility of infinite recursion (global non-termination), nor the possibility of the computation reaching some intermediate state which leads to local non-termination.

This concludes our explanation of theorem 8.47 and brings the section on derivatives to a close.

Exercises

8.1. Explain the remark on the (non-)ambiguity of $b_1 \leftarrow b_2$ following definition 8.5.

8.2. Prove the fact stated in the proof of lemma 8.8a.
(Hint: let $S \equiv x{:=}0;\mu X[x{:=}x+1;X \cup D]$. Take $\phi = \mathcal{M}(S)(\gamma)$ for some γ, and $\pi_i = \lambda\sigma\cdot\underline{if}\ \sigma{=}\bot\ \underline{then}\ ff\ \underline{else}\ \sigma(x) \le i\ \underline{fi}$, $i = 0,1,\ldots$.)

8.3. Prove

a. $\models (p_1 \supset p_2) \Rightarrow (S \leftarrow p_1) \supset (S \leftarrow p_2)$
$\models (S_1 \sqsubseteq S_2) \Rightarrow (S_1 \leftarrow p) \supset (S_2 \leftarrow p)$

b. $\models \neg(\Omega \leftarrow p)$, $\models \neg(\underline{false} \leftarrow p)$, $\models \underline{true} \leftarrow p = p$, $\models \neg(S \leftarrow \underline{false})$

c. $\mathcal{T}(S \leftarrow \underline{true})(\gamma)(\sigma) = tt$ whenever γ and σ are such that $(\sigma \ne \bot$ and) $\mathcal{M}(S)(\gamma)(\sigma)$ contains at least one state $\ne \bot$

d. $\models \neg(S \triangleright p) = \neg(S \triangleright \underline{true}) \vee (S \leftarrow \neg p)$.

e. $p \in sc(X) \Rightarrow (S \leftarrow p) \in sc(X)$.

8.4. a. Prove

(i) $\models S \rightarrow (p_1 \wedge p_2) = (S \rightarrow p_1) \wedge (S \rightarrow p_2)$
$\models (p_1 \vee p_2) \leftarrow S = (p_1 \leftarrow S) \vee (p_2 \leftarrow S)$
$\models S \triangleright (p_1 \wedge p_2) = (S \triangleright p_1) \wedge (S \triangleright p_2)$

(ii) $\models (S \rightarrow p_1) \vee (S \rightarrow p_2) \sqsubseteq (S \rightarrow (p_1 \vee p_2))$
$\models ((p_1 \wedge p_2) \leftarrow S) \sqsubseteq (p_1 \leftarrow S) \wedge (p_2 \leftarrow S)$
$\models (S \triangleright p_1) \vee (S \triangleright p_2) \sqsubseteq (S \triangleright (p_1 \vee p_2))$

b. Find counterexamples to " = " in part a(ii).

8.5. Determine $\underline{if}\ b_1 \rightarrow S_1 \square \ldots \square b_n \rightarrow S_n\ \underline{fi} \triangleright p$
$\underline{do}\ b_1 \rightarrow S_1 \square \ldots \square b_n \rightarrow S_n\ \underline{od} \triangleright p$.

8.6. Let $S \equiv \underline{\text{if}}\ b_1 \to S_1 \,\square\, \ldots \,\square\, b_n \to S_n\ \underline{\text{fi}}$

$b \equiv b_1 \vee \ldots \vee b_n$.

a. Prove

$$\frac{[p \wedge b]S[p]}{p \wedge (\underline{\text{do}}\ S\ \underline{\text{od}} \rhd \underline{\text{true}}) \supset (\underline{\text{do}}\ S\ \underline{\text{od}} \rhd (p \wedge \neg b))}$$

b. Compare part a with theorem 3.31 (and infer that $\{p \wedge b\}S\{p\}$ suffices as premise).

8.7. Let $f\colon C \to D$, with C and D complete lattices. We call f downward continuous if, for each descending chain $x_0 \sqsupseteq x_1 \sqsupseteq \ldots$, $f(\sqcap_i x_i) = \sqcap_i f(x_i)$

a. Prove that, for each ϕ, $\lambda\pi\cdot(\phi \to \pi)$ $(\in \Pi \to \Pi)$ is downward continuous

b. Prove that, if C is a complete lattice and $f\colon C \to C$ is downward continuous, then $\nu f = \sqcap_i f^i(\top)$, where $\top = \sqcup C$

c. Compare part b and the proof of theorem 3.35.

8.8. Define

(i) for $\tau_1, \tau_2 \in T$, $\tau_1 \le \tau_2$ iff either $\bot \in \tau$, or $\tau_1 \supseteq \tau_2$

(ii) for $\phi_1, \phi_2 \in M$, $\phi_1 \le \phi_2$ iff, for all σ, $\phi_1(\sigma) \le \phi_2(\sigma)$

Prove that $\phi_1 \le \phi_2$ iff, for all π, $\pi \circ \phi_1 \sqsubseteq \pi \circ \phi_2$.

8.9. Investigate the analog of section 8.3 for *partial* correctness.

8.10. Prove remark 3 after definition 8.20.

8.11. Let $Cond_0$, with typical elements p,..., be defined by

$p ::= \underline{\text{true}} \,|\, \underline{\text{false}} \,|\, s_1 = s_2 \,|\, \neg p \,|\, p_1 \supset p_2 \,|\, \exists x[p] \,|\, Z \,|\, \mu Z[p] \,|\, \nu Z[p]$
(where $p \in sm(Z)$)

Let $Cond_1$, with typical elements q,..., be defined by

$q ::= \underline{\text{true}} \,|\, \underline{\text{false}} \,|\, s_1 = s_2 \,|\, \neg q \,|\, q_1 \supset q_2 \,|\, \exists x[q] \,|\, Z$

(I.e. $Cond_0$ contains all conditions without "$\to$", "$\leftarrow$", or "$\rhd$", and $Cond_1$ is like $Cond_0$, but without $\mu Z[\ldots]$ and $\nu Z[\ldots]$.)

Prove

a. For each $q \in \mathit{Cond}_1$, with $q \in sm(Z)$, there exist $q', q'' \in \mathit{Cond}_1$ such that $\models \mu Z[q] = q'$, $\models \nu Z[q] = q''$

(Hint: show that, for each $q \in \mathit{Cond}_1$,

if $q \in sm(Z)$ then

$\models q = (Z \wedge q_1) \vee q_2$, for some q_1, q_2, $Z \notin \mathit{cndv}(q_1, q_2)$

if $q \in sa(Z)$ then

$\models q = \neg((Z \wedge q_1) \vee q_2)$, for some q_1, q_2, $Z \notin \mathit{cndv}(q_1, q_2)$

and use $\models \mu Z[(Z \wedge q_1) \vee q_2] = q_2$, etc.)

b. For each $p \in \mathit{Cond}_0$ there exists $q \in \mathit{Cond}_1$ such that $\models p = q$.

8.12. Prove

$$\frac{p[\Omega/X],\ ((X \sqsubseteq \mu X[S]) \wedge p) \Rightarrow p[S/X]}{p[\mu X[S]/X]}$$

provided that p is semantically anti-continuous in X

8.13. Let, for each $\pi \in \Pi$, $\pi^+ \in M$ be defined by

$\pi^+ = \lambda\sigma \cdot \underline{if}\ \sigma = \bot\ \underline{then}\ \{\bot\}\ \underline{else}\ \underline{if}\ \pi(\sigma)\ \underline{then}\ \{\sigma\}\ \underline{else}\ \emptyset\ \underline{fi}\ \underline{fi}$

Prove that, for each ϕ and π,

$\mu[\lambda\pi' \cdot ((\phi \to \pi') \wedge \pi)] = \mu[\lambda\pi' \cdot ((\phi \cup (\neg\pi)^+) \to \pi')]$.

8.14. Prove that, if $S \cong S'$, then $\models \frac{dS}{dX} = \frac{dS'}{dX}$ (but not, in general, $\frac{dS}{dX} \cong \frac{dS'}{dX}$).

8.15. Prove

$$\frac{[p \wedge b]S[p],\ p \supset \mu Z[(b;S) \to Z]}{[p]\mu X[b;S;X \cup \neg b][p \wedge \neg b]}$$

provided that $X \notin \mathit{stmv}(S)$

8.16. Let us call a statement S *divergent* if, for all γ and $\sigma \neq \bot$, there exists an infinite sequence $\sigma_0 = \sigma, \sigma_1, \sigma_2, \ldots$, such that $\sigma_{i+1} \in M(S)(\gamma)(\sigma_i)$, $i = 0, 1, \ldots$. Prove that $\models \nu Z[S \leftarrow Z]$ iff S is divergent.

Chapter 9

PARAMETER MECHANISMS

9.1. Introduction

The spectrum of ALGOL-like languages exhibits a wide variety of parameter mechanisms, a detailed treatment of all of which seems neither feasible, nor in line with the purposes of our treatise. Therefore, we have decided to restrict ourselves in this chapter to two well-known cases, viz. those of *value parameters* (referred to by the same term in e.g. ALGOL 60 and PASCAL) and of *address parameters* (which is our term for the PASCAL "variable parameters" and FORTRAN "reference parameters"). A few further mechanisms are mentioned in the exercises, and, moreover, in the bibliographical remarks concerning this chapter we shall provide some references to investigations of other parameter mechanisms found in the literature.

Recall that in chapter 5 on parameterless procedures, we used the syntactic format $R \equiv \langle\langle P_i \Leftarrow S_i\rangle_{i=1}^{n} | S\rangle$ for our programs. In this chapter we shall be concerned with programs of the form $R \equiv \langle\langle P_i \Leftarrow B_i\rangle_{i=1}^{n} | S\rangle$, with P_i, S as usual, and B_i a *procedure body* of the form $\langle \underline{val}\ x, \underline{add}\ y | S_i\rangle$, with formal value parameter x and formal address parameter y. (The declaration $P \Leftarrow \langle \underline{val}\ x, \underline{add}\ y | S\rangle$ in our formalism corresponds to a declaration in PASCAL of the form <u>procedure</u> P(x:integer,<u>var</u> y:integer);<u>begin</u> S <u>end</u>.) *Calls* of a procedure now take the form P(t,v), with t the actual value parameter and v the actual address parameter.

The organization of the chapter is the usual one, section 9.2 being devoted to semantics, section 9.3 to correctness and the introduction of a sound proof system, and section 9.4 to the proof of the completeness of that system. In general, the mathematical theory as developed in this chapter is a synthesis of the ideas of chapter 5 and 6, to which certain features stemming from the introduction of parameters are added.

Since our way of defining the meaning of a call P(t,v) may be frowned upon by purists in denotational semantics, we devote a few words to this issue. Our approach - to be presented in detail in section 9.2 - consists in the following: for a procedure P declared by P ⇐ B, we define P(t,v) by means of a technique we call *syntactic application,* in which we replace the construct P(t,v) by a new piece of program text B(t,v), the definition of which embodies the usual effect ascribed to the value and address parameters t and v. It would conform more to the general principles of denotational semantics if another method was adopted, viz. to compose the meaning of P(t,v) from the meanings of respectively P (yielding some suitable function), t (yielding some integer), and v (yielding some address). Though we admit that the latter approach adheres to the basic philosophy of denotational semantics in that the meaning of the whole is composed from the meanings of its constituent parts, we nonetheless prefer our syntactic application device since it substantially alleviates our task in the correctness considerations for programs with parameters. As we shall see, the proof system to be proposed in section 9.3 is obtained essentially by merging the systems of sections 5.5 and 6.3, provided a quite simple modification is made to the induction rule. Roughly speaking, the technique of syntactic application defines the parameters away, and we are left with the constructs obtained by combining the syntax of chapters 5 and 6. So much for the apology.

Sections 9.2 and 9.3 of this chapter should be reasonably clear to the reader who has digested the ideas of chapters 5 and 6. In particular, the notion of initialization reappears in a somewhat more complex form, and the definition of validity requires a refinement of the "$\gamma \in \Gamma^E$" idea of section 5.5. We are as unhappy now as fairly soon the reader will no doubt be about the somewhat perplexingly complicated new definition of Γ^E. The only comfort we have to offer is that the details of the definition are needed only for a short while in section 9.3; once the counterparts of various basic results of section 6.3 have been established, the definition of Γ^E may be forgotten entirely. The completeness theorem of section 9.4 follows the same lines as that of section 5.5, but, again, some unfortunate additional complexities have to be faced.

9.2. Semantics

We present the (syntax and) semantics of programs with blocks and procedures with parameters, by combining the least-fixed-point approach of chapter 5 with the use of environments as introduced in chapter 6, taking care of parameters through syntactic application. We begin with the new syntax:

DEFINITION 9.1 (syntax of programs with blocks and procedures with parameters).
Let x,y ∈ *Svar*, v ∈ *Ivar*, t ∈ *Iexp*, b ∈ *Bexp*, and P ∈ *Pvar* be as usual.

a. The class of statements *Stat*, with typical elements S,..., is defined by

$$S ::= v{:=}t \mid S_1;S_2 \mid \underline{\text{if}}\ b\ \underline{\text{then}}\ S_1\ \underline{\text{else}}\ S_2\ \underline{\text{fi}} \mid \underline{\text{begin}}\ \underline{\text{new}}\ x;S\ \underline{\text{end}} \mid P(t,v)$$

b. The class of procedure bodies *Pbod*, with typical elements B,..., is defined by

$$B ::= \langle \underline{\text{val}}\ x, \underline{\text{add}}\ y\text{: } S\rangle, \quad x \not\equiv y$$

c. The class of declarations *Decl*, with typical elements E,..., is defined by

$$E ::= P_1 \Leftarrow B_1,\ldots,P_n \Leftarrow B_n, \quad n \geq 0, \text{ and, for } 1 \leq i < j \leq n,\ P_i \not\equiv P_j$$

d. The class of programs *Prog*, with typical elements R,..., is defined by

R::= <E:S>

END 9.1.

Remarks

1. As usual, we replace " : " by " | " (in procedure bodies and programs).
2. Again, a program R ≡ <E|S>, E ≡ $<P_i \Leftarrow B_i>_{i=1}^{n}$, is called *closed* if it satisfies: *pvar*($B_1,\dots,B_n$,S) $\subseteq \{P_1,\dots,P_n\}$.
3. For later use (definition 9.2) we adopt the convention that, for x_i, $1 \le i \le n$, all different, <u>begin</u> <u>new</u> $x_1,x_2,\dots,x_n$;S <u>end</u> abbreviates <u>begin</u> <u>new</u> x_1; <u>begin</u> <u>new</u> x_2; ... <u>begin</u> <u>new</u> x_n;S <u>end</u> ... <u>end</u> <u>end</u>.

Example. <P ⇐ <<u>val</u> x,<u>add</u> y|<u>if</u> x=0 <u>then</u> a[0]:=1 <u>else</u>
x:=x-1; P(x,a[x]); y:=(x+1)×a[x] <u>fi</u>>
|<u>begin</u> <u>new</u> z; P(4,z) <u>end</u>>

In the procedure call P(t,v), t is the actual value parameter, and v the actual address parameter. For P declared as P ⇐ <<u>val</u> x, <u>add</u> y|S>, the actual t corresponds to the formal x, and the actual v to the formal y. For simplicity's sake, we do not introduce parameter *lists* (in calls P($t_1,\dots,t_n,v_1,\dots,v_m$) or bodies <<u>val</u> $x_1,\dots,x_n$, <u>add</u> $y_1,\dots,y_m$|S>, n > 1 or m > 1), since their treatment is a straightforward generalization of that of single parameters presented below.

Two syntactic tools play an important role in this chapter. First, we have the familiar operation of *substitution*. *svar*(S) is as before for S not a procedure call, and *svar*(P(t,v)) = *svar*(t,v). S[v/x] is defined as in chapter 6 for S not a procedure call, and P(t,w)[v/x] ≡ P(t[v/x],w[v/x]). We emphasize that substitution in a call does not affect the body (possibly) associated with P in its declaration. For later use, we introduce, for

$$E \equiv \langle P_i \Leftarrow B_i \rangle_{i=1}^{n},$$

the set *svar*(E) by:

$$svar(E) = \bigcup_{i=1}^{n} svar(B_i),$$

where, for $B \equiv$ <val x,add y|S>, *svar*(B) = *svar*(S)\{x,y}. Thus, formal parameters are bound in procedure bodies. The notion of *congruence* between statements will also be used again. This is defined as in definition 6.2, where clause a is extended with P(t,v) ≅ P(t,v).

The second syntactic tool is that of *syntactic application*. As announced in the introduction, this is a technique of associating with a procedure body B and two actual parameters t and v, a piece of program text B(t,v) such that, for B the body of a procedure P, B(t,v) embodies the meaning of P(t,v) according to the customary semantics of the parameter mechanisms of call by value and call by address.

DEFINITION 9.2 (syntactic application).
Let B ≡ <<u>val</u> x,<u>add</u> y|S>. In the definition of B(t,v) we distinguish two cases:

a. v ≡ z

<<u>val</u> x,<u>add</u> y|S>(t,z) $\overset{df.}{\equiv}$

<u>begin</u> <u>new</u> u; u:=t; S[u/x][z/y] <u>end</u>,

where u is the first simple variable ∉ *svar*(y,S,t,z)

b. v ≡ a[s]

<<u>val</u> x, <u>add</u> y|S>(t,a[s]) $\overset{df.}{\equiv}$

<u>begin</u> <u>new</u> u_1,u_2; u_1:=t; u_2:=s; S[u_1/x][a[u_2]/y] <u>end</u>,

where u_1 (u_2) is the first (second) simple variable ∉ *svar*(y,S,t,s).

END 9.2.

Example. Let B ≡ <<u>val</u> x,<u>add</u> y|<u>if</u> x=0 <u>then</u> a[0]:=1 <u>else</u> x:=x-1;
P(x,a[x]); y:=(x+1)×a[x] <u>fi</u>>.

Then B(x+3,a[x+4]) ≡

<u>begin</u> <u>new</u> u_1,u_2; u_1:=x+3; u_2:=x+4;
    <u>if</u> u_1=0 <u>then</u> a[0]:=1
    <u>else</u> $u_1:=u_1-1$; P(u_1,a[u_1]); a[u_2]:=(u_1+1)×a[u_1] <u>fi</u>
<u>end</u>,

where u_1 (u_2) is the first (second) simple variable $\notin$ *svar*(x,y).

Observe that

- Our definition of syntactic application implies that the actual value parameter t and the subscript s of the actual address parameter v (in the case that v ≡ a[s]) are evaluated before execution of S.
- The precaution with the fresh u is necessary since the simpler definition (for v ≡ z) B(t,z) ≡ <u>begin</u> <u>new</u> x; x:=t; S[z/y] <u>end</u> does not work because there might be a clash between the local x introduced in this block and possible occurrences of some (non-local) x in the actual t (cf., for example, section 4.7.3.2 of the ALGOL 60 report).
- The two possibilities for the actual address parameter v are:
  - v ≡ z, a simple variable. Call by address then coincides with the ALGOL 60 call by name, and is dealt with by the substitution S[z/y]
  - v ≡ a[s], a subscripted variable. Then s is evaluated and stored in u_2, before execution of S (with a[u_2] substituted for y).

After these syntactic preparations, we proceed with the semantic definitions. Environments, states, and the functions L, R and W are as in chapter 6. For the semantics of statements and programs, we first have to (re)define some sets:

$$M \overset{\text{df.}}{=} Env \to (\Sigma \to_s \Sigma) \text{ , with typical elements } \phi,\ldots$$

$$H \overset{\text{df.}}{=} Iexp \times Ivar \to M\text{, with typical elements } \eta,\ldots$$

$$\Gamma \overset{\text{df.}}{=} Pvar \to H \qquad \text{, with typical elements } \gamma,\ldots$$

The definition of H (and, accordingly, of Γ) stems from the fact that procedure calls always have an actual parameter pair <t,v>, which belongs to the set $\mathit{Iexp} \times \mathit{Ivar}$.

DEFINITION 9.3 (semantics of statements and programs).

a. The function N is of type: $\mathit{Stat} \to (\Gamma \to M)$, and is defined by:

$N(S)(\gamma)(\varepsilon)(\sigma) = \bot$, if $intv(S) \nsubseteq dom(\varepsilon)$ or $\sigma = \bot$. Otherwise

(i) $N(v{:=}t)(\gamma)(\varepsilon)(\sigma) = \sigma\{R(t)(\varepsilon)(\sigma)/L(v)(\varepsilon)(\sigma)\}$

(ii) $N(S_1;S_2)(\gamma)(\varepsilon)(\sigma) = N(S_2)(\gamma)(\varepsilon)(N(S_1)(\gamma)(\varepsilon)(\sigma))$

(iii) $N(\underline{\text{if}}\ b\ \underline{\text{then}}\ S_1\ \underline{\text{else}}\ S_2\ \underline{\text{fi}})(\gamma)(\varepsilon)(\sigma) =$
$\underline{\text{if}}\ W(b)(\varepsilon)(\sigma)\ \underline{\text{then}}\ N(S_1)(\gamma)(\varepsilon)(\sigma)\ \underline{\text{else}}\ N(S_2)(\gamma)(\varepsilon)(\sigma)\ \underline{\text{fi}}$

(iv) $N(\underline{\text{begin}}\ \underline{\text{new}}\ x;S\ \underline{\text{end}})(\gamma)(\varepsilon)(\sigma) = N(S[y/x])(\gamma)(\varepsilon \cup \langle y,e\rangle)(\sigma)$, where y is the first simple variable $\notin dom(\varepsilon)$, and e the first address $\notin range(\varepsilon)$

(v) $N(P(t,v))(\gamma)(\varepsilon)(\sigma) = \gamma(P)(t,v)(\varepsilon)(\sigma)$

b. The function M is of the type: $\mathit{Prog} \to (\Gamma \to M)$, and is defined by:

$M(\langle E|S\rangle)(\gamma)(\varepsilon)(\sigma) = \bot$, if $intv(E,S) \nsubseteq dom(\varepsilon)$ or $\sigma = \bot$. Otherwise,

let $E \equiv \langle P_i \Leftarrow B_i\rangle_{i=1}^n$.

$M(\langle E|S\rangle)(\gamma)(\varepsilon)(\sigma) = N(S)(\gamma\{\eta_i/P_i\}_{i=1}^n)(\varepsilon)(\sigma)$, where

$$\langle \eta_1,\ldots,\eta_n\rangle = \mu[\Upsilon_1,\ldots,\Upsilon_n]$$

and, for j = 1,...,n, Υ_j is a function: $H^n \to H$, defined by

$$\Upsilon_j = \lambda\eta_1'\cdot\ldots\cdot\lambda\eta_n'\cdot\lambda t\cdot\lambda v\cdot N(B_j(t,v))(\gamma\{\eta_i'/P_i\}_{i=1}^n)$$

END 9.3.

Example. Let ∅ stand for the nowhere defined environment.

$M(\langle P \Leftarrow \langle \underline{\text{val}}\ x,\underline{\text{add}}\ y|y{:=}x+1\rangle|\underline{\text{begin}}\ \underline{\text{new}}\ z;\ P(2,z)\ \underline{\text{end}}\rangle)(\gamma)(\emptyset)(\sigma) =$

$N(\underline{\text{begin}}\ \underline{\text{new}}\ z;\ P(2,z)\ \underline{\text{end}})(\gamma\{\eta/P\})(\emptyset)(\sigma) =$ (for η see below)

$N(P(2,u))(\gamma\{\eta/P\})(\langle u,e\rangle)(\sigma)$ (where u is the first simple variable and e the first address) =

$\eta(2,u)(\langle u,e\rangle)(\sigma)$ =

$\mu[\lambda\eta'\cdot\lambda t\cdot\lambda v\cdot N(\langle \underline{\text{val}}\ x,\underline{\text{add}}\ y \mid y{:=}x{+}1\rangle(t,v))(\gamma\{\eta'/P\})](2,u)(\langle u,e\rangle)(\sigma)$ =

(by *fpp*)

$\lambda t\cdot\lambda v\cdot N(\langle \underline{\text{val}}\ x,\underline{\text{add}}\ y \mid y{:=}x{+}1\rangle(t,v))(\gamma\{\mu[\ldots]/P\})(2,u)(\langle u,e\rangle)(\sigma)$ =

$N(\langle \underline{\text{val}}\ x,\underline{\text{add}}\ y \mid y{:=}x{+}1\rangle(2,u))(\gamma\{\cdot\})(\langle u,e\rangle)(\sigma)$ =

$N(\underline{\text{begin}}\ \underline{\text{new}}\ \bar{u};\ \bar{u}{:=}2;\ u{:=}\bar{u}{+}1\ \underline{\text{end}})(\gamma\{\cdot\})(\langle u,e\rangle)(\sigma)$

(where $\bar{u}$ is the first simple variable $\notin$ *svar*(y,u)) =

$N(\bar{\bar{u}}{:=}2;\ u{:=}\bar{\bar{u}}{+}1)(\gamma\{\cdot\})(\langle u,e\rangle,\langle\bar{\bar{u}},\bar{e}\rangle)(\sigma)$

(where $\bar{\bar{u}}$ is the first simple variable $\neq$ u, and

$\bar{e}$ the first address $\neq$ e) =

$N(u{:=}\bar{\bar{u}}{+}1)(\gamma\{\cdot\})(\langle u,e\rangle,\langle\bar{\bar{u}},\bar{e}\rangle)(N(\bar{\bar{u}}{:=}2)(\gamma\{\cdot\})(\langle u,e\rangle,\langle\bar{\bar{u}},\bar{e}\rangle)(\sigma))$ =

$N(u{:=}\bar{\bar{u}}{+}1)(\gamma\{\cdot\})(\langle u,e\rangle,\langle\bar{\bar{u}},\bar{e}\rangle)(\sigma\{2/\bar{e}\})$ =

$\sigma\{2/\bar{e}\}\{3/e\}$.

Remarks.

1. In our definition of $M(\langle\langle P_i \Leftarrow B_i\rangle_{i=1}^{n} \mid S\rangle)(\gamma)$, we use a combination of the familiar least-fixed-point technique (storing in γ the meaning $\langle\eta_1,\ldots,\eta_n\rangle$ of the $\langle P_1,\ldots,P_n\rangle$, obtained as simultaneous least fixed point of the n-tuple of operators $\langle\Upsilon_1,\ldots,\Upsilon_n\rangle$) with the syntactic application construction $B_j(t,v)$ contained in the formula for Υ_j. Thus, we observe as an advantage of this definition the what one might call orthogonal treatment of recursion on the one hand - the least fixed point definition has exactly the same structure as the one given in chapter 5 - and of the parameter mechanisms - which are completely taken care of by syntactic application - on the other hand.
2. It is possible to give the semantics of programs with procedures containing call-by-value parameters only, in a way more in keeping

with the spirit of denotational semantics, and avoiding the use of syntactic application (see the discussion in section 9.1) as follows. Let $\mathit{Pbod}^{(v)}$, with typical elements $B^{(v)}, \ldots$, be the class of procedure bodies containing call-by-value parameters only:

$$B^{(v)} ::= \ <\underline{val}\ x|S>$$

The class Stat of statements is now defined by (cf. definition 9.1):

$$S ::= \ \ldots|P(t)$$

and for convenience we restrict attention to the class Prog_0 of programs containing a single declaration

$$R ::= \ <P_0 \Leftarrow B^{(v)}|S>.$$

Note that H (cf. earlier definition) is now given by $H = \mathit{Iexp} \rightarrow M$, and syntactic application (cf. definition 9.2) by

$$<\underline{val}\ x|S>(t) \equiv \underline{begin}\ \underline{new}\ u;\ u{:=}t;\ S[u/x]\ \underline{end},$$

where u is the first simple variable $\notin \mathit{svar}(S,t)$. Now define

$$\tilde{H} \overset{df.}{=} V_0 \rightarrow M \quad \text{, with typical elements } \tilde{\eta}, \ldots$$

$$\tilde{\Gamma} \overset{df.}{=} \mathit{Pvar} \rightarrow \tilde{H} \text{ , with typical elements } \tilde{\gamma}, \ldots$$

Then define $\tilde{N}$: $\mathit{Stat} \rightarrow (\tilde{\Gamma} \rightarrow M)$ as in definition 9.3(a), but with clause (v) replaced by

$$\tilde{N}(P(t))(\tilde{\gamma})(\varepsilon)(\sigma) = \tilde{\gamma}(P)(\mathcal{R}(t)(\varepsilon)(\sigma))(\varepsilon)(\sigma).$$

Next define $\tilde{P}$: $\mathit{Pbod}^{(v)} \rightarrow (V_0 \rightarrow (\tilde{\Gamma} \rightarrow M))$ by

$$\tilde{P}(<\underline{val}\ x|S>)(\alpha)(\tilde{\gamma})(\varepsilon)(\sigma) = \tilde{N}(S[u/x])(\tilde{\gamma})(\varepsilon \cup <u,e>)(\sigma\{\alpha/e\})$$

where u is the first simple variable $\notin$ dom(ε) and e the first address $\notin$ range(ε). (Think of $\tilde{P}(B^{(v)})(\mathcal{R}(t)(\varepsilon)(\sigma))(\cdot)(\varepsilon)(\sigma)$ as corresponding to $N(B^{(v)}(t))(\cdot)(\varepsilon)(\sigma)$.) Finally, define $\tilde{M}$: $Prog_0 \to (\tilde{\Gamma} \to M)$ by (cf. definition 9.3(b))

$$\tilde{M}(\langle P_0 \Leftarrow B^{(v)} \mid S\rangle)(\tilde{\gamma})(\varepsilon)(\sigma)$$

$$= \begin{cases} \perp, \text{ if } intv(B^{(v)},S) \not\subseteq \text{dom}(\varepsilon) \text{ or } \sigma = \perp \\ \tilde{N}(S)(\tilde{\gamma}\{\tilde{\eta}_0/P_0\})(\varepsilon)(\sigma), \text{ otherwise} \end{cases}$$

where $\tilde{\eta}_0 = \mu[\lambda\tilde{\eta}\cdot\lambda\alpha\cdot\tilde{P}(B^{(v)})(\alpha)(\tilde{\gamma}\{\tilde{\eta}/P_0\})]$.

$\tilde{M}$ is equivalent to M, in the sense that for any closed program R and any γ, $\tilde{\gamma}$:

$$\tilde{M}(R)(\tilde{\gamma}) = M(R)(\gamma).$$

(See exercise 9.2, and also exercise 9.6. We do not know how to obtain a similar result for procedures with call-by-address parameters.)

3. We can now elaborate on the comments following definition 6.5, concerning the definition of the semantics of blocks. Let us consider the following simpler variant of definition 9.3a(iv):
N(<u>begin</u> <u>new</u> x;S <u>end</u>)$(\gamma)(\varepsilon)(\sigma) \overset{(*)}{=} N(S)(\gamma)(\varepsilon[e/x])(\sigma)$, where e is the first address $\notin$ range(ε), and $\varepsilon[e/x]$ is an ad-hoc notation for (i) $\varepsilon \cup \langle x,e\rangle$, if $x \notin$ dom(ε) (ii) $\varepsilon\{e/x\}$, if $x \in$ dom(ε). The reason we did not adopt (*) has to do with the question of so-called static versus dynamic scope for procedures. Consider a program $R \equiv \langle P \Leftarrow \langle\ldots\mid\ldots z\ldots\rangle \mid \ldots$ <u>begin</u> <u>new</u> z; ...z...P(...)...<u>end</u>...$\rangle$, where the z in the procedure body is some global (i.e. non-local) simple variable. Now let us find out what happens with this occurrence of z at the moment of the indicated call of P. According to the dynamic scope rule, z would then be identified with the locally declared simple variable z, whereas, according to the static scope rule, z remains global. Standard practice in ALGOL-like languages is to adopt the static scope rule. We show that this rule is indeed

captured by our definition 9.3a(iv), whereas the (rejected) alternative (*) would yield dynamic scope. Let us take some ε which is defined on all elements of *intv*(R). In particular, it is defined on the global z, i.e. $\varepsilon = \varepsilon_1 \cup \langle z,e_1\rangle$, say. According to 9.3a(iv), N(begin new z; ...z...P(...)...end)(γ)($\varepsilon_1 \cup \langle z,e_1\rangle$)($\sigma$) = N(...u...P(...)...)(γ)($\varepsilon_1 \cup \langle z,e_1\rangle \cup \langle u,e\rangle$)($\sigma$), where u is the first simple variable $\notin \text{dom}(\varepsilon_1) \cup \{z\}$, and e is the first address $\notin \text{range}(\varepsilon_1) \cup \{e_1\}$. At the subsequent evaluation of P(...), the current environment is $\varepsilon_1 \cup \langle z,e_1\rangle \cup \langle u,e\rangle$; hence, during the evaluation of P(...), the z occurring in the procedure body associated with P is indeed treated as a global variable (the value of which is reached through address e_1), and no clashes with the local z occur (since this has been replaced by the fresh u). On the other hand, let us see what would happen if strategy (*) were to be chosen. Then N(begin new z; ...z...P(...)...end)(γ)($\varepsilon_1 \cup \langle z,e_1\rangle$)($\sigma$) = N(...z...P(...)...)(γ)($\varepsilon_1 \cup \langle z,e\rangle$)($\sigma$) (the address e_1 for z is overwritten by the new address e), so that in the subsequent evaluation of P(...), the z occurring in its body is now treated in the same way (i.e. associated with the same address) as the *local* z.

4. However, there *is* a way to adopt variant (*) given in the previous remark for the meaning of blocks, and still preserve static scope; namely by making further changes in the definition of N and M, as follows. For simplicity, we will consider the language with blocks and procedure calls, but without parameters (i.e. a combination of the languages of chapters 5 and 6), and we will restrict attention to the class *Stat* of statements containing a single procedure variable P_0: thus (cf. definition 9.1)

   $S ::= \ \ldots | P_0$

   The class $Prog_0$ of programs is given by

   $R ::= \ \langle P_0 \Leftarrow S_0 | S\rangle$.

Now define (cf. the earlier definitions of M and Γ)

$$M_1 \overset{\text{df.}}{=} Env \to (\Sigma \to_s \Sigma), \text{ with typical elements } \eta_1, \ldots$$

$$\Gamma_1 \overset{\text{df.}}{=} Pvar \to M_1 \quad , \text{ with typical elements } \gamma_1, \ldots$$

The function N_1: $Stat_0 \to (\Gamma_1 \to M_1)$ is defined like N in definition 9.3(a), with clause (v) replaced by

$$N_1(P_0)(\gamma_1)(\varepsilon)(\sigma) = \gamma_1(P_0)(\varepsilon)(\sigma) \qquad (v)_1$$

and the function M_1: $Prog_0 \to (\Gamma_1 \to M_1)$ like M in definition 9.3(b) (or 5.19(b)):

$$M_1(<P_0 \Leftarrow S_0|S>)(\gamma_1)(\varepsilon)(\sigma) = N_1(S)(\gamma_1\{\eta_1/P\})(\varepsilon)(\sigma)$$

(assuming $intv(S_0,S) \subseteq \text{dom}(\varepsilon)$), where

$$\eta_1 = \mu[\lambda\eta_1'\cdot N_1(S_0)(\gamma_1\{\eta_1'/P_0\})] \qquad (fp)_1$$

M_1 is essentially the semantics M for programs given in this chapter. For the alternative semantics, let

$$M_2 \overset{\text{df.}}{=} \Sigma \to_s \Sigma \quad , \text{ with typical elements } \eta_2, \ldots$$

$$\Gamma_2 \overset{\text{df.}}{=} Pvar \to M_2, \text{ with typical elements } \gamma_2, \ldots$$

The function N_2: $Stat_0 \to (\Gamma_2 \to M_2)$ is defined like N, but with clauses (iv) and (v) now replaced by (cf. exercise 6.12)

N_2(begin new x;S end)$(\gamma_2)(\varepsilon)(\sigma)$ =
$N_2(S)(\gamma_2)(\varepsilon[e/x])(\sigma\{<\sigma(e)_1,->/e\})$ $(iv)_2$
where e is the first address $\notin$ range(ε) such that $\sigma(e)_2 = +$

$$N_2(P_0)(\gamma_2)(\varepsilon)(\sigma) = \gamma_2(P_0)(\sigma) \qquad (v)_2$$

The function M_2: $Prog_0 \to (\Gamma_2 \to M_2)$ is defined by

$$M_2(<P_0 \Leftarrow S_0|S>)(\gamma_2)(\varepsilon)(\sigma) = N_2(S)(\gamma_2\{\eta_2/P_0\})(\varepsilon)(\sigma)$$

(assuming $intv(S_0,S) \subseteq \mathrm{dom}(\varepsilon)$), where

$$\eta_2 = \mu[\lambda\eta_1' \cdot N_2(S_0)(\gamma_2\{\eta_2'/P_0\})(\varepsilon)] \qquad (\mathrm{fp})_2$$

Notice how M_2 differs from M_1: not only in clause $(\mathrm{iv})_2$ in the definition of N_2, but also in the role of the environment ε, which is absent from the right-hand side of equation (v_2), but present in the right-hand side of $(\mathrm{fp})_2$. In short, for the M_2-semantics, the meaning of P_0 uses the environment at the moment of its declaration and not of its call.

With this M_2-semantics, which is used by many authors in denotational semantics, we again have static scope for procedures.

The development of the theory of the M_2-semantics would entail various modifications in the theory developed in this chapter (for example, lemma 9.4 no longer holds in general). Furthermore (not having checked the details, we can only state a conjecture here) we expect that M_2 is not completely equivalent to M_1, but rather equivalent "up to matching". That is, under a suitable initialization condition (similar to the one stated after definition 9.6), we have that, for any closed program R and any γ_1,γ_2, if $\sigma_1 = M_1(R)(\gamma_1)(\varepsilon)(\sigma) \neq \bot$, $\sigma_2 = M_2(R)(\gamma_2)(\varepsilon)(\sigma) \neq \bot$, and $\delta = \mathrm{dom}(\varepsilon)\setminus\{x_i\}_{i=1}^n$, where R contains blocks of the form <u>begin</u> <u>new</u> $x_i;S_i$ <u>end</u>, $i = 1,\dots,n$, then $(\sigma_1\circ\varepsilon)|\delta = (\sigma_2\circ\varepsilon)|\delta$. (See exercise 9.3.)

We now discuss a number of consequences of our semantic definitions, most of which are generalizations of corresponding results in chapter 6. We begin with

<u>LEMMA 9.4</u>. $S \cong S' \Rightarrow N(S) = N(S')$.

<u>PROOF</u>. See lemma 6.6.

END 9.4.

The next theorem states an *invariance* property of our programs. Roughly, we assert that a closed program R does not change the value of any intermediate variable $\notin$ *intv*(R). This property is used - after extension to non-closed programs - in the validity proof of the invariance rule of section 9.3 (and, also, in corollary 9.8b).

THEOREM 9.5. Let $R \equiv \langle E|S\rangle$ be a closed program, with $E \equiv \langle P_i \Leftarrow B_i\rangle_{i=1}^n$. Let $\gamma \in \Gamma$, let η_i, $i = 1,\ldots,n$, be as in definition 9.3, and let $\bar{\gamma} \overset{df.}{=} \gamma\{\eta_i/P_i\}_{i=1}^n$. If

(i) $intv(R) \subseteq dom(\varepsilon)$

(ii) $\sigma' = N(S)(\bar{\gamma})(\varepsilon)(\sigma)$, $\sigma' \neq \bot$

then

(iii) $(\sigma'\circ\varepsilon)|(dom(\varepsilon)\backslash intv(R)) = (\sigma\circ\varepsilon)|(dom(\varepsilon)\backslash intv(R))$.

PROOF. Let, for $k = 0,1,\ldots$, $\gamma^k \overset{df.}{=} \gamma\{\eta_i^k/P_i\}_{i=1}^n$, where, with a natural extension of the ϕ_i^k definition of the preceding chapters, for $i = 1,\ldots,n$,

$$\eta_i^0 = \lambda t\cdot\lambda v\cdot\lambda\varepsilon\cdot\lambda\sigma\cdot\bot$$

$$\eta_i^{k+1} = \Upsilon_i(\eta_1^k,\ldots,\eta_n^k), \quad k = 0,1,\ldots$$

Clearly, $\eta_i = \bigsqcup_k \eta_i^k$, $i = 1,\ldots,n$. It is now sufficient to prove, by the usual induction on $\langle k,\ell(S)\rangle$, that if

(i) $intv(R) \subseteq dom(\varepsilon)$

(ii) $\sigma' = N(S)(\gamma^k)(\varepsilon)(\sigma)$, $\sigma' \neq \bot$

(iii) $\xi \in dom(\varepsilon)\backslash intv(R)$

then

(iv) $\sigma'(\varepsilon(\xi)) = \sigma(\varepsilon(\xi))$.

We distinguish several cases.

1. $S \equiv (v:=s)$. Then $\sigma' = \sigma\{R(s)(\varepsilon)(\sigma)/L(v)(\varepsilon)(\sigma)\}$. Since $\xi \notin intv(R)$, we have that $\xi \notin intv(v:=s)$. From the fact that ε is 1-1 on its domain, it follows that $\varepsilon(\xi) \neq L(v)(\varepsilon)(\sigma)$. Hence, $\sigma'(\varepsilon(\xi)) = \sigma(\varepsilon(\xi))$.

2. $S \equiv S_1;S_2$ or $S \equiv$ <u>if</u> b <u>then</u> S_1 <u>else</u> S_2 <u>fi</u>. Easy by induction.
3. $S \equiv$ <u>begin</u> <u>new</u> x;S_1 <u>end</u>. We have that
   $N(\underline{\text{begin}}\ \underline{\text{new}}\ x;S_1\ \underline{\text{end}})(\gamma^k)(\varepsilon)(\sigma)(\varepsilon(\xi))$ = (<y,e> as usual)
   $N(S_1[y/x])(\gamma^k)(\varepsilon\cup\langle y,e\rangle)(\sigma)(\varepsilon(\xi))$ = (since $\xi \in dom(\varepsilon)$, $\xi \neq y$)
   $N(S_1[y/x])(\gamma^k)(\varepsilon\cup\langle y,e\rangle)(\sigma)((\varepsilon\cup\langle y,e\rangle)(\xi))$ = (induction)
   $\sigma((\varepsilon\cup\langle y,e\rangle)(\xi)) = \sigma(\varepsilon(\xi))$.
4. $S \equiv P(t,v)$, with $P \equiv P_j$, for some j, $1 \le j \le n$. If $k = 0$, we have nothing to prove. Otherwise, $N(P_j(t,v))(\gamma^k)(\varepsilon)(\sigma) = N(B_j(t,v))(\gamma^{k-1})(\varepsilon)(\sigma)$, and the desired result follows by induction, since $\langle k-1,\ell(B_j(t,v))\rangle \prec \langle k,\ell(P_j(t,v))\rangle$.

END 9.5.

The remainder of this section is devoted to definition and consequences of the initialization requirement. We begin with an adaptation of definition 6.11 to a framework involving procedures. Note that some care has to be taken in that procedures can only initialize local simple variables through the call by address parameter mechanism. (This is a consequence of the static scope rule: in the program $\langle P \Leftarrow \langle \ldots | z:=0\rangle |$<u>begin</u> <u>new</u> z;P(...) <u>end</u>>, the local z is not initialized.)

<u>DEFINITION 9.6</u> (initialization).

a. For each $R \in$ *Prog*, *init*(R) is the smallest subset of *Svar* satisfying
   (i) If $x \notin$ *svar*(s), then $x \in$ *init*(<E|x:=s>)
   (ii) If $x \in$ *init*(<E|S_1>), or $x \notin$ *svar*(S_1) and $x \in$ *init*(<E|S_2>), then $x \in$ *init*(<E|$S_1;S_2$>)
   (iii) If $x \notin$ *svar*(b), $x \in$ *init*(<E|S_i>), i = 1,2, then $x \in$ *init*(<E|<u>if</u> b <u>then</u> S_1 <u>else</u> S_2 <u>fi</u>>)
   (iv) If $x \not\equiv y$, $x \in$ *init*(<E|S>), then $x \in$ *init*(<E|<u>begin</u> <u>new</u> y;S <u>end</u>>)
   (v) If $E \equiv \langle P_i \Leftarrow B_i\rangle_{i=1}^n$, with $B_i \equiv \langle$<u>val</u> x_i,<u>add</u> $y_i|S_i\rangle$, i = 1,...,n, if $x \notin$ *svar*(t), $x \equiv v$, and $y_i \in$ *init*(<E|S_i>), then $x \in$ *init*(<E|P_i(t,v)>).

b. We say that all local simple variables of a program $R \equiv \langle E|S\rangle$, with $E \equiv \langle P_i \Leftarrow \langle \underline{val}\ x_i, \underline{add}\ y_i | S_i\rangle\rangle_{i=1}^n$, are initialized whenever, for each block $\underline{begin}\ \underline{new}\ x; S_0\ \underline{end}$ occurring as substatement of S or any of the S_i, $i = 1,\ldots,n$, we have that $x \in init(\langle E|S_0\rangle)$ or $x \notin svar(S_0)$.

END 9.6.

Examples

a. $x \notin init(\langle\ |P(0,x)\rangle)$, $z \in init(\langle P \Leftarrow \langle \underline{val}\ x, \underline{add}\ y|y:=x\rangle|P(0,z)\rangle)$,

$init(\langle P_1 \Leftarrow \langle \underline{val}\ x_1, \underline{add}\ y_1|P_2(0,y_1)\rangle,$
$\quad \langle P_2 \Leftarrow \langle \underline{val}\ x_2, \underline{add}\ y_2|P_1(0,y_2)\rangle|P_1(0,x)\rangle) = \emptyset$

b. All local simple variables are initialized in

$\langle P \Leftarrow \langle \underline{val}\ \bar{x}, \underline{add}\ \bar{y}|\underline{begin}\ \underline{new}\ z; \bar{y}:=1; z:=\bar{x}+\bar{y}\ \underline{end}\rangle$
$|\underline{begin}\ \underline{new}\ u; P(0,u)\ \underline{end}\rangle$,

but not in

$\langle P \Leftarrow \langle \underline{val}\ \bar{x}, \underline{add}\ \bar{y}|\underline{begin}\ \underline{new}\ z; \bar{y}:=1; z:=\bar{x}+\bar{y}\ \underline{end}\rangle$
$|\underline{begin}\ \underline{new}\ u; P(u+1,u)\ \underline{end}\rangle$,

nor in

$\langle P \Leftarrow \langle \underline{val}\ \bar{x}, \underline{add}\ \bar{y}|\underline{begin}\ \underline{new}\ z; z:=\bar{x}+\bar{y}; \bar{y}:=1\ \underline{end}\rangle$
$|\underline{begin}\ \underline{new}\ u; P(0,u)\ \underline{end}\rangle$.

As in chapter 6, from now on we require that all our programs satisfy the requirement that all their local simple variables are initialized.

As a consequence of this requirement we obtain the following theorem, which generalizes theorem 6.12:

THEOREM 9.7. Let $R \equiv \langle E|S\rangle$ be a closed program, with $E \equiv \langle P_i \Leftarrow B_i\rangle_{i=1}^n$. Let $\gamma \in \Gamma$, let η_i, $i = 1,\ldots,n$, be as in definition 9.3, and let $\bar{\gamma} = \gamma\{\eta_i/P_i\}_{i=1}^n$. Let $m \geq 0$. If

(i) $intv(E) \cup (intv(S)\backslash\{x_j\}_{j=1}^m) \subseteq \delta \subseteq dom(\varepsilon) \cap dom(\bar{\varepsilon})$, $\sigma \neq \bot$, $\bar{\sigma} \neq \bot$

(ii) $(\sigma\circ\varepsilon)|\delta = (\bar{\sigma}\circ\ddot{\varepsilon})|\delta$

(iii) For all $j = 1,\ldots,m$, $\sigma(e_j) = \bar{\sigma}(\bar{e}_j)$, or $x_j \in init(\langle E|S\rangle)$, or $x_j \notin svar(S)$

(iv) $\sigma' = N(S[y_j/x_j]_{j=1}^{m})(\bar{\gamma})(\varepsilon \cup \langle y_j,e_j\rangle_{j=1}^{m})(\sigma)$

$\bar{\sigma}' = N(S[z_j/x_j]_{j=1}^{m})(\bar{\gamma})(\bar{\varepsilon} \cup \langle z_j,\bar{e}_j\rangle_{j=1}^{m})(\bar{\sigma})$

then *either* $\sigma' = \bot$, $\bar{\sigma}' = \bot$, *or* $\sigma' \neq \bot$, $\bar{\sigma}' \neq \bot$, and

(v) $(\sigma' \circ \varepsilon)|\delta = (\bar{\sigma}' \circ \bar{\varepsilon})|\delta$

(vi) For all $j = 1,\ldots,m$, if $\sigma(e_j) = \bar{\sigma}(\bar{e}_j)$ or $x_j \in init(\langle E|S\rangle)$ then $\sigma'(e_j) = \bar{\sigma}'(\bar{e}_j)$.

PROOF. Let, for $k = 0,1,\ldots$, γ^k be as in the proof of theorem 9.5. By discreteness, it is sufficient to prove, by the usual induction on $\langle k,\ell(S)\rangle$, that the theorem, with, in (iv), $\bar{\gamma}$ replaced by γ^k, holds for all S. We distinguish two cases:

1. S not a procedure call. Then the argument is exactly as in the proof of theorem 6.12.
2. $S \equiv P(t,v)$, with $P \equiv P_h$, for some h, $1 \leq h \leq n$. If $k = 0$, then the desired result is immediate from the definitions. Otherwise, we have to show that, under the assumptions (i), (ii), (iii), if

$$\sigma' = N(B_h(t[y_j/x_j]_j, v[y_j/x_j]_j))(\gamma^{k-1})(\varepsilon \cup \langle y_j,e_j\rangle_j)(\sigma)$$

$$\bar{\sigma}' = N(B_h(t[z_j/x_j]_j, v[z_j/x_j]_j))(\gamma^{k-1})(\bar{\varepsilon} \cup \langle z_j,\bar{e}_j\rangle_j)(\bar{\sigma})$$

then either $\sigma' = \bot$, $\bar{\sigma}' = \bot$, *or* $\sigma' \neq \bot$, $\bar{\sigma}' \neq \bot$, and $\sigma',\bar{\sigma}'$ satisfy (v), (vi). We distinguish various possibilities for v: $v \equiv u \not\equiv x_j$, $1 \leq j \leq m$, $v \equiv x_\ell$ for some ℓ, $1 \leq \ell \leq m$, and $v \equiv a[s]$. We only treat the case that $v \equiv x_\ell$ for some ℓ, $1 \leq \ell \leq m$, and leave the treatment of the other two cases to the reader. Let $B_h \equiv \langle$<u>val</u> x,<u>add</u> y$|S_h\rangle$. By the definition of syntactic application

$$\sigma' = N(\underline{\text{begin}}\ \underline{\text{new}}\ u; u:=t[\,]_j; S_h[u/x][y_\ell/y]\ \underline{\text{end}})(\gamma^{k-1})(\varepsilon \cup \langle y_j,e_j\rangle_j)(\sigma)$$

$$\bar{\sigma}' = N(\underline{\text{begin}}\ \underline{\text{new}}\ \bar{u};\bar{u}:=t[\,]_j;S_h[\bar{u}/x][z_\ell/y]\ \underline{\text{end}})(\gamma^{k-1})(\bar{\varepsilon}\cup\langle z_j,\bar{e}_j\rangle_j)(\bar{\sigma})$$

where u ($\bar{u}$) is the first simple variable $\notin$ *svar*$(y,S_h,t[y_j/x_j]_j,y_\ell)$ (*svar*$(y,S_h,t[z_j/x_j]_j,z_\ell)$). By properties of " $\cong$ ", we may assume that $u \equiv \bar{u}$. Let $u_1,\ldots,u_n$ be completely fresh simple variables. We have, using properties of substitution and of " $\cong$ ":

$$\sigma' = N(\underline{\text{begin}}\ \underline{\text{new}}\ u;u:=t[u_j/x_j]_j;S_h[u/x][u_\ell/y]\ \underline{\text{end}}$$

$$[y_j/u_j]_j)(\gamma^{k-1})(\varepsilon\cup\langle y_j,e_j\rangle_j)(\sigma)$$

$$\bar{\sigma}' = N(\underline{\text{begin}}\ \underline{\text{new}}\ u;u:=t[u_j/x_j]_j;S_h[u/x][u_\ell/y]\ \underline{\text{end}}$$

$$[z_j/u_j]_j)(\gamma^{k-1})(\bar{\varepsilon}\cup\langle z_j,\bar{e}_j\rangle_j)(\bar{\sigma})$$

Now, by assumption (iii), for $j = 1,\ldots,m$, at least one of the following is satisfied:

1. $\sigma(e_j) = \bar{\sigma}(\bar{e}_j)$
2. $x_j \in$ *init*$(\langle E|P_h(t,x_\ell)\rangle)$. Thus, by definition 9.6a(v), $j = \ell$, $x_\ell \notin$ *svar*(t), and $y \in$ *init*$(\langle E|S_h\rangle)$, from which it follows that $u_\ell \notin$ *svar*$(t[u_j/x_j]_j)$, and $u_\ell \in$ *init*$(\langle E|S_h[u/x][u_\ell/y]\rangle)$. Thus, we may conclude that $u_\ell \in$ *init*$(\langle E|\underline{\text{begin}}\ \underline{\text{new}}\ u;u:=t[u_j/x_j]_j;$ $S_h[u/x][u_\ell/y]\ \underline{\text{end}}\rangle)$.
3. $x_j \notin$ *svar*$(P_h(t,x_\ell))$. Then, clearly, $j \neq \ell$, and $u_j \notin$ *svar*$(\underline{\text{begin}}\ \underline{\text{new}}\ u;u:=t[u_j/x_j]_j;S_h[u/x][u_\ell/y]\ \underline{\text{end}})$.

By the induction hypothesis - which we may apply since $\langle k-1,\ell(\ldots)\rangle \prec \langle k,\ell(P_h(t,v))\rangle$ - we obtain that either $\sigma' = \bot$, $\bar{\sigma}' = \bot$, *or* $\sigma' \neq \bot$ $\bar{\sigma}' \neq \bot$, $(\sigma'\circ\varepsilon)|\delta = (\bar{\sigma}'\circ\bar{\varepsilon})|\delta$, and, for $j = 1,\ldots,m$, if

(*): $\sigma(e_j) = \bar{\sigma}(\bar{e}_j)$ or

(**): $u_j \in$ *init*$(\langle E|\underline{\text{begin}}\ \underline{\text{new}}\ u;u:=t[u_j/x_j]_j;S_h[u/x][u_\ell/y]\ \underline{\text{end}}\rangle)$

then (***): $\sigma'(e_j) = \bar{\sigma}'(\bar{e}_j)$. In order to complete the induction, we have to verify whether conclusion (vi) of the theorem holds for $S \equiv P_h(t,x_\ell)$, i.e. whether, for $j = 1,\ldots,m$, if ($\star$) or (#): $x_j \in$ *init*$(<E|P_h(t,x_\ell)>)$ then (***). Since, as we just saw, (**) can be inferred from (#), the proof is complete.

END 9.7.

As in chapter 6, this theorem has the following corollary which we shall apply in the next sections:

COROLLARY 9.8. Let $R \equiv <E|S>$ be a closed program, and let γ, $\bar{\gamma}$ be as in theorem 9.7.

a. If

(i) $intv(R) \subseteq \delta \subseteq dom(\varepsilon) \cap dom(\bar{\varepsilon})$, $\sigma \neq \bot$, $\bar{\sigma} \neq \bot$

(ii) $(\sigma \circ \varepsilon)|\delta = (\bar{\sigma} \circ \bar{\varepsilon})|\delta$

(iii) $\sigma' = N(S)(\bar{\gamma})(\varepsilon)(\sigma)$, $\bar{\sigma}' = N(S)(\bar{\gamma})(\bar{\varepsilon})(\bar{\sigma})$

then *either* $\sigma' = \bot$, $\bar{\sigma}' = \bot$, *or* $\sigma' \neq \bot$, $\bar{\sigma}' \neq \bot$ and

(iv) $(\sigma' \circ \varepsilon)|\delta = (\bar{\sigma}' \circ \bar{\varepsilon})|\delta$

b. If

(i) $intv(E) \cup (intv(S)\backslash\{x\}) \subseteq \delta = dom(\varepsilon)$, $\sigma \neq \bot$

(ii) $\sigma' = N(S[y/x])(\bar{\gamma})(\varepsilon \cup <y,e>)(\sigma)$

$\sigma'' = N(S[z/x])(\bar{\gamma})(\varepsilon \cup <z,e>)(\sigma)$

then *either* $\sigma' = \bot$, $\bar{\sigma}' = \bot$, *or* $\sigma' \neq \bot$, $\bar{\sigma}' \neq \bot$, and

(iii) $(\sigma' \circ \varepsilon)|\delta = (\sigma'' \circ \varepsilon)|\delta$

(iv) $\sigma'(e) = \sigma''(e)$.

PROOF. Cf. corollary 6.13. As to part b(iv), if $x \in svar(S)$, this is clear by theorem 9.7(vi). Otherwise, $x \notin svar(S)$, and, by theorem 9.5, $\sigma'(e) = \sigma(e)$, $\sigma''(e) = \sigma(e)$.

END 9.8.

Remark. Conclusion b(iv) is used (only) in the proof of theorem 9.23c.

As before, we even may replace conclusion b(iii),(iv) by $\sigma' = \sigma''$, but this needs a separate proof which is not immediate from theorem 9.7.

9.3. Correctness

In this section we are concerned with correctness of programs as introduced in section 9.2. More specifically, we shall present a definition of validity, and a proof system for partial correctness for which we prove soundness in the present section, and completeness in the next one. Much of the material to be developed is a refinement of that of section 5.5, necessitated by the addition of blocks to our language. In particular, the proof system is obtained by extending that of section 5.5 with the block rule of chapter 6, generalizing Scott's induction rule to deal with procedures with parameters, and adding two simple rules of technical nature. Also, in the definition of validity of a correctness formula we encounter problems of a similar kind as those dealt with in section 5.5 - caused by the presence of non-closed programs - and a solution continuing the ideas of that section will be proposed. Again, all programs are assumed to satisfy the initialization requirement stated in section 9.2.

As usual, our correctness considerations involve the classes of assertions Assn, of correctness formulae Form (as in chapter 6, we omit inclusions $S_1 \sqsubseteq S_2$ from this class), and of generalized correctness formulae Gfor. Syntax and semantics of assertions are as in definition 6.14; for correctness formulae we have

DEFINITION 9.9 (syntax and semantics of (generalized) correctness formulae).

a. The class of correctness formulae Form, with typical elements f,..., is defined by

$$f ::= p \mid \{p\}S\{q\} \mid f_1 \wedge f_2$$

b. The class of generalized correctness formulae Gfor, with typical elements g,..., is defined by

$$g ::= \langle E : f_1 \Rightarrow f_2 \rangle$$

(As before, " | " replaces " : ", and $\langle E|f\rangle$ is short for $\langle E|\underline{\text{true}} \Rightarrow f\rangle$.)

c. The function F: $Form \to (\Gamma \to (Env \to (\Sigma \to_s T)))$ is defined by
$F(f)(\gamma)(\varepsilon)(\sigma) = ff$ if $intv(f) \nsubseteq dom(\varepsilon)$ or $\sigma = \bot$. Otherwise

(i) $F(p)(\gamma)(\varepsilon)(\sigma) = T(p)(\varepsilon)(\sigma)$

(ii) $F(\{p\}S\{q\})(\gamma)(\varepsilon)(\sigma) =$
$\forall\sigma'[T(p)(\varepsilon)(\sigma) \wedge \sigma' = N(S)(\gamma)(\varepsilon)(\sigma) \wedge \sigma' \neq \bot \Rightarrow T(q)(\varepsilon)(\sigma')]$

(iii) $F(f_1 \wedge f_2)(\gamma)(\varepsilon)(\sigma) = F(f_1)(\gamma)(\varepsilon)(\sigma) \wedge F(f_2)(\gamma)(\varepsilon)(\sigma)$

d. The function G: $Gfor \to (\Gamma \to T)$ is defined by: let $g \equiv \langle E|f_1 \Rightarrow f_2\rangle$, with $E \equiv \langle P_i \Leftarrow B_i\rangle_{i=1}^n$. Let $\gamma \in \Gamma$, η_i, $i = 1,\ldots,n$, be as in definition 9.3, and let $\bar{\gamma} = \gamma\{\eta_i/P_i\}_{i=1}^n$. Then

$G(g)(\gamma) =$

[For all ε such that $intv(E,f_1) \subseteq dom(\varepsilon)$, all $\sigma\neq\bot[F(f_1)(\bar{\gamma})(\varepsilon)(\sigma)]$

$\Rightarrow$

For all ε such that $intv(E,f_2) \subseteq dom(\varepsilon)$, all $\sigma\neq\bot[F(f_2)(\bar{\gamma})(\varepsilon)(\sigma)]]$

END 9.9.

Remark. Compare definitions 5.24, 5.25 and 6.20.

We now present the proof system for partial correctness. The system coincides with that of section 5.5, apart from

- an obvious rule for "strengthening" formulae which is included only for technical reasons (cf. lemma 9.21); also, the weakening rule is slightly expanded
- the block rule
- a version of the induction rule adapted to the presence of parameters
- a rule which allows us to replace a statement by a congruent one.

1. $\langle E \mid f \Rightarrow \underline{true} \rangle$ (strengthening)

2. $\dfrac{\langle E \mid f_1 \Rightarrow f_2 \rangle}{\langle E \mid f_1 \wedge f_3 \Rightarrow f_2 \rangle}$ (weakening)

3. $\dfrac{\langle E \mid f_1 \Rightarrow f_2 \rangle, \langle E \mid f_2 \Rightarrow f_3 \rangle}{\langle E \mid f_1 \Rightarrow f_3 \rangle}$ (transitivity)

4. $\dfrac{\langle E \mid f \Rightarrow f_1 \rangle, \langle E \mid f \Rightarrow f_2 \rangle}{\langle E \mid f \Rightarrow f_1 \wedge f_2 \rangle}$ (collection)

5. $\langle E \mid f_1 \wedge \ldots \wedge f_n \Rightarrow f_i \rangle, \quad n \geq 1,\ 1 \leq i \leq n$ (selection)

6. $\langle E \mid \{p[t/v]\} v{:=}t \{p\} \rangle$ (assignment)

7. $\langle E \mid \{p\} S_1 \{q\} \wedge \{q\} S_2 \{r\} \Rightarrow \{p\} S_1 ; S_2 \{r\} \rangle$ (composition)

8. $\langle E \mid \{p \wedge b\} S_1 \{q\} \wedge \{p \wedge \neg b\} S_2 \{q\} \Rightarrow$
   $\{p\}\ \underline{if}\ b\ \underline{then}\ S_1\ \underline{else}\ S_2\ \underline{fi}\ \{q\} \rangle$ (conditionals)

9. $\langle E \mid \{p\} S[y/x] \{q\} \Rightarrow \{p\}\ \underline{begin}\ \underline{new}\ x; S\ \underline{end}\ \{q\} \rangle$
   provided that $y \notin \mathit{svar}(E,p,S,q)$ (blocks)

10. $\langle E \mid (p \supset p_1) \wedge \{p_1\} S \{q_1\} \wedge (q_1 \supset q) \Rightarrow \{p\} S \{q\} \rangle$ (consequence)

For the formulation of the induction rule we need two preparations:

a. We introduce the procedure constant Ω, which may syntactically appear in a statement wherever a procedure variable may appear, and which has as its meaning: $N(\Omega(t,v)) = \lambda\gamma\cdot\lambda\varepsilon\cdot\lambda\sigma\cdot\bot$, for all t,v. Ω is the "undefined procedure"; the present chapter does not use Ω as the "undefined statement", as in the previous chapters.

b. We assume the constructs $S[B_i/P_i]_{i=1}^n$ and $f[B_i/P_i]_{i=1}^n$ to be defined in the natural way. As to $S[B_i/P_i]_{i=1}^n$, all clauses are evident but for, maybe, the case $S \equiv P(t,v)$, where $P \equiv P_j$ for some j, $1 \leq j \leq n$. Then $P(t,v)[B_i/P_i]_{i=1}^n \equiv B_j(t,v)$, with $B_j(t,v)$ as in definition 9.2.

This brings us to

11. $$\frac{\langle\langle P_i \Leftarrow B_i\rangle_{i=1}^n \mid f_0 \Rightarrow f[\Omega/Q_i]_{i=1}^n,\ \langle\langle P_i \Leftarrow B_i\rangle_{i=1}^n \mid f_0 \wedge f \Rightarrow f[B_i'/Q_i]_{i=1}^n\rangle}{\langle\langle P_i \Leftarrow B_i\rangle_{i=1}^n \mid f_0 \Rightarrow f[P_i/Q_i]_{i=1}^n\rangle}$$ (induction)

where, for i = 1,...,n,

(i) $Q_i \notin \mathit{pvar}(f_0,P_1,\ldots,P_n,B_1,\ldots,B_n)$

(ii) $B_i' \equiv B_i[Q_j/P_j]_{j=1}^n$

We see that a major advantage of the device of syntactic application is that the induction rule for procedures with parameters is an immediate extension of the same rule for parameterless procedures (cf. theorem 5.37). (A version of the rule which is structured along the lines of rule 9 of section 5.5 is possible, but quite tedious to formulate, which is why we prefer the above general version.)

12. $$\frac{\langle\langle P_i \Leftarrow B_i\rangle_{i=1}^n \mid (f_1 \Rightarrow f_2)[Q_i/P_i]_{i=1}^n\rangle}{\langle\langle P_i \Leftarrow B_i\rangle_{i=1}^n \mid f_1 \Rightarrow f_2\rangle}$$ (instantiation)

where, for i = 1,...,n, $Q_i \notin \mathit{pvar}(P_1,\ldots,P_n,f_1,f_2)$

13. $\langle E \mid \{p\}S\{q_1\} \wedge \{p\}S\{q_2\} \Rightarrow \{p\}S\{q_1 \wedge q_2\}\rangle$ (conjunction)

14. $\langle E \mid \{p\}S\{p\}\rangle$ (invariance)

provided that $\mathit{intv}(p) \cap \mathit{intv}(E,S) = \emptyset$

15. $\langle E \mid \{p\}S\{q\} \Rightarrow \{p[y/x][a'/a]\}S\{q\}\rangle$ (substitution, I)

provided that $x \notin \mathit{svar}(E,S,q)$, $a \notin \mathit{avar}(E,S,q)$

16. $\langle E \mid \{p\}S\{q\} \Rightarrow$

$\{p[y/x][a'/a]\}S[y/x][a'/a]\{q[y/x][a'/a]\}\rangle$ (substitution, II)

provided that

- either $x \equiv y$, or $x \notin \mathit{svar}(E)$, $y \notin \mathit{svar}(E,S,q)$
- either $a \equiv a'$, or $a \notin \mathit{avar}(E)$, $a' \notin \mathit{avar}(E,S,q)$

17. $\langle E \mid \{p\}S\{q\} \Rightarrow \{p\}S'\{q\}\rangle$ (congruence)

provided that $S \cong S'$

We proceed with a discussion of how to define validity of a correctness formula (and soundness of an inference) in such a way that the above proof system can be shown to be sound. Just as in section 5.5, it does not work to put (*): $\models g$ iff, for all $\gamma \in \Gamma$, $\mathcal{G}(g)(\gamma)$. E.g. the invariance rule can be shown to be invalid in exactly the same way as in section 5.5. However, the situation is even worse in that a number of rules which were still valid with respect to (*) in the framework of section 5.5, are now invalid with respect to that definition. For example, this holds for the rule of consequence (and, in general, for each of the above formulae $\langle E|f_1 \Rightarrow f_2\rangle$ such that $intv(f_1) \supsetneq intv(f_2)$). The difficulty underlying this is that, in order to prove the validity of this rule, we want to argue as in the proof of lemma 6.27, which, in turn, requires the analog of lemma 6.21 allowing us, in evaluating $\mathcal{F}(f)(\bar{\gamma})(\varepsilon)(\sigma)$, to arbitrarily extend ε without affecting the outcome, as long as $intv(E,f) \subseteq dom(\varepsilon)$ remains satisfied. Now since the proof of lemma 6.21 is based on corollary 6.13a, it seems natural to formulate and prove an analog of lemma 6.21 in the present setting based on corollary 9.8a. However, this will not work, since corollary 9.8a was derived only for *closed* programs, and, just as in section 5.5, we want the rules of our proof system to be sound as well for non-closed programs. Before continuing with the developments to remedy this difficulty, we show by an example that the rule of consequence is indeed invalid with respect to definition (*), by treating the following special case: take E empty, $S \equiv P(t,v)$, $p \equiv q \equiv q_1$, and $p_1 \equiv p \wedge (x=x)$, for some $x \notin svar(p,t,v)$. We obtain

$$\langle |(p \supset p \wedge (x=x)) \wedge \{p \wedge (x=x)\}P(t,v)\{p\} \wedge (p \supset p)$$
$$\Rightarrow \{p\}P(t,v)\{p\}\rangle,$$

the validity of which is clearly equivalent with that of

$$\langle |\{p \wedge (x=x)\}P(t,v)\{p\} \Rightarrow \{p\}P(t,v)\{p\}\rangle.$$

Call the last formula g, and let γ be arbitrary. By definition 9.9,

$\mathcal{G}$(g)(γ) holds iff

For all ε such that $intv(p,t,v) \cup \{x\} \subseteq dom(\varepsilon)$, all $\sigma \neq \bot$

$$\forall\sigma'[\mathcal{T}(p \wedge (x=x))(\varepsilon)(\sigma) \wedge \sigma' = \gamma(P)(t,v)(\varepsilon)(\sigma) \wedge \sigma' \neq \bot \Rightarrow \mathcal{T}(p)(\varepsilon)(\sigma')] \tag{9.1}$$

$\Rightarrow$

For all ε such that $intv(p,t,v) \subseteq dom(\varepsilon)$, all $\sigma \neq \bot$

$$\forall\sigma''[\mathcal{T}(p)(\varepsilon)(\sigma) \wedge \sigma'' = \gamma(P)(t,v)(\varepsilon)(\sigma) \wedge \sigma'' \neq \bot \Rightarrow \mathcal{T}(p)(\varepsilon)(\sigma'')] \tag{9.2}$$

Observe that (cf. the discussion after example 2 following definition 6.22) the set of ε over which we quantify in (9.1) is properly contained in the set over which we quantify in (9.2). This allows us to construct the following counterexample to the implication (9.1) ⇒ (9.2). Let ε_0, $\sigma_0 \neq \bot$, $\sigma_1 \neq \bot$ be such that $dom(\varepsilon_0) = intv(p,t,v)$, $\mathcal{T}(p)(\varepsilon_0)(\sigma_0) = tt$, $\mathcal{T}(p)(\varepsilon_0)(\sigma_1) = ff$, and let $\gamma_0(P)$ be such that, for all $t,v,\bar{\varepsilon},\bar{\sigma}$,

1. $\gamma_0(P)(t,v)(\bar{\varepsilon})(\bar{\sigma}) = \bar{\sigma}$, if $intv(p,t,v) \subseteq dom(\bar{\varepsilon})$ and $x \in dom(\bar{\varepsilon})$
2. $\gamma_0(P)(t,v)(\bar{\varepsilon})(\bar{\sigma}) = \sigma_1$, if $intv(p,t,v) \subseteq dom(\bar{\varepsilon})$ and $x \notin dom(\bar{\varepsilon})$

We infer that (9.1) is satisfied for this choice of γ_0, whereas (9.2) is not: take $\varepsilon = \varepsilon_0$, $\sigma = \sigma_0$. Then

3. $\mathcal{T}(p)(\varepsilon_0)(\sigma_0) = tt$
4. $\sigma_1 = \gamma_0(P)(t,v)(\varepsilon_0)(\sigma_0)$ (since $x \notin dom(\varepsilon_0)$), $\sigma_1 \neq \bot$

but

5. $\mathcal{T}(p)(\varepsilon_0)(\sigma_1) = ff$.

The example of the invalidity of the rule of consequence (with respect to definition (*)) indicates that we are faced with a harder problem than that of section 5.5. It is not sufficient to restrict γ to range over a class Γ^E, such that, for $\gamma \in \Gamma^E$ and all P,t,v, γ(P)(t,v) uses no variables not in *intv*(E). Rather, it is necessary to restrict γ such that γ(P)(t,v) does not allow the construction just given, nor some further constructions invalidating other rules (the problem as exemplified by the rule of consequence is not the only one encountered in the soundness proof of the above system). However, the restrictions we are going to impose upon γ in a moment will take care of all problems simultaneously. Now which form do these restrictions take? In order to prepare the way for their - rather complicated - definition, we recall theorems 9.5 and 9.7. It will turn out that if the programs $<E|S>$ occurring in the above proof system were to satisfy these two theorems, we can indeed prove soundness of the system. As noted above, we have derived these theorems only for *closed* programs, whereas, due to the presence of the induction rule, we have to account for the possibility of encountering non-closed programs as well. Thus, what we do is to *postulate* the analogs of theorems 9.5, 9.7 for undeclared procedures, by restricting γ to range over a subset $\Gamma^E \subsetneq \Gamma$ such that, for all $\gamma \in \Gamma^E$ and P,t,v, $\gamma(P)(t,v)$ has the desired properties. Before we can give the definition of Γ^E, there is one further complication we have to deal with. Owing to the array substitutions occurring in the substitution rules (15,16), we have to generalize our previous results (theorem 9.7 and the lemma used in its proof) to also cover array substitution. First, let us introduce the notation

$$\varepsilon \cup <y_i,e_i>_{i=1}^{n} \cup <<a_j,\alpha>,e_{j,\alpha}>_{j=1,\alpha\in V_0}^{m}$$

with the obvious meaning. We now restate lemma 6.7, theorem 9.7 and lemma 6.15 (for subsequent use):

THEOREM 9.10.

a. Let $n,m \geq 0$. If

(i) $intv(s) \backslash \{x_i\}_{i=1}^{n} \backslash \{<a_j,\alpha>\}_{j=1,\alpha\in V_0}^{m} \subseteq \delta \subseteq dom(\varepsilon) \cap dom(\bar{\varepsilon})$, $\sigma \neq \bot$, $\bar{\sigma} \neq \bot$

(ii) $(\sigma\circ\varepsilon)|\delta = (\bar{\sigma}\circ\bar{\varepsilon})|\delta$

(iii) For $i = 1,\ldots,n$, either $\sigma(e_i) = \bar{\sigma}(\bar{e}_i)$, or $x_i \notin svar(s)$

For $j = 1,\ldots,m$, either, for all $\alpha \in V_0$, $\sigma(e_{j,\alpha}) = \bar{\sigma}(\bar{e}_{j,\alpha})$, or $a_j \notin avar(s)$,

then

(iv) $R(s[y_i/x_i]_i[a'_j/a_j]_j)(\varepsilon\cup\langle y_i,e_i\rangle_i\cup\langle\langle a'_j,\alpha\rangle,e_{j,\alpha}\rangle_{j,\alpha})(\sigma) =$

$R(s[z_i/x_i]_i[a''_j/a_j]_j)(\bar{\varepsilon}\cup\langle z_i,\bar{e}_i\rangle_i\cup\langle\langle a''_j,\alpha\rangle,\bar{e}_{j,\alpha}\rangle_{j,\alpha})(\bar{\sigma})$

b. Similarly for $b \in$ *Bexp*

c. Similarly for $p \in$ *Assn*

d. Let $n,m \geq 0$. Let $R \equiv \langle E|S\rangle$ be a closed program, and let $\gamma \in \Gamma$, $\bar{\gamma}$ be as usual. If

(i) $intv(E) \cup (intv(S)\backslash\{x_i\}_i\backslash\{\langle a_j,\alpha\rangle\}_{j,\alpha}) \subseteq \delta \subseteq dom(\varepsilon) \cap dom(\bar{\varepsilon})$,

$\sigma \neq \bot$, $\bar{\sigma} \neq \bot$

(ii) $(\sigma\circ\varepsilon)|\delta = (\bar{\sigma}\circ\bar{\varepsilon})|\delta$

(iii) For $i = 1,\ldots,n$, either $\sigma(e_i) = \bar{\sigma}(\bar{e}_i)$, or $x_i \in init(\langle E|S\rangle)$ or $x_i \notin svar(S)$

For $j = 1,\ldots,m$, either, for all $\alpha \in V_0$, $\sigma(e_{j,\alpha}) = \bar{\sigma}(\bar{e}_{j,\alpha})$, or $a_j \notin avar(S)$

(iv) $\sigma' = N(S[y_i/x_i]_i[a'_j/a_j]_j)(\bar{\gamma})(\varepsilon\cup\langle y_i,e_i\rangle_i\cup\langle\langle a'_j,\alpha\rangle,e_{j,\alpha}\rangle_{j,\alpha})(\sigma)$

$\bar{\sigma}' = N(S[z_i/x_i]_i[a''_j/a_j]_j)(\bar{\gamma})(\bar{\varepsilon}\cup\langle z_i,\bar{e}_i\rangle_i\cup\langle\langle a''_j,\alpha\rangle,\bar{e}_{j,\alpha}\rangle_{j,\alpha})(\bar{\sigma})$

then *either* $\sigma' = \bot$, $\bar{\sigma}' = \bot$, *or* $\sigma' \neq \bot$, $\bar{\sigma}' \neq \bot$, and

(v) $(\sigma'\circ\varepsilon)|\delta = (\bar{\sigma}'\circ\bar{\varepsilon})|\delta$

(vi) For $i = 1,\ldots,n$, if $\sigma(e_i) = \bar{\sigma}(\bar{e}_i)$ or $x_i \in init(\langle E|S\rangle)$ then $\sigma'(e_i) = \bar{\sigma}'(\bar{e}_i)$

For $j = 1,\ldots,m$, if, for all $\alpha \in V_0$, $\sigma(e_{j,\alpha}) = \bar{\sigma}(\bar{e}_{j,\alpha})$, then for all $\alpha \in V_0$, $\sigma'(e_{j,\alpha}) = \bar{\sigma}'(\bar{e}_{j,\alpha})$.

PROOF. Follows by a straightforward extension of the proofs of lemmas 6.7, 6.15 and theorem 9.7 with array substitution. Details are left to the reader.

END 9.10.

We now give the definition of Γ^E which will ensure that theorems 9.5 and 9.10d hold for arbitrary (i.e. closed or non-closed) programs, provided $\gamma \in \Gamma^E$ is satisfied:

DEFINITION 9.11 (Γ^E).

Γ^E is the set of all $\gamma \in \Gamma$ which satisfy the following two postulates for each P,t,v,:

a. If

(i) $intv(E,t,v) \subseteq dom(\varepsilon)$

(ii) $\gamma(P)(t,v)(\varepsilon)(\sigma) = \sigma', \ \sigma' \neq \perp$

then

(iii) $(\sigma' \circ \varepsilon) | (dom(\varepsilon) \backslash intv(E,t,v)) =$
$(\sigma \circ \varepsilon) | (dom(\varepsilon) \backslash intv(E,t,v))$

b. Let n,m ≥ 0. If

(i) $intv(E) \cup (intv(t,v) \backslash \{x_i\} \backslash \{<a_j,\alpha>\}_{j,\alpha}) \subseteq \delta \subseteq dom(\varepsilon) \cap dom(\bar{\varepsilon})$,
$\sigma \neq \perp, \ \bar{\sigma} \neq \perp$

(ii) $(\sigma \circ \varepsilon) | \delta = (\bar{\sigma} \circ \bar{\varepsilon}) | \delta$

(iii) For i = 1,...,n, either $\sigma(e_i) = \bar{\sigma}(\bar{e}_i)$, or $x_i \notin svar(t,v)$
For j = 1,...,m, either, for all $\alpha \in V_0$, $\sigma(e_{j,\alpha}) = \bar{\sigma}(\bar{e}_{j,\alpha})$,
or $a_j \notin avar(t,v)$

(iv) $\sigma' = \gamma(P)((t,v)[y_i/x_i]_i[a'_j/a_j]_j)(\varepsilon \cup <y_i,e_i>_i$
$\cup <<a'_j,\alpha>,e_{j,\alpha}>_{j,\alpha})(\sigma)$
$\bar{\sigma}' = \gamma(P)((t,v)[z_i/x_i]_i[a''_j/a_j]_j)(\bar{\varepsilon} \cup <z_i,\bar{e}_i>_i$
$\cup <<a''_j,\alpha>,\bar{e}_{j,\alpha}>_{j,\alpha})(\bar{\sigma})$

then *either* $\sigma' = \perp$, $\bar{\sigma}' = \perp$, *or* $\sigma' \neq \perp$, $\bar{\sigma}' \neq \perp$, and

(v) $(\sigma' \circ \varepsilon) | \delta = (\bar{\sigma}' \circ \bar{\varepsilon}) | \delta$

(vi) For i = 1,...,n, if $\sigma(e_i) = \bar{\sigma}(\bar{e}_i)$ then $\sigma'(e_i) = \bar{\sigma}'(\bar{e}_i)$
For j = 1,...,m, if, for all $\alpha \in V_0$, $\sigma(e_{j,\alpha}) = \bar{\sigma}(\bar{e}_{j,\alpha})$, then,

for all $\alpha \in V_0$, $\sigma'(e_{j,\alpha}) = \bar{\sigma}'(\bar{e}_{j,\alpha})$.

END 9.11.

It is not difficult to prove that theorems 9.5, 9.10d hold for *all* programs $\langle E|S\rangle$ (whether closed or not), provided that we restrict γ to range over Γ^E as in definition 9.11. In fact, the proofs of theorem 9.5, 9.10d as given before may be taken over literally, but for an extension with an additional clause dealing with undeclared procedure variables which case is taken care of by definition 9.11 (also using the fact that, if P is not declared in E, then *init*($\langle E|P(t,v)\rangle$) = $\emptyset$ by definition 9.6). Accordingly, we now have corollary 9.8 available for *arbitrary* programs. In the next theorem (9.12) we repeat theorem 9.5 and this corollary. In the soundness proof to be given presently, we shall only appeal to theorem 9.12; the complications of theorem 9.10d and definition 9.11 may be forgotten for the remainder of this section.

THEOREM 9.12. Let $R \equiv \langle E|S\rangle$ be an arbitrary program with $E \equiv \langle P_h \Leftarrow B_h\rangle_{h=1}^{\ell}$, and let $\gamma \in \Gamma^E$, $\bar{\gamma} = \gamma\{\eta_h/P_h\}_{h=1}^{\ell}$, with η_h, $h = 1,\dots,\ell$, as usual. Then

a. If

(i) $intv(R) \subseteq dom(\varepsilon)$

(ii) $\sigma' = N(S)(\bar{\gamma})(\varepsilon)(\sigma)$, $\sigma' \neq \bot$

then

(iii) $(\sigma'\circ\varepsilon)|(dom(\varepsilon)\backslash intv(R)) =$
$(\sigma\circ\varepsilon)|(dom(\varepsilon)\backslash intv(R))$

b. If

(i) $intv(R) \subseteq \delta \subseteq dom(\varepsilon) \cap dom(\bar{\varepsilon})$, $\sigma \neq \bot$, $\bar{\sigma} \neq \bot$

(ii) $(\sigma\circ\varepsilon)|\delta = (\bar{\sigma}\circ\bar{\varepsilon})|\delta$

(iii) $\sigma' = N(S)(\bar{\gamma})(\varepsilon)(\sigma)$, $\bar{\sigma}' = N(S)(\bar{\gamma})(\bar{\varepsilon})(\bar{\sigma})$

then *either* $\sigma' = \bot$, $\bar{\sigma}' = \bot$, *or* $\sigma' \neq \bot$, $\bar{\sigma}' \neq \bot$, and

(iv) $(\sigma'\circ\varepsilon)|\delta = (\bar{\sigma}'\circ\bar{\varepsilon})|\delta$

c. Let m = 0 or m = 1. If

(i) $intv(E) \cup (intv(S)\backslash\{x\}\backslash\{<a_j,\alpha>\}^m_{j=1,\alpha\in V_0}) \subseteq \delta = dom(\varepsilon),\ \sigma \neq \bot$

(ii) $\sigma' = N(S[y/x][a'_j/a_j]_j)(\bar{\gamma})(\varepsilon\cup<y,e>\cup<<a'_j,\alpha>,e_{j,\alpha}>_{j,\alpha})(\sigma)$

$\sigma'' = N(S[z/x][a''_j/a_j]_j)(\bar{\gamma})(\varepsilon\cup<z,e>\cup<<a''_j,\alpha>,e_{j,\alpha}>_{j,\alpha})(\sigma)$

then *either* $\sigma' = \bot$, $\sigma'' = \bot$, *or* $\sigma' \neq \bot$, $\sigma'' \neq \bot$, and

(iii) $(\sigma'\circ\varepsilon)|\delta = (\sigma''\circ\varepsilon)|\delta$.

PROOF. By the argument preceding the theorem.

END 9.12.

Remark. As to part c of the theorem, the case m = 0 is used to prove soundness of the block rule, and the case m = 1 to prove soundness of substitution rule II.

The remainder of this section is devoted to the soundness proof for the system of rules 1 to 17. First, for completeness' sake, we give

DEFINITION 9.13 (validity and soundness).

a. A correctness formula $g \equiv <E|f_1 \Rightarrow f_2>$ is called *valid* ($\models g$) whenever, for all $\gamma \in \Gamma^E$, $G(g)(\gamma)$ holds.

b. An inference $\frac{g_1,\ldots,g_n}{g}$ is called *sound* whenever validity of each of g_i, i = 1,...,n, implies validity of g.

END 9.13.

A major part of the soundness proof follows by arguments encountered already in either section 5.5 or section 6.3. In particular, the following analog of lemma 6.21 which played a crucial part in section 6.3, will be needed:

LEMMA 9.14. Let $\gamma \in \Gamma^E$, $\bar{\gamma}$ as usual. If

(i) $intv(E,f) \subseteq \delta \subseteq dom(\varepsilon) \cap dom(\bar{\varepsilon})$, $\sigma \neq \bot$, $\bar{\sigma} \neq \bot$

(ii) $(\sigma \circ \varepsilon)|\delta = (\bar{\sigma} \circ \bar{\varepsilon})|\delta$

then

(iii) $F(f)(\bar{\gamma})(\varepsilon)(\sigma) = F(f)(\bar{\gamma})(\bar{\varepsilon})(\bar{\sigma})$.

PROOF. Similar to the proof of lemma 6.21, but now based on theorem 9.10c and theorem 9.12b.
END 9.14.

We now first collect all rules the soundness proof of which requires no arguments beyond those encountered previously:

LEMMA 9.15.

a. The correctness formulae 1,5,6,7,8,9,10,13,17 of the above proof system are valid.
b. The inferences 2,3,4,11,12 of the above proof system are sound.

PROOF. For rules 1,3,4 and 13, the desired result is obvious from the definitions. For rules 2 and 5 we use the same trick about extending environments (now based on lemma 9.14) as encountered in the proof of lemma 6.24. Rules 6,7,8,9,10 follow by a straightforward adaptation of the arguments used in the proofs of lemma 6.23 to 6.27 (for rule 9, use theorem 9.12c with m = 0). For rules 11 and 12 compare theorem 5.37 and lemma 5.38. Finally, rule 17 is immediate by lemma 9.4.
END 9.15.

There remains the proof of the soundness of rules 14,15 and 16. First we deal with the invariance rule:

LEMMA 9.16. $\models$ <E|{p}S{p}>, provided $intv(p) \cap intv(E,S) = \emptyset$.

PROOF. Let $\gamma \in \Gamma^E$, $\bar{\gamma}$ as usual. We have to show that, if $intv(p) \cap intv(E,S) = \emptyset$, then

For all ε such that *intv*(E,p,S) $\subseteq$ dom(ε), all $\sigma \neq \bot$

$\forall\sigma'[T(p)(\varepsilon)(\sigma) \wedge \sigma' = N(S)(\bar{\gamma})(\varepsilon)(\sigma) \wedge \sigma' \neq \bot \Rightarrow T(p)(\varepsilon)(\sigma')]$

Choose ε, $\sigma \neq \bot$, σ' such that

1. *intv*(E,p,S) $\subseteq$ dom(ε)
2. $T(p)(\varepsilon)(\sigma)$
3. $\sigma' = N(S)(\bar{\gamma})(\varepsilon)(\sigma)$, $\sigma' \neq \bot$.

To show

4. $T(p)(\varepsilon)(\sigma')$.

By theorem 9.12a, for all $\xi \in$ dom(ε)*intv*(E,S), we have that $\sigma'(\varepsilon(\xi))= \sigma(\varepsilon(\xi))$. By the assumption on *intv*(p) this means, in particular, that, for all $\xi \in$ *intv*(p), $\sigma'(\varepsilon(\xi)) = \sigma(\varepsilon(\xi))$. Thus, by theorem 9.10c (with $n = m = 0$, $\bar{\varepsilon} = \varepsilon$, $\bar{\sigma} = \sigma'$, δ = dom(ε)) we obtain that $T(p)(\varepsilon)(\sigma) = T(p)(\varepsilon)(\sigma')$, and we see that 4 follows from 2.
END 9.16.

Next, we prove the validity of the first substitution rule. The proof of this requires an extension of lemma 6.18 with

LEMMA 9.17. If *intv*(p,s,v) $\cup$ $\{\langle a,\alpha\rangle,\langle a',\alpha\rangle\}_{\alpha\in V_0} \subseteq$ dom(ε) then

$$T(p[s/v][a'/a])(\varepsilon)(\sigma) =$$
$$T(p)(\varepsilon)(\sigma\{R(s)(\varepsilon)(\sigma)/L(v)(\varepsilon)(\sigma)\}\{\sigma(\varepsilon(a',\alpha))/\varepsilon(a,\alpha)\}_{\alpha})$$

PROOF. Left to the reader. (Note that the proof requires corresponding extensions to lemmas 6.9, 6.17.)
END 9.17.

We now prove

LEMMA 9.18. $\models$ $\langle E|\{p\}S\{q\} \Rightarrow \{p[y/x][a'/a]\}S\{q\}\rangle$, provided that $x \notin$ *svar*(E,S,q), $a \notin$ *avar*(E,S,q).

PROOF. Let $\gamma \in \Gamma^E$, $\bar{\gamma}$ as usual. We have to show that, under the given assumptions,

For all ε such that $intv(E,p,S,q) \subseteq dom(\varepsilon)$, all $\sigma \neq \bot$

$$\forall\sigma'[T(p)(\varepsilon)(\sigma) \wedge \sigma' = N(S)(\bar{\gamma})(\varepsilon)(\sigma) \wedge \sigma' \neq \bot \Rightarrow T(q)(\varepsilon)(\sigma')] \tag{9.3}$$

$\Rightarrow$

For all ε such that $intv(E,p[y/x][a'/a],S,q) \subseteq dom(\varepsilon)$, all $\sigma \neq \bot$

$$\forall\sigma''[T(p[y/x][a'/a])(\varepsilon)(\sigma) \wedge \sigma'' = N(S)(\bar{\gamma})(\varepsilon)(\sigma) \wedge \sigma'' \neq \bot \Rightarrow T(q)(\varepsilon)(\sigma'')] \tag{9.4}$$

Choose some ε, $\sigma \neq \bot$, σ'' such that

1. $intv(E,p[y/x][a'/a],S,q) \subseteq dom(\varepsilon)$
2. $T(p[y/x][a'/a])(\varepsilon)(\sigma)$
3. $\sigma'' = N(S)(\bar{\gamma})(\varepsilon)(\sigma)$, $\sigma'' \neq \bot$.

To show

4. $T(q)(\varepsilon)(\sigma'')$.

By lemma 9.14, we may assume, without loss of generality, that $intv(E,p,S,q) \cup \{x,y\} \cup \{\langle a,\alpha\rangle,\langle a',\alpha\rangle\}_\alpha \subseteq dom(\varepsilon)$.

By 2 and lemma 9.17

5. $T(p)(\varepsilon)(\sigma_1)$, where $\sigma_1 = \sigma\{\sigma(\varepsilon(y))/\varepsilon(x)\}\{\sigma(\varepsilon(a',\alpha))/\varepsilon(a,\alpha)\}_\alpha$.

Let

6. $\sigma' = N(s)(\bar{\gamma})(\varepsilon)(\sigma_1)$.

Since x, $\langle a,\alpha\rangle_\alpha \in dom(\varepsilon)$, we may write $\varepsilon = \varepsilon_1 \cup \langle x,e\rangle \cup \langle\langle a,\alpha\rangle,e_\alpha\rangle_\alpha$, for some ε_1,e,e_α. Let $\delta = dom(\varepsilon_1)$. Since $x \notin svar(E,S)$, $a \notin avar(E,S)$, we have that $intv(E,S) \subseteq \delta \subseteq dom(\varepsilon)$. Also, $(\sigma\circ\varepsilon)|\delta = (\sigma_1\circ\varepsilon)|\delta$, by the definition of σ_1. Thus, by theorem 9.12b, we obtain that $\sigma' \neq \bot$ (since $\sigma'' \neq \bot$), and (*): $(\sigma''\circ\varepsilon)|\delta = (\sigma'\circ\varepsilon)|\delta$. By 5, 6 and (9.3), $T(q)(\varepsilon)(\sigma')$. Since $x \notin svar(q)$, $a \notin avar(q)$, we have (**): $intv(q) \subseteq \delta$. Finally, from (*), (**), $T(q)(\varepsilon)(\sigma')$ and theorem 9.10c, we obtain that $T(q)(\varepsilon)(\sigma'')$, as was to be shown.

The last validity result is

<u>LEMMA 9.19.</u>

$$\models \langle E|\{p\}S\{q\} \Rightarrow \{p[y/x][a'/a]\}S[y/x][a'/a]\{q[y/x][a'/a]\}\rangle,$$

provided that

- either $x \equiv y$, or $x \notin svar(E)$, $y \notin svar(E,S,q)$
- either $a \equiv a'$, or $a \notin avar(E)$, $a' \notin avar(E,S,q)$.

PROOF. We first prove the desired result under the additional assumption that $y \notin svar(p)$, $a' \notin avar(p)$, and, at the end of the proof, show how this assumption may be dropped again. Let $\gamma \in \Gamma^E$, $\bar{\gamma}$ be as usual. We show that, under the given assumptions (9.3) ⇒ (9.5), with

$$\begin{aligned}&\text{For all } \varepsilon \text{ such that } intv(E,(p,S,q)[y/x][a'/a]) \subseteq \mathrm{dom}(\varepsilon), \text{ all } \sigma \neq \bot\\ &\forall\sigma''[T(p[y/x][a'/a])(\varepsilon)(\sigma) \wedge \sigma'' = N(S[y/x][a'/a])(\bar{\gamma})(\varepsilon)(\sigma) \wedge \sigma'' \neq \bot\\ &\quad \Rightarrow T(q[y/x][a'/a])(\varepsilon)(\sigma'')] \qquad (9.5)\end{aligned}$$

Choose ε such that

1. $intv(E,(p,S,q)[y/x][a'/a]) \subseteq \mathrm{dom}(\varepsilon)$.

Without loss of generality (lemma 9.14) we may assume that ε is of the form $\varepsilon = \varepsilon_1 \cup \langle y,e\rangle \cup \langle\langle a',\alpha\rangle,e_\alpha\rangle_\alpha$, for some $\varepsilon_1, e, e_\alpha$, and such that, for $\delta = \mathrm{dom}(\varepsilon_1)$, $x \notin \delta$, $\langle a,\alpha\rangle_\alpha \not\subseteq \delta$. (Note that this moreover uses that $x \notin svar(E)$, $a \notin avar(E)$.)

Let $\sigma \neq \bot$, σ'' be such that

2. $T(p[y/x][a'/a])(\varepsilon_1 \cup \langle y,e\rangle \cup \langle\langle a',\alpha\rangle,e_\alpha\rangle_\alpha)(\sigma)$
3. $\sigma'' = N(S[y/x][a'/a])(\bar{\gamma})(\varepsilon_1 \cup \langle y,e\rangle \cup \langle\langle a',\alpha\rangle,e_\alpha\rangle_\alpha)(\sigma)$, $\sigma'' \neq \bot$

To show

4. $T(q[y/x][a'/a])(\varepsilon_1 \cup \langle y,e\rangle \cup \langle\langle a',\alpha\rangle,e_\alpha\rangle_\alpha)(\sigma'')$

From 2 and theorem 9.10c (with n=m=1, $z \equiv x$, $a'' \equiv a$, $\varepsilon = \bar{\varepsilon} = \varepsilon_1$, $\sigma = \bar{\sigma}$, $e = \bar{e}$, $e_\alpha = \bar{e}_\alpha$) which we may apply since $y \notin intv(p)$, $\langle a',\alpha\rangle_\alpha \not\subseteq intv(p)$, we obtain

5. $T(p)(\varepsilon_1 \cup \langle x,e\rangle \cup \langle\langle a,\alpha\rangle,e_\alpha\rangle_\alpha)(\sigma)$.

Now let

6. $\sigma' = N(S)(\bar{\gamma})(\varepsilon_1 \cup \langle x,e\rangle \cup \langle\langle a,\alpha\rangle,e_\alpha\rangle_\alpha)(\sigma)$.

From 3 and theorem 9.12c (with m=1, $z \equiv x$, $a'' \equiv a$ etc.) which we may apply since $y \notin intv(E,S)$, $\langle a',\alpha\rangle_\alpha \not\subseteq intv(E,S)$, we obtain $\sigma' \neq \bot$ (since $\sigma'' \neq \bot$), and

7. $(\sigma''\circ\varepsilon_1)|\delta = (\sigma'\circ\varepsilon_1)|\delta$.

Thus, from 5,6 and (9.3),

8. $\mathcal{T}(q)(\varepsilon_1 \cup \langle x,e\rangle \cup \langle\langle a,\alpha\rangle,e_\alpha\rangle_\alpha)(\sigma')$

Since $y \notin$ *intv*(q), $\langle a',\alpha\rangle_\alpha \notin$ *intv*(q), we infer from this, using the same argument as the one just applied to p, that 4 indeed holds. This completes the proof of (*): $\models \langle E|\{p\}S\{q\} \Rightarrow \{p[y/x][a'/a]\}S[y/x][a'/a]\{q[y/x][a'/a]\}\rangle$, for the case $x \notin$ *svar*(E), $a \notin$ *avar*(E), $y \notin$ *svar*(E,p,S,q), $a' \notin$ *avar*(E,p,S,q). We next show how the assumptions $y \notin$ *svar*(p), $a' \notin$ *avar*(p), may be dropped. From now on we consider only simple-variable-substitution, leaving the treatment of the completely analogous array-variable-substitution to the reader. First, by lemma 9.18, $\models \langle E|\{p\}S\{q\} \Rightarrow \{p[y'/y]\}S\{q\}\rangle$, where y' is a completely fresh simple variable. Next, by (*), $\models \langle E|\{p[y'/y]\}S\{q\} \Rightarrow \{p[y'/y][y/x]\}S[y/x]\{q[y/x]\}\rangle$ follows, since $y \notin$ *svar*(p[y'/y]). Furthermore, again by lemma 9.18, $\models \langle E|\{p[y'/y][y/x]\}S[y/x]\{q[y/x]\} \Rightarrow \{p[y'/y][y/x][y/y']\}S[y/x]\{q[y/x]\}\rangle$ holds, since $y' \notin$ *svar*(E,S[y/x], q[y/x]). Combining these results with $\models \langle E|p[y'/y][y/x][y/y'] = p[y/x]\rangle$ and the rules of consequence and transitivity then yields the desired conclusion.

END 9.19.

With the last lemma we have concluded our list of validity and soundness results. Altogether, we have established:

THEOREM 9.20 (soundness theorem).

The proof system consisting of rules 1 to 17 is sound.

PROOF. By lemmas 9.15, 9.16, 9.18 and 9.19.

END 9.20.

Thus, we have achieved the goal of this section.

9.4. Completeness

We present a completeness proof for the proof system introduced in section 9.3 for the restricted case that E consists of one procedure declaration only, using a version of the induction rule adapted to this situation. The proof of the general case is, in principle, a straightforward extension of the argument to be given below, but involves a rather heavy indexing machinery on the occurrences of procedure calls in E and S, and we prefer not to obscure the main line of thought of the already intricate proof of the restricted case by this additional complexity. The structure of the proof is a refinement of that of section 5.5. Complications are caused by the presence of parameters, dealt with, if we may say so, by stretching the syntactic application technique to its limits (cf. lemma 9.26). The section concludes with an extended example of a partial correctness proof using direct means, i.e. without recourse to the general strategy of the completeness proof.

Let Ax consist of all formulae $\langle E|p\rangle$, such that $\models \langle E|p\rangle$, together with the correctness formulae 1,5,6,7,8,9,10,13,14,15,16,17, and let Pr consist of the inferences 2,3,4,11' (11' is a special case of the induction rule, and will be presented shortly), 12. As usual $\vdash_{\mathit{Ax},\mathit{Pr}}$ will be abbreviated to $\vdash$. We begin with a very simple lemma:

<u>LEMMA 9.21</u>.

a. If $\vdash \langle E|f_1 \Rightarrow f_2\rangle$ and $\vdash \langle E|f_3 \Rightarrow f_4\rangle$, then $\vdash \langle E|f_1 \wedge f_3 \Rightarrow f_2 \wedge f_4\rangle$

b. If $\vdash \langle E|f\rangle$, then $\vdash \langle E|f_1 \Rightarrow f\rangle$.

<u>PROOF</u>.

a. If $\vdash \langle E|f_1 \Rightarrow f_2\rangle$, then $\vdash \langle E|f_1 \wedge f_3 \Rightarrow f_2\rangle$, by weakening. Similarly, $\vdash \langle E|f_1 \wedge f_3 \Rightarrow f_4\rangle$, and the desired result follows by the collection rule.

b. If $\vdash \langle E|f\rangle$, then $\vdash \langle E|\underline{\mathrm{true}} \Rightarrow f\rangle$ by definition. Furthermore, $\vdash \langle E|f_1 \Rightarrow \underline{\mathrm{true}}\rangle$ by strengthening, and the desired result follows by the transitivity rule.

END 9.21.

The next lemma is the counterpart of lemma 6.29, adapted to the presence of procedures:

LEMMA 9.22.

a. $\models$ <E|{p} if b then S_1 else S_2 fi {q} $\Rightarrow$ {p$\wedge$b}S_1{q} $\wedge$ {p$\wedge\neg$b}S_2{q}>

b. $\models$ <E|{p} begin new x;S end {q} $\Rightarrow$ {p}S[y/x]{q}>, provided $y \notin$ *svar*(E,p,S,q).

PROOF. Part a is obvious. For part b, we argue as in the proof of lemma 6.29b, replacing an appeal to theorem 6.12 by one to theorem 9.10d (with n=1, m=0, $\varepsilon=\bar{\varepsilon}$, $\sigma=\bar{\sigma}$).

END 9.22.

Just as in the completeness proof of sections 3.6 and 5.5, we need an expressibility result. Weakest preconditions playing no role in the proof, we consider only strongest postconditions. We recall from chapter 6 that there are two ways of introducing strongest postconditions, viz. by a *syntactic*, and by a *semantic* characterization. It is convenient to start with the latter, and, accordingly, we use the following

PROPOSITION. For each assertion p and closed program R there exists an assertion r such that *intv*(r) $\subseteq$ *intv*(p,R) and, moreover

$$\text{For all } \varepsilon \text{ such that } intv(p,R) \subseteq \delta \overset{df.}{=} dom(\varepsilon), \text{ all } \sigma \neq \perp$$
$$T(r)(\varepsilon)(\sigma) = \exists\sigma'[T(p)(\varepsilon)(\sigma') \wedge (\sigma\circ\varepsilon)|\delta = (M(R)(\gamma)(\varepsilon)(\sigma')\circ\varepsilon)|\delta] \tag{9.6}$$

where γ is arbitrary.

END.

Remarks.

1. Recall that, for R closed, $M(R)(\gamma)$ does not depend on γ.

2. An assertion r satisfying $intv(r) \subseteq intv(p,R)$ and (9.6) will be denoted by {p}R. (Note that we actually have a slight abuse of language here, in that (9.6) does not determine r uniquely as a syntactic object.)
3. Compare definition 6.34 and lemma 6.36.

The following lemma shows that {p}R satisfies a number of familiar properties, viz.

- it also expresses the syntactic strongest postcondition
- it can be used to express intermediate assertions
- it is preserved by substitution of a fresh simple variable.

LEMMA 9.23.

a. Let $R \equiv \langle E|S\rangle$ be closed. For all p,q

$$\models \langle E|\{p\}S\{q\}\rangle \quad \text{iff} \quad \models \langle E|(\{p\}R) \supset q\rangle$$

b. Let $R \equiv \langle E|S_1;S_2\rangle$ be closed. For all p,q there exists r such that

$$\models \langle E|\{p\}S_1;S_2\{q\}\rangle \text{ iff } \models \langle E|\{p\}S_1\{r\} \wedge \{r\}S_2\{q\}\rangle$$

c. Let $R \equiv \langle E|S\rangle$ be closed, let $x \notin svar(E)$ and $y \notin svar(E,p,S)$. Then

$$\models \langle E|(\{p\}R)[y/x] = \{p[y/x]\}\langle E|S[y/x]\rangle\rangle.$$

PROOF.

a. By the definition of $\models \langle E|\{p\}S\{q\}\rangle$ and by (9.6), it is sufficient to prove the following equivalence (cf. lemma 6.33):

$$\text{For all } \varepsilon \text{ such that } intv(E,p,S,q) \subseteq \text{dom}(\varepsilon), \text{ all } \sigma \neq \bot$$
$$\exists\sigma'[\mathcal{T}(p)(\varepsilon)(\sigma') \wedge \sigma = \mathcal{N}(S)(\bar{\gamma})(\varepsilon)(\sigma')] \Rightarrow \mathcal{T}(q)(\varepsilon)(\sigma)$$
$$\Longleftrightarrow$$
$$\text{For all } \varepsilon \text{ such that } intv(E,p,S,q) \subseteq \delta \overset{\text{df.}}{=} \text{dom}(\varepsilon), \text{ all } \sigma \neq \bot$$
$$\exists\sigma''[\mathcal{T}(p)(\varepsilon)(\sigma'') \wedge (\sigma\circ\varepsilon)|\delta = (\mathcal{N}(S)(\bar{\gamma})(\varepsilon)(\sigma'')\circ\varepsilon)|\delta] \Rightarrow \mathcal{T}(q)(\varepsilon)(\sigma)$$

where γ is arbitrary and $\bar{\gamma}$ as usual. Now this is shown just as in the proof of lemma 6.33.

b. " $\Leftarrow$ " is obvious. For " $\Rightarrow$ ", assume (*): $\models$ $<E|\{p\}S_1;S_2\{q\}>$, and take $r \equiv \{p\}<E|S_1>$. Clearly, $\models$ $<E|\{p\}S_1\{\{p\}<E|S_1>\}>$. There remains the proof of $\models$ $<E|\{\{p\}<E|S_1>\}S_2\{q\}>$. By (*) and (9.6), also using some familiar manipulations with quantifiers, we have to show that (for γ, $\bar{\gamma}$ as usual)

$$\begin{array}{l}\text{For all } \varepsilon \text{ such that } intv(E,p,S_1,S_2,q) \subseteq dom(\varepsilon), \text{ all } \sigma \neq \bot \\ \forall\sigma',\sigma''[T(p)(\varepsilon)(\sigma) \wedge \sigma' = N(S_1)(\bar{\gamma})(\varepsilon)(\sigma) \wedge \sigma'' = \\ \qquad N(S_2)(\bar{\gamma})(\varepsilon)(\sigma') \wedge \sigma'' \neq \bot \Rightarrow T(q)(\varepsilon)(\sigma'')]\end{array}$$

$$\Rightarrow$$

$$\begin{array}{l}\text{For all } \varepsilon \text{ such that } intv(E,p,S_1,S_2,q) \subseteq \delta \overset{df.}{=} dom(\varepsilon), \text{ all } \sigma \neq \bot \\ \forall\bar{\sigma},\bar{\bar{\sigma}}[T(p)(\varepsilon)(\sigma) \wedge (\bar{\sigma}\circ\varepsilon)|\delta = (N(S_1)(\bar{\gamma})(\varepsilon)(\sigma)\circ\varepsilon)|\delta \wedge \\ \qquad \bar{\bar{\sigma}} = N(S_2)(\bar{\gamma})(\varepsilon)(\bar{\sigma}) \wedge \bar{\bar{\sigma}} \neq \bot \Rightarrow T(q)(\varepsilon)(\bar{\bar{\sigma}})]\end{array}$$

Since, by theorem 9.12b, if $(\bar{\sigma}\circ\varepsilon)|\delta = (\sigma'\circ\varepsilon)|\delta$ then $(\bar{\bar{\sigma}}\circ\varepsilon)|\delta = (\sigma''\circ\varepsilon)|\delta$, the desired result is immediate from theorem 9.10c.

c. We have to show that, if r satisfies (9.6) and $\bar{r}$ is an assertion satisfying $intv(\bar{r}) \subseteq intv(E,p[y/x],S[y/x])$ and

$$\begin{array}{l}\text{For all } \varepsilon \text{ such that } intv(E,p[y/x],S[y/x]) \subseteq \delta \overset{df.}{=} dom(\varepsilon), \text{ all } \sigma\neq\bot \\ T(\bar{r})(\varepsilon)(\sigma) = \exists\sigma''[T(p[y/x])(\varepsilon)(\sigma'') \wedge \\ \qquad (\sigma\circ\varepsilon)|\delta = (N(S[y/x])(\bar{\gamma})(\varepsilon)(\sigma'')\circ\varepsilon)|\delta]\end{array} \tag{9.7}$$

where $\bar{\gamma}$ is as usual, then, for all ε such that (**): $intv(E,r[y/x],\bar{r}) \subseteq dom(\varepsilon)$, all $\sigma \neq \bot$, $T(r[y/x])(\varepsilon)(\sigma) = T(\bar{r})(\varepsilon)(\sigma)$.

Choose ε satisfying (**). Without loss of generality we may assume that ε is of the form $\varepsilon_1 \cup <y,e>$, for some ε_1, e with $x \notin dom(\varepsilon_1)$ (which is possible since $x \notin svar(E) \cup (svar(r[y/x],\bar{r})\setminus\{y\})$). Let $\delta_1 \overset{df.}{=} dom(\varepsilon_1)$. Note that $intv(E) \subseteq \delta_1$, $intv(r) \subseteq \delta_1 \cup \{x\}$ (since $intv(r[y/x]) \subseteq \delta_1 \cup \{y\}$ and $y \notin svar(r)\setminus\{x\}$), and $intv(\bar{r}) \subseteq \delta_1 \cup \{y\}$ (by (**))). Let $\bar{\varepsilon}_1$ be an extension of ε_1 such that $intv(E,p[y/x],S[y/x]) \subseteq dom(\bar{\varepsilon}_1 \cup <y,e>)$, with $x \notin dom(\bar{\varepsilon}_1)$. Let

$\bar{\delta}_1 \stackrel{\text{df.}}{=} dom(\bar{\varepsilon}_1)$. Note that $intv(E) \cup (intv(p,S)\backslash\{x\}) \subseteq \bar{\delta}_1$. Now

$T(\bar{r})(\varepsilon_1 \cup <y,e>)(\sigma) = T(\bar{r})(\bar{\varepsilon}_1 \cup <y,e>)(\sigma) =$ (by (9.7))

$\exists\sigma''[T(p[y/x])(\bar{\varepsilon}_1 \cup <y,e>)(\sigma'') \wedge (\sigma \circ (\bar{\varepsilon}_1 \cup <y,e>))|(\bar{\delta}_1 \cup \{y\}) =$

$(N(S[y/x])(\bar{\gamma})(\bar{\varepsilon}_1 \cup <y,e>)(\sigma'') \circ (\bar{\varepsilon}_1 \cup <y,e>))|(\bar{\delta}_1 \cup \{y\})] =$

(corollary 9.8b (iii,(iv), theorem 9.10c)

$\exists\sigma''[T(p)(\bar{\varepsilon}_1 \cup <x,e>)(\sigma'') \cup (\sigma \circ (\bar{\varepsilon}_1 \cup <x,e>))|(\bar{\delta}_1 \cup \{x\}) =$

$(N(S)(\bar{\gamma})(\bar{\varepsilon}_1 \cup <x,e>)(\sigma'') \circ (\bar{\varepsilon}_1 \cup <x,e>))|(\bar{\delta}_1 \cup \{x\})] =$ (by 9.6))

$T(r)(\bar{\varepsilon}_1 \cup <x,e>)(\sigma) = T(r)(\varepsilon_1 \cup <x,e>)(\sigma) = T(r[y/x])(\varepsilon_1 \cup <y,e>)(\sigma)$.

END 9.23.

From now on - till the end of the completeness proof - we assume that $E \equiv P \Leftarrow B$. We can then specialize the induction rule 11 to rule 11':

$$11'.\ \frac{<P \Leftarrow B|\{p_1\}Q(t_1,v_1)\{q_1\} \wedge\ldots\wedge \{p_m\}Q(t_m,v_m)\{q_m\} \Rightarrow \{p_1\}B'(t_1,v_1)\{q_1\}\wedge\ldots\wedge \{p_m\}B'(t_m,v_m)\{q_m\}>}{<P \Leftarrow B|\{p_1\}P(t_1,v_1)\{q_1\} \wedge\ldots\wedge \{p_m\}P(t_m,v_m)\{q_m\}>}$$

where $m \geq 1$, $Q \notin pvar(P,B)$, and $B' \equiv B[Q/P]$.

The soundness of this rule follows straightforwardly from that of rule 11.

We now proceed with the proof that the proof system *Ax,Pr* as defined at the beginning of this section is complete. The structure of the proof is an extension of that of section 5.5; a key lemma (lemma 9.25) similar to lemma 5.48 is the first main step in the proof. Before we can give lemma 9.25, we need some notational preparations and an auxiliary result.

First, it is convenient to introduce two classes of *auxiliary* simple and array variables. These are infinite subsets of *Svar* and *Avar*, with typical elements $z_1,z_2,\ldots$, $a'_1,a'_2,\ldots$, respectively, such that no program R contains an occurrence (either bound or free) of any z_i or a'_j. (Note that we do not prohibit the occurrence of an auxiliary variable in an assertion.) The introduction of the z_i, a'_j is motivated by the wish to avoid all clashes between program variables and fresh variables used in the construction of various assertions below. A *vector* of auxiliary simple or array variables $\langle z_1,\dots,z_k\rangle$, $\langle a'_1,\dots,a'_\ell\rangle$ will mostly be denoted by $\vec{z}$ or $\vec{a}'$, where the length of the vector will be clear from the context.

LEMMA 9.24. Let E ($\equiv P \Leftarrow B$), t,v be as usual, and let *svar*(E,t,v) = $\{x_1,\dots,x_k\}$, *avar*(E,t,v) = $\{a_1,\dots,a_\ell\}$. Let $\langle x_1,\dots,x_k\rangle,\langle a_1,\dots,a_\ell\rangle$ be the ordered lists of elements of *svar*(E,t,v) and *avar*(E,t,v), respectively, determined by the ordering of *Svar* and *Avar*. Let $\vec{z} \equiv \langle z_1,\dots,z_k\rangle$, $\vec{a}' \equiv \langle a'_1,\dots,a'_\ell\rangle$, with z_i, $i = 1,\dots,k$, and a'_j, $j = 1,\dots,\ell$, distinct auxiliary variables. We define

1. $p_E(t,v)(\vec{z},\vec{a}') \equiv (x_1=z_1)\wedge\dots\wedge(x_k=z_k) \wedge (a_1=a'_1)\wedge\dots\wedge(a_\ell=a'_\ell)$

   (where, for any a_1,a_2, $a_1=a_2$ is defined as in chapter 5)

2. $r_E(t,v)(\vec{z},\vec{a}') \equiv \{p_E(t,v)(\vec{z},\vec{a}')\}\langle E|P(t,v)\rangle$.

We have

a. $\models \langle E|p_E(t,v)(\vec{z},\vec{a}')[y/x] = p_E(t[y/x],v[y/x])(\vec{z}',\vec{a}')\rangle$

b. $\models \langle E|r_E(t,v)(z,a')[y/x] = r_E(t[y/x],v[y/x])(\vec{z}',\vec{a}')\rangle$

   where (both for a and b)

   (i) $x \notin$ *svar*(E), $y \notin$ *svar*(E,t,v)

   (ii) $\vec{z}'$ is some suitable permutation of $\vec{z} \equiv \langle z_1,\dots,z_k\rangle$.

PROOF. Throughout, we forget about the array-variable-part of the formulae, which is not affected by the substitutions.

a. We do not give the full proof, but consider a representative case. Let, e.g., *svar*(E,t,v) consist of three elements, occurring in *Svar* in the order $\langle x_5,x_7,x_{19}\rangle$, and let $x \equiv x_7$, $y \equiv x_{21}$. Let $\vec{z} \equiv \langle z_1,z_2,z_3\rangle$ consist of three (arbitrary and distinct) auxiliary variables. Then

$$p_E(t,v)(\vec{z}) \equiv (x_5=z_1) \wedge (x_7=z_2) \wedge (x_{19}=z_3),$$

$$p_E(t,v)(\vec{z})[y/x] \equiv (x_5=z_1) \wedge (x_{21}=z_2) \wedge (x_{19}=z_3)$$

Now we take the permutation $\vec{z}' \equiv \langle z_1,z_3,z_2\rangle$. Then

$$p_E(t[y/x],v[y/x])(\vec{z}') \equiv (x_5=z_1)\wedge(x_{19}=z_3)\wedge(x_{21}=z_2),$$

and we see that, apart from the ordering in the conjuctions, the formulae for $p_E(t,v)(\vec{z})[y/x]$ and $p_E(t[y/x],v[y/x])(\vec{z}')$ are identical, thus yielding the desired validity result.

b. Follows from part a and lemma 9.23c.

END 9.24.

LEMMA 9.25. Let $R \equiv \langle E|S\rangle$ be a closed program (with $E \equiv P\Leftarrow B$). Let $\tilde{S}$ be a statement congruent with S such that

(i) no bound variable of $\tilde{S}$ occurs free in E

(ii) $\tilde{S}$ has no substatements of the form begin new x;... begin new x; ... end ... end (i.e. no nested bindings using the same variable).

Let $P(t_1,v_1),\ldots,P(t_m,v_m)$, $m \geq 0$, be the occurrences of procedure calls (of P, since by closedness no other calls are possible) in $\tilde{S}$. For $i = 1,\ldots,m$, let $\vec{z}^{(i)},\vec{a}'^{(i)}$ be vectors of auxiliary variables, all components of which are distinct, such that the number of components in $\vec{z}^{(i)}$ ($\vec{a}'^{(i)}$) equals the number of elements in *svar*(E,t_i,v_i) (*avar*(E,t_i,v_i)). Let $\vec{z} \equiv \vec{z}^{(1)},\ldots,\vec{z}^{(m)}$, and $\vec{a}' \equiv \vec{a}'^{(1)},\ldots,\vec{a}'^{(m)}$.

Let, furthermore,

$$f_{\tilde{S}}(\vec{z},\vec{a}') \stackrel{df.}{\equiv} \{p_E(t_1,v_1)(\vec{z}^{(1)},\vec{a}'^{(1)})\}Q(t_1,v_1)\{r_E(t_1,v_1)(\vec{z}^{(1)},\vec{a}'^{(1)})\}$$

$$\wedge \ldots \wedge$$

$$\{p_E(t_m,v_m)(\vec{z}^{(m)},\vec{a}'^{(m)})\}Q(t_m,v_m)\{r_E(t_m,v_m)(\vec{z}^{(m)},\vec{a}'^{(m)})\}$$

where $f_{\tilde{S}}(\vec{z},\vec{a}') \equiv$ true if $m = 0$.

We have: for all $p,q \in \mathit{Assn}$, for all $\vec{z},\vec{a}'$, if

$$\models \langle E|\{p\}S\{q\}\rangle$$

then

$$\vdash \langle E|f_{\tilde{S}}(\vec{z},\vec{a}') \Rightarrow \{p\}\tilde{S}[Q/P]\{q\}\rangle.$$

PROOF. Again, we suppress the $\vec{a}'$-arguments; also, we drop the E-subscripts on p and r. We use induction on the complexity of S (and use $bv(S)$ to denote the set of bound variables of S).

a. $S \equiv v:=t$. Exercise.

b. $S \equiv S_1;S_2$. By lemma 9.23b, there exists an assertion r such that $\models \langle E|\{p\}S_1\{r\}\rangle$ and $\models \langle E|\{r\}S_2\{q\}\rangle$. Clearly, we can put $\tilde{S} \equiv \tilde{S}_1;\tilde{S}_2$. Also, we can divide the auxiliary variables in $\vec{z}$ into two groups $\vec{z}_1,\vec{z}_2$, such that $f_{\tilde{S}}(\vec{z}) \equiv f_{\tilde{S}_1}(\vec{z}_1) \wedge f_{\tilde{S}_2}(\vec{z}_2)$.
By the induction hypothesis, we have that $\vdash \langle E|f_{\tilde{S}_1}(\vec{z}_1) \Rightarrow \{p\}\tilde{S}_1[Q/P]\{r\}\rangle$ and $\vdash \langle E|f_{\tilde{S}_2}(\vec{z}_2) \Rightarrow \{r\}\tilde{S}_2[Q/P]\{q\}\rangle$, and the desired result follows by lemma 9.21a and the composition rule.

c. $S \equiv$ if b then S_1 else S_2 fi. Exercise.

d. $S \equiv$ begin new x; S_1 end. Then $\tilde{S}$ is of the form begin new y; $\tilde{S}_1$ end, where $y \notin \mathit{svar}(S_1)\backslash\{x\}$, $\tilde{S}_1 \cong S_1[y/x]$, $\tilde{S}_1$ satisfies assumptions (i) and (ii) of the lemma, and
(iii) $y \notin \mathit{svar}(E)$ (this follows from assumption (i))
(iv) $y \notin bv(\tilde{S}_1)$ (this follows from assumption (ii)).
Clearly, (*): $f_{\tilde{S}}(\vec{z}) \equiv f_{\tilde{S}_1}(\vec{z})$. Now choose $\bar{y}$ such that $\bar{y} \notin \mathit{svar}(E,p,\tilde{S}_1,q,f_{\tilde{S}_1}(\vec{z})) \cup bv(\tilde{S}_1)$. By lemma 9.22b, $\models \langle E|\{p\}\tilde{S}_1[\bar{y}/y]\{q\}\rangle$. Since $\bar{y} \notin bv(\tilde{S}_1)$, the substitution $\tilde{S}_1[\bar{y}/y]$ does not lead to a renaming of the bound variables of $\tilde{S}_1$, and so we can assume that $\tilde{S}_1[\bar{y}/y]^{\sim} \equiv \tilde{S}_1[\bar{y}/y]$. Hence, by the induction hypothesis, (**): $\vdash \langle E|f_{\tilde{S}_1[\bar{y}/y]}(\vec{z}) \Rightarrow \{p\}\tilde{S}_1[\bar{y}/y][Q/P]\{q\}\rangle$.

Furthermore, by substitution rule II we have, for $i = 1,\ldots,m$,

$$\vdash \langle E \mid \{p(t_i,v_i)(\vec{z}^{(i)})\}Q(t_i,v_i)\{r(t_i,v_i)(\vec{z}^{(i)})\} \Rightarrow \{p(t_i,v_i)(\vec{z}^{(i)})[\bar{y}/y]\}Q(t_i,v_i)[\bar{y}/y]\{r(t_i,v_i)(\vec{z}^{(i)})[\bar{y}/y]\}\rangle$$

(here we use (iii)), from which, by lemma 9.24 (again using (iii)) and the rules of consequence and transitivity, we obtain, for some suitable permutation $\vec{z}'^{(i)}$ of the $\vec{z}^{(i)}$:

$$\begin{aligned}\vdash \langle E \mid &\{p(t_i,v_i)(\vec{z}^{(i)})\}Q(t_i,v_i)\{r(t_i,v_i)(\vec{z}^{(i)})\}\\ &\Rightarrow \\ &\{p(t_i[\bar{y}/y],v_i[\bar{y}/y])(\vec{z}'^{(i)})\}Q(t_i[\bar{y}/y],v_i[\bar{y}/y])\\ &\{r(t_i[\bar{y}/y],v_i[\bar{y}/y])(\vec{z}'^{(i)})\}\rangle\end{aligned} \qquad (9.8)$$

Also, if the procedure calls in $\tilde{S}_1$ are $P(t_1,v_1),\ldots,P(t_m,v_m)$, then the procedure calls in $\tilde{S}_1[\bar{y}/y]$ are $P(t_1[\bar{y}/y],v_1[\bar{y}/y]),\ldots,$ $P(t_m[\bar{y}/y],v_m[\bar{y}/y])$ (here we use (iv)). From this and (9.8) (and repeated use of lemma 9.21a) we obtain

$$\vdash \langle E \mid f_{\tilde{S}_1}(\vec{z}) \Rightarrow f_{\tilde{S}_1[\bar{y}/y]}(\vec{z}')\rangle$$

From this, (*), and (**) (with $\vec{z}'$ replacing $\vec{z}$) we obtain
$\vdash \langle E \mid f_{\tilde{S}}(\vec{z}) \Rightarrow \{p\}\tilde{S}_1[\bar{y}/y][Q/P]\{q\}\rangle$. By the block rule
$\vdash \langle E \mid \{p\}\tilde{S}_1[\bar{y}/y][Q/P]\{q\} \Rightarrow \{p\}$ <u>begin</u> <u>new</u> y; $\tilde{S}_1[Q/P]$ <u>end</u> $\{q\}\rangle$
Thus, combining the last two results, we finally obtain that
$\vdash \langle E \mid f_{\tilde{S}}(\vec{z}) \Rightarrow \{p\}\tilde{S}[Q/P]\{q\}\rangle$.

e. $S \equiv P(t,v)$. Then $m = 1$ and $(t_1,v_1) \equiv (t,v)$. We have to show that from $\models \langle E \mid \{p\}P(t_1,v_1)\{q\}\rangle$ it follows that $\vdash \langle E \mid \{p(t_1,v_1)(\vec{z})\}$ $Q(t_1,v_1)\{r(t_1,v_1)(\vec{z})\} \Rightarrow \{p\}Q(t_1,v_1)\{q\}\rangle$. Now argue as in the proof of lemma 5.48, case d, also assuming the counterpart of lemma 5.49, the proof of which we leave to the reader.

END 9.25.

Now that we have, with this lemma, established the counterpart of lemma 5.48 for procedures with parameters, the next step in the completeness proof which suggests itself is, analogous to the argument of theorem 5.47, the following: Assume $\models$ <E|{p}S{q}>, let, using the notation of lemma 9.25, $P(t_i,v_i)$, i = 1,...,m, be the occurrences of a procedure call in $\tilde{S}$, and let $p_E(t_i,v_i)(\vec{z},\vec{a}')$,$r_E(t_i,v_i)(\vec{z},\vec{a}')$ be as defined there. In order to further ease the notation, from now on we also suppress the $\vec{z}$-arguments and simply write $p(t_i,v_i)$, etc. We want to establish that $\vdash$ <E|{$p(t_i,v_i)$}$P(t_i,v_i)$ {$r(t_i,v_i)$}>, i = 1,...,m, (cf. formula (5.20)). However, contrary to the parameterless case, this is not an easy consequence of the preceding lemma, but needs additional analysis, which is why we devote a separate lemma to it.

LEMMA 9.26. Let E ≡ P⇐B, t,v arbitrary, and let p(t,v), r(t,v) be defined as in lemma 9.24. Then

$\vdash$ <E|{p(t,v)}P(t,v){r(t,v)}>.

PROOF. By the definition of r(t,v), $\models$ <E|{p(t,v)}P(t,v){r(t,v)}>, from which, by *fpp*, (*): $\models$ <E|{p(t,v)}B(t,v){r(t,v)}>. One might now be tempted to argue as in the proof of theorem 5.47, i.e. to assert that, by lemma 9.25, (**): $\vdash$ <E|{p(t,v)}Q(t,v){r(t,v)} ⇒ {p(t,v)}$\widetilde{B(t,v)}$[Q/P]{r(t,v)}>, from which the desired result then follows by the congruence and induction rules. However, this would be incorrect, since (**) is not instance of lemma 9.25: For S ≡ B(t,v), the antecedens of "⇒" in (**) is not of the form $f_{\tilde{S}}$, since it does not refer to all procedure calls in $\tilde{S}$. Neither can this easily be remedied by extending the antecedent with constructs referring to all calls of P in $\tilde{S}$, since the parameters of the inner calls of P in B change owing to the syntactic application B(t,v). Therefore, we need a more complex way of reasoning. In general, B will have the form B ≡ <val x,add y|... $P(t_1,v_1)$...$P(t_n,v_n)$...>, say, for some n ≥ 0, and the occurrences of P(...,...) in $\tilde{S}$ ≡ $\widetilde{B(t,v)}$ are to be derived from (t_i,v_i), i = 1,...,n, and (t,v) through syntactic application. We first restrict ourselves to the case $n = 1$, and at the end of the proof sketch how the general case may be dealt with. So let us assume that $B \equiv$ <u>val</u> x,<u>add</u> y$|S_0$>, where S_0 has one occurrence of a call of P. Now let $\tilde{S}_0$ satisfy: (i) $\tilde{S}_0 \cong S_0$, (ii) no bound variable of $\tilde{S}_0$ occurs free in E or {x,y}, (iii) $\tilde{S}_0$ contains no substatements of the form <u>begin</u> <u>new</u> x; ... <u>begin</u> <u>new</u> x; ... <u>end</u> ... <u>end</u>. Let $P(t_1,v_1)$ be the occurrence of a call of P in $\tilde{S}_0$. We distinguish various subcases (eight altogether): $v \equiv z$ and $v \equiv a[s]$, and $v_1 \equiv x$, $v_1 \equiv y$, $v_1 \equiv z_1$ ($\not\equiv x,y$; we are not using z_1 any longer as auxiliary simple variable), $v_1 \equiv a_1[s_1]$. We treat only two subcases, viz. $v \equiv z$ and $v_1 \equiv x$, $v \equiv z$ and $v_1 \equiv a_1[s_1]$, leaving the remaining ones (which have similar proofs) to the reader.

Subcase (i). $v \equiv z$, $v_1 \equiv x$. Let us recall what we want to show: $\vdash$ <E|{p(t,v)}P(t,v){r(t,v)}>. As indicated already, if we would be able to establish that (**): $\vdash$ <E|{p(t,v)}Q(t,v){r(t,v)} $\Rightarrow$ {p(t,v)}$B(t,v)^\sim$[Q/P]{r(t,v)}> - where $B(t,v)^\sim$ satisfies the usual properties - we would be done by the (congruence and) induction rule. We shall now modify (**) in a number of steps so that we obtain successive formulae to which lemma 9.25 is applicable, and the combination of which eventually leads to a form which allows application of the induction rule. In addition to the constraints already imposed upon $\tilde{S}_0$, we moreover assume that no bound variable of $\tilde{S}_0$ is equal to z. Now choose $B(t,z)^\sim \equiv$ <u>begin</u> <u>new</u> u; u:=t; $\tilde{S}_0$[u/x][z/y] <u>end</u> for suitable u (since no bound variable of $\tilde{S}_0$ is equal to z, the substitution $\tilde{S}_0$[u/x][z/y] (for suitable u) does not lead to a renaming of bound variables). We then have $B(t,z)^\sim \equiv \ldots P(t_1$[u/x][z/y], x[u/x][z/y]) ... $\equiv$ ... $P(t_1$[u/x][z/y],u) ... $\equiv$ ... $P(t_2,v_2)$ ..., say. By lemma 9.25 we may infer that $\vdash$ <E|{$p(t_2,v_2)$}$Q(t_2,v_2)${$r(t_2,v_2)$} $\Rightarrow$ {p(t,v)}$B(t,v)^\sim$[Q/P]{r(t,v)}>. Let $f \overset{df.}{\equiv}$ {p(t,v)}Q(t,v){r(t,v)}, $f_2 \overset{df.}{\equiv}$ {$p(t_2,v_2)$}$Q(t_2,v_2)${$r(t_2,v_2)$}. By weakening we have that (***): $\vdash$ <E|$f \wedge f_2 \Rightarrow f[B'/Q]^\sim$>, with $B' \overset{df.}{\equiv}$ B[Q/P] (and, by definition,

$\{p\}S\{q\}^{\sim} \equiv \{p\}\tilde{S}\{q\}$, $(f'\wedge f'')^{\sim} \equiv \tilde{f}'\wedge\tilde{f}'')$. As next step we try to modify (***) so that the induction rule becomes applicable, i.e. we try to establish that $\vdash \langle E|f\wedge f_2 \Rightarrow (f\wedge f_2)[B'/Q]^{\sim}\rangle$. Once more, we want to apply lemma 9.25, and therefore choose $B(t_2,v_2)^{\sim} \equiv \langle$ <u>val</u> x, <u>add</u> y$|\ldots$ $P(t_1,x)\ldots\rangle(t_1[u/x][z/y],u)^{\sim} \equiv \ldots P(t_1[\bar{u}/x][u/y],\bar{u})\ldots$, with $\bar{u}$ suitably chosen. Let $(t_3,v_3) \equiv (t_1[\bar{u}/x][u/y],\bar{u})$, and let f_3 be defined accordingly. By lemma 9.25 we have that $\vdash \langle E|f_3 \Rightarrow f_2[B'/Q]^{\sim}\rangle$, from which, by lemma 9.21a and (***), $\vdash \langle E|f\wedge f_2\wedge f_3 \Rightarrow (f\wedge f_2)[B'/Q]^{\sim}\rangle$. Let, continuing the above definitions, $(t_4,v_4) \equiv (t_1[\bar{\bar{u}}/x][\bar{u}/y],\bar{\bar{u}})$, and let f_4 be defined accordingly. We are now in a position to terminate the argument, since we can derive f_4 from f_3. By substitution rule II we have that $\vdash \langle E|f_3 \Rightarrow f_3[\bar{\bar{u}}/\bar{u}]\rangle$, and $\vdash \langle E|f_3[\bar{\bar{u}}/\bar{u}] \Rightarrow f_3[\bar{\bar{u}}/\bar{u}][\bar{u}/u]\rangle$. Since $\vdash \langle E|f_3[\bar{\bar{u}}/\bar{u}][\bar{u}/u] \Rightarrow f_4\rangle$ (by lemma 9.23c and the rule of consequence), we have that $\vdash \langle E|f_3 \Rightarrow f_4\rangle$. (Note that we have to be careful with these substitutions: $\vdash \langle E|f_3 \Rightarrow f_3[\bar{u}/u]\rangle$ is not an instance of substitution rule II, since $\bar{u} \in$ *svar*(t_3,v_3).) Since, again by lemma 9.25, $\vdash \langle E|f_4 \Rightarrow f_3[B'/Q]^{\sim}\rangle$, we obtain, combining the previous results, that $\vdash \langle E|f\wedge f_2\wedge f_3 \Rightarrow (f\wedge f_2\wedge f_3)[B'/Q]^{\sim}\rangle$. From this and the congruence rule we get $\vdash \langle E|f\wedge f_2\wedge f_3 \Rightarrow (f\wedge f_2\wedge f_3)[B'/Q]\rangle$, which, finally, allows us to apply the induction rule, with as result that $\vdash \langle E|(f\wedge f_2\wedge f_3)[P/Q]\rangle$, implying that $\vdash \langle E|f[P/Q]\rangle$ i.e. that $\vdash \langle E|\{p(t,v)\}P(t,v)\{r(t,v)\}\rangle$, as was to be shown.

Subcase (ii). $v \equiv z$, $v_1 \equiv a_1[s_1]$. The argument has the same structure as that used in subcase (i). In fact, we can take $B(t,a_1[s])^{\sim} \equiv$ <u>begin</u> <u>new</u> u_1,u_2; $u_1{:=}t$; $u_2{:=}s$; $\tilde{S}_0[u_1/x][a_1[u_2]/y]$ <u>end</u>, for suitable

u_1, u_2. We list only the various parameters occurring here. Let

$(t,v) \equiv (t,z)$, $(t_1,v_1) \equiv (t_1,a_1[s_1])$. Then

$(t_2,v_2) \equiv (t_1[u/x][z/y],a_1[s_1[u/x][z/y]])$,

$(t_3,v_3) \equiv (t_1[\bar{u}_1/x][a_1[\bar{u}_2]/y],a_1[s_1[\bar{u}_1/x][a_1[\bar{u}_2]/y]])$,

$(t_4,v_4) \equiv (t_1[\bar{\bar{u}}_1/x][a_1[\bar{\bar{u}}_2]/y],a_1[s_1[\bar{\bar{u}}_1/x][a_1[\bar{\bar{u}}_2]/y]])$.

Since $(t_4,v_4) \equiv (t_3,v_3)[\bar{\bar{u}}_1/\bar{u}_1][\bar{\bar{u}}_2/\bar{u}_2]$, we again have ($f_3$ and f_4 as in subcase (i)) $\vdash \langle E|f_3 \Rightarrow f_4\rangle$, and the desired result is obtained just as in subcase (i).

We conclude the proof with a few remarks on the general case (remember that subcases (i), (ii) dealt with the case that S_0 has only one inner recursive call of P). There is, for arbitrary $n \geq 2$, a proliferation of intermediate parameter pairs arising when we follow the argument as given for the case $n = 1$, whence a full treatement of the general case is notationally complicated. Therefore, we restrict ourselves to a typical subcase, viz. $n = 2$, $(t,v) \equiv (t,z)$, $(t_1,v_1) \equiv (t_1,x)$, and $(t_2,v_2) \equiv (t_2,a[s_2])$, where (t_1,v_1), (t_2,v_2) are the parameters of the two inner calls of P in $\tilde{S}_0$. As in subcase (ii), we list only the various intermediate parameter pairs, and also show how the argument terminates by indicating how the third group of parameters can be obtained by suitable substitutions from the second group. Let, for $s,\bar{t},\bar{\bar{t}}$ arbitrary, $s(\bar{t},\bar{\bar{t}})$ be an (ad-hoc) notation for $s[\bar{t}/x][\bar{\bar{t}}/y]$.

(α) Parameters corresponding to the (t_2,v_2) level of subcase (i), (ii) above

1. $(t_1(u,z),u)$
2. $(t_2(u,z),a[s_2(u,z)])$

(β) Parameters corresponding to the (t_3,v_3) level

1.1. $(t_1(\bar{u},u),\bar{u})$

2.1. $(t_2(\bar{u},u),a[s_2(\bar{u},u)])$

1.2. $(t_1(\bar{u}_1,a[\bar{u}_2]),\bar{u}_1)$

2.2. $(t_2(\bar{u}_1,a[\bar{u}_2]),a[s_2(\bar{u}_1,a[\bar{u}_2])])$

(γ) Parameters corresponding to the (t_4,v_4) level

1.1.1. $(t_1(\bar{\bar{u}},\bar{u}),\bar{\bar{u}})$

2.1.1. $(t_2(\bar{\bar{u}},\bar{u}),a[s_2(\bar{\bar{u}},\ddot{u})])$

1.2.1. $(t_1(\bar{\bar{u}}_1,a[\bar{\bar{u}}_2]),\bar{\bar{u}}_1)$

2.2.1. $(t_2(\bar{\bar{u}}_1,a[\bar{\bar{u}}_2]),a[s_2(\bar{\bar{u}}_1,a[\bar{\bar{u}}_2])])$

1.1.2. $(t_1(\bar{\bar{\bar{u}}},u_1),\bar{\bar{\bar{u}}})$

2.1.2. $(t_2(\bar{\bar{\bar{u}}},\bar{u}_1),a[s_2(\bar{\bar{\bar{u}}},\bar{u}_1)])$

1.2.2. $(t_1(\bar{\bar{\bar{u}}}_1,a[\bar{\bar{\bar{u}}}_2]),\bar{\bar{\bar{u}}}_1)$

2.2.2. $(t_2(\bar{\bar{\bar{u}}}_1,a[\bar{\bar{\bar{u}}}_2]),a[s_2(\bar{\bar{\bar{u}}}_1,a[\bar{\bar{\bar{u}}}_2])])$

Now (1.1) $[\bar{\bar{u}}/\bar{u}][\bar{u}/u] \equiv$ (1.1.1),...,(1.1)$[\bar{\bar{\bar{u}}}/\bar{u}][\bar{u}_1/u] \equiv$ (1.1.2),..., (2.2)$[\bar{\bar{\bar{u}}}_1/\bar{u}_1][\bar{\bar{\bar{u}}}_2/\bar{u}_2] \equiv$ (2.2.2), and we see that, indeed, in the notation of the case $n = 1$, $\vdash$ <E$|f_3 \Rightarrow f_4$> follows by substitution rule II.

END 9.26.

We are finally ready for the proof of

<u>THEOREM 9.27</u> (completeness theorem). Let <E|S> be a closed program with $E \equiv P \Leftarrow B$. Then

$$\models \langle E|\{p\}S\{q\}\rangle \;\Rightarrow\; \vdash \langle E|\{p\}S\{q\}\rangle.$$

<u>PROOF</u>. Assume $\models$ <E|{p}S{q}>, and let $P(t_1,v_1),\ldots,P(t_m,v_m)$ be the occurrences of a call of P in $\tilde{S}$ (notation as in lemma 9.25). By lemma 9.26, $\vdash \langle E|\{p(t_i,v_i)\}P(t_i,v_i)\{r(t_i,v_i)\}\rangle$, $i = 1,\ldots,m$, from which we infer that (*): $\vdash \langle E|\{p(t_1,v_1)\}P(t_1,v_1)\{r(t_1,v_1)\}\wedge\ldots\wedge \{p(t_m,v_m)\}P(t_m,v_m)\{r(t_m,v_m)\}\rangle$. Also, by lemma 9.25 and the congruence rule, $\vdash \langle E|\{p(t_1,v_1)\}Q(t_1,v_1)\{r(t_1,v_1)\}\wedge\ldots\wedge\{p(t_m,v_m)\}Q(t_m,v_m)$

$\{r(t_m,v_m)\} \Rightarrow \{p\}S[Q/P]\{q\}>$, from which, by instantiation, (**):
$\vdash$ $<E|\{p(t_1,v_1)\}P(t_1,v_1)\{r(t_1,v_1)\}\wedge\ldots\wedge\{p(t_m,v_m)\}P(t_m,v_m)\{r(t_m,v_m)\} \Rightarrow$
$\{p\}S\{q\}>$. From (*) and (**) we obtain, by transitivity, that
$\vdash$ $<E|\{p\}S\{q\}>$, as was to be shown.
END 9.27.

We close this section with an example of a partial correctness result which, though it has some of the flavor of the techniques of the completeness proof, does not fully follow its general strategy (thus illustrating that in specific cases the full complexity of the completeness proof may well be unnecessary). We show that

$$\vdash <P \Leftarrow B|\{u\geq 0\}P(u,a[u])\{\forall\bar{u}[(0\leq\bar{u}) \wedge (\bar{u}\leq u) \supset (a[\bar{u}]=\bar{u}!)]\}>,$$

where $B \equiv$ <<u>val</u> x,<u>add</u> y|<u>if</u> x=0 <u>then</u> a[0]:=1 <u>else</u>
x:=x-1; P(x,a[x]); y:=(x+1)×a[x] <u>fi</u>>

We first prove that

$$\vdash <P \Leftarrow B|\{p\}P(x,a[x])\{q\}>, \tag{9.9}$$

where $p \equiv (x=z) \wedge (z\geq 0)$
$q \equiv \forall\bar{u}[(0\leq\bar{u}) \wedge (\bar{u}\leq x) \supset (a[\bar{u}]=\bar{u}!)] \wedge (x=z)$
(In order for the inductive argument to go through, the pair p,q has to express that the value of x is not changed by the call P(x,a[x]), and this is done by using the assertion x = z.) By rule 11' it is sufficient to prove

$$\vdash <P \Leftarrow B|\{p\}Q(x,a[x])\{q\} \Rightarrow \{p\}B'(x,a[x])\{q\}>, \tag{9.10}$$

where $B' \equiv B[Q/P]$. We have: $B'(x,a[x]) \equiv$ <u>begin</u> <u>new</u> $u_1,u_2;S_0$ <u>end</u>,
where $S_0 \equiv u_1$:=x; u_2:=x; <u>if</u> u_1 = 0 <u>then</u> S_1 <u>else</u> S_2 <u>fi</u>
$S_1 \equiv$ a[0]:=1
$S_2 \equiv u_1:=u_1-1;\ Q(u_1,a[u_1]);\ a[u_2]:=(u_1+1)\times a[u_1]$
By the block rule, in order to prove (9.10) we have to show that

$$\vdash \langle P \Leftarrow B \mid \{p\}Q(x,a[x])\{q\} \Rightarrow \{p\}\bar{S}_0\{q\}\rangle,$$

where $\bar{S}_i \equiv S_i[\bar{u}_1/u_1][\bar{u}_2/u_2]$, $i = 0,1,2$, for some fresh $\bar{u}_1,\bar{u}_2$. It is sufficient to prove that $\vdash \langle P \Leftarrow B \mid \{p\}Q(x,a[x])\{q\} \Rightarrow \{p \wedge (\bar{u}_1{=}x) \wedge (\bar{u}_2{=}x) \wedge (\bar{u}_1{=}0)\}\ a[0]{:=}1\ \{q\}\rangle$, which is left as exercise, and

$$\vdash \langle P \Leftarrow B \mid \{p\}Q(x,a[x])\{q\} \Rightarrow \{p \wedge (\bar{u}_1{=}x) \wedge (\bar{u}_2{=}x) \wedge (\bar{u}_1 > 0)\}\bar{S}_2\{q\}\rangle.$$

Let $p_0 \equiv p \wedge (\bar{u}_1 = x-1) \wedge (\bar{u}_2{=}x) \wedge (\bar{u}_1{+}1 > 0)$. Clearly,
(*): $\vdash \langle P \Leftarrow B \mid \{p\}\ \bar{u}_1{:=}\bar{u}_1{-}1\ \{p_0\}\rangle$.

There remains to be shown that $\vdash \langle P \Leftarrow B \mid \{p\}Q(x,a[x])\{q\} \Rightarrow \{p_0\}Q(\bar{u}_1,a[\bar{u}_1]);a[\bar{u}_2]{:=}(\bar{u}_1{+}1) \times a[\bar{u}_1]\{q\}\rangle$ holds. If we can show that

$$\vdash \langle P \Leftarrow B \mid \{p\}Q(x,a[x])\{q\} \Rightarrow \{p_0\}Q(\bar{u}_1,a[\bar{u}_1])\{q_1\}\rangle \qquad (9.12)$$

where $q_1 \equiv \forall \bar{u}[(0{\le}\bar{u}) \wedge (\bar{u}{\le}\bar{u}_1) \supset (a[\bar{u}]{=}\bar{u}!)] \wedge (x{=}z) \wedge (x{=}\bar{u}_2) \wedge (\bar{u}_1 = x-1)$, then we are ready, because $\vdash \langle P \Leftarrow B \mid \{q_1\}a[\bar{u}_2]{:=}(\bar{u}_1{+}1) \times a[\bar{u}_1]\{q\}\rangle$ can be shown straightforwardly. Now using the invariance rule one shows easily

$$\vdash \langle P \Leftarrow B \mid \{(x{=}z) \wedge (x{=}\bar{u}_2)\}Q(\bar{u}_1,a[\bar{u}_1])\{(x{=}z) \wedge (x{=}\bar{u}_2)\}\rangle \qquad (9.13)$$

Furthermore one can use substitution rule II to prove

$$\vdash \langle P \Leftarrow B \mid \{p\}Q(x,a[x])\{q\} \Rightarrow \{p[\bar{u}_1/x]\}Q(\bar{u}_1,a[\bar{u}_1])\{q[\bar{u}_1/x]\}\rangle \qquad (9.14)$$

However, it is not straightforward to show that $\vdash \langle P \Leftarrow B \mid \{p\}Q(x,a[x])\{q\} \Rightarrow \{\bar{u}_1{=}x{-}1\}Q(\bar{u}_1,a[\bar{u}_1])\{\bar{u}_1{=}x{-}1\}\rangle$, since this is not an instance of the invariance rule. It is here that we have to use the claim $x = z$ occurring in the induction hypothesis $\{p\}Q(x,a[x])\{q\}$. Notice that this claim is transformed by the substitution $[\bar{u}_1/x]$ into $\bar{u}_1 = z$. Notice furthermore that we do not want the formula in this form either. In fact, before the call $Q(\bar{u}_1,a[\bar{u}_1])$ it does not even hold (as one can see from p_0): the invariant value of $\bar{u}_1$ must be equal to x-1. So we might try to apply substitution rule II once more to get

$$\vdash \langle P \Leftarrow B \mid \{p[\bar{u}_1/x]\}Q(\bar{u}_1,a[\bar{u}_1])\{q[\bar{u}_1/x]\} \Rightarrow \{p[\bar{u}_1/x][x-1/z]\}Q(\bar{u}_1,a[\bar{u}_1])\{q[\bar{u}_1/x][x-1/z]\}\rangle.$$

Unfortunately, this is not an instance of substitution rule II (since x-1 is an expression and not a variable). Therefore, we have to obtain the desired result in a different way. Choose an arbitrary fresh variable $\bar{z}$. Then, by (9.14) and substitution rule II,

$$\vdash \langle P \Leftarrow B \mid \{p\}Q(x,a[x])\{q\} \Rightarrow \{p[\bar{u}_1/x][\bar{z}/z]\}Q(\bar{u}_1,a[\bar{u}_1])\{q[\bar{u}_1/x][\bar{z}/z]\}\rangle \quad (9.15)$$

By invariance, we have

$$\vdash \langle P \Leftarrow B \mid \{\bar{z}=x-1\}Q(\bar{u}_1,a[\bar{u}_1])\{\bar{z}=x-1\}\rangle \quad (9.16)$$

(Note that this is where we give the variable $\bar{z}$ the "right value".) Now we can combine (9.13), (9.15) and (9.16) into

$$\vdash \langle P \Leftarrow B \mid \{p\}Q(x,a[x])\{q\} \Rightarrow \{p_2\}Q(\bar{u}_1,a[\bar{u}_1])\{q_2\}\rangle \quad (9.17)$$

where $p_2 \equiv (x=z) \wedge (x=\bar{u}_2) \wedge (\bar{u}_1=\bar{z}) \wedge (\bar{z}\geq 0) \wedge (\bar{z} = x-1)$,

$q_2 \equiv (x=z) \wedge (x=\bar{u}_2) \wedge \forall\bar{u}[(0\leq\bar{u}) \wedge (\bar{u}\leq\bar{u}_1) \supset (a[\bar{u}]=\bar{u}!)] \wedge \wedge (\bar{u}_1=z) \wedge (\bar{z} = x-1)$.

In order to be able to fit this formula into the rest of the formal proof we have to get rid of the occurrences of $\bar{z}$ in p_2 and q_2. This is easy for q_2, since we have that $\vdash \langle P \Leftarrow B \mid q_2 \supset q_1\rangle$. Now this can be combined with (9.17) yielding that $\vdash \langle P \Leftarrow B \mid \{p\}Q(x,a[x])\{q\} \Rightarrow \{p_2\}Q(\bar{u}_1,a[\bar{u}_1])\{q_1\}\rangle$. Next, we substitute $\bar{u}_1$ for $\bar{z}$ in p_2 using substitution rule I (which is allowed since $\bar{z} \notin svar(q_1)$). Thus, we obtain $\vdash \langle P \Leftarrow B \mid \{p\}Q(x,a[x])\{q\} \Rightarrow \{p_2[\bar{u}_1/\bar{z}]Q(\bar{u}_1,a[\bar{u}_1])\{q_1\}\rangle$. This formula, together with $\vdash \langle P \Leftarrow B \mid p_0 \supset p_2[\bar{u}_1/\bar{z}]\rangle$, finally leads to (9.12), which in turn proves (9.9). By substitution rule II and the rule of consequence we infer from (9.9) that

$$\vdash \langle P \Leftarrow B \mid \{(u=z) \wedge (z\geq 0)\}P(u,a[u])\{\forall\bar{u}[(0\leq\bar{u}) \wedge (\bar{u}\leq u) \supset (a[\bar{u}]=\bar{u}!)]\}\rangle$$

Finally, we use substitution rule I with substitution [u/z], and we conclude that

$$\vdash \langle P \Leftarrow B \mid \{u \geq 0\} P(u, a[u]) \{\forall \bar{u}[(0 \leq \bar{u}) \wedge (\bar{u} \leq u) \supset (a[\bar{u}] = \bar{u}!)]\}\rangle$$

as was to be shown.

Exercises

9.1. Prove or disprove

$\models \langle E \mid \{p[y/x]\} S \{q[y/x]\} \Rightarrow \{p\}$ <u>begin</u> <u>new</u> $x; S$ <u>end</u> $\{q\}\rangle$

where $y \notin$ *svar*(E,p,S,q).

9.2. Prove the equivalence of the semantics given by $\tilde{M}$ and M, as described in remark 2 following definition 9.3, for programs with procedures containing call-by-value parameters only, as follows (using the notation of that remark). Define the pair $\langle\tilde{\gamma},\gamma\rangle$ (with $\tilde{\gamma} \in \tilde{\Gamma}$, $\gamma \in \Gamma$) to be *consistent* if, for any P,t,ε,σ, if *intv*$(t) \subseteq \mathrm{dom}(\varepsilon)$ and $\sigma \neq \bot$ then $\tilde{\gamma}(P)(R(t)(\varepsilon)(\sigma))(\varepsilon)(\sigma) = \gamma(P)(t)(\varepsilon)(\sigma)$. Now prove the following:

a. For any $S,\tilde{\gamma},\gamma,\varepsilon,\sigma$, if $\langle\tilde{\gamma},\gamma\rangle$ is consistent, *intv*$(S) \subseteq \mathrm{dom}(\varepsilon)$ and $\sigma \neq \bot$, then $\tilde{N}(S)(\tilde{\gamma})(\varepsilon)(\sigma) = N(S)(\gamma)(\varepsilon)(\sigma)$

b. For any R and consistent $\langle\tilde{\gamma},\gamma\rangle$,

$$\tilde{M}(R)(\tilde{\gamma}) = M(R)(\gamma)$$

c. For any closed R and any $\langle\tilde{\gamma},\gamma\rangle$

$$\tilde{M}(R)(\tilde{\gamma}) = M(R)(\gamma).$$

9.3. Investigate the alternative (M_2-)semantics described in remark 4 following definition 9.3, and determine to what extent it is equivalent to the (M_1-)semantics of this chapter. Also, use the example (*): $\langle P \Leftarrow$ <u>begin</u> <u>new</u> y; y:=1 <u>end</u> | <u>begin</u> <u>new</u> z; z:=0; P <u>end</u>$\rangle$ to explain why clause $(\mathrm{iv})_2$ could not simply be formulated as

N_2(<u>begin</u> <u>new</u> x;S <u>end</u>)(γ_2)(ε)(σ) = N_2(S)(γ_2)(ε[e/x])(σ)

where e is the first address $\notin$ range(ε) (iv)$_3$

(Hint: take $\varepsilon = \emptyset$ in evaluating (*) with (iv)$_3$, and determine the value(s) stored at the first (free) address.)

9.4. Show that the definition 9.11 of Γ^E could be replaced by the following:

Γ^E is the set of all $\gamma \in \Gamma$ such that, for all P, there is a declaration E' $\equiv$ <P$\Leftarrow$B,$P_1 \Leftarrow B_1,\ldots,P_n \Leftarrow B_n$>, with *pvar*(E') = {P,$P_1,\ldots,P_n$} and *intv*(E') = *intv*(E), and such that γ(P) = M(<E'|P>)($\bar{\gamma}$) for arbitrary $\bar{\gamma}$.

(In other words, any γ satisfying the above condition will also satisfy the postulates listed in definition 9.11.)

9.5. a (call-by-result). Let us consider procedure bodies with only one formal parameter, *called-by-result*, denoted by B $\equiv$ <<u>res</u> x|S>. As actual parameter we have an integer variable v, and syntactic application is defined by

<<u>res</u> x|S>(z) $\equiv$ <u>begin</u> <u>new</u> u;S[u/x];z:=u <u>end</u>

<<u>res</u> x|S>(a[s]) $\equiv$ <u>begin</u> <u>new</u> u_1,u_2;u_1:=s;S[u_2/x];a[u_1]:=u_2 <u>end</u>

for u,u_1,u_2 as usual. Assuming a corresponding change in the induction rule (rule 11' of section 9.4), investigate whether the resulting proof system is complete.

b (call-by-value-result). Same question for call-by-value-result, with syntactic application (for simple variables as actual parameters) defined by

<<u>vre</u> x|S>(z) $\equiv$ <u>begin</u> <u>new</u> u;u:=z;S[u/x];z:=u <u>end</u>

with u as usual.

9.6. Repeat exercise 9.2 for procedures of the type described in exercise 9.5. For example, let $Pbod^{(r)}$, with typical elements

$B^{(r)}$,..., be the class of procedure bodies containing call-by-result parameters only. Define a function $\tilde{P}$: $Pbod^{(r)} \to (Addr_0 \to (\tilde{\Gamma} \to M))$ (where now $\tilde{\Gamma} = Pvar \to (Addr_0 \to M)$), so that $\tilde{P}(B^{(r)}(L(v)(\varepsilon)(\sigma))(\tilde{\gamma})(\varepsilon)(\sigma) = N(B^{(r)}(v))(\gamma)(\varepsilon)(\sigma)$, for a (suitably defined) consistent pair $<\tilde{\gamma},\gamma>$. Show again that this gives rise to a semantics equivalent to the one which uses syntactic application. Similarly with call-by-value-result.

Chapter 10

GOTO STATEMENTS

A. de Bruin

10.1. Introduction

The somewhat debatable role of goto statements in practical programming is reflected in their theoretical properties, in that in the treatment both of their semantics and their correctness we are confronted with difficulties of a nature not previously encountered.

In order not to complicate matters unduly, we restrict ourselves to a simple language: no procedures and no nesting of labels. As before, in our choice of how complex we allow our language to be, we are guided not so much by the expressive power of denotational semantics (which can certainly deal with all the concepts discussed in this treatise simultaneously in full generality), but rather by the wish to provide no more concepts than necessary to understand why methods of proving program correctness are valid or sound.

In what way are goto statements more difficult than the statements of the previous chapters? Consider a sequential composition $S \equiv S_1;S_2$. Up to now, the meaning of this was always easy to determine: it was straightforwardly defined as the mathematical composition " $\circ$ " of the two functions $M(S_2)$ and $M(S_1)$ (or $N(S_2)$ and $N(S_1)$). However, this is no longer possible in the case that our statements are, or contain goto's. Consider the case that $S \equiv$ goto L;S'. Whatever function ϕ we would ascribe as meaning to goto L, we cannot simply put $M($goto L;S$) = M(S)\circ\phi$, since this would amount to an interpretation of goto's which resumes execution of S after the effect of goto L has been taken care of, and this is contrary to the very meaning of goto's: execution of S should not be resumed after the jump to L has been completed.

Thus we have to resort to a new strategy, the essence of which is that the meaning of a statement is no longer given as a function from states σ to states σ' (i.e. as an element of M), but as an operator from functions ϕ to functions ϕ' (i.e. as an element of $[M \to M]$). For reasons which will become clear below, in the present context these functions ϕ are called *continuations*, thus explaining why the semantics of goto's is usually referred to as "continuation semantics". Let us moreover announce already that least-fixed-point techniques which are a slight variant on those of chapter 5 will also play a part in the definition of the mathematical semantics of goto's.

As in chapters 3 and 5, we precede the definition of $\mathcal{M}(S)$ by that of $\mathcal{O}(S)$, the *operational* meaning of a statement S. This is more or less straightforward, using techniques similar to those developed in chapter 5. The difficult part is, again, how to define $\mathcal{O}(S_1;S_2)$; as we shall see, this is done by induction on the complexity of S_1. We also remark that, analogously to what we had in chapter 5, where in order to determine $\mathcal{C}omp(P)(\sigma)$ we had to carry along the set of declarations E - to ensure that $\mathcal{C}omp$ was defined on arguments of the form $<\ldots,P_i \Leftarrow S_i,\ldots \mid P_i>(\sigma)$ - we now define $\mathcal{C}omp$ on arguments which are of the form $<L_1:S_1;\ldots;L_n:S_n|S>(\sigma)$. (Since the precise syntactic definitions are not yet available, this rough indication has to suffice for the moment.)

The main theorem of section 10.2 states the equivalence of $\mathcal{O}$ and $\mathcal{M}$. Its proof is similar to that of theorem 5.22, but for a number of complications caused by the additional structure in the definitions of $\mathcal{O}$ and $\mathcal{M}$.

After that we will discuss correctness issues concerning programs with goto statements. We will establish a proof system and prove its soundness and completeness. In this system, partial correctness formulae $\{p\}R\{q\}$ for programs $R \equiv L_1:S_1;\ldots;L_n:S_n$ with labels and goto statements can be deduced in a way resembling the method of chapter 5 used for recursive procedures, where we had the rule (here simplified):

$$\frac{\langle \mid \{p\}P\{q\} \Rightarrow \{p\}S\{q\}\rangle}{\langle P \Leftarrow S \mid \{p\}P\{q\}\rangle}$$

or in words: "if {p}S{q} is true under the assumption that {p}P{q} holds, then {p}P{q} is true with respect to the declaration $P \Leftarrow S$". The validity of rules of this type can be proved in essence by induction on the number of procedure calls occurring in an arbitrary evaluation of type $\langle P \Leftarrow S \mid P\rangle$.

An analogous approach (i.e. the use of assumptions in a formal proof) will be used for programs with labels and goto's. However, the correctness formulae which are to be used as assumptions are less obvious, as can be seen from the following rule (for programs with one label only):

$$\frac{\{p\}\ \underline{\text{goto}}\ L\ \{\underline{\text{false}}\} \Rightarrow \{p\}S\{q\}}{\{p\}\ L{:}S\ \{q\}}$$

Now this rule is not easily justified, either intuitively or formally. The main problem is that we have to refine the definition of validity of formulae like {p}S{q} now that S can contain goto statements. The intuitive description of its meaning used up till now "if p holds before evaluation of S and if this evaluation terminates then afterwards q is correct" cannot be maintained any more, because evaluation of S can terminate by execution of a substatement which is a goto statement. So there can be more classes of final states than the usual one, and it is not clear whether q should hold for all final states, and if not, whether there should be a restriction on the final states for which q does not have to be true.

In section 10.3 a validity definition will be given which is based on the continuation semantics and which can be used to demonstrate soundness and completeness of the proof system. As this validity definition will be rather intricate, the proofs will also tend to be complicated, though the main lines of reasoning are straightforward.

To make the whole argument more perspicuous we will adopt the following strategy. We first state a more direct validity definition using a new semantics. Soundness and completeness can now be shown more straightforwardly, and this will be done. After that we will show that both validity definitions are equivalent. These results taken together will then form a proof of soundness and completeness of the proof system, with respect to our original validity definition.

10.2. Semantics

First of all we define the syntax of our language. As a starting point for this we take the classes *Ivar*, *Iexp*, *Bexp* and *Assn* as defined in chapter 4. We also need a set *Lvar*, the class of *label variables*, with typical elements L,... . Furthermore, we will define besides the class *Stat* of *statements*, the class *Unst* of *unlabelled statements*, with typical elements A,... .

DEFINITION 10.1.

a. The class *Unst* is defined by

A::= v:=t|(A';A")|<u>if</u> b <u>then</u> A' <u>else</u> A" <u>fi</u>|<u>goto</u> L

b. The class *Stat* is defined by

$S::= L_1:A_1;\ldots;L_n:A_n$

where $n \geq 1$, and $L_i \neq L_j$ for $1 \leq i < j \leq n$.

END 10.1.

Remarks

1. Parentheses have been inserted in clause (A';A") of the definition of *Unst*, because it is not yet clear whether the syntactic operator " ; " is associative now that functional composition (" ∘ ") is no longer the semantical counterpart of sequential composition (" ; "). That we have to be careful can be seen from the fact that we have:

$$Comp(((A;A');A'') \neq Comp((A;(A';A'')))$$

(cf. definition 10.2). To limit the number of parentheses in the expressions, we adopt the convention that " ; " associates to the right; i.e. $A_1;A_2;\ldots;A_n$ should be read as $(A_1;(A_2(\ldots;A_n)\ldots))$.

2. In the sequel we will use the abbreviation $[L_i:A_i]_{i=1}^n$ for the statement $L_1:A_1;\ldots;L_n:A_n$;
3. A statement $[L_i:A_i]_{i=1}^n$ will be called *closed* if all labels in it are declared, i.e. for all A_i and for all substatements goto L of A_i we have that $L \equiv L_j$ for some j ($1 \leq j \leq n$). A pair $<S,A> \in$ *Stat* × *Unst* is called closed if S is closed and all labels in A are declared in S.

We now define an operational semantics for *Stat* in a way analogous to what has been done in chapter 5. We assume that the semantical domains Σ, V and W, and the semantical functions *L*, *R* and *W* are defined as in chapter 5. Furthermore, we adopt from that chapter the notions Σ^+, Σ^ω, the tail function κ, and the concatenation operator $^\frown$.

The first step is to define the auxiliary function *Comp* which is meant to yield the computation sequence which is the result of evaluation of an unlabelled statement. As has been mentioned earlier, this function cannot straightforwardly be defined on statements of the form (A';A") owing to the fact that in A' goto statements can occur. We have to know how evaluation will proceed once such a substatement has been executed, that is, we need a declaration of the labels. Therefore, we give the function *Comp* a second argument (the analog of the declaration E in $<E|S>$ in chapter 5), namely a statement from *Stat*.

DEFINITION 10.2. The function *Comp*: $Stat \times Unst \xrightarrow[part]{} (\Sigma \to (\Sigma^+ \cup \Sigma^\omega))$ is defined as follows. If $\sigma = \bot$ then $Comp(<S,A>)(\sigma) = <\bot>$. If $\sigma \neq \bot$ we have (where $S \equiv [L_i:A_i]_{i=1}^n$)

a. $Comp(<S,v:=t>)(\sigma) = <\sigma\{R(t)(\sigma)/L(v)(\sigma)\}>$

b. $Comp(\langle S, \underline{\text{goto}}\ L\rangle)(\sigma) = \begin{cases} \langle\sigma\rangle^{\frown}\ Comp(\langle S, A_i; A_{i+1}; \ldots; A_n\rangle)(\sigma), & \text{if } L \equiv L_i \\ \text{undefined, otherwise} \end{cases}$

c. $Comp(\langle S,\ \underline{\text{if}}\ b\ \underline{\text{then}}\ A'\ \underline{\text{else}}\ A''\ \underline{\text{fi}}\rangle)(\sigma) =$

$\underline{\text{if}}\ W(b)(\sigma)\ \underline{\text{then}}\ \langle\sigma\rangle^{\frown}\ Comp(\langle S,A'\rangle)(\sigma)\ \underline{\text{else}}\ \langle\sigma\rangle^{\frown}\ Comp(\langle S,A''\rangle)(\sigma)\ \underline{\text{fi}}$

d. $Comp(\langle S,v:=t;A'\rangle)(\sigma) =$

$\langle\sigma\{R(t)(\sigma)/L(v)(\sigma)\}\rangle^{\frown}\ Comp(\langle S,A'\rangle)(\sigma\{R(t)(\sigma)/L(v)(\sigma)\})$

e. $Comp(\langle S,\ \underline{\text{goto}}\ L;A'\rangle)(\sigma) = \langle\sigma\rangle^{\frown}\ Comp(\langle S,\ \underline{\text{goto}}\ L\rangle)(\sigma)$

f. $Comp(\langle S,\ \underline{\text{if}}\ b\ \underline{\text{then}}\ A''\ \underline{\text{else}}\ A'''\ \underline{\text{fi}};A'\rangle)(\sigma) =$

$\underline{\text{if}}\ W(b)(\sigma)\ \underline{\text{then}}\ \langle\sigma\rangle^{\frown}\ Comp(\langle S,A'';A'\rangle)(\sigma)$

$\underline{\text{else}}\ \langle\sigma\rangle^{\frown}\ Comp(\langle S,A''';A'\rangle)(\sigma)\ \underline{\text{fi}}$

g. $Comp(\langle S,((A'';A''');A')\rangle)(\sigma) = \langle\sigma\rangle^{\frown}\ Comp(\langle S,(A'';(A''';A'))\rangle)(\sigma)$

END 10.2.

Remarks

1. It should be clear that clauses a to g cover all possibilities for the syntactic structure of A.
2. As in chapter 5, we should view this definition as a sequence-generating scheme, the intuitive meaning of which is straightforward, though a completely rigorous specification of it would require substantial effort.
3. If we restrict *Comp* to the domain of all closed pairs <S,A> then it is a total function.
4. The problem concerning the definition of *Comp* for statements of the form (A';A") has been solved as follows. As long as it is unclear whether the first atomic statement in A' is an assignment or a goto statement, the statement A' is decomposed, applying rule f or g. After that rule d or e can be used.

Using definition 10.2 we can now define the function O.

<u>DEFINITION 10.3</u>. The function O: $Stat \xrightarrow[\text{part}]{} M$ is defined by

$$O([L_i:A_i]_{i=1}^n) = \kappa \circ Comp(\langle [L_i:A_i]_{i=1}^n, A_1; \ldots; A_n\rangle)$$

END 10.3.

Examples

1. $\mathcal{O}(L_1$:x:=0; goto L_2; L_2:x:=x)(σ) =

   κ(*Comp*(<L_1:x:=0; goto L_2; L_2:x:=x, (x:=0; goto L_2); x:=x>)(σ)) =

   κ(<σ>$^\frown$ *Comp*(L_1:x:=0; goto L_2; L_2:x:=x, x:=0; goto L_2; x:=x>)(σ)) =

   κ(<σ,σ{0/x}>$^\frown$ *Comp*(<L_1:x:=0; goto L_2; L_2:x:=x,

   goto L_2; x:=x>)(σ{0/x})) =

   κ(<σ,σ{0/x},σ{0/x}>$^\frown$ *Comp*(<L_1:x:=0; goto L_2; L_2:x:=x,

   goto L_2>)(σ{0/x})) =

   κ(<σ,σ{0/x},σ{0/x},σ{0/x}>$^\frown$ *Comp*(<L_1:x:=0;

   goto L_2; L_2:x:=x, x:=x>)(σ{0/x})) =

   κ(<σ,σ{0/x},σ{0/x},σ{0/x},σ{0/x}>) = σ{0/x}.

   Note that the convention in remark 1 after definition 10.1 has been used here.

2. $\mathcal{O}$(L:goto L)(σ) = κ(*Comp*(<L:goto L, goto L>)(σ)) =

   κ(<σ>$^\frown$ *Comp*(<L:goto L, goto L>)(σ)) =

   κ(<σ,σ>$^\frown$ *Comp*(<L:goto L, goto L>)(σ)) =

   κ(<σ,σ,...>) = ⊥, as it should be.

We now discuss the denotational semantics for unlabeled statements from *Unst*. Again we are faced with problems about what to do with substatements of the form goto L. In the operational semantics this was solved by giving *Comp* an extra argument S ≡ $[L_i:A_i]_{i=1}^n$, which was used in essence to associate with each label L_i the statement $A_i;\ldots;A_n$. The value of *Comp* for the unlabelled statement goto L_i was practically the same as its value for $A_i;\ldots;A_n$, which could be reduced to a state transformation (i.e. κ ∘ *Comp*(<S,$A_i;\ldots;A_n$>)). This function, applied to a state σ, yields a final state σ' which corresponds to the result of evaluation of the rest of the program, i.e. that part of statement S ≡ $[L_i:A_i]_{i=1}^n$ that will be executed after goto L_i has been evaluated.

The denotational semantics uses the same approach but in a more abstract way. Instead of giving for each label L_i a statement $A_i;\ldots;A_n$ that specifies a state transformation, we now provide this transformation directly. This is organized analogous to chapter 5, namely by giving the semantic function N an extra argument γ which now is a function form *Lvar* to $(\Sigma \to_s \Sigma)$. In the definition of N we then will have the clause N(goto L)(γ) = γ(L). How this γ(L) is obtained from the declaration of L in a statement S will be discussed later when we come to define the meaning of statements from *Stat*.

Thus we see that the meaning γ(L) of the statement goto L with respect to γ is a state transformation that does not describe the evaluation of goto L only, but also of the rest of the program to be evaluated once goto L has been executed. But then the same must be true for an arbitrary statement A as well. In the operational semantics care was taken of this, because the other statements which had to be evaluated afterwards remained available (see clauses d - g in definition 10.2). Here we will use an abstraction of this idea resembling the approach of the goto statement. Instead of keeping track of a text defining a state transformation, we supply this transformation as an extra argument of N. This transformation ϕ is called a *continuation*, and it is meant to describe the effect of evaluation of the "rest of the program" textually following the statement being defined. Summarizing: if ϕ specifies how evaluation of the program will continue once the right-hand end of A has been reached, and if γ specifies for every label L how evaluation of the program proceeds once we have reached L, then we want $N(A)(\gamma)(\phi)$ to specify the evaluation of the program starting from the left-hand end of A.

This approach also solves the problem how to define the meaning of (A';A") in terms of the meanings of A' and A". The meaning $N((A';A''))(\gamma)(\phi)$ of (A';A") with labels defined by γ and continuation ϕ, will be equal to the meaning of A' with labels defined by γ, but now with a new continuation ϕ'. For, if evaluation of A' terminates normally (i.e. not through execution of a goto statement), then afterwards the statement A" has to be evaluated. Thus the continuation ϕ' must be equal to the meaning of A" with labels defined by γ and with continuation ϕ, i.e. we have $N((A';A''))(\gamma)(\phi) = N(A')(\gamma)(N(A'')(\gamma)(\phi))$.

Now if A' happens to be the statement goto L, we arrive at the following: $N((\underline{\text{goto}}\ L;A''))(\gamma)(\phi) = N((\underline{\text{goto}}\ L)(\gamma)(N(A'')(\gamma)(\phi)) = \gamma(L)$. Thus, we obtain the desired result, namely that evaluation of (goto L;A") is dependent only on the meaning of L and not on the meaning of A" or the continuation ϕ.

In order to be able to give the definition of the semantic function N, we first have to introduce the domain of all label definitions. This domain is (again) denoted by Γ, has typical elements $\gamma,\ldots$, but now is defined as $\Gamma = Lvar \to M$ with M defined as in chapter 5. From that chapter we also adopt the notion of a variant $\gamma\{\phi/L\}$ and a simultaneous variant $\gamma\{\phi_i/L_i\}_{i=1}^{n}$ of γ.

DEFINITION 10.4. The semantic function N with functionality N: $Unst \to (\Gamma \to [M \to M])$ is defined inductively by:

(i) $N(v:=t)(\gamma)(\phi) = \lambda\sigma\cdot\phi(\sigma\{R(t)(\sigma)/L(v)(\sigma)\})$

(ii) $N((A';A''))(\gamma)(\phi) = N(A')(\gamma)(N(A'')(\gamma)(\phi))$

(iii) $N(\underline{\text{if}}\ b\ \underline{\text{then}}\ A'\ \underline{\text{else}}\ A''\ \underline{\text{fi}})(\gamma)(\phi) =$

$\lambda\sigma\cdot\underline{\text{if}}\ W(b)(\sigma)\ \underline{\text{then}}\ N(A')(\gamma)(\phi)(\sigma)\ \underline{\text{else}}\ N(A'')(\gamma)(\phi)(\sigma)\ \underline{\text{fi}}$

(iv) $N(\underline{\text{goto}}\ L)(\gamma)(\phi) = \gamma(L)$

END 10.4.

Remark. The claim on the functionality of N in the above definition has to be justified. However, in the first place one can easily show that $\forall A \in Unst\ \forall\gamma \in \Gamma\ \forall\phi \in M$ we have $N(A)(\gamma)(\phi) \in M$, i.e. it is a strict function. Furthermore, one can use lemma 5.7 to prove that $\lambda\phi_1\cdot\lambda\phi_2\cdot\ldots\cdot\lambda\phi_n\cdot\lambda\phi\cdot N(A)(\gamma\{\phi_i/L_i\}_{i=1}^{n})(\phi) \in [M^{n+1} \to M]$ from which it follows that $\lambda\phi\cdot N(A)(\gamma)(\phi) \in [M \to M]$.

We now discuss, as a preparation to the definition of the denotational semantics for statements from *Stat*, how the continuations $\phi_i = \gamma(L_i)$ $(i = 1,\ldots,n)$ can be obtained from their declaration in $S \equiv [L_i:A_i]_{i=1}^{n}$. We have explained that the continuation ϕ_i associated with label L_i is such that it describes what remains to be done until completion of the execution of S, once this execution has reached label L_i. In particular, we have that ϕ_1 coincides with the meaning of S itself.

We develop some relations between the ϕ_i $(i = 1,\ldots,n)$. First of all, we have that

$$\phi_n = N(A_n)(\gamma\{\phi_i/L_i\}_{i=1}^n)(\lambda\sigma\cdot\sigma).$$

For, if L_n has been reached during evaluation of S, we then have to execute statement A_n, and if this execution terminates normally (i.e. not by execution of a goto statement) then the computation is finished, so the appropriate continuation here is $\lambda\sigma\cdot\sigma$, the identity function. Notice that A_n can contain backward jumps (substatements of the form <u>goto</u> L_i) and therefore the continuations $\phi_1,\ldots,\phi_n$ have to be available in γ. Analogously we have

$$\phi_{n-1} = N(A_{n-1})(\gamma\{\phi_i/L_i\}_{i=1}^n)(\phi_n):$$

once label L_{n-1} has been reached, what remains to be done is the execution of A_{n-1} and, if this execution terminates at the right-hand end of A_{n-1}, it has to be followed by that what remains to be done once label L_n has been reached, i.e. the continuation ϕ_n.

We thus arrive at the following equations:

$$\phi_i = N(A_i)(\gamma\{\phi_i/L_i\}_{i=1}^n)(\phi_{i+1})$$

for $i = 1,\ldots,n$, where $\phi_{n+1} = \lambda\sigma\cdot\sigma$. Or, stated otherwise, the n-tuple $<\phi_1,\ldots,\phi_n>$ must be a fixed point of the operator $<\Phi_1,\ldots,\Phi_n>$, where Φ_i is defined by

$$\Phi_i = \lambda\psi_1\cdot\lambda\psi_2\cdot\ldots\cdot\lambda\psi_n\cdot N(A_i)(\gamma\{\psi_i/L_i\}_{i=1}^n)(\psi_{i+1})$$

for $i = 1,\ldots,n$ ($\psi_{n+1} = \lambda\sigma\cdot\sigma$). In fact, the required fixed point must be the least one $\mu[\Phi_1,\ldots,\Phi_n]$. The main reason for this is that we can approximate $\mu[\Phi_1,\ldots,\Phi_n]$ with the functions $<\Phi_1,\ldots,\Phi_n>^k(\bot)$ (see also theorem 5.8) and these approximations are in some sense equivalent to those evaluations in $[L_i:A_i]_{i=1}^n$ during which the total number of labels encountered is not more than k (compare exercise 10.5).

All this leads to the following definition.

DEFINITION 10.5. The function M: *Stat* $\to (\Gamma \to M)$ is defined by

$$M([L_i:A_i]_{i=1}^n)(\gamma) = \phi_1,$$

where $<\phi_1,\ldots,\phi_n> = \mu[\Phi_1,\ldots,\Phi_n]$, and for each j, $1 \le j \le n$,

$\Phi_j = \lambda\psi_1\cdot\ldots\cdot\lambda\psi_n\cdot N(A_j)(\gamma\{\psi_i/L_i\}_{i=1}^n)(\psi_{j+1})$, with $\psi_{n+1} = \lambda\sigma\cdot\sigma$.

END 10.5.

Examples

1. $M(L{:}\underline{\text{goto}}\ L)(\gamma) = \phi_1$, with $\phi_1 = \mu\Phi_1$, and

   $\Phi_1 = \lambda\psi_1\cdot N(\underline{\text{goto}}\ L)(\gamma\{\psi_1/L\})(\lambda\sigma\cdot\sigma) = \lambda\psi_1\cdot\psi_1$. Thus,

   $\mu\Phi_1 = \mu[\lambda\psi_1\cdot\psi_1] = \lambda\sigma\cdot\bot$, as it should be.

2. Let $A \in$ *Unst* be without goto statements and let $D \equiv x:=x$.

   Then $M(L{:}\underline{\text{if}}\ b\ \underline{\text{then}}\ (A;\underline{\text{goto}}\ L)\ \underline{\text{else}}\ D\ \underline{\text{fi}})(\gamma) = \phi_1$, where

   $\phi_1 = \mu\Phi_1$, and $\Phi_1 =$

   $\lambda\psi_1\cdot N(\underline{\text{if}}\ b\ \underline{\text{then}}\ (A;\underline{\text{goto}}\ L)\ \underline{\text{else}}\ D\ \underline{\text{fi}})(\gamma\{\psi_1/L\})(\lambda\sigma\cdot\sigma) =$

   $\lambda\psi_1\cdot\lambda\sigma\cdot\underline{\text{if}}\ W(b)(\sigma)\ \underline{\text{then}}\ N((A;\underline{\text{goto}}\ L))(\gamma\{\psi_1/L\})(\lambda\sigma\cdot\sigma)(\sigma)$
   $\qquad\underline{\text{else}}\ N(D)(\gamma\{\psi_1/L\})(\lambda\sigma\cdot\sigma)(\sigma)\ \underline{\text{fi}} =$

   $\lambda\psi_1\cdot\lambda\sigma\cdot\underline{\text{if}}\ W(b)(\sigma)\ \underline{\text{then}}\ N(A)(\gamma\{\psi_1/L\})(N(\underline{\text{goto}}\ L)(\gamma\{\psi_1/L\})(\lambda\sigma\cdot\sigma))(\sigma)$
   $\qquad\underline{\text{else}}\ (\lambda\sigma\cdot\sigma)(\sigma\{R(x)(\sigma)/L(x)(\sigma)\})\ \underline{\text{fi}} =$

   $\lambda\psi_1\cdot\lambda\sigma\cdot\underline{\text{if}}\ W(b)(\sigma)\ \underline{\text{then}}\ N(A)(\gamma\{\psi_1/L\})(\psi_1)(\sigma)\ \underline{\text{else}}\ \sigma\ \underline{\text{fi}} =$

   (applying exercise 10.1)

   $\lambda\psi_1\cdot\lambda\sigma\cdot\underline{\text{if}}\ W(b)(\sigma)\ \underline{\text{then}}\ \psi_1(N(A)(\gamma\{\psi_1/L\})(\lambda\sigma\cdot\sigma)(\sigma))\ \underline{\text{else}}\ \sigma\ \underline{\text{fi}}.$

   If A contains no goto statements then $N(A)(\gamma\{\psi_1/L\})(\lambda\sigma\cdot\sigma) = M(A)$, with $M(A)$ as in chapter 4 (exercise 10.2), and we finally obtain that $M(L{:}\underline{if}\ b\ \underline{then}\ (A;\underline{goto}\ L)\ \underline{else}\ D\ \underline{fi})(\gamma) = \mu[\lambda\psi_1\cdot\lambda\sigma\cdot\underline{if}\ W(b)(\sigma)\ \underline{then}\ \psi_1(M(A)(\sigma))\ \underline{else}\ \sigma\ \underline{fi}]$, i.e. we have shown (using theorem 3.26) that L:<u>if</u> b <u>then</u> (A;<u>goto</u> L) <u>else</u> D <u>fi</u> is equivalent to <u>while</u> b <u>do</u> A <u>od</u>.

Remarks

1. The least fixed point referred to in the above definition actually exists, because the operators Φ_i are continuous (use the remark on 10.4) and, therefore, $<\Phi_1,\ldots,\Phi_n> \in [M^n \to M^n]$.
2. If $S \equiv [L_i{:}A_i]_{i=1}^n$ is a closed program, then the operators Φ_i and consequently also the least fixed point $<\phi_1,\ldots,\phi_n>$ are not dependent on the γ chosen.

Before the proof of the main theorem 10.7, stating the equivalence of the two functions M and O, we collect some useful facts in the following lemma.

<u>LEMMA 10.6</u>. Let $S \equiv [L_i{:}A_i]_{i=1}^n \in Stat$, let $\gamma \in \Gamma$ and let Φ_i and ϕ_i be derived from S and γ as in the definition of M $(i = 1,\ldots,n)$. Let ϕ_i^k and γ^k be defined inductively by:

$$\phi_i^0 = \lambda\sigma\cdot\bot \quad , i = 1,\ldots,n$$

$$\phi_{n+1}^k = \lambda\sigma\cdot\sigma \quad , k = 0,1,\ldots$$

$$\gamma^k = \gamma\{\phi_j^k/L_j\}_{j=1}^n \quad , k = 0,1,\ldots$$

$$\phi_i^{k+1} = \Phi_i(\phi_i^k,\ldots,\phi_n^k) = N(A_i)(\gamma^k)(\phi_{i+1}^k),\ i = 1,\ldots,n,\ k = 0,1,\ldots$$

Then

a. $\phi_i = \bigsqcup_k \phi_i^k$, $i = 1,\ldots,n$

b. $\phi_i = N(A_i;\ldots;A_n)(\gamma\{\phi_j/L_j\}_{j=1}^n)(\lambda\sigma\cdot\sigma)$, $i = 1,\ldots,n$

c. $\phi_i^k \sqsubseteq N(A_i;\ldots;A_n)(\gamma^{k-1})(\lambda\sigma\cdot\sigma)$, $1 \le i \le n$, $k = 1,2,\ldots$

PROOF.

a. This is a straightforward analog of results in chapter 5 (see for example corollary 5.10)

b. We have (by *ffp*)

$\phi_n = N(A_n)(\gamma\{\phi_i/L_i\}_{i=1}^n)(\lambda\sigma\cdot\sigma)$, and also

$$\begin{aligned}\phi_{n-1} &= N(A_{n-1})(\gamma\{\phi_i/L_i\}_{i=1}^n)(\phi_n) = \\ &\quad N(A_{n-1})(\gamma\{\phi_i/L_i\}_{i=1}^n)(N(A_n)(\gamma\{\phi_i/L_i\}_{i=1}^n)(\lambda\sigma\cdot\sigma)) = \\ &\quad N(A_{n-1};A_n)(\gamma\{\phi_i/L_i\}_{i=1}^n)(\lambda\sigma\cdot\sigma),\end{aligned}$$

etc.

c. Induction on k. The basic step (k = 1) can be proved using the fact that $\lambda\phi\cdot N(A)(\gamma)(\phi)$ is monotonic in ϕ and that $N(A_i;\ldots;A_n)(\gamma)(\phi) = N(A_i)(\gamma)(N(A_{i+1};\ldots;A_n)(\gamma)(\phi))$. The induction step is proved as follows.

$$\phi_i^k = N(A_i)(\gamma^{k-1})(\phi_{i+1}^{k-1}) = N(A_i)(\gamma^{k-1})(N(A_{i+1})(\gamma^{k-2})(\phi_{i+2}^{k-2})) = (\#)$$

Now we use the remark on definition 10.4, and the fact that continuous functions are by definition monotonic to show that

$$N(A_{i+1})(\gamma^{k-2})(\phi_{i+2}^{k-2}) \sqsubseteq N(A_{i+1})(\gamma^{k-1})(\phi_{i+2}^{k-1})$$

and thus, using this remark again:

$$\begin{aligned}(\#) &\sqsubseteq N(A_i)(\gamma^{k-1})(N(A_{i+1})(\gamma^{k-1})(\phi_{i+2}^{k-1})) = \\ &\quad N(A_i;A_{i+1})(\gamma^{k-1})(\phi_{i+2}^{k-1}).\end{aligned}$$

Repeating the argument, we get

$$\phi_i^k \sqsubseteq N((\ldots(A_i;A_{i+1});\ldots);A_n))(\gamma^{k-1})(\lambda\sigma\cdot\sigma) =$$

$$N(A_i;A_{i+1};\ldots;A_n)(\gamma^{k-1})(\lambda\sigma\cdot\sigma),$$

where the last identity can be proved easily from the definition of N.

END 10.6.

THEOREM 10.7. For each closed statement $S \in \mathit{Stat}$, and for all $\gamma \in \Gamma$, we have

$$O(S) = M(S)(\gamma)$$

PROOF. Note that $O(S)$ cannot be undefined, because S is closed (compare remark 3 after definition 10.2).

a. $O(S) \sqsubseteq M(S)(\gamma)$. Let $S \equiv [L_i:A_i]_{i=1}^n$. It is sufficient to show that, for all A and σ, $\kappa(\mathit{Comp}(\langle S,A\rangle)(\sigma)) \sqsubseteq N(A)(\gamma\{\phi_i/L_i\}_{i=1}^n)(\lambda\sigma\cdot\sigma)(\sigma)$, with ϕ_i, $i = 1,\ldots,n$, as in definition 10.5. In fact, taking $A \equiv A_1;A_2;\ldots;A_{n-1};A_n$ this leads to the desired result, since $O(S) = \kappa \circ \mathit{Comp}(\langle S,A_1;\ldots;A_n\rangle)$ by definition 10.3, and $N(A_1;\ldots;A_n)(\gamma')(\lambda\sigma\cdot\sigma) = \phi_1 = M(S)(\gamma)$ by lemma 10.6b (putting $\gamma' = \gamma\{\phi_i/L_i\}_{i=1}^n$). If $\sigma = \bot$, the result is obvious. Also, if $\mathit{Comp}(\langle S,A\rangle)(\sigma) \in \Sigma^\omega$, applying κ to it yields $\bot$, and the result is clear. There remains the case that $\sigma \neq \bot$ and $\mathit{Comp}(\langle S,A\rangle)(\sigma) \in \Sigma^+$. We then apply induction on the length of the sequence $\mathit{Comp}(\langle S,A\rangle)(\sigma)$. We distinguish various cases for the structure of A.

1. $A \equiv v:=t$. $\kappa(\mathit{Comp}(\langle S,v:=t\rangle)(\sigma)) = \kappa(\langle\sigma\{R(t)(\sigma)/L(v)(\sigma)\}\rangle) =$
$\sigma\{R(t)(\sigma)/L(v)(\sigma)\} = (\lambda\sigma\cdot\sigma)(\sigma\{R(t)(\sigma)/L(v)(\sigma)\}) =$
$N(v:=t)(\gamma')(\lambda\sigma\cdot\sigma)(\sigma)$.

2. A ≡ <u>goto</u> L. Let L ≡ L_j, for some j, 1 ≤ j ≤ n.

$\kappa(Comp(<S,\underline{goto}\ L_j>)(\sigma)) = \kappa(Comp(<S,A_j;\ldots;A_n>)(\sigma)) \sqsubseteq$ (the length of $Comp(<S,\underline{goto}\ L_j>)(\sigma)$ is one more than that of $Comp(<S,A_j;\ldots;A_n>)(\sigma)$, so we may apply the induction hypothesis) $N(A_j;A_{j+1};\ldots;A_n)(\gamma')(\lambda\sigma\cdot\sigma)(\sigma)$ = (lemma 10.6b) $\phi_j(\sigma) = \gamma\{\phi_i/L_i\}_{i=1}^n(L_j)(\sigma) = N(\underline{goto}\ L_j)(\gamma')(\lambda\sigma\cdot\sigma)(\sigma)$.

3. A ≡ <u>if</u> b <u>then</u> A' <u>else</u> A" <u>fi</u>. This is easy by induction, since the length of the computation sequence for <u>if</u> b <u>then</u> A' <u>else</u> A" <u>fi</u> is one more than that for A' or that for A".

4. A ≡ (v:=t;A'). $\kappa(Comp(<S,v:=t;A'>)(\sigma)) =$ $\kappa(Comp(<S,A'>)(\sigma\{R(t)(\sigma)/L(v)(\sigma)\})) \sqsubseteq$ (by the usual induction argument) $N(A')(\gamma')(\lambda\sigma\cdot\sigma)(\sigma\{R(t)(\sigma)/L(v)(\sigma)\}) =$ $N(v:=t;A')(\gamma')(\lambda\sigma\cdot\sigma)(\sigma)$.

5. A ≡ (<u>goto</u> L;A'). Similar to case 2, using the fact that $N(\underline{goto}\ L;A')(\gamma')(\lambda\sigma\cdot\sigma) = N(\underline{goto}\ L)(\gamma')(\lambda\sigma\cdot\sigma)$.

6. A ≡ (<u>if</u> b <u>then</u> A" <u>else</u> A‴ <u>fi</u>;A'). Exercise.

7. A ≡ ((A";A‴);A'). Again easy by induction, using the facts that the length of $Comp(<S,((A'';A''');A')>)(\sigma)$ is one more than that of $Comp(<S,(A'';(A''';A'))>)(\sigma)$, and that $N(((A'';A''');A')) =$ $N((A'';(A''';A')))$ (which follows directly from definition 10.4).

b. $M(S)(\gamma) \sqsubseteq O(S)$. Let Φ_i, ϕ_i, ϕ^k and γ^k be as in lemma 10.6. Similar to part a, and the proof of theorem 5.22, it is sufficient to show that, for all k and A, $N(A)(\gamma^k)(\lambda\sigma\cdot\sigma)(\sigma) \sqsubseteq \kappa(Comp(<S,A>)(\sigma))$. We use induction on the entity <k,c(A)> - ordered as in the proof of theorem 5.22 - with c(A) defined not simply as the complexity of A, but as follows: c(v:=t) = c(goto L) = 1, c((A';A")) = 2×c(A')+c(A") and c(if b then A' else A" fi) = c(A') + c(A"). (The anomaly in the definition of c((A';A")) is necessary to make the induction argument go through. Observe that c(((A';A");A‴)) > c((A';(A";A‴))), a property which we shall need below.)

1. A ≡ v:=t, or A ≡ if b then A' else A" fi. Exercises.
2. A ≡ goto L_j. N(goto L_j)$(\gamma^k)(\lambda\sigma\cdot\sigma)$ = $\phi_j^k \sqsubseteq$ (by 10.6c) $N(A_j;\ldots;A_n)(\gamma^{k-1})(\lambda\sigma\cdot\sigma) \sqsubseteq$ (induction, since $\langle k-1, c(A_j;\ldots;A_n)\rangle \prec \langle k, c(\text{goto } L_j)\rangle$) $\kappa \circ Comp(\langle S, A_j;\ldots;A_n\rangle) = \kappa \circ Comp(\langle S, \text{goto } L_j\rangle)$.
3. A ≡ (v:=t;A') or A ≡ (if b then A" else A‴ fi;A'). Exercises. (Notice that c((v:=t;A')) > c(A'), and c((if b then A" else A‴ fi;A')) > max(c((A";A')),c((A‴;A'))).)
4. A ≡ (goto L_j;A'). Since N((goto L_j;A')) = N(goto L_j) and $\kappa \circ Comp(\langle S,(\text{goto } L_j;A')\rangle) = \kappa \circ Comp(\langle S, \text{goto } L_j\rangle)$, we can use the induction hypothesis.
5. A ≡ ((A";A‴);A'). $N(((A";A‴);A'))(\gamma^k)(\lambda\sigma\cdot\sigma)$ = $N(A")(\gamma^k)(N(A‴)(\gamma^k)(N(A')(\gamma^k)(\lambda\sigma\cdot\sigma)))$ = $N((A";(A‴;A')))(\gamma^k)(\lambda\sigma\cdot\sigma) \sqsubseteq$ (by induction, since c((A";(A‴;A'))) < c(((A";A‴);A'))) $\kappa \circ Comp(\langle S,(A";(A‴;A'))\rangle)$ = (def. $Comp$) $\kappa \circ Comp(\langle S,((A";A‴);A')\rangle)$.

END 10.7.

We will close this section by taking another look at the meaning of unlabeled statements A. We saw that the function N(A) essentially yields a continuation as a result. This result depends on a number of continuations, which are supplied to N(A) either directly as an argument (the ϕ in $N(A)(\gamma)(\phi)$) or implicitly through γ, as meaning of the labels occurring in A. In exercise 10.2 we describe a method called "continuation removal" to dispose of the ϕ in the above formula, yielding a more direct approach: the meaning of a statement is again a state transformation instead of a continuation transformation. This method can only be applied to unlabeled statements A which do not contain goto statements as substatements.

We now take one further step: we show that an analogous method can be applied if there are goto-substatements. We will define a function A giving the meaning of a statement A as a (total) function from Σ_0 to $\Sigma_0 \cup (\Sigma_0 \times Lvar)$, where $\Sigma_0 = \Sigma \backslash \{\bot\}$, such that $A(A)(\sigma) = \sigma'$ means that evaluation of A terminates normally in state σ' (i.e. not as the result of an execution of a goto statement), and $A(A)(\sigma) = \langle\sigma',L\rangle$ means that evaluation of A terminates by execution of a substatement <u>goto</u> L in state σ'.

Put another way, a statement A containing goto-substatements can be viewed as a statement with one *entry point* (where evaluation of A starts) but with several *exit points*, namely the *normal exit point* (the right-hand end of the statement) and the *special exit points* (the substatements <u>goto</u> L). We call an exit point determined by a substatement <u>goto</u> L an L-*exit point*. The function A then specifies for every initial state σ the kind of exit point which will be reached and the final state in which this exit point will be reached.

The function A, applied to a statement A and an initial state σ, yields a final state σ' which is the result of evaluation of A, and not of evaluation of A followed by some continuation (as was the case in $N(A)(\gamma)(\phi)(\sigma)$). Since, in the proof systems to be discussed in the next section, we deal with formulae {p}A{q}, where q is a predicate on the final state at the normal exit point, we can expect that the function A will be more useful there than N.

We now give the definition of A.

DEFINITION 10.8. The function A with functionality
A: $Unst \to (\Sigma_0 \to (\Sigma_0 \cup (\Sigma_0 \times Lvar)))$ is inductively defined by

(i) $A(v{:=}t)(\sigma) = \sigma\{R(t)(\sigma)/L(v)(\sigma)\}$

(ii) $A((A';A''))(\sigma) = \begin{cases} A(A'')(A(A')(\sigma)), & \text{if } A(A')(\sigma) \in \Sigma_0 \\ A(A')(\sigma) & \text{, otherwise} \end{cases}$

(iii) $A(\underline{\text{if}}\ b\ \underline{\text{then}}\ A'\ \underline{\text{else}}\ A''\ \underline{\text{fi}})(\sigma) = \begin{cases} A(A')(\sigma), & \text{if } W(b)(\sigma) = tt \\ A(A'')(\sigma), & \text{if } W(b)(\sigma) = ff \end{cases}$

(iv) $A\ (\underline{\text{goto}}\ L)(\sigma) = \langle\sigma, L\rangle$

END 10.8.

We have the following lemma on the relation between A and N.

LEMMA 10.9.

1. $A(A)(\sigma) = \sigma' \iff \forall\gamma\in\Gamma\forall\phi\in M[N(A)(\gamma)(\phi)(\sigma) = \phi(\sigma')]$
2. $A(A)(\sigma) = \langle\sigma', L\rangle \iff \forall\gamma\in\Gamma\forall\phi\in M[N(A)(\gamma)(\phi)(\sigma) = \gamma(L)(\sigma')]$.

PROOF. The $\Rightarrow$ - parts of 1 and 2 are straightforward by induction on the complexity of A. The $\Leftarrow$ - parts can be proven by contradiction. For instance, proving 2 " $\Leftarrow$ ", suppose $\forall\gamma\in\Gamma\forall\phi\in M[N(A)(\gamma)(\phi)(\sigma) = \gamma(L)(\sigma')]$, and $A(A)(\sigma) \neq \langle\sigma', L\rangle$. Then we have two possibilities.

The first one is $A(A)(\sigma) = \langle\sigma'', L'\rangle$ (where $\sigma' \neq \sigma''$ or $L \not\equiv L'$) and thus, using 2 " $\Rightarrow$ ", $\forall\gamma\in\Gamma\forall\phi\in M[N(A)(\gamma)(\phi)(\sigma) = \gamma(L')(\sigma'')]$. Now choose γ such that $\gamma(L)(\sigma') \neq \gamma(L')(\sigma'')$ and we have a contradiction.

The other possibility is $A(A)(\sigma) = \sigma''$. Then we have (1 " $\Rightarrow$ ") $\forall\gamma\in\Gamma\forall\phi\in M[N(A)(\gamma)(\phi)(\sigma) = \phi(\sigma'')]$, and we reach a contradiction by choosing γ and ϕ such that $\gamma(L)(\sigma') \neq \phi(\sigma'')$.

END 10.9.

10.3. Correctness and completeness

In this section we will discuss a proof system which can handle goto statements. This system will be introduced by re-examining correctness formulae like {p}A{q}, and in particular by investigating how validity of such constructs must be defined.

Let $S \equiv [L_i:A_i]_{i=1}^n$ be a closed statement, and suppose we want to build up a formal proof of the correctness formula $\{p\}S\{q\}$. Notice that the meaning of this formula can be formulated as has been done up till now in this book. This is due to the fact that S is closed, i.e. all its labels are declared, and therefore S has only one exit point, namely the normal one. If we want to build a formal proof of the formula $\{p\}S\{q\}$ using the rule of composition, then we have to construct proofs of the formulae $\{p\}A_1\{p_2\},\{p_2\}A_2\{p_3\},\ldots,\{p_n\}A_n\{q\}$.

Now, as has been remarked already in the introduction, the notion of validity for formulae of this type has to be refined. Consider, for example, the case that $A_1 \equiv (A';A'')$. We would like to derive $\{p\}(A';A'')\{p_2\}$ from proofs of $\{p\}A'\{p'\}$ and of $\{p'\}A''\{p_2\}$ using the rule of composition

$$\frac{\{p\}A'\{p'\},\{p'\}A''\{q\}}{\{p\}A';A''\{q\}}$$

However, this rule is not valid anymore, if we take as informal definition of validity of $\{p\}A\{q\}$ the usual notion "if p holds before evaluation of A and this evaluation terminates, then q holds after this evaluation". Take for instance, in the above rule, $A' \equiv$ goto L and for A" an arbitrary unlabeled statement. Then, after evaluation of A';A" as well as after evaluation of A', the assertion p' will hold, and in general q will not be true.

The following refinement of the notion of validity looks promising to solve this difficulty. Let us reformulate the meaning of $\{p_1\}A\{p_2\}$ as "if A is evaluated beginning in a state where p_1 holds, and if evaluation of A terminates *at the normal exit point,* then p_2 holds in the final state". After all, an intermediate assertion in a program can be viewed as a condition which should be true at a certain point in the program text or, stated otherwise, an intermediate assertion at a certain point in a program is supposed to be valid every time evaluation of the program reaches this point.

Now, according to the new informal validity definition, the formula

$$\{p\}\ \underline{\text{goto}}\ L\ \{q\} \tag{\#}$$

would be valid for every assertion p and q, for evaluation of goto L always terminates by "jumping away". However, this brings up new problems. For instance the formula

$$\{\underline{\text{true}}\}\ L_1{:}x{:=}1;\ \underline{\text{goto}}\ L_2;\ L_2{:}x{:=}x\ \{x=0\}$$

would now be derivable, by the following steps:

1. $\{\underline{\text{true}}\}\ L_1{:}x{:=}1\ \{x=1\}$ (assignment)
2. $\{x=1\}\ \underline{\text{goto}}\ L_2\ \{x=0\}$ (#)
3. $\{x=0\}\ L_2{:}x{:=}x\ \{x=0\}$ (assignment)
4. $\{\underline{\text{true}}\}\ L_1{:}x{:=}1;\ \underline{\text{goto}}\ L_2;\ L_2{:}x{:=}x\ \{x=0\}$ (composition)

But clearly, after evaluation of $L_1{:}x{:=}1;\ \underline{\text{goto}}\ L_2;\ L_2{:}x{:=}x$, the postcondition $x = 1$ holds.

These difficulties can be solved by putting a restriction on the preconditions p allowed in (#), in the following way. Suppose we want to prove $\{p\}S\{q\}$, where $S \equiv L_1{:}A_1;\ldots;L_n{:}A_n$. Now assume that we can find a list of *label invariants* $p_1,\ldots,p_n$. These p_i are assertions which we assume to be true every time label L_i is reached during execution of S, starting in initial state satisfying p. We now refine our notion of validity once more, and define validity with respect to the invariants p_i at L_i for $i = 1,\ldots,n$, informally as follows:

> The formula $\{p\}A\{q\}$ is called valid iff for every evaluation of A the following holds: if p holds for the initial state, then
>
> (*) either evaluation terminates at the normal exit point of A and q holds, or evaluation terminates at an L_i-exit point of A and p_i holds.

One can see that, according to (*), the formulae $\{p\}\ \underline{\text{goto}}\ L_i\ \{q\}$ are no longer valid for all p. Validity holds however for all preconditions p such that $p \supset p_i$. In particular $\{p_i\}$ goto L_i $\{false\}$ is valid ($i = 1,\ldots,n$). Notice also that the usual inference rules and the axioms are all valid according to (*).

Now if we can *derive* $\{p_i\}A_i\{p_{i+1}\}$ using valid rules and axioms, and also using the formulae $\{p_j\}$ goto L_j $\{false\}$, then we know that $\{p_i\}A_i\{p_{i+1}\}$ must be valid according to (*). This means the following: if we consider evaluation of A_i as a substatement of $S \equiv [L_i:A_i]_{i=1}^{n}$, starting in an initial state for which p_i holds, then we can infer from the validity of $\{p_i\}A_i\{p_{i+1}\}$ that at the normal exit point p_{i+1} holds, and that at every L_j-exit point p_j holds. In other words: when evaluation of A_i terminates because label L_j has been reached, then the corresponding invariant p_j must hold ($1 \leq j \leq n$).

But from this we can infer that $\{p_1\}S\{p_{n+1}\}$ holds. For, consider an evaluation of S with initial state satisfying p_1, and suppose that this evaluation terminates. Then this evaluation can be split up in a finite number of subsequent evaluations of substatements A_i, and since, by the above considerations, we are assured that at all "links" labeled L_j the corresponding invariant p_j holds, we can infer that p_{n+1} is true when the last evaluation of substatement A_n terminates (necessarily at the normal exit point).

The above considerations suggest the following inference rule:

> if we can derive $\{p_i\}A_i\{p_{i+1}\}$ ($i = 1,\ldots,n$) from the assumptions $\{p_j\}$ goto L_j $\{false\}$ ($j = 1,\ldots,n$), then we may infer $\{p_1\}\ L_1:A_1;\ldots;L_n:A_n\ \{p_{n+1}\}$.

Now the formula $\{true\}S\{x=0\}$, where $S \equiv L_1$:x:=1; goto L_2; L_2:x:=x (see the above incorrect derivation) cannot be derived anymore, but a derivation of $\{true\}S\{x=1\}$ can be made straightforwardly (take $p_1 \equiv$ true, $p_2 \equiv x=1$).

Thus we arrive at an inference rule of the same type as Scott's induction rule, in that assumptions are used in the premise which are discharged in the conclusion. The proof system to be defined will therefore be framed in a way resembling the system of chapter 5.

DEFINITION 10.10 (syntax of correctness formulae).

a. The class *Assn* of the *assertions* is defined as in chapter 3.
b. The class *Asmp* of the *assumptions*, with typical elements h,... is defined by

$$h ::= \{p\}\ \underline{\text{goto}}\ L\ \{\underline{\text{false}}\} \mid h_1 \wedge h_2$$

c. The class *Afor* of *atomic correctness formulae*, with typical elements f,... is defined by

$$f ::= \{p\}A\{q\} \mid f_1 \wedge f_2$$

d. The class *Gfor* of *generalized correctness formulae*, with typical elements g,... is defined by

$$g ::= p \mid h \Rightarrow \{p\}A\{q\} \mid \{p\}S\{q\}$$

END 10.10.

Remarks

1. The only assumptions which are needed to derive results like {p}S{q} are assumptions of the form {p} goto L {false}. Therefore, we do not allow other assumptions (see also exercise 10.7).
2. A generalized correctness formula g is called *closed* if either
   a. g is an assertion, or
   b. $g \equiv h \Rightarrow \{p\}A\{q\}$, with $h \equiv \{p_1\}\ \underline{\text{goto}}\ L_1\ \{\underline{\text{false}}\} \wedge \ldots \wedge$ $\{p_k\}\ \underline{\text{goto}}\ L_k\ \{\underline{\text{false}}\}$ such that $L_i \not\equiv L_j$ for $1 \le i < j \le k$ and every label in A is an L_i $(1 \le i \le k)$
   c. $g \equiv \{p\}S\{q\}$, where S is a closed statement

   A pair $\langle h,A\rangle \in$ *Asmp* × *Unst* is called *closed* if the correctness formula $h \Rightarrow \{\underline{\text{true}}\}A\{\underline{\text{true}}\}$ is closed.
3. We will not need the class *Afor* for the present. Use of it will be

made when we come to define validity using the semantic function N (definition 10.23 and following).

DEFINITION 10.11. The proof system H has the following axioms and inference rules.

1. $h \Rightarrow \{p[t/v]\}\ v{:=}t\ \{p\}$ (assignment)
2. $h_1 \wedge \ldots \wedge h_n \Rightarrow h_i \quad (n \geq 1,\ 1 \leq i \leq n)$ (selection)
3. Every valid assertion is an axiom (assertion)
4. $$\frac{p \supset p_1, \{p_1\}S\{q_1\}, q_1 \supset q}{\{p\}S\{q\}}$$ (consequence I)
5. $$\frac{p \supset p_1,\ h \Rightarrow \{p_1\}A\{q_1\},\ q_1 \supset q}{h \Rightarrow \{p\}A\{q\}}$$ (consequence II)
6. $$\frac{h \Rightarrow \{p\}A\{q\},\ h \Rightarrow \{q\}A'\{r\}}{h \Rightarrow \{p\}A;A'\{r\}}$$ (composition)
7. $$\frac{h \Rightarrow \{p \wedge b\}A\{q\},\ h \Rightarrow \{p \wedge \neg b\}A'\{q\}}{h \Rightarrow \{p\}\ \underline{\text{if}}\ b\ \underline{\text{then}}\ A\ \underline{\text{else}}\ A'\ \underline{\text{fi}}\ \{q\}}$$ (conditional)
8. $$\frac{h \Rightarrow \{p_1\}A_1\{p_2\}, \ldots, h \Rightarrow \{p_n\}A_n\{p_{n+1}\}}{\{p_1\}[L_i : A_i]_{i=1}^{n}\{p_{n+1}\}}$$ (labelling)

provided $h \equiv \{p_1\}\ \underline{\text{goto}}\ L_1\ \{\underline{\text{false}}\} \wedge \ldots \wedge \{p_n\}\ \underline{\text{goto}}\ L_n\ \{\underline{\text{false}}\}$.

END 10.11.

Remarks

1. In the above definition (2 and 8) as well as in remark 2b on definition 10.10, we have tacitly assumed that the operator $\wedge$ is associative. From the way assumptions of the form $h_1 \wedge \ldots \wedge h_n$ are used in the system (axiom 2 and rule 8), it is clear that this is indeed the case (the way the expression is built as a conjunction of subexpressions is not relevant). However, notice that it follows from rule 8 that we cannot assume that the operator is commutative (i.e. the order of the formulae in $h_1 \wedge \ldots \wedge h_n$ is relevant).
2. The *closed fragment* of H is denoted by H_C and defined as the system in which only closed correctness formulae occur. One easily establishes that system H is conservative over H_C (i.e. every

closed formula derivable in H has a proof in H_C) using the fact that every inference rule that has a closed conclusion must have closed premises.

3. We cannot do without rule 4, i.e. the formulae which are derivable in system H without rule 4 form a proper subset of the class of formulae derivable in H. However, this rule can be weakened to

   4'. $\dfrac{p \supset p_1, \{p_1\}S\{q\}}{\{p\}S\{q\}}$

   i.e. every formula that can be derived in H can also be derived in H with rule 4' instead of rule 4.

Examples

1. (Formal proof of {true}S{x=1}, where $S \equiv L_1$:x:=1; goto L_2; L_2:x:=x. Compare the discussion preceding definition 10.10.) We denote the assumption {true} goto L_1 {false} ∧ {x=1} goto L_2 {false} by h.

1. true ⊃ 1=1	(assertion)
2. h ⇒ {1=1} x:=1 {x=1}	(assignment)
3. h ⇒ {true} x:=1 {x=1}	(1,2, consequence II)
4. false ⊃ x=1	(assertion)
5. h ⇒ {x=1} goto L_2 {false}	(selection)
6. h ⇒ {x=1} goto L_2 {x=1}	(4,5, consequence II)
7. h ⇒ {true} x:=1; goto L_2 {x=1}	(3,6, composition)
8. h ⇒ {x=1} x:=x {x=1}	(assignment)
9. {true} L_1:x:=1; goto L_2; L_2:x:=x {x=1}	(7,8, labelling)

2. We have derived that for unlabeled statements A not containing goto statements, the statements while b do A od and L: if b then A; goto L else x:=x fi are equivalent (example 2 on definition 10.5). Moreover, we have the inference rule

   $$\frac{\{p \wedge b\}A\{p\}}{\{p\}\ \underline{\text{while}}\ b\ \underline{\text{do}}\ A\ \underline{\text{od}}\ \{p \wedge \neg b\}}$$

   Suppose now that, for arbitrary h, we have a formal proof in H of the formula h ⇒ {p∧b}A{p}. Notice that the condition that h be arbitrary is not a real restriction since every proof of

$h \Rightarrow \{p \wedge b\}A\{p\}$ is independent of h because there are no labels in A. Moreover, each formal proof in the system of chapter 3 can be reformulated in our system, provided the statements in it do not contain while statements. We now show that we can build a proof of {p} L: <u>if</u> b <u>then</u> A; <u>goto</u> L <u>else</u> x:=x <u>fi</u> $\{p \wedge \neg b\}$. Clearly, we have to choose p as the invariant at L, p being the assumption that will always be true at L. Take $h \equiv \{p\}$ <u>goto</u> L {<u>false</u>}. Then we have

1. $h \Rightarrow \{p \wedge b\}A\{p\}$ (assumption)
2. $h \Rightarrow \{p\}$ <u>goto</u> L {<u>false</u>} (selection)
3. <u>false</u> $\supset p \wedge \neg b$ (assertion)
4. $h \Rightarrow \{p\}$ <u>goto</u> L $\{p \wedge \neg b\}$ (2,3, consequence II)
5. $h \Rightarrow \{p \wedge b\}$ A; <u>goto</u> L $\{p \wedge \neg b\}$ (1,4 composition)
6. $h \Rightarrow \{p \wedge \neg b\}$ x:=x $\{p \wedge \neg b\}$ (assignment)
7. $h \Rightarrow \{p\}$ <u>if</u> b <u>then</u> A; <u>goto</u> L
   <u>else</u> x:=x <u>fi</u> $\{p \wedge \neg b\}$ (5,6, conditional)
8. {p} L: <u>if</u> b <u>then</u> A; <u>goto</u> L
   <u>else</u> x:=x <u>fi</u> $\{p \wedge \neg b\}$ (7, labelling)

In order to be able to justify the proof system 10.11, we have to give a definition of validity of generalized correctness formulae. Reasoning along the lines laid out in chapter 5, we would come to a design like the following.

1. Validity of a formula of the form {p}S{q} can be defined in the usual way: $\forall\gamma\in\Gamma\forall\sigma,\sigma'\in\Sigma_0[\mathcal{T}(p)(\sigma) \wedge \mathcal{M}(S)(\gamma)(\sigma) = \sigma' \Rightarrow \mathcal{T}(q)(\sigma')]$.
2. Validity of a formula of the form $h \Rightarrow \{p\}A\{q\}$ can be defined using a function $\mathcal{F}$: $\mathcal{A}for \rightarrow (\Gamma \rightarrow T)$, taking $\models h \Rightarrow \{p\}A\{q\}$ if and only if $\forall\gamma\in\Gamma[\mathcal{F}(h)(\gamma) \Rightarrow \mathcal{F}(\{p\}A\{q\})(\gamma)]$ (see also definitions 5.25 and 5.26; also, it is exactly for this definition that we introduced the class $\mathcal{A}for$, see remark 3 on definition 10.10). Notice that we cannot simply take $\mathcal{F}$ as a function in $\mathcal{A}for \rightarrow T$ because of the possible occurrences of undeclared labels in formulae from $\mathcal{A}for$, the meaning of which has to be provided in some form or another. Therefore, if we take this approach we will have to use a definition of the

meaning of unlabeled statements A which depends on a function γ as well, and this suggests that we have to use the function N for this purpose.

Now such a system can, and in fact will, be given but we postpone this for a while. The reason for this is that a definition along the above lines cannot be used in a natural way to formalize the notion of validity that we have developed in the discussion preceding definition 10.10. Therefore, we will first give another approach.

We again state this notion of validity: a formula {p}A{q} is called valid with respect to the label invariants p_i at L_i for i = 1,...,n, if and only if for every evaluation of A the following holds: if p holds in the initial state, then either evaluation terminates at the normal exit point of A and q holds, or evaluation terminates at an L_i-exit point of A and p_i holds (for some i, $1 \leq i \leq n$).

Now notice that the assertions q and $p_1,\ldots,p_n$ apply to the final states at the various exit points of A. This suggests that we use the semantic function A in the definition of validity. Using this function, we can formalize this notion of validity in the following natural way: {p}A{q} is valid with respect to p_i at L_i (i = 1,...,n) if and only if:

$$\forall\sigma\in\Sigma_0\colon\ T(p)(\sigma) \Rightarrow \begin{bmatrix} (\exists\sigma'\in\Sigma_0[A(A)(\sigma) = \sigma' \wedge T(q)(\sigma')]) \vee \\ (\exists\sigma'\in\Sigma_0[A(A)(\sigma) = \langle\sigma', L_i\rangle \wedge T(p_i)(\sigma')]) \end{bmatrix}$$

Notice furthermore that in the proof system (notably in the rule of labelling) assumptions like $\{p_i\}$ <u>goto</u> L_i {<u>false</u>} are used to indicate which label invariant corresponds to which label. Thus it can be seen that validity of {p}A{q} with respect to p_i at L_i (i = 1,...,n) must mean the same as validity of the generalized correctness formula $\{p_1\}$ <u>goto</u> L_1 {<u>false</u>} $\wedge \ldots \wedge$ $\{p_n\}$ <u>goto</u> L_n {<u>false</u>} $\Rightarrow$ {p}A{q}. All these considerations then lead to the following definition.

<u>DEFINITION 10.12</u> (validity, first definition).

Validity of a closed correctness formula g, notation $\Vdash g$, is defined by

a. $\Vdash p$, if $\forall\sigma\in\Sigma_0: \mathcal{T}(p)(\sigma)$

b. $\Vdash \{p_1\}\ \underline{\text{goto}}\ L_1\ \{\underline{\text{false}}\} \wedge \ldots \wedge \{p_n\}\ \underline{\text{goto}}\ L_n\ \{\underline{\text{false}}\} \Rightarrow \{p\}A\{q\}$, if

$$\forall\sigma\in\Sigma_0: \mathcal{T}(p)(\sigma) \Rightarrow \left[\begin{array}{l}(\exists\sigma'\in\Sigma_0[\mathcal{A}(A)(\sigma) = \sigma' \wedge \mathcal{T}(q)(\sigma')]) \vee \\ (\exists\sigma'\in\Sigma_0[\mathcal{A}(A)(\sigma) = \langle\sigma', L_i\rangle \wedge \mathcal{T}(p_i)(\sigma')])\end{array}\right]$$

c. $\Vdash \{p\}S\{q\}$, if $\forall\gamma\in\Gamma\forall\sigma,\sigma'\in\Sigma_0[\mathcal{T}(p)(\sigma) \wedge \mathcal{M}(S)(\gamma)(\sigma) = \sigma' \Rightarrow \mathcal{T}(q)(\sigma')]$

END 10.12.

Remarks

1. We will use the symbol $\Vdash$ to denote the above notion of validity instead of the more usual $\models$, because we view the above definition as an auxiliary one. A notion of validity which is better adapted to the form of the proof system $\mathcal{H}$ will be introduced in definition 10.24, and we reserve the symbol $\models$ for the latter notion.
2. Soundness of an inference rule (with respect to the above notion of validity) is defined in the usual way. We will use a somewhat loose terminology, speaking of soundness (instead of validity) of axioms too.
3. The way the label invariants $p_1,\ldots,p_n$ corresponding to the labels $L_1,\ldots,L_n$ are derived from an assumption $h \equiv \{p_1\}\ \underline{\text{goto}}\ L_1\ \{\underline{\text{false}}\} \wedge \ldots \wedge \{p_n\}\ \underline{\text{goto}}\ L_n\ \{\underline{\text{false}}\}$ is not too elegant. The presentation could be ameliorated by introducing a new class of correctness formulae, say of the form $\langle L_1:p_1,\ldots,L_n:p_n | \{p\}A\{q\}\rangle$, with the same meaning as $\{p_1\}\ \underline{\text{goto}}\ L_1\ \{\underline{\text{false}}\} \wedge \ldots \wedge \{p_n\}\ \underline{\text{goto}}\ L_n\ \{\underline{\text{false}}\} \Rightarrow \{p\}A\{q\}$. However, as the above validity definition is only an auxiliary one, we will leave the situation as it is now.

<u>THEOREM 10.13</u> (soundness).

The closed fragment $\mathcal{H}_C$ of the proof system defined by 10.10 and 10.11 is sound with respect to validity definition 10.12. Or, in other words, for every closed generalized correctness formula g we have $\vdash g \Rightarrow \Vdash g$.

PROOF. It is sufficient to prove that the axioms and rules in definition 10.11 are all sound.

1. We have to prove $\Vdash h \Rightarrow \{p[t/v]\}\ v:=t\ \{p\}$. We now have for all $\sigma \in \Sigma_0$ that $\mathcal{A}(v:=t)(\sigma) = \sigma\{\mathcal{R}(t)(\sigma)/\mathcal{L}(v)(\sigma)\}$. Thus we see from definition 10.12 that we have to prove $\forall\sigma\in\Sigma_0[\mathcal{T}(p[t/v])(\sigma) \Rightarrow \mathcal{T}(p)(\sigma\{\mathcal{R}(t)(\sigma)/\mathcal{L}(v)(\sigma)\})]$, but this has been derived in the proof of theorem 4.6.
2. We have to prove $\Vdash h_1 \wedge \ldots \wedge h_n \Rightarrow h_i$. Now $h_j \equiv \{p_j\}$ goto L_j {false} for $j = 1,\ldots,n$. Suppose $\mathcal{T}(p_i)(\sigma) = tt$. For all $\sigma \in \Sigma_0$ we have $\mathcal{A}(\text{goto } L_i)(\sigma) = \langle\sigma, L_i\rangle$. Then definition 10.12 yields that we have to show that $\mathcal{T}(p_i)(\sigma) = tt$, and this is true.
3. Trivial.
4. 4, 5 and 7 are exercises.
6. Suppose $\Vdash h \Rightarrow \{p\}A\{q\}$ and $\Vdash h \Rightarrow \{q\}A'\{r\}$, and let $h \equiv \{p_1\}$ goto L_1 {false} $\wedge \ldots \wedge \{p_n\}$ goto L_n {false}. We have to prove $\Vdash h \Rightarrow \{p\}A;A'\{r\}$. Choose a $\sigma \in \Sigma_0$ such that $\mathcal{T}(p)(\sigma) = tt$. From $\Vdash h \Rightarrow \{p\}A\{q\}$ we infer that

   either $\mathcal{A}(A)(\sigma) = \sigma' \wedge \mathcal{T}(q)(\sigma')$ for some $\sigma' \in \Sigma_0$, ... (1)

   or $\mathcal{A}(A)(\sigma) = \langle\sigma', L_i\rangle \wedge \mathcal{T}(p)(\sigma')$ for some $\sigma' \in \Sigma_0$ $(1 \le i \le n)$ ... (2)

   re (1) $\Vdash h \Rightarrow \{p\}A'\{r\}$ and $\mathcal{T}(q)(\sigma')$ give us

   either $\mathcal{A}(A)(\sigma') = \sigma'' \wedge \mathcal{T}(r)(\sigma'')$ for some $\sigma'' \in \Sigma_0$. But in that case we have from $\mathcal{A}(A)(\sigma) = \sigma'$ that $\mathcal{A}(A;A')(\sigma) = \sigma''$ and furthermore $\mathcal{T}(r)(\sigma'')$,

   or $\mathcal{A}(A)(\sigma') = \langle\sigma'', L_j\rangle \wedge \mathcal{T}(p_j)(\sigma'')$ for some $\sigma'' \in \Sigma_0$. But then we derive from $\mathcal{A}(A)(\sigma) = \sigma'$ and $\mathcal{A}(A')(\sigma') = \langle\sigma'', L_j\rangle$ that $\mathcal{A}(A;A')(\sigma) = \langle\sigma'', L_j\rangle$ and $\mathcal{T}(p_j)(\sigma'')$.

   re (2) From $\mathcal{A}(A)(\sigma) = \langle\sigma', L_i\rangle$ we have $\mathcal{A}(A;A')(\sigma) = \langle\sigma', L_i\rangle$ and $\mathcal{T}(p_i)(\sigma)$.

   The conclusion is that, for every choice of σ, the conditions imposed by the definition of $\Vdash h \Rightarrow \{p\}A;A'\{r\}$ are met.

8. Suppose $h \equiv \{p_1\}$ goto L_1 $\{$false$\} \wedge \ldots \wedge \{p_n\}$ goto L_n $\{$false$\}$, and suppose $\Vdash h \Rightarrow \{p_1\}A_1\{p_2\},\ldots,\Vdash h \Rightarrow \{p_n\}A_n\{p_{n+1}\}$. We have to prove $\Vdash \{p_1\}[L_i:A_i]_{i=1}^{n}\{p_{n+1}\}$, or equivalently $\forall\gamma\in\Gamma\forall\sigma,\sigma'\in\Sigma_0[\mathcal{T}(p_1)(\sigma) \wedge \mathcal{M}([L_i:A_i]_{i=1}^{n})(\gamma)(\sigma)=\sigma' \Rightarrow \mathcal{T}(p_{n+1})(\sigma')]$. So, choose $\gamma \in \Gamma$, and let ϕ_i, ϕ_i^k and γ^k be derived from $[L_i:A_i]_{i=1}^{n}$ and γ as in lemma 10.6. We first prove the following lemma.

<u>LEMMA 10.14</u>. $\forall k\in\mathbb{N}[\forall\sigma,\sigma'\in\Sigma_0[\mathcal{T}(p_i)(\sigma) \wedge \sigma' = \phi_i^k(\sigma) \Rightarrow \mathcal{T}(p_{n+1})(\sigma')]]$ for $i = 1,\ldots,n+1$.

<u>PROOF</u> (induction on k). The basis ($k=0$) is easy, because (i) $\phi_i^0 = \lambda\sigma\cdot\bot$ for $i = 1,\ldots,n$ and therefore there is no $\sigma'\in\Sigma_0$ such that $\sigma' = \phi_i^0(\sigma)$; (ii) $\phi_{n+1}^i = \lambda\sigma\cdot\sigma$, but then the assumption reduces to $\mathcal{T}(p_{n+1})(\sigma) \wedge \sigma' = (\lambda\sigma\cdot\sigma)(\sigma)$, and thus the conclusion $\mathcal{T}(p_{n+1})(\sigma')$ holds.
(Induction step). Choose an i ($1 \le i \le n$; the case $i = n+1$ is again easy) and choose $\sigma,\sigma' \in \Sigma_0$ such that $\mathcal{T}(p_i)(\sigma) = tt$ and $\sigma' = \phi_i^{k+1}(\sigma)$. Now $\phi_i^{k+1}(\sigma) = \mathcal{N}(A_i)(\gamma^k)(\phi_{i+1}^k)(\sigma)$. From $\Vdash h \Rightarrow \{p_i\}A_i\{p_{i+1}\}$ we know that
<u>either</u> $\mathcal{A}(A_i)(\sigma) = \sigma''$ and $\mathcal{T}(p_{i+1})(\sigma'') = tt$ for some $\sigma'' \in \Sigma_0$. But then we have $\sigma' = \phi_i^{k+1}(\sigma) = \phi_{i+1}^k(\sigma'')$ (by 10.9.1). The induction hypothesis then yields $\mathcal{T}(p_{n+1})(\sigma') = tt$.
<u>or</u> $\mathcal{A}(A_i)(\sigma) = \langle\sigma'',L_j\rangle$ and $\mathcal{T}(p_j)(\sigma'') = tt$ for some $\sigma'' \in \Sigma_0$ and some j between 1 and n. Now $\sigma' = \phi_i^{k+1}(\sigma) = \mathcal{A}(A_i)(\gamma^k)(\phi_{i+1}^k)(\sigma) = \gamma^k(L_j)(\sigma'') = \phi_j^k(\sigma'')$ (using 10.9.2). The induction hypothesis then yields $\mathcal{T}(p_{n+1})(\sigma') = tt$.

END 10.14.

Now, returning to the proof of $\Vdash \{p_1\}[L_i:A_i]_{i=1}^n\{p_{n+1}\}$, we have by definition 10.5 that $M([L_i:A_i]_{i=1}^n)(\gamma) = \phi_1$, and $\phi_1 = \bigsqcup_k \phi_1^k$, by lemma 10.6a. Choose $\sigma,\sigma' \in \Sigma_0$ such that $T(p_1)(\sigma) = tt$ and $\sigma' = \phi_1(\sigma)$. Then, because $\phi_1(\sigma) = \bigsqcup_k \phi_1^k(\sigma) = \bigsqcup_k(\phi_1^k(\sigma))$, there is a $\bar{k}$ such that $\sigma' = \phi_1^{\bar{k}}(\sigma)$, and the lemma gives us $T(p_{n+1})(\sigma') = tt$.

END 10.13.

We now turn our attention towards the question of completeness of the proof system, i.e. $\Vdash g \Rightarrow \vdash g$. If g is an assertion, then we can simply use the assertion axiom 10.11.3, so there is no problem here.

The next possibility is $g \equiv h \Rightarrow \{p\}A\{q\}$. Suppose this g is valid. We then want to construct a formal proof of this formula. In chapters 3, 5 and 9, we needed for this purpose propositions which stated that there exist assertions expressing the weakest preconditions and strongest postconditions needed in the formal proofs. We will need such a proposition too, but not yet in this stage. Later on, when dealing with formulae $g \equiv \{p\}S\{q\}$, such a proposition has to be used, but the proof system, restricted to (closed) formulae of the form $h \Rightarrow \{p\}A\{q\}$ is simple enough to allow us to effectively construct the weakest preconditions needed, as was the case in chapters 2 and 6.

Following the lines of reasoning from chapter 6 (definition 6.30 and lemma 6.32) we establish the fact that, for every closed pair $\langle h,A\rangle$ and for every assertion q, we can construct an assertion r satisfying

$$\forall p \in \mathit{Assn}[(\Vdash h \Rightarrow \{p\}A\{q\}) \Leftrightarrow \Vdash p \supset r].$$

We first define which assertion corresponds in the above sense to a pair $\langle h,A\rangle$ and an assertion q.

DEFINITION 10.15. For each A, q and h such that $\langle h,A\rangle$ is closed we define an assertion, denoted by $A\{q,h\}$, by induction on the structure of A as follows:

a. $v:=t\{q,h\} \equiv q[t/v]$

v. $(A';A'')\{q,h\} \equiv A'\{A''\{q,h\},h\}$

c. $\underline{\text{if}}$ b $\underline{\text{then}}$ A' $\underline{\text{else}}$ A" $\underline{\text{fi}}$ $\{q,h\} \equiv$ $\underline{\text{if}}$ b $\underline{\text{then}}$ $A'\{q,h\}$ $\underline{\text{else}}$ $A''\{q,h\}$ $\underline{\text{fi}}$

d. $\underline{\text{goto}}\ L_i\{q,h\} \equiv p_i$

(where $h \equiv \{p_1\}\ \underline{\text{goto}}\ L_1\ \{\underline{\text{false}}\} \wedge \ldots \wedge \{p_n\}\ \underline{\text{goto}}\ L_n\ \{\underline{\text{false}}\}$)

END 10.15.

Next we show that the assertion $A\{q,h\}$ defined as above is the weakest precondition of A with respect to q and h in the following (semantical) sense (compare also validity definition 10.12).

<u>LEMMA 10.16</u>. For all $A \in \mathit{Unst}$, $q \in \mathit{Assn}$ and $h \equiv \{p_1\}\ \underline{\text{goto}}\ L_1\ \{\underline{\text{false}}\} \wedge \ldots \wedge \{p_n\}\ \underline{\text{goto}}\ L_n\ \{\underline{\text{false}}\} \in \mathit{Asmp}$ such that $\langle h,A\rangle$ is closed we have

$$\forall\sigma\in\Sigma_0:\ \mathcal{T}(A\{q,h\})(\sigma) \Longleftrightarrow \begin{bmatrix}(\exists\sigma'\in\Sigma_0[\mathcal{A}(A)(\sigma)=\sigma' \wedge \mathcal{T}(q)(\sigma')]) \vee \\ (\exists\sigma'\in\Sigma_0[\mathcal{A}(A)(\sigma)=\langle\sigma',L_i\rangle \wedge \mathcal{T}(p_i)(\sigma')])\end{bmatrix}$$

<u>PROOF</u>. By induction on the structure of A. We distinguish four cases.

1. $A \equiv v:=t$. Choose $q \in \mathit{Assn}$ and $h \in \mathit{Asmp}$. Now $(v:=t)\{q,h\} \equiv q[t/v]$. Choose $\sigma \in \Sigma_0$. We have to show

$$\mathcal{T}(q[t/v])(\sigma) \Longleftrightarrow \begin{bmatrix}(\exists\sigma'\in\Sigma_0[\mathcal{A}(v:=t)(\sigma)=\sigma' \wedge \mathcal{T}(q)(\sigma')]) \vee \\ (\exists\sigma'\in\Sigma_0[\mathcal{A}(v:=t)(\sigma)=\langle\sigma',L_i\rangle \wedge \mathcal{T}(p_i)(\sigma')])\end{bmatrix}$$

Now $\mathcal{A}(v:=t)(\sigma) = \sigma\{\mathcal{R}(t)(\sigma)/\mathcal{L}(v)(\sigma)\} \in \Sigma_0$, so the above equivalence comes down to $\mathcal{T}(q[t/v])(\sigma) \Longleftrightarrow \exists\sigma'\in\Sigma_0[\mathcal{A}(v:=t)(\sigma)=\sigma' \wedge \mathcal{T}(q)(\sigma')] \Longleftrightarrow \mathcal{T}(q)(\sigma\{\mathcal{R}(t)(\sigma)/\mathcal{L}(v)(\sigma)\})$, and this has been derived in the proof of theorem 4.6.

2. $A \equiv A';A''$. Choose $q \in \mathit{Assn}$ and $h \equiv \{p_1\}\ \underline{\text{goto}}\ L_1\ \{\underline{\text{false}}\} \wedge \ldots \wedge \{p_n\}\ \underline{\text{goto}}\ L_n\ \{\underline{\text{false}}\} \in \mathit{Asmp}$ such that $\langle h,A\rangle$ is closed. We will show that $A'\{A''\{q,h\},h\}$ has the desired property. Choose $\sigma \in \Sigma_0$. We have to prove

$\mathcal{T}$(A'{A"{q,h},h})(σ) ⟺

$$\begin{bmatrix}(\exists\sigma'\in\Sigma_0[\mathcal{A}(A';A")(\sigma)=\sigma' \wedge \mathcal{T}(q)(\sigma')]) \vee \\ (\exists\sigma'\in\Sigma_0[\mathcal{A}(A';A")(\sigma)=<\sigma',L_i> \wedge \mathcal{T}(p_i)(\sigma')])\end{bmatrix}$$

We distinguish two cases.

a. $\mathcal{A}$(A')(σ) = σ". We then have $\mathcal{A}$(A';A")(σ) = $\mathcal{A}$(A")(σ") by definition of $\mathcal{A}$. Using this the above equivalence reduces to

$\mathcal{T}$(A'{A"{q,h},h})(σ) ⟺

$$\begin{bmatrix}(\exists\sigma'\in\Sigma_0[\mathcal{A}(A")(\sigma")=\sigma' \wedge \mathcal{T}(q)(\sigma')]) \vee \\ (\exists\sigma'\in\Sigma_0[\mathcal{A}(A")(\sigma")=<\sigma',L_i> \wedge \mathcal{T}(p_i)(\sigma')])\end{bmatrix}$$

and by induction this is equivalent to $\mathcal{T}$(A'{A"{q,h},h})(σ) ⟺ $\mathcal{T}$(A"{q,h})(σ").

Now we have, again by induction

$\mathcal{T}$(A'{A"{q,h},h})(σ) ⟺

$$\begin{bmatrix}(\exists\sigma'\in\Sigma_0[\mathcal{A}(A')(\sigma)=\sigma' \wedge \mathcal{T}(A"\{q,h\})(\sigma')]) \vee \\ (\exists\sigma'\in\Sigma_0[\mathcal{A}(A')(\sigma)=<\sigma',L_i> \wedge \mathcal{T}(p_i)(\sigma')])\end{bmatrix}$$

Substituting σ" for $\mathcal{A}$(A')(σ) (that is the assumption) the right-hand side of the equivalence reduces to $\mathcal{T}$(A"{q,h})(σ") and we are ready.

b. $\mathcal{A}$(A')(σ) = $<\sigma",L_i>$. We then have also that $\mathcal{A}$(A';A")(σ) = $<\sigma",L_i>$, so there remains to be proved $\mathcal{T}$(A'{A"{q,h},h})(σ) ⟺ $\mathcal{T}(p_i)(\sigma")$. Now by induction we have the fact that, for every assertion p, $\mathcal{T}$(A'{p,h})(σ) ⟺ $\mathcal{T}(p_i)(\sigma")$, so we are ready.

3 en 4 are left to the reader as exercises.

END 10.16.

This lemma now leads immediately to the result announced in the discussion preceding definition 10.15:

<u>LEMMA 10.17</u>. For all A ∈ *Unst*, q ∈ *Assn* and h ∈ *Asmp* such that <h,A> is closed, we have

$$\forall p \in \mathit{Assn}[(\Vdash h \Rightarrow \{p\}A\{q\}) \Longleftrightarrow \Vdash p \supset A\{q,h\}].$$

<u>PROOF</u>. Immediate from definition 10.12 and lemma 10.16.

END 10.17.

We have now enough results to prove a lemma on completeness for formulae of the form $h \Rightarrow \{p\}A\{q\}$.

LEMMA 10.18. For all $A \in \mathit{Unst}$, $p,q \in \mathit{Assn}$ and $h \in \mathit{Asmp}$ such that $h \Rightarrow \{p\}A\{q\}$ is closed, we have

$$(\Vdash h \Rightarrow \{p\}A\{q\}) \Rightarrow (\vdash h \Rightarrow \{p\}A\{q\}).$$

PROOF. First of all one proves easily by induction on the complexity of A that, for every $A \in \mathit{Unst}$, $q \in \mathit{Assn}$ and $h \in \mathit{Asmp}$ such that $\langle h,A \rangle$ is closed, we have $\vdash h \Rightarrow \{A\{q,h\}\}A\{q\}$.

Now assume $h \Rightarrow \{p\}A\{q\}$ is closed and valid according to definition 10.12. Then we have by lemma 10.17 that $\Vdash p \supset A\{q,h\}$, and thus (axiom 10.11.3) $\vdash p \supset A\{q,h\}$. We then only have to use rule 10.11.5 to get $\vdash h \Rightarrow \{p\}A\{q\}$.
END 10.18.

We now turn our attention towards completeness as regards formulae of the form $\{p\}S\{q\}$. If we want to formally prove such a formula, we have to find suitable label invariants for all labels declared in S. It is here that we need a proposition like the ones in chapters 3, 5 and 9, stating that such invariants can be formulated as assertions. These invariants will be weakest preconditions; it is convenient to define them as in

DEFINITION 10.19 (weakest precondition of a transformation from M). Let $\phi \in M$, $\pi \in \Pi(=\Sigma \to_s T)$. We say that q *expresses the weakest precondition of* ϕ *with respect to* π iff

$$\forall \sigma \in \Sigma_0 [\mathcal{T}(q)(\sigma) \iff \forall \sigma' \in \Sigma_0 [\phi(\sigma) = \sigma' \Rightarrow \pi(\sigma')]]$$

END 10.19.

PROPOSITION. For all closed statements $S \equiv [L_i : A_i]_{i=1}^n \in \mathit{Stat}$, and for all assertions $p \in \mathit{Assn}$, there exist assertions $p_1, \ldots, p_n$ such

that p_i expresses the weakest precondition of ϕ_i with respect to $T(p)$, where the ϕ_i are derived from S as in the definition of M.
END.

Remarks

1. From the fact that S is closed, one sees that the ϕ_i in the above proposition are uniquely determined by S (see remark 2 on definition 10.5).
2. The above proposition can be justified in a way which is analogous to what has been done in the appendix for the corresponding proposition from chapter 5. It can also be derived directly from the results proved there (more precisely from theorem A.34) using exercise 10.6.

LEMMA 10.20. Let $S \equiv [L_i:A_i]_{i=1}^n \in \mathit{Stat}$ be a closed statement, let $p \in \mathit{Assn}$ and ϕ_i be derived from S, and p_i be derived from ϕ_i and p as in the above proposition. Let $h \equiv \{p_1\}$ goto L_1 $\{$false$\} \wedge \ldots \wedge \{p_n\}$ goto L_n $\{$false$\}$ and let $p_{n+1} \equiv p$. Then we have for $i = 1,\ldots,n$,

$$\Vdash h \Rightarrow \{p_i\}A_i\{p_{i+1}\}.$$

PROOF. Choose i ($1 \leq i \leq n$) and $\sigma \in \Sigma_0$ such that $T(p_i)(\sigma) = tt$. We distinguish two cases.

a. $A(A_i)(\sigma) = \sigma'$. Then, according to the definition of $\Vdash h \Rightarrow \{p_i\}A_i\{p_{i+1}\}$, we have to prove that $T(p_{i+1})(\sigma') = tt$. By assumption on p_i and by definition 10.19, we have $T(p_i)(\sigma) \Longleftrightarrow \forall\sigma''\in\Sigma_0[\phi_i(\sigma) = \sigma'' \Rightarrow T(p)(\sigma'')]$. Also $\phi_i(\sigma) = \phi_{i+1}(\sigma')$ (by 10.9.1, using $A(A_i)(\sigma) = \sigma'$ and $\phi_i(\sigma) = N(A_i)(\gamma\{\phi_j/L_j\}_{j=1}^n)(\phi_{i+1})(\sigma))$. Combining these results, we get $T(p_i)(\sigma) \Longleftrightarrow \forall\sigma''\in\Sigma_0[\phi_{i+1}(\sigma')=\sigma'' \Rightarrow T(p)(\sigma'')] \Longleftrightarrow T(p_{i+1})(\sigma')$, where the last equivalence follows immediately from definition 10.19.

b. $A(A_i)(\sigma) = \langle\sigma',L\rangle$. From the fact that S is closed, we infer that

$L \equiv L_k$ for some k $(1 \le k \le n)$. By definition of $\Vdash h \Rightarrow \{p_i\}A_i\{p_{i+1}\}$ we then have to prove that $T(p_k)(\sigma') = tt$. Similarly as in a, we have $T(p_i)(\sigma) \Longleftrightarrow \forall\sigma''\in\Sigma_0[\phi_i(\sigma) = \sigma'' \Rightarrow T(p)(\sigma'')]$, and now we have $\phi_i(\sigma) = \phi_k(\sigma')$ (by 10.9.2), which together give $T(p_i)(\sigma) \Longleftrightarrow$ $\forall\sigma''\in\Sigma_0[\phi_k(\sigma') = \sigma'' \Rightarrow T(p)(\sigma'')] \Longleftrightarrow T(p_k)(\sigma')$.

END 10.20.

We now can collect our results in the following completeness theorem.

<u>THEOREM 10.21</u> (completeness).

The closed fragment H_C of the proof system defined by 10.11 is complete with respect to the validity definition 10.12. Or, in other words, for every closed generalized correctness formula g, we have $\Vdash g \Rightarrow \vdash g$.

<u>PROOF</u>. If $g \equiv p \in \mathit{Assn}$, then $\Vdash g \Rightarrow \vdash g$ by axiom 10.11.3 and if $g \equiv h \Rightarrow \{p\}A\{q\}$, then we can apply lemma 10.18. So let $g \equiv \{p\}S\{q\}$ be a closed formula, and let ϕ_i be derived from S, and p_i from ϕ_i and q as in the proposition. Lemma 10.20 then yields that $\Vdash h \Rightarrow \{p_i\}A_i\{p_{i+1}\}$ $(i = 1,\dots,n)$, where $p_{n+1} \equiv q$ and $h \equiv \{p_1\}$ <u>goto</u> L_1 {<u>false</u>} $\wedge \dots \wedge$ $\{p_n\}$ <u>goto</u> L_n {<u>false</u>}. Notice that these correctness formulae are closed by the fact that S is closed. Lemma 10.18 then yields $\vdash h \Rightarrow \{p_i\}A_i\{p_{i+1}\}$ for $i = 1,\dots,n$. Now we can apply rule 10.11.8 (labelling) to derive $\vdash \{p_1\}S\{p_{n+1}\}$.

We have $p_{n+1} \equiv q$. Moreover $\Vdash p \supset p_1$. For assume $T(p)(\sigma) = tt$ for some $\sigma \in \Sigma_0$. Then by $\Vdash \{p\}S\{q\}$ we have $\forall\gamma\in\Gamma\forall\sigma'\in\Sigma_0[\sigma' = M(S)(\gamma)(\sigma) \Rightarrow T(q)(\sigma')]$. But (by definition 10.5) $M(S)(\gamma) = \phi_1$. Thus $\forall\sigma'\in\Sigma_0[\phi_1(\sigma) = \sigma' \Rightarrow T(q)(\sigma')]$ and this is equivalent to $T(p_1)(\sigma) = tt$ by definition 10.19. We now combine $\vdash \{p_1\}S\{p_{n+1}\}$ and $\Vdash p \supset p_1$, using axiom 10.11.3 and rule 10.11.4, to $\vdash \{p\}S\{q\}$.

END 10.21.

We now return to a discussion and a definition of validity which uses the semantic function N instead of A, as we already announced in the discussion preceding definition 10.12. Notice that this is not really necessary because the proof system has been justified completely by now (theorems 10.13 and 10.21). However, the forthcoming definition of validity is better adapted to the proof system in the form as it has been stated here and, moreover, fits more easily in the general framework which has been developed in the other chapters of this book.

So we have to find a function $\mathcal{F}$: $\mathcal{A}for \to (\Gamma \to T)$ which leads to a satisfactory definition of validity. The main problem in defining the value of $\mathcal{F}(\{p\}A\{q\})$ for some γ is that $\mathcal{N}(A)(\gamma)(\phi)$ is not a function that transforms states just before evaluation of A into states immediately after this evaluation, while q is an assertion describing the latter states.

We can however say something about the states of the normal exit point of A in the following indirect way. Consider the formula $\{p\}A\{q\}$ and choose a predicate $\pi \in \Pi$ which we want to be true in every final state $\sigma' = \mathcal{N}(A)(\gamma)(\phi)(\sigma)$ corresponding to an initial state σ satisfying $\mathcal{T}(p)(\sigma) = tt$. That is, we want

$$\forall\sigma,\sigma'\in\Sigma_0[\mathcal{T}(p)(\sigma) \wedge \sigma' = \mathcal{N}(A)(\gamma)(\phi)(\sigma) \Rightarrow \pi(\sigma')].$$

We will abbreviate this partial correctness condition to

$$\{\mathcal{T}(p)\}\mathcal{N}(A)(\gamma)(\phi)\{\pi\}.$$

Now, as this formula has to correspond to $\{p\}A\{q\}$, there must be some relation between q, the continuation ϕ chosen and the predicate π. It is reasonable to demand that $\pi(\phi(\sigma''))$ holds for every (intermediate) state σ'' satisfying $\mathcal{T}(q)(\sigma'')$ (provided $\phi(\sigma'') \neq \perp$). For the continuation ϕ is the state transformation describing what happens after evaluation of A has terminated at the normal exit point. So we want q, ϕ and π to be related through $\{\mathcal{T}(q)\}\phi\{\pi\}$. It turns out that this constraint on ϕ and π is sufficient to lead to a satisfactory validity definition.

DEFINITION 10.22 (partial correctness, semantic level).
For any $\pi,\pi' \in \Pi$ and $\phi \in M$ we define

$$\{\pi\}\phi\{\pi'\} \Leftrightarrow \forall\sigma,\sigma'\in\Sigma_0[(\pi(\sigma) \wedge \sigma' = \phi(\sigma)) \Rightarrow \pi'(\sigma')]$$

END 10.22.

DEFINITION 10.23. The function F with functionality $F\colon \mathcal{A}for \rightarrow (\Gamma \rightarrow T)$ is defined by

1. $F(\{p\}A\{q\})(\gamma) \Leftrightarrow \forall\pi\in\Pi\forall\phi\in M[\{T(q)\}\phi\{\pi\} \Rightarrow \{T(p)\}N(A)(\gamma)(\phi)\{\pi\}]$
2. $F(f_1 \wedge f_2)(\gamma) \Leftrightarrow F(f_1)(\gamma)$ and $F(f_2)(\gamma)$

END 10.23.

DEFINITION 10.24 (validity, second definition).
A closed correctness formula g is *valid* (written $\models g$) if

1. $g \equiv p$ and $\forall\sigma\in\Sigma_0\colon T(p)(\sigma)$, or
2. $g \equiv h \Rightarrow \{p\}A\{q\}$ and $\forall\gamma\in\Gamma[F(h)(\gamma) \Rightarrow F(\{p\}A\{q\})(\gamma)]$, or
3. $g \equiv \{p\}S\{q\}$ and $\forall\gamma\in\Gamma[\{T(p)\}(M(S)(\gamma))\{T(q)\}]$

END 10.24.

Remarks

1. Notice that 1 and 3 of the above definition are equivalent to the corresponding clauses in definition 10.12 (validity, first definition).
2. The restriction to closed formulae in 10.24 is not necessary. However, since $\Vdash$-validity is defined only for closed formulae, and since we want to compare the two definitions, we restrict ourselves to closed formulae. It can be proven (exercise 10.7) that the proof system, not restricted to closed formulae, is sound with respect to (an extension of) $\models$-validity. However, the system is not complete anymore. For instance, we would have $\models$ {p} goto L {false} $\Rightarrow$ {true} if true then x:=x else goto L' fi {true}, but there is no way to formally prove this formula (if L $\not\equiv$ L').

We now will prove the equivalence of the two validity definitions.

<u>LEMMA 10.25</u>. Suppose $g \equiv h \Rightarrow \{p\}A\{q\}$, where $h \equiv \{p_1\}$ <u>goto</u> L_1 {<u>false</u>} $\wedge \ldots \wedge \{p_n\}$ <u>goto</u> L_n {<u>false</u>}, is a correctness formula that is closed and valid. Then the following holds:

a. $\forall\sigma,\sigma'\in\Sigma_0[(\mathcal{A}(A)(\sigma) = \sigma' \wedge \mathcal{T}(p)(\sigma)) \Rightarrow \mathcal{T}(q)(\sigma')]$

b. $\forall\sigma,\sigma'\in\Sigma_0[(\mathcal{A}(A)(\sigma) = \langle\sigma',L_i\rangle \wedge \mathcal{T}(p)(\sigma)) \Rightarrow \mathcal{T}(p_i)(\sigma')]$ $(i = 1,\ldots,n)$.

<u>PROOF</u>.

a. Choose $\sigma,\sigma' \in \Sigma_0$ such that $\mathcal{T}(p)(\sigma) = tt$ and $\mathcal{A}(A)(\sigma) = \sigma'$. Choose γ_0 such that $\gamma_0(L_i) = \lambda\sigma\cdot\bot$ for $i = 1,\ldots,n$. Then we can check that $\mathcal{F}(\{p_i\}$ <u>goto</u> L_i {<u>false</u>}$)(\gamma_0)$ holds for $i = 1,\ldots,n$ and thus from validity of g we have

$$\forall\pi\in\Pi\forall\phi\in M[\{\mathcal{T}(q)\}\phi\{\pi\} \Rightarrow \{\mathcal{T}(p)\}(\mathcal{N}(A)(\gamma_0)(\phi))\{\pi\}].$$

If we choose $\pi = \mathcal{T}(q)$ and $\phi = \lambda\sigma\cdot\sigma$, we can deduce from this

$$\{\mathcal{T}(p)\}(\mathcal{N}(A)(\gamma_0)(\lambda\sigma\cdot\sigma))\{\mathcal{T}(q)\}.$$

Combining this with $\mathcal{N}(A)(\gamma_0)(\lambda\sigma\cdot\sigma)(\sigma) = \sigma'$ (lemma 10.9.1) and $\mathcal{T}(p)(\sigma) = tt$, we get $\mathcal{T}(q)(\sigma') = tt$.

b. Choose $\sigma,\sigma' \in \Sigma_0$ and i $(1 \le i \le n)$ such that $\mathcal{T}(p)(\sigma) = tt$ and $\mathcal{A}(A)(\sigma) = \langle\sigma',L_i\rangle$. Now if we take γ_0 such that

$$\gamma_0(L_j)(\sigma) = \begin{cases} \sigma & \text{if } \sigma \ne \bot \text{ and } \mathcal{T}(p_j)(\sigma) = ff \\ \bot & \text{otherwise} \end{cases}$$

for $j = 1,\ldots,m$, we again have that $\mathcal{F}(\{p_j\}$ <u>goto</u> L_j {<u>false</u>}$)(\gamma_0) = tt$ $(j = 1,\ldots,n)$. Arguing the same way as in the proof of a, we come to

$$\forall\pi\in\Pi\forall\phi\in M[\{\mathcal{T}(q)\}\phi\{\pi\} \Rightarrow \{\mathcal{T}(p)\}(\mathcal{N}(A)(\gamma_0)(\phi))\{\pi\}].$$

Now we choose $\phi = \lambda\sigma\cdot\bot$ and $\pi = \lambda\sigma\cdot ff$. We then derive

$$\{\mathcal{T}(p)\}(\mathcal{N}(A)(\gamma_0)(\lambda\sigma\cdot\bot))\{\lambda\sigma\cdot ff\}.$$

Combining this with $\mathcal{N}(A)(\gamma_0)(\lambda\sigma\cdot\bot)(\sigma) = \gamma_0(L_i)(\sigma')$ (lemma 10.9.2) and with $T(p)(\sigma) = tt$ we have that

$$\gamma_0(L_i)(\sigma') \neq \bot \Rightarrow (\lambda\sigma\cdot ff)(\gamma_0(L_i)(\sigma')) = tt.$$

So we must have $\gamma_0(L_i)(\sigma') = \bot$, but this is equivalent (by definition of γ_0 and the fact that $\sigma' \neq \bot$) to $T(p_i)(\sigma') = tt$.

END 10.25.

LEMMA 10.26. Suppose $g \equiv h \Rightarrow \{p\}A\{q\}$, where $h \equiv \{p_1\}$ goto L_1 {false} $\wedge \ldots \wedge$ $\{p_n\}$ goto L_n {false} is a closed correctness formula. Then

$$\models g \Longleftrightarrow \forall\sigma\in\Sigma_0: T(p)(\sigma) \Rightarrow \begin{bmatrix} (\exists\sigma'\in\Sigma_0[A(A)(\sigma) = \sigma' \wedge T(q)(\sigma')]) \vee \\ (\exists\sigma'\in\Sigma_0[A(A)(\sigma) = <\sigma',L_i> \wedge T(p_i)(\sigma')]) \end{bmatrix}$$

PROOF. " $\Rightarrow$ ". Suppose $\models g$ and $T(p)(\sigma) = tt$. There are two possibilities (by definition of A).

a. $A(A)(\sigma) = \sigma' \in \Sigma_0$, and lemma 10.25a yields $T(q')(\sigma) = tt$

b. $A(A)(\sigma) = <\sigma',L>$. Since g is closed, we have $L \equiv L_i$ $(1 \leq i \leq n)$. We then can apply 10.25b to obtain $T(p_i)(\sigma') = tt$.

" $\Leftarrow$ ". Choose $\gamma \in \Gamma$ such that $F(\{p_i\}$ goto L_i {false})$(\gamma) = tt$ for $i = 1,\ldots,n$. Then we must derive $F(\{p\}A\{q\})(\gamma) = tt$, or equivalently

$$\forall\pi\in\Pi\forall\phi\in M[\{T(q)\}\phi\{\pi\} \Rightarrow \{T(p)\}(N(A)(\gamma)(\phi))\{\pi\}].$$

So choose π_0 and ϕ_0 such that $\{T(q)\}\phi_0\{\pi_0\}$ holds, and choose σ such that $T(p)(\sigma) = tt$. We have to prove $(\sigma'' = N(A)(\gamma)(\phi_0)(\sigma) \wedge \sigma'' \neq \bot) \Rightarrow \pi_0(\sigma'')$. Again we distinguish two possibilities:

a. $A(A)(\sigma) = \sigma'$. Then by assumption $T(q)(\sigma') = tt$, and by lemma 10.9.1: $\sigma'' = N(A)(\gamma)(\phi_0)(\sigma) = \phi_0(\sigma')$. From $\{T(q)\}\phi_0\{\pi_0\}$ we then have $\sigma'' \neq \bot \Rightarrow \pi_0(\sigma'')$.

b. $A(A)(\sigma) = <\sigma',L_i>$. By assumption $T(p_i)(\sigma') = tt$, and by lemma 10.9.2: $\sigma'' = N(A)(\gamma)(\phi_0)(\sigma) = \gamma(L_i)(\sigma')$. Now we use the fact $F(\{p_i\}$ goto L_i {false})$(\gamma) = tt$ or $\forall\pi\in\Pi\forall\phi\in M[\{T(false)\}\phi\{\pi\} \Rightarrow \{T(p_i)\}(\gamma(L_i))\{\pi\}]$. Taking $\pi = \pi_0$ and $\phi = \lambda\sigma\cdot\bot$, we get

$\{T(p_i)\}(\gamma(L_i))\{\pi_0\}$, and from this we prove $\sigma" \neq \bot \Rightarrow \pi_0(\sigma")$.
END 10.26.

THEOREM 10.27. The two validity definitions for closed generalized correctness formulae given in this chapter are equivalent. Stated otherwise, for every closed $g \in \mathit{Gfor}$, we have $\models g \Leftrightarrow \Vdash g$.

PROOF. Immediate from remark 1 on definition 10.24 and lemma 10.26.
END 10.27.

COROLLARY 10.28. The proof system H_C is sound and complete with respect to validity definition 10.24.

PROOF. Immediate from theorems 10.13, 10.21 and 10.27.
END 10.28.

Exercises

10.1. Prove the following: if an unlabeled statement A does not contain goto statements, then, for all $\gamma \in \Gamma$, $\phi \in M$ and $\sigma \in \Sigma$, we have $N(A)(\gamma)(\phi)(\sigma) = \phi(N(A)(\gamma)(\lambda\sigma\cdot\sigma)(\sigma))$.

10.2. This exercise, together with the preceding one, describes a technique called *continuation removal*. Suppose $A \in \mathit{Unst}$ does not contain goto statements, and suppose also that the function N' is defined as M in chapter 4. Then we have $N(A)(\gamma)(\lambda\sigma\cdot\sigma) = N'(A)$ for all γ. In other words, if A does not contain goto statements then $N(A)(\gamma)(\lambda\sigma\cdot\sigma)$ is the state transformation which has been associated with A until this chapter.

10.3. Let $S \equiv [L_i:A_i]_{i=1}^{n}$ be a closed statement. Define $M'(S)$ as the least fixed point of an operator $[\Phi_1',\ldots,\Phi_n']$, where the Φ_i' are defined from A_i, but now not using the semantic function N but the function A instead.

10.4. Combine the semantics given in this chapter with that of chapter 5. That is, we define the following syntax:

Unst $A ::= v:=t \mid A';A'' \mid \underline{\text{if}}\ b\ \underline{\text{then}}\ A'\ \underline{\text{else}}\ A''\ \underline{\text{fi}} \mid \underline{\text{goto}}\ L \mid P$

Stat $S ::= L_1:A_1;\ldots;L_n:A_n$, where $L_i \not\equiv L_j$ for $i \neq j$

Decl $E ::= P_1 \Leftarrow A_1,\ldots,P_n \Leftarrow A_n$, where $P_i \not\equiv P_j$ for $i \neq j$

Prog $R ::= \langle E:S \rangle$

Define functions *Comp*, *O*, *N* and *M* for this language and show that $\mathcal{O} = \mathcal{M}$.

10.5. For this exercise we redefine the functions *Comp* and *O* somewhat, namely as follows:

a. $Comp^*(\langle S,A\rangle)$ is defined analogous to $Comp(\langle S,A\rangle)$ if A is not a goto statement

b. $Comp^*(\langle [L_i:A_i]_{i=1}^n, \underline{\text{goto}}\ L_j\rangle)(\sigma) =$

$\langle\sigma\rangle^\frown\ Comp(\langle [L_i:A_i]_{i=1}^n, (A_j;\ \underline{\text{goto}}\ L_{j+1})\rangle)(\sigma)$ if $j < n$ and

$\langle\sigma\rangle^\frown\ Comp(\langle [L_i:A_i]_{i=1}^n, A_j\rangle)(\sigma)$ if $j = n$

c. $\mathcal{O}^*([L_i:A_i]_{i=1}^n) = \kappa \circ Comp^*(\langle [L_i:A_i]_{i=1}^n, \underline{\text{goto}}\ L_1\rangle)$.

We define the *number of labels encountered in a finite computation sequence* $Comp^*(\langle S,A\rangle)(\sigma)$ (notation: $nl(Comp^*(\langle S,A\rangle)(\sigma))$) as the number of steps of type b executed in this computation sequence.

1. Define *nl* formally (see exercise 5.7)
2. Let ϕ_i^k be derived from the closed statement $S \equiv [L_i:A_i]_{i=1}^n$ as in lemma 10.6. Prove

a. $\phi_i^k(\sigma) = \sigma' \in \Sigma_0 \Longleftrightarrow \kappa(Comp^*\langle S,\underline{\text{goto}}\ L_i\rangle)(\sigma)) = \sigma'$ and $nl(Comp^*(\langle S,\underline{\text{goto}}\ L_i\rangle)(\sigma)) \leq k$

b. for all closed statements $S \in$ *Stat* and all $\gamma \in \Gamma$ we have $\mathcal{O}^*(S) = \mathcal{M}(S)(\gamma)$

c. $\mathcal{O}^* = \mathcal{O}$

10.6. An unlabeled statement A is called *regular* if

a. A $\equiv$ v:=t, or A $\equiv$ goto L

b. A $\equiv$ (A';A") where A" is regular and A' does not contain goto statements

c. A $\equiv$ if b then A' else A" fi where A' and A" are regular.

1. Let $S \equiv [L_i:A_i]_{i=1}^n$ be a closed statement. Show that

$\lambda\psi_1\cdot\ldots\cdot\lambda\psi_n\cdot N(A_j;\ \underline{\text{goto}}\ L_{j+1})(\gamma\{\psi_i/L_i\}_{i=1}^n)(\lambda\sigma\cdot\sigma) =$

$\lambda\psi_1\cdot\ldots\cdot\lambda\psi_n\cdot N(A_j)(\gamma\{\psi_i/L_i\}_{i=1}^n)(\psi_{j+1})$, for $j = 1,\ldots,n-1$.

2. For all A $\in$ *Unst*, there exist a regular A' $\in$ *Unst* such that

$\lambda\psi_1\cdot\ldots\cdot\lambda\psi_n\cdot N(A')(\gamma\{\psi_i/L_i\}_{i=1}^n)(\lambda\sigma\cdot\sigma) =$

$\lambda\psi_1\cdot\ldots\cdot\lambda\psi_n\cdot N(A)(\gamma\{\psi_i/L_i\}_{i=1}^n)(\lambda\sigma\cdot\sigma)$.

3. Let *Pvar* be defined as in chapter 5, and let $P_1,\ldots,P_n \in Pvar$ be such that $1 \le i < j \le n \Rightarrow P_i \not\equiv P_j$. Let $A[P_i/\underline{\text{goto}}\ L_i]_{i=1}^n$ be derived from A by simultaneously substituting the variables P_i for the substatements of the form goto L_i $(i = 1, \ldots, n)$. It is clear that if A is regular then $A[P_i/\underline{\text{goto}}\ L_i]_{i=1}^n$ is regular according to the definition in exercise 5.18.
Now let $\bar{\Gamma}$, $\bar{N}$ and $\bar{M}$ be the functions Γ, N and M as defined in chapter 5. Show that for all regular A we have

$$\forall\bar{\gamma}\in\bar{\Gamma}\forall\gamma\in\Gamma: [\lambda\psi_1\cdot\ldots\cdot\lambda\psi_n\cdot\bar{N}(A[P_i/\underline{\text{goto}}\ L_i]_{i=1}^n)(\bar{\gamma}\{\psi_i/P_i\}_{i=1}^n) = \lambda\psi_1\cdot\ldots\cdot\lambda\psi_n\cdot N(A)(\gamma\{\psi_i/L_i\}_{i=1}^n)(\lambda\sigma\cdot\sigma)]$$

(where $L_1,\ldots,L_n$ are all labels occurring in A).
(Hint: use induction on the structure of A, and exercise 10.1.)

4. Using 1, 2 and 3, we show that for every closed $S \equiv [L_i:A_i]_{i=1}^n \in$ *Stat*, there exist regular statements $S_1,\ldots,S_n \in$ *Stat* (as defined in 5.18) such that

$\forall\gamma\in\bar{\Gamma}[\phi_i = \bar{M}(<P_1 \Leftarrow S_1,\ldots,P_n \Leftarrow S_n | P_i>)(\bar{\gamma})]$, for i = 1,...,n, where $\phi_i \in M$ is derived from S as in definition 10.5.

10.7. Allow arbitrary atomic formulae as assumptions in the correctness formulae defined in 10.10, that is define $\mathcal{Gfor}$ by

$$g ::= \ p \,|\, f \Rightarrow \{p\}A\{q\} \,|\, \{p\}S\{q\}.$$

Define validity as follows:

$$\models p \iff \forall\sigma\in\Sigma_0 \colon \mathcal{T}(p)(\sigma)$$

$$(\models f \Rightarrow \{p\}A\{q\}) \iff \forall\gamma\in\Gamma[\mathcal{F}(f)(\gamma) \Rightarrow \mathcal{F}(\{p\}A\{q\})(\gamma)]$$

$$\models \{p\}S\{q\} \iff \forall\gamma\in\Gamma[\{\mathcal{T}(p)\}\mathcal{M}(S)(\gamma)\{\mathcal{T}(q)\}].$$

Prove that the new proof system is sound.

Notice that this system is not complete. A counterexample has already been given in remark 2 on definition 10.24. Even a restriction to formulae $f \Rightarrow \{p\}A\{q\}$ which have the property that all labels in A also occur in f does not work, as the following example shows. For $g \equiv \{p\}(x{:=}x;\underline{\text{goto}}\ L)\{\underline{\text{false}}\} \Rightarrow \{p\}\ \underline{\text{goto}}\ L\ \{\underline{\text{false}}\}$, we have $\models g$ but not $\vdash g$.

APPENDIX

EXPRESSIBILITY OF PRE- AND POSTCONDITIONS

J.I. Zucker

A.1. Introduction

Let *L* be the language of (first order) Peano arithmetic, including array variables. The *formulae* of *L* (*L-formulae*) are just the *assertions* of chapter 5.

Remark. This is not quite accurate, since the individual variables of chapter 5 range over integers, rather than natural numbers. However, this distinction is quite unimportant for our purposes, and will be ignored below, since the integers can easily be coded as natural numbers (by e.g. the enumeration 0,1,-1,2,-2...), in such a way that the arithmetical operations and relations on the integers +,-,×,<,... correspond to primitive recursive operations and relations on the natural numbers.

The aim of this appendix is to prove the proposition in chapter 5 (section 5.5) stating that the weakest precondition and strongest postcondition are expressible in *L*. This is given below in corollaries A.35 and A.39, where Precond(R,p) and Postcond(p,R) (defined in A.33 and A.37) are the required *L*-formulae (i.e. the assertions r_1 and r_2 of the proposition).

We will refer below to the books of Kleene [1952] and Rogers [1967], as [K] and [R] respectively.

We assume the reader knows a little recursion theory, e.g. the material in chapters 1 and 5 of [R], and also:

(i) The fact that all primitive recursive - or general recursive, or recursively enumerable - predicates and relations on the natural numbers are *arithmetical*, i.e. expressible in L (see [R,§14.4] or [K,§49]). In other words, if R is a primitive recursive (or recursively enumerable) k-ary relation, then there is an L-formula $R(x_1,\ldots,x_k)$ with k free number variables, such that for all numbers $n_1,\ldots,n_k$:

$$R(n_1,\ldots,n_k) \iff \models R(\bar{n}_1,\ldots,\bar{n}_k)$$

(where $\bar{n}$ denotes the numeral for n, and " $\models$ " means truth in the standard model for arithmetic).

(ii) The notion of *arithmetization* (coding, Gödel numbering) of syntactic objects of various kinds [K,chapter 10].

(iii) The *recursion theorem*: if f is a total recursive function, then there is a number n such that $\phi_n = \phi_{f(n)}$ (where ϕ_x is the partial recursive function with index x) (see [R,§11.2, theorem 1] or [K,p.352,theorem XXVII]).

Remark. Because of (i) above, we may as well assume that L contains symbols for any (or all) of the primitive recursive functions.

Some terminology and notation

We let i,j,m,n,... range over the natural numbers 0,1,2,... . By "number" we will mean natural number.

If ϕ is a k-ary partial recursive function and $\vec{m}$ is a k-tuple of numbers, then we write $\phi(\vec{m})\downarrow n$ for: $\phi(\vec{m})$ converges to n, or has value n, i.e., $\exists y[T_k(e,\vec{m},y) \wedge U(y)=n]$, where e is an index for ϕ, T_k is Kleene's T-predicate for k arguments, and U is the "result-extracting function" [K,§63]. T_k and U are primitive recursive, and so this relation is arithmetical. Similarly, we write $\phi(\vec{m})\uparrow$, or $\phi(\vec{m})=\infty$, for: $\phi(\vec{m})$ diverges, or is undefined, i.e. $\neg\exists y T_k(e,\vec{m},y)$.

If t is an expression containing symbols for partial recursive functions, then t$\downarrow$ means that all the subexpressions of t denoting partial recursive function application converge, and hence t has a value; and t$\downarrow$n means that this value is n. For two such expressions t and t', $t \simeq t'$ means that t and t' either both converge to the same number, or both diverge.

Code of finite objects as numbers

(i) Finite sets. A finite set of numbers $\{n_0, n_1, \ldots, n_{k-1}\}$ can be coded as the number $2^{n_0}+2^{n_1}+\ldots+2^{n_{k-1}}$ [R, §5.6]. The coding is surjective.

$\mathcal{E\ell t}(m,n)$ is the binary relation: "m is an element of the finite set coded by n". It is primitive recursive. Note that $\mathcal{E\ell t}(m,n)$ implies $m < n$.

Remark. Here and below, we often point out that certain relations and functions are primitive recursive, although in general all we really need to know, for the main result, is that these relations and functions (i.e. their graphs) are arithmetical.

(ii) Finite sequences. We assume a standard coding of finite sequences of numbers as numbers: "sequence numbers". Assume for convenience that the coding is surjective (so that in fact every number is a sequence number).

For example, we can take the following simple coding, due to A. van Wijngaarden. The code of the empty sequence $\langle\ \rangle$ is 0, and $\langle n_0, n_1, \ldots, n_{k-1}\rangle$ $(k \geq 1)$ is the number with the *binary representation* $10^{n_0}10^{n_1}1 \ldots 0^{n_{k-2}}10^{n_{k-1}}$ (where 0^n denotes a string of n consecutive 0's). Thus $\langle 0\rangle$ is the number 1, and $\langle 1,3,0,2\rangle$ is the number $(1010001100)_2 = 1304$.

For a sequence number $m = \langle n_0, \ldots, n_{k-1}\rangle$, we define $\ell h(m) = k$ and $(m)_i = n_i$ for $i < k$. ($\ell h(m)$ is the "length of m" and the $(m)_i$ are the *components* of m. If $i > \ell h(m)$, we may take e.g. $(m)_i = 0$.)

Further definitions: $\mathcal{end}(m)$ is the *last component* of m (if m is a nonempty sequence number): $(m)_{\ell h(m)-1}$. And $m^\frown m'$ is (the code for) the sequence formed by *concatenating* m and m'.

The functions *ℓh*, $(m)_i$ (as a function of m and i), *end* and $^\frown$ are all primitive recursive.

A.2. State numbers

CONVENTION A.1. Assume we have enumerations $x_0, x_1, \ldots$ and $a_0, a_1, \ldots$ of all simple and array variables of L. For ease of exposition, we also assume given two (arbitrary but) fixed numbers N_0 and N_1 such that, writing $X = \{x_i \mid i < N_0\}$ and $A = \{a_i \mid i < N_1\}$, all the programs with which we deal have free variables among X and A only. END A.1.

DEFINITION A.2.

(1) An *Intv-number* (*intermediate variable number*) is (a code for) a pair $\langle 0,i\rangle$ (for $i < N_0$) or a triple $\langle 1,i,j\rangle$ (for $i < N_1$, any j). (These will function as codes for intermediate variables: $\langle 0,i\rangle$ for x_i and $\langle 1,i,j\rangle$ for $\langle a_i,j\rangle$.)

(2) A *domain* is a finite set of *Intv*-numbers.

(3) A *state number* is (a code for) a finite function from *Intv*-numbers to numbers. (These will function as representations of states.)

(4) Given a state number s, *dom*(s) is its domain (where s is taken as a function). (Note that *dom*(s) is indeed a domain, in the sense of (2) above.)

END A.2.

Notation: d,d',... for *Intv*-numbers,
δ,... for domains,
s,... for state numbers.

DEFINITION A.3.

$$(1)\quad s\langle d\rangle = \begin{cases} \text{value of } s \text{ at } d \text{ if } d \in dom(s), \\ 0 \text{ (say) otherwise.} \end{cases}$$

We write $s\langle 0,i\rangle$ or $s\langle 1,i,j\rangle$ for $s\langle d\rangle$ when $d = \langle 0,i\rangle$ or $\langle 1,i,j\rangle$, respectively.

(2) $s \preceq s'$ (s' is an *extension* of s) means: $dom(s) \subseteq dom(s')$ and $\forall d \in dom(s)\ s\langle d\rangle = s'\langle d\rangle$.

END A.3.

Remark. Our coding is such that the following predicates are primitive recursive:

(a) *IntvNo*(n), "n is an *Intv*-number":

$$\forall i < \ell h(n)[(\ell h((n)_i) = 2 \wedge (n)_{i,0} = 0 \wedge (n)_{i,1} < N_0) \vee (\ell h((n)_i) = 3 \wedge (n)_{i,0} = 1 \wedge (n)_{i,1} < N_1)].$$

(b) *StateNo*(n), "n is a state number":

$$\forall m < n[Elt(m,n) \supset (\ell h(m) = 2 \wedge IntvNo((m)_0) \wedge \forall m' < n(Elt(m',n) \wedge m' \neq m \supset (m')_0 \neq (m)_0))].$$

Also, for example, the following relations and functions are primitive recursive, as the reader can easily check:

$\{(d,s) \mid d \in dom(s)\}$, i.e., $\{(m,n) \mid IntvNo(m) \wedge StateNo(n) \wedge m \in dom(n)\}$,

$\{(i,s) \mid \langle 0,i\rangle \in dom(s)\}$,

$\{(i,j,s) \mid \langle 1,i,j\rangle \in dom(s)\}$,

$\{(s,s') \mid s \preceq s'\}$.

State numbers are intended as *finite approximations* of states, in the following sense. (Note: when we refer to a state σ below, we will generally assume that $\sigma \neq \bot$. We also assume, for convenience, that states σ have natural numbers as values, rather than integers: see the remark in section A.1.)

DEFINITION A.4.

(1) ξ_d (the intermediate variable coded by d) is defined by:

$\xi_{<0,i>} \equiv x_i$, and $\xi_{<1,i,j>} \equiv <a_i,j>$.

(2) s *approx* σ means: for all $d \in dom(s)$, $s<d> = \sigma(\xi_d)$.

(3) $\sigma \upharpoonright \delta$ (the "restriction of σ to δ") is the unique state number s such that s *approx* σ and $dom(s) = \delta$.

END A.4.

DEFINITION A.5 (*variant* of a state number).
Given s, $d \in dom(s)$ and n, s[n/d] is the state number s_1 defined by

(i) $dom(s_1) = dom(s)$, and

(ii) $s_1<d'> = s<d'>$ for $d' \in dom(s)$, $d' \neq d$, and $s_1<d> = n$.

END A.5.

PROPOSITION A.6. If s *approx* σ and $d \in dom(s)$ then s[n/d] *approx* $\sigma\{n/\xi_d\}$.

END A.6.

A.3. Computation numbers

DEFINITION A.7.

(1) A *computation number* is a code for a finite, non-empty sequence of state numbers, all with the *same domain*.

Remark. The predicate "m is a computation number" is primitive recursive:

$$CompNo(m) := \ell h(m) > 0 \wedge \forall i < \ell h(m)[StateNo((m)_i) \wedge dom((m)_i) = dom((m)_0)].$$

Notation: c,c',... for computation numbers.

(2) cdom(c) (the "component domain" of a computation number c) is just the domain of any of the components of c (= $dom((c)_i)$ for any $i < \ell h(c)$, or simply $dom((c)_0)$).

Note. If c, c' are computation numbers, then so is $c^\frown c'$, provided $cdom(c) = cdom(c')$.

(3) $c \underline{\langle}\,\underline{\langle}\, c'$ (c' is a "componentwise extension" of c) means: $\ell h(c) = \ell h(c')$ and $\forall i < \ell h(c)$, $(c)_i \underline{\langle}\, (c')_i$.

(4) <s> is the computation number of length 1, with single component s.

END A.7.

We think of computation numbers as finite approximations to (finite) *computation sequences* (see chapter 5.3), in the following sense.

Notation. $\vec{\sigma}$ denotes a finite computation sequence $(\sigma_0,\ldots,\sigma_{m-1})$, with $length(\vec{\sigma}) = m$.

DEFINITION A.8.

(1) c *approx* $\vec{\sigma}$ if $\ell h(c) = length(\vec{\sigma})$ and $\forall i < \ell h(c)$ $(c)_i$ *approx* σ_i.

(2) $\vec{\sigma}\restriction\delta$ is the unique computation number c such that c *approx* $\vec{\sigma}$ and $cdom(c) = \delta$.

END A.8.

A.4. Coding of the programming language

DEFINITION A.9.

(1) *Cl.Prog* is the class of *closed programs*.

(2) $Ivar_N$ is the syntactic class $\{v \in Ivar \mid svar(v) \subseteq X,\ avar(v) \subseteq \mathcal{a}\}$, where $X = \{x_i \mid i < N_0\}$ and $\mathcal{a} = \{a_i \mid i < N_1\}$ and $N = \langle N_0, N_1\rangle$ (see convention A.1).

$Iexp_N$, $Cl.Prog_N$, etc., are defined similarly.

(3) *Synt* is the class of all our syntactic objects (=*Iexp* ∪ *Bexp* ∪ *Stat* ∪ *Cl.Prog* ∪ ...). We let X,... range over *Synt*.

(4) We assume a numerical *coding* (Gödel numbering) of *Synt* satisfying certain (obvious) desirable properties, e.g. (denoting the code of X by $\ulcorner X \urcorner$):

- $\ulcorner X \urcorner$ increases strictly with the complexity of X,
- sets such as $\{\ulcorner t \urcorner \mid t \in \mathit{Iexp}\}$ and $\{\ulcorner t \urcorner \mid t \in \mathit{Iexp}_N\}$ are primitive recursive,
- $\ulcorner t_1 + t_2 \urcorner$ is primitive recursive in $\ulcorner t_1 \urcorner$ and $\ulcorner t_2 \urcorner$,
- $\ulcorner S_1 ; S_2 \urcorner$ is primitive recursive in $\ulcorner S_1 \urcorner$ and $\ulcorner S_2 \urcorner$, etc.

(5) An Iexp_N-number is a code for a member of Iexp_N.
Similarly for Bexp_N-numbers, etc.

END A.9.

Remark. We are interested only in *closed programs* in this appendix, and, moreover, only in programs in $\mathit{Cl.Prog}_N$, and take "program" to mean: member of $\mathit{Cl.Prog}_N$, and "program number" to mean: code for a member of $\mathit{Cl.Prog}_N$.

DEFINITION A.10 (valuations).

We define (partial) recursive valuations L', R' and W' of Ivar_N-, Iexp_N- and Bexp_N-numbers $\ulcorner X \urcorner$ respectively, relative to state numbers (cf. definition 4.2c). The definition is by (simultaneous) induction on $\ulcorner X \urcorner$ (or the complexity of X).

First, $L'(m,n)$, $R'(m,n)$ and $W'(m,n)$ are undefined if n is *not* a state number, or if m is *not* an Ivar_N-, Iexp_N- or Bexp_N-number respectively. Otherwise:

(i) $L'(\ulcorner x_i \urcorner, s) = \langle 0, i \rangle$ (where $i < N_0$),
$L'(\ulcorner a_i[t] \urcorner, s) \simeq \langle 1, i, R'(\ulcorner t \urcorner, s) \rangle$ (where $i < N_1$).
(Note that $L'(\ulcorner v \urcorner, s)$, when defined, is an Intv_N-number.)

(ii) $$R'(\ulcorner v \urcorner, s) = \begin{cases} s\langle d \rangle & \text{if } L'(\ulcorner v \urcorner, s)\downarrow d \text{ and } d \in \mathit{dom}(s), \\ \infty & \text{otherwise.} \end{cases}$$

$$R'(\ulcorner \underline{\text{if}}\ b\ \underline{\text{then}}\ t_1\ \underline{\text{else}}\ t_2\ \underline{\text{fi}} \urcorner, s) \simeq \begin{cases} R'(\ulcorner t_1 \urcorner, s) & \text{if } W'(\ulcorner b \urcorner, s)\downarrow 1, \\ R'(\ulcorner t_2 \urcorner, s) & \text{if } W'(\ulcorner b \urcorner, s)\downarrow 2, \\ \infty & \text{otherwise.} \end{cases}$$

$R'(\ulcorner t_1 + t_2 \urcorner, s) \simeq R'(\ulcorner t_1 \urcorner, s) + R'(\ulcorner t_2 \urcorner, s)$, etc.

(iii) $W'(\ulcorner \underline{\text{true}} \urcorner, s) = 1$
$W'(\ulcorner \underline{\text{false}} \urcorner, s) = 2$

$$\mathcal{W}'(\ulcorner t_1 = t_2 \urcorner, s) = \begin{cases} 1 \text{ if } \mathcal{R}'(\ulcorner t_1 \urcorner, s)\downarrow n \text{ and } \mathcal{R}'(\ulcorner t_2 \urcorner, s)\downarrow n \text{ for some } n, \\ 2 \text{ if } \mathcal{R}'(\ulcorner t_1 \urcorner, s)\downarrow m \text{ and } \mathcal{R}'(\ulcorner t_2 \urcorner, s)\downarrow n \text{ for some } m,n \\ \qquad \text{with } m \neq n, \\ \infty \text{ otherwise.} \end{cases}$$

$$\mathcal{W}'(\ulcorner b_1 \supset b_2 \urcorner, s) = \begin{cases} 1 \text{ if } \mathcal{W}'(\ulcorner b_1 \urcorner, s)\downarrow i \text{ and } \mathcal{W}'(\ulcorner b_2 \urcorner, s)\downarrow j, \text{ where} \\ \qquad j \leq i (<\infty), \\ 2 \text{ if } \mathcal{W}'(\ulcorner b_1 \urcorner, s)\downarrow 1 \text{ and } \mathcal{W}'(\ulcorner b_2 \urcorner, s)\downarrow 2, \\ \infty \text{ otherwise,} \end{cases}$$

etc.

(Note that $\mathcal{W}'(\ulcorner b \urcorner, s)$, when defined, is 1 or 2.)

END A.10.

PROPOSITION A.11 (upward persistence of valuation relative to s). Suppose $s \preceq s'$.

a. If $\mathcal{L}'(\ulcorner v \urcorner, s)\downarrow d$ then $\mathcal{L}'(\ulcorner v \urcorner, s')\downarrow d$

b. If $\mathcal{R}'(\ulcorner t \urcorner, s)\downarrow n$ then $\mathcal{R}'(\ulcorner t \urcorner, s')\downarrow n$

c. If $\mathcal{W}'(\ulcorner b \urcorner, s)\downarrow i$ then $\mathcal{W}'(\ulcorner b \urcorner, s')\downarrow i$.

PROOF. Simultaneous induction on the complexity of v, t and b.

END A.11.

The following two propositions show that these valuation functions really do give a representation of the corresponding functions $\mathcal{L}$, $\mathcal{R}$, $\mathcal{W}$ (cf. definition 4.2).

PROPOSITION A.12. Suppose s *approx* σ.

a. If $\mathcal{L}'(\ulcorner v \urcorner, s)\downarrow d$ then $\mathcal{L}(v)(\sigma) = \xi_d$

b. If $\mathcal{R}'(\ulcorner t \urcorner, s)\downarrow n$ then $\mathcal{R}(t)(\sigma) = n$

c. If $\mathcal{W}'(\ulcorner b \urcorner, s)\downarrow 1$ then $\mathcal{W}(b)(\sigma) = tt$, and if $\mathcal{W}'(\ulcorner b \urcorner, s)\downarrow 2$ then $\mathcal{W}(b)(\sigma) = ff$.

PROOF. Simultaneous induction on v, t and b (following the inductive definition (A.10) of $\mathcal{L}'$, $\mathcal{R}'$, $\mathcal{W}'$).

END A.12.

Conversely:

PROPOSITION A.13. Suppose $\sigma \neq \bot$ and $v \in \mathit{Ivar}_N$, $t \in \mathit{Iexp}_N$ and $b \in \mathit{Bexp}_N$. Then there exists δ such that if $s = \sigma \vdash \delta$ then

a. $L'(\ulcorner v \urcorner, s) \downarrow d$, where $\xi_d = L(v)(\sigma)$

b. $R'(\ulcorner t \urcorner, s) \downarrow R(t)(\sigma)$

c. $W'(\ulcorner b \urcorner, s) \downarrow i$, where $i = \begin{cases} 1 & \text{if } W(b)(\sigma) = tt, \\ 2 & \text{if } W(b)(\sigma) = ff. \end{cases}$

PROOF. Simultaneous induction on v, t, b. We give two cases as examples (both in part b).

(i) t is a variable v. Assume (induction hypothesis) there exists δ_1 such that $L'(\ulcorner v \urcorner, \sigma \vdash \delta_1) \downarrow d$, where $\xi_d = L(v)(\sigma)$. Now let $\delta = \delta_1 \cup \{d\}$ and $s = \sigma \vdash \delta$. By proposition A.11, $L'(\ulcorner v \urcorner, s) \downarrow d$, and moreover $d \in \mathit{dom}(s)$. Hence

$$R'(\ulcorner v \urcorner, s) \downarrow s\langle d \rangle = \sigma(\xi_d) = R(v)(\sigma).$$

(ii) $t \equiv t_1 + t_2$. By induction hypothesis there exist δ_1, δ_2 which work for t_1, t_2 resp. Now take $\delta = \delta_1 \cup \delta_2$.

END A.13.

A.5. The computation function

DEFINITION A.14 (simple statements).

A statement is *simple* if it is *not* of the form $S_1;S_2$.

END A.14.

(Note: a program such as: if b then $S_1;S_2$ else $S_3;S_4$ fi, is simple!)

DEFINITION A.15 (computation function).

Suppose ψ is a partial recursive function of two arguments. (Think of the first argument as a program number, the second as a state number, and the value (when convergent) as a computation number.) ψ is called a *computation function* if it satisfies the following conditions (cf. definition 5.16):

(0) $\psi(m,n)\uparrow$ if m is not a program number, or n is not a state number. Otherwise (writing $\ulcorner E|S \urcorner$ for $\ulcorner <E|S> \urcorner$):

(1) $\psi(\ulcorner E|v{:=}t \urcorner, s) \simeq \langle s[n/d]\rangle$ if $L'(\ulcorner v \urcorner, s)\downarrow d$ and $d \in dom(s)$ and $R'(\ulcorner t \urcorner, s)\downarrow n$ (and ∞ otherwise).

(2) $\psi(\ulcorner E|\underline{\text{if}}\ b\ \underline{\text{then}}\ S_1\ \underline{\text{else}}\ S_2\ \underline{\text{fi}} \urcorner, s) \simeq \begin{cases} s^\frown\psi(\ulcorner E|S_1 \urcorner, s) & \text{if } W'(\ulcorner b \urcorner, s)\downarrow 1, \\ s^\frown\psi(\ulcorner E|S_2 \urcorner, s) & \text{if } W'(\ulcorner b \urcorner, s)\downarrow 2. \end{cases}$

(3) $\psi(\ulcorner E|S_1;S_2 \urcorner, s) \simeq \psi(\ulcorner E|S_1 \urcorner, s)^\frown\psi(\ulcorner E|S_2 \urcorner, end(\psi(\ulcorner E|S_1 \urcorner, s)))$, where S_1 is simple.

(4) $\psi(\ulcorner E|P_i \urcorner, s) \simeq \langle s\rangle^\frown\psi(\ulcorner E|S_i \urcorner, s)$, where $E \equiv \langle P_j \Leftarrow S_j\rangle_{j=1}^n$.

END A.15.

Let ψ be a computation function.

PROPOSITION A.16. If $\psi(\ulcorner R \urcorner, s)\downarrow n$, then n is a computation number with $cdom(n) = dom(s)$.

PROOF. Induction on $\ell h(n)$.

END A.16.

PROPOSITION A.17. Suppose $R \equiv \langle E|S_1;S_2;\ldots;S_n\rangle$ where the S_i are simple, and $c_1,\ldots,c_n$ are such that $\psi(\ulcorner E|S_1 \urcorner, s)\downarrow c_1$, and for all $i < n$, $\psi(\ulcorner E|S_{i+1} \urcorner, end(c_i))\downarrow c_{i+1}$. Then $\psi(\ulcorner R \urcorner, s)\downarrow c_1{}^\frown c_2{}^\frown\ldots{}^\frown c_n$.

PROOF. Apply clause (3) in definition A.15 repeatedly.

END A.17.

COROLLARY A.18.

(a) Clause (3) in definition A.15 holds for computation functions even when S_1 is not simple.

(b) More generally, proposition A.17 holds even when the S_i are not simple.

END A.18.

THEOREM A.19 (existence of computation function).
There exists a computation function.

PROOF. Use the *recursion theorem* ([R,§11.2,theorem 1] or [K,p.352, theorem XXVII]).

In detail (using the notation of [R]): define a partial recursive function θ of three arguments as follows.

$\theta(z,x,y)\uparrow$ if x is not a program number or y is not a state number. Otherwise, $\theta(z,\ulcorner R\urcorner,s)$ is defined, according to the form of R, just as in clauses (1) to (5) of definition A.15, except that "ψ" on the *right-hand side* is replaced throughout by "ϕ_z" (the partial recursive function with index z). The conditions in these clauses are clearly (partial) effective, so θ is a partial recursive function. By the S^m_n theorem ([R,§1.8, theorem 5] or [K,p.342, theorem XXIII]) there is a total recursive function g such that for all z,x,y

$$\phi_{g(z)}(x,y) \simeq \theta(z,x,y).$$

By the recursion theorem, we can find an index n such that $\phi_{g(n)} = \phi_n$. Then ϕ_n is the desired computation function.
END A.19.

THEOREM A.20 (uniqueness of computation function).
Suppose ψ and ψ' are computation functions and $\psi(\ulcorner R\urcorner,s)\downarrow c$. Then $\psi'(\ulcorner R\urcorner,s)\downarrow c$.

PROOF. Induction on $\ell h(c)$.
END A.20.

DEFINITION A.21. ψ_0 is the (unique) computation function given by theorems A.19 and A.20.
END A.21.

PROPOSITION A.22 (upward persistence of computation number relative to s).

Suppose $\psi_0(\ulcorner R \urcorner, s){\downarrow}c$ and $s \preceq s_1$. Then $\psi_0(\ulcorner R \urcorner, s_1){\downarrow}c_1$, where c_1 is such that $c \preceq\preceq c_1$ and $(c_1)_i\langle d\rangle = s_1\langle d\rangle$ for $d \in \mathit{dom}(s_1)\backslash\mathit{dom}(s)$ (and $i < \ell h(c)$).

PROOF. Induction on $\ell h(c)$.

END A.22.

A.6. The computation relation

DEFINITION A.23 (the computation relation).
Compu(m,s,c,s') is the relation:

$$\psi_0(m,s){\downarrow}c \text{ and } \mathit{end}(c) = s'.$$

END A.23.

Compu$(\ulcorner R \urcorner, s, c, s')$ says that program R, starting with state (coded by) s, produces computation (coded by) c, which ends with state (coded by) s'.

Note that, if *Compu*$(\ulcorner R \urcorner, s, c, s')$, then $\mathit{dom}(s) = \mathit{cdom}(c) = \mathit{dom}(s')$.

Proposition A.22 can now be re-stated:

THEOREM A.24. Suppose *Compu*$(\ulcorner R \urcorner, s, c, s')$ and $s \preceq s_1$. Then *Compu*$(\ulcorner R \urcorner, s_1, c_1, s_1')$, where c_1 and s_1' are such that $c \preceq\preceq c_1$, $s' \preceq s_1'$ and $(c_1)_i\langle d\rangle = s_1'\langle d\rangle = s_1\langle d\rangle$ for $d \in \mathit{dom}(s_1)\backslash\mathit{dom}(s)$ (and $i < \ell h(c)$).
END A.24.

The following two theorems show that ψ_0 (and hence *Compu*) really does give a representation of *operational semantics* for programs (in the sense of definitions 5.16 and 5.17).

DEFINITION A.25. $\sigma =_\delta \sigma'$ ("σ equals σ' off δ") means: for all $d \notin \delta$, $\sigma(\xi_d) = \sigma'(\xi_d)$.
END A.25.

THEOREM A.26. Suppose *Compu*(⌜R⌝,s,c,s') and s *approx* σ. Then *Comp*(R)(σ) is a finite computation sequence $\vec{\sigma} = (\sigma_i)_{i<\ell h(c)}$ such that c *approx* $\vec{\sigma}$ and (hence) s' *approx* $\kappa(\vec{\sigma})$ (= $\mathcal{O}$(R)(σ), cf. definition 5.17). Moreover, for all i < ℓh(c), $\sigma_i =_\delta \sigma$ (where δ = *dom*(σ)).

PROOF. Induction on ℓh(c). (Use propositions A.12 and A.6.)
END A.26.

Conversely:

THEOREM A.27. Suppose *Comp*(R)(σ) is a finite computation sequence, and $\sigma' = \mathcal{O}$(R)(σ). Then there exists δ such that for s = $\sigma \upharpoonright \delta$, c = *Comp*(R)($\sigma$)$\upharpoonright\delta$ and s' = $\sigma' \upharpoonright \delta$, we have: *Compu*(⌜R⌝,s,c,s'). Moreover (for such δ) $\sigma =_\delta \sigma'$.

PROOF. Induction on length of *Comp*(R)(σ). Consider cases according to the form of R. We give two cases as examples.

(i) R ≡ <E|v:=t>. By proposition A.13 there are δ_1,δ_2 such that L'(⌜v⌝,$\sigma\upharpoonright\delta_1$)↓d and R'(⌜t⌝,$\sigma\upharpoonright\delta_2$)↓n where $\xi_d = L(v)(\sigma)$ and n = R(t)(σ). Take $\delta = \delta_1 \cup \delta_2$, s = $\sigma\upharpoonright\delta$, s' = s[n/d] and c = <s'>. The result follows by propositions A.11 and A.6, and definitions A.15 clause (1) and 5.16 clause (a).

(ii) R ≡ <E|S_1;S_2>, with S_1 simple. By induction hypothesis there are δ_1,δ_2 which work for <E|S_1> and <E|S_2> respectively. Take $\delta = \delta_1 \cup \delta_2$, and apply theorem A.24 and definitions A.15 clause (3) and 5.16 clause (b).

END A.27.

Remark. Theorems A.24, A.26 and A.27 can be taken as giving a *justification* for the definition (5.16) of *Comp*, at least in the case that *Comp*(R)(σ) is finite; for then *Comp*(R)(σ) is the unique finite sequence $\vec{\sigma}$ such that for some δ_0 and all $\delta \supseteq \delta_0$,

$$\psi_0(⌜R⌝, \sigma\upharpoonright\delta) \text{ converges to } \vec{\sigma}\upharpoonright\delta.$$

(Of course, the above theorems would have to be re-worded to show that we were busy (re-)*defining* "*Comp*".)

The non-trivial step in this approach to the definition of *Comp* is the use of the recursion theorem in proving the existence of a computation function (theorem A.19).

A.7. Satisfaction of assertions by state numbers

NOTATION A.28 (formalized predicates).

(1) We have seen that many of the predicates and relations we have defined are (primitive recursive, and hence) arithmetical; for example *StateNo*(n), "n is a state number", and *CompNo*(n), "n is a computation number". Again, the relation *Compu* (definition A.23) is (recursively enumerable, hence) arithmetical. We denote the *L*-formulae which express these relations by a change of typeface, thus: StateNo(x), CompNo(x), Compu(x,y,z,u). Thus, for example

$$Compu(\ulcorner R\urcorner,s,c,s') \iff \models \mathrm{Compu}(\overline{\ulcorner R\urcorner},\bar{s},\bar{c},\bar{s}')$$

(where $\bar{n}$ is the numeral for n).

As a further example, the relation d $\in$ *dom*(s) (being primitive recursive in d,s) is arithmetical. We write the *L*-formula expressing it as "x $\in$ dom(y)".

(2) We let *s*,*s'*,... denote simple variables ranging over state numbers numbers, and assume *s*,... $\notin \chi$. (In other words, $\forall$s(...s...) stands for the formula $\forall$y(StateNo(y) $\supset$ ...y...) and $\exists$*s*(...*s*...) for the formula $\exists$y(StateNo(y) $\wedge$ ...y...), where y $\notin \chi$.)

Similarly, *c* denotes a simple variable ranging over computation numbers.

END A.28.

Now we cannot define a partial recursive valuation $T'(\ulcorner p\urcorner,s)$ of two numerical arguments (a code $\ulcorner p\urcorner$ for an assertion p, and a state number s), which would reflect the definition (2.9) of T, as we did for L, R and W (definition A.10), since this would contradict Tarski's theorem on the inexpressibility of arithmetical truth within arithmetic (see [R,exercise 11-45] or [K,p.501]). (If we try to extend the definition of W' in A.10 so as to have codes of arbitrary assertions, not just booleans, as arguments, we will see that the difficulty comes with numerical quantification, i.e. the condition in clause (f) of definition 2.9, which is not effectively decidable.)

Instead, we proceed as follows, taking a *fixed* assertion (= L-formula) p.

<u>DEFINITION A.29</u> (satisfaction of an assertion by a state number). Sat(p,s) is the L-formula formed by replacing each occurrence of a term t in p by a term t^*, which is defined inductively as follows.

$$x_i^* \equiv \begin{cases} \underline{\text{if}}\ \langle 0,\bar{i}\rangle \in \text{dom}(s)\ \underline{\text{then}}\ s\langle 0,\bar{i}\rangle\ \underline{\text{else}}\ x_i\ \underline{\text{fi}} & \\ & \text{if } x_i \text{ is free in p,} \\ x_i & \text{if } x_i \text{ is bound in p,} \end{cases}$$

$$a_i[t]^* \equiv \underline{\text{if}}\ \langle 1,\bar{i},t\rangle \in \text{dom}(s)\ \underline{\text{then}}\ s\langle 1,\bar{i},t^*\rangle\ \underline{\text{else}}\ a_i[t^*]\ \underline{\text{fi}}$$

$$0^* \equiv 0,\quad (t_1+t_2)^* \equiv t_1^*+t_2^*,\ \text{etc.}$$

END A.29.

Remarks (on definition A.29).

(1) We are assuming that $s \notin$ *intv*(p)

(2) *svar* (Sat(p,s)) = *svar* (p) ∪ {s}, and *avar*(Sat(p,s)) = *avar*(p).

(3) Now we still cannot give a full representation for T (definition 2.9) by means of Sat, as we did for L, R, W by means of L', R', W' (propositions A.12 and A.13), or computation sequences by means of *Compu* (theorems A.26 and A.27). This is because T(p)(σ), unlike these other operations, is not continuous in σ (where "continuous" here means: determined by a finite approximation to σ). In fact, analogs of these results would imply

$$\mathcal{T}(p)(\sigma) = tt \iff \exists\delta \models \mathsf{Sat}(p,\overline{\sigma{\restriction}\delta})$$
$$\iff \exists\delta\forall\sigma'(\sigma' =_\delta \sigma \Rightarrow \mathcal{T}(p)(\sigma') = tt),$$

which is clearly false for e.g. $p \equiv \forall x(a[x] = 0)$.

However, $\mathsf{Sat}(p,s)$ does give a "local representation" of $\mathcal{T}(p)(\sigma)$, in the sense that

if s *approx* σ, then $\mathcal{T}(\mathsf{Sat}(p,\bar{s}))(\sigma) = \mathcal{T}(p)(\sigma)$.

More generally:

THEOREM A.30. If $s = \sigma{\restriction}\delta$ and $\sigma =_\delta \sigma'$ then $\mathcal{T}(\mathsf{Sat}(p,\bar{s}))(\sigma') = \mathcal{T}(p)(\sigma)$.

PROOF (outline). Define a (more general) formula $\mathsf{Sat}_I(p,s)$, where I is an arbitrary (finite) set of indices, using the modified condition that $x_i^* \equiv x_i$ if $i \in I$ (or if x_i is bound in p). (So our Sat is $\mathsf{Sat}_\emptyset$.) Then prove that (under the stated assumptions) $\mathcal{T}(\mathsf{Sat}_I(p,\bar{s}))(\sigma') = \mathcal{T}(p)(\sigma)$ for arbitrary I, by induction on the complexity of p. Note (for the induction step) that

$$\mathsf{Sat}_I(\exists x_i p,\bar{s}) \equiv \exists x_i\ \mathsf{Sat}_{I\cup\{i\}}(p,\bar{s}).$$

END A.30.

A.8. Weakest precondition

DEFINITION A.31. $\mathsf{Val}(s,x,a)$ ("s has values given by x and a") is the $\mathcal{L}$-formula

$$\bigwedge_{i<N_0} (\langle 0,\bar{i}\rangle \in \mathsf{dom}(s) \supset s\langle 0,\bar{i}\rangle = x_i) \wedge$$

$$\bigwedge_{i<N_1} \forall y(\langle 1,\bar{i},y\rangle \in \mathsf{dom}(s) \supset s\langle 1,\bar{i},y\rangle = a_i[y])$$

(where " $\bigwedge$ " denotes a finite conjuction).

END A.31.

Remark. $svar(\mathsf{Val}(s,X,A)) = X \cup \{s\}$, and $avar(\mathsf{Val}(s,X,A)) = A$.

PROPOSITION A.32. $T(\mathsf{Val}(\bar{s},X,A))(\sigma) \iff s$ *approx* σ.
END A.32.

Let R be a (fixed) program.

DEFINITION A.33 (formula expressing weakest precondition).
Precond(R,p) is the *L*-formula

$$\forall s,c,s'[\mathsf{Val}(s,X,A) \wedge \mathsf{Compu}(\ulcorner R \urcorner,s,c,s') \supset \mathsf{Sat}(p,s')].$$

END A.33.

Remark (on definition A.33). Note that the formula Precond(R,p) depends on the variables X and A occurring in $\mathsf{Val}(s,X,A)$; we can make this explicit by writing $\mathsf{Precond}_{X,A}(R,p)$. Now we have been assuming that $svar(R) \subseteq X$ and $avar(R) \subseteq A$ (see remark after definition A.9; this was necessary for theorem A.27); but no such assumption is necessary with regard to the assertion p (for e.g. theorem A.30 to hold). Thus (by remark (2) following definition A.29)

$$var(\mathsf{Precond}_{X,A}(R,p)) = X \cup A \cup var(p)$$

(where $var(X) = svar(X) \cup avar(X)$).

Finally, we may assume that, *starting with* an arbitrary closed program R, we *define* X and A by: $X = svar(R)$, $A = avar(R)$. In this case we will have:

$$var(\mathsf{Precond}(R,p)) = var(R,p).$$

THEOREM A.34 (semantic characterization of weakest precondition).
For all $\sigma \neq \perp$

$$T(\mathsf{Precond}(R,p))(\sigma) \iff \forall \sigma' \neq \perp (\mathcal{O}(R)(\sigma) = \sigma' \Rightarrow T(p)(\sigma')).$$

PROOF. Take $\sigma \neq \bot$, and put $r \equiv \mathsf{Precond}(R,p)$. Note that by proposition A.32, (lhs) $\Longleftrightarrow$

$$\forall s,c,s'[s \; \mathit{approx} \; \sigma \text{ and } \mathit{Compu}(\ulcorner R \urcorner,s,c,s') \Rightarrow \mathcal{T}(\mathsf{Sat}(p,\bar{s}'))(\sigma)]. \quad (A.1)$$

We must show: (A.1) $\Longleftrightarrow$ (rhs).

$\Rightarrow$: Assume (A.1), and let $\sigma' = \mathcal{O}(R)(\sigma) \neq \bot$. Show $\mathcal{T}(p)(\sigma')$. Since $\sigma' \neq \bot$, $\mathit{Comp}(R)(\sigma)$ is finite. So by theorem A.27 there exist δ,s,c,s' such that $s = \sigma \restriction \delta$, $c = \mathit{Comp}(R)(\sigma) \restriction \delta$, $s' = \sigma' \restriction \delta$, $\mathit{Compu}(\ulcorner R \urcorner,s,c,s')$, and $\sigma =_\delta \sigma'$. Hence, by (A.1), $\mathcal{T}(\mathsf{Sat}(p,\bar{s}'))(\sigma)$, and so, by theorem A.30, $\mathcal{T}(p)(\sigma')$.

$\Leftarrow$: Assume (rhs), and suppose, for given s,c,s', that $s \; \mathit{approx} \; \sigma$ and $\mathit{Compu}(\ulcorner R \urcorner,s,c,s')$. We must show $\mathcal{T}(\mathsf{Sat}(p,\bar{s}'))(\sigma)$. Let $\sigma' = \mathcal{O}(R)(\sigma)$. By theorem A.26, $\mathit{Comp}(R)(\sigma)$ is finite, and so $\sigma' \neq \bot$. Hence (by (rhs)) $\mathcal{T}(p)(\sigma')$. Again by theorem A.26, $s' \; \mathit{approx} \; \sigma'$, and $\sigma' =_\delta \sigma$, where $\delta = \mathit{dom}(s)$. Hence, again by theorem A.30, $\mathcal{T}(\mathsf{Sat}(p,\bar{s}'))(\sigma)$.
END A.34.

From theorem A.34 we easily get the corollaries:

COROLLARY A.35.
(a) $\models$ $<E|\{\mathsf{Precond}(R,p)\}S\{p\}>$
(b) $\models$ $<E|\{q\}S\{p\} \Rightarrow q \supset \mathsf{Precond}(R,p)>$, where $R \equiv <E|S>$.

PROOF. Directly from the definitions (5.24-26). Use (of course) theorem 5.22: $\mathcal{O}(R)(\sigma) = \mathcal{M}(R)(\gamma)(\sigma)$ for any $\gamma \in \Gamma$.
END A.35.

COROLLARY A.36 (intermediate assertion).
(a) $\models$ $\mathsf{Precond}(<E|S_1;S_2>,p) \leftrightarrow \mathsf{Precond}(<E|S_1>,\mathsf{Precond}(<E|S_2>,p))$
(b) $\models$ $<E|\{q\}S_1;S_2\{p\} \Rightarrow \{q\}S_1\{\mathsf{Precond}(<E|S_2>,p)\}>$.
END A.36.

A.9. Strongest postcondition

Now we can be quite brief. (See A.33-A.36.)

DEFINITION A.37 (formula expressing strongest postcondition).
Postcond(p,R) is the L-formula

$$\exists s',c,s[\mathrm{Sat}(p,s') \wedge \mathrm{Compu}(\ulcorner \overline{R} \urcorner,s',c,s) \wedge \mathrm{Val}(s,x,a)].$$

END A.37.

THEOREM A.38 (semantic characterization of strongest postcondition).
For all $\sigma \neq \perp$,

$$T(\mathrm{Postcond}\ (p,R))(\sigma) \Longleftrightarrow \exists\sigma'(\mathcal{O}(R)(\sigma') = \sigma \wedge T(p)(\sigma')).$$

END A.38.

COROLLARY A.39.

(a) $\models$ <E|{p}S{Postcond(p,R)}>

(b) $\models$ <E|{p}S{q} $\Rightarrow$ Postcond(p,R) $\supset$ q>, where R $\equiv$ <E|S>.

END A.39.

COROLLARY A.40 (intermediate assertion).

(a) $\models$ Postcond(p,<E|S_1;S_2>) $\leftrightarrow$ Postcond(Postcond(p,<E|S_1>),<E|S_2>).

(b) $\models$ <E|{p}S_1;S_2{q} $\Rightarrow$ {Postcond(p,<E|S_1>)}S_2{q}>.

END A.40.

A.10. Some concluding remarks

From corollary A.35 we can infer:

$$\models \text{<E|\{p\}S\{q\}>} \quad \text{iff} \quad \models \text{<E|p} \supset \text{Precond(<E|S>,q)>}. \qquad \text{(A.2)}$$

Two points emerge from a consideration of this equivalence.

(1) Suppose we add the following valid inference rule to our proof

system:

$$\frac{\langle E | p \supset \text{Precond}(\langle E | S\rangle, q)\rangle}{\langle E | \{p\}S\{q\}\rangle} \tag{A.3}$$

Then we obtain a system which is trivially complete! (Remember that all valid assertions are axioms.)

However such a system would not conform to the spirit of the proof systems considered in this book, in the following sense. All of the axioms and rules in (say) the system of chapter 5 (other than the valid assertions; cf. section 5.5) fall into two categories: either they reflect the *meanings* (so to speak) of the *particular constructions* used in building up statements (rule 5 for assignments, 6 for composition, 7 for conditionals and 9 for recursive procedure calls), or they express *basic semantic properties* of the correctness formulae $\{p\}S\{q\}$ for arbitrary statements S (rules 1-4, 8 and 10-14). Now rule (A.3) above falls into neither of these categories; it is highly artificial from the viewpoint of program semantics, depending as it does on the machinery of Gödel numbering. We conclude that the trivialization of the completeness theorem obtained by adjoining a rule like (A.3) in no way detracts from the interest of the investigation of completeness properties for the proof systems considered in this book.

(2) Given two sets of numbers A and B, we say that A is 1-*reducible* to B if there is a one-to-one total recursive function f such that $\forall n(n \in A \Leftrightarrow f(n) \in B)$. Intuitively, this implies that the "problem" of membership of A can be reduced to the "problem" of membership of B, via the effective map f.

Consider now the two sets of numbers:

$$A \overset{\text{df.}}{=} \{ \ulcorner p \urcorner \mid \models \langle E|p\rangle \},$$

$$B \overset{\text{df.}}{=} \{ \ulcorner \{p\}S\{q\} \urcorner \mid \models \langle E|\{p\}S\{q\}\rangle \}.$$

A is the set of codes of valid assertions (essentially the "truth set" for arithmetic), and B is the set of codes of valid correctness formulae. It is clear that A is 1-reducible to B, via the effective map $\ulcorner p \urcorner \mapsto \ulcorner\{\underline{\text{true}}\}x:=x\{p\}\urcorner$. It follows from the equivalence (A.2), however, that B is also 1-reducible to A, via the map $\ulcorner\{p\}S\{q\}\urcorner \mapsto \ulcorner p \supset \text{Precond}(\langle E|S\rangle,q)\urcorner$. Thus B has the same *degree of unsolvability* as A (namely $0^{(\omega)}$; cf. [R,§14.7,theorem X]). This means, intuitively, that the two "problems" of deciding the validity of arithmetical assertions, and of correctness formulae, have the same degree of difficulty, since each is effectively reducible to the other.

REFERENCES AND BIBLIOGRAPHICAL NOTES

The first section of this chapter contains a brief outline of the history of the research which led to the mathematical theory of program correctness as developed in the preceding chapters. In the second section, we provide some general references on semantics, program correctness and logic, which together establish the context in which our work should be situated. Though we have attempted to give a fair presentation of what we see as the major sources and related investigations, we know that we have also been guided by our personal taste, and limited by restrictions in the available time and space, and in our knowledge. In particular, in our discussion of related work where the connection between denotational semantics and the theory of program correctness is not the central theme, our aim has been no more than to supply the reader with enough references to enable him to find his own way into the relevant literature.

In section 3, we present the references which more specifically correspond to each of the chapters 2 to 10.

R.1. Historical references

Ever since the advent of the first electronic computers, their users have been concerned with program correctness. This can be seen, e.g. from the paper by Goldstine & Von Neumann [1963,p.92] and, in a very clear form, from Turing's "On checking a large routine" (Turing [1949]), where assertions are employed to ascertain correctness just as one does this at the present time. However, the development of a *mathematical theory* of program correctness was initiated only in the sixties. As a starting point of this we see the pioneering papers by McCarthy [1963a,b], who was the first to systematically study the mathematical properties of various fundamental concepts in the theory of computation, including the notion of state, properties of conditionals and recursion, and abstract syntax (which, if one insists, may be used to justify the neglect of syntactic questions in our book). After McCarthy's work most attention was paid for a number of years to semantics rather than to program correctness, and a vigorous activity in methods for formally defining full programming languages such as ALGOL 60 or PL/I evolved. The best source for the state of the art at that time is Steel [1966]. Though a few contributions to Steel's book foreshadow denotational semantics (in particular Strachey [1966]), the majority of the methods then in use were *operational*, essentially assuming an abstract machine which grinds out state transformations as prescribed by the respective programming constructs. An impressive representative of this approach is the Vienna Definition Language, culminating in the formal definition of PL/I (Lucas & Walk [1971], cf. also Wegner [1972]). Another important example of a semantic definition with strong operational flavor - though exhibiting, on the other hand, vast differences with the VDL effort - is that of ALGOL 68 (Van Wijngaarden (ed.) et al. [1969], Van Wijngaarden et al. (eds) [1975]).

In the second half of the sixties the situation changed drastically. In fact, all the major ideas of our book can be traced back to developments of these years. First, there appeared the fundamental paper by Floyd (Floyd [1967], see also Naur [1966]), which reawakened the use of assertions which had been dormant for many years, and caused a breakthrough in the treatment of program correctness, raising it to a subject which nowadays appears in some form in virtually all computer science curricula, and which pervades current concern about the design of reliable software. Instrumental in this breakthrough were furthermore the paper by Hoare (Hoare [1969]), where the use of assertions was systematized for ALGOL-like-languages - rather than for flowcharts as was the case with Floyd's paper - and the work of Dijkstra (culminating in Dijkstra [1976]), who eloquently advocated that a program should be proved correct not after, but concurrently with, its design, and who also was the first to recognize the importance of the notion of weakest precondition.

Simultaneously with these developments in correctness the theory of denotational semantics was started. Fixed points entered the scene in 1969 (Scott & De Bakker [1969], and, independently, Park [1970] and Bekic [1969]). In subsequent years from a very fruitful cooperation between Scott and Strachey in Oxford, with Scott mainly responsible for the mathematical foundations and Strachey for the applications to programming languages, the essential ideas from denotational semantics originated (described in Scott [1970, 1972a, 1972b, 1972c, 1976, 1977], Scott & Strachey [1971]).

R.2. General references

R.2.1. Semantics

The main references for denotational semantics are Stoy's textbook (Stoy [1977]), and the monograph by Milne & Strachey [1976]. Gordon [1979] is an introductory text with a non-mathematical approach. A very nice tutorial on denotational semantics in general is Tennent [1976], while Milne [1978] gives a tutorial on weakest preconditions in denotational semantics. From the various applications of the method to the definition of full programming languages, we mention only Mosses [1974].

Lest the reader thinks that denotational semantics as employed in our book covers (almost) all of it, we emphasize that there is much more to this theory than he has been exposed to. For example, we have not dealt at all with the so-called reflexive domain structures (sets D such that, in some suitable sense, $D = [D \to D]$), needed to deal, e.g., with the concept of self-application as encountered in the λ-calculus ($\lambda x \cdot xx$) or ALGOL 60 (f(f)). An introduction to these problems is to be found in Stoy [1977]; mathematical details are given in Scott [1972a,1976].

Many further references on denotational semantics are contained in the bibliographies of the books by Stoy and Milne & Strachey, and in the chapter references in section 3 below.

Besides the operational approach already referred to in section R.1, there is a substantial further variety of semantical methods. Here we mention only two, viz. the method of attribute grammars (Knuth [1968], see also Marcotty et al. [1976]), and that of algebraic semantics, which is built upon notions from universal algebra and category theory. Examples of the latter are the work of the ADJ-group (e.g. Goguen et al. [1977], Thatcher et al. [1979]), and of the French school of semantics (see Nivat [1973, 1975]). Though this research partly covers the same ground as our sections on semantics, it is much less oriented toward program correctness in our sense. Also, it often deals with constructs which are outside the scope of our treatise, such as flow charts, recursive function schemes, or abstract data types.

R.2.2. *Correctness*

In Hoare & Wirth [1973] an axiomatic definition - a proof system in our terminology - for most of the language PASCAL is given. A text-book elaborating these ideas - to be recommended for the reader who is interested in how to design correct programs - is Alagić & Arbib [1978]. Manna's book (Manna [1974]) is an excellent introduction to program verification. It puts rather less emphasis on mathematical rigor than ours, but, on the other hand, covers a much broader range of topics. For example, it complements our work as a source of many examples of applying Scott's induction rule to recursive function procedures (in the sense of the factorial function mentioned in section 5.1). Another book with goals somewhat similar to those of Manna is Greibach [1975]. For the reader who understands French we mention Livercy [1978], which, besides program verification, is also concerned with program schemes and semantics (including fixed point semantics and attribute grammars).

Though a few of the investigations listed so far include discussion of the relationship between semantics and correctness (e.g. chapter 14 of Stoy [1977], various places in Milne & Strachey [1976], chapter 5 of Manna [1974]), it seems fair to say that the main emphasis in them is either on semantics, or on correctness. We now mention some further publications where, just as we have done in our book, the authors stress the relationship between the two: Hoare & Lauer [1974] (see also Greif & Meyer [1979]), Ligler [1975a, 1975b], Donahue [1976], and Constable & O'Donnell [1978]. In particular Donahue [1976] addresses problems which are similar to ours. However, there are also a number of differences in the mathematical apparatus and choice of concepts dealt with; moreover, completeness issues are not dealt with in Donahue's monograph. Fixed point techniques, used as a tool to analyze the correctness of (mostly regular) programs, have been investigated extensively by the Polish school of semantics (see, e.g., Blikle [1977, 1979], and references mentioned there).

Finally, we mention Apt's survey paper (Apt [1979]) on "Ten years of Hoare's logic", which could be used by a reader who has already some understanding of the problem area as a quick introduction, mostly without detailed proofs, to our book.

R.2.3. *Logic*

Besides the partial correctness formalism which forms the main object of study of the preceding chapters, a number of further logical systems motivated by program correctness have been studied in the past decade. We mention the algorithmic logic of Engeler (see e.g. Engeler [1975]) and of the Polish group of Salwicki et al. (e.g. Banachowski et al. [1977]). Recently, interest in this approach has increased sharply owing to the contributions of the MIT school (see Pratt [1976, 1979], Harel [1979], and references contained in these papers). No doubt, there are various overlaps between the approach of what is nowadays mostly called dynamic logic and our results, and we consider it an important topic for future study to clarify these relationships.

Though our book - with the exception of the appendix - uses no technical results from mathematical logic, the reader would certainly benefit from some familiarity with elementary predicate calculus (e.g. Mendelson [1964], Robbin [1969], or Shoenfield [1967]). Also, we have often omitted full proofs concerning substitution, congruent constructs and the like; if necessary, the reader may consult Curry & Feys [1974] or Hindley et al. [1972], where details of very similar problems are provided.

R.3. Chapter references

R.3.1. *References for chapter* 2

This chapter contains (our version of) a number of basic ideas from denotational semantics (introduction of states, the functions $\mathcal{V}$, $\mathcal{W}$, $\mathcal{M}$, $\mathcal{T}$ (etc.)) and proof theory. A tutorial paper partly covering the same material is De Bakker [1977]. For the notions of substitution, validity, formal proof, soundness and completeness of a proof system in general, compare any textbook on mathematical logic (see references in R.2.3). The definition of completeness as used in section 2.6 (where all valid assertions are taken as axioms) is due to Cook [1978]. The rules for assignment (theorem 2.15a), composition and consequence are from Hoare [1969], and the rule for conditionals is from Lauer [1971]. Theorem 2.15b is due to Floyd [1967]. The concept of a function (not) setting or using a variable was inspired by work of Maurer [1966]. Some of the examples on conditional expressions following definition 2.12 are from McCarthy [1963b]. Exercise 2.20 is from De Bakker [1971a]; further results on an axiomatic treatment of program equivalence are described in Igarashi [1971].

R.3.2. *References for chapter* 3

Cpo's and (least) fixed points are fundamental notions in denotational semantics. The while rule is from Hoare [1969]. Theorem 3.35 is related to results from Clarke [1977]; theorem 3.36 is a reformulation of an example from De Bakker & De Roever [1973]. The completeness theorem of section 3.6 follows a suggestion of Clarke [1979] to simplify the proof of Cook [1978]. A purely semantic version of the proof appeared in De Bakker & Meertens [1975]. For exercises 3.14, 3.15, compare De Bakker [1975b], Knuth [1974], and Wirth [1974]. Many further results clarifying the relationships between semantics and deductive systems for the while statement are described in Greif & Meyer [1979].

R.3.3. *References for chapter* 4

Left-hand values and right-hand values first appeared in Strachey [1966]. The problem with formula (?) was pointed out to us by Peter van Emde Boas, and the idea of solving this by refining the definition of substitution was proposed in De Bakker [1976c]. An alternative solution (exercise 4.10) is from Hoare & Wirth [1973]. Other treatments of assignment to a subscripted variable are described in Gries [1978], Janssen & Van Emde Boas [1977], and Pratt [1976].

R.3.4. *References for chapter* 5

Least fixed points as a tool in the mathematical theory of recursive procedures were anticipated in the work of Landin and of McCarthy [1963a,b], and started playing a central role from 1969 onwards, when some of the essential ideas of this chapter were first reported in Scott & De Bakker [1969], Park [1970], and Bekić [1969]. In general, much of the mathematics of chapter 5 (with the exception of section 5.5, but including some of the exercises) is due to Scott (e.g. Scott & De Bakker [1969], Scott [1972b], private communications to the author). This holds for the results on least fixed points and the induction rule, and in particular for the notion of continuity, which is fundamental in all of denotational semantics and is used extensively in its advanced theory (e.g. Scott [1972a,1976]). Prior versions of our approach to the material in parts of this chapter were given in De Bakker [1971b,1975a].

Theorem 5.13 is in fact an old result from set theory (Knaster [1928]), generalized in a lattice-theoretic setting by Tarski [1955]. Theorem 5.14 (which is from Scott & De Bakker [1969]) was obtained independently by Bekić [1969] and Leszczylowski [1971].

The operational semantics of section 5.3 was inspired by Cook [1978], theorem 5.22 uses techniques first proposed in De Bakker [1976b]. An extension of theorem 5.22 to programs with local variable and procedure declarations is proved in Apt [1978a].

Example 2b after definition 5.27 is Hoare's rule for recursive procedures (Hoare [1971]). Scott's rule can also be applied fruitfully to prove properties of recursive functions (in the sense of the procedure for the factorial mentioned in section 5.1). Many examples of this are given in Manna [1974]. Another formal system embodying the induction rule is LCF (e.g. Milner [1972,1976], Gordon et al. [1979]).

The problem with the validity definition discussed in section 5.5 was pointed out to us by Krzysztof Apt; the structure of the completeness proof, in particular lemma 5.48, follows Gorelick [1975]. A what may be called semantic completeness result concerning partial correctness of recursive procedures is described in De Bakker & Meertens [1975]; related questions are dealt with in Apt & Meertens [1977], Gallier [1978], and Harel, Pnueli & Stavi [1977]. Clarke [1977] uses greatest fixed points to investigate the connection between the syntactic and semantic completeness theorems.

Exercise 5.2 is due to David Park, exercise 5.6 to Jean Vuillemin. A survey of proof methods for regular (cf. exercise 5.18) programs is given by Harel [to appear, a]. Exercise 5.21 is from De Bakker [1975b], exercise 5.22 from De Bakker & Meertens [1975], and exercise 5.24 is due to Regis Pliuskevicius.

R.3.5. *References for chapter* 6

Environments are a standard tool in denotational semantics (see, e.g., Stoy [1977], chapter 12). Our definition of the semantics of a block is taken from Apt & De Bakker [1977]; a similar use of substitution to define the meaning of a block appears in Clarke [1979]. Details about properties of the congruence relation can be found, for example, in Hindley, Lercher & Seldin [1972]. The problem expressed by (6.1) was brought to our attention by Krzysztof Apt; also, the paper Apt [1978b] formed the starting point for section 6.3. Our notion of matching is a simplification of his fits-relation; corresponding simplifications - with respect to the arguments from Apt's paper - were obtained for the soundness proof of section 6.3 and the proof of lemma 6.29b (albeit at the cost of the initialization requirement, for a discussion of which we also refer to Dijkstra [1976]). The block rule is from Hoare [1971]. Exercise 6.6 is due to Lauer [1971]; exercise 6.11 is based on Apt [1978b] (and also relates to the techniques employed in Cook [1978] and used there to prove the soundness theorem), and exercise 6.12 presents an idea of Robert Milne.

R.3.6. *References for chapter* 7

The Egli-Milner ordering is due to Egli [1975] and Robin Milner. Our way of using this ordering was first described in De Bakker [1976a]; the need for the condition of bounded nondeterminacy (i.e. definition 7.2) was pointed out to us by John Reynolds, thus correcting an error in De Bakker [1976a]. Most of the results of section 7.2 were stated (without proof) in De Bakker [1978]. Guarded commands were proposed in Dijkstra [1975] and further exploited in Dijkstra [1976].

The μ-calculus dates back to Scott & De Bakker [1969]. Early papers on the calculus are De Bakker [1971b], Hitchcock & Park [1973] and De Bakker & De Roever [1973]; cf. also Park [1970], De Bakker [1975a], and Livercy [1978]. Much of the material in section 7.3 and the exercises is in fact a reformulation of results from these papers in the framework of denotational semantics.

Lemma 7.15 and exercise 7.12 are from De Roever [1976a], examples 7.13, 7.14 and exercise 7.10 are from De Bakker & De Roever [1973], exercises 7.7, 7.8, 7.9 are from De Bakker [1971b]. Exercises 7.11 and 7.15 arose from an attempt at understanding Cooper [1966]; the hint from exercise 7.15 is due to Robin Milner. The language of exercise 7.18 is Dijkstra's guarded command language.

For a different treatment of denotational semantics of nondeterminacy see Plotkin [1976]. There is a substantial variety of approaches to its operational semantics, from which we mention those of Harel [to appear, b], Hoare [1978], and Nivat [1979]. Further investigations of the μ-calculus include Courcelle & Vuillemin [1976], Kfoury & Park [1975], Park [1976], and De Roever [1974,1976a]. The proof theory of nondeterministic programs - including a number of completeness results - is investigated extensively in dynamic logic (Harel [1979]).

R.3.7. *References for chapter* 8

The notion of weakest precondition (for total correctness) forms the foundation of Dijkstra's approach to program correctness (Dijkstra [1975,1976]). Our interpretation of " $\triangleright$ " by " $\circ$ ", and the result on continuity of " $\circ$ " with respect to the Egli-Milner ordering were inspired by De Roever [1976b] and made precise in De Bakker [1978]. The notion of a semantically anti-continuous condition is related to that of an inclusive predicate (cf. Stoy [1977]). Section 8.3 is based on De Bakker [1978]. The use of greatest fixed points was proposed by Hitchcock & Park [1973] and Mazurkiewicz [1973]. Lemma 8.29 is from Hitchcock & Park [1973]; other applications of greatest fixed points are described in De Roever [1977]. For theorem 8.27a and exercise 8.9 compare Clarke [1977]; for theorem 8.27b see De Bakker & De Roever [1973], and for theorem 8.27c and exercises 8.5, 8.6a compare Dijkstra [1975].

The notion of derivative was introduced by Hitchcock & Park

[1973], and investigated in the setting of denotational semantics in De Bakker [1976a] where also the definition of $\tilde{S}$ first appeared.

The ordering " ≤ " from exercise 8.8 is the so-called Smyth-ordering. The result of the exercise is due independently to Gordon Plotkin and to Back [1978], where " ≤ " is used to model program refinement. Exercise 8.15 is from De Bakker [1975b].

Wand [1977] introduces some mathematical properties which together characterize the weakest precondition for total correctness.

Many of the results of sections 8.2 and 8.4 have counterparts in dynamic logic (Harel [1979], Pratt [1976,1979]) where also proof systems for total correctness - a topic not discussed at all in chapter 8 - are considered.

R.3.8. *References for chapter* 9

Section 9.2 - excluding the initialization requirement - is based on Apt & De Bakker [1976,1977]. The main source for section 9.3 is Apt [1978b]. Though the material as presented here differs considerably from that of his paper, e.g. in the addition of parameter mechanisms and the initialization requirement, the basic philosophy has remained the same; in particular, there are many traces of Apt's work in our definition of validity and our soundness proof. Related questions are addressed in Olderog [1979]. A brief summary of chapter 9 appeared in De Bakker [1979]. The example concluding section 9.4 was provided by Krzysztof Apt.

Langmaack & Olderog [1980] presents a survey of many results on proof systems for procedures, also addressing various questions not dealt with in our treatment. A survey of proof systems for various parameter mechanisms is contained in Apt [1979]. Many of these systems take the rule from Hoare [1971] as their starting point. Call-by-name is discussed in Cook [1978] and Gorelick [1975]. Further references include Igarashi, London & Luckham [1975], London et al. [1978], Cartwright & Oppen [1978] and Schwartz [1979]. Clarke [1979] contains both completeness results, and a discussion of incompleteness due to the addition of new constructs (such as the use of procedures as parameters). Incompleteness is also studied in Lipton [1977] and Wand [1978]. These papers, as well as those on dynamic logic referred to above, are concerned with interpretations over arbitrary structures (instead of over the integers, as used throughout our book); the fundamental expressibility results - i.e. the propositions of sections 3.6, 5.5 and 9.4, see also the appendix - then no longer necessarily hold, and various new kinds of problems arise.

R.3.9. *References for chapter* 10

The use of continuations in the denotational semantics of goto statements was inspired by work of Mazurkiewicz [1971], and has been published in the form as given here by Strachey & Wadsworth [1974]. The proof system, more precisely the inference rule on labelling (10.11.8) stems from Clint & Hoare [1972]. Arbib & Alagić [1979] give proof rules in a form that reflects more clearly the ideas developed in the discussion preceding definition 10.10 (in particular the concept of a statement with more than one exit point). The second validity definition (10.24) appears also in a more elaborate form in Milne & Strachey [1976, section 3.7.8]. The justification of the proof system, as well as the proof of the equivalence of M and O, is given in De Bruin [1979] in a more general setting where the language can be interpreted in arbitrary structures. Also, exercise 10.7 is elaborated there.

R.4. Bibliography

ALAGIC, S. & M.A. ARBIB, *The Design of Well-Structured and Correct Programs*, Springer, 1978.

APT, K.R., *Equivalence of denotational and operational semantics for a fragment of PASCAL*, in Proc. IFIP TC-2 Working Conference on Formal Description of Programming Concepts (E.J. Neuhold, ed.), pp. 139-163, North-Holland, 1978a.

APT, K.R., *A sound and complete Hoare-like system for a fragment of PASCAL,* Report IW 97/78, Mathematisch Centrum, 1978b.

APT, K.R., *Ten years of Hoare's logic, a survey,* in Proc. 5th Scandinavian Logic Symposium (F.V. Jensen, B.H. Mayoh, K.K. Møller, eds), pp. 1-44, Aalborg University Press, 1979.

APT, K.R. & J.W. DE BAKKER, *Exercises in denotational semantics,* in Proc. 5th Symp. Mathematical Foundations of Computer Science (A. Mazurkiewicz, ed.), pp. 1-11, Lecture Notes in Computer Science 45, Springer, 1976.

APT, K.R. & J.W. DE BAKKER, *Semantics and proof theory of PASCAL procedures,* in Proc. 4th Coll. Automata, Languages and Programming (A. Salomaa & M. Steinby, eds), pp. 30-44, Lecture Notes in Computer Science 52, Springer, 1977.

APT, K.R. & L.G.L.T. MEERTENS, *Completeness with finite systems of intermediate assertions for recursive program schemes,* Report IW 84/77, Mathematisch Centrum 1977 (to appear in SIAM J. on Computing).

ARBIB, M.A. & S. ALAGIC, *Proof rules for gotos*, Acta Informatica, 11, pp. 139-148, 1979.

BACK, R.J. *On the correctness of refinement steps in program development,* Ph.D. Thesis, University of Helsinki, 1978.

DE BAKKER, J.W., *Semantics of programming languages,* in Advances in Information Systems Science (J.T. Tou, ed.), Vol. 2, pp. 173-227, Plenum Press, 1969.

DE BAKKER, J.W., *Axiom systems for simple assignment statements,* in Symp. on Semantics of Algorithmic Languages (E. Engeler, ed.), pp. 1-22, Lecture Notes in Mathematics 188, Springer, 1971a.

DE BAKKER, J.W., *Recursive Procedures*, Mathematical Centre Tracts 24, Mathematisch Centrum, 1971b.

DE BAKKER, J.W., *The fixed point approach in semantics: theory and applications,* in Foundations of Computer Science (J.W. de Bakker, ed.), pp. 3-53, Mathematical Centre Tracts 63, Mathematisch Centrum, 1975a.

DE BAKKER, J.W., *Flow of control in the proof theory of structured programming,* in Proc. 16th IEEE Symp. Foundations of Computer Science, pp. 29-33, Berkeley, 1975b.

DE BAKKER, J.W., *Semantics and termination of nondeterministic recursive programs,* in Proc. 3rd Coll. Automata, Languages and Programming (S. Michaelson & R. Milner, eds), pp. 435-477, Edinburgh University Press, 1976a.

DE BAKKER, J.W., *Least fixed points revisited,* Theoretical Computer Science, 2, pp. 155-181, 1976b.

DE BAKKER, J.W., *Correctness proofs for assignment statements,* Report IW 55/76, Mathematisch Centrum, 1976c.

DE BAKKER, J.W., *Semantics and the foundations of program proving,* in Proc. IFIP Congress 77 (B. Gilchrist, ed.), pp. 279-284, North-Holland, 1977.

DE BAKKER, J.W., *Recursive programs as predicate transformers,* in Proc. IFIP TC-2 Working Conference on Formal Description of Programming Concepts (E.J. Neuhold, ed.), pp. 165-181, North-Holland, 1978.

DE BAKKER, J.W., *A sound and complete proof system for partial program correctness,* in Proc. 8th Symp. Mathematical Foundations of Computer Science (J. Bečvář, ed.), pp. 1-12, Lecture Notes in Computer Science 74, Springer, 1979.

DE BAKKER, J.W. & L.G.L.T. MEERTENS, *On the completeness of the inductive assertion method,* Journal of Computer and System Sciences, 11, pp. 323-357, 1975.

DE BAKKER, J.W. & W.P. DE ROEVER, *A calculus for recursive program schemes,* in Proc. 1st Coll. Automata, Languages and Programming (M. Nivat, ed.), pp. 167-196, North-Holland, 1973.

BANACHOWSKI, L., A. KRECZMAR, G. MIRKOWSKA, H. RASIOWA & A. SALWICKI, *An introduction to algorithmic logic; metamathematial investigations in the theory of programs,* in Mathematical Foundations of Computer Science Banach Center Publications (A. Mazurkiewicz & Z. Pawlak, eds), pp. 7-99, Warsaw, 1977.

BEKIĆ, H., *Definable operations in general algebras, and the theory of automata and flow charts* (typescript), IBM Laboratory, Vienna, 1969.

BLIKLE, A., *A comparative review of some program verification methods,* Proc. 6th Symp. Mathematical Foundations of Computer Science (J. Gruska, ed.), pp. 17-33, Lecture Notes in Computer Science 53, Springer, 1977.

BLIKLE, A., *A survey of input-output semantics and program verification,* Institute of Computer Science Report 344, Polish Academy of Science, Warsaw, 1979.

DE BRUIN, A., *Goto statements: semantics and deduction systems,* Report IW 74/79, Mathematisch Centrum, 1979.

CARTWRIGHT, R. & D. OPPEN, *Unrestricted procedure calls in Hoare's logic,* in Proc. 5th ACM Symp. on Principles of Programming Languages, pp. 131-140, 1978.

CLARKE, E.M., *Program invariants as fixed points,* in Proc. 18th IEEE Symp. Foundations of Computer Science, pp. 18-29, Providence, 1977.

CLARKE, E.M., *Programming language constructs for which it is impossible to obtain good Hoare-like axioms,* Journal ACM, 26, pp. 129-147, 1979.

CLINT, M. & C.A.R. HOARE, *Program proving: jumps and functions,* Acta Informatica, 1, pp. 214-224, 1972.

CONSTABLE, R.L. & M.J. O'DONNELL, *A Programming Logic*, Winthrop, 1978.

COOK, S.A., *Soundness and completeness of an axiom system for program verification*, SIAM J. on Computing, 7, pp. 70-90, 1978.

COOPER, D.C., *The equivalence of certain computations*, Computer Journal, 9, pp. 45-52, 1966.

COURCELLE, B. & J. VUILLEMIN, *Completeness results for the equivalence of recursive schemes*, Journal of Computer and System Sciences, 12, pp. 179-197, 1976.

CURRY, H.B. & R. FEYS, *Combinatory Logic*, Vol. I, North-Holland, 1974.

DONAHUE, J.E., *Complementary Definitions of Programming Language Semantics*, Lecture Notes in Computer Science 42, Springer, 1976.

DIJKSTRA, E.W., *Guarded commands, nondeterminacy and formal derivations of programs*, Communications ACM, 18, pp. 453-457, 1975.

DIJKSTRA, E.W., *A Discipline of Programming*, Prentice-Hall, 1976.

EGLI, H., *A mathematical model for nondeterministic computations*, ETH, Zürich, 1975.

VAN EMDE BOAS, P., *The connection between modal logic and algorithmic logics*, in Proc. 7th Symp. Mathematical Foundations of Computer Science (J. Winkowski, ed.), pp. 1-15, Lecture Notes in Computer Science 64, Springer, 1978.

ENGELER, E., *Algorithmic logic*, in Foundations of Computer Science (J.W. de Bakker, ed.), pp. 57-85, Mathematical Centre Tracts 63, Mathematisch Centrum, 1975.

FLOYD, R.W., *Assigning meanings to programs*, in Proc. Symp. in Applied Mathematics, 19- Mathematical Aspects of Computer Science (J.T. Schwartz, ed.), pp. 19-32, AMS, 1967.

GALLIER, J., *Semantics and correctness of nondeterministic flowchart programs with recursive procedures*, in Proc. 5th Coll. Automata, Languages and Programming (G. Ausiello & C. Böhm, eds), pp. 251-267, Lecture Notes in Computer Science 62, Springer, 1978.

GOGUEN, J.A., J.W. THATCHER, E.G. WAGNER & J.B. WRIGHT, *Initial algebra semantics and continuous algebras*, Journal ACM, 24, pp. 68-95, 1977.

GOLDSTINE, H.H. & J. VON NEUMANN, *Planning and coding problems for an electronic computer instrument*, John von Neumann Collected Works, Vol. 5 (A.M. Taub, ed.), pp. 80-235, Pergamon Press, 1963.

GORDON, M., *The Denotational Description of Programming Languages*, Springer, 1979.

GORDON, M., R. MILNER & C. WADSWORTH, *Edinburgh LCF*, Lecture Notes in Computer Science 78, Springer, 1979.

GORELICK, G.A., *A complete axiomatic system for proving assertions about recursive and non-recursive programs*, Technical Report 75, Department of Computer Science, University of Toronto, 1975.

GREIBACH, S.A., *Theory of Program Structures: Schemes, Semantics, Verification*, Lecture Notes in Computer Science 36, Springer, 1975.

GREIF, I. & A.R. MEYER, *Specifying the semantics of while-programs: A tutorial and critique of a paper by Hoare and Lauer*, MIT Report MIT/LCS/TM-130, 1979.

GRIES, D., *The multiple assignment statement*, IEEE Transactions on Software Engineering, 4, pp. 89-93, 1978.

HAREL, D., *First-Order Dynamic Logic*, Lecture Notes in Computer Science 68, Springer, 1979.

HAREL, D., *Proving the correctness of regular deterministic programs; a unified survey using dynamic logic*, Theoretical Computer Science, to appear, a.

HAREL, D., *On the total correctness of nondeterministic programs*,

Theoretical Computer Science, to appear b.

HAREL, D., A. Pnueli & J. STAVI, *A complete axiom system for proving deductions about recursive programs*, in Proc. 9th ACM Symp. Theory of Computing, Boulder, 1977.

HINDLEY, J.R., B. LERCHER & J.P. SELDIN, *Introduction to Combinatory Logic*, Cambridge University Press, 1972.

HITCHCOCK, P. & D.M.R. PARK, *Induction rules and termination proofs*, in Proc. 1st Coll. Automata, Languages and Programming (M. Nivat, ed.), pp. 225-251, North-Holland, 1973.

HOARE, C.A.R., *An axiomatic basis for computer programming*, Communications ACM, 12, pp. 576-580, 1969.

HOARE, C.A.R., *Procedures and parameters: an axiomatic approach*, in Symp. on Semantics of Algorithmic Languages (E. Engeler, ed.), pp. 102-116, Lecture Notes in Mathematics 188, Springer, 1971.

HOARE, C.A.R., *Some properties of predicate transformers*, Journal ACM, 25, pp. 461-480, 1978.

HOARE, C.A.R. & P.E. LAUER, *Consistent and complementary formal theories of the semantics of programming languages*, Acta Informatica, 3, pp. 135-153, 1974.

HOARE, C.A.R. & N. WIRTH, *An axiomatic definition of the programming language PASCAL*, Acta Informatica, 2, pp. 335-355, 1973.

IGARASHI, S., *Semantics of ALGOL-like statements*, in Symp. on Semantics of Algorithmic Languages (E. Engeler, ed.), pp. 117-188, Lecture Notes in Mathematics 188, Springer, 1971.

IGARASHI, S., R.L. LONDON & D.C. LUCKHAM, *Automatic program verification I: a logical basic and its implementation*, Acta Informatica, 4, pp. 145-182, 1975.

JANSSEN, T.M.V. & P. VAN EMDE BOAS, *On the proper treatment of referencing, dereferencing and assignment*, in Proc. 4th Coll.

Automata, Languages and Programming (A. Salomaa & M. Steinby, eds), pp. 282-300, Lecture Notes in Computer Science 52, Springer, 1977.

KFOURY, A.J. & D.M.R. PARK, *On the termination of programs*, Information and Control, 29, pp. 243-251, 1975.

KLEENE, S.C., *Introduction to Metamathematics*, Van Nostrand, 1952.

KNASTER, B., *Un théorème sur les fonctions d'ensembles*, Ann. Soc. Pol. Math., 6, pp. 133-134, 1928.

KNUTH, D., *Semantics of context-free languages*, Mathematical Systems Theory, 2, pp. 127-145, 1968.

KNUTH, D., *Structured programming with goto statements*, Computing Surveys, 6, pp. 261-302, 1974.

LANGMAACK, H. & E.R. OLDEROG, *Present-day Hoare-like systems for programming languages with procedures: power, limits and most likely extensions*, in Proc. 7th Coll. Automata, Languages and Programming (J.W. de Bakker & J. van Leeuwen, eds), Lecture Notes in Computer Science, Springer, 1980.

LAUER, P.E., *Consistent formal theories of the semantics of programming languages*, Technical Report TR.25.121, IBM Laboratory, Vienna, 1971.

LESZCZYLOWSKI, J., *A theorem on resolving equations in the space of languages*, Bull. Acad. Polon. Sci., Ser. Sci. Math. Astr. Phys., 19, pp. 967-970, 1971.

LIGLER, G.T., *A mathematical approach to language design*, in Proc 2nd ACM Symp. on Principles of Programming Languages, pp. 41-53, 1975a.

LIGLER, G.T., *Surface properties of programming language constructs*, in Proc. Symp. on Proving and Improving Programs (G. Huet & G. Kahn, eds), pp. 299-323, IRIA, 1975b.

LIPTON, R.J., *A necessary and sufficient condition for the existence of Hoare logics,* in Proc. 18th IEEE Symp. on Foundations of Computer Science, pp. 1-6, 1977.

LIVERCY, C., *Théorie des Programmes,* DUNOD, 1978.

LONDON, R.L. J.V. GUTTAG, J.J. HORNING, B.W. LAMPSON, J.G. MITCHELL & G.J. POPEK, *Proof rules for the programming language Euclid,* Acta Informatica, 10, pp. 1-26, 1978.

LUCAS, P. & K. WALK, *On the formal description of PL/I,* Annual Review in Automatic Programming, 6, pp. 105-182, 1971.

MCCARTHY, J., *Towards a mathematical science of computation,* in Proc. IFIP Congress 62 (C.M. Popplewell, ed.), pp. 21-28, North-Holland, 1963a.

MCCARTHY, J., *A basis for a mathematical theory of computation,* in Computer Programming and Formal Systems (P. Braffort & D. Hirschberg, eds), pp. 33-70, North-Holland, 1963b.

MANNA, Z., *Mathematical Theory of Computation,* McGraw-Hill, 1974.

MARCOTTY, M., H.F. LEDGARD & G.C. BOCHMANN, *A sampler of formal definitions,* Computing Surveys, 8, pp. 191-276, 1976.

MAURER, W.D., *A theory of computer instructions,* Journal ACM, 2, pp. 226-235, 1966.

MAZURKIEWICZ, A., *Proving algorithms by tail functions,* Information and Control, 18, pp. 220-226, 1971.

MAZURKIEWICZ, A., *Proving properties of processes,* Report 134, Computation Centre, Polish Academy of Sciences, Warsaw, 1973.

MENDELSON, E., *Introduction to Mathematical Logic,* Van Nostrand, 1964.

MILNE, R.E., *Transforming predicate transformers,* in Proc. IFIP TC-2 Working Conference on Formal Description of Programming Concepts (E.J. Neuhold, ed.), pp. 31-65, North-Holland, 1978.

MILNE, R.E. & C. STRACHEY, *A Theory of Programming Language Semantics,* 2 Vols, Chapman and Hall, 1976.

MILNER, R., *Implementation and applications of Scott's logic for computable functions,* in Proc. ACM Conf. on Proving Assertions about Programs, pp. 1-6, ACM, 1972.

MILNER, R., *Program semantics and mechanized proof,* in Foundations of Computer Science II, part 2 (K.R. Apt & J.W. de Bakker, eds), pp. 3-44, Mathematical Centre Tracts 82, Mathematisch Centrum, 1976.

MOSSES, P.D., *The mathematical semantics of ALGOL 60,* Technical Monograph PRG-12, Programming Research Group, University of Oxford, 1974.

NAUR, P., *Proof of algorithms by general snapshots,* BIT, 6, pp. 310-316, 1966.

NIVAT, M., *Langages algébriques sur le magma libre et semantique des schèmes de programmes,* in Proc. 1st Coll. Automata, Languages and Programming (M. Nivat, ed.), pp. 293-308, North-Holland, 1973.

NIVAT, M., *On the interpretation of recursive polyadic program schemes,* in Symposia Mathematica, Vol. 15, pp. 256-281, 1975.

NIVAT, M., *Infinite words, infinite trees, infinite computations,* in Foundations of Computer Science III, part 2 (J.W. de Bakker & J. van Leeuwen, eds), pp. 1-52, Mathematical Centre Tracts 109, Mathematisch Centrum, 1979.

OLDEROG, E.R., *Korrektheits- und Vollständigkeitsaussagen über Hoaresche Ableitungskalküle,* Diplomarbeit, Department of Computer Science, University of Kiel, 1979.

PARK, D.M.R., *Fixpoint induction and proofs of program semantics,* in Machine Intelligence, Vol. 5 (B. Meltzer & D. Michie, eds), pp. 59-78, Edinburgh University Press, 1970.

PARK, D.M.R., *Finiteness is mu-ineffable,* Theoretical Computer Science, 3, pp. 173-182, 1976.

PLOTKIN, G.D., *A powerdomain construction,* SIAM J. on Computing, 5, pp. 452-487, 1976.

PRATT, V.R., *Semantical considerations on Floyd-Hoare logic,* in Proc. 17th IEEE Symp. Foundations of Computer Science, pp. 109-121, 1976.

PRATT, V.R., *Dynamic logic,* in Foundations of Computer Science III, part 2 (J.W. de Bakker & J. van Leeuwen, eds), pp. 53-82, Mathematical Centre Tracts 109, Mathematisch Centrum, 1979.

DE ROEVER, W.P., *Recursion and parameter mechanisms: an axiomatic approach,* in Proc. 2nd Coll. Automata, Languages and Programming (J. Loeckx, ed.), pp. 34-65, Lecture Notes in Computer Science 14, Springer, 1974.

DE ROEVER, W.P., *Recursive Program Schemes: Semantics and Proof Theory,* Mathematical Centre Tracts 70, Mathematisch Centrum, 1976a.

DE ROEVER, W.P., *Dijkstra's predicate transformer, nondeterminism, recursion and termination,* in Proc. 5th Symp. Mathematical Foundations of Computer Science (A. Mazurkiewicz, ed.), pp. 472-481, Lecture Notes in Computer Science 45, Springer, 1976b.

DE ROEVER, W.P., *On backtracking and greatest fixed points,* in Proc. 4th Coll. Automata, Languages and Programming (A. Salomaa & M. Steinby, eds), pp. 412-429, Lecture Notes in Computer Science 52, Springer, 1977.

ROBBIN, J.W., *Mathematical Logic,* Benjamin, 1969.

ROGERS, Jr., H., *Theory of Recursive Functions and Effective Computability,* McGraw-Hill, 1967.

SCHWARTZ, R.L., *An axiomatic treatment of ALGOL 68 routines*, in Proc. 6th Coll. Automata, Languages and Programming (H.A. Maurer, ed.), pp. 530-545, Lecture Notes in Computer Science 71, Springer, 1979.

SCOTT, D.S., *Outline of a mathematical theory of computation*, in Proc. 4th Ann. Princeton Conf. on Information Sciences and Systems, pp. 169-176, Princeton, 1970.

SCOTT, D.S., *Continuous lattices*, in Toposes, Algebraic Geometry and Logic (F.W. Lawvere, ed.), pp. 97-136, Lecture Notes in Mathematics 274, Springer, 1972a.

SCOTT, D.S., *Data types as lattices*, unpublished lecture notes, Amsterdam, 1972b.

SCOTT, D.S., *Lattice theory, data types and semantics*, in Symp. Formal Semantics (R. Rustin, ed.), pp. 64-106, Prentice-Hall, 1972c.

SCOTT, D.S., *Data types as lattices*, SIAM J. on Computing, 5, pp. 522-587, 1976.

SCOTT, D.S., *Logic and programming language*, Communications ACM, 20, pp. 634-641, 1977.

SCOTT, D.S. & J.W. DE BAKKER, *A theory of programs*, unpublished seminar notes, IBM, Vienna, 1969.

SCOTT, D.S. & C. STRACHEY, *Toward a mathematical semantics for computer languages*, in Proc. Symp. Computers and Automata (J. Fox, ed.), pp. 19-46, Polytechnic Institute of Brooklyn Press, 1971.

SHOENFIELD, J.R., *Mathematical Logic*, Addison-Wesley, 1967.

STEEL, Jr., T.B., *Formal Language Description Languages for Computer Programming*, Proc. IFIP Working Conference on Formal Language Description Languages, North-Holland, 1966.

STOY, J., *Denotational Semantics: The Scott-Strachey Approach to Programming Language Theory*, MIT Press, 1977.

STRACHEY, C., *Towards a formal semantics*, in Formal Language

Description Languages for Computer Programming (T.B. Steel Jr., ed.), pp. 198-220, North-Holland, 1966.

STRACHEY, C. & C.P. WADSWORTH, *Continuations: a mathematical semantics for handling full jumps*, Technical Monograph PRG-11, Programming Research Group, University of Oxford, 1974.

TARSKI, A., *A lattice-theoretical fixpoint theorem and its applications*, Pacific J. of Mathematics, 5, pp. 285-309, 1955.

TENNENT, R.D., *The denotational semantics of programming languages*, Communications ACM, 19, pp. 437-453, 1976.

THATCHER, J.W., E.G. WAGNER & J.B. WRIGHT, *Notes on algebraic fundamentals for theoretical computer science*, in Foundations of Computer Science III, part 2 (J.W. de Bakker & J. van Leeuwen, eds), pp. 83-163, Mathematical Centre Tracts 109, Mathematisch Centrum, 1979.

TURING, A.M., *On checking a large routine*, Report of a Conference on high-speed automatic calculating machines, pp. 67-69, University Mathematical Laboratory, Cambridge, 1949.

WAND, M., *A characterization of weakest preconditions*, J. Computer and System Sciences, 15, pp. 209-212, 1977.

WAND, M., *A new incompleteness result for Hoare's system*, Journal ACM, 25, pp. 168-175, 1978.

WEGNER, P., *The Vienna Definition Language*, Computing Surveys, 4, pp. 5-63, 1972.

WIRTH, N., *On the composition of well-structured programs*, Computing Surveys, 6, pp. 247-260, 1974.

VAN WIJNGAARDEN, A. (ed.), B.J. MAILLOUX, J.E.L. PECK & C.H.A. KOSTER, *Report on the Algorithmic Language ALGOL 68*, Numerische Mathematik, 14, pp. 79-218, 1969.

VAN WIJNGAARDEN, A., B.J. MAILLOUX, J.E.L. PECK, C.H.A. KOSTER,

M. SINTZOFF, C.H. LINDSEY, L.G.L.T. MEERTENS & R.G. FISKER (eds), *Revised Report on the Algorithmic Language ALGOL 68*, Acta Informatica, 5, pp. 1-236, 1975.

SUBJECT INDEX

A

B

C

INDEX OF NOTATIONS

A reference such as "2.1" refers to definition 2.1, and "p.23" refers to page 23. Notations of the appendix are not included in the index.